Introduction to Philosophical Thinking

Readings and Commentary

Introduction to Philosophical Thinking

Readings and Commentary

Ralph W. Clark
West Virginia University

West Publishing Company
St. Paul New York Los Angeles San Francisco

Copyediting—Mary Hoff
Design—Paula Shuhert
Cover Design—Theresa Jensen
Cover Art—René Magritte, *Les Promenades d'Euclide,* The Minneapolis Institute of Arts

COPYRIGHT © 1987 By WEST PUBLISHING COMPANY
50 W. Kellogg Boulevard
P.O. Box 64526
St. Paul, MN 55164–1003

All rights reserved

Printed in the United States of America

Library of Congress Cataloging-in-Publication Data

Clark, Ralph W.
Introduction to philosophical thinking.

1. Philosophy—Introductions. I. Title.
BD41.C53 1987 100 86–15822
ISBN 0–314–29524–0

To Myrtle Dodge, for her unfailing service during 19 years to the Philosophy Department at West Virginia University.

Contents

Preface **xi**

CHAPTER 1
Why Is Philosophical Thinking Unique? 1
Cameo: Bertrand Russell 6

CHAPTER 2
Writing Philosophy 7
Cameo: Plato 18

CHAPTER 3
God's Existence 19
Cameo: William James 22
Thomas Huxley *Agnosticism* 23
Saint Anselm *The Ontological Argument* 27
Gaunilo *On Behalf of the Fool* 28
George Bowles *Anselm's Ontological Argument for the Existence of God* 32
Samuel Clarke *A Demonstration of the Being and Attributes of God* 40
William Rowe *The Cosmological Argument* 44
Ernest Nagel *Philosophical Concepts of Atheism* 58
William James *Mysticism* 67
Jonathan Edwards *The Sense of the Heart* 76
Readings 78

CHAPTER 4

Evil 79
Cameo: Gottfried Wilhelm Leibniz 82
Martin Gardner *Evil: Why We Don't Know Why* 83
Gottfried Wilhelm Leibniz *The Best of All Possible Worlds* 97
Bertrand Russell *The Free Man's Worship* 100
John Hick *The Infinite Future Good* 108
J. L. Mackie *Evil and Omnipotence* 113
Readings 125

CHAPTER 5

Free Will and Determinism 126
Cameo: Jean-Paul Sartre 131
Nicholas J. Dixon *A "Slippery Slope" Argument in Defense of Hard Determinism* 132
Jean-Paul Sartre *Existentialism and Freedom* 137
Kai Nielsen *The Compatibility of Freedom and Determinism* 146
Fred Alan Wolf *Determinism, Indeterminism, and Science* 155
Susan Leigh Anderson *The Libertarian Conception of Freedom* 166
Readings 175

CHAPTER 6

The Philosophy of Mind 176
Cameo: René Descartes 182
René Descartes *Meditations* 183
Gilbert Ryle *Descartes' Myth* 186
David M. Armstrong *Identification of the Mental with the Physical* 193
William James *On the Theory of the Soul* 203
James E. Royce *Nature of the Human Soul* 207
Jerome A. Shaffer *The Identity Theory* 213
Keith Campbell *A New Epiphenomenalism* 220
Paul Ziff *The Feelings of Robots* 224
Readings 229

CHAPTER 7

Life after Death 230
Cameo: John Locke 234
John Locke *On Personal Identity* 235
H. H. Price *What Kind of "Next World"?* 238
Bertrand Russell *Do We Survive Death?* 245

Martin Ebon *The Moody Phenomena* 249
James E. Alcock *Psychology and Near-Death Experiences* 253
Paul and Linda Badham *Claimed Memories of Former Lives* 260
Readings 271

CHAPTER 8

The Foundations of Morality 272
Cameo: Immanuel Kant 276
William James *Conditions Required for the Application of Value Terms* 277
Plato *The Good* 281
Bertrand Russell *Science and Ethics* 288
A. C. Ewing *The Objectivity of Moral Judgements* 295
James Rachels *The Challenge of Cultural Relativism* 304
Immanuel Kant *The Categorical Imperative and the Practical Imperative* 315
John Stuart Mill *Utilitarianism* 322
Readings 328

CHAPTER 9

Egoism and Altruism 329
Cameo: Josiah Royce 333
Gardner Williams *Individual, Social, and Universal Ethics* 334
James Rachels *Egoism and Moral Scepticism* 344
Saint Matthew *The Sermon on the Mount* 354
Josiah Royce *The Moral Insight* 360
Bernard Mayo *Doing and Being* 364
Ralph W. Clark *The Concept of Altruism* 369
Susan Wolf, *Moral Saints* 378
Readings 386

CHAPTER 10

Knowledge and Perception 387
Cameo: David Hume 391
John Locke *The Distinction Between Primary and Secondary Qualities* 392
George Berkeley *To Be Is to Be Perceived* 399
John Stuart Mill *The Permanent Possibility of Sensation* 406
Frank Jackson *Color and Science* 412
Eugene Valberg *A Theory of Secondary Qualities* 418
David Hume *The Limitations of Experience* 426
A. C. Ewing *The "A Priori" and the Empirical* 434
Readings 443

CHAPTER 11

Technology and Values 445
Cameo: René Dubos 449
Peter Pringle and James Spigelman *The Beginnings of the Nuclear Age* 450
William Godfrey-Smith *The Value of Wilderness* 456
René Dubos *The Crisis of Man in His Environment* 467
Stephen P. Stich *The Recombinant DNA Debate* 477
Carl Sagan *In Praise of Science and Technology* 486
Readings 493

CHAPTER 12

Cross-Cultural Understanding 495
Cameo: John Stuart Mill 498
N.L. Gifford *Relativism and Knowledge* 499
Henry L. Ruf *Cultural Pluralism: A Philosophical Investigation* 509
John Stuart Mill *Necessity and Inconceivability* 516
Roger Trigg *The Sociobiological View of Man* 518
Po-keung Ip *Taoism and the Foundations of Environmental Ethics* 524
Ahmed M. Abou-Zeid *The Concept of Time in Peasant Society* 532
Readings 536

CHAPTER 13

Science versus Pseudoscience 537
Cameo: J. B. Rhine 541
J. B. Rhine *The Science of Nonphysical Nature* 542
Paul Kurtz *Is Parapsychology a Science?* 552
Paul E. Meehl and Michael Scriven *Compatibility of Science and ESP* 566
John D. McGervey *A Statistical Test of Sun-Sign Astrology* 570
Readings 575

CHAPTER 14

Time 576
Cameo: Saint Augustine 581
Saint Augustine *What Is Time?* 582
H. G. Wells *The Time Machine* 586
Nigel Calder *Methuselah in a Spaceship* 593
James Otten *The Passage of Time* 599
Readings 604

Glossary 607

Preface

This book is a combination text/anthology—a type of book that has become popular in recent years for introductory philosophy courses. Such books differ considerably among themselves, depending on what their function is conceived to be. The present book is based on the belief that the most effective text/anthology excels in the following ways:

1. *It provides introductory and support materials that are user-friendly.* Because philosophical readings in themselves are often a major challenge in introductory courses, students need help and encouragement, and they will find both in chapters 1 and 2, in the opening essays for chapters 3 through 14, and in a variety of other study aids. At the same time, the reading selections are allowed to speak for themselves.
2. *It is skills oriented.* Some introductory textbooks have a section or a chapter on logic; extended treatment of logic, however, is probably better left to separate texts and courses. This book does have a brief discussion of the nature of arguments in chapter 2 and in the opening essay for chapter 3. Its focus, however, is on the most important *general* skill in philosophy, namely the ability to write philosophically. Chapter 2 provides guidelines for writing both term papers and short in-class essays.
3. *It contains readings selected and edited for easy accessibility to beginning students, while also presenting a balanced treatment of the issues.* Readings in this book are taken from all possible sources: the history of philosophy, books and articles by current philosophers, and the work of writers who are not professional philosophers.
4. *It covers topics of value and interest to its readers.* There is no best way to do this; several different approaches may work well. This book offers a

somewhat greater diversity of topics than usual in order to cover a number of contemporary issues in addition to many classical ones.

The following chapters concern classical issues:

- God's Existence
- Evil
- Free Will and Determinism
- The Philosophy of Mind
- Life After Death
- The Foundations of Morality
- Egoism and Altruism
- Knowledge and Perception

The following chapters concern contemporary issues:

- Technology and Values (reflecting philosophical response to the ecological crisis and to the threat of nuclear war)
- Cross-Cultural Understanding (reflecting philosophical response to an awareness of the world's great cultural diversity)
- Science vs. Pseudoscience (reflecting philosophical response to parapsychology and astrology)
- The Nature of Time (reflecting philosophical response to relativity theory and other developments in science that have made people more aware of the puzzling nature of time)

As would be expected, the reading selections in the contemporary chapters are almost entirely from works that have recently been published. The classical chapters also contain many contemporary, up-to-date selections, in addition to ones from noted historical figures.

This book takes special care to define philosophy in a way that will help students the most. Chapter 1 is an overview of some particularly interesting characteristics of philosophy as a discipline. Chapter 2 discusses the aims of philosophy in the context of describing good philosophical writing. Each of the opening essays for chapters 3 through 14 briefly describes a specific aspect of philosophy that can be illustrated effectively by the subject matter of the chapter. The advantage of this book's approach is that students are not presented with a lengthy discussion of the nature of philosophy before they have been exposed to actual examples of philosophical writing. At the same time, they are told enough early on to be able to appreciate the unique contributions that philosophy makes.

The "Comments and Questions" section that follows each reading selection contains summaries of potentially difficult key points. These summaries are selective, not comprehensive, and help and encourage students to read each selection carefully.

As much as possible, each chapter is self-contained, and consequently the chapters need not be assigned in order. For example, even though the issues addressed in chapter 6, "The Philosophy of Mind," are for the most part more fundamental than the issues addressed in chapter 7, "Life After Death," chapter 7 can be assigned first as a somewhat easier introduction to the philosophy of mind. As another possibility, one or more of the contemporary chapters (11–14) can be covered first to stimulate interest in the more traditional topics of the earlier chapters. Or, it may be helpful to assign chapter 2, "Writing Philosophy," *after* assigning a chapter with substantive material to write about. Other combinations of chapters are also useful.

Regardless of the order in which chapters are read, students will be reminded how the chapters are interrelated by the many cross references given in the opening essays and in the "Comments and Questions" section following each reading selection.

Many people have helped in preparing this book. I would especially like to thank: my wife Suzanne, the students who over the years have taken my introductory philosophy courses and told me what they liked and did not like about them, my colleagues Roderick Stewart and Theodore Drange for looking at parts of the manuscript, Clark Baxter and Nancy Roth of West Publishing Company for their encouragement and consistently very helpful editorial advice, and Mary Hoff for her excellent copyediting. Most importantly, I would like to thank the following reviewers: Nicholas J. Dixon, Central Michigan University; Steve Sapontzis, University of California-Hayward; Jon Moran, Southwest Missouri State University; Mary Sirridge, Louisiana State University; Gray Cox, Middle Tennessee State University; and William Jones, Eastern Kentucky University. Finally, the book could not have been completed on schedule if Kellie Vankirk had not typed, retyped, and copied everything quickly and accurately.

Introduction to Philosophical Thinking

Readings and Commentary

C H A P T E R   O N E

Why Is Philosophical Thinking Unique?

Philosophical thinking differs from ordinary thinking. It also differs from the thinking found in business, engineering, and the sciences and from the creative thought of novelists and poets.

Perhaps the best way to describe philosophical thinking is to give examples of the questions that philosophers ask and contrast them with those that nonphilosophers ask. As an example, consider the study of time. An astronomer may ask about different ways that time is measured—by the rotation of the earth, by the earth's revolution around the sun, by the movement of the sun against the stars. A physicist may ask questions about the movements of atoms that are the basis for the universe's so-called atomic clocks. An engineer may inquire about using quartz crystals and solid state electronic circuits to construct more accurate clocks and watches. A philosopher would not ask about any of these aspects of time, but would ask the following instead:

- What is time itself?
- Is time relative to the existence of changing things, or is time an absolute that exists independently of everything else in the universe?
- Does the idea of "time travel" make sense?
- How "long" is the present moment?
- Does it even make sense to ask how long the present moment is?
- Does time have a beginning or an end?

In all important areas of life philosophers ask questions that go beyond those asked by nonphilosophers. Philosophers and nonphilosophers may start with the same questions, but philosophers are never content to stop with such questions. While no sharp lines separate the philosophical from the nonphilosophical, the following sets of questions should help to distinguish the two.

Nonphilosophical questions: Have I picked the right career? Did I marry the right person? Is my life going well?
Philosophical questions: What does it mean to have picked the right career? What is personal happiness? How does one know when life is going well? What is the meaning of life?

Nonphilosophical: Am I a good person?
Philosophical: What does it mean to be a good person? What are the most important values in life? What makes a person virtuous? What is moral virtue?

Nonphilosophical: Are the prisons and the court system doing a good job?
Philosophical: How can punishment be justified? What is the nature of moral responsibility? In what sense is anyone free to choose or not choose a life of crime?

Nonphilosophical: At what distances and under what lighting conditions can the normal human eye make out certain figures? How do glasses correct visual problems?
Philosophical: Do we see things as they really are "in themselves"? Is color an "objective" feature of the world or does its perception depend on the ways our eyes are constructed or the ways our brains interpret messages received from the optic nerve?

Nonphilosophical: Does God care about me?
Philosophical: Can God's existence be proven? If not, can it be shown to be probable? What does, or could, the word *God* really mean? What kind of knowledge about God could ever be possible?

Nonphilosophical: Is there hope for life after death?
Philosophical: Is life after death conceivable? Is the existence of life after death a probable hypothesis? Is the world purely material, or is it also spiritual? Is human consciousness the activity of the brain, or does it belong to an immaterial soul? What is consciousness?

Nonphilosophical: Will medical science find new cures for serious illnesses such as arterial disease?
Philosophical: What enables science to be successful at all? Can the inductive method of science be justified? What is the nature of scientific knowledge?

Why would anyone want to raise philosophical questions such as these? The answer is that without philosophy life is lived on the *intellectual surface* of things. People may live intense lives without philosophy. They may devote themselves happily to their careers, love their families, care deeply about social causes, have interesting hobbies, and travel to beautiful faraway places. Their lives may be rich in experiences and beneficial to themselves and their fellow human beings. But their lives will not be *deep* because they will not ask truly probing questions about life. I am not saying that a life without philosophy is a bad thing. (Besides, almost everyone's life has *some* philosophy in it.) I am saying that a life that does not include serious and extensive philosophical probing of itself has left an important and rewarding dimension untouched and unfulfilled.

Each of you, *in addition* to your other aspirations, has the capacity to dig beneath the intellectual surface of your life. As a discipline, philosophy is often frustrating because it leaves so much unanswered. One of the truly marvelous things about philosophy, however, is that it takes nothing away from the other areas of life except a little time. Even in this respect, the loss need not be great because the time for philosophizing can be picked up here and there at little cost to other activities. The odd moment when you are waiting to meet someone; the time spent taking a walk; the occasion when you need a good book to fill up an evening; the time when you are at a party talking with friends—all of these can be spent pursuing philosophical questions. Please keep this point in mind as you undertake the study of philosophy—philosophical thinking complements other important thinking. It need not take its place.

Philosophy can and should be added to most other areas of life. To a large extent, philosophers themselves perceive philosophy in this way, as the names of some of the important areas of study in philosophy make clear: the philosophy *of* science, the philosophy *of* art, the philosophy *of* law, the philosophy *of* language, and so on. Of course, philosophers are not content to stop with the philosophy *of* something else. Philosophy also has its own special areas of investigation, such as epistemology, the study of knowledge, and metaphysics, the study of the basic nature of reality. There is even the philosophy *of* philosophy—philosophizing about the very activity of raising basic philosophical questions. In philosophy everything is fair game. Nothing is left unchallenged.

I do not mean to suggest that philosophers only raise questions. That would not be at all satisfactory. It is philosophy's job to give us answers—if and when they can be given. But a book or course or even a lifetime devoted to the study of philosophy cannot be expected to provide final answers to philosophical questions. To state *any* answer is immediately to raise further questions about it. This is of course not to say that the discipline of philosophy has made no progress or that those who study philosophy make no progress.

It is true that the *content* of the answers to philosophical questions is in some important respects unsettled because the search for answers is an ongoing process. But the *method* of philosophizing is rigorous and requires strict rules and procedures. Philosophy demands *clarity* in thinking, speaking, and writing. It also demands *logical support* for philosophical claims. Philosophers spend considerable time constructing and analyzing arguments. The insistence upon high standards for clarity and logical rigor may be a response in part to the unsettled nature of philosophical answers to questions: because philosophers are always asking questions about questions and take absolutely nothing for granted, they have a special need to set high standards for the conduct of philosophical thinking. Anyone interested in philosophy must pay heed to the following advice:

> Don't just say it, say what you mean. Define your terms. Analyze your concepts. Whenever possible, illustrate what you mean with concrete examples. Give your reasons or arguments. Anticipate all possible objections to what you are saying in order to answer them. Ask yourself: How might someone misunderstand what I am saying or my reasons for saying it? What can I do to guard against being misunderstood?

Philosophers always think of themselves as walking on thin ice—moving out ahead of everyone else to ask the most basic and difficult questions—and thus always in danger of losing their footing. Philosophers therefore proceed very cautiously, testing the ice before stepping out onto it. They are always on guard against saying things that are unclear or misleading.

In philosophy, it is true that *anything can be questioned*. It is not true that *anything goes*.

Because philosophy is an exacting discipline, students sometimes become discouraged. Perhaps you will be somewhat comforted to know that philosophy is difficult for professors as well. Enjoyable (usually), but difficult. Even the most famous and respected philosophers have found philosophy challenging.

Something else may be of comfort to you as you wrestle with the issues in this book: namely, the fact that there is really no such thing as introductory philosophy. No easy or elementary questions can be covered first, and then mastered, before the really difficult questions are addressed. All of the questions in philosophy almost immediately open up the most far-reaching puzzles. Whether the questions are about knowledge, perception, time, free will, God's existence, life after death, the nature of human consciousness, or values, they are all "advanced" questions. Philosophy is like a deep pool that you must plunge into, with no shallow end for wading.

To bring order into their world of open-ended questioning, philosophers have introduced many new concepts. Three of the most important follow:

1. The concept of *epistemology*, or the study of knowledge in general. Epistemology is a major branch of philosophy that raises questions such as these: Can anything be known with certainty? What is the nature of probabilistic knowledge (something known that is more likely true than false, but not true for sure)? Does all knowledge derive from the experiences of the five senses? What is the nature of truth? Can anything in the world be known as it exists in itself (assuming that it even makes sense to talk about something "existing in itself")?
2. The concept of *metaphysics*, or the study of the basic nature of existence or reality in general. Another major branch of philosophy, metaphysics raises questions such as these: Is there a single cause, such as God, for everything that exists in the universe? Is the universe completely material, or does it have a spiritual dimension? Do souls exist in addition to bodies? Is space infinite or finite? What is the nature of time? of causality? of freedom?
3. The concept of *axiology*, or the study of basic values. The third major branch of philosophy, axiology is divided into two further branches—ethics, the study of moral values, and aesthetics, the study of values in art and the beauty of nature. The following are some of the questions that axiology raises: Are any moral values true for everyone, or are moral values all relative to societies or to individuals? What roles are played in morality by conscience, compassion, love for self, love for others, rights, and justice? What is the nature of beauty? Is beauty subjective or objective?

If you check the table of contents and the biographical sketches for some of the authors whose works are included in this book, you will see that philosophers have been selected from many different historical periods. The majority are contemporary, but some go back as far as ancient Greece, some are from medieval Europe, some are from the sixteenth, seventeenth, eighteenth, and nineteenth centuries. A diversity of historical figures are included for several reasons. The first is that philosophy is devoted to the analysis of conflicts among ideas and theories. Hence, if a clear statement of a particular point of view comes from ancient Greece or medieval Europe, its use is as valid as that of a more modern statement. More importantly, some philosophers from earlier times were truly outstanding in formulating possible answers to philosophical questions; as a consequence, their answers have become identified with their names. Contemporary philosophers speak, for example, of the *Platonic* position, the *Humean* position, the *Thomistic* position, and so on.

Because philosophy is so open-ended it is fair to say that it depends on historical traditions to give the field some stability and continuity over time. Philosophers like to use arguments and theories from the history of philosophy as convenient "landmarks" or points of departure for their own views. For this reason alone a beginning survey course must refer to historical figures and traditions.

Up to this point, I have emphasized the ways in which philosophical thinking is unique. It does not differ in every possible way from other types of thinking, however. When properly done, *all* types of thinking—whether philosophical, scientific, or everyday problem solving—have the following in common: all are clear and logical. Therefore, a study of good philosophical thinking helps us to understand what is required for good thinking in other areas as well. Indeed, the study of philosophy is self-conscious and self-reflexive, that is, devoted to a scrutiny of its own answers to questions, its own foundations, and its own standards for success and failure.

Not surprisingly, the discipline of logic was invented by Aristotle, a philosopher who lived in ancient Greece. Philosophers have always taken the lead in setting standards for clarity and logical rigor that can be applied in other areas.

BERTRAND RUSSELL

The man who has no tincture of philosophy goes through life imprisoned in the prejudices derived from common sense, from the habitual beliefs of his age or his nation, and from convictions which have grown up in his mind without the cooperation or consent of his deliberate reason. . . .

—*Problems of Philosophy*

Bertrand Russell, who died in 1970 at the age of ninety-eight, was probably the best known and most influential of twentieth century philosophers. He wrote a great many books on a wide variety of topics. His *Principia Mathematica* (written with Alfred North Whitehead) gave much of contemporary philosophy its emphasis on logical analysis. During World War I Russell was jailed as a pacifist and lost his position at Cambridge University. In the 1930s and 1940s he was a very controversial spokesman for such social causes as greater sexual freedom. In his very old age, he was an activist opposed to the Vietnam War and to nuclear weapons. Among the many honors that he received were the Order of Merit in 1949 and the Nobel Prize for literature in 1950.

CHAPTER TWO

Writing Philosophy

Being able to write philosophy well is a valuable skill for at least two reasons. The first is purely pragmatic; the grades in most philosophy courses are largely based on how well the student expresses an understanding of philosophy in writing. Term papers are frequently assigned, and examinations are often the essay type. The second reason is closely related to the first; skill at writing down one's ideas helps immensely to clarify them—or to expose their lack of clarity. Indeed, many philosophy instructors would go so far as to say that:

> If you can't write it,
> You don't know it.

It would be impossible to overestimate the importance of writing to the discipline of philosophy.

A single, broad description of philosophy would indicate that its purpose is to *clarify* our basic concepts and ways of looking at the world. Consider, for example, some of the basic issues in epistemology (theory of knowledge). Nearly all philosophers agree that *in some sense* we have knowledge of a world that *in some sense* is "out there," and that *in some sense* knowledge is based upon sensory experience, which *in some sense* depends on the nature of eyesight, hearing, the human brain, language, and so on. The major goal of philosophy is to state the *exact* sense in which all of these things are true. To do this, we must put our ideas in writing.

All of us have fuzzy concepts that rest comfortably in the back of our minds while we are speaking to others or occupying ourselves with our own thoughts. We may have in our minds several different ways to describe something, and be forced to choose only when we attempt to put our ideas in writing. At that point we can no longer be content with the thought that *somehow* we will be able to say precisely what we mean.

Philosophy is a complex discipline, which is reason enough for writing it out. By putting our views and arguments in writing, we have a chance to notice whether important points have been overlooked. However, there is also a special need for writing because philosophy so often deals with questions that most people think about at some time in their lives, but usually not in the self-conscious and thoroughly critical way that the discipline of philosophy requires. Everyone thinks about such concepts as freedom, the existence of God, knowledge, and moral responsibility. Before undertaking the disciplined study of philosophy, however, we may be inclined to believe that we have clear ideas about these matters, when in fact we do not.

Probably the best known figure in the history of philosophy is Socrates, who lived in Athens in the fourth century B.C. Socrates took it upon himself to be a gadfly to the citizens of Athens, often engaging them in philosophical conversation just to show them how little they knew. We have an opportunity to be our own gadfly by attempting to write down our philosophical beliefs. Almost surely, this will show us that we do not know as much as we think. Not only will we learn that our ideas need work, but putting them in writing will allow us to solicit the opinions of others in the most effective way.

Writing Papers for Philosophy Classes

Clarity, vigor, conciseness, smoothness, and the capacity to generate and sustain interest characterize good writing wherever it may be found. But good philosophical writing has additional unique characteristics that often give students problems in writing papers for philosophy classes.

My purpose is not to define *the* way to write a good paper. Writing styles and perspectives on philosophy vary from person to person. Therefore, there is no single way to write a good philosophical paper.

The many different kinds of philosophical papers include critical essays, historical interpretations, book reviews, papers restricted to analyzing the logical structure of arguments, and so on. I will discuss only one kind of paper—the critical essay that requires sorting through conflicting points of view to determine which is closest to being true. All of the issues covered in this book are appropriate subjects for such a paper.

To write a critical essay you must do some philosophizing of your own. You must determine what you believe to be the correct position on a controversial philosophical topic and then present arguments to defend your position. This cannot take place in a vacuum. It is absolutely essential for you to include the most important things that other writers have said on the topic. Your instructor will probably give you some idea of how extensive this section of your paper should be. For a relatively short paper on, for example, the existence of God, it may be sufficient for you to summarize the major points in the articles from the present book or a similar collection. For a longer paper you would need additional material.

If you are writing on a topic that is covered in your textbook, you absolutely must take into account (1) the assigned readings in the text that are relevant to your paper and (2) additional arguments that have been presented in class lectures or discussion. You should prepare careful notes for all of this material and any additional readings, and only after you have assembled your notes should you decide what to include in the paper.

Special requirements for writing a good critical essay are fairness, open-mindedness, and a degree of personal commitment to your position. You must be open-minded in order to see what the opposing viewpoints are. At the same time, you must have some commitment to make the assignment worthwhile to you and also to help you make your presentation compelling to those who read it.

At the heart of any critical essay is the tension between opposing viewpoints. Philosophers do not shy away from conflicts of ideas, but do insist upon clarity and fairness in presenting these conflicts. As philosophers see it—and they are not alone in this regard—the way to make progress toward the truth is to begin by presenting all sides to a controversy as fairly and completely as possible, and only then to set about discussing the strengths and weaknesses of each. You cannot determine how strong your own position is without examining opposing positions and stacking yours against them. A famous quotation from the nineteenth century philosopher John Stuart Mill aptly sums up this viewpoint: "He who knows only his own side of the case knows little of that."

The following are general guidelines for writing philosophical papers.

Rule 1. You must state clearly and precisely the goals and limitations of your paper. Good philosophical writing is self-conscious in a way that is not true of writing in other areas. You must deliberate about what you intend to cover in your paper, and then do your best to tell the reader exactly what that is. I do not mean that you must follow the old rubric, "Say what you are going to say, say it, then say what you have said." Some professors may suggest following this guideline, particularly for long compositions, but other professors may tell you *not* to follow it. For short papers (anything under six pages) space will be too limited for you to follow this guideline.

Thus you must set clear limits for your topic and its treatment. For example, in a paper on God's existence, you must state whether you are restricting your discussion to the Judeo-Christian concept of God. You must also say whether you will be discussing all of the important arguments for and against God's existence or only some of them. If you are discussing some of the arguments, or only one, you must explain why you have restricted the scope of your paper in just this way. All of this should be done as concisely as possible.

Some shortcuts are available for specifying the scope of a paper, but a person just beginning the study of philosophy may find them difficult to use. For example, professional philosophers often set the scene in their papers by referring to recent philosophical work in books or journals: "My intention in this paper is to comment on the controversy between Smith and Jones in their recent articles on free will. I shall give a new argument to show that Jones can after all defend himself against the objections raised by Smith." This procedure must be used with caution because its success requires extensive knowledge of the books and articles bearing on your topic. You need to know that the controversy between Smith and

Jones is still open and that Smith and Jones have particularly important things to say.

In addition to letting the reader know the exact goals and limitations of your paper at the beginning, you must also say why your presentation matters. You must motivate the reader to be interested in the outcome of your paper. Again, this needs to be done concisely.

Rule 2. Everything in your paper must be tied together into a logically coherent whole. Almost everything in a good philosophical paper has a role in the logical presentation of ideas. Therefore, practically nothing should be presented that is not part of (1) the statement of a philosophical position or question or (2) an argument for or against a philosophical position or answer to a question. This means that you should omit or minimize, for example, remarks about the lives of philosophers or about the times in which they lived. Aside from the logical irrelevance of such material, the typical paper for a philosophy class has no room for the extraneous—the space is needed to state precisely and completely the bare essentials.

Whenever possible, use conclusion indicators, such as "therefore," "consequently," and "it follows that," and premise indicators, such as "since," "for," and "because." Conclusion and premise indicators tell the reader explicitly that you are presenting an argument. For example, if I say, "Even toxic chemicals buried deep in the earth may eventually seep into ground water and therefore are dangerous," the statement that precedes the word "*therefore*" is the premise of a brief argument and the statement that follows the word "*therefore*" is the conclusion. The word "*therefore*" tells the reader that the conclusion of an argument is about to be given. Whenever possible, you should telegraph to the reader what you are doing in the paper.

Now, I could have said, "Even toxic chemicals buried deep in the earth are dangerous because they may eventually seep into the ground water." Here the word "because" tells the reader that a premise for an argument is about to follow. Most of your arguments will be more complex than this because they will have more than one premise to support the conclusion. Moreover, arguments are often tied together into argument chains, in which the conclusion of one argument is the premise of another. Conclusion indicators and premise indicators help the reader know exactly how an argument chain has been put together.

Rule 3. When you are criticizing a position, be sure to state that position as clearly, persuasively, and sympathetically as you can. It is unfair to state someone's position in a way that weakens it and then attack it in its altered state. Philosophers call this attacking a straw man (a substitute for the true man, that is, the true argument). The best way to avoid presenting a straw man is not to be too brief in describing a position that you are about to attack.

Rule 4. Whatever you write should be in your own words, but you should also give credit when it is due for the ideas that you include in your paper. You should use direct quotes sparingly and only if they are short. Anything quoted directly must be cited either in the body of the paper by indicating the author, work, and page numbers, or in a footnote at the bottom of the page or at the end of the paper. Citations are standardized for various disciplines, and your instructor may tell you which form is required for your class.

If you are stating a position associated with the name of a philosopher, you should mention the name. For example, "I will now discuss Saint Augustine's theory of time." However, mentioning a name should never be a substitute for clearly stating the issue. For example, the reader may not know what Augustine said about time. Moreover, what Augustine said may not be entirely clear anyway, even to someone familiar with his writings; therefore you must state what *you* believe Augustine said.

Whenever you use someone else's ideas—whether or not you quote directly—you must indicate the source of the ideas in some way. This can be done by means of a citation in a footnote or in the body of a paper, or it can sometimes be accomplished in a less formal way. For example, you could write in the body of the paper, "I will now summarize the views of James Rachels on ethical egoism from the assigned paper in the course textbook." Or you could say, "In raising objections against the position of Keith Campbell on the mind-body question, I have drawn heavily upon the works of C. D. Broad." Books and articles that you have used in writing your paper should be listed in a bibliography at the end of the paper.

Rule 5. A good philosophical paper almost always has been rewritten at least once. Philosophical thinking is difficult for everyone; there are no easy formulas and no shortcuts. Because a paper is practically never right the first time, you will almost surely need a second draft. Be sure to keep a photocopy of the final draft. Students often keep their rough drafts and hand in the only copy of the final draft. If the paper is somehow lost much work has to be done over.

In preparing to write a second draft, you should read through the first draft slowly and carefully and ask yourself the following questions:

- Is the paper free of mistakes in spelling and grammar?
- Does it read smoothly?
- Have I defined all important words whose meanings are not clear and obvious?
- Will the reader easily see why each sentence and paragraph follows the one before it?
- Is the presentation fair?
- Is it complete?
- Have enough examples been used to clarify the meaning and especially to show how general ideas are applied to specific cases?
- In stating my own view or in evaluating someone else's, have I given good reasons in defense of what I say?

In answering the last question, you need not be concerned as to whether the reader will be convinced by what you say. All you must do is to present arguments that appear to carry weight from a reasonable perspective. Your instructor, or whoever else is assigned to read your paper, may not share your perspective on a particular topic. But this should not matter at all, because your job is to demonstrate your knowledge of a good defense.

You may be wondering when and how it is appropriate to seek help in writing your paper. Your instructor may give you somewhat different guidelines, but the general rule here is that the actual writing of the first draft should be entirely your own. It is not only permissible but a good idea for you to discuss the topic with others before you sit down to write. You may appropriately ask someone to read your first draft and make comments that you can respond to in the second draft. In the final analysis, all philosophy is a cooperative enterprise between people responding to each other's arguments and counterarguments.

What follows is a short student essay that for the most part is well written. It is focused on the major competing theories in the philosophy of mind. It does not contain any extraneous material. It presents arguments in defense of the major competing theories and it presents counterarguments against some of these arguments. Real-life examples are used to illustrate points. References are given for the philosophers whose views are mentioned.

The instructor's comments in brackets contain suggestions for ways that the paper could be improved. The paper's main shortcoming is that its arguments are incomplete and it proceeds too quickly to its conclusion. These problems are difficult to avoid entirely in a short paper, but they can be diminished considerably if care is taken to state conclusions that do not go beyond the evidence, or the arguments, that are presented.

WHAT IS THE MIND

by

Todd Scherich

There are many different theories about the mind of a human being. Some philosophers claim that the mind is material while others say that the mind is immaterial and that it is separate from the body. What the mind is exactly may never be known, but some logical conclusions can be reached by observing the minds of ourselves and of others. There are two major classifications of the ways philosophers suppose the mind is related to the body. Those who believe that the mind is a material part of the body are called monists. Those who feel that the mind is separate from the body are called dualists. This paper will discuss some of the theories included in monism and dualism and attempt to defend the most logical theory. *[A good introductory paragraph]*

Monism

It does seem conceivable that the mind is an inseparable part of the body. Modern science complements *[A better choice of words is needed here]* this theory in many ways. Electrical charges can be measured in the brain and can be related to bodily movements. Chemical changes in the brain have been shown to produce certain feelings. The brain seems to have certain physical structures for each thought or feeling. A German biologist described thoughts as a secretion from

---

This paper was written for a course entitled "Introduction to the Problems of Philosophy", given at West Virginia University, Summer 1986. Used by permission of Todd Scherich.

the brain. *[A reference should be given.]* These scientific arguments do hold a lot of merit, but they cannot stand alone. *[The arguments should be stated more explicitly as arguments.]* The monistic or materialistic view gives us a picture according to which everything we do and each thought we think is an effect resulting from a physical causal antecedent. It is true that if I touch a hot kettle my reaction would be to release it quickly. The nerves in my hand would send a signal to my brain telling it that my hand is being burned. Then my brain would send a signal to the reflex muscles in my hand making it release that kettle. So far this supports the materialistic view. But, this reaction can be overriden. After I have been burnt I can decide to place my hand back on the kettle and hold it there, regardless of the pain. This would seem to be foolish, but it is true that I can take control of my bodily movements in this manner. There seems to be more to a person than physical parts.

Someone defending the monistic view would still want to debate the issue. David Hume argues that every person has a group of perceptions or impressions that rise to the occasion when a certain action takes place.[1] Pain, pleasure, and other thoughts and feelings never occur at the same time so a person does not have a particular state of mind. *[This sentence is not clear. It should be rewritten or followed by a sentence that explains it more adequately.]* A person's mind is a bundle or collection of thoughts and feelings that succeed each other and dwindle away. Hume says that the mind is not a single indivisible substance. He says that no one percept can be called the mind. *[The word "percept" should be defined, and the ideas in this paragraph should be explained further].*

I would tend to disagree with Hume. It does seem conceivable that the mind is a stream of perceptions, but there is also a factor that is above this stream. Any time I am placed in a situation I can decide what my actions are going to be. This decision making process or thought process stays with me. Feelings of pain and joy come and go but there is something inside of me that stays. Hume would describe this as memories of who I perceive myself to be, but this is not always the case. I can think about what I am going to do today and make plans for tomorrow regardless of what I remember about the past. *[This paragraph needs to be "wrapped up" with a concluding sentence.]*

Another theory of the mind that is related to materialism is epiphenomenalism. This theory is materialistic in a broad sense according to which matter or physical material is the *primary* reality but perhaps not the only reality. *[A more complete definition of "epiphenomenalism" needs to be given.]*

Epiphenomenalism states that the mind is distinct from any physical movements of the body. Thomas Huxley [2] gives the example of an experiment with a frog. The frog's spinal cord was severed so that part of its body was separated from its brain. The frog was then subjected to tests of movement. If the frog was touched it reacted the same as an uninjured frog. If it was tossed into the water, it swam like a normal frog. Huxley then concluded that the frog was a machine and would react the same if uninjured. However, this conclusion does not follow from the rest of the experiment. It was noted that if the anterior portion of the brain was removed the frog would sit unmoved forever if no irritation was provided. It seems to me that this proves that epiphenomenalism is false. If the mind is completely separate from bodily actions, why would the frog sit for such a long time when the mind is cut off, when it is clear that the frog would normally be very active? *[The author should probably note that the frog experiment can be interpreted in several different ways.]*

Dualism

Dualism is the theory that the mind is separate from the body.[3] There are two major types of dualism, parallelism and interactionism.

Parallelism is the view that the mind and body are separate and also do not interact with each other. The mind and body run side by side like two clocks on the wall. They are both reacting to the same situation, but they are independent of each other. One way the view is defined is by saying that God watches everything that happens to us and feeds our minds with the proper information. Therefore the mind does not need to receive the information from the body. Another view having to do with God is that our minds are fed when we are born and they play through our situations like a tape recording that is synchronized with a movie projector. If the philosopher defending parallelism is an atheist, he will describe the mind and body as two different aspects of reality. The mind and body view the same situation and reveal it in different ways. *[This sentence needs to be explained.]*

Parallelism cannot be taken seriously when scientific proofs are brought into the picture. It has been argued in this paper that the body affects the mind, and this rules out the parallelistic view. The philosophers that hold the parallelistic theory do so because they know that there is a separate mind and body, but they cannot find where they link. However, just because a meeting place between the mind and body cannot be found, it doesn't mean the place is nonexistent.

If parallelism can be ruled out, then we can proceed to interactionism. Interactionism is the belief that the mind and body are separate, but can interact with each other. The first type of interactionism is one-sided. This means that either the mind acts only on the body or the body acts only on the mind. We know already that the body acts on the mind. *[The author is proceeding too quickly here. This sentence seems to imply that the truth of dualism has been established. At most, the author should say something to the effect that some reason has been given to support dualism.]* Just touch something hot or soft and the sensations of pain or comfort will enter your mind. We also can perceive that our minds act upon our bodies. If we decide to move our arm or to go jogging, we will; thus we cause the body to move in a certain way.

These arguments lead us to two-sided interactionism. This form of dualism is the belief that the mind and body interact with each other. Two-sided interactionism and the concept of dualism are hard to defend and perhaps impossible to prove, but they have the advantage over the other theories stated in this paper thus far by not trying to define the mind in a limited way. *[This is a good way for the author to state the position that he wishes to defend.]*

The best way to understand dualism and to find support for it is through introspection. We can look inside ourselves and know that we have certain thoughts and feelings and also that we have power over them. The thoughts and feelings and even the power over them seem to be immaterial. They cannot be bottled or weighed. They rise above and beyond any part of our body. The power of the mind is superior to and can overcome the effects on our body. Even though the mind is perceived to be separate from the body, interaction still takes place. The place of contact cannot now be defined by scientists, but this does not show that it does not exist.

In conclusion, it seems that materialism, epiphenomenalism, parallelism, and one-sided interactionism are all inadequate as definitions of the mind. The mind can best be described in the dualistic, two-sided interactionistic manner. Although this theory lacks a specific description of the mind, it does lead us to the most correct view of the mind.

Notes

1. David Hume, *A Treatise of Human Nature*, Book I, Part IV, Section 6. *[A good way to give references to classical works that have appeared in many editions.]*

2. Thomas Huxley, "On the Hypothesis that Animals are Automata and Its History" in *Methods and Results*. New York: D. Appleton and Co.

3. Some of the arguments regarding dualism are taken from chapter 3 of C. D. Broad, *The Mind and Its Place in Nature*. London: Routledge and Kegan Paul, 1925.

The Process of Writing

Individuals differ in the way they actually write their papers. For some, writing a detailed outline ahead of time is helpful. Others write out a list of sentences that capture various points to be made in the paper; these sentences are then reworked and incorporated into the paper. Still others focus on arguments, listing premises and conclusions. Some writers find that a series of short quotations or paraphrases from the relevant readings "inspire" them to put their own ideas down on paper.

You may need to experiment a bit to see what works best for you. The only rule (unless you are an absolute genius with a photographic memory) is that you *must* begin with an outline or extensive notes of some kind. You cannot sit down with a blank sheet of paper in front of you and simply start to write your paper. Don't even attempt to do this—it can be an unnerving experience! In contrast, if you start out with a sufficient number of notes or with an outline, and if you have spent time beforehand thinking about the subject of your paper and perhaps discussing it with others, you will find that the actual writing is not particularly difficult.

Some people find that the process of writing is the most satisfying when they try to write a polished first draft. If you follow this method, you will proceed more slowly, but you will probably have less to do in the second draft. Others feel better about writing if it proceeds more quickly, even if less perfectly. At least they have gotten something down that can be revised extensively in the next draft.

In writing both first and second drafts, you will probably find that you need to shift around sections of your paper, add new sections, change the order of or rewrite sentences, and so on. If you have access to a word processor and the skills to use it, making changes in your paper will be relatively easy. If you do not have the use of a word processor, you should work out a notational system for rearranging parts of your paper. A suggestion: put sections in brackets, or circle them, and give each a number; then place the number in the manuscript where the section is to be inserted. These numbers serve as markers when your paper is typed.

Writing Short In-Class Essays

Most students agree that writing in-class essays for a philosophy course is difficult. It is like writing a term paper in miniature, except for a major difference—only an extremely brief amount of time is available.

Does the taking of essay tests need to be as threatening and unpleasant as it often is? Very likely not. Students often fail to appreciate the fact that philosophy is a highly organized and integrated discipline. Almost nothing in philosophy is arbitrary; therefore, preparing for an essay test in philosophy is not like preparing for an essay test in a discipline such as history, where sheer memory is often needed to bring things together. In philosophy, logical relevance ties things together—philosophers say things for reasons, and other philosophers object to these things for reasons. You need not rely upon sheer memory because you can follow the *internal order* of philosophy in reconstructing positions and arguments.

Although two basic types of questions may appear on an essay test, the preparation is similar for each.

In *historical* (or *personality-oriented*) questions, you may be asked:

- What was Berkeley's theory of perception?
- In what ways can Berkeley's theory of perception be seen as a development of Locke's theory?
- State the views of some philosophers who rejected Berkeley's theory of perception.

In *topical* questions you may be asked:

- What is meant by soft determinism?
- What are all of the arguments in defense of soft determinism?
- What are all of the arguments against soft determinism?

Philosophy instructors want a concise statement of everything that is logically relevant to an answer, *and nothing more*. They are not impressed by the quantity of material written. They definitely do not want you to write down everything that you can think of that might have to do with the question. Therefore, taking a test should not cause anxiety as long as you understand the positions and arguments beforehand. Everything will then tie together, and the necessary information will not be especially difficult to memorize. If you are not sure whether you understand the material for a test, try writing it out ahead of time. If you are unable to do this, you need help. Ask questions in or out of class that will clarify the material. Do not hesitate to do this. Almost all instructors welcome questions from students who have made good efforts on their own to read and understand the material.

A piece of practical advice. Even though time is short for essay tests, you should allow a few minutes at the end of the period to read over both the questions and what you have written. Careless mistakes are easy to make when writing hurriedly. You may leave out things that you thought you had put in, you may have misread a question and consequently not answered all parts completely, you may have transposed the names of philosophers, and so on. These mistakes can often be corrected in a very small amount of time.

The Philosophical Spirit in Writing

The mark of a rational person is the ability to change his or her mind when confronted with good reasons to do so. Obviously true? No doubt you will agree that it is. But living up to this ideal is not as easy as it may seem; giving up any beliefs that one has a commitment to is difficult.

The philosophical spirit requires that you be prepared, while writing a paper, to change your mind after examining arguments in support of views contrary to your own. The philosophical spirit requires that you not be an advocate, that is, someone who presents only the affirmative case, not the negative one. Good examples of advocates are defense attorneys and writers of advertisements.

The true philosopher follows the trail of argument wherever it may lead. (You could call this the "Philosopher's Hippocratic Oath.") If the argument reinforces beliefs fondly held, fine. If the argument undermines these beliefs, so be it.

PLATO

Is not this the most reprehensible form of ignorance, that of thinking one knows what one does not know?

—*Apology*

If the just man is good, the business of harming people, whether friends or not, must belong to his opposite, the unjust . . . . It is never right to harm anyone.

—*Republic*

As the soul is immortal, has been born often and has seen all things here and in the underworld, there is nothing that it has not learned; so it is in no way surprising that it can recollect the things it knew before.

Meno

Plato lived from 427 to 347 B.C. in Athens. If a single philosopher can be chosen as the most important and influential of all philosophers, Plato is the one. As a young man, he knew Socrates and was very much influenced by the example of Socrates' life. In turn, Plato was the teacher of Aristotle, whose philosophy has also been extremely influential. During his long life, Plato was a writer, a teacher at the Academy that he founded, and, for several years, a political advisor to the ruler of the city of Syracuse.

Plato believed in the existence of an unseen world that "transcends" the material world. He believed in the existence of a human soul that can survive the death of the body. He believed in the possibility of an ideal type of society that would be ruled by a "philosopher king," and in which the lives of everyone would be oriented toward Beauty, Truth, Harmony, and the "Form of the Good." Most of Plato's writings are in dialogue form, with Socrates as the principal speaker.

CHAPTER THREE

The existence of mystical states absolutely overthrows the pretension of non-mystical states to be the sole and ultimate dictators of what we may believe.

—*William James*

In matters of the intellect, follow your reason as far as it will take you.

—*Thomas Huxley*

God's Existence

Because philosophy asks the most basic questions about the world and human life, the question of whether God exists necessarily belongs at its heart. What could make a greater difference to our understanding of ourselves and the world we live in? The *kind* of difference in question will depend upon the meaning that we attach to the word "God". The reading selections in this chapter are confined for the most part to the Judeo-Christian concept of God, in which God is thought of as the "all-powerful," "all knowing," "completely good" "creator of the world." (Some other concepts of God are referred to in the opening reading selection for chapter 4.) For the sake of simplicity in what follows, "God" should be understood to mean "Judeo-Christian God."

If God exists, human life belongs within a purposeful moral framework of a kind that it otherwise lacks, and the world we inhabit has a cause and a destiny that otherwise do not belong to it. Such contemporary concerns as the threat of nuclear war and the possibility of genetic restructuring of the human race take on very different meanings from what they have if God does not exist. Indeed, if God does *not* exist, the implications are profound for a great many traditionally held beliefs in ethics, the philosophy of mind, and other areas. Practically everyone has at some time very much wanted an answer to the following question: As members of the human race are we, or are we not, all alone in having to solve our most difficult problems and in having to give ultimate direction to our lives?

In philosophical discussions of the question of whether God exists, one of three basic positions may be defended:

1. Theism, the belief that God exists
2. Atheism, the belief that God does not exist
3. Agnosticism, a withholding of judgment as to whether God exists, or the belief that God's existence can neither be proven nor disproven

The distinctions between theism, atheism, and agnosticism have to do with the *content* of one's beliefs. Another set of distinctions have to do with the *grounds* for one's beliefs. These are (1) belief grounded on arguments or reasons and (2) belief grounded on faith.

Philosophers have been concerned primarily with the first of these, belief grounded on arguments or reasons. They distinguish between the following kinds of arguments that may be offered in defense of the belief that God exists:

1. Arguments based purely on analysis of concepts, such as the concept of an all-perfect being
2. Arguments based on analysis of what is taken to be an important feature of the world, such as order or design (such arguments typically involve analysis of concepts as well)
3. Arguments based on the experiences of people, such as when someone seems to feel the presence of God or some other supernatural (or spiritual) being (such arguments may also involve analysis of concepts or examination of important features of the world)

In the reading selections for this chapter, the one from Saint Anselm is of the first type; it is purely an analysis of concepts, especially the concept of God. According to Anselm, if we "unpack" the concept of God—"a being than which nothing greater can be conceived"—we will see that God must exist. That is, we will see that the concept of God is necessarily not a "mere concept" like the concept of a unicorn, but instead really refers to an actual being in the world, namely God. Gaunilo, a contemporary of Anselm in the eleventh century, responds to Anselm's version of what has become known as the Ontological Argument. The selection from George Bowles examines several possible objections to the Ontological Argument.

The selection from Samuel Clarke contains an argument of the second type, which has come to be known as the Cosmological Argument. William Rowe responds to it. The selections from both William James and Jonathan Edwards contain discussions of arguments of the third type, all of which have come to be known among contemporary philosophers as Arguments from Religious Experience.

The first reading selection is from a famous late nineteenth century writer, Thomas Huxley, who defends agnosticism.

Because the present chapter focuses on discussions of arguments, it may be helpful to say a few words about arguments in general. Those of you who have taken logic or some other course in philosophy are likely to be thoroughly acquainted with the points that immediately follow, but those of you who are studying philosophy for the first time should find them of some interest.

The word *argument* has a *non*philosophical meaning that calls up images of shouting and quarreling, for example, "He was shot to death in a tavern during an argument." In the philosophical sense, an argument is an *intended statement of reasons for believing something to be true*. In a good argument, the reasons meet the following conditions:

1. The statement or statements that contain the reasons are true. These statements are called the premises of the argument.
2. The premises logically support the conclusion of the argument.

Two different types of argument can be identified, depending on how strong is the logical support that the premises give to the conclusion. Consider the following examples:

Argument A

Premise 1. All grizzly bears are vicious.
Premise 2. Vicious animals should not be given as pets.
Conclusion. You should not give a grizzly bear cub to your baby sister as a pet.

In this argument the premises give very strong logical support to the conclusion.

Argument B

Premise 1. Most, but not all, cocker spaniel puppies grow up to be good-natured pets.
Premise 2. John has given a cocker spaniel puppy to his sister.
Conclusion. John has given a good-natured pet to his sister.

The logical support provided by the premises in argument B is weaker than the logical support provided in argument A. In A, the truth of the premises *guarantees* the truth of the conclusion. In B, the truth of the premises does not guarantee the truth of the conclusion, but instead makes it *probable*. Arguments intended to be like A are called *deductive*, while arguments intended to be like B are called *inductive*.

I have included the phrase "intended to be like" in the above descriptions of deductive and inductive arguments because both types of arguments obviously may fail. In analyzing arguments for God's existence, your job is to determine whether they are successful—whether the deductive ones really do guarantee that God exists and whether the inductive ones really do make God's existence probable.

WILLIAM JAMES

Conceived objects must show sensible effects or else be disbelieved.

—*Principles of Psychology*

Pragmatism . . . asks its usual question, "Grant an idea or belief to be true," it says, "what concrete difference will its being true make in any one's actual life?" How will the truth be realized? What experiences will be different from those which would obtain if the belief were false? What, in short, is the truth's cash-value in experiential terms?

—*Pragmatism*

William James (1842–1910), a noted American philosopher and psychologist whose work has greatly influenced both the academic and nonacademic world, was one of the founders of the philosophy of pragmatism. He studied in European universities and obtained a degree from Harvard Medical School. He taught physiology, then psychology and philosophy at a time when Josiah Royce and George Santayana were also teaching at Harvard. James was interested in and wrote about a wide range of issues in both psychology and philosophy: mental illness, the theories of Sigmund Freud, the experience of religious conversion, the experiences of mystics, the free will question, the nature of truth, the nature of the human soul, and many others. The movement called *spiritualism* was active during James' lifetime, and he carried out extensive investigations of claims by spiritualists. James was very popular as a public lecturer. To his friends and colleagues he was energetic and enthusiastic, but privately he suffered from depression and self-doubt. Several of his books have become classics, including *Principles of Psychology, The Will to Believe, Varieties of Religious Experience,* and *Pragmatism*.

THOMAS HUXLEY

Agnosticism

* * * * *

Looking back nearly fifty years, I see myself as a boy, whose education has been interrupted, and who, intellectually, was left, for some years, altogether to his own devices. At that time, I was a voracious and omnivorous reader; a dreamer and speculator of the first water, well endowed with that splendid courage in attacking any and every subject, which is the blessed compensation of youth and inexperience.

* * * * *

When I reached intellectual maturity and began to ask myself whether I was an atheist, a theist, or a pantheist; a materialist or an idealist; a Christian or a freethinker; I found that the more I learned and reflected, the less ready was the answer; until, at last, I came to the conclusion that I had neither art nor part with any of these denominations, except the last. The one thing in which most of these good people were agreed was the one thing in which I differed from them. They were quite sure they had attained a certain "gnosis," [knowledge] had, more or less successfully, solved the problem of existence; while I was quite sure I had not, and had a pretty strong conviction that the problem was insoluble. And, with Hume and Kant on my side, I could not think myself presumptuous in holding fast by that opinion.

* * * * *

This was my situation when I had the good fortune to find a place among the members of that remarkable confraternity of antagonists, long since deceased, but of green and pious memory, the Metaphysicial Society. Every variety of philosophical and theological opinion was represented there, and expressed itself with entire openness; most of my colleagues were *-ists* of one sort or another; and, however kind and friendly they might be, I, the man without a rag of a label to cover himself with, could not fail to have some of the uneasy feelings which must have beset the historical fox when, after leaving the trap in which his tail remained, he presented himself to his normally elongated companions. So I took thought, and

---

Thomas Huxley (1825–1895) was an English biologist who made many important discoveries. As a popular writer, he became known for his defense of the theory of evolution, but he also wrote on a number of philosophical topics, including the mind-body problem. His most important books are Evidence as to Man's Place in Nature, The Physical Basis of Life, *and* Evolution and Ethics.

From *Science and Christian Tradition*, 1898.

invented what I conceived to be the appropriate title of "agnostic." It came into my head as suggestively antithetic to the "gnostic" of Church history, who professed to know so much about the very things of which I was ignorant; and I took the earliest opportunity of parading it at our Society, to show that I, too, had a tail, like the other foxes. To my great satisfaction, the term took; and when the *Spectator* had stood godfather to it, any suspicion in the minds of respectable people, that a knowledge of its parentage might have awakened was, of course, completely lulled.

That is the history of the origin of the terms "agnostic" and "agnosticism"; and it will be observed that it does not quite agree with the confident assertion of the reverend Principal of King's College, that "the adoption of the term agnostic is only an attempt to shift the issue, and that it involves a mere evasion" in relation to the Church and Christianity.[1]

The last objection (I rejoice as much as my readers must do, that it is the last) which I have to take to Dr. Wace's deliverance before the Church Congress arises, I am sorry to say, on a question of morality.

"It is, and it ought to be," authoritatively declares this official representative of Christian ethics, "an unpleasant thing for a man to have to say plainly that he does not believe in Jesus Christ" (*l.c.* p. 254).

Whether it is so depends, I imagine, a good deal on whether the man was brought up in a Christian household or not. I do not see why it should be "unpleasant" for a Mahommedan or Buddhist to say so. But that "it ought to be" unpleasant for any man to say anything which he sincerely, and after due deliberation, believes, is, to my mind, a proposition of the most profoundly immoral character. I verily believe that the great good which has been effected in the world by Christianity has been largely counteracted by the pestilent doctrine on which all the Churches have insisted, that honest disbelief in their more or less astonishing creeds is a moral offence, indeed a sin of the deepest dye, deserving and involving the same future retribution as murder and robbery. If we could only see, in one view, the torrents of hypocrisy and cruelty, the lies, the slaughter, the violations of every obligation of humanity, which have flowed from this source along the course of the history of Christian nations, our worst imaginations of Hell would pale beside the vision.

A thousand times, no! It ought *not* to be unpleasant to say that which one honestly believes or disbelieves. That it so constantly is painful to do so, is quite enough obstacle to the progress of mankind in that most valuable of all qualities, honesty of word or of deed, without erecting a sad concomitant of human weakness into something to be admired and cherished. The bravest of soldiers often, and very naturally, "feel it unpleasant" to go into action; but a court-martial which did its duty would make short work of the officer who promulgated the doctrine that his men *ought* to feel their duty unpleasant.

* * * * *

It is quite true that the ground of

1. *Report of the Church Congress*, Manchester, 1888, p. 252.

every one of our actions, and the validity of all our reasonings, rest upon the great act of faith, which leads us to take the experience of the past as a safe guide in our dealings with the present and the future. From the nature of ratiocination, it is obvious that the axioms, on which it is based, cannot be demonstrated by ratiocination. It is also a trite observation that, in the business of life, we constantly take the most serious action upon evidence of an utterly insufficient character. But it is surely plain that faith is not necessarily entitled to dispense with ratiocination because ratiocination cannot dispense with faith as a starting-point; and that because we are often obliged, by the pressure of events, to act on very bad evidence, it does not follow that it is proper to act on such evidence when the pressure is absent.

The writer of the epistle to the Hebrews tells us that "faith is the assurance of things hoped for, the proving of things not seen." In the authorised version, "substance" stands for "assurance," and "evidence" for "proving."

I fancy we shall be not far from the mark if we take the writer to have had in his mind the profound psychological truth, that men constantly feel certain about things for which they strongly hope, but have no evidence, in the legal or logical sense of the word; and he calls this feeling "faith." I may have the most absolute faith that a friend has not committed the crime of which he is accused. In the early days of English history, if my friend could have obtained a few more compurgators of a like robust faith, he would have been acquitted. At the present day, if I tendered myself as a witness on that score, the judge would tell me to stand down, and the youngest barrister would smile at my simplicity. Miserable indeed is the man who has not such faith in some of his fellow-men—only less miserable than the man who allows himself to forget that such faith is not, strictly speaking, evidence; and when his faith is disappointed, as will happen now and again, turns Timon and blames the universe for his own blunders. And so, if a man can find a friend, the hypostasis of all his hopes, the mirror of his ethical ideal, in the Jesus of any, or all, of the Gospels, let him live by faith in that ideal. Who shall or can forbid him? But let him not delude himself with the notion that his faith is evidence of the objective reality of that in which he trusts. Such evidence is to be obtained only by the use of the methods of science, as applied to history and to literature, and it amounts at present to very little.

* * * * *

Agnosticism, in fact, is not a creed, but a method, the essence of which lies in the rigorous application of a single principle. That principle is of great antiquity; it is as old as Socrates; as old as the writer who said, "Try all things, hold fast by that which is good;" it is the foundation of the Reformation, which simply illustrated the axiom that every man should be able to give a reason for the faith that is in him; it is the great principle of Descartes; it is the fundamental axiom of modern science. Positively the principle may be expressed: In matters of the intellect, follow your reason as far as it will take you, without regard to any other consideration. And negatively: In matters of the intellect do not pretend that conclusions are certain which are not demonstrated or demonstrable. That I take to be the agnostic faith, which if a man keep whole and undefiled, he shall not be ashamed to look the universe in the face, whatever the future may have in store for him.

COMMENTS ■ QUESTIONS

1. Huxley tells the story of how he came to coin the word "agnosticism," which has since become a part of our vocabulary along with the terms "atheist," "theist," and "pantheist" (the last means "one who believes that God is the entire universe"). Are more terms needed? Or are you content to apply to yourself one of the above terms as an adequate label for your beliefs regarding the question of God's existence?
2. According to Huxley, agnosticism is based upon a single, supremely important principle. He writes, "In matters of the intellect, follow your reason as far as it will take you, without regard for any other consideration [and] do not pretend that conclusions are certain which are not demonstrable." Is this principle as important as Huxley believes it is?
3. Huxley distinguishes between two senses of the word "faith": (a) belief in the most basic principles of reasoning (he calls them axioms), which themselves cannot be demonstrated by reason, and (b) belief in something that has not been proven but which *is* open to investigation (He says: "I do not very much care to speak of anything as 'unknowable' "). As Huxley sees it, faith in the first sense is quite acceptable, but faith in the second sense is an "abomination." Do you accept Huxley's view of these matters? As an agnostic, he holds that most of the beliefs of Christianity are examples of faith in the second sense. Do you believe that Huxley's agnosticism is defensible?

SAINT ANSELM

The Ontological Argument

And so, Lord, do thou, who dost give understanding to faith, give me, so far as thou knowest it to be profitable, to understand that thou art as we believe; and that thou art that which we believe. And, indeed, we believe that thou art a being than which nothing greater can be conceived. Or is there no such nature, since the fool hath said in his heart, there is no God? (Psalms xiv. 1). But, at any rate, this very fool, when he hears of this being of which I speak—a being than which nothing greater can be conceived—understands what he hears, and what he understands is in his understanding; although he does not understand it to exist.

For, it is one thing for an object to be in the understanding, and another to understand that the object exists. When a painter first conceives of what he will afterwards perform, he has it in his understanding, but he does not yet understand it to be, because he has not yet performed it. But after he has made the painting, he both has it in his understanding, and he understands that it exists, because he has made it.

Hence, even the fool is convinced that something exists in the understanding, at least, than which nothing greater can be conceived. For, when he hears of this, he understands it. And whatever is understood, exists in the understanding. And assuredly that, than which nothing greater can be conceived, cannot exist in the understanding alone. For, suppose it exists in the understanding alone: then it can be conceived to exist in reality; which is greater.

Therefore, if that, than which nothing greater can be conceived, exists in the understanding alone, the very being, than which nothing greater can be conceived, is one, than which a greater can be conceived. But obviously this is impossible. Hence, there is no doubt that there exists a being, than which nothing greater can be conceived, and it exists both in the understanding and in reality.

Saint Anselm (1033–1109) was archbishop of Canterbury and one of the greatest of the medieval philosophers.

From *St. Anselm: Basic Writings*, translated by S. N. Deane, 1903. Anselm's *Proslogion* was written in the eleventh century.

GAUNILO

On Behalf of the Fool

If one doubts or denies the existence of a being of such a nature that nothing greater than it can be conceived, he receives this answer:

The existence of this being is proved, in the first place, by the fact that he himself, in his doubt or denial regarding this being, already has it in his understanding; for in hearing it spoken of he understands what is spoken of. It is proved, therefore, by the fact that what he understands must exist not only in his understanding, but in reality also.

And the proof of this is as follows.—It is a greater thing to exist both in the understanding and in reality than to be in the understanding alone. And if this being is in the understanding alone, whatever has even in the past existed in reality will be greater than this being. And so that which was greater than all beings will be less than some being, and will not be greater than all: which is a manifest contradiction.

And hence, that which is greater than all, already proved to be in the understanding, must exist not only in the understanding, but also in reality: for otherwise it will not be greater than all other beings.

The fool might make this reply:

This being is said to be in my understanding already, only because I understand what is said. Now could it not with equal justice be said that I have in my understanding all manner of unreal objects, having absolutely no existence in themselves, because I understand these things if one speaks of them, whatever they may be?

Unless indeed it is shown that this being is of such a character that it cannot be held in concept like all unreal objects, or objects whose existence is uncertain: and hence I am not able to conceive of it when I hear of it, or to hold it in concept; but I must understand it and have it in my understanding; because, it seems, I cannot conceive of it in any other way than by understanding it, that is, by comprehending in my knowledge its existence in reality.

* * * * *

Let us notice also the point touched on above, with regard to this being which is greater than all which can be conceived, and which, it is said, can be none other than God himself. I, so far as actual knowledge of the object, either from its specific or general character, is concerned, am as little able to con-

Gaunilo was an eleventh century Benedictine monk of Marmoutier.

From *St. Anselm: Basic Writings*, translated by S. N. Deane, 1903. Guanilo's "On Behalf of the Fool" was written in the eleventh century.

ceive of this being when I hear of it, or to have it in my understanding, as I am to conceive of or understand God himself: whom, indeed, for this very reason I can conceive not to exist. For I do not know that reality itself which God is, nor can I form a conjecture of that reality from some other like reality. For you yourself assert that that reality is such that there can be nothing else like it.

For, suppose that I should hear something said of a man absolutely unknown to me, of whose very existence I was unaware. Through that special or general knowledge by which I know what man is, or what men are, I could conceive of him also, according to the reality itself, which man is. And yet it would be possible, if the person who told me of him deceived me, that the man himself, of whom I conceived, did not exist; since that reality according to which I conceived of him, though a no less indisputable fact, was not that man, but any man.

Hence, I am not able, in the way in which I should have this unreal being in concept or in understanding, to have that being of which you speak in concept or in understanding, when I hear the word *God* or the words, *a being greater than all other beings*. For I can conceive of the man according to a fact that is real and familiar to me: but of God, or a being greater than all others, I could not conceive at all, except merely according to the word. And an object can hardly or never be conceived according to the word alone.

For when it is so conceived, it is not so much the word itself (which is, indeed, a real thing—that is, the sound of the letters and syllables) as the signification of the word, when heard, that is conceived. But it is not conceived as by one who knows what is generally signified by the word; by whom, that is, it is conceived according to a reality and in true conception alone. It is conceived as by a man who does not know the object, and conceives of it only in accordance with the movement of his mind produced by hearing the word, the mind attempting to image for itself the signification of the word that is heard. And it would be surprising if in the reality of fact it could ever attain to this.

Thus, it appears, and in no other way, this being is also in my understanding, when I hear and understand a person who says that there is a being greater than all conceivable beings. So much for the assertion that this supreme nature already is in my understanding.

But that this being must exist, not only in the understanding but also in reality, is thus proved to me:

If it did not so exist, whatever exists in reality would be greater than it. And so the being which has been already proved to exist in my understanding, will not be greater than all other beings.

I still answer: if it should be said that a being which cannot be even conceived in terms of any fact, is in the understanding, I do not deny that this being is, accordingly, in my understanding. But since through this fact it can in no wise attain to real existence also, I do not yet concede to it that existence at all, until some certain proof of it shall be given.

For he who says that this being exists, because otherwise the being which is greater than all will not be greater than all, does not attend strictly enough to what he is saying. For I do not yet say, no, I even deny or doubt that this being is greater than any real object. Nor do I concede to it any other existence than this (if it should be called existence) which it has when the mind, according to a word merely heard, tries to form the image of an object absolutely unknown to it.

How, then, is the veritable existence of that being proved to me from the assumption, by hypothesis, that it is greater than all other beings? For I should still deny this, or doubt your demonstration of it, to this extent, that I should not admit that this being is in my understanding and concept even in the way in which many objects whose real existence is uncertain and doubtful, are in my understanding and concept. For it should be proved first that this being itself really exists somewhere; and then, from the fact that it is greater than all, we shall not hesitate to infer that it also subsists in itself.

For example: it is said that somewhere in the ocean is an island, which, because of the difficulty, or rather the impossibility, of discovering what does not exist, is called the lost island. And they say that this island has an inestimable wealth of all manner of riches and delicacies in greater abundance than is told of the Islands of the Blest; and that having no owner or inhabitant, it is more excellent than all other countries, which are inhabited by mankind, in the abundance with which it is stored.

Now if some one should tell me that there is such an island, I should easily understand his words, in which there is no difficulty. But suppose that he went on to say, as if by a logical inference: "You can no longer doubt that this island which is more excellent than all lands exists somewhere, since you have no doubt that it is in your understanding. And since it is more excellent not to be in the understanding alone, but to exist both in the understanding and in reality, for this reason it must exist. For if it does not exist, any land which really exists will be more excellent than it; and so the island already understood by you to be more excellent will not be more excellent."

If a man should try to prove to me by such reasoning that this island truly exists, and that its existence should no longer be doubted, either I should believe that he was jesting, or I know not which I ought to regard as the greater fool: myself, supposing that I should allow this proof; or him, if he should suppose that he had established with any certainty the existence of this island. For he ought to show first that the hypothetical excellence of this island exists as a real and indubitable fact, and in no wise as any unreal object, or one whose existence is uncertain, in my understanding.

COMMENTS ■ QUESTIONS

1. Before deciding whether you accept Anselm's argument or Gaunilo's objection to it, you should read the following selection by George Bowles, which contains an analysis of both Anselm's argument and Gaunilo's objections. Once you have read Bowles's analysis you should ask yourself whether Anselm's Ontological Argument is sound. If you believe that it is not, is this because you believe that one or more of its premises are false? Which ones? What are your reasons for believing them false? If you believe that the premises are all true but that the conclusion does not follow from the premises, what are your reasons for believing thusly?
2. Gaunilo objects to Anselm's claim that "a being than which nothing greater can be conceived exists in the understanding at least." The first of Gaunilo's objections is that he believes there is no clear concept of God. He can, he says, think clearly the *words* "that which is greater than everything," but cannot think clearly what is *signified* by these words. Therefore, according to Gaunilo, it is not correct to say that the "supreme nature" exists already in the mind. What is your response to these remarks?
3. Gaunilo's second line of attack against Anselm is by way of analogy. He claims his strategy is to produce an argument that has the same structure as Anselm's but is obviously unsound (Anselm would deny that Gaunilo succeeds). Because the analogous argument is unsound, Gaunilo says that *Anselm's* argument must be unsound:—if you *could* show that God exists in the way that Anselm attempts to do it, you could as well show that a most perfect island exists. But that is absurd. Therefore Anselm's argument cannot be a good argument. Do you believe that Gaunilo's strategy is successful? Are there philosophically relevant *differences* between the concept of God and the concept of a most perfect island that one might appeal to in defending Anselm's Ontological Argument?

GEORGE BOWLES

Anselm's Ontological Argument for the Existence of God

Anselm's Ontological Argument for the existence of God is probably the most controversial of all arguments for God's existence. I shall first analyze the argument and then present objections and replies, proceeding from the more naive to the more sophisticated. The objections and replies should help you better to understand and appreciate Anselm's argument.

I Analysis

Anselm's argument is like some of the proofs you probably did in geometry, in that it is an indirect proof (also called a "*reductio ad absurdum*"). That means that, instead of trying to prove God's existence directly, Anselm tries to show that the supposition that God does *not* exist leads logically to a contradiction. Since nothing true logically entails a contradiction, Anselm indirectly reaches the conclusion that God exists. (In the following analysis of the argument, all quotations are from the Deane translation.)

1. (Premise) God is something "than which nothing greater can be conceived".

2. (Conclusion from lines 2a and 2b) ". . . something exists in the understanding, at least, than which nothing greater can be conceived." Proof:

 2a. (Premise) All men (believers and unbelievers alike) understand when they hear of something than which nothing greater can be conceived.

 2b. (Premise) ". . . whatever is understood, exists in the understanding."

3. (Premise) Something that existed *both* in the understanding *and* in reality would be greater (as a being) than an otherwise identical thing that existed in the understanding but not in reality.

4. (Conclusion from 4a–d) If something than which nothing greater can be conceived exists in the understanding but not in reality, then it is something than which something greater can be conceived. Proof:

 4a. (Hypothetical premise) Suppose something (call it "G1") than which nothing greater can be conceived exists in the understanding but not in reality.

 4b. (Conclusion from 4a) It can be conceived to exist in reali-

---

George Bowles holds a doctorate in philosophy from Stanford University. He teaches philosophy at George Washington University.

Used by permission of the author.

ty also. That is, an otherwise identical thing (call it "G2") can be conceived to exist in reality as well as in the understanding.

4c. (Conclusion from 4b and 3) The thing we conceive to exist both in the understanding and in reality is greater (as a being) than the otherwise identical thing that exists in the understanding but not in reality. That is, G2 is greater (as a being) than G1.

4d. (Conclusion from 4c) The thing than which nothing greater can be conceived is something than which something greater can be conceived. That is, G1 is a thing than which something greater (namely, G2) can be conceived.

5. (Premise) It is impossible that something than which nothing greater can be conceived is something than which a greater thing can be conceived.

6. (Conclusion from 4 and 5) It is *false* that something than which nothing greater can be conceived exists in the understanding but not in reality.

7. (Conclusion from 2 and 6) There exists something than which nothing greater can be conceived.

8. (Conclusion from 1 and 7) God exists.

II Objections and Replies

Objection 1. Among the earliest objections that occur to students when they first encounter Anselm's Ontological Argument is the following. "From the fact that you can think of something, it doesn't follow that it exists. Therefore, from the fact that we can think of something than which nothing greater can be conceived, it does not follow that it exists. So, Anselm's argument fails." [1]

Reply. This objection attacks the argument—

1. (Premise) We can think of something than which nothing greater can be conceived.

2. (Conclusion from 1) There exists something than which nothing greater can be conceived.

—, which is obviously invalid (that is, its conclusion does not follow from its premise). But it is not Anselm's argument. For, although its premise is equivalent to line 2a of the Ontological Argument, Anselm's proof does not try to show that God exists merely on the grounds that we can think of Him. It has several more premises and a more complicated structure than the argument that Objection 1 attacks. And so, it is untouched by Objection 1.

Objection 2. A similar objection is this: "All the Ontological Argument proves is that if you conceive of something than which a greater cannot be conceived, then you must also conceive of it as existing. But from the fact that you must conceive of something as existing, it does not follow that that thing does in fact exist. Therefore, the argument does not prove the existence of anything." [2]

Reply. What Anselm's argument proves, if it proves anything at all, is its conclusion. And its conclusion is

1. Cf. Gaunilon, "On Behalf of the Fool", in Anselm, *St. Anselm: Basic Writings*, tr. S. N. Deane (La Salle, Illinois: Open Court Publishing Company, 1962), Para. 5, pp. 149–50.

2. Cf. Wilhelm Windleband, *A History of Philosophy*, tr. James H. Tufts (New York: Harper & Row, 1901), Vol. I, p. 293.

that God exists. Therefore, if the proof is sound—that is, if its premises are true and its conclusion follows from them—, then Anselm has proved not merely that God must be conceived as existing but that He actually does exist.

Objection 3. The next objection says that Anselm's argument is unsound because it presupposes that we can conceive God. For it says (line 2a) that even the unbeliever understands what is meant by "something than which nothing greater can be conceived". And it also says (line 4b) that something than which nothing greater can be conceived can be conceived to exist both in the understanding and in reality, which would be impossible if that than which nothing greater can be conceived were inconceivable. But that presupposition is false, as Anselm himself says later (*Proslogion*, Chapter 15): "thou art a being greater than can be conceived." So, God cannot be conceived. Hence, lines 2a and 4b are false.[3]

Reply. There is something to this objection. It is true that Anselm's Ontological Argument requires that we be able to conceive God. It is also true that Anselm later denies that God is conceivable. In responding to Gaunilon, Anselm tried to resolve this apparent contradiction by saying that, although God is not *comprehensively* conceivable, we can conceive Him to the extent that we can understand the phrase "something than which nothing greater can be conceived". That phrase is not nonsense to us: we understand it. Hence, to that degree, we understand the being to which it refers.[4]

Objection 4. This objection says that the argument is unsound, because lines 2 and 2b are both false premises. For if something is understood, then there is an understanding of it; but the thing that is understood need not exist, even in the understanding. It is not something than which nothing greater can be conceived, but the understanding *of* such a being, that exists in the understanding. In other words, if anything exists in the understanding when we understand such a being, it is not that being itself but the idea, or concept, *of* it. So, Anselm's claims that (2b) "... whatever is understood, exists in the understanding" and (2) "... something exists in the understanding, at least, than which nothing greater can be conceived" are both false. The argument, therefore, is unsound.

Reply. To this objection one might reply as follows. The objection presupposes that, when Anselm says that something than which nothing greater can be conceived exists "in the understanding", he means that it exists in the mind; for that, presumably, is where ideas or concepts would exist. But this is untrue: Anselm "does not mean this to be taken in any psychological sense, as though there were existents of two distinct kinds, real existents and mental existents."[5] What he means, rather, is that something than which nothing greater can be conceived exists *as an object of the understanding*—that is, as something that is under-

3. Based on Gaunilon, op. cit., Para. 4, pp. 148–9.

4. Anselm, "Anselm's Apologetic"; in Anselm, op. cit., I, p. 156 and IX, pp. 168–9.

5. M. J. Charlesworth, *St. Anselm's* Proslogion (London: Oxford University Press, 1965), p. 63.

stood.[6] Even if such a being does not exist in the mind, it may still exist as an object that is understood. And so lines 2 and 2b may not be false after all.

But this reply depends on the assumption that every object that is understood exists, and this assumption seems to be false. For we can understand impossible objects, like round squares, although they do not exist.

Objection 5. This objection challenges the soundness of the argument by trying to show that line 3 is a false premise. It says that line 3 is false, because nothing can be greater, as a being, than anything else. For a thing either exists or not. If each of two things exists, then they are equal, as beings, in that they both exist: neither is greater, as a being, than the other. If one of the two things exists, and the other does not, then the existent one is not greater, as a being, than the other, since the other is not a being at all and consequently cannot be compared, as a being, with anything else. And if neither exists, then, for the same reason, neither can be compared, as a being, with the other. From this, it follows that there is no way for one thing to be greater, as a being, than any other thing.

Reply. For Anselm, the objection's premise 'A thing either exists or not' is false. For there are two ways, not just one, in which something can exist: it can exist *in reality* or *in the understanding*. And these two ways of existing are compatible: something can exist *both* in reality *and* in the understanding. Hence, instead of "A thing either exists or not", Anselm would say, "A thing either exists both in reality and in the understanding, or it exists in reality but not in the understanding, or it exists in the understanding but not in reality, or it exists neither in reality nor in the understanding".

Given all this, it is possible, from Anselm's point of view, for one thing to be greater, as a being, than another thing. Something that exists both in the understanding and in reality is greater, as a being, than something that exists in the understanding but not in reality, since it exists in both of these two ways rather than in only one. Similarly, something that existed both in the understanding and in reality would be greater, as a being, than one that existed in reality alone.

This explains why, at several points in my analysis of Anselm's argument, I added the phrase 'as a being', which does not appear in Anselm's text. As I understand him, when he says in the argument that one thing would be greater than another, Anselm means that it would be greater (that is, better) *in some respect*, or *as* something. Something that exists both in the understanding and in reality would be greater with respect to *existence*, or *as a being*, than some otherwise identical thing existing in the understanding alone.

Objection 6. This objection says that Anselm's argument is not clearly sound, since lines 2, 4b, 6, and 7 of the proof presuppose that "something than which nothing greater (as a being) can be conceived" is possi-

6. See Arthur C. McGill, translation of Anselm's *Proslogion*, in *The Manyfaced Argument*, ed. John H. Hick and Arthur C. McGill (New York: The Macmillan Company, 1967), p. 4, n. 10; Arthur C. McGill, "Recent Discussions of Anselm's Argument", in Hick and McGill, p. 82.

ble. It assumes that the scale of things that are greater or less than each other (as beings) has a highest point. Now, in fact that scale may be like the scale of natural numbers, which has no highest point. No matter how large a number is, it is always possible to conceive of a larger number, so that "the largest natural number" is impossible. Perhaps, likewise, no matter how great something is (as a being), it is always possible to conceive of one greater, so that "something than which nothing greater (as a being) can be conceived" is impossible. Until it is demonstrated that this notion *is* possible, Anselm's argument is not clearly sound.[7]

Reply. Although I cannot supply the demonstration that the objection asks for, I can at least offer a judgment on the question. It seems that "something than which nothing greater (as a being) can be conceived" differs from "the largest natural number" in that it is possible. For, although it is always possible to conceive of a larger natural number, it seems that it is not always possible to conceive of another thing greater (as a being) than the last. Once we have conceived of something that exists not only in the understanding but also in reality and in whatever other ways there are to exist (assuming those ways to be finitely numerous), that seems to be as far as there is to go along those lines. And once we have added that the same thing exists in such a way that it cannot be conceived not to exist; [8] that it is "whatever it is better to be than not to be"; [9] that it is omniscient, omnipotent, and so on: [10] there doesn't seem to be any way for it to be any greater.[11] Consequently, it seems that "something than which nothing greater (as a being) can be conceived" is possible.

Objection 7. This objection is more sophisticated than the preceding ones. It says that Anselm's argument is invalid because it is just like arguing in the following way for a perfect island, which we know does not exist:

1. (Premise) The Perfect Island is an island than which no greater island can be conceived.

2. (Conclusion from 2a and 2b) An island than which no greater island can be conceived exists in the understanding, at least. Proof:

    2a. (Premise) All men understand when they hear of an island than which no greater island can be conceived.

    2b. (Premise) ". . . whatever is understood, exists in the understanding."

3. (Premise) An island that existed *both* in the understanding *and* in reality would be greater (as an island) than an otherwise identical island that existed in the understanding but not in reality.

4. (Conclusion from 4a–d) If an island than which no greater island can be conceived exists in the understanding but not in reality, then it is an island than which a greater island

---

7. Cf. Thomas Aquinas, *Summa Theologica*, I, Q. 2, Art. 1, Rep. Obj. 2; G. W. Leibniz, *New Essays on Human Understanding*, IV, 10.

8. Anselm, "Proslogion"; in Anselm, op. cit., III, pp. 8–9.

9. Ibid., V, pp. 10–11.

10. Ibid., passim.

11. Alvin Plantinga, *God and Other Minds* (Ithaca: Cornell University Press, 1967), p. 66.

can be conceived. Proof:

4a. (Hypothetical premise) Suppose an island (call it "I1") than which no greater island can be conceived exists in the understanding but not in reality.

4b. (Conclusion from 4a) It can be conceived to exist in reality also. That is, an otherwise identical island (call it "I2") can be conceived to exist in reality as well as in the understanding.

4c. (Conclusion from 4b and 3) The island we conceive to exist both in the understanding and in reality is greater (as an island) than the otherwise identical island that exists in the understanding but not in reality. That is, I2 is greater (as an island) than I1.

4d. (Conclusion from 4c) The island than which no greater island can be conceived is an island than which a greater island can be conceived. That is, I1 is an island than which a greater island (namely, I2) can be conceived.

5. (Premise) It is impossible that an island than which no greater island can be conceived is an island than which a greater island can be conceived.

6. (Conclusion from 4 and 5) It is *false* that an island than which no greater island can be conceived exists in the understanding but not in reality.

7. (Conclusion from 2 and 6) There exists an island than which no greater island can be conceived.

8. (Conclusion from 1 and 7) The Perfect Island exists.

This new argument has the same logical form as Anselm's: it is producible from Anselm's argument by substituting "Perfect Island" for "God" and "island" for "something", for "thing", and for "being" throughout. Moreover, its premises, this objection claims, are true, although its conclusion is false. If Anselm's argument had been formally valid—that is, if its logical form had been such that any argument having that form would have a true conclusion whenever it had true premises—, we would not have been able to construct another argument, possessing the old one's form, true premises, and a false conclusion. Therefore, Anselm's argument is not formally valid.[12]

Reply. The new argument about the Perfect Island fails to show that Anselm's original argument is not formally valid. For in order to do that, all the new argument's premises would have to be true, whereas line 3 is a false premise. It is false because existing in reality as well as in the understanding does not increase the greatness of an island, *as an island*. An island that exists both in the understanding and in reality is no greater *as an island* than an otherwise identical island that exists in the understanding alone. The first has all the "riches and delicacies" and other advantages of the second, and it is only such things as these that are relevant to the greatness of an island, *as an island*. So, this objection also fails.

Objection 8. This objection says that Anselm's argument is unsound, because line 3 falsely presupposes that existence is a real predicate. Let's see what this means. You know what a grammatical predicate is: it is something that is said about a sub-

12. Gaunilon, op. cit., Para. 6; pp. 150–1.

ject. For instance, in the sentence "Anselm thinks", "thinks" is the predicate; for "thinks" is what the sentence says about Anselm, its subject. Now, something is a real, as contrasted with a grammatical, predicate, if it can actually be an attribute of something. "Thinks" can be an attribute of Anselm, and so it is not only a grammatical but a real predicate. This objection, while admitting not only that things exist but also that "exists" is a grammatical predicate, denies that it is a real one. That is, it denies that existence can be an attribute of anything.

Why does it deny that? Two arguments have been given, one by Immanuel Kant, the other by Bertrand Russell. Kant says that existence is not a real predicate because if it were, then when we say that something exists, we would be adding another attribute to the thing, so that it would no longer be the original thing that we say exists. For instance, if existence were a real predicate, then when we say that a golden mountain exists, we would be adding the attribute "existence" to the original concept, "a golden mountain", so that it would no longer be "a golden mountain" that we say exists but "an existent golden mountain". But this is absurd: when we say that something exists, we say that the *original* thing, not the thing augmented by another attribute, exists. Therefore, Kant concludes, existence is not a real predicate.[13]

Russell says that the proper way to analyze a statement like "A golden mountain exists" is not to say that "A golden mountain" is its subject and "exists" its predicate (for that would presuppose that a golden mountain somehow exists, so that it can be a constituent of the proposition "A golden mountain exists") but to break it down into "(x is a golden mountain) is sometimes true", or "There exists an x such that x is a golden mountain". This analysis, Russell thinks, relieves us of the presupposition that a golden mountain somehow exists, and makes it easy to see that existence is not a predicate.[14]

So, since existence is not a predicate, line 3 of Anselm's proof is false. For it says that something that existed *both* in the understanding *and* in reality would be greater (as a being) than an otherwise identical thing that existed in the understanding but not in reality; and this, the objection contends, presupposes that existence is a predicate.

Reply. There are two avenues of reply to this objection. The first is to refuse to accept the claim that existence is not a real predicate, and the second is to reject the claim that line 3 of Anselm's argument requires that existence be such a predicate.

1. We may refuse to accept the claim that existence is not a real predicate on the grounds that we have not been given good enough reasons in its favor. Kant's argument is too strong: it would prove that "thinks", or "red", or anything else

13. *Critique of Pure Reason*, A592, B620–A602, B630.

14. *Principia Mathematica*, I, Introduction, Ch. I, and Part I, Section B, p. 14; "The Philosophy of Logical Atomism", V and VI; *Introduction to Mathematical Philosophy*, Ch. 16; *History of Western Philosophy*, Ch. XXXI. Russell denies that existence is a predicate of individuals but affirms that it is a predicate of propositional functions, like "x is a golden mountain", and of classes.

we ordinarily think is a real predicate in fact is not. For, following Kant's argument, we could say that if "red", for instance, were a real predicate, when we say that a rose is red, the thing we say is red is not merely a rose but a red rose. If Kant's argument shows that existence is not a real predicate, then this argument shows that red is not a real predicate either. But, of course, red is a real predicate, and so Kant's argument fails.[15]

And Russell's reason for analyzing "A golden mountain exists" as he proposes rests on the mistaken assumption that we cannot attribute a predicate to a non-existent subject. But we can. For instance, when we say, "A positive integer less than 0 is odd", we attribute oddness to a positive integer less than 0, even though we know that no such integer exists, in any sense. Something need not exist in order to be a constituent—more precisely, a subject—of a proposition.

2. And we may reject the claim that line 3 of Anselm's argument presupposes that existence is a predicate, on the grounds that it might be paraphrased (rather awkwardly, I admit) according to Russell's preferences without making any difference to the argument. We require only two concessions: (a) that we be able to say not merely "There is an x such that" but "There is in reality an x such that" and "There is in the understanding an x such that"; and (b) that we be able to say that one thing is greater (as a being) than another. Given these concessions, we might paraphrase line 3 thus: "If there is in reality an x, and in the understanding a y, such that x is identical with y; and if there is in the understanding a z, and there is not in reality a w, such that z is identical with w; then x is greater (as a being) than z".

15. Jerome Schaffer, "Existence, Predication and the Ontological Argument", *Mind*, Vol. LXXI, N.S., No. 283 (July 1962), pp. 309–10.

COMMENTS ■ QUESTIONS

1. Bowles begins by reconstructing Anselm's argument in a way that makes its premises explicit. From your reading of the relevant passages in Anselm, would you say that Bowles has accurately stated the argument that Anselm had in mind?
2. Bowles' strategy is to consider possible objections to Anselm's argument—eight of them in all—and to argue that there is a possible reason not to accept each of the objections. Do you believe that Bowles is successful in carrying this out? If not, then which one, or more, of the *objections* do you believe is successful?
3. Perhaps the most difficult of the points made by Bowles is to be found in his reply to objection 5, where he says that, according to

Anselm, "there are two ways, not just one, in which something can exist: it can exist *in reality* or *in the understanding*." Would you say that these two concepts of existence are sufficiently clear to do the job that Anselm requires of them?

SAMUEL CLARKE

A Demonstration of the Being and Attributes of God

All those who either are, or pretend to be *Atheists*; who either disbelieve the Being of God, or would be thought to do so; or, which is all one, who deny the Principal Attributes of the Divine Nature, and suppose God to be an Unintelligent Being, which acts merely by Necessity; that is, which, in any tolerable Propriety of Speech, acts not at all, but is only acted upon: All Men that are *Atheists*, I say, in this Sense, must be so upon one or other of these three Accounts.

Either, *First*, Because being extremely ignorant and stupid, they have *never duly considered* any thing, nor made any just use of their natural Reason, to discover even the plainest and most obvious Truths; but have spent their Time in a manner of Life very little Superiour to that of Beasts.

Or, *Secondly*, Because being totally debauched and corrupted in their *Practice*, they have, by a vicious and degenerate Life, corrupted the Principles of their Nature, and defaced the Reason of their own Minds; and, instead of fairly and impartially enquiring into the Rules and Obligations of Nature, and the Reason and Fitness of Things, have accustomed themselves only to mock and scoff at Religion; and, being under the Power of Evil Habits, and the Slavery of Unreasonable and Indulged Lusts, are resolved not to hearken to any Reasoning which would oblige them to forsake their beloved Vices.

Or, *Thirdly*, Because in the way of *Speculative Reasoning*, and upon the Principles of Philosophy, they pretend that the Arguments used Against the Being or Attributes of God, seem to them, after the strictest and fullest inquiry, to be more

Samuel Clarke (1675–1729) was an English philosopher and theologian. His work is known for its careful analysis and forceful style.

From *A Demonstration of the Being and Attributes of God*, 1705.

strong and conclusive, than those by which we endeavour to prove these great Truths.

These seem the only Causes that can be imagined, of any Man's disbelieving the Being or Attributes of God; and no Man can be supposed to be an Atheist, but upon one or other of these three Accounts. Now to the *two former* of these three sorts of Men; namely, to such as are wholly ignorant and stupid, or to such as through habitual Debauchery have brought themselves to a Custom of mocking and scoffing at all Religion, and will not hearken to any fair Reasoning; it is *not* my *present* Business to apply my self. The One of these, wants to be instructed in the first Principles of *Reason*, as well as of *Religion*. The Other disbelieves only for a present false *Interest*, and because he is desirous that the Thing should not be true. The One has *not yet arrived* to the use of his natural Faculties: The Other has *renounced* them; and declares he will not be argued with, as a rational Creature. 'Tis therefore the *third sort* of Atheists only (namely those who in the way of Speculative *Reasoning*, and upon the Principles of Philosophy, pretend that the Arguments brought Against the Being or Attributes of God, do, upon the strictest and fullest Examination, appear to them to be more strong and conclusive, than those by which these great Truths are attempted to be proved;) These, I say, are the only Atheistical Persons, to whom my present Discourse can be supposed to be directed, or indeed who are capable of being reasoned with at all.

* * * * *

I. First then, it is Absolutely and Undeniably certain, that *Something has existed from all Eternity.* This is so evident and Undeniable a Proposition, that no Atheist in any Age has ever presumed to assert the contrary; and therefore there is little need of being particular in the proof of it. For since Something now Is, 'tis evident that Something always Was: Otherwise the Things that Now Are, must have been produced out of Nothing, absolutely and without Cause: Which is a plain Contradiction in Terms. For, to say a Thing is *produced*, and yet that there is no *Cause* at all of that Production, is to say that Something is *Effected*, when it is *Effected by Nothing;* that is, at the same time when it is *not Effected at all*. Whatever Exists, has a Cause, or Reason, a Ground of its Existence; (a Foundation, on which its Existence relies; a Ground or Reason why it doth *exist*, rather than *not exist*;) either in the Necessity of its own Nature, and then it must have been *of it self Eternal*. Or in the Will of some Other Being; and then That Other Being must, at least in the order of Nature and Causality, have Existed before it.

That *Something* therefore *has really Existed from Eternity*, is one of the certainest and most evident Truths in the World; acknowledged by all Men, and disputed by none. Yet as to the *Manner* how it can be; there is nothing in Nature more difficult for the Mind of Man to conceive, than this very first Plain and Self-evident Truth. For, *How any thing can have existed eternally*, that is, *How an Eternal Duration can be now actually Past*; is a thing utterly as impossible for our narrow Understandings to comprehend, as any thing that is not an express Contradiction in terms can be imagined to be.

* * * * *

II. *There has Existed from Eternity, Some One Unchangeable and Independent Being.* For since Something must needs have been from Eternity; as has been already proved, and is granted on all hands: Either there has always Existed some one Unchangeable and *Independent* Being, from which all other Beings that are or ever were in the Universe, have received their Original; or else there has been an infinite Succession of changeable and *dependent* Beings produced one from another in an endless Progression, *without* any Original Cause at all. Now this latter Supposition is so very absurd, that tho' all Atheism must in its Account of most things (as shall be shewn hereafter) terminate in it, yet I think very few Atheists ever were so weak as openly and directly to defend it. For it is plainly impossible, and *contradictory* to itself. I shall not argue against it from the *Supposed* Impossibility of Infinite Succession, *barely* and *absolutely considered in itself*; for a Reason which shall be mentioned hereafter. But, if we consider such an infinite Progression, as *One* entire endless *Series of Dependent* Beings; 'tis plain this *whole Series of Beings* can have no Cause *from without* of its Existence; because in it are supposed to be included *all Things* that are or ever were in the Universe: And 'tis plain it can have no Reason *within itself* of its Existence; because no one Being in this Infinite Succession is supposed to be Self-existent or *Necessary*, (which is the only Ground or Reason of Existence of any thing, that can be imagined *within the thing itself*, as will presently more fully appear,) but every one *Dependent* on the foregoing: And where *no Part* is necessary, 'tis manifest *the Whole* cannot be necessary: Absolute Necessity of Existence, not being an *extrinsick, relative*, and *accidental* Denomination; but an *inward and essential* Property of the Nature of the Thing which so Exists. An infinite Succession therefore of merely *Dependent* Beings, without any Original Independent Cause; is a *Series* of Beings, that has neither Necessity, nor Cause, nor any Reason or Ground *at all* of its Existence, either *within itself* or *from without*: That is, 'tis an express Contradiction and Impossibility; 'tis a supposing *Something* to be *caused*, (because it is granted in every one of its Stages of Succession, *not* to be *necessarily and of itself*;) and yet that, in the whole, 'tis caused *absolutely by Nothing*. Which every Man knows is a Contradiction to imagine done *in Time*, and, because Duration in this Case makes no Difference, 'tis equally a Contradiction to suppose it done *from Eternity*. And consequently there must, *on the contrary*, of necessity have existed from Eternity, *some One* Immutable and *Independent* Being: Which, *what* it is, remains in the next place to be inquired.

III. *That unchangeable and Independent Being, which has Existed from Eternity, without any external Cause of its Existence; must be Self-Existent, that is, Necessarily-existing.* For whatever Exists, must either have come into Being out of Nothing, absolutely without Cause; or it must have been produced by some External Cause; or it must be Self-Existent. Now to arise out of Nothing, absolutely without any Cause; has been already shown to be a plain Contradiction. To have been produced by some External Cause, cannot possibly be true of every thing; but something must have existed Eternally and Independently; As has likewise been shown already. It remains therefore, that That Being which has existed Independently from Eternity, must of Necessity be Self-existent. Now to be *Self-existent*, is not, to be *Produced by itself*; for that is an express Contradiction. But it is, (which is the only Idea we can frame of Self-existence; and without which, the word seems to have no Signification at all:) It is, I say, to *exist by an Absolute Necessity originally in the Nature of the Thing itself*. And this Necessity, must be *Antecedent*; not indeed in Time, to the Existence of the Being itself; because That is Eternal; But it must be *Antecedent* in the Natural Order of our Ideas, to our *Supposition* of its Being. That is; This Necessity must not barely be *consequent* upon our Supposition of the Existence of such a Being; (For then it would not be a Necessity *Absolutely* such in itself, nor be the Ground or Foundation of the Existence of any thing, being on the contrary only a Consequent of it;) But it must *antecedently* force itself upon us, whether we will or no, even when we are endeavouring to suppose that no such Being Exists: The attempting which very supposition, because it in an impossible one, does of all other ways the most clearly evidence to us the Absoluteness of this Necessity Antecedent to any Supposition whatsoever: For when we are endeavouring to suppose, that there is *no Being* in the Universe that exists Necessarily; we always find in our Minds, (besides the foregoing Demonstration of Something being Self-existent, from the *Impossibility of every Thing's being dependent;) We always find in our Minds, I say, some Ideas, as of Infinity and Eternity*; which to remove, that is, to suppose that there is no Being, no Substance in the Universe, to which these Attributes or Modes of Existence are necessarily inherent, is a Contradiction in the very Terms. [Modes and Attributes exist only by the Existence of the Substance to which they belong.] For He that can suppose Eternity and Immensity (and consequently the Substance by whose Existence these Modes or Attributes exist,) removed out of the Universe; may, if he please, as easily remove the Relation of Equality between twice two and four.

COMMENTS ■ QUESTIONS

1. For an analysis of Clarke's major arguments you should turn to the selection from William Rowe which follows this one.
2. Do you accept Clarke's account of what he says are the only three possible causes for a person becoming an atheist?

WILLIAM ROWE

The Cosmological Argument

Since ancient times thoughtful people have sought to justify their religious beliefs. Perhaps the most basic belief for which justification has been sought is the belief that there is a God. The effort to justify belief in the existence of God has generally started either from facts available to believers and nonbelievers alike or from facts, such as the experience of God, normally available only to believers. In this and the next two chapters, we shall consider some major attempts to justify belief in God by appealing to facts supposedly available to any rational person, whether religious or not. By starting from such facts theologians and philosophers have developed arguments for the existence of God, arguments which, they have claimed, prove beyond reasonable doubt that there is a God.

Stating the Argument

Arguments for the existence of God are commonly divided into *a posteriori* arguments and *a priori* arguments. An *a posteriori* argument depends on a principle or premise that can be known only by means of our experience of the world. An *a priori* argument, on the other hand, purports to rest on principles all of which can be known independently

William Rowe, a professor of philosophy at Purdue University, is widely known for his books and articles on the philosophy of religion.

From *Philosophy of Religion: An Introduction* by William L. Rowe, (c) 1978 by Dickenson Publishing Company, Inc. Used by permission of Wadsworth Inc.

of our experience of the world, by just reflecting on and understanding them. Of the three major arguments for the existence of God—the Cosmological, the Teleological, and the Ontological—only the last of these is entirely *a priori*. In the Cosmological Argument one starts from some simple fact about the world, such as that it contains things which are caused to exist by other things. In the Teleological Argument a somewhat more complicated fact about the world serves as a starting point, the fact that the world exhibits order and design. In the Ontological Argument, however, one begins simply with a concept of God. In this chapter we shall consider the Cosmological Argument; in the next two chapters we shall examine the Ontological Argument and the Teleological Argument.

Before we state the Cosmological Argument itself, we shall consider some rather general points about the argument. Historically, it can be traced to the writings of the Greek philosophers, Plato and Aristotle, but the major developments in the argument took place in the thirteenth and in the eighteenth centuries. In the thirteenth century, Aquinas put forth five distinct arguments for the existence of God, and of these, the first three are versions of the Cosmological Argument.[1] In the first of these he started from the fact that there are things in the world undergoing change and reasoned to the conclusion that there must be some ultimate cause of change that is itself unchanging. In the second he started from the fact that there are things in the world that clearly are caused to exist by other things and reasoned to the conclusion that there must be some ultimate cause of existence whose own existence is itself uncaused. And in the third argument he started from the fact that there are things in the world which need not have existed at all, things which do exist but which we can easily imagine might not, and reasoned to the conclusion that there must be some being that had to be, that exists and could not have failed to exist. Now it might be objected that even if Aquinas' arguments do prove beyond doubt the existence of an unchanging changer, an uncaused cause, and a being that could not have failed to exist, the arguments fail to prove the existence of the theistic God. For the theistic God, as we saw, is supremely good, omnipotent, omniscient, and creator of but separate from and independent of the world. How do we know, for example, that the unchanging changer isn't evil or slightly ignorant? The answer to this objection is that the Cosmological Argument has two parts. In the first part the effort is to prove the existence of a special sort of being, for example, a being that could not have failed to exist, or a being that causes change in other things but is itself unchanging. In the second part of the argument the effort is to prove that the special sort of being whose existence has been established in the first part has, and must have, the features—perfect goodness, omnipotence, omniscience, and so on—which go together to make up the theistic idea of God. What this means, then, is that Aquinas' three arguments are differ-

1. See St. Thomas Aquinas, *Summa Theologica*, 1a. 2, 3.

ent versions of only the first part of the Cosmological Argument. Indeed, in later sections of his *Summa Theologica* Aquinas undertakes to show that the unchanging changer, the uncaused cause of existence, and the being which had to exist are one and the same being and that this single being has all of the attributes of the theistic God.

We noted above that a second major development in the Cosmological Argument took place in the eighteenth century, a development reflected in the writings of the German philosopher, Gottfried Leibniz (1646–1716), and especially in the writings of the English theologian and philosopher, Samuel Clarke (1675–1729). In 1704 Clarke gave a series of lectures, later published under the title *A Demonstration of the Being and Attributes of God*. These lectures constitute, perhaps, the most complete, forceful, and cogent presentation of the Cosmological Argument we possess. The lectures were read by the major skeptical philosopher of the century, David Hume (1711–1776), and in his brilliant attack on the attempt to justify religion in the court of reason, his *Dialogues Concerning Natural Religion*, Hume advanced several penetrating criticisms of Clarke's arguments, criticisms which have persuaded many philosophers in the modern period to reject the Cosmological Argument. In our study of the argument we shall concentrate our attention largely on its eighteenth century form and try to assess its strengths and weaknesses in the light of the criticisms which Hume and others have advanced against it.

The first part of the eighteenth-century form of the Cosmological Argument seeks to establish the existence of a self-existent being. The second part of the argument attempts to prove that the self-existent being is the theistic God, that is, has the features which we have noted to be basic elements in the theistic idea of God. We shall consider mainly the first part of the argument, for it is against the first part that philosophers from Hume to Russell have advanced very important objections.

In stating the first part of the Cosmological Argument we shall make use of two important concepts, the concept of a *dependent being* and the concept of a *self-existent being*. By "a dependent being" we mean *a being whose existence is accounted for by the causal activity of other things*. Recalling Anselm's division into the three cases: "explained by another," "explained by nothing," and "explained by itself," it's clear that a dependent being is a being whose existence is explained by another. By "a self-existent being" we mean *a being whose existence is accounted for by its own nature*. This idea, as we saw in the preceding chapter, is an essential element in the theistic concept of God. Again, in terms of Anselm's three cases, a self-existence being is a being whose existence is explained by itself. Armed with these two concepts, the concept of a dependent being and the concept of a self-existent being we can now state the first part of the Cosmological Argument.

1. Every being (that exists or ever did exist) is either a dependent being or a self-existent being.

2. Not every being can be a dependent being. Therefore,

3. There exists a self-existent being.

Deductive Validity

Before we look critically at each of the premises of this argument, we should note that this argument is, to use an expression from the logician's vocabulary, *deductively valid*. To find out whether an argument is deductively valid we need only ask the question: If its premises were true would its conclusion have to be true? If the answer is yes, the argument is deductively valid. If the answer is no, the argument is deductively invalid. Notice that the question of the validity of an argument is entirely different from the question of whether its premises are in fact true. The following argument is made up entirely of false statements, but it is deductively valid.

1. Babe Ruth is the President of the U.S.
2. The President of the U.S. is from Indiana. Therefore,
3. Babe Ruth is from Indiana.

The argument is deductively valid because even though its premises are false, if they were true its conclusion would have to be true. Even God, Aquinas would say, cannot bring it about that the premises of this argument are true and yet its conclusion is false, for God's power extends only to what is possible, and it is an absolute impossibility that Babe Ruth be the President, the President be from Indiana, and yet Babe Ruth not be from Indiana.

The Cosmological Argument (that is, its first part) is a deductively valid argument. If its premises are or were true its conclusion would have to be true. It's clear from our example about Babe Ruth, however, that the fact that an argument is deductively valid is insufficient to establish the truth of its conclusion. What else is required? Clearly that we know or have rational grounds for believing that the premises are true. If we know that the Cosmological Argument is deductively valid and can establish that its premises are true, we shall thereby have proved that its conclusion is true. Are, then, the premises of the Cosmological Argument true? To this more difficult question we must now turn.

PSR and the First Premise

At first glance the first premise might appear to be an obvious or even trivial truth. But it is neither obvious nor trivial. And if it appears to be obvious or trivial, we must be confusing the idea of a self-existent being with the idea of a being that is not a dependent being. Clearly, it is obviously true that any being is either a dependent being (explained by other things) or it is not a dependent being (not explained by other things). But what our premise says is that any being is either a dependent being (explained by other things) or it is a self-existent being (explained by itself). Consider again Anselm's three cases.

a. explained by another,
b. explained by nothing,
c. explained by itself.

What our first premise asserts is that each being that exists (or ever did exist) is either of sort *a* or of sort *c*. It denies that any being is of sort *b*. And it is this denial that makes the first premise both significant and controversial. The obvious truth we must not confuse it with is the truth that any being is either of sort *a* or not of sort *a*. While this is true it is neither very significant nor controversial.

Earlier we saw that Anselm accepted as a basic principle that whatever exists has an explanation of its existence. Since this basic principle denies that any thing of sort *b* exists or ever did exist, it's clear that Anselm would believe the first premise of our Cosmological Argument. The eighteenth-century proponents of the argument also were convinced of the truth of the basic principle we attributed to Anselm. And because they were convinced of its truth, they readily accepted the first premise of the Cosmological Argument. But by the eighteenth century, Anselm's basic principle had been more fully elaborated and had received a name, "the Principle of Sufficient Reason." Since this principle (PSR, as we shall call it) plays such an important role in justifying the premises of the Cosmological Argument, it will help us to consider it for a moment before we continue our enquiry into the truth or falsity of the premises of the Cosmological Argument.

The Principle of Sufficient Reason (PSR), as it was expressed by both Leibniz and Samuel Clarke, is a very general principle and is best understood as having two parts. In its first part it is simply a restatement of Anselm's principle that there must be an explanation of the existence of any being whatever. Thus if we come upon a man in a room, PSR implies that there must be an explanation of the fact that that particular man exists. A moment's reflection, however, reveals that there are many facts about the man other than the mere fact that he exists. There is the fact that the man in question is in the room he's in, rather than somewhere else, the fact that he is in good health, and the fact that he is at the moment thinking of Paris, rather than, say, London. Now the purpose of the second part of PSR is to require an explanation of these facts as well. We may state PSR, therefore, as the principle that *there must be an explanation (a) of the existence of any being, and (b) of any positive fact whatever*. We are now in a position to study the role this very important principle plays in the Cosmological Argument.

Since the proponent of the Cosmological Argument accepts PSR in both its parts, it is clear that he will appeal to its first part, PSRa, as justification for the first premise of the Cosmological Argument. Of course, we can and should enquire into the deeper question of whether the proponent of the argument is rationally justified in accepting PSR itself. But we shall put this question aside for the moment. What we need to see first is whether he is correct in thinking that *if* PSR is true then both of the premises of the Cosmological Argument are true. And what we have just seen is that if only the first part of PSR, that is, PSRa, is true, the first premise of the Cosmological Argument will be true. But what of the second premise of the Argument? For what reasons does the proponent think that it must be true?

The Second Premise

According to the second premise, not every being that exists can be a dependent being, that is, can have the explanation of its existence in some other being or beings. Presumably, the proponent of the argument thinks there is something fundamentally wrong with the idea that every being that exists is dependent, that each existing being was caused by some other being which in turn was caused by some other being, and so on. But just what does he think is wrong with it? To help us in understanding his thinking, let's simplify things by supposing that there exists only one thing now, A_1, a living thing perhaps, that was brought into existence by something else A_2, which perished shortly after it brought A_1 into existence. Suppose further that A_2 was brought into existence in similar fashion some time ago by A_3, and A_3 by A_4, and so forth back into the past. Each of these beings is a *dependent* being, it owes its existence to the preceding thing in the series. Now if nothing else ever existed but these beings, then what the second premise says would not be true. For if every being that exists or ever did exist is an A and was produced by a preceding A, then every being that exists or ever did exist would be dependent and, accordingly, premise two of the Cosmological Argument would be false. If the proponent of the Cosmological Argument is correct there must, then, be something wrong with the idea that every being that exists or did exist is an A and that they form a causal series, A_1 caused by A_2, A_2 caused by A_3, A_3 caused by A_4, ... A_n caused by A_{n+1}. How does the proponent of the Cosmological Argument propose to how us that there is something wrong with this view?

A popular but mistaken idea of how the proponent tries to show that something is wrong with the view that every being might be dependent is that he uses the following argument to reject it.

1. There must be a *first being* to start any causal series.

2. If every being were dependent there would be no *first being* to start the causal series.

Therefore,

3. Not every being can be a dependent being.

Although this argument is deductively valid and its second premise is true, its first premise overlooks the distinct possibility that a causal series might be *infinite*, with no first member at all. Thus if we go back to our series of A beings, where each A is dependent, having been produced by the preceding A in the causal series, it's clear that if the series existed it would have no first member, for every A in the series there would be a preceding A which produced it, *ad infinitum*. The first premise of the argument just given assumes that a causal series must stop with a first member somewhere in the distant past. But there seems to be no good reason for making that assumption.

The eighteenth-century proponents of the Cosmological Argument recognized that the causal series of dependent beings could be infinite, without a first member to start the series. They rejected the idea that every being that is or ever was is dependent not because there would then be no first member to the series of dependent beings, but because there would then be no explanation for the fact that there are and have always been dependent beings. To see their reasoning let's return to our simplification of the supposition that the only things that exist or ever did exist are dependent beings. In our simplification of that supposition only one of the dependent beings exists at a time, each one perishing as it produces the next in the series. Perhaps the first thing to note about this supposition is that there is no individual A in the causal series of dependent beings whose existence is unexplained—A_1 is explained by A_2, A_2 by A_3, and A_n by A_{n+1}. So the first part of PSR, PSRa, appears to be satisfied. There is no particular being whose existence lacks an explanation. What, then, is it that lacks an explanation, if every particular A in the causal series of dependent beings has an explanation? It is the *series itself* that lacks an explanation. Or, as I've chosen to express it, *the fact that there are and have always been dependent beings*. For suppose we ask why it is that there are and have always been As in existence. It won't do to say that As have always been producing other As—we can't explain why there have always been As by saying there always have been As. Nor, on the supposition that only As have ever existed, can we explain the fact that there have always been As by appealing to something other than an A—for no such thing would have existed. Thus the supposition that the only things that exist or ever existed are dependent things leaves us with a fact for which there can be no explanation; namely, the fact that there are and have always been dependent beings.

Questioning the Justification of the Second Premise

Critics of the Cosmological Argument have raised several important objections against the claim that if every being is dependent the series or collection of those beings would have no explanation. Our understanding of the Cosmological Argument, as well as of its strengths and weaknesses, will be deepened by a careful consideration of these criticisms.

The first criticism is that the proponent of the Cosmological Argument makes the mistake of treating the collection or series of dependent beings as though it were itself a dependent being, and, therefore, requires an explanation of its existence. But, so the objection goes, the collection of dependent beings is not itself a dependent being any more than a collection of stamps is itself a stamp.

A second criticism is that the proponent makes the mistake of inferring that because each member of the collection of dependent beings has a cause the collection itself must have a cause. But, as Bertrand Russell noted, such reasoning is as fallacious as to infer that the human race (that is, the collection of human beings) must have a mother because each member of the collection (each human being) has a mother.

A third criticism is that the proponent of the argument fails to realize that for there to be an explanation of a collection of things is nothing more than for there to be an explanation of each of the things making up the collection. Since in the infinite collection (or series) of dependent beings, each being in the collection does have an explanation—by virtue of having been caused by some preceding member of the collection—the explanation of the collection, so the criticism goes, has already been given. As David Hume remarked, "Did I show you the particular causes of each individual in a collection of twenty particles of matter, I should think it very unreasonable, should you afterwards ask me, what was the cause of the whole twenty. This is sufficiently explained in explaining the cause of the parts." [2]

Finally, even if the proponent of the Cosmological Argument can satisfactorily answer these objections, he must face one last objection to his ingenious attempt to justify premise two of the Cosmological Argument. For someone may agree that if nothing exists but an infinite collection of dependent beings, the infinite collection will have no explanation of its existence, and still refuse to conclude from this that there is something wrong with the idea that every being is a dependent being. Why, he might ask, should we think that everything has to have an explanation? What's wrong with admitting that the fact that there are and have always been dependent beings is a *brute fact*, a fact having no explanation whatever? Why does everything have to have an explanation anyway? We must now see what can be said in response to these several objections.

Responses to Criticism

It is certainly a mistake to think that a collection of stamps is itself a stamp, and very likely a mistake to think that the collection of dependent beings is itself a dependent being. But the mere fact that the proponent of the argument thinks that there must be an explanation not only for each member of the collection of dependent beings but for the collection itself is not sufficient grounds for concluding that he must view the collection as itself a dependent being. The collection of human beings, for example, is certainly not itself a human being. Admitting this, however, we might still seek an explanation of why there is a collection of human beings, of why there are such things as human beings at all. So the mere fact that an explanation is demanded for the collection of dependent beings is no proof that the person who demands the explanation must be supposing that the collection itself is just another dependent being.

The second criticism attributes to the proponent of the Cosmological Argument the following bit of reasoning:

1. Every member of the collection of dependent beings has a cause or explanation.

Therefore,

2. The collection of dependent beings has a cause or explanation.

As we noted in setting forth this criticism, arguments of this sort are often unreliable. It would be a mistake to conclude that a collection of objects is light in weight simply because each object in the collection is light in weight, for if there were many objects in the collection it might be quite heavy. On the other hand, if we know that each marble weighs more than one ounce we could infer validly that the collection

2. David Hume, *Dialogues Concerning Natural Religion*, Part IX, ed. H. D. Aiken (New York: Hafner Publishing Company, 1948), pp. 59–60.

of marbles weighs more than an ounce. Fortunately, however, we don't need to decide whether the inference from (1.) to (2.) is valid or invalid. We need not decide this question because the proponent of the Cosmological Argument need not use this inference to establish that there must be an explanation of the collection of dependent beings. He need not use this inference because he has in PSR a principle from which it follows immediately that the collection of dependent beings has a cause or explanation. For according to PSR every positive fact must have an explanation. If it is a fact that there exists a collection of dependent beings then, according to PSR, that fact too must have an explanation. So it is PSR that the proponent of the Cosmological Argument appeals to in concluding that there must be an explanation of the collection of dependent beings, and not some dubious inference from the premise that each member of the collection has an explanation. It seems, then, that neither of the first two criticisms is strong enough to do any serious damage to the reasoning used to support the second premise of the Cosmological Argument.

The third objection contends that to explain the existence of a collection of things is the same thing as to explain the existence of each of its members. If we consider a collection of dependent beings where each being in the collection is explained by the preceding member which caused it, it's clear that no member of the collection will lack an explanation of its existence. But, so the criticism goes, if we've explained the existence of every member of a collection we've explained the existence of the collection—there's nothing left over to be explained. This forceful criticism, originally advanced by David Hume, has gained considerable support in the modern period. But the criticism rests on an assumption that the proponent of the Cosmological Argument would not accept. The assumption is that to explain the existence of a collection of things it is *sufficient* to explain the existence of every member in the collection. To see what is wrong with this assumption is to understand the basic issue in the reasoning by which the proponent of the Cosmological Argument seeks to establish that not every being can be a dependent being.

In order for there to be an explanation of the existence of the collection of dependent beings, it's clear that the eighteenth-century proponents would require that the following two conditions be satisfied:

C1. There is an explanation of the existence of each of the members of the collection of dependent beings.

C2. There is an explanation of why there are *any* dependent beings.

According to the proponents of the Cosmological Argument if every being that exists or ever did exist is a dependent being—that is, if the whole of reality consists of nothing more than a collection of dependent beings—C1 will be satisfied, but C2 will not be satisfied. And since C2 won't be satisfied there will be no explanation of the collection of dependent beings. The third criticism, therefore, says in effect that if C1 is satisfied C2 will be satisfied, and, since in a collection of dependent beings each member will have an explanation in whatever it was that produced it, C1 will be satisfied. So, therefore, C2 will be satisfied and the collection of dependent beings will have an explanation.

Although the issue is a complicated one, I think it is possible to see that the third criticism rests on a mistake: the mistake of thinking that if C1 is satisfied C2 must also be satisfied. The mistake is a natural one to make for it is easy to imagine circumstances in which if C1 is satisfied C2 also will be satisfied. Suppose, for example, that the whole of reality includes not just a collection of dependent beings but also a self-existent being. Suppose further that instead of each dependent being having been produced by some other dependent being every dependent being was produced by the self-existent being. Finally, let us consider both the possibility that the collection of dependent beings is finite in time and has a first member and the possibility that the collection of dependent beings is infinite in past time, having no first member. Using "G" for the self-existent being, the first possibility may be diagramed as follows:

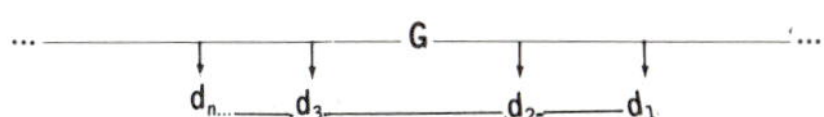

G, we shall say, has always existed and always will. We can think of d_1 as some presently existing dependent being, d_2, d_3, and so forth as dependent beings that existed at some time in the past, and d_n as the first dependent being to exist. The second possibility may be portrayed as follows:

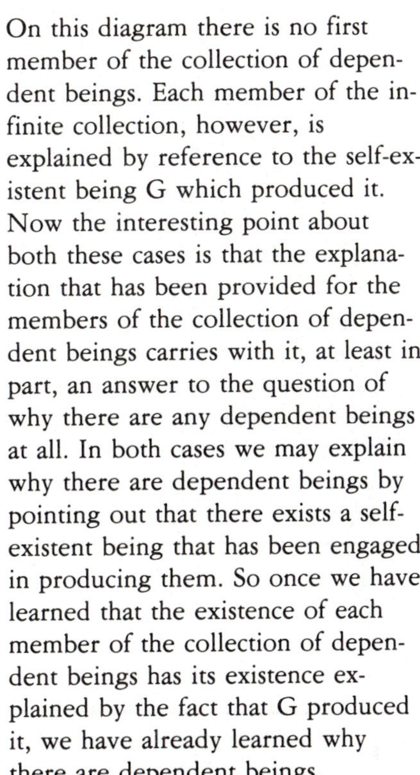

On this diagram there is no first member of the collection of dependent beings. Each member of the infinite collection, however, is explained by reference to the self-existent being G which produced it. Now the interesting point about both these cases is that the explanation that has been provided for the members of the collection of dependent beings carries with it, at least in part, an answer to the question of why there are any dependent beings at all. In both cases we may explain why there are dependent beings by pointing out that there exists a self-existent being that has been engaged in producing them. So once we have learned that the existence of each member of the collection of dependent beings has its existence explained by the fact that G produced it, we have already learned why there are dependent beings.

Someone might object that we haven't really learned why there are dependent beings until we also learn *why* G has been producing them. But, of course, we could also say that we haven't really explained the existence of a particular dependent being, say d_3, until we also learn not just that G produced it but *why* G produced it. The point we need to grasp, however, is that once we admit that every dependent being's existence is explained by G, we must admit that the fact that there are dependent beings has also been explained. So it is not unnatural that someone should think that to explain the existence of the collection of dependent beings is nothing more than to explain the existence of its members. For, as we've seen, to explain the collection's existence is to explain each member's existence and to explain why there are any dependent beings at all. And in the examples we've considered, in doing the one (explaining why each dependent being exists) we've already done the other (explained why there are any dependent beings at all). We must now see, however, that on the supposition that the whole of reality consists *only* of a collection of dependent beings, to give an explanation of each member's existence is not to provide an explanation of why there are dependent beings.

In the examples we've considered we have gone *outside* of the collection of dependent beings in order to explain the members' existence. But if the only beings that exist or ever existed are dependent beings then each dependent being will be explained by some other dependent being, ad infinitum. This does not mean that there will be some particular dependent being whose existence is unaccounted for. Each dependent being has an explanation of its existence; namely, in the dependent being which preceded it and produced it. So C1 is satisfied; there is an explanation of the existence of each member of the collection of dependent beings. Turning to C2, however, we can see that it will not be satisfied. We cannot explain why there are (or have ever been) dependent beings by appealing to all the members of the infinite collection of dependent beings. For if the question to be answered is why there are (or have ever been) any dependent beings at all, we cannot answer that question by noting that there always have been dependent beings, each one accounting for the existence of some other dependent being. Thus on the supposition that every being is dependent it seems there will be no explanation of why there are dependent beings. C2 will not be satisfied. Therefore, on the supposition that every being is dependent there will be no explanation of the existence of the collection of dependent beings.

The Truth of PSR

We come now to the final criticism of the reasoning supporting the second premise of the Cosmological Argument. According to this criticism, it is admitted that the supposition that every being is dependent implies that there will be a *brute fact* in the universe, a fact, that is, for which there can be no explanation whatever. For there will be no explanation of the fact that dependent beings exist and have always been in existence. It is this brute fact that the proponents of the argument were describing when they pointed out that if every being is dependent the series or collection of dependent beings would lack an explanation of its existence. The final criticism asks what is wrong with admitting that the universe contains such a brute, unintelligible fact. In asking this question the critic challenges the fundamental principle, PSR, on which the Cosmological Argument rests. For, as we've seen, the first premise of the argument denies that there exists a being whose existence has no explanation. In support of this premise the proponent appeals to the first part of PSR. The second premise of the argument claims that not every being can be dependent.

In support of this premise the proponent appeals to the second part of PSR, the part which states that there must be an explanation of any positive fact whatever.

The proponent reasons that if every being were a dependent being then although the first part of PSR would be satisfied—every being would have an explanation—the second part would be violated, there would be no explanation for the positive fact that there are and have always been dependent beings. For first, since every being is supposed to be dependent, there would be nothing outside of the collection of dependent beings to explain the collection's existence. Second, the fact that each member of the collection has an explanation in some other dependent being is insufficient to explain why there are and have always been dependent beings. And, finally, there is nothing about the collection of dependent beings that would suggest that it is a self-existent collection. Consequently, if every being were dependent, the fact that there are and have always been dependent beings would have no explanation. But this violates the second part of PSR. So the second premise of the Cosmological Argument must be true, not every being can be a dependent being. This conclusion, however, is no better than the principle, PSR, on which it rests. And it is the point of the final criticism to question the truth of PSR. Why, after all, should we accept the idea that every being and every positive fact must have an explanation? Why, in short, should we believe PSR? These are important questions, and any final judgment of the Cosmological Argument depends on how they are answered.

Most of the theologians and philosophers who accept PSR have tried to defend it in either of two ways. Some have held that PSR is (or can be) known *intuitively* to be true. By this they mean that if we fully understand and reflect on what is said by PSR we can see that it must be true. Now, undoubtedly, there are statements which are known intuitively to be true. "Every triangle has exactly three angles" or "No physical object can be in two different places in space at one and the same time" are examples of statements whose truth we can apprehend just by understanding and reflecting on them. The difficulty with the claim that PSR is intuitively true, however, is that a number of very able philosophers fail to apprehend its truth, and some even claim that the principle is false. It is doubtful, therefore, that many of us, if any, know intuitively that PSR is true.

The second way philosophers and theologians who accept PSR have sought to defend it is by claiming that although it is not known to be true, it is, nevertheless, a presupposition of reason, a basic assumption that rational people make, whether or not they reflect sufficiently to become aware of the assumption. It's probably true that there are some assumptions we all make about our world, assumptions which are so basic that most of us are unaware of them. And, I suppose, it might be true that PSR is such an assumption. What bearing would this view of PSR have on the Cosmological Argument? Perhaps the main point to note is that even if PSR is a presupposition we all share, the premises of the Cosmological Argument could still be false. For PSR itself could still be false. The fact, if it is a fact, that all of us *presuppose* that every existing being and every positive fact has an explanation does not imply that no being exists, and no positive fact obtains, without an explanation. Nature is not bound to satisfy our presuppositions. As the American philosopher, William James, once remarked in another connection, "In the great boarding house of nature, the cakes and the butter and the syrup seldom come out so even and leave the plates so clear."

Our study of the first part of the Cosmological Argument has led us to the fundamental principle on which its premises rest, the Principle of Sufficient Reason. Since we do not seem to know that PSR is true we cannot reasonably claim to know that the premises of the Cosmological Argument are true. They might be true. But unless we do know them to be true they cannot *establish* for us the conclusion that there exists a being that has the explanation of its existence within its own nature. If it were shown, however, that even though we do not *know* that PSR is true we all, nevertheless, *presuppose* PSR to be true, then, whether PSR is true or not, to be consistent we should accept the Cosmological Argument. For, as we've seen, its premises imply its conclusion and its premises do seem to follow from PSR. But no one has succeeded in *showing* that PSR is an assumption that most or all of us share. So our final conclusion must be that although the Cosmological Argument might be a *sound* argument (valid with true premises), it does not provide us with good rational grounds for believing that among those beings that exist there is one whose existence is accounted for by its own nature. Having come to this conclusion we may safely put aside the second part of the argument. For even if it succeeded in showing that a self-existent being would have the other attributes of the theistic God, the Cosmological Argument would still not provide us with good rational grounds for belief in God, having failed in its first part to provide us with good rational grounds for believing that there is a self-existent being.

COMMENTS ■ QUESTIONS

1. Near the beginning of this selection, Rowe refers to three versions of the Cosmological Argument defended by Saint Thomas Aquinas in the thirteenth century. Because Aquinas's arguments are widely discussed, it may be helpful to present them here.

First Argument

Premise 1. "In the world some things are in motion."
Premise 2. "Whatever is moved is moved by another."
Proof:
Premise 2a. "Nothing can be moved except it is in potentiality to that toward which it is moved."
Premise 2b. "A thing moves inasmuch as it is in act."
Premise 2c. "It is not possible that the same thing should be at once in actuality and potentiality in the same respect."
Premise 3. There cannot be an infinite regress of things moved and movers.
Conclusion. There must be a first mover, and "This everyone understands to be God."

Second Argument

Premise 1. "In the world of sensible things . . . there is an order of efficient causes."
Premise 2. A thing cannot be the efficient cause of itself (since then it would be prior to itself, which is impossible).
Premise 3. There cannot be an infinite regress of efficient causes.
Proof:
Premise 3a. "If there be no first cause among efficient causes, there will be no ultimate, nor any intermediate cause."
Conclusion. There must be a first efficient cause, "to which everyone gives the name of God."

Third Argument

Premise 1. "We find in nature things that are possible to be and not to be."
Premise 2. "It is impossible for these always to exist for that which can not-be at some time is not."
Premise 3. "If everything can not-be, then at one time there was nothing in existence."
Premise 4. Nothing comes from nothing.
Conclusion. There must be a necessary being, "This all men speak of as God."

2. In his statement of what he refers to as the eighteenth century version of the Cosmological Argument—which comes from Samuel Clarke—Rowe makes use of the expression "self-existent being," which he defines as follows: "a being whose existence is accounted for by its own nature." Do you believe that this concept is sufficiently clear to function as intended in the Cosmological Argument? In answering this question, please bear in mind that concepts pertaining to the nature and existence of God are notoriously difficult.
3. Rowe has responded in turn to each one of the major objections

to the Cosmological Argument. Do you accept the conclusion that he reaches, namely, that *if* the Principle of Sufficient Reason (which says that "there must be an explanation (a) of the existence of any being, and (b) of any positive fact whatever") is accepted as being true, then the premises of the Cosmological Argument must be accepted as being true, and, *if* the premises of the argument are accepted as being true, then the conclusion of the argument must be accepted as being true? Do you agree with Rowe also when he says "we do not seem to know that the Principle of Sufficient Reason is true"?

ERNEST NAGEL

Philosophical Concepts of Atheism

1

I must begin by stating what sense I am attaching to the word "atheism," and how I am construing the theme of this paper. I shall understand by "atheism" a critique and a denial of the major claims of all varieties of theism. And by theism I shall mean the view which holds, as one writer has expressed it, "that the heavens and the earth and all that they contain owe their existence and continuance in existence to the wisdom and will of a supreme, self-consistent, omnipotent, omniscient, righteous, and benevolent being, who is distinct from, and independent of, what he has created." Several things immediately follow from these definitions.

In the first place, atheism is not necessarily an irreligious concept, for theism is just one among many views concerning the nature and origin of the world. The denial of theism is logically compatible with a religious outlook upon life, and is in fact characteristic of some of the great historical religions. For as readers of this volume will know,

Ernest Nagel, who died in 1985, was a world-renowned philosopher of science. He taught at Columbia University for more than 40 years, where he was most recently University Professor Emeritus.

From Ernest Nagel, "Philosophical Concepts of Atheism." In J. E. Fairchild (ed.), *Basic Beliefs*. N.Y.: Sheridan House, Inc., 1959.

early Buddhism is a religion which does not subscribe to any doctrine about a god; and there are pantheistic religions and philosophies which, because they deny that God is a being separate from and independent of the world, are not theistic in the sense of the word explained above.

The second point to note is that atheism is not to be identified with sheer unbelief, or with disbelief in some particular creed of a religious group. Thus, a child who has received no religious instruction and has never heard about God, is not an atheist—for he is not denying any theistic claims. Similarly in the case of an adult who, if he has withdrawn from the faith of his fathers without reflection or because of frank indifference to any theological issue, is also not an atheist—for such an adult is not challenging theism and is not professing any views on the subject. Moreover, though the term "atheist" has been used historically as an abusive label for those who do not happen to subscribe to some regnant orthodoxy (for example, the ancient Romans called the early Christians atheists, because the latter denied the Roman divinities), or for those who engage in conduct regarded as immoral it is not in this sense that I am discussing atheism.

One final word of preliminary explanation. I propose to examine some *philosophic* concepts of atheism, and I am not interested in the slightest in the many considerations atheists have advanced against the evidences for some particular religious and theological doctrine—for example, against the truth of the Christian story. What I mean by "philosophical" in the present context is that the views I shall consider are directed against any form of theism, and have their origin and basis in a logical analysis of the theistic position, and in a comprehensive account of the world believed to be wholly intelligible without the adoption of a theistic hypothesis.

Theism as I conceive it is a theological proposition, not a statement of a position that belongs primarily to religion. On my view, religion as a historical and social phenomenon is primarily an institutionalized *cultus* or practice, which possesses identifiable social functions and which expresses certain attitudes men take toward their world. Although it is doubtful whether men ever engage in religious practices or assume religious attitudes without some more or less explicit interpretation of their ritual or some rationale for their attitude, it is still the case that it is possible to distinguish religion as a social and personal phenomenon from the theological doctrines which may be developed as justifications for religious practices. Indeed, in some of the great religions of the world the profession of a creed plays a relatively minor role. In short, religion is a form of social communion, a participation in certain kinds of ritual (whether it be a dance, worship, prayer, or the like), and a form of experience (sometimes, though not invariably, directed to a personal confrontation with divine and holy things). Theology is an articulated and, at its best, a rational attempt at understanding these feelings and practices, in the light of their relation to other parts of human experience, and in terms of some hypothesis concerning the nature of things entire.

2

As I see it, atheistic philosophies fall into two major groups: 1) those which hold that the theistic doctrine is meaningful, but reject it either on the ground that, (a) the positive evidence for it is insufficient, or (b) the negative evidence is quite overwhelming; and 2) those who hold that the theistic thesis is not even meaningful, and reject it (a) as just nonsense or (b) as literally meaningless but interpreting it as a symbolic rendering of human ideals, thus reading the theistic thesis in a sense that most believers in theism would disavow. It will not be possible in the limited space at my disposal to discuss the second category of atheistic critiques; and in any event, most of the traditional atheistic critiques of theism belong to the first group.

But before turning to the philosophical examination of the major classical arguments for theism, it is well to note that such philosophical critiques do not quite convey the passion with which atheists have often carried on their analyses of theistic views. For historically, atheism has been, and indeed continues to be, a form of social and political protest, directed as much against institutionalized religion as against theistic doctrine. Atheism has been, in effect, a moral revulsion against the undoubted abuses of the secular power exercised by religious leaders and religious institutions.

Religious authorities have opposed the correction of glaring injustices, and encouraged politically and socially reactionary policies. Religious institutions have been havens of obscurantist thought and centers for the dissemination of intolerance. Religious creeds have been used to set limits to free inquiry, to perpetuate inhumane treatment of the ill and the underprivileged, and to support moral doctrines insensitive to human suffering.

These indictments may not tell the whole story about the historical significance of religion; but they are at least an important part of the story. The refutation of theism has thus seemed to many as an indispensible step not only towards liberating men's minds from superstitution, but also towards achieving a more equitable reordering of society. And no account of even the more philosophical aspects of atheistic thought is adequate, which does not give proper recognition to the powerful social motives that actuate many atheistic arguments.

But however this may be, I want now to discuss three classical arguments for the existence of God, arguments which have constituted at least a partial basis for theistic commitments. As long as theism is defended simply as a dogma, asserted as a matter of direct revelation or as the deliverance of authority, belief in the dogma is impregnable to rational argument. In fact, however, reasons are frequently advanced in support of the theistic creed, and these reasons have been the subject of acute philosophical critiques.

One of the oldest intellectual defenses of theism is the cosmological argument, also known as the argument from a first cause. Briefly put, the argument runs as follows. Every event must have a cause. Hence an event A must have as cause some event B, which in turn must have a cause C, and so on. But if there is no end to this backward progression of causes, the progression will be infinite; and in the opinion of those who use this argument, an infinite series of actual events is unintelligible and absurd. Hence there must be a first cause, and this first cause is God, the initiator of all change in the universe.

The argument is an ancient one, and is especially effective when stated within the framework of assumptions of Aristotelian physics; and it has impressed many generations of exceptionally keen minds. The argument is nonetheless a weak reed on which to rest the theistic thesis. Let us waive any question concerning the validity of the principle that every event has a cause, for though the question is important its discussion would lead us far afield. However, if the principle is assumed, it is surely incongruous to postulate a first cause as a way of escaping from the coils of an infinite series. For if everything must have a cause, why does not God require one for His own existence? The standard answer is that He does not need any, because He is self-caused. But if God can be self-caused, why cannot the world itself be self-caused? Why do we require a God transcending the world to bring the world into existence and to initiate changes in it? On the other hand, the supposed inconceivability and absurdity of an infinite series of regressive causes will be admitted by no one who has competent familiarity with the modern mathematical analysis of infinity. The cosmological argument does not stand up under scrutiny.

The second "proof" of God's existence is usually called the ontological argument. It too has a long history going back to early Christian days, though it acquired great prominence only in medieval times. The argument can be stated in several ways, one of which is the following. Since God is conceived to be omnipotent, he is a perfect being. A perfect being is defined as one whose essence or nature lacks no attributes (or properties) whatsoever, one whose nature is complete in every respect. But it is evident that we have an idea of a perfect being, for we have just defined the idea; and since this is so, the argument continues, God who is the perfect being must exist. Why must he? Because his existence follows from his defined nature. For if God lacked the attribute of existence, he would be lacking at least one attribute, and would therefore not be perfect. To sum up, since we have an idea of God as a perfect being, God must exist.

There are several ways of approaching this argument, but I shall consider only one. The argument was exploded by the 18th century philosopher Immanuel Kant. The substance of Kant's criticism is that it is just a confusion to say that existence is an attribute, and that though the *word* "existence" may occur as the grammatical predicate in a sentence no attribute is being predicated of a thing when we say that the thing exists or has existence. Thus, to use Kant's example, when we think of $100 we are thinking of the nature of this sum of money; but the nature of $100 remains the same whether we have $100 in our pockets or not. Accordingly, we are confounding grammar with logic if we suppose that some characteristic is being attributed to the nature of $100 when we say that a hundred dollar bill exists in someone's pocket.

To make the point clearer, consider another example. When we say that a lion has a tawny color, we are predicating a certain attribute of the animal, and similarly when we say that the lion is fierce or is hungry. But when we say the lion exists, all that we are saying is that something is (or has the nature of) a lion; we are not specifying an attribute which belongs to the nature of anything that is a lion. In short, the word "existence" does not signify any attribute, and in consequence no attribute that belongs to the nature of anything. Accordingly, it does not follow from the assumption that we have an idea of a perfect being that such a being exists. For the idea of a perfect being does not involve the attribute of existence as a constituent of that idea, since there is no such attribute. The ontological argument thus has a serious leak, and it can hold no water.

3

The two arguments discussed thus far are purely dialectical, and attempt to establish God's existence without any appeal to empirical data. The next argument, called the argument from design, is different in character, for it is based on what purports to be empirical evidence. I wish to examine two forms of this argument.

One variant of it calls attention to the remarkable way in which different things and processes in the world are integrated with each other, and concludes that this mutual "fitness" of things can be explained only by the assumption of a divine architect who planned the world and everything in it. For example, living organisms can maintain themselves in a variety of environments, and do so in virtue of their delicate mechanisms which adapt the organisms to all sorts of environmental changes. There is thus an intricate pattern of means and ends throughout the animate world. But the existence of this pattern is unintelligible, so the argument runs, except on the hypothesis that the pattern has been deliberately instituted by a Supreme Designer. If we find a watch in some deserted spot, we do not think it came into existence by chance, and we do not hesitate to conclude that an intelligent creature designed and made it. But the world and all its contents exhibit mechanisms and mutual adjustments that are far more complicated and subtle than are those of a watch. Must we not therefore conclude that these things too have a Creator?

The conclusion of this argument is based on an inference from analogy: the watch and the world are alike in possessing a congruence of parts and an adjustment of means to ends; the watch has a watch-maker; hence the world has a world-maker. But is the analogy a good one? Let us once more waive some important issues, in particular the issue whether the universe is the unified system such as the watch admittedly is. And let us concentrate on the question what is the ground for our assurance that watches do not come into existence except through the operations of intelligent manufacturers. The answer is plain. We have never run across a watch which has not been deliberately made by someone. But the situation is nothing like this in the case of the innumerable animate and inanimate systems with which we are familiar. Even in the case of living organisms, though they are generated by their parent organisms, the parents do not "make" their progeny in the same sense in which watchmakers make watches. And once this point is clear, the inference from the existence of living organisms to the existence of a supreme designer no longer appears credible.

Moreover, the argument loses all its force if the facts which the hypothesis of a divine designer is supposed to explain can be understood on the basis of a better supported assumption. And indeed, such an alternative explanation is one of the achievements of Darwinian biology. For Darwin showed that one can account for the variety of biological species, as well as for their adaptations to their environments, without invoking a divine creator and acts of special creation. The Darwinian theory explains the diversity of biological species in terms of chance variations in the structure of organisms, and of a mechanism of selection which retains those variant forms that possess some advantages for survival. The evidence for these assumptions is considerable; and developments subsequent to Darwin have only strengthened the case for a thoroughly naturalistic explanation of the facts of biological adaptation. In any event, this version of the argument from design has nothing to recommend it.

A second form of this argument has been recently revived in the speculations of some modern physicsts. No one who is familiar with the facts, can fail to be impressed by the success with which the use of mathematical methods has enabled us to obtain intellectual mastery of many parts of nature. But some thinkers have therefore concluded that since the book of nature is ostensibly written in mathematical language, nature must be the creation of a divine mathematician. However, the argument is most dubious. For it rests, among other things, on the assumption that mathematical tools can be successfully used only if the events of nature exhibit some *special* kind of order, and on the further assumption that if the structure of things were different from what they are mathematical language would be inadequate for describing such structure. But it can be shown that no matter what the world were like—even if it impressed us as being utterly chaotic—it would still possess some order, and would in principle be amenable to a mathematical description. In point of fact, it makes no sense to say that there is absolutely *no* pattern in any conceivable subject matter. To be sure, there are differences in complexities of structure, and if the patterns of events were sufficiently complex we might not be able to unravel them. But however that may be, the success of mathematical physics in giving us some understanding of the world around us does not yield the conclusion that only a mathematician could have devised the patterns of order we have discovered in nature.

4

The inconclusiveness of the three classical arguments for the existence of God was already made evident by Kant, in a manner substantially not different from the above discussion. There are, however, other types of arguments for theism that have been influential in the history of thought, two of which I wish to consider, even if only briefly.

Indeed, though Kant destroyed the classical intellectual foundations for theism, he himself invented a fresh argument for it. Kant's attempted proof is not intended to be a purely theoretical demonstration, and is based on the supposed facts of our moral nature. It has exerted an enormous influence on subsequent theological speculation. In barest outline, the argument is as follows. According to Kant, we are subject not only to physical laws like the rest of nature, but also to moral ones. These moral laws are categorical imperatives, which we must heed not because of their utilitarian consequences, but simply because as autonomous moral agents it is our duty to accept them as binding. However, Kant was keenly aware that though virtue may be its reward, the virtuous man (that is, the man who acts out of a sense of duty and in conformity with the moral law) does not always receive his just desserts in this world; nor did he shut his eyes to the fact that evil men frequently enjoy the best things this world has to offer. In short, virtue does not always reap happiness. Nevertheless, the highest human good is the realization of happiness commensurate with one's virtue; and Kant believed that it is a practical postulate of the moral life to promote this good. But what can guarantee that the highest good is realizable? Such a guarantee can be found only in God, who must therefore exist if the highest good is not to be a fatuous ideal. The existence of an omnipotent, omniscient, and omnibenevolent God is thus postulated as a necessary condition for the possibility of a moral life.

Despite the prestige this argument has acquired, it is difficult to grant it any force. It is easy enough to postulate God's existence. But as Bertrand Russell observed in another connection, postulation has all the advantages of theft over honest toil. No postulation carries with it any assurance that what is postulated is actually the case. And though we may postulate God's existence as a means to guaranteeing the possibility of realizing happiness together with virtue, the postulation establishes neither the actual realizability of this ideal nor the fact of his existence. Moreover, the argument is not made more cogent when we recognize that it is based squarely on the highly dubious conception that considerations of utility and human happiness must not enter into the determination of what is morally obligatory. Having built his moral theory on a radical separation of means from ends, Kant was driven to the desperate postulation of God's existence in order to relate them again. The argument is thus at best a *tour de force*, contrived to remedy a fatal flaw in Kant's initial moral assumptions. It carries no conviction to anyone who does not commit Kant's initial blunder.

One further type of argument, pervasive in much Protestant theological literature, deserves brief mention. Arguments of this type take their point of departure from the psychology of religious and mystical experience. Those who have undergone such experiences, often report that during the experience they feel themselves to be in the presence of the divine and holy, that they lose their sense of self-identity and become merged with some fundamental reality, or that they enjoy a feeling of total dependence upon some ultimate power. The overwhelming sense of transcending one's finitude which characterizes such vivid periods of life, and of coalescing with some ultimate source of all existence, is then taken to be compelling evidence for the existence of a supreme being. In a variant form of this argument, other theologians have identified God as the object which satisfies the commonly experienced need for integrating one's scattered and conflicting impulses into a coherent unity, or as the subject which is of ultimate concern to us. In short, a proof of God's existence is found in the occurrence of certain distinctive experiences.

It would be flying in the face of well-attested facts were one to deny that such experiences frequently occur. But do these facts constitute evidence for the conclusion based on them? Does the fact, for example, that an individual experiences a profound sense of direct contract with an alleged transcendent ground of all reality, constitute competent evidence for the claim that there is such a ground and that it is the immediate cause of the experience? If well-established canons for evaluating evidence are accepted, the answer is surely negative. No one will dispute that many men do have vivid experiences in which such things as ghosts or pink elephants appear before them; but only the hopelessly credulous will without further ado count such experiences as establishing the existence of ghosts and pink elephants. To establish the existence of such things, evidence is required that is obtained under controlled conditions and that can be confirmed by independent inquirers. Again, though a man's report that he is suffering pain may be taken at face value, one cannot take at face value the claim, were he to make it, that it is the food he ate which is the cause (or a contributory cause) of his felt pain—not even if the man were to report a vivid feeling of abdominal disturbance. And similarly, an overwhelming feeling of being in the presence of the Divine is evidence enough for admitting the genuineness of such feeling; it is no evidence for the claim that a supreme being with a substantial existence independent of the experience is the cause of the experience.

COMMENTS ■ QUESTIONS

1. In this paper Nagel sets out to present reasons for rejecting belief in the traditional Judeo-Christian concept of God—that is, belief in "a supreme, self-consistent, ommipotent, omniscient, righteous, and benevolent being" who has created the world but is independent of it. Do you believe that the traditional Judeo-Christian concept of God is the most defensible *concept* of God? That is, is it the best starting point for discussions of whether God exists?
2. Nagel mentions in passing that atheists typically take a dim view of the historical influences of religion: "religious authorities have opposed the correction of glaring injustices, and encouraged politically and socially reactionary policies. Religious institutions have been havens of obscurantist thought and centers for the dissemination of intolerance. Religious creeds have been used to set limits to free inquiry, to perpetuate inhumane treatment of the ill and the underprivileged, and to support moral doctrines insensitive to human suffering." Does this quotation express a fair appraisal of the historical effects of religion? (This is a broad question, of course, but is worth thinking about.)
3. Nagel presents succinct statements of the Cosmological Argument and the Ontological Argument. In light of what has been said in the preceding selections from Saint Anselm, Gaunilo, George Bowles, Samuel Clarke, and William Rowe, would you say that Nagel's statements of these arguments are adequate? Has he stated the essential points for each argument? If you believe that he has, would you say also that Nagel presents good reasons for rejecting both the Cosmological Argument and the Ontological Argument?
4. Do you accept Nagel's reasons for rejecting the Argument from Design? In particular, do you believe that the Darwinian theory of evaluation provides the best explanation for the origin of plants and animals?
5. You may wish to defer your evaluation of the Argument from Morality (God must exist if there is to be a foundation for the highest moral good) until after you have read the selections in chapter 8.

WILLIAM JAMES

Mysticism

* * * * *

One may say truly, I think, that personal religious experience has its root and centre in mystical states of consciousness; so for us, who in these lectures are treating personal experience as the exclusive subject of our study, such states of consciousness ought to form the vital chapter from which the other chapters get their light. Whether my treatment of mystical states will shed more light or darkness, I do not know, for my own constitution shuts me out from their enjoyment almost entirely, and I can speak of them only at second hand. But though forced to look upon the subject so externally, I will be as objective and receptive as I can; and I think I shall at least succeed in convincing you of the reality of the states in question, and of the paramount importance of their function.

First of all, then, I ask, What does the expression "mystical states of consciousness" mean? How do we part off mystical states from other states?

The words "mysticism" and "mystical" are often used as terms of mere reproach, to throw at any opinion which we regard as vague and vast and sentimental, and without a base in either facts or logic. For some writers a "mystic" is any person who believes in thought-transference, or spirit-return. Employed in this way the word has little value: there are too many less ambiguous synonyms. So, to keep it useful by restricting it, I will do what I did in the case of the word "religion," and simply propose to you four marks which, when an experience has them, may justify us in calling it mystical for the purpose of the present lectures. In this way we shall save verbal disputation, and the recriminations that generally go therewith.

1. *Ineffability.* The handiest of the marks by which I classify a state of mind as mystical is negative. The subject of it immediately says that it defies expression, that no adequate report of its contents can be given in words. It follows from this that its quality must be directly experienced; it cannot be imparted or transferred to others. In this peculiarity mystical states are more like states of feeling than like states of intellect. No one can make clear to another who has never had a certain feeling, in what the quality or worth of it consists. One must have musical ears to know the value of a symphony; one must have been in love one's self to un-

A biographical sketch of William James is to be found earlier in this chapter.

From *The Varieties of Religious Experience*, 1902.

derstand a lover's state of mind. Lacking the heart or ear, we cannot interpret the musician or the lover justly, and are even likely to consider him weak-minded or absurd. The mystic finds that most of us accord to his experiences an equally incompetent treatment.

2. *Noetic quality.* Although so similar to states of feeling, mystical states seem to those who experience them to be also states of knowledge. They are states of insight into depths of truth unplumbed by the discursive intellect. They are illuminations, revelations, full of significance and importance, all inarticulate though they remain; and as a rule they carry with them a curious sense of authority for aftertime.

These two characters will entitle any state to be called mystical, in the sense in which I use the word. Two other qualities are less sharply marked, but are usually found. These are:

3. *Transiency.* Mystical states cannot be sustained for long. Except in rare instances, half an hour, or at most an hour or two, seems to be the limit beyond which they fade into the light of common day. Often, when faded, their quality can but imperfectly be reproduced in memory; but when they recur it is recognized; and from one recurrence to another it is susceptible of continuous development in what is felt as inner richness and importance.

4. *Passivity.* Although the oncoming of mystical states may be facilitated by preliminary voluntary operations, as by fixing the attention, or going through certain bodily performances, or in other ways which manuals of mysticism prescribe; yet when the characteristic sort of consciousness once has set in, the mystic feels as if his own will were in abeyance, and indeed sometimes as if he were grasped and held by a superior power. This latter peculiarity connects mystical states with certain definite phenomena of secondary or alternative personality, such as prophetic speech, automatic writing, or the mediumistic trance. When these latter conditions are well pronounced, however, there may be no recollection whatever of the phenomenon, and it may have no significance for the subject's usual inner life, to which, as it were, it makes a mere interruption. Mystical states, strictly so-called, are never merely interruptive. Some memory of their content always remains, and a profound sense of their importance. They modify the inner life of the subject between the times of their recurrence. Sharp divisions in this region are, however, difficult to make, and we find all sorts of gradations and mixtures.

These four characteristics are sufficient to mark out a group of states of consciousness peculiar enough to deserve a special name and to call for careful study. Let it then be called the mystical group.

* * * * *

The simplest rudiment of mystical experience would seem to be that deepened sense of the significance of a maxim or formula which occasionally sweeps over one. "I've heard that said all my life," we exclaim, "but I never realized its full meaning until now." "When a fellow-monk," said Luther, "one day repeated the words of the Creed: 'I believe in the forgiveness of sins,' I saw the Scripture in an entirely new light; and straightway I felt as if I were born anew. It was as if I had found the door of paradise thrown wide open." This sense of deeper significance is not confined to rational propositions. Single words, and conjunctions of words, effects of light on land and sea, odors and musical sounds, all bring it when the mind is tuned aright. Most of us can remember the strangely moving power of passages in certain poems read when we were young, irrational doorways as they were through which the mystery of fact, the wildness and the pang of life, stole into our hearts and thrilled them. The words have now perhaps become mere polished surfaces for us; but lyric poetry and music are alive and significant only in proportion as they fetch these vague vistas of a life continuous with our own, beckoning and inviting, yet ever eluding our pursuit. We are alive or dead to the eternal inner message of the arts according as we have kept or lost this mystical susceptibility.

A more pronounced step forward on the mystical ladder is found in an extremely frequent phenomenon, that sudden feeling, namely, which sometimes sweeps over us, of having "been here before," as if at some indefinite past time, in just this place, with just these people, we were already saying just these things. As Tennyson writes:

> "Moreover, something is or seems
> That touches me with mystic gleams,
> Like glimpses of forgotten dreams—
>
> "Of something felt, like something here;
> Of something done, I know not where;
> Such as no language may declare." [1]

1. The Two Voices.

Sir James Crichton-Browne has given the technical name of "dreamy states" to these sudden invasions of vaguely reminiscent consciousness.[2] They bring a sense of mystery and of the metaphysical duality of things, and the feeling of an enlargement of perception which seems imminent but which never completes itself. In Dr. Crichton-Browne's opinion they connect themselves with the perplexed and scared disturbances of self-consciousness which occasionally precede epileptic attacks. I think that this learned alienist takes a rather absurdly alarmist view of an intrinsically insignificant phenomenon. He follows it along the downward ladder, to insanity; our path pursues the upward ladder chiefly. The divergence shows how important it is to neglect no part of a phenomenon's connections, for we make it appear admirable or dreadful according to the context by which we set it off.

Somewhat deeper plunges into mystical consciousness are met with in yet other dreamy states. Such feelings as these which Charles Kingsley describes are surely far from being uncommon, especially in youth:

> "When I walk the fields, I am oppressed now and then with an innate feeling that everything I see has a meaning, if I could but understand it. And this feeling of being surrounded with truths which I cannot grasp amounts to indescribable awe sometimes.... Have you not felt that your real soul was imperceptible to your mental vision, except in a few

2. The Lancet, July 6 and 13, 1895, reprinted as the Cavendish Lecture, on Dreamy Mental States, London, Baillière, 1895.

hallowed moments?"[3]

A much more extreme state of mystical consciousness is described by J. A. Symonds; and probably more persons than we suspect could give parallels to it from their own experience.

> "Suddenly," writes Symonds, "at church, or in company, or when I was reading, and always, I think, when my muscles were at rest, I felt the approach of the mood. Irresistibly it took possession of my mind and will, lasted what seemed an eternity, and disappeared in a series of rapid sensations which resembled the awakening from anæsthetic influence. One reason why I disliked this kind of trance was that I could not describe it to myself. I cannot even now find words to render it intelligible. It consisted in a gradual but swiftly progressive obliteration of space, time, sensation, and the multitudinous factors of experience which seem to qualify what we are pleased to call our Self. In proportion as these conditions of ordinary consciousness were subtracted, the sense of an underlying or essential consciousness acquired intensity. At last nothing remained but a pure, absolute, abstract Self. The universe became without form and void of content. But Self persisted, formidable in its vivid keenness, feeling the most poignant doubt about reality, ready, as it seemed, to find existence break as breaks a bubble round about it. And what then? The apprehension of a coming dissolution, the grim conviction that this state was the last state of the conscious Self, the sense that I had followed the last thread of being to the verge of the abyss, and had arrived at demonstration of eternal Maya or illusion, stirred or seemed to stir me up again. The return to ordinary conditions of sentient existence began by my first recovering the power of touch, and then by the gradual though rapid influx of familiar impressions and diurnal interests. At last I felt myself once more a human being; and though the riddle of what is meant by life remained unsolved, I was thankful for this return from the abyss—this deliverance from so awful an initiation into the mysteries of skepticism.
>
> "This trance recurred with diminishing frequency until I reached the age of twenty-eight. It served to impress upon my growing nature the phantasmal unreality of all the circumstances which contribute to a merely phenomenal consciousness. Often have I asked myself with anguish, on waking from that formless state of denuded, keenly sentient being, Which is the unreality—the trance of fiery, vacant, apprehensive, skeptical Self from which I issue, or these surrounding phenomena and habits which veil that inner Self and build a self of flesh-and-blood conventionality? Again, are men the factors of some dream, the dream-like unsubstantiality of which they comprehend at such eventful moments? What would happen if the final stage of the trance were reached?"

* * * * *

Certain aspects of nature seem to have a peculiar power of awakening such mystical moods. Most of the striking cases which I have collected have occurred out of doors. Literature has commemorated this fact in many passages of great beauty—this extract, for example, from Amiel's Journal Intime:

> "Shall I ever again have any of those prodigious reveries which sometimes came to me in former days? One day, in youth, at sunrise,

3. Charles Kingsley's Life, i. 55, quoted by Inge: Christian Mysticism, London, 1899, p. 341.

> sitting in the ruins of the castle of Faucigny; and again in the mountains, under the noonday sun, above Lavey, lying at the foot of a tree and visited by three butterflies; once more at night upon the shingly shore of the Northern Ocean, my back upon the sand and my vision ranging through the milky way;—such grand and spacious, immortal, cosmogonic reveries, when one reaches to the stars, when one owns the innite! Moments divine, ecstatic hours; in which our thought flies from world to world, pierces the great enigma, breathes with a respiration broad, tranquil, and deep as the respiration of the ocean, serene and limitless as the blue firmament; . . . instants of irresistible intuition in which one feels one's self great as the universe, and calm as a god. . . . What hours, what memories! The vestiges they leave behind are enough to fill us with belief and enthusiasm, as if they were visits of the Holy Ghost."[4]

Here is a similar record from the memoirs of that interesting German idealist, Malwida von Meysenbug:

> "I was alone upon the seashore as all these thoughts flowed over me, liberating and reconciling; and now again, as once before in distant days in the Alps of Dauphiné, I was impelled to kneel down, this time before the illimitable ocean, symbol of the Infinite. I felt that I prayed as I had never prayed before, and knew now what prayer really is: to return from the solitude of individuation into the consciousness of unity with all that is, to kneel down as one that passes away, and to rise up as one imperishable. Earth, heaven, and sea resounded as in one vast world-encircling harmony. It was as if the chorus of all the great who had ever lived were about me. I felt myself one with them, and it appeared as if I heard their greeting: 'Thou too belongest to the company of those who overcome.' "[5]

4. Op. cit., i. 43–44.

* * * * *

I have now sketched with extreme brevity and insufficiency, but as fairly as I am able in the time allowed, the general traits of the mystic range of consciousness. *It is on the whole pantheistic and optimistic, or at least the opposite of pessimistic. It is anti-naturalistic, and harmonizes best with twice-bornness and so-called other-worldly states of mind.*

My next task is to inquire whether we can invoke it as authoritative. Does it furnish any *warrant for the truth* of the twice-bornness and supernaturality and pantheism which it favors? I must give my answer to this question as concisely as I can.

In brief my answer is this—and I will divide it into three parts:

(1) Mystical states, when well developed, usually are, and have the right to be, absolutely authoritative over the individuals to whom they come.

(2) No authority emanates from them which should make it a duty for those who stand outside of them to accept their revelations uncritically.

(3) They break down the authority of the non-mystical or rationalistic consciousness, based upon the understanding and the senses alone. They show it to be only one kind of consciousness. They open out the possibility of other orders of truth, in which, so far as anything in us vitally responds to them, we may free-

5. Memoiren einer Idealistin, 5te Auflage, 1900, iii. 166. For years she had been unable to pray, owing to materialistic belief.

ly continue to have faith.

I will take up these points one by one.

1

As a matter of psychological fact, mystical states of a well-pronounced and emphatic sort *are* usually authoritative over those who have them.[6] They have been "there," and know. It is vain for rationalism to grumble about this. If the mystical truth that comes to a man proves to be a force that he can live by, what mandate have we of the majority to order him to live in another way? We can throw him into a prison or a madhouse, but we cannot change his mind—we commonly attach it only the more stubbornly to its beliefs.[7] It mocks our utmost efforts, as a matter of fact, and in point of logic it absolutely escapes our jurisdiction. Our own more "rational" beliefs are based on evidence exactly similar in nature to that which mystics quote for theirs. Our senses, namely, have assured us of certain states of fact; but mystical experiences are as direct perceptions of fact for those who have them as any sensations ever were for us. The records show that even though the five senses be in abeyance in them, they are absolutely sensational in their epistemological quality, if I may be pardoned the barbarous expression—that is, they are face to face presentations of what seems immediately to exist.

The mystic is, in short, *invulnerable*, and must be left, whether we relish it or not, in undisturbed enjoyment of his creed. Faith, says Tolstoy, is that by which men live. And faith-state and mystic state are practically convertible terms.

2

But I now proceed to add that mystics have no right to claim that we ought to accept the deliverance of their peculiar experiences, if we are ourselves outsiders and feel no private call thereto. The utmost they can ever ask of us in this life is to admit that they establish a presumption. They form a consensus and have an unequivocal outcome; and it would be odd, mystics might say, if such a unanimous type of experience should prove to be altogether wrong. At bottom, however, this would only be an appeal to numbers, like the appeal of rationalism the other way; and the appeal to numbers has no logical force. If we acknowledge it, it is for "suggestive," not for logical reasons: we follow the majority because to do so suits our life.

But even this presumption from the unanimity of mystics is far from being strong. In characterizing mystic states as pantheistic, optimistic, etc., I am afraid I over-simplified the truth. I did so for expository reasons, and to keep the closer to the

6. I abstract from weaker states, and from those cases of which the books are full, where the director (but usually not the subject) remains in doubt whether the experience may not have proceeded from the demon.

7. Example: Mr. John Nelson writes of his imprisonment for preaching Methodism: "My soul was as a watered garden, and I could sing praises to God all day long; for he turned my captivity into joy, and gave me to rest as well on the boards, as if I had been on a bed of down. Now could I say, 'God's service is perfect freedom,' and I was carried out much in prayer that my enemies might drink of the same river of peace which my God gave so largely to me." Journal, London, no date, p. 172.

classic mystical tradition. The classic religious mysticism, it now must be confessed, is only a "privileged case." It is an *extract*, kept true to type by the selection of the fittest specimens and their preservation in "schools." It is carved out from a much larger mass; and if we take the larger mass as seriously as religious mysticism has historically taken itself, we find that the supposed unanimity largely disappears. To begin with, even religious mysticism itself, the kind that accumulates traditions and makes schools, is much less unanimous than I have allowed. It has been both ascetic and antinomianly self-indulgent within the Christian church.[8] It is dualistic in Sankhya, and monistic in Vedanta philosophy. I called it pantheistic; but the great Spanish mystics are anything but pantheists. They are with few exceptions non-metaphysical minds, for whom "the category of personality" is absolute. The "union" of man with God is for them much more like an occasional miracle than like an original identity.[9] How different again, apart from the happiness common to all, is the mysticism of Walt Whitman, Edward Carpenter, Richard Jefferies, and other naturalistic pantheists, from the more distinctively Christian sort.[10] The fact is that the mystical feeling of enlargement, union, and emancipation has no specific intellectual content whatever of its own. It is capable of forming matrimonial alliances with material furnished by the most diverse philosophies and theologies, provided only they can find a place in their framework for its peculiar emotional mood. We have no right, therefore, to invoke its prestige as distinctively in favor of any special belief, such as that in absolute idealism, or in the absolute monistic identity, or in the absolute goodness, of the world. It is only relatively in favor of all these things—it passes out of common human consciousness in the direction in which they lie.

So much for religious mysticism proper. But more remains to be told, for religious mysticism is only one half of mysticism. The other half has no accumulated traditions except those which the text-books on insanity supply. Open any one of these, and you will find abundant cases in which "mystical ideas" are cited as characteristic symptoms of enfeebled or deluded states of mind. In delusional insanity, paranoia, as they sometimes call it, we may have a *diabolical* mysticism, a sort of religious mysticism turned upside down. The same sense of ineffable importance in the smallest events, the same texts and words coming with new meanings, the same voices and visions and leadings and missions, the same controlling by extraneous powers; only this time the emotion is pessimistic: instead of consolations we have desolations; the meanings are dreadful; and the powers are ene-

---

8. Ruysbroeck, in the work which Maeterlinck has translated, has a chapter against the antinomianism of disciples. H. Delacroix's book (Essai sur le mysticisme spéculatif en Allemagne au XIVme Siècle, Paris, 1900) is full of antinomian material. Compare also A. Jundt: *Les Amis de Dieu au XIV Siécle, These de Strasbourg*, 1879.

9. Compare Paul Rousselot: *Les Mystiques Espagnols*, Paris, 1869, ch. xii.

10. See Carpenter's *Towards Democracy*, especially the latter parts, and Jefferies's wonderful and splendid mystic rhapsody, *The Story of my Heart*.

mies to life. It is evident that from the point of view of their psychological mechanism, the classic mysticism and these lower mysticisms spring from the same mental level, from that great subliminal or transmarginal region of which science is beginning to admit the existence, but of which so little is really known. That region contains every kind of matter: "seraph and snake" abide there side by side. To come from thence is no infallible credential. What comes must be sifted and tested, and run the gauntlet of confrontation with the total context of experience, just like what comes from the outer world of sense. Its value must be ascertained by empirical methods, so long as we are not mystics ourselves.

Once more, then, I repeat that non-mystics are under no obligation to acknowledge in mystical states a superior authority conferred on them by their intrinsic nature.[11]

11. In chapter i. of book ii. of his work Degeneration, "Max Nordau" seeks to undermine all mysticism by exposing the weakness of the lower kinds. Mysticism for him means any sudden perception of hidden significance in things. He explains such perception by the abundant uncompleted associations which experiences may arouse in a degenerate brain. These give to him who has the experience a vague and vast sense of its leading further, yet they awaken no definite or useful consequent in his thought. The explanation is a plausible one for certain sorts of feeling of significance; and other alienists (Wernicke, for example, in his *Grundriss der Psychiatrie*, Theil ii., Leipzig, 1896) have explained "paranoiac" conditions by a laming of the association-organ. But the higher mystical flights, with their positiveness and abruptness, are surely products of no such merely negative condition. It seems far more reasonable to ascribe them to inroads from the subconscious life, of the cerebral activity correlative to which we as yet know nothing.

3

Yet, I repeat once more, the existence of mystical states absolutely overthrows the pretension of non-mystical states to be the sole and ultimate dictators of what we may believe. As a rule, mystical states merely add a supersensuous meaning to the ordinary outward data of consciousness. They are excitements like the emotions of love or ambition, gifts to our spirit by means of which facts already objectively before us fall into a new expressiveness and make a new connection with our active life. They do not contradict these facts as such, or deny anything that our senses have immediately seized.[12] It is the rationalistic critic rather who plays the part of denier in the controversy, and his denials have no strength, for there never can be a state of facts to which new meaning may not truthfully be added, provided the mind ascend to a more enveloping point of view. It must always remain an open question whether mystical states may not possibly be such superior points of view, windows through which the mind looks out upon a more extensive and inclusive world. The difference of the views seen from the different mystical windows need not prevent us from entertaining this supposition. The wider world would in that case prove to have a mixed constitution like that of this world, that is all. It would have its celestial and its infernal regions, its tempting and its saving moments, its valid experiences and its counterfeit ones,

12. They sometimes add subjective *audita et visa* to the facts, but as these are usually interpreted as transmundane, they oblige no alteration in the facts of sense.

just as our world has them; but it would be a wider world all the same. We should have to use its experiences by selecting and subordinating and substituting just as is our custom in this ordinary naturalistic world; we should be liable to error just as we are now; yet the counting in of that wider world of meanings, and the serious dealing with it, might, in spite of all the perplexity, be indispensable stages in our approach to the final fullness of the truth.

COMMENTS ■ QUESTIONS

1. "One may say truly [says James] that personal religious experience has its roots and center in mystical states of consciousness." James goes on to describe what he takes to be the essential characteristics of mystical experience—ineffability, noetic quality, transiency, and passivity. Remember that there are experiences other than mystical ones proper that many people call religious or believe put them in contact with a "world beyond." These include, among others, seeming to hear disembodied voices, seeming to see apparitions, seeming to feel that one is not alone when no other person is present, seeming to leave one's body temporarily in a near-death experience, and seeming to have memories of "past lives." Some of these sorts of experiences are discussed elsewhere in the book from which the present selection is taken, James's *The Varieties of Religious Experience*. Others are discussed in more recent books, such as Raymond Moody's *Life After Life* and Ian Stevenson's *Twenty Cases Suggestive of Reincarnation*. Do you believe that reports of these experiences should be taken seriously? If so, which should be taken the most seriously?
2. "We pass into mystical states from out of ordinary consciousness as from a less into a more, as from a smallness into a vastness, and at the same time as from an unrest to a rest." Much of the literature on mystical experience is couched in such vague but suggestive words as these. Such writing does not have the clarity or precision of science or philosophical analysis at its best. Does this mean that it should not be taken seriously? Or does it mean that we should take it all the more seriously as pointing to "higher realities" that necessarily are difficult to describe?
3. Do you agree with James's evaluation of mystical experiences when they are taken all altogether—that at most they establish a weak "presumption" in favor of certain religious ideas?
4. What do you suppose Thomas Huxley would have said about James's account of mystical experience?

JONATHAN EDWARDS

The Sense of the Heart

* * * * *

There is such a thing, if the Scriptures are of any use to teach us anything, as a spiritual, supernatural understanding of divine things, that is peculiar to the saints, and which those who are not saints have nothing of. 'Tis certainly a kind of understanding, apprehending or discerning of divine things, that natural men have nothing of.

* * * * *

From hence it may be surely inferred, wherein spiritual understanding consists. For if there be in the saints a kind of apprehension or perception, which is in its nature, perfectly diverse from all that natural men have, or that it is possible they should have, till they have a new nature; it must consist in their having a certain kind of ideas or sensations of mind, which are simply diverse from all that is or can be in the minds of natural men. And that is the same thing as to say, that it consists in the sensations of a new spiritual sense, which the souls of natural men have not; as is evident by what has been before, once and again observed. But I have already shown what that new spiritual sense is, which the saints have given them in regeneration, and what is the object of it. I have shown that the immediate object of it is the supreme beauty and excellency of the nature of divine things, as they are in themselves. And this is agreeable to the Scripture: the Apostle very plainly teaches that the great thing discovered by spiritual light, and understood by spiritual knowledge, is the glory of divine things, (2 Cor. 4:3, 4). "But if our gospel be hid, it is hid to them that are lost; in whom the God of this world hath blinded the minds of them that believe not, lest the light of the glorious gospel of Christ, who is the image of God, should shine unto them;" together with 4:6: "For God who commanded the light to shine out of darkness, hath shined in our hearts, to give the light of the knowledge of the glory of God in the face of Jesus Christ;" and 3:18 preceding: "But we all, with open face, beholding as in a glass, the glory of the Lord, are changed into the same image, from glory to glory, even as by the Spirit of the Lord." And it must needs be so, for as has been before observed,

---

Jonathan Edwards (1703–1758), the best known eighteenth century American philosopher, was influenced by John Locke. Edwards was also a theologian and preacher. Two major themes of his works are human sinfulness and the orderly, deterministic workings of nature.

From *Treatise Concerning Religious Affections*, 1746.

the Scripture often teaches that all true religion summarily consists in the love of divine things. And therefore that kind of understanding or knowledge, which is the proper foundation of true religion, must be the knowledge of the loveliness of divine things. For doubtless, that knowledge which is the proper foundation of love, is the knowledge of loveliness. What that beauty or loveliness of divine things is, which is the proper and immediate object of a spiritual sense of mind, was showed under the last head insisted on, viz. that it is the beauty of their moral perfection. Therefore it is in the view or sense of this, that Spiritual understanding does more immediately and primarily consist. And indeed it is plain it can be nothing else; for (as has been shown) there is nothing pertaining to divine things besides the beauty of their moral excellency, and those properties and qualities of divine things which this beauty is the foundation of, but what natural men and devils can see and know, and will know fully and clearly to all eternity.

From what has been said, therefore, we come necessarily to this conclusion, concerning that wherein spiritual understanding consists; viz. that it consists in a sense of the heart, of the supreme beauty and sweetness of the holiness or moral perfection of divine things, together with all that discerning and knowledge of things of religion, that depends upon, and flows from such a sense.

COMMENTS ■ QUESTIONS

1. One major objection that philosophers raise regarding religious experience is that, for the most part, it appears not to come through any of the five senses. Many philosophers believe that sensory experience is the only source of knowledge. (For discussions of this issue, see chapter ten.) In the eighteenth century, Jonathan Edwards agreed—but wished to add that certain persons ("saints") have a special sense, a "sense of the heart," by which they acquire knowledge of divine things. Do you believe that the "sense of the heart" as Edwards describes it can properly be referred to as being (in any sense!) a sense?
2. Do you believe that Edwards is correct in saying that only a few people, namely those he refers to as saints, have the "sense of the heart"? Is there any reason to believe that this sense is possessed by a great number of people or by anyone at all?

READINGS

Angeles, Peter, ed. *Critiques of God.* Buffalo, N.Y.: Prometheus Books, 1976. A very useful collection representing skeptical and atheistic viewpoints.

Burrill, Donald. *The Cosmological Argument.* New York: Doubleday, Anchor Books, 1967. A good collection of critical essays.

Hick, John. *Faith and Knowledge.* 2d ed. Ithaca, N.Y.: Cornell University Press, 1960. One of the best defenses of religious faith.

———, ed. *The Existence of God.* New York: Macmillan, 1964. A very good collection of readings, both classical and contemporary, on the main arguments for God's existence.

Kaufman, Walter. *The Faith of a Heretic.* Ithaca, N.Y.: Cornell University Press, 1961. One of the best presentations of the case against religious faith.

Klemke, E. D., ed. *The Meaning of Life.* New York: Oxford University Press, 1981. Contains readings that discuss three different perspectives on the meaning of life: theistic, nontheistic, and the view that is critical of the concept of the meaning of life.

Leuba, J. H. *The Psychology of Religious Mysticism.* New York: Harcourt, Brace and World, 1925. Discusses mysticism from an unsympathetic perspective.

Mitchell, Basil, ed. *Philosophy of Religion.* Oxford: Oxford University Press, 1971. A collection of papers on faith, religious language, and related topics. Perhaps somewhat more difficult to read than other collections.

Plantinga, Alvin, ed. *The Ontological Argument.* New York: Doubleday, Anchor Books, 1965. A good collection of papers and excerpts. Contemporary treatments of the ontological argument are somewhat dated, but the classical excerpts are well chosen and comprehensive.

Rowe, William L., and William J. Wainwright, eds. *Philosophy of Religion: Selected Readings.* New York: Harcourt Brace Jovanovich, 1973. One of the best general anthologies. Includes important readings on religious language and the concept of God.

Smith, H. George. *Atheism: The Case Against God.* Los Angeles: Nash, 1974. Extensive criticism of religion and arguments for God's existence.

Stace, W. T. *Mysticism and Philosophy.* Philadelphia: Lippincott, 1960. Discusses mysticism from a sympathetic point of view.

C H A P T E R F O U R

[The] law of justice ... declares that each should participate in the perfection of the universe and in a happiness of his own in proportion to his own virtue and to the degree in which his will has regard to the common good.

—Gottfried Wilhelm Leibniz

A baby who drowns accidentally in a flood is just as incomprehensibly dead as a baby tossed by someone into the sea.

—Martin Gardner

Evil

One popular view of philosophy is really quite unfair. According to this view, philosophy is too abstract to be concerned with the things in life that matter most. For example, consider the writings of philosophers on the subject of evil. Most philosophical books and articles on the "problem of evil" treat it primarily as a *conceptual* problem. By this is meant a problem having to do with the logical relations among concepts, specifically the concept of God and the concept of evil. Philosophers ask: Is the concept of God compatible with the concept of evil? If the concepts are compatible, God could exist despite the evil in the world; if the concepts are not compatible, then God could not exist along with the evil in the world.

People who are not philosophers may ask: Isn't the question of evil considerably more than a conceptual problem? How can we actually live out our lives in a world that contains so much evil? How can evil be lessened or eliminated? These may appear to be the most important questions having to do with evil. Thus, it may appear that philosophy has taken an issue that is live and full of urgency and made it cold and abstract.

In reality, many of life's problems are essentially conceptual in the sense that resolution must come primarily at the level of human thought, not at the level of human action. How we think about the world and the evil in it matters a great deal, and it matters apart from doing practical things that may prevent evil or produce good. How we think about evil bears directly on many important beliefs, such as the belief (or disbelief) in the existence of God and the belief (or disbelief) in the existence of a world that one can view optimistically. These "foundational" beliefs in turn bear directly on the ways that we live our lives. "The thought is father of the deed."

It would be nice if we *could* solve the problem of evil by taking direct action. However, large amounts of evil will doubtless remain in the world—at least within the foreseeable future—regardless of what people do. If we cannot solve the problem of evil directly, the only apparent recourse is to *think about evil* in an attempt to come to terms with it.

For thousands of years, philosophers have been thinking about the human condition from all conceivable perspectives. They have thought about their own personal disappointments, unhappiness, and impending death; as sensitive individuals (in most cases), they have felt the pain that comes from contemplating the misery of others. They have tried to find ways to think of evil that would make it easier to bear, and in pursuing this goal they have come back again and again to the age-old question: Does evil serve good? That is, in the final analysis, is it not a good thing to have evil in the world?

Philosophers have asked this question most often in the context of their religious beliefs, or in the context of raising challenges to religious beliefs. If God is all-good, all-knowing, and all-powerful, then it would seem that God would not permit evil—unless evil does serve good. If a way can be found to think of evil as serving good, then it cannot be argued that the existence of evil precludes the existence of God. In other words, the concept of God would be compatible with the concept of evil (or, more exactly, with the concept of the kind and quantity of evil that exist in the world). If the two concepts are compatible, we can take a different view of suffering, pain, and disappointment than we could otherwise. If the concept of God is *not* compatible with the concept of evil in the world, the implications again are far-reaching.

The first reading selection in this chapter, from a recent book by Martin Gardner, contains a particularly clear and vivid statement of the so-called Argument from Evil, plus a discussion of some of the responses to the argument. The Argument from Evil attempts to show that the evil in the world is such that God's existence is impossible. As Gardner sees it, the only way to refute the argument is through an appeal to faith in the mysteries of God's ways.

In contrast, the second selection in the chapter, from the famous seventeenth century philosopher Gottfried Wilhelm Leibniz, defends a refutation of the Argument from Evil that is based entirely upon reason. According to Leibniz, we have good reason to believe that we live in the "best of all possible worlds"—a world that, despite the evil in it, a supremely powerful, wise, and good being could have created.

John Hick, a contemporary philosopher, rejects the Argument from Evil in a somewhat different way, by appealing to a belief in life after death. Hick argues that the existence of God is not compatible with the existence of evil in *this life* when this life is considered by itself. However, that is a shortsighted view of things. Let us suppose instead that lessons learned from suffering in this life will bear fruit in the next life, and that there will then be recompense for the suffering of the innocent. Let us suppose that there will be "no personal life that is unperfected and no suffering that has not eventually become a phase in the fulfillment of God's good purpose." This is not to say that, according to Hick, the present life is only a "preparation for eternity"; the "soul-making" that is made possible by the presence of evil that must be responded to can be thought of as increasing the value and significance of *this life* as well as being preparation for the next life.

In "The Free Man's Worship," Bertrand Russell speaks for an heroic attitude toward the great imperfections of the world. For Russell, the material world is not good, but human existence is limited to it. "Brief and powerless is Man's life; on him and all his race the slow, sure doom falls pitiless and dark."

The final selection, from J. L. Mackie, is perhaps the most difficult to read. It is a careful, step-by-step analysis of the major responses to the Argument from Evil.

The readings in this chapter represent all major positions in Western philosophy regarding the problem of evil. In addition, Martin Gardner makes reference to the doctrine of *karma*, which plays a major role in Eastern philosophy. According to the doctrine of karma, all, or at least most, of the evil in the world can be explained in terms of a belief in reincarnation. People can live more than one life (that is, their souls or spirits may return after death to a new human life in a different body). Therefore, a person who appears to be innocent may in reality deserve to suffer as punishment for misdeeds in an earlier life. In other cases, suffering may be necessary preparation for living a better future life. (The final reading selection in chapter 7 contains a discussion of some arguments for the existence of reincarnation.)

As you read through the chapters in this book, you will notice again and again that the basic problems of philosophy are all closely linked to each other. You will become aware that the divisions among chapters are somewhat artificial. We have seen that the problem of evil is closely tied to the question of God's existence and to the question of whether there is life after death (and if so, in what form). Although we have not yet mentioned it, the problem of evil is also closely tied to the question of free will (the subject for chapter 5). This connection is discussed at some length by Mackie in section B4 of his paper (he argues that linking together human free will and evil will not establish that God's existence is compatible with the evil in the world). The problem of evil is also linked to questions about the foundations for moral values (taken up in chapter 8) and to the conflict between egoism and altruism (taken up in chapter 9). More and more as you examine arguments for and against a diversity of different philosophical claims, you will find that you need to evaluate entire *networks* of views. You will find that you cannot accept or reject a particular view by itself but only in the context of interrelated philosophical claims.

GOTTFRIED WILHELM LEIBNIZ

[Consider] the Principle of Sufficient Reason, in virtue of which we believe that no fact can be real and no statement true unless it has a sufficient reason why it should be thus and not otherwise. Most frequently, however, these reasons cannot be known to us.

If we were able to understand sufficiently well the order of the universe, we should find that it surpasses all the desires of the wisest of us, and that it is impossible to render it better than it is, not only for all in general, but also for each one of us in particular.

—*Monadology*

Gottfried Wilhelm Leibniz (1646–1716) was born in Leipzig and spent most of his life in major European cities. His life is a most impressive example of self-motivation. His father, a professor of law and philosophy, had a large library. When Leibniz was six, his father died and Leibniz's mother took him away from a dull teacher and gave him the run of his father's library. By the time he was fifteen, not only was Leibniz prepared for the university, but he had read more widely than many mature scholars. By the time he was twenty, he had earned a doctorate and was offered a professorship at the University of Altdorf. He declined this to pursue a diplomatic career, which he combined over the course of a long life with his interests in philosophy, mathematics, and physics. Very energetic and enthusiastic, Leibnitz pursued political ideals that were not much appreciated in his day: a vision of a world society of nations founded upon science and culture and guided by Christian ethics. With his wide intellectual interests and great number of friends in high places, Leibniz lived a very satisfying life.

MARTIN GARDNER

Evil: Why We Don't Know Why

* * * * *

It is customary to distinguish moral evil or sin from what is usually called physical or natural evil, but unless I say otherwise, or the context implies it, I shall use the word to mean every kind of pain and suffering regardless of the cause. A baby who drowns accidentally in a flood is just as incomprehensibly dead as a baby tossed by someone into the sea. If a madman fires a gun at a crowd, killing ten people at random, they are just as needlessly dead as if they had been killed by an earthquake. It is this kind of senseless, irrational evil that is such a monstrous stumbling block for a theist. . . . To the atheist, or to the pantheist who is almost an atheist, there is no problem of evil. Evil is just part of how things are.

Occasionally one encounters the notion that an atheist faces an equally difficult problem in explaining goodness. It is a foolish notion because the atheist has no need to explain either good or evil. Of course if one could muster up a belief that God is supremely evil, then a problem of good might arise. It could be justified (as atheists sometimes do in jest) by asserting that all the good we experience is necessary to make possible greater pain. What better means could a Supreme Devil use for maximizing evil than allowing his creatures to enjoy life for a brief time, even to live with hope for another life, only to meet with final annihilation or perpetual torment in hell? But for the atheist or pantheist there is no problem of good or evil. The world is simply the absurd mixture that it is.

Evil is not even a problem for polytheism unless the gods form a hierarchy with a deity of supreme power and goodness at the top. In Greek mythology the gods who have power over human lives are themselves mixtures of good and evil impulses, but even in ancient Greece the problem of evil arose whenever the power of Zeus was emphasized. Epicurus seems to have been the first philosopher to state clearly the atheist's most formidable argument. Either Zeus is unable to prevent suffering, in which case he is not powerful enough to be called a supreme God, or Zeus has the

---

Martin Gardner has for many years written the "Mathematical Games" section of Scientific American. *He has written many books about science, and one on pseudoscience that has become a classic*—Fads and Fallacies in the Name of Science.

From pp. 242–244, 254–263, and 268–272 in *The Whys of a Philosophical Scrivener* by Martin Gardner. By permission of William Morrow & Company.

power to prevent suffering but doesn't wish to exercise it, in which case he is not moral enough to be worshiped as a supreme deity. Here is how Philo, in David Hume's *Dialogues Concerning Natural Religion*, phrases the argument: "Is he [God] willing to prevent evil, but not able? Then is he impotent. Is he able, but not willing? Then is he malevolent. Is he both able and willing? Whence then is evil?"

This argument, deadly and incisive, has been repeated endlessly by philosophers of all persuasions. I suspect that in every age and place, if you asked an ordinary atheist why he or she did not believe in God you would get some version of Epicurus's argument. If suffering were only a minor aspect of the human scene, the argument might have less force, but the plain truth is that the amount of needless, irrational misery inflicted on humanity passes all comprehension. No one has expressed this with more painful honesty than John Stuart Mill in his essay "Nature." The paragraph is too long to quote in full, but here is how it begins:

> In sober truth, nearly all the things which men are hanged or imprisoned for doing to one another are nature's everyday performances. Killing, the most criminal act recognized by human laws, nature does once to every being that lives, and in a large proportion of cases after protracted tortures such as only the greatest monsters whom we read of ever purposely inflicted on their living fellow creatures. If by an arbitrary reservation we refuse to account anything murder but what abridges a certain term supposed to be allotted to human life, nature also does this to all but a small percentage of lives, and does it in all the modes, violent or insidious, in which the worst human beings take the lives of one another. Nature impales men, breaks them as if on the wheel, casts them to be devoured by wild beasts, burns them to death, crushes them with stones like the first Christian martyr, starves them with hunger, freezes them with cold, poisons them by the quick or slow venom of her exhalations, and has hundreds of other hideous deaths in reserve such as the ingenious cruelty of a Nabis or a Domitian never surpassed. All this nature does with the most supercilious disregard both of mercy and of justice. . . .

Emily Dickinson said it ironically:

> *Apparently with no surprise*
> *To any happy flower*
> *The frost beheads it at its play—*
> *In accidental power—*
> *The blonde assassin passes on—*
> *The sun proceeds unmoved*
> *To measure off another day*
> *For an approving God.*[1]

* * * * *

In no way will this chapter solve the enigma of evil. As a theist I believe by faith, and by faith alone, that there is an answer. But I do not know the answer. At the end of the chapter I will defend the view, also supported only by faith, that God does not want us to know the answer.

Let us build some models. One, the model of choice for most of those today who believe in an afterlife, is that the evils that befall us are punishments for sins in previous lives. The doctrines of reincarnation and karma, which this model presupposes, are suggested in Plato (is

1. *The Complete Poems of Emily Dickinson*, Thomas H. Johnson, ed. (1960), Poem 1624.

there anything Plato does not suggest?), defended by Pythagoras and Plotinus, and by some Greek and Roman mystery religions. The model is taken for granted in almost every Hindu sect and in most forms of Buddhism. Today in the United States it is a fundamental dogma of such cults as theosophy, Rosicrucianism, and Scientology.[2] It is popular among many who belong to no organized church or cult, but who are caught up in current enthusiasms for Eastern religions and the paranormal.

Although the doctrine can be found in some minor strands of old Judaism (parts of the Talmud, the Kabbala, the writings of Philo), even in some early Christian heresies such as Gnosticism and Manicheanism, it has played almost no role in Christian theology. The reason surely is that Jesus did not teach it. It is as unsupported by the New Testament as it is omnipresent in Hindu sacred literature.

The model is logically flawless, incapable of empirical refutation, and like the hypothesis of life after death it could be confirmed by experiments. There is now a considerable literature about individuals who claim to recall details of their past lives. In recent decades experimenters such as Ian Stevenson have reported such recall by persons who have been "regressed" under hypnosis and hypnotic drugs. This is not the place to examine such extraordinary claims. I will say only that I find the evidence as shaky, and the experiments as poorly controlled, as the "evidential" claims of Spiritualism.

The often encountered argument from moments of *déjà vu* is valueless because there are adequate explanations that do not assume previous lives, and because *déjà vu* is counterbalanced by the less common but equally eerie experience of *jamais vu*—a peculiar strangeness about a familiar scene. I recall a startling occasion a few years ago when my wife and I were driving home late at night along a New York parkway we had traversed a hundred times, yet both of us suddenly felt as if we had taken a wrong turn and were on a road we had never traveled before. The feeling lasted several minutes. No doubt something in the environment of which we were unconscious was affecting us, but we never found out what it was.

Occasionally it is argued that our sufferings cannot result from bad karma because we have no recall of past sins and therefore the punishment is useless. It is a poor argument. Believers can reply that lack of memory is essential for the punishment, and that a time will come when our recall will be complete. Perhaps our souls remember past cycles in the intervals between earthly reincarnations. In any case, at some future date we may be able to see the entire pattern, to appreciate the impeccable justice behind it all.

I cannot say this model is wrong. In spite of its singular beauty, and the grandeur it adds to the spectacle of evolution (if one believes that our souls began their pilgrimage in lowly forms of life), in spite of the sim-

---

2. I did not include the Unity movement, because it professes to have no dogmas. However, both Charles and Myrtle Fillmore, who founded this New Thought cult in Kansas City in the 1890s, were passionate believers in reincarnation, and today most of Unity's ministers and members share that belief.

ple solution it offers for the problem of evil, I cannot say I find the model satisfying. Because I have no memory of a previous life, I tend to rule it out by the principle of Occam's razor. I readily confess that my having been brought up a Christian may play a strong role in this sentiment. Had I spent my childhood in India, with Hindu parents, perhaps I would now find the doctrine more attractive. Another reason I am not now attracted to reincarnation is that in cultures where it is widely believed, it is constantly invoked to condone extreme intolerance. In India, for example, the misery of the untouchables has repeatedly been justified by other castes on the grounds that the unclean are being punished for their sins in a previous life. In any case, my heart has no need for the doctrine. I do not know if it is false. I only feel it is false.

The mathematician I. J. Good, in his entertaining anthology of "partly-baked" ideas, *The Scientist Speculates*, proposes a curious variant of the reincarnation model. Good calls it "a theory which is impossible to believe if true." We are on earth as punishment for crimes committed in heaven, and part of the punishment is that we cannot believe the theory. "For if we did, the punishment would not be effective." Good makes clear that he himself does not believe this. How could he if it were true? [3] And there are other curious models that justify irrational evil on grounds less fantastic to Eastern minds than ours. You'll find some choice examples in Raymond Smullyan's book *5000 B. C. and Other Philosophical Fantasies*.

The models that have dominated theism in the West, in or out of the Judaic-Christian tradition, all have one central and incredible idea in common. They assert that, in some fashion we can now comprehend only dimly (if at all), the evils we suffer are permitted by God because they contribute, in the long run, to the highest obtainable good.

The model is suggested in Plato, by some of Plato's followers, by the Stoics, and by other pre-Christian thinkers. But it was Saint Augustine who placed the greatest stress on it, who stamped it indelibly with its orthodox Christian form.

In Augustine's model, moral evil is the price we and the angels must pay for having been given the gift of free will, and natural evil, in a less direct way, is also a consequence of this freedom. Although God could make angels and human beings incapable of choosing evil, they would not then be fully conscious creatures who are in some respect images of himself. There is a paradox here, for if God has free will but never chooses to do evil, could he not create images of himself that also would always choose to do good? At any rate, so goes the argument, the nature of an angel includes the freedom to do evil, and although most angels remained loyal to their creator, a few, led by Satan, chose to rebel. Since God is outside of time, he knew this would occur. Why then did he permit it? Because only by doing so could he achieve the greater good that comes from letting evil have its hour, of allowing it to display for all time the hideous consequences of rebellion against God.

This rebellion, on a lower plane

3. I. J. Good, *The Scientist Speculates* (1962).

of creation, is still taking place on earth. Adam and Eve were given free wills like the angels, but, tempted by Satan, they, too, used their freedom to defy their creator. Had they not done so, according to Augustine, they would have lived in a Paradise free of death, aging, disease, and all other natural evils. This, too, was foreseen by God. He permitted the fall of humanity for the same reason he permitted the fall of Satan. It was all part of the same vast plan in which human history, alongside the ultimate fate of Satan and his followers, would become the great lesson-book of the universe.

Although there are complicated side issues and many subtle variations, it is astonishing how closely later Christian theologians, including the leaders of the Protestant Reformation, adhered to Augustine's model. One can easily see why, for clearly it is the model that best conforms to biblical mythology. Today it is still the accepted model for Catholics and for all traditional Protestants who believe in Satan and original sin. It is a model on which the Pope and Billy Graham can agree.

Jump to the early eighteenth century. The queen of Prussia is distressed by the writings of the French fideist Pierre Bayle. Faith, said Bayle (as Unamuno would later say) is not only unsupported by reason and experience, it is contrary to reason and experience. The unnecessary evil we see around us is so immense that it strongly implies a world that is not under the control of an all-powerful, all-good deity. Could Leibniz, the queen wanted to know, ease her mind on this point? Leibniz responded with his famous *Théodicée*, the only important book he published in his lifetime. Written in French, printed in Amsterdam in 1710, and later translated into Latin, it became enormously popular and influential.

Leibniz's model is essentially Augustinian, but elaborated so as to bring out more clearly that evil cannot be justified by theists unless they recognize that the power of God is severely limited by logic. As we have seen, this notion was familiar to the Schoolmen. Thomas Aquinas readily admitted that omnipotence cannot include the ability to do logically absurd things. Rather than say there are things God cannot do, said Saint Thomas, it is best to say there are things that cannot be done. For example, it is not possible for a creature to be completely a horse and at the same time be completely a human being.

Let us make the point mathematically. If we define a triangle as a polygon of three sides, it makes no sense to say God could create a triangle with four sides. This does not limit God's power. It only limits our ability to find meaning in a meaningless sentence. A four-sided triangle is as meaningless as a married bachelor. To say that God could do something that can be expressed in our syntax only as a self-contradictory string of symbols is simply to utter nonsense.

This applies to the physical world as well as to our mental concepts. We use what Rudolf Carnap called correspondence rules to establish isomorphisms between purely mathematical ideas and physical things. A bead on an abacus, for example, is not made of putty. It is a wooden object that keeps its size and shape as it slides back and forth along a rod. We take each bead as a model of the number one, and posit a one-to-one correspondence between the laws of arithmetic and the way the sliding beads group themselves into sets. To ask if God could slide two beads up a rod, then two more beads up the same rod, and (without creating another bead) produce five beads at the top of the rod, is to ask for something that is logically impossible. This is not a limitation on God's power. It is a limitation on our ability to make sense of what it would mean to say that two beads plus two beads equal five beads. As long as the beads remain what we mean by beads, "four beads" is another name for "two beads plus two beads," just as "yard" is another name for "three feet." Can God make a valley that is not between two mountains? No, because our language defines a valley as something between two mountains. To expect God to do impossible things is to expect something that cannot be done.

In creating a physical universe, said Leibniz, and covering its planets with intelligent creatures, God's power, though infinitely great, is limited (as the Schoolmen had perceived) by laws of logic and mathematics. The universe must be *possible.* We have a dim understanding of trivial ways in which a universe would be impossible because of logical contradictions, but from God's transcendent perspective there are infinitely many other ways we cannot comprehend. Leibniz used the term *compossible* for those elements of a universe that can go together without contradiction. From our finite point of view there is a distinction between logically impossible and what our experience tells us is physically impossible. We cannot conceive of a world in which the number of pigs in a pen depends on our choice of the pig where we first start our count. We *can* conceive of a world in which pigs fly. However, from God's point of view there are higher laws of logic and mathematics, unknown to us, which severely restrict the structure of any universe capable of existing.

Imagine, said Leibniz, an immense pyramid in which God has piled the abstract models of all possible worlds—worlds that contain no contradictions. There are infinitely many such models. God has arranged them so that as you go down the pyramid you encounter structures with less and less total goodness for its creatures—hence with more evil—than the models above. At the apex of the pyramid is the structure that maximizes good and minimizes evil. In his infinite wisdom God perceives that no better world is possible. Being also infinitely good, he selects this as the model for the universe he conjures into existence.

How does this vision justify evil? Moral evil is explained along Augustinian lines. It is the inevitable consequence of free will. God could have created angels and human beings unable to sin, but they would not then have been angels or human beings. They would have been automata of the sort that Thomas Huxley, in a careless moment, said he would like to be. The question is obviously intertwined with the mystery of human will and how it differs from the will of God.

As a Christian, Leibniz believed

in the rewards and punishments of an afterlife, and the reality of hell, though his hell was considerably less populous than Augustine's. Leibniz objected vigorously to the belief that hell contains the souls of unbaptized infants, or adults who had no way of knowing about Jesus. Nevertheless he argued (in a passage so offensive to William James that he quotes it at length in *Pragmatism*) that even if a majority of human beings were destined for eternal torment it would be only a minute fraction of the intelligent creatures in the universe who had chosen to obey God. Our universe has many suns, said Leibniz, and presumably many planets, all of which may be inhabited by happy, sinless creatures. And beyond our universe may be a vaster region "replete with happiness and glory." Thus the number of earthlings who are damned are but an infinitesimal part of the number of intelligent beings in the universe who are not. Perhaps only on earth was the Fall necessary to display the terrible consequences of rebellion.

Leibniz's justification of natural evils, such as diseases and earthquakes, follows a similar line. It is not possible for human beings with free wills to exist except in a physical world with an environment structured by natural laws. The price we pay for our structured world is precisely those physical evils we see around us. Besides, these natural evils contribute in numerous ways to higher goods, especially in light of the rewards that await the saved in heaven. Without natural evils there would be less compassion, less opportunity for doing good, less incentive to improve the lot of mankind, and so on.

The reaction to Leibniz's vision, with its central dogma that this is the best of all possible worlds, was understandably mixed. One admirer, Alexander Pope, though himself crippled by nature, summed up the vision in these oft-quoted lines from his *Essay on Man:*

> *All nature is but art, unknown to thee;*
> *All chance, direction, which thou canst not see;*
> *All discord, harmony not understood;*
> *All partial evil, universal good:*
> *And, spite of pride, in erring reason's spite,*
> *One truth is clear*, Whatever is, is Right.

To a skeptic like Voltaire, Leibniz's *Theodicy* seemed so outrageous that he mercilessly caricatured it through the simpleminded remarks of Dr. Pangloss in *Candide*.[4] For a modern theist who is not a Christian there are indeed aspects of the *Theodicy*, and of Augustine's earlier efforts to justify evil, that are ugly and offensive. The belief in Satan, the doctrine of the Fall of man, the need for preserving the unsaved in perpetual torment—none of these doctrines press themselves on modern theists unless they believe that the Bible contains a special Revelation from the Creator. Augustine's belief that natural evils, like famines and floods, would not have existed

4. John Stuart Mill, in his essay "Nature," expresses surprise that Leibniz's *Theodicy* was "so strangely mistaken for a system of optimism and, as such, satirized by Voltaire on grounds which do not even touch the author's argument." The main point of *Candide* is that at this stage of history we live in what is not the best possible world, a point so obvious that Leibniz took it for granted. It is as trivial as asserting that a teen-ager is not the best possible adult. Leibniz's world is the best possible only in its incomprehensible totality, and in the long run, which of course includes an afterlife.

on earth had Satan not rebelled, seems incredibly naïve to a philosophical theist.

In preparation for this chapter I read for the first time C. S. Lewis's much-admired book *The Problem of Pain*. As always in reading Lewis I found many estimable things, but I read with acute embarrassment for the author the chapter in which he imagines a possible scenario for what happened at the Fall. Although Lewis makes clear that his account is only a "myth," nevertheless he presents it seriously as a "not unlikely tale" of what actually may have happened. Let me summarize:

For millions of years God used evolution to shape the animal form that would become the image of himself. When the right moment arrived he "caused to descend upon this organism" a new kind of consciousness. The bestial form became human. Lewis does not tell us whether the first human beings were a single pair or many men and women, nor does he mention the odd fact that these first humans would have been brought up and nurtured by parents who were beasts. In any case, the first men and women were sinless and had such marvelous control over their bodies' functions that they experienced no pain. They did not grow old and die. Like the inhabitants of Oz, they could live as long as they pleased. All animals, even the fiercest, were obedient to them.

Enter Satan. Actually, as Lewis suggests in a later chapter on animal pain, Satan had long been "at work for ill on the material universe, or the solar system, or, at least, the planet Earth, before ever man came on the scene. . . . " Lewis believes that this malevolent angel may have corrupted the animal world in the early stages of evolution. As a result, animals became carnivorous and began to eat one another. Disease-producing microbes became part of earth's life-forms. Lewis reminds us that Jesus (Luke 13:16) attributed a woman's infirmity explicitly to her having been "bound by Satan" for eighteen years. Thus does Lewis follow his mentor Augustine in tracing all natural evil, as well as moral evil, back to the machinations of fallen angels.

The paradise God had planned for humanity was shattered when the first humans were tempted by Satan. Like the Evil One, they exercised their free wills to commit the sin of pride, the sin of thinking they knew better than God what was good for them. "For all I can see," writes Lewis in a sentence I had to read several times before I believed it was there, "it might have concerned the literal eating of a fruit. . . . " Fruit or not, the Fall brought into being a new species, not the spotless creatures God had intended but a fallen race that had "sinned itself into existence." This new condition "was transmitted by heredity to all later generations." Of course God, being outside of time, saw the Fall and the Atonement in his timeless Now, allowing it all to happen as part of his unfathomable Plan. The plan may well be confined to Earth. Lewis agrees with Leibniz that if there are rational creatures on other planets there is no reason to assume they too have fallen.

I can find nothing in Lewis's scenario with which Augustine would have taken issue except for those passages that reflect an acceptance of the evolution of life and of man's body, but we certainly can't fault Augustine for not knowing what Darwin knew. The only chapter in *The Problem of Pain* that I found sadder than the chapter on "The Fall of Man" is the chapter on "Hell." But of course Lewis, being an orthodox believer in the Church of England, had no alternative except to defend these monstrous doctrines. To have denied them would have entailed finding fault with the teachings of Jesus, and Lewis was too honest to suppose that he could give up such doctrines and still call himself a Christian.

For the philosophical theist who does not believe in hell, Satan, or the Fall, is there anything in the Augustine-Leibniz way of justifying evil that can be preserved and made more credible? I think there is. Let us call it the revised version of Leibniz's model. You will find it defended by some very early fathers of the Church who were influenced by Greek philosophy, by large numbers of liberal Protestant theologians of recent times, and by many theists outside of Christianity altogether.

Charles Peirce, for instance, regarded the revised version as an "obvious solution," adding that "Columbus's egg was not simpler." [5] For Peirce, evil is necessary because God is "perpetually creating us." The struggle against evil, on the part of both individuals and the race, is essential to the process of what Christians have called "soul-making." Evil exists to be overcome, to make life a genuine battle. As to whether ours is the best possible world, Peirce took the sensible Thomist view. Although we believe God to be omnipotent and omniscient and infinitely good, these words are used vaguely because we cannot know what any human trait is like when raised to God's level. We have no clear notion of what omniscience means, Peirce wrote: "Not the faintest! The question is gabble." Perhaps this is the best possible universe. Perhaps it is the *only* possible universe (as Arthur Stanley Eddington would later speculate). "Perhaps others do exist. But we only wildly gabble about such things." [6]

Peirce often referred to a book called *Substance and Shadow*, by Henry James, Sr., the father of his good friend William, for having clearly presented the "obvious solution." The book is hard to read today, saturated as it is with misty Swedenborgian theology. Perhaps the best expression of the elder James's view of evil is in one of his letters, part of which reads as follows:

> Think of a spiritual existence so wan, so colourless, so miserably dreary and lifeless as this; an existence presided over by a sentimental deity, a deity so narrow-hearted, so brittle-brained, and putty-fingered as to be unable to make godlike men with hands and feet to do their own work and go their own errands, and content himself, therefore, with making spiritual animals with no functions but those of deglutition, digestation, assimilation.... These creatures could have no *life*. At the very most they would barely *exist*. Life means individuality or character; and individuality or character can never be *conferred*, can never be *communicated* by one to an-

5. *Collected Papers of Charles Sanders Peirce*, edited by Charles Hartshorne and Paul Weiss, Vol. 6 (1935), paragraph 507.

6. Ibid, paragraphs 508–510.

> other, but must be inwardly wrought out by the diligent and painful subjugation of evil to good in the sphere of one's proper activity. If God made spiritual sacks, merely, which he might fill out with his own breath to all eternity, why then of course evil might have been left out of the creature's experience. But he abhors sacks, and loves only men, made in his own image of heart, head and hand.[7]

This notion that suffering is required to make life a genuine adventure, to make history an authentic struggle, reverberates through all of William James's writings about evil. In *Pragmatism*, James compares the world to a football game. If the aim of the game is merely to get the ball over a certain goal line, said James, the team "would simply get up on some dark night and place it there." But of course the aim is to get it there according to fixed rules. "The aim of God is not merely . . . to make men and to save them, but rather to get this done through the sole agency of nature's vast machinery. Without nature's stupendous laws and counter-forces, man's creation and perfection, we might suppose, would be too insipid achievements for God to have proposed them."

One essential condition of the game, according to James, is that human beings have free wills that are unpredictable even by God. "I want a world of anarchy" was how he put it in a letter.

* * * * *

It is clear that this model [according to which one of the causes of evil is human free will] imposes severe logical restraints on God. Does this mean one must speak of a "finite God"? Here, I think, we move into a language dispute which I find profitless. My own preference is to speak of God as infinite, as did Aquinas and Leibniz, never forgetting that we have no conception, none whatever, of what words like *infinite* and *omniscient* mean when applied to God. It seems to me that the differences between Leibniz's model in its revised version and similar models that have been put forth in more recent times by non-Christian theists who use the term *finite God* are differences mainly of language and emphasis.

The modern notion of a God whose attributes are finite is usually credited to David Hume, who was probably an atheist, although the first detailed defense was made later by John Stuart Mill. Mill did not think it necessary to combine his theism with belief in an afterlife, though he was open to the possibility. Since Mill, the concept of a finite God, with or without an afterlife, has been set forth by William James, F.C.S. Schiller, Alfred North Whitehead, William Pepperell Montague, Samuel Alexander, Edgar Sheffield Brightman, Charles Hartshorne, and many others. H. G. Wells, of all people, went through a brief phase of interest in the finite-God idea. He even wrote a book about it—the first ever devoted to the topic, *God the Invisible King*—before he concluded he was really an atheist.

Like most concepts, the finite-God idea is on various continua, a fact that leads to all sorts of curious and obscure debates among finite-God philosophers over the best way to talk about justifying evil. In the previous chapter we considered

---

7. Ralph Barton Perry, *The Thought and Character of William James*, Vol. 1 (1935).

briefly the "process" theologians who like to think of God as developing in time as he struggles to remove defects from the human scene. My own view, to repeat, is that I do not know what it means to say God is in or out of time. But I do not like a language that speaks of God as undergoing growth, because it reduces God's transcendence, because it suggests a deity who is more like a demigod or a superhumanoid than the God of traditional theism. It is one thing to say that God is limited in certain ways, quite another thing to say that God is finite. A circle cannot be a triangle, and its length is finite, but it contains an uncountable infinity of points. Because I do not know what it means to say that God is finite, and because I feel uncomfortable in applying this adjective to God, I find the debates among finite-God theologians over the precise degrees of God's powers to be unproductive wrangling—gabbling, as Peirce would say—over words that have only the cloudiest meaning when applied to God. To me the topic is too dreary to pursue further.

As for the notion of "best of all possible worlds," the phrase seems to me as useless as the adjective *finite*. How can we know whether there is one possible universe, or seven, or a countable infinity, or an uncountable infinity, or perhaps even a higher aleph number? And what does "best" mean? For all I know there could be an infinity of existing worlds, no two alike, all as real as ours, all equally good. To speak of the best possible world may be as absurd as speaking of the best possible bird. Leibniz strikes me as naïve in this respect. As a mathematician who invented the calculus he should have remembered that equations can have no solution, one solution, any finite number, or an infinite number. If two cities, with widely differing customs, can be equally good in maximizing the happiness of their citizens (whatever that means), why not two universes? We gabble nonsense when we talk about such things.

Although a theist can justify evil by making it an inescapable aspect of any physical world capable of sustaining such fantastic creatures as you and I, without a belief in an afterlife the justification surely fails to counter the argument of Epicurus. A God capable of creating a universe that is in turn capable of producing you and me is certainly capable of providing another life for us. And if there is no such afterlife, we are back to the terrible questions that tormented Job, and to the arguments of Immanuel Kant's *Critique of Practical Reason*. We live in a world in which children die of cancer, or are born insane, while wicked persons prosper. Every theist I have cited as a defender of the revised version of Leibniz's model, even some of the finite theists, recognized that their model gives no satisfying answer to the riddle of evil unless it is accompanied (as it was not for Job) by belief in a future life.

Such belief is, of course, part of the irrational leap of faith. From our perspective we obviously cannot see God's final pattern in which injustices are remedied. Thornton Wilder's Brother Juniper charted the relative goodness and badness of fifteen people who died in a pestilence with those of fifteen who survived, and found that the dead were "five times more worth saving." His study of the five who perished when the bridge in Peru collapsed comes to no firm conclusion, and Wilder, who knows so much more about the five than Brother Juniper, ends his novel by recognizing the futility of such investigations.[8] When a tower in Siloam collapsed and killed eighteen people (Luke: 13:4–5), were they killed because they were great sinners? Jesus' answer was: "I tell you, Nay." In his last novel, *The Eighth Day*, Wilder compares history to a vast tapestry. We think we see dim designs in tiny portions, but the Grand Design is known only to God.

Believers in Revelation claim to trace certain features of the Grand Design. Although Judas's betrayal of Jesus was an act of moral evil, Leibniz tells us, it made possible the crucifixion that redeems us all. The betrayal was a *felix culpa*—a happy sin, as an old medieval hymn has it. But even to orthodox Christians such details as the needless suffering of a child are as incomprehensible as they are for any non-Christian theist. Lewis Carroll, a devout Anglican, in a letter to an invalid tried to justify the suffering of children by asking: "May it not be to raise to *higher* glory the soul that is already glorious? To make the good yet better, the pure *more* pure, the saint *more* saintly?"[9] Carroll repeats the words of Jesus (John 15:2), "and every branch that beareth fruit, He purgeth it, that it may bring forth more fruit." Guesses, guesses! But believers have to guess, even though they know they cannot know the answer.

Why cannot we know the answer? I have already mentioned one hypothesis—that if we could see clearly how evils contribute to higher goods, we would become indifferent toward them. Evil, said Royce, is the dirt we must wash out of the universe. This is the symbolic meaning behind the myth of Satan and his angels, behind the devils and lesser demons of other faiths. Evil must somehow be hated by God, even though he permits and uses it. In itself no evil is good. In a sense it is something apart from God, something God is trying to expunge. "Evil is as real as the good . . . " said James in a letter. "It must be accepted and hated and resisted. . . . " Obviosities! As Batman put it on a poster I saw in the mid-sixties, "It is well to remember that evil is a pretty bad thing!" If it is true that evil contributes to ultimate good, it may be part of God's mercy that he has hidden the details from us, that we are in no better position today to answer the enigma of evil than long-suffering Job, or his bitter wife, or his long-winded friends.

There is a still deeper reason, fideists believe, or at least I so believe, why we cannot solve the problem of evil. "Verily thou art a God that hidest thyself, O God of Israel, the Saviour" (Isaiah 45:15). The mystery of evil is part of the larger mystery of why God chooses to remain concealed. The only answer a fideist can give is that God wants uncompelled love, love that springs from a free turning of the heart. If God could be proved by reason, every rational person would

---

8. Thornton Wilder, *The Bridge of San Luis Rey* (1927).

9. *The Letters of Lewis Carroll* (1979), edited by Morton N. Cohen, Vol. 2.

believe. If God could be established empirically, every person with respect for science would believe. To formulate a convincing answer to the riddle of evil would require knowing things we cannot know, that we may not have the capacity to know. If we could understand the reason for suffering, God would no longer be hidden. And only if God remains concealed, remains a *deus abscondus*, can faith escape contamination by coercion.[10]

No one has said this more eloquently than Blaise Pascal in his *Pensées:*

> It was not then right that He should appear in a manner manifestly divine, and completely capable of convincing all men; but it was also not right that He should come in so hidden a manner that He could not be known by those who should sincerely seek Him. He has willed to make Himself quite recognizable by those; and thus, willing to appear openly to those who seek Him with all their heart, and to be hidden from those who flee from Him with all their heart. He so regulates the knowledge of Himself that He has given signs of Himself, visible to those who seek Him, and not to those who seek Him not. There is enough light for those who only desire to see, and enough obscurity for those who have a contrary disposition.

Pascal is speaking of God's appearance on earth as Jesus, and he is making the point that even with respect to the Incarnation the Creator concealed himself sufficiently so that no one would be forced to believe. Did not Jesus even thank God that the truths of faith were hidden from the wise and prudent, and revealed only to babes? Innumerable theologians before and after Pascal have sounded this theme. For Sören Kierkegaard, Jesus was God's "Incognito." Not even Jesus' contemporaries who witnessed his miracles could be certain of who he was, for cannot miracles be counterfeited by fallen angels?

A non-Christian fideist may find it hard to believe that anyone could witness, say, the raising of Lazarus and remain in a state of neutrality with respect to Jesus' claim of divinity, but Pascal's point can be applied to evidence for God's existence quite apart from belief in the Incarnation. Indeed, Pascal himself so applied it. Here is another passage from the *Pensées*:

> This is what I see and what troubles me. I look on all sides, and see nothing but obscurity, nature offers me nothing but matter for doubt and disquiet. Did I see nothing there which marked a Divinity I should decide not to believe in him. Did I see every where the marks of a Creator, I should rest peacefully in faith. But seeing too much to deny, and too lit-

10. It is possible to give this argument in a game-theoretic framework. See Steven J. Brams, *Superior Beings: Game-Theoretic Implications of Omniscience, Omnipotence, Immortality, and Incomprehensibility*, a forthcoming book. In Chapter 13, Note 1, I referred to Brams's earlier work, *Biblical Games*. I have not yet decided just what to make of these two books. They may be significant contributions to theology, or little more than ingenious attempts to apply game and decision theory in areas where such applications are unproductive. Brams concerns himself exclusively with Old Testament myths, but clearly his approach is just as applicable (or inapplicable) to myths in the New Testament, Homer, the Koran, or the sacred books of any other religious tradition. It is Brams's view that it may be rational for a god who wants to be believed to adopt a mixed strategy in which there is genuinely random behavior of the sort that would appear to us as irrational.

tle to affirm, my state is pitiful, and I have a hundred times wished that if God upheld nature, he would mark the fact unequivocally, but that if the signs which she gives of a God are fallacious, she would wholly suppress them, that she would either say all or say nothing, that I might see what part I should take. While in my present state, ignorant of what I am, and of what I ought to do, I know neither my condition nor my duty, my heart is wholly bent to know where is the true good in order to follow it, nothing would seem to me too costly for eternity.

COMMENTS ■ QUESTIONS

1. Gardner does not put much weight on the distinction between moral evil (sin) and physical or natural evil. "If a madman fires a gun at a crowd, killing ten people at random, they are just as needlessly dead as if they had been killed by an earthquake." Is Gardner correct to downplay the distinction between moral evil and physical evil?
2. Gardner takes the position that there is no way, using reason and arguments, to solve the problem of evil. Instead, he says: "As a theist I believe by faith, and by faith alone, that there is an answer. But I do not know the answer." A belief that is based on faith alone is not in itself a philosophical belief. However, the claim that certain things can be known only by faith is a philosophical claim if arguments are given in its defense. Has Gardner given good reasons for believing that the problem of evil can be solved only on the basis of beliefs that are held on faith alone?
3. "We live in a world in which children die of cancer, or are born insane, while wicked persons prosper." Therefore, says Gardner, the problem of evil cannot be solved without a belief in an afterlife in which injustices are remedied. Do you accept this argument?

GOTTFRIED WILHELM LEIBNIZ

The Best of All Possible Worlds

* * * * *

Lest any one should think that we are here confounding moral perfection or goodness with metaphysical perfection or greatness and, allowing the latter, should deny the former, it is to be observed that it follows from what has been said not only that the world is most perfect physically, or, if you prefer it, metaphysically, that is to say, that that series of things has come into existence in which the greatest amount of reality is actually manifested, but also that the world is most perfect morally because genuine moral perfection is physical perfection in minds themselves. Wherefore the world is not only the most admirable mechanism, but it is also, in so far as it is made up of minds the best commonwealth, through which there is bestowed upon minds the greatest possible happiness or joy, in which their physical perfection consists.

But, you will say, we find that the opposite of this takes place in the world, for very often the best people suffer the worst things, and those who are innocent, both animals and men, are afflicted and put to death even with torture; and indeed the world, especially if we consider the government of the human race, seems rather a confused chaos than anything directed by a supreme wisdom. So, I confess, it seems at a first glance, but when we look at it more closely the opposite conclusion manifestly follows *a priori* from those very considerations which have been adduced, the conclusion, namely, that the highest possible perfection of all things, and therefore of all minds, is brought about.

And indeed, as the lawyers say, it is not proper to judge unless we have examined the whole law. We know a very small part of eternity which is immeasureable in its extent; for what a little thing is the record of a few thousand years, which history transmits to us! Nevertheless, from so slight an experience we rashly judge regarding the immeasureable and eternal, like men who, having been born and brought up in prison or, perhaps, in the subterranean salt-mines of the Sarmatians, should think that there is no other light in the world than that of

A biographical sketch of Gottfried Wilhelm Leibniz is to be found earlier in this chapter.

From *On The Ultimate Origination of Things*, translated by Robert Latta, 1898. This paper was originally written in 1697.

the feeble lamp which hardly suffices to direct their steps. If you look at a very beautiful picture, having covered up the whole of it except a very small part, what will it present to your sight, however thoroughly you examine it (nay, so much the more, the more closely you inspect it), but a confused mass of colours laid on without selection and without art? Yet if you remove the covering and look at the whole picture from the right point of view, you will see that what appeared to have been carelessly daubed on the canvas was really done by the painter with very great art. The experience of the eyes in painting corresponds to that of the ears in music. Eminent composers very often mingle discords with harmonies so as to stimulate and, as it were, to prick the hearer, who becomes anxious as to what is going to happen, and is so much the more pleased when presently all is restored to order; just as we take pleasure in small dangers or risks of mishap, merely from the consciousness of our power or our luck or from a desire to make a display of them; or, again, as we delight in the show of danger that is connected with performances on the tight-rope or sword-dancing; and as we ourselves in jest half let go a little boy, as if about to throw him from us, like the ape which carried Christiern, King of Denmark, while still an infant in swaddling-clothes, to the top of the roof, and then, as in jest, relieved the anxiety of every one by bringing him safely back to his cradle. On the same principle sweet things become insipid if we eat nothing else; sharp, tart, and even bitter things must be combined with them, so as to stimulate the taste. He who has not tasted bitter things does not deserve sweet things and, indeed, will not appreciate them. This is the very law of enjoyment, that pleasure does not have an even tenor, for this begets loathing and makes us dull, not happy.

But as to our saying that a part may be disturbed without destroying harmony in the whole, this must not be understood as meaning that no account is taken of the parts or that it is enough for the world as a whole to be perfect, although it may be that the human race is wretched, and that there is in the universe no regard for justice and no care for us, as is the opinion of some whose judgment regarding the totality of things is not quite just. For it is to be observed that, as in a thoroughly well-constituted commonwealth care is taken, as far as may be, for the good of individuals, so the universe will not be sufficiently perfect unless the interests of individuals are attended to, while the universal harmony is preserved. And for this no better standard could be set up than the very law of justice which declares that each should participate in the perfection of the universe and in a happiness of his own in proportion to his own virtue and to the degree in which his will has regard to the common good; and by this is fulfilled that which we call charity and the love of God, in which alone, in the opinion of wise theologians, consists the force and power even of the Christian religion. Nor ought it to appear wonderful that so great a place should be given to minds in the universe, since they most closely resemble the image of the Supreme Author; they are related to Him, not (like other things) as machines to their constructor, but as citizens to their prince; they are to last as long as the universe itself, and in a manner they express and concentrate the whole in themselves, so that it may be said that minds are whole parts.

But as to the special question of the afflictions of good men, it is to be held as certain that these afflictions have as their result the greater good of those who are afflicted, and this is true not only theologically but also naturally, as the grain cast into the earth suffers before it bears fruit. And in general it may be said that afflictions are for the time evil but in the end good, since they are short ways to greater perfection. So in physics, liquids which ferment slowly take also a longer time to purify, while those which undergo a greater agitation throw off certain of their ingredients with greater force, and are thus more quickly rectified. And this is what you might call going back in order that you may put more force into your leap forward. Wherefore these things are to be regarded not only as agreeable and comforting, but also as most true. And in general I think there is nothing more true than happiness, and nothing more happy and pleasant than truth.

Further, to realize in its completeness the universal beauty and perfection of the works of God, we must recognize a certain perpetual and very free progress of the whole universe, such that it is always going forward to greater improvement. So even now a great part of our earth has received cultivation *[cultura]* and will receive it more and more. And although it is true that sometimes certain parts of it grow wild again, or again suffer destruction or degeneration, yet this is to be understood in the way in which affliction was explained above, that is to say, that this very destruction and degeneration leads to some greater end, so that somehow we profit by the loss itself.

And to the possible objection that, if this were so, the world ought long ago to have become a paradise, there is a ready answer. Although many substances have already attained a great perfection, yet on account of the infinite divisibility of the continuous, there always remain in the abyss of things slumbering parts which have yet to be awakened, to grow in size and worth, and, in a word, to advance to a more perfect state. And hence no end of progress is ever reached.

COMMENTS ■ QUESTIONS

1. "Sweet things become insipid if we eat nothing else; sharp, tart, and even bitter things must be combined with them, so as to stimulate the taste." Few would disagree with the claim that Leibniz's point (expressed in these words) helps to show that *some* of the evil or bad things in the world are necessary for the existence of good things. To what extent is this true? Is it true to the extent that Leibniz believes it is?
2. In a world where good people suffer, Leibniz asks us to take a long view of things: "Afflictions are for the time evil but in the end good, since they are short ways to greater perfection." Because Leibniz presupposes the existence of life after death, the argument has been made that his attempt to solve the problem of evil fails because it is an appeal to the existence of something unknowable. Is this criticism fair? (Arguments both for and against the existence of life after death are considered in chapter 7.)

BERTRAND RUSSELL

The Free Man's Worship

o Dr. Faustus in his study Mephistopheles told the history of the Creation, saying:

"The endless praises of the choirs of angels had begun to grow wearisome; for, after all, did he not deserve their praise? Had he not given them endless joy? Would it not be more amusing to obtain undeserved praise, to be worshipped by beings whom he tortured? He smiled inwardly, and resolved that the great drama should be performed.

"For countless ages the hot nebula whirled aimlessly through space.

A biographical sketch of Bertrand Russell is to be found in chapter 1.

From *Philosophical Essays*, 1910. This article was originally published in the *Independent Review*, Dec., 1903.

At length it began to take shape, the central mass threw off planets, the planets cooled, boiling seas and burning mountains heaved and tossed, from black masses of cloud hot sheets of rain deluged the barely solid crust. And now the first germ of life grew in the depths of the ocean, and developed rapidly in the fructifying warmth into vast forest trees, huge ferns springing from the damp mould, sea monsters breeding, fighting, devouring, and passing away. And from the monsters, as the play unfolded itself, Man was born, with the power of thought, the knowledge of good and evil, and the cruel thirst for worship. And Man saw that all is passing in this mad, monstrous world, that all is struggling to snatch, at any cost, a few brief moments of life before Death's inexorable decree. And Man said: 'There is a hidden purpose, could we but fathom it, and the purpose is good; for we must reverence something, and in the visible world there is nothing worthy of reverence.' And Man stood aside from the struggle, resolving that God intended harmony to come out of chaos by human efforts. And when he followed the instincts which God had transmitted to him from his ancestry of beasts of prey, he called it Sin, and asked God to forgive him. But he doubted whether he could be justly forgiven, until he invented a divine Plan by which God's wrath was to have been appeased. And seeing the present was bad, he made it yet worse, that thereby the future might be better. And he gave God thanks for the strength that enabled him to forego even the joys that were possible. And God smiled; and when he saw that Man had become perfect in renunciation and worship, he sent another sun through the sky, which crashed into Man's sun; and all returned again to nebula.

" 'Yes,' he murmured, 'it was a good play; I will have it performed again.' "

Such, in outline, but even more purposeless, more void of meaning, is the world which Science presents for our belief. Amid such a world, if anywhere, our ideals henceforward must find a home. That Man is the product of causes which had no prevision of the end they were achieving; that his origin, his growth, his hopes and fears, his loves and his beliefs, are but the outcome of accidental collocations of atoms; that no fire, no heroism, no intensity of thought and feeling, can preserve an individual life beyond the grave; that all the labours of the ages, all the devotion, all the inspiration, all the noonday brightness of human genius, are destined to extinction in the vast death of the solar system, and that the whole temple of Man's achievement must inevitably be buried beneath the débris of a universe in ruins—all these things, if not quite beyond dispute, are yet so nearly certain, that no philosophy which rejects them can hope to stand. Only within the scaffolding of these truths, only on the firm foundation of unyielding despair, can the soul's habitation henceforth be safely built.

How, in such an alien and inhuman world, can so powerless a creature as Man preserve his aspirations untarnished? A strange mystery it is that Nature, omnipotent but blind, in the revolutions of her secular hurryings through the abysses of space, has brought forth at last a child, subject still to her power, but gifted with sight, with knowledge of good and evil, with the capacity of judging all the works of his unthinking Mother. In spite of Death, the mark and seal of the parental control, Man is yet free, during his brief years, to examine, to criticise, to know, and in imagination to create. To him alone, in the world with which he is acquainted, this freedom belongs; and in this lies his superiority to the resistless forces that control his outward life.

The savage, like ourselves, feels the oppression of his impotence before the powers of Nature; but having in himself nothing that he respects more than Power, he is willing to prostrate himself before his gods, without inquiring whether they are worthy of his worship. Pathetic and very terrible is the long history of cruelty and torture, of degradation and human sacrifice, endured in the hope of placating the jealous gods: surely, the trembling believer thinks, when what is most precious has been freely given, their lust for blood must be appeased, and more will not be required. The religion of Moloch—as such creeds may be generically called—is in essence the cringing submission of the slave, who dare not, even in his heart, allow the thought that his master deserves no adulation. Since the independence of ideals is not yet acknowledged, Power may be freely worshipped, and receive an unlimited respect, despite its wanton infliction of pain.

But gradually, as morality grows bolder, the claim of the ideal world begins to be felt; and worship, if it is not to cease, must be given to gods of another kind than those created by the savage. Some, though they feel the demands of the ideal, will still consciously reject them, still urging that naked Power is worthy of worship. Such is the attitude inculcated in God's answer to Job out of the whirlwind: the divine power and knowledge are paraded, but of the divine goodness there is no hint. Such also is the attitude of those who, in our own day, base their morality upon the struggle for survival, maintaining that the survivors are necessarily the fittest. But others, not content with an answer so repugnant to the moral sense, will adopt the position which we have become accustomed to regard as specially religious, maintaining that, in some hidden manner, the world of fact is really harmonious with the world of ideals. Thus Man creates God, all-powerful and all-good, the mystic unity of what is and what should be.

But the world of fact, after all, is not good; and, in submitting our judgment to it, there is an element of slavishness from which our thoughts must be purged. For in all things it is well to exalt the dignity of Man, by freeing him, as far as possible, from the tyranny of non-human Power. When we have realised that Power is largely bad, that man, with his knowledge of good and evil, is but a helpless atom in a world which has no such knowledge, the choice is again presented to us: Shall we worship Force, or shall we worship Goodness? Shall our God exist and be evil, or shall he be recognised as the creation of our own conscience?

The answer to this question is very momentous, and affects profoundly our whole morality. The worship of Force, to which Carlyle and Nietzsche and the creed of Militarism have accustomed us, is the result of failure to maintain our own ideals against a hostile universe: it is itself a prostrate submission to evil, a sacrifice of our best to Moloch. If strength indeed is to be respected, let us respect rather the strength of those who refuse that false "recognition of facts" which fails to recognise that facts are often bad. Let us admit that, in the world we know, there are many things that would be better otherwise, and that the ideals to which we do and must adhere are not realised in the realm of matter. Let us preserve our respect for truth, for beauty, for the ideal of perfection which life does not permit us to attain, though none of these things meet with the approval of the unconscious universe. If Power is bad, as it seems to be, let us reject it from our hearts. In this lies Man's true freedom: in determination to worship only the God created by our own love of the good, to respect only the heaven which inspires the insight of our best moments. In action, in desire, we must submit perpetually to the tyranny of outside forces; but in thought, in aspiration, we are free, free from our fellow-men, free from the petty planet on which our bodies impotently crawl, free even, while we live, from the tyranny of death. Let us learn, then, that energy of faith which enables us to live constantly in the vision of the good; and let us descend, in action, into the world of fact, with that vision always before us.

When first the opposition of fact and ideal grows fully visible, a spirit of fiery revolt, of fierce hatred of the gods, seems necessary to the assertion of freedom. To defy with Promethean constancy a hostile universe, to keep its evil always in view, always actively hated, to refuse no pain that the malice of Power can invent, appears to be the duty of all who will not bow before the inevitable. But indignation is still a bondage, for it compels our thoughts to be occupied with an evil world; and in the fierceness of desire from which rebellion springs there is a kind of self-assertion which it is necessary for the wise to overcome. Indignation is a submission of our thoughts, but not of our desires; the Stoic freedom in which wisdom consists is found in the submission of our desires, but not of our thoughts. From the submission of our desires springs the virtue of resignation; from the freedom of our thoughts springs the whole world of art and philosophy, and the vision of beauty by which, at last, we half reconquer the reluctant world. But the vision of beauty is possible only to unfettered contemplation, to thoughts not weighted by the load of eager wishes; and thus Freedom comes only to those who no longer ask of life that it shall yield them any of those personal goods that are subject to the mutations of Time.

Although the necessity of renunciation is evidence of the existence of evil, yet Christianity, in preaching it, has shown a wisdom exceeding that of the Promethean philosophy of rebellion. It must be admitted that, of the things we desire, some, though they prove impossible, are yet real goods; others, however, as ardently longed for, do not form part of a fully purified ideal. The belief that what must be renounced is bad, though sometimes false, is far less often false than untamed passion supposes; and the creed of religion, by providing a reason for proving that it is never false, has been the means of purifying our hopes by the discovery of many austere truths.

But there is in resignation a further good element: even real goods, when they are unattainable, ought not to be fretfully desired. To every man comes, sooner or later, the great renunciation. For the young, there is nothing unattainable; a good thing desired with the whole force of a passionate will, and yet impossible, is to them not credible. Yet, by death, by illness, by poverty, or by the voice of duty, we must learn, each one of us, that the world was not made for us, and that, however beautiful may be the things we crave, Fate may nevertheless forbid them. It is the part of courage, when misfortune comes, to bear without repining the ruin of our hopes, to turn away our thoughts from vain regrets. This degree of submission to Power is not only just and right: it is the very gate of wisdom.

But passive renunciation is not the whole of wisdom; for not by renunciation alone can we build a temple for the worship of our own ideals. Haunting foreshadowings of the temple appear in the realm of imagination, in music, in architecture, in the untroubled kingdom of reason, and in the golden sunset magic of lyrics, where beauty shines and glows, remote from the touch of sorrow, remote from the fear of change, remote from the failures and disenchantments of the world of fact. In the contemplation of these things the vision of heaven will shape itself in our hearts, giving at once a touchstone to judge the world about us, and an inspiration by which to fashion to our needs whatever is not incapable of serving as a stone in the sacred temple.

Except for those rare spirits that are born without sin, there is a cavern of darkness to be traversed before that temple can be entered. The gate of the cavern is despair, and its floor is paved with the gravestones of abandoned hopes. There Self must die; there the eagerness, the greed of untamed desire must be slain, for only so can the soul be freed from the empire of Fate. But out of the cavern the Gate of Renunciation leads again to the daylight of wisdom, by whose radiance a new insight, a new joy, a new tenderness, shine forth to gladden the pilgrim's heart.

When, without the bitterness of impotent rebellion, we have learnt both to resign ourselves to the outward rule of Fate and to recognise that the non-human world is unworthy of our worship, it becomes possible at last so to transform and refashion the unconscious universe, so to transmute it in the crucible of imagination, that a new image of shining gold replaces the old idol of clay. In all the multiform facts of the world—in the visual shapes of trees and mountains and clouds, in the events of the life of man, even in the very omnipotence of Death—the insight of creative idealism can find the reflection of a beauty which its own thoughts first made. In this way mind asserts its subtle mastery over the thoughtless forces of Nature. The more evil the material with which it deals, the more thwarting to untrained desire, the greater is its achievement in inducing the reluctant rock to yield up its hidden treasures, the prouder its victory in compelling the opposing forces to swell the pageant of its triumph. Of all the arts, Tragedy is the proudest, the most triumphant; for it builds its shining citadel in the very centre of the enemy's country, on the very summit of his highest mountain; from its impregnable watch-towers, his camps and arsenals, his columns and forts, are all revealed; within its walls the free life continues, while the legions of Death and Pain and Despair, and all the servile captains of tyrant Fate, afford the burghers of that dauntless city new spectacles of beauty. Happy those sacred ramparts, thrice happy the dwellers on that all-seeing eminence. Honour to those brave warriors who, through countless ages of warfare, have preserved for us the priceless heritage of liberty, and have kept undefiled by sacrilegious invaders the home of the unsubdued.

But the beauty of Tragedy does but make visible a quality which, in more or less obvious shapes, is present always and everywhere in life. In the spectacle of Death, in the endurance of intolerable pain, and in the irrevocableness of a vanished past, there is a sacredness, an overpowering awe, a feeling of the vastness, the depth, the inexhaustible mystery of existence, in which, as by some strange marriage of pain, the sufferer is bound to the world by bonds of sorrow. In these moments of insight, we lose all eagerness of temporary desire, all struggling and striving for petty ends, all care for the little trivial things that, to a superficial view, make up the common life of day by day; we see, surrounding the narrow raft illumined by the flickering light of human comradeship, the dark ocean on whose rolling waves we toss for a brief hour; from the great night without, a chill blast breaks in upon our refuge; all the loneliness of humanity amid hostile forces is concentrated upon the individual soul, which must struggle alone, with what of courage it can command, against the whole weight of a universe that cares nothing for its hopes and fears. Victory, in this struggle with the powers of darkness, is the true baptism into the glorious company of heroes, the true initiation into the overmastering beauty of human existence. From that awful encounter of the soul with the outer world, renunciation, wisdom, and charity are born; and with their birth a new life begins. To take into the inmost shrine of the soul the irresistible forces whose puppets we seem to be—Death and change, the irrevocableness of the past, and the powerlessness of man before the blind hurry of the universe from vanity to vanity—to feel these things and know them is to conquer them.

This is the reason why the Past has such magical power. The beauty of its motionless and silent pictures is like the enchanted purity of last autumn, when the leaves, though one breath would make them fall, still glow against the sky in golden glory. The Past does not change or strive; like Duncan, after life's fitful fever it sleeps well; what was eager and grasping, what was petty and transitory, has faded away, the things that were beautiful and eternal shine out of it like stars in the night. Its beauty, to a soul not worthy of it, is unendurable; but to a soul which has conquered Fate it is the key of religion.

The life of Man, viewed outwardly, is but a small thing in comparison with the forces of Nature. The slave is doomed to worship Time and Fate and Death, because they are greater than anything he finds in himself, and because all his thoughts are of things which they devour. But, great as they are, to think of them greatly, to feel their passionless splendour, is greater still. And such thought makes us free men; we no longer bow before the inevitable in oriental subjection, but we absorb it, and make it a part of ourselves. To abandon the struggle for private happiness, to expel all eagerness of temporary desire, to burn with passion for eternal things—this is emancipation, and this is the free man's worship. And this liberation is effected by a contemplation of Fate; for Fate itself is subdued by the mind which leaves nothing to be purged by the purifying fire of Time.

United with his fellow-men by the strongest of all ties, the tie of a common doom, the free man finds that a new vision is with him always, shedding over every daily task the light of love. The life of Man is a long march through the night, surrounded by invisible foes, tortured by weariness and pain, towards a goal that few can hope to reach, and where none may tarry long. One by one, as they march, our comrades vanish from our sight, seized by the silent orders of omnipotent Death. Very brief is the time in which we can help them, in which their happiness or misery is decided. Be it ours to shed sunshine on their path, to lighten their sorrows by the balm of sympathy, to give them the pure joy of a never-tiring affection, to strengthen failing courage, to instil faith in hours of despair. Let us not weigh in grudging scales their merits and demerits, but let us think only of their need—of the sorrows, the difficulties, perhaps the blindnesses, that make the misery of their lives; let us remember that they are fellow-sufferers in the same darkness, actors in the same tragedy with ourselves. And so, when their day is over, when their good and their evil have become eternal by the immortality of the past, be it ours to feel that, where they suffered, where they failed, no deed of ours was the cause; but wherever a spark of the divine fire kindled in their hearts, we were ready with encouragement, with sympathy, with brave words in which high courage glowed.

Brief and powerless is Man's life; on him and all his race the slow, sure doom falls pitiless and dark. Blind to good and evil, reckless of destruction, omnipotent matter rolls on its relentless way; for Man, condemned to-day to lose his dearest, to-morrow himself to pass through the gate of darkness, it remains only to cherish, ere yet the blow falls, the lofty thoughts that ennoble his little day; disdaining the coward terrors of the slave of Fate, to worship at the shrine that his own hands have built; undismayed by the empire of chance, to preserve a mind free from the wanton tyranny that rules his outward life; proudly defiant of the irresistible forces that tolerate, for a moment, his knowledge and his condemnation, to sustain alone, a weary but unyielding Atlas, the world that his own ideals have fashioned despite the trampling march of unconscious power.

COMMENTS ■ QUESTIONS

1. Do you agree with Russell when he says that "the world which Science presents for our belief" is purposeless and devoid of meaning? If not, why not?
2. Russell makes two major points regarding religion: (a) that some religions (those of "Moloch," as he calls them) have been very bad because they have called for sacrifice, suffering, and cruelty; (b) that other religions, such as Christianity, have benefited the human race by calling for the renunciation of many things that are bad. In describing religion as he does, Russell has assumed the falsity of religious beliefs regarding God's existence, heaven and hell, and so on. Hence, he is interested only in describing what he takes to be the actual effects (some good, some bad) that religious beliefs have had upon the lives of believers. Is Russell's perspective on religion the best one to have? If not, why not?
3. In place of religious belief, Russell advocates that the human mind assert a "subtle mastery over the thoughtless forces of nature" by finding beauty in the very fact that human life is tragic and that all human hopes are ultimately vain. Recognizing these facts makes it all the more possible, says Russell, for us to express our love and sympathy for our fellow human beings who are as doomed as we are. Perhaps you will reject Russell's starting point, that is, his belief that the world "rolls on its relentless way" completely blind to good and evil. But if you accept Russell's starting point, would you say that Russell's view expresses a profound wisdom? Or is it merely an exercise in trying to make something out of nothing? Is it a case of whistling in the dark? Can Russell's position be described in a better way?

JOHN HICK

The Infinite Future Good

It is a commonplace that the prevailing modes of thought in our contemporary Western world are naturalistic. That is to say, the categories of the sciences are today regarded as ultimate, rather than those of religion. In consequence it is widely assumed that God can exist only as an idea in the human mind. Even within the Christian Churches this presupposition is evident in various forms of religious naturalism, or naturalistic religion, according to which statements about God, instead of referring to a transcendent divine Being, are expressions of ethical policies,[1] or of ways of seeing and feeling about the world,[2] or of convictional (as distinct from cognitive) stances,[3] or of one's existential situation.[4] Neither the general naturalistic or positivistic climate of our culture as a whole nor the growing enclave of naturalistic religion within Christianity has any use for the idea of an after-life. From the point of view of secular naturalism, human survival after death is a scientific impossibility of which only the superstitious still allow themselves to dream. For religious naturalism the notion of the life everlasting remains as a symbol of the worth of human personality, with its capacity to appreciate timeless truths and values. But for

1. R. B. Braithwaite, *An Empiricist's View of the Nature of Religious Belief* (Cambridge: Cambridge University Press, 1955); Peter Munz, *Problems of Religious Knowledge* (London: The S.C.M. Press, 1959); T. R. Miles, *Religion and the Scientific Outlook* (London: George Allen & Unwin, 1959); Paul F. Schmidt, *Religious Knowledge* (Glencoe: The Free Press, 1961).

2. John Wisdom, 'Gods' (*Proceedings of the Aristotelian Society*, 1944–5. Reprinted in *Essays on Logic and Language*, i, ed. by Antony Flew, Oxford: Basil Blackwell, 1951, and in *Classical and Contemporary Readings in the Philosophy of Religion*, ed. John Hick, Englewood-Cliffs, N.J.: Prentice-Hall, Inc., 1964) and 'The Modes of Thought and the Logic of God' (*The Existence of God*, ed. John Hick, New York: The Macmillan Co., 1964); J. H. Randall, Jr., *The Role of Knowledge in Western Religion* (Boston: The Beacon Press, 1958), chap. 4.

3. Willem Zuurdeeg, *An Analytical Philosophy of Religion* (Nashville, Tenn.: Abingdon Press, 1958).

4. Paul Van Buren, *The Secular Meaning of the Gospel* (London: S.C.M. Press, 1964).

John Hick, who is a professor in the Department of Religion at Claremont Graduate School in California, has also taught at Cambridge University and served as H. G. Wood Professor of Theology at the University of Birmingham. He has written widely in the philosophy of religion.

Pp. 373–387 from *Evil and the God of Love* by John Hick. Copyright © 1966, 1978 by John Hick. Reprinted by permission of Harper & Row, Publishers, and Macmillan, London and Basingstoke.

historic Christian faith, the expectation of a life after death is a part of the total organism of Christian belief. It is a constantly recurring theme of our Lord's teaching, primarily in the form of encouragements and warnings derived from the consequences in the next world of good or evil done in this. It is likewise prominent in the thought of St. Paul and the other New Testament writers. It is supported by the belief in Christ's resurrection and by the *discensus ad infernos* clause in the Apostles' Creed. Further, belief in an after-life has its roots in religious reasoning as well as in the biblical revelation, as a corollary of belief in a transcendent personal God who has created finite persons for fellowship with Himself. Would it not contradict God's love for the creatures made in His image if He caused them to pass out of existence whilst His purpose for them was still so largely unfulfilled?

The expectation of a life after death thus constitutes an important crux between naturalism (whether secular or religious) and historic Christianity. In an age dominated by naturalistic presuppositions it stands out as a stubborn pocket of belief in the supernatural, decisively distinguishing a faith directed to an eternal and transcendent God from one that terminates in man himself as an intelligent animal, uniquely valuable in his own eyes but nevertheless destined to perish with the beasts and plants.

Belief in an after-life is no less crucial for theodicy [a justification of God's ways in permitting evil to exist]. We have seen that whilst from our human point of view evil is equivalent to the disvalued or unwelcome, from a theological standpoint it means that which frustrates or tends to frustrate God's purpose for His creation; and that conversely, for theology, good is that which serves the divine purpose. In the light of these definitions, the question whether human sin and suffering are finally evil and inimical to good depends upon their eventual furtherance or prevention of the fulfilment of God's plan for His creation. If man's pain and sin are revealed in the final reckoning, at the end of human time, as having frustrated God's purpose for His creatures, then in that ultimate perspective they have been evil. If, on the other hand, they have played a part in the fulfilment of that purpose, then in the ultimate perspective they have contributed to good. In considering the nature of the divine purpose for man by reference to which, accordingly, good and evil are defined, we have adopted the Irenaean view that God is gradually forming perfected members of the humanity whose fuller nature we glimpse in Christ. Now so far as we can see, such a purpose is at best only begun in the present life, whilst at worst there is a marked retrogressive development. Sometimes we see good being created out of evil: we see sin ending in repentance and obstacles breeding strength of character, dangers evoking courage and unselfishness, or calamities producing patience and moral steadfastness. But too often we see the opposite of this in wickedness multiplying and in the disintegration of personalities under the impact of suffering: we see good turned to evil, kindness to bitterness, hope to despair. And from our own observations, even when supplemented by the entire scroll of recorded history, we are not entitled to say either that all sin leads to redemption or that all suffering is used for good in its final issue. We have to say simply that the incomprehensible mingling in human experience of good and evil, virtue and vice, pain and pleasure, grief and laughter, continues in all its characteristic and baffling ambiguity throughout life and ends only with death.

If, then, the evil in human life finally reveals its nature according as it becomes or fails to become a phase in the fulfilment of God's purpose, we must conclude, so far as the present life is concerned, that there are both good and evil suffering, and that there are redeemed and unredeemed sinners. Any revision of the verdict must depend upon lengthening the perspective out until it reaches a new and better conclusion. If there is any eventual resolution of the interplay between good and evil, any decisive bringing of good out of evil, it must lie beyond this world and beyond the enigma of death. Therefore we cannot hope to state a Christian theodicy without taking seriously the doctrine of a life beyond the grave. This doctrine is not, of course, based upon any theory of natural immortality, but upon the hope that beyond death God will resurrect or recreate or reconstitute the human personality in both its inner and its outer aspects. The Christian claim is that the ultimate life of man—after what further scenes of "soul-making" we do not know—lies in that Kingdom of God which is depicted in the teaching of Jesus as a state of exultant and blissful happiness, symbolized as a joyous banquet in which all and sundry, having accepted God's gracious invitation, rejoice together. And Christian theodicy must point forward to that final blessedness, and claim that this infinite future good will render worth while all the pain and travail and wickedness that has occurred on the way to it. Theodicy cannot be content to look to the past, seeking an explanation of evil in its origins, but must look towards the future, expecting a triumphant resolution in the eventual perfect fulfilment of God's good purpose. We cannot, of course, concretely picture to ourselves the nature of this fulfilment; we can only say that it represents the best gift of God's infinite love for His children. But no other acceptable possibility of Christian theodicy offers itself than that in the human creature's joyous participation in the completed creation his sufferings, struggles, and failures will be seen to be justified by their outcome.[5] We must thus affirm in faith that there will in the final accounting be no personal life that is unperfected and no suffering that has not eventually become a phase in the fulfilment of God's good purpose. Only so, I suggest, is it possible to believe both in the perfect goodness of God and in His unlimited capacity to perform His will. For if there are finally wasted lives and finally unredeemed sufferings, either God is not perfect in love or He is not sovereign in rule over His creation.

It is perhaps worth pointing out here the difference between this po-

5. Cf. Emil Brunner, *Man in Revolt*, trans. Olive Wyon (London: Lutterworth Press, 1939), p. 454.

sition and another to which it is in some ways similar, namely the view that the promised joys of heaven are to be related to man's earthly travails as a compensation or reward. This suggests a divine arrangement equitably proportioning compensation to injury, so that the more an individual has suffered beyond his desert the more intense or the more prolonged will be the heavenly bliss that he experiences. Thus those who have suffered most will subsequently have cause to rejoice most; and presumably, if the just proportion is to be preserved, none will enjoy an endless or infinite bliss, since none will have suffered an unending or unlimited injury. As distinct from such a book-keeping view, what is being suggested here, so far as men's sufferings are concerned, is that these sufferings—which for some people are immense and for others relatively slight—will in the end lead to the enjoyment of a common good which will be unending and therefore unlimited, and which will be seen by its participants as justifying all that has been endured on the way to it. The 'good eschaton' will not be a reward or a compensation proportioned to each individual's trials, but an infinite good that would render worth while *any* finite suffering endured in the course of attaining to it.

* * * * *

Christian theodicy claims, then, that the end to which God is leading us is a good so great as to justify all the failures and suffering and sorrow that will have been endured on the way to it. The life of the Kingdom of God will be an infinite, because eternal, good, outweighing all temporal and therefore finite evils. We cannot visualize the life of the redeemed and perfected creation, for all our imagery is necessarily drawn from our present "fallen" world. We can think only in very general terms of the opening up before us of new dimensions of reality "which eye hath not seen nor ear heard nor the heart of man conceived";[6] a new intensity and vividness of experience; of expanded capacities for fulfilment in personal relationships, artistic and other forms of creativity, knowledge, wonder, the enjoyment of beauty, and yet other goods and kinds of goods at present beyond our ken.

But, having said this, questions and difficulties at once arise. Could even an endless heavenly joy ever heal the scars of deep human suffering? It has been said (by Leon Bloy) that "Souffrir passe; avoir souffert ne passe jamais." Physical pain is quickly forgotten; but the memory and the effects of mental and emotional anguish can remain with us throughout our lives and presumably beyond this life so long as there is continuity of personal identity. Would not, then, the recollection of past miseries, shames, crimes, injustices, hatreds, and agonies—including the recollection of witnessing the sufferings of others—destroy the happiness of heaven?[7]

It is very difficult indeed to resolve such a question; for we do not know what is possible, let alone what is probable, in realms of being so far beyond our present experience. We can think only in terms of

6. I Corinthians ii. 9.

7. For a powerful underlining of this question, see Dostoievski's *The Brothers Karamazov*, pt. II, bk. v, chap. 4.

what Plato called "likely tales". It may be that the personal scars and memories of evil remain for ever, but are transfigured in the light of the universal mutual forgiveness and reconciliation on which the life of heaven is based. Or it may be that the journey to the heavenly Kingdom is so long, and traverses such varied spheres of existence, involving so many new and transforming experiences, that in the end the memory of our earthly life is dimmed to the point of extinction. There is no evident ground or need to decide between such possibilities, and I mention them only to suggest that the puzzle that was raised, although not at present soluble, is also not such as to overthrow the theodicy that we have been developing.

COMMENTS ■ QUESTIONS

1. According to Hick, the only way to solve the problem of evil is to suppose that there is life after death. Some people have argued that Hick's solution is a "last resort," a desperate attempt to solve the problem of evil by appealing to the existence of something unknowable. Is this criticism fair?
2. Would you say that the problem of evil is *necessarily* solved if there *is* life after death? (See arguments and counterarguments in chapter 7.) If not, why not?

J. L. MACKIE

Evil and Omnipotence

The traditional arguments for the existence of God have been fairly thoroughly criticised by philosophers. But the theologian can, if he wishes, accept this criticism. He can admit that no rational proof of God's existence is possible. And he can still retain all that is essential to his position, by holding that God's existence is known in some other, non-rational way. I think, however, that a more telling criticism can be made by way of the traditional problem of evil. Here it can be shown, not that religious beliefs lack rational support, but that they are positively irrational, that the several parts of the essential theological doctrine are inconsistent with one another, so that the theologian can maintain his position as a whole only by a much more extreme rejection of reason than in the former case. He must now be prepared to believe, not merely what cannot be proved, but what can be *disproved* from other beliefs that he also holds.

The problem of evil, in the sense in which I shall be using the phrase, is a problem only for someone who believes that there is a God who is both omnipotent and wholly good. And it is a logical problem, the problem of clarifying and reconciling a number of beliefs: it is not a scientific problem that might be solved by further observations, or a practical problem that might be solved by a decision or an action. These points are obvious; I mention them only because they are sometimes ignored by theologians, who sometimes parry a statement of the problem with such remarks as "Well, can you solve the problem yourself?" or "This is a mystery which may be revealed to us later" or "Evil is something to be faced and overcome, not to be merely discussed".

In its simplest form the problem is this: God is omnipotent; God is wholly good; and yet evil exists. There seems to be some contradiction between these three propositions, so that if any two of them were true the third would be false. But at the same time all three are essential parts of most theological positions: the theologian, it seems, at once *must* adhere and *cannot consistently* adhere to all three. (The problem does not arise only for theists,

J. L. Mackie (1917–1981), who taught philosophy at Oxford University, wrote several books and many journal articles that were widely read. They include The Cement of the Universe *and* Ethics: Inventing Right and Wrong.

J. L. Mackie: "Evil and Omnipotence." Reprinted from *Mind*, volume 16, number 254 (1955). By permission of Oxford University Press and Mrs. Joan Mackie.

but I shall discuss it in the form in which it presents itself for ordinary theism.)

However, the contradiction does not arise immediately; to show it we need some additional premises, or perhaps some quasi-logical rules connecting the terms "good", "evil", and "omnipotent". These additional principles are that good is opposed to evil, in such a way that a good thing always eliminates evil as far as it can, and that there are no limits to what an omnipotent thing can do. From these it follows that a good omnipotent thing eliminates evil completely, and then the propositions that a good omnipotent thing exists, and that evil exists, are incompatible.

A. Adequate Solutions

Now once the problem is fully stated it is clear that it can be solved, in the sense that the problem will not arise if one gives up at least one of the propositions that constitute it. If you are prepared to say that God is not wholly good, or not quite omnipotent, or that evil does not exist, or that good is not opposed to the kind of evil that exists, or that there are limits to what an omnipotent thing can do, then the problem of evil will not arise for you.

There are, then, quite a number of adequate solutions of the problem of evil, and some of these have been adopted, or almost adopted, by various thinkers. For example, a few have been prepared to deny God's omnipotence, and rather more have been prepared to keep the term "omnipotence" but severely to restrict its meaning, recording quite a number of things that an omnipotent being cannot do. Some have said that evil is an illusion, perhaps because they held that the whole world of temporal, changing things is an illusion, and that what we call evil belongs only to this world, or perhaps because they held that although temporal things *are* much as we see them, those that we call evil are not really evil. Some have said that what we call evil is merely the privation of good, that evil in a positive sense, evil that would really be opposed to good, does not exist. Many have agreed with Pope that disorder is harmony not understood, and that partial evil is universal good. Whether any of these views is *true* is, of course, another question. But each of them gives an adequate solution of the problem of evil in the sense that if you accept it this problem does not arise for you, though you may, of course, have *other* problems to face.

But often enough these adequate solutions are only *almost* adopted. The thinkers who restrict God's power, but keep the term 'omnipotence', may reasonably be suspected of thinking, in other contexts, that his power is really unlimited. Those who say that evil is an illusion may also be thinking, inconsistently, that this illusion is itself an evil. Those who say that "evil" is merely privation of good may also be thinking, inconsistently, that privation of good is an evil. (The fallacy here is akin to some forms of the "naturalistic fallacy" in ethics, where some think, for example, that "good" is just what contributes to evolutionary progress, and that evolutionary progress is itself good.) If Pope meant what he said in the first line of his couplet, that "disorder" is only harmony not understood, the "partial evil" of the second line must, for consistency, mean "that which, taken in isolation, falsely appears to be evil", but it would more naturally mean "that which, in isolation, really is evil". The second line, in fact, hesitates between two views, that "partial evil" isn't really evil, since only the universal quality is real, and that "partial evil" is really an evil, but only a little one.

In addition, therefore, to adequate solutions, we must recognise unsatisfactory inconsistent solutions, in which there is only a half-hearted or temporary rejection of one of the propositions which together constitute the problem. In these, one of the constituent propositions is explicitly rejected, but it is covertly re-asserted or assumed elsewhere in the system.

B. *Fallacious Solutions*

Besides these half-hearted solutions, which explicitly reject but implicitly assert one of the constituent propositions, there are definitely fallacious solutions which explicitly maintain all the constituent propositions, but implicitly reject at least one of them in the course of the argument that explains away the problem of evil.

There are, in fact, many so-called solutions which purport to remove the contradiction without abandoning any of its constituent propositions. These must be fallacious, as we can see from the very statement of the problem, but it is not so easy to see in each case precisely where the fallacy lies. I suggest that in all cases the fallacy has the general form suggested above: in order to solve the problem one (or perhaps more) of its constituent propositions is given up, but in such a way that it appears to have been retained, and can therefore be asserted without qualification in other contexts. Sometimes there is a further complication: the supposed solution moves to and fro between, say, two of the constituent propositions, at one point asserting the first of these but covertly abandoning the second, at another point asserting the second but covertly abandoning the first. These fallacious solutions often turn upon some equivocation with the words "good" and "evil", or upon some vagueness about the way in which good and evil are opposed to one another, or about how much is meant by "omnipotence". I propose to examine some of these so-called solutions, and to exhibit their fallacies in detail. Incidentally, I shall also be considering whether an adequate solution could be reached by a minor modification of one or more of the constituent propositions, which would, however, still satisfy all the essential requirements of ordinary theism.

1. "Good Cannot Exist Without Evil" or "Evil Is Necessary as a Counterpart to Good"

It is sometimes suggested that evil is necessary as a counterpart to good, that if there were no evil there could be no good either, and that this solves the problem of evil. It is true that it points to an answer to the question "Why should there be evil?" But it does so only by qualifying some of the propositions that constitute the problem.

First, it sets a limit to what God can do, saying that God *cannot* create good without simultaneously creating evil, and this means either that God is not omnipotent or that there are *some* limits to what an omnipotent thing can do. It may be replied that these limits are always presupposed, that omnipotence has never meant the power to do what is logically impossible, and on the present view the existence of good without evil would be a logical impossibility. This interpretation of omnipotence may, indeed, be accepted as a modification of our original account which does not reject anything that is essential to theism, and I shall in general assume it in the subsequent discussion. It is, perhaps, the most common theistic view, but I think that some theists at least have maintained that God can do what is logically impossible. Many theists, at any rate, have held that logic itself is created or laid down by God, that logic is the way in which God arbitrarily chooses to think. (This is, of course, parallel to the ethical view that morally right actions are those which God arbitrarily chooses to command, and the two views encounter similar difficulties.) And *this* account of logic is clearly inconsistent with the view that God is bound by logical necessities—unless it is possible for an omnipotent being to bind himself, an issue which we shall consider later, when we come to the Paradox of Omnipotence. This solution of the problem of evil cannot, therefore, be consistently adopted along with the view that logic is itself created by God.

But, secondly, this solution denies that evil is opposed to good in our original sense. If good and evil are counterparts, a good thing will not "eliminate evil as far as it can". Indeed, this view suggests that good and evil are not strictly qualities of things at all. Perhaps the suggestion is that good and evil are related in much the same way as great and small. Certainly, when the term "great" is used relatively as a condensation of "greater than so-and-so", and "small" is used correspondingly, greatness and smallness are counterparts and cannot exist without each other. But in this sense greatness is not a quality, not an intrinsic feature of anything; and it would be absurd to think of a movement in favour of greatness and against smallness in this sense. Such a movement would be self-defeating, since relative greatness can be promoted only by a simultaneous promotion of relative smallness. I feel sure that no theists would be content to regard God's goodness as analogous to this—as if what he supports were not the *good* but the *better*, and as if he had the paradoxical aim that all things should be better than other things.

This point is obscured by the fact that "great" and "small" seem to have an absolute as well as a relative sense. I cannot discuss here whether there is absolute magnitude or not, but if there is, there could be an absolute sense for "great", it could mean of at least a certain size, and it would make sense to speak of all things getting bigger, of a universe that was expanding all over, and therefore it would make sense to speak of promoting greatness. But in *this* sense great and small are not logically necessary counterparts: either quality could exist without the other. There would be no logical impossibility in everything's being small or in everything's being great.

Neither in the absolute nor in the

relative sense, then, of "great" and "small" do these terms provide an analogy of the sort that would be needed to support this solution of the problem of evil. In neither case are greatness and smallness *both* necessary counterparts *and* mutually opposed forces or possible objects for support and attack.

It may be replied that good and evil are necessary counterparts in the same way as any quality and its logical opposite: redness can occur, it is suggested, only if non-redness also occurs. But unless evil is merely the privation of good, they are not logical opposites, and some further argument would be needed to show that they are counterparts in the same way as genuine logical opposites. Let us assume that this could be given. There is still doubt of the correctness of the metaphysical principle that a quality must have a real opposite: I suggest that it is not really impossible that everything should be, say, red, that the truth is merely that if everything were red we should not notice redness, and so we should have no word "red"; we observe and give names to qualities only if they have real opposites. If so, the principle that a term must have an opposite would belong only to our language or to our thought, and would not be an ontological principle, and, correspondingly, the rule that good cannot exist without evil would not state a logical necessity of a sort that God would just have to put up with. God might have made everything good, though *we* should not have noticed it if he had.

But, finally, even if we concede that this *is* an ontological principle, it will provide a solution for the problem of evil only if one is prepared to say, "Evil exists, but only just enough evil to serve as the counterpart of good". I doubt whether any theist will accept this. After all, the *ontological* requirement that non-redness should occur would be satisfied even if all the universe, except for a minute speck, were red, and, if there were a corresponding requirement for evil as a counterpart to good, a minute dose of evil would presumably do. But theists are not usually willing to say, in all contexts, that all the evil that occurs is a minute and necessary dose.

2. "Evil Is Necessary as a Means to Good"

It is sometimes suggested that evil is necessary for good not as a counterpart but as a means. In its simple form this has little plausibility as a solution of the problem of evil, since it obviously implies a severe restriction of God's power. It would be a *causal* law that you cannot have a certain end without a certain means, so that if God has to introduce evil as a means to good, he must be subject to at least some causal laws. This certainly conflicts with what a theist normally means by omnipotence. This view of God as limited by causal laws also conflicts with the view that causal laws are themselves made by God, which is more widely held than the corresponding view about the laws of logic. This conflict would, indeed, be resolved if it were possible for an omnipotent being to bind himself, and this possibility has still to be considered. Unless a favourable answer can be given to this question, the suggestion that evil is necessary as a means to good solves the problem of evil only by denying one of its constituent propositions, either that God is omnipotent or that "omnipotent" means what it says.

3. "The Universe Is Better With Some Evil in It Than It Could Be If There Were No Evil"

Much more important is a solution which at first seems to be a mere variant of the previous one, that evil may contribute to the goodness of a whole in which it is found, so that the universe as a whole is better as it is, with some evil in it, than it would be if there were no evil. This solution may be developed in either of two ways. It may be supported by an aesthetic analogy, by the fact that contrasts heighten beauty, that in a musical work, for example, there may occur discords which somehow add to the beauty of the work as a whole. Alternatively, it may be worked out in connexion with the notion of progress, that the best possible organisation of the universe will not be static, but progressive, that the gradual overcoming of evil by good is really a finer thing than would be the eternal unchallenged supremacy of good.

In either case, this solution usually starts from the assumption that the evil whose existence gives rise to the problem of evil is primarily what is called physical evil, that is to say, pain. In Hume's rather half-hearted presentation of the problem of evil, the evils that he stresses are pain and disease, and those who reply to him argue that the existence of pain and disease makes possible the existence of sympathy, benevolence, heroism, and the gradually successful struggle of doctors and reformers to overcome these evils. In fact, theists often seize the opportunity to accuse those who stress the problem of evil of taking a low, materialistic view of good and evil, equating these with pleasure and pain, and of ignoring the more spiritual goods which can arise in the struggle against evils.

But let us see exactly what is being done here. Let us call pain and misery "first order evil" or "evil (1)". What contrasts with this, namely, pleasure and happiness, will be called "first order good" or "good (1)". Distinct from this is "second order good" or "good (2)" which somehow emerges in a complex situation in which evil (1) is a necessary component—logically, not merely causally, necessary. (Exactly *how* it emerges does not matter: in the crudest version of this solution good (2) is simply the heightening of happiness by the contrast with misery, in other versions it includes sympathy with suffering, heroism in facing danger, and the gradual decrease of first order evil and increase of first order good.) It is also being assumed that second order good is more important than first order good or evil, in particular that it more than outweighs the first order evil it involves.

Now this is a particularly subtle attempt to solve the problem of evil. It defends God's goodness and omnipotence on the ground that (on a sufficiently long view) this is the best of all logically possible worlds, because it includes the important second order goods, and yet it admits that real evils, namely first order evils, exist. But does it still hold that good and evil are opposed? Not, clearly, in the sense that we set out originally: good does not tend to eliminate evil in general. Instead, we have a modified, a more complex pattern. First order good (*e.g.* happiness) *contrasts with* first order evil (*e.g.* misery): these two are opposed in a fairly mechanical way; some second order goods (*e.g.* benevolence) try to maximise first order good and minimise first order evil; but God's goodness is not this, it is rather the will to maximise *second* order good. We might, therefore, call God's goodness an example of a third order goodness, or good (3). While this account is different from our original one, it might well be held to be an improvement on it, to give a more accurate description of the way in which good is opposed to evil, and to be consistent with the essential theist position.

There might, however, be several objections to this solution.

First, some might argue that such qualities as benevolence—and *a fortiori* the third order goodness which promotes benevolence—have a merely derivative value, that they are not higher sorts of good, but merely means to good (1), that is, to happiness, so that it would be absurd for God to keep misery in existence in order to make possible the virtues of benevolence, heroism, etc. The theist who adopts the present solution must, of course, deny this, but he can do so with some plausibility, so I should not press this objection.

Secondly, it follows from this solution that God is not in our sense benevolent or sympathetic: he is not concerned to minimise evil (1), but only to promote good (2); and this might be a disturbing conclusion for some theists.

But, thirdly, the fatal objection is this. Our analysis shows clearly the possibility of the existence of a *second* order evil, an evil (2) contrasting with good (2) as evil (1) contrasts with good (1). This would include malevolence, cruelty, callousness, cowardice, and states in which good (1) is decreasing and evil (1) increasing. And just as good (2) is held to be the important kind of good, the kind that God is concerned to promote, so evil (2) will, by analogy, be the important kind of evil, the kind which God, if he were wholly good and omnipotent, would eliminate. And yet evil (2) plainly exists, and indeed most theists (in other contexts) stress its existence more than that of evil (1). We should, therefore, state the problem of evil in terms of second order evil, and against this form of the problem the present solution is useless.

An attempt might be made to use this solution again, at a higher level, to explain the occurrence of evil (2): indeed the next main solution that we shall examine does just this, with the help of some new notions. Without any fresh notions, such a solution would have little plausibility: for example, we could hardly say that the really important good was a good (3), such as the increase of benevolence in proportion to cruelty, which logically required for its occurrence the occurrence of some second order evil. But even if evil (2) could be explained in this way, it is fairly clear that there would be third order evils contrasting with this third order good: and we should be well on the way to an infinite regress, where the solution of a problem of evil, stated in terms of evil (n), indicated the existence of an evil ($n + 1$), and a further problem to be solved.

4. "Evil Is Due to Human Freewill"

Perhaps the most important proposed solution of the problem of evil is that evil is not to be ascribed to God at all, but to the independent actions of human beings, supposed to have been endowed by God with freedom of the will. This solution may be combined with the preceding one: first order evil (*e.g.* pain) may be justified as a logically necessary component in second order good (*e.g.* sympathy) while second order evil (*e.g.* cruelty) is not *justified*, but is so ascribed to human beings that God cannot be held responsible for it. This combination evades my third criticism of the preceding solution.

The freewill solution also involves the preceding solution at a higher level. To explain why a wholly good God gave men freewill although it would lead to some important evils, it must be argued that it is better on the whole that men should act freely, and sometimes err, than that they should be innocent automata, acting rightly in a wholly determined way. Freedom, that is to say, is now treated as a third order good, and as being more valuable than second order goods (such as sympathy and heroism) would be if they were deterministically produced, and it is being assumed that second order evils, such as cruelty, are logically necessary accompaniments of freedom, just as pain is a logically necessary precondition of sympathy.

I think that this solution is unsatisfactory primarily because of the incoherence of the notion of freedom of the will: but I cannot discuss this topic adequately here, although some of my criticisms will touch upon it.

First I should query the assumption that second order evils are logically necessary accompaniments of freedom. I should ask this: if God has made men such that in their free choices they sometimes prefer what is good and sometimes what is evil, why could he not have made men such that they always freely choose the good? If there is no logical impossibility in a man's freely choosing the good on one, or on several, occasions, there cannot be a logical impossibility in his freely choosing the good on every occasion. God was not, then, faced with a choice between making innocent automata and making beings who, in acting freely, would sometimes go wrong: there was open to him the obviously better possibility of making beings who would act freely but always go right. Clearly, his failure to avail himself of this possibility is inconsistent with his being both omnipotent and wholly good.

If it is replied that this objection is absurd, that the making of some wrong choices is logically necessary for freedom, it would seem that "freedom" must here mean complete randomness or indeterminacy, including randomness with regard to the alternatives good and evil, in other words that men's choices and consequent actions can be "free" only if they are not determined by their characters. Only on this assumption can God escape the responsibility for men's actions; for if he made them as they are, but did not determine their wrong choices, this can only be because the wrong choices are not determined by men as they are. But then if freedom is randomness, how can it be a characteristic of *will*? And, still more, how can it be the most important good? What value or merit would there be in free choices if these were random actions which were not determined by the nature of the agent?

I conclude that to make this solution plausible two different senses of "freedom" must be confused, one sense which will justify the view that freedom is a third order good, more valuable than other goods would be without it, and another sense, sheer randomness, to prevent us from ascribing to God a decision to make men such that they sometimes go wrong when he might have made them such that they would always freely go right.

This criticism is sufficient to dispose of this solution. But besides this there is a fundamental difficulty in the notion of an omnipotent God creating men with free will, for if men's wills are really free this must mean that even God cannot control them, that is, that God is no longer omnipotent. It may be objected that God's gift of freedom to men does not mean that he *cannot* control their wills, but that he always *refrains* from controlling their wills. But why, we may ask, should God refrain from controlling evil wills? Why should he not leave men free to will rightly, but intervene when he sees them beginning to will wrongly? If God could do this, but does not, and if he is wholly good, the only explanation could be that even a wrong free act of will is not really evil, that its freedom is a value which outweighs its wrongness, so that there would be a loss of value if God took away the wrongness and the freedom together. But this is utterly opposed to what theists say about sin in other contexts. The present solution of the problem of evil, then, can be maintained only in the form that God has made men so free that he *cannot* control their wills.

This leads us to what I call the Paradox of Omnipotence: can an omnipotent being make things which he cannot subsequently control? Or, what is practically equivalent to this, can an omnipotent being make rules which then bind himself? (These are practically equivalent because any such rules could be regarded as setting certain things beyond his control, and *vice versa*.) The second of these formulations is relevant to the suggestions that we have already met, that an omnipotent God creates the rules of logic or causal laws, and is then bound by them.

It is clear that this is a paradox: the questions cannot be answered satisfactorily either in the affirmative or in the negative. If we answer "Yes", it follows that if God actually makes things which he cannot control, or makes rules which bind himself, he is not omnipotent once he has made them: there are *then* things which he cannot do. But if we answer "No", we are immediately asserting that there are things which he cannot do, that is to say that he is already not omnipotent.

It cannot be replied that the question which sets this paradox is not a proper question. It would make perfectly good sense to say that a human mechanic has made a machine which he cannot control: if there is any difficulty about the question it lies in the notion of omnipotence itself.

This, incidentally, shows that although we have approached this paradox from the free will theory, it is equally a problem for a theological determinist. No one thinks that machines have free will, yet they may well be beyond the control of their makers. The determinist might reply that anyone who makes anything determines its ways of acting, and so determines its subsequent behaviour: even the human mechanic does this by his *choice* of materials and structure for his machine, though he does not know all about either of these: the mechanic thus determines, though he may not foresee, his machine's actions. And since God is omniscient, and since his creation of things is total, he both determines and foresees the ways in which his creatures will act. We may grant this, but it is beside the point. The question is not whether God *originally* determined the future actions of his creatures, but whether he can *subsequently* control their actions, or whether he was able in his original creation to put things beyond his subsequent control. Even on determinist principles the answers "Yes" and "No" are equally irreconcilable with God's omnipotence.

Before suggesting a solution of this paradox, I would point out that there is a parallel Paradox of Sovereignty. Can a legal sovereign make a law restricting its own future legislative power? For example, could the British parliament make a law forbidding any future parliament to socialise banking, and also forbidding the future repeal of this law itself? Or could the British parliament, which was legally sovereign in Australia in, say, 1899, pass a valid law, or series of laws, which made it no longer sovereign in 1933? Again, neither the affirmative nor the negative answer is really satisfactory. If we were to answer "Yes", we should be admitting the validity of a law which, if it were actually made, would mean that parliament was no longer sovereign. If we were to answer "No", we should be admitting that there is a law, not logically absurd, which parliament cannot validly make, that is, that parliament is not now a legal sovereign. This paradox can be solved in the following way. We should distinguish between first order laws, that is laws governing the actions of individuals and bodies other than the legislature, and second order laws, that is laws about laws, laws governing the actions of the legislature itself. Correspondingly, we should distinguish two orders of sovereignty, first order sovereignty (sovereignty (1)) which is unlimited authority to make first order laws, and second order sovereignty (sovereignty (2)) which is unlimited authority to make second order laws. If we say that parliament is sovereign we might mean that any parliament at any time has sovereignty (1), or we might mean that parliament has both sovereignty (1) and sovereignty (2) at present, but we cannot without contradiction mean both that the present parliament has sovereignty (2) and that every parliament at every time has sovereignty (1), for if the present parliament has sovereignty (2) it may use it to take away the sovereignty (1) of later parliaments. What the paradox shows is that we cannot ascribe to any continuing institution legal sovereignty in an inclusive sense.

The analogy between omnipotence and sovereignty shows that the paradox of omnipotence can be solved in a similar way. We must distinguish between first order omnipotence (omnipotence (1)), that is unlimited power to act, and second order omnipotence (omnipotence (2)), that is unlimited power to determine what powers to act things shall have. Then we could consistently say that God all the time has omnipotence (1), but if so no beings at any time have powers to act independently of God. Or we could say that God at one time had omnipotence (2), and used it to assign independent powers to act to certain things, so that God thereafter did not have omnipotence (1). But what the paradox shows is that we cannot consistently ascribe to any continuing being omnipotence in an inclusive sense.

An alternative solution of this paradox would be simply to deny that God is a continuing being, that any times can be assigned to his actions at all. But on this assumption (which also has difficulties of its own) no meaning can be given to the assertion that God made men with wills so free that he could not control them. The paradox of omnipotence can be avoided by putting God outside time, but the freewill solution of the problem of evil cannot be saved in this way, and equally it remains impossible to hold that an omnipotent God *binds himself* by causal or logical laws.

Conclusion

Of the proposed solutions of the problem of evil which we have examined, none has stood up to criticism. There may be other solutions which require examination, but this study strongly suggests that there is no valid solution of the problem which does not modify at least one of the constituent propositions in a way which would seriously affect the essential core of the theistic position.

Quite apart from the problem of evil, the paradox of omnipotence has shown that God's omnipotence must in any case be restricted in one way or another, that unqualified omnipotence cannot be ascribed to any being that continues through time. And if God and his actions are not in time, can omnipotence, or power of any sort, be meaningfully ascribed to him?

COMMENTS ■ QUESTIONS

1. In analyzing the problem of evil, Mackie begins by discussing what he calls "adequate solutions" to the problem. Keep in mind that he means *logically adequate*; he means adequate in the sense that such solutions do not involve the contradiction that (Mackie argues) arises when the following three statements are asserted together: God is omnipotent; God is wholly good; evil exists. In adequate solutions, says Mackie, one (or more) of these three statements is rejected. Mackie himself does not actually claim

that any of these statements *should* be rejected. Do you believe that any of them should be rejected?

2. By "fallacious solutions" to the problem of evil, Mackie means attempts to show that the three statements referred to in question 1 above can be asserted together without any contradiction. Mackie argues that this simply cannot be done, and that therefore in each one of these attempted solutions, one of the three statements is *implicitly* rejected. Mackie's discussion of each of these attempts is complex and needs to be read (or reread) carefully. You need to ask yourself at each step in Mackie's arguments whether he has made a logically valid point. Is Mackie's way of stating the matter the only possible way, or is there an alternative that has a different logical consequence?
3. One attempted solution to the problem of evil has been written about by philosophers more than the others. This is the claim that much evil is a result of human free will. For this solution to seem plausible at all there first must be reason to believe that free will exists (for an examination of free will, see chapter 5). Second, there must be reason to believe that free will is necessary for the sort of "soul-making" that John Hick refers to in the preceding reading selection. Mackie's rejection of the "free will solution" has to do with the way that Mackie analyzes the concept of free will. Do you believe that Mackie is correct? In particular, do you agree with Mackie when he says that if "the making of some wrong choices is logically necessary for freedom, it would seem that 'freedom' must here mean complete randomness or indeterminacy"?

READINGS

Abernethy, George L., and Thomas A. Langford, eds. *Philosophy of Religion: A Book of Readings.* New York: Macmillan, 1968. Chapter 6 of this widely used anthology is on the problem of evil.

Ahern, M. B. *The Problem of Evil.* London: Routledge & Kegan Paul, 1971. Defends the theistic position against the argument from evil.

Bible, Book of Job.

Camus, Albert. *The Myth of Sisyphus.* New York: Vintage, 1955. Argues against suicide in an "absurd world."

Leibniz, Gottfried Wilhelm. *Theodicy.* Indianapolis: Bobbs-Merrill, 1966. (First published in 1710.) Elaborates upon the view presented in this chapter, but is difficult to read.

Madden, E. H., and Hare, P. H. *Evil and the Concept of God.* Springfield, Ill.: Charles C Thomas, 1968. One of the most comprehensive recent treatments.

Pike, Nelson, ed. *God and Evil.* Englewood Cliffs, N.J.: Prentice-Hall, 1964. A very useful collection of classical and contemporary works on the problem of evil.

Sartre, Jean-Paul. *Being and Nothingness.* New York: Citadel, 1956. This difficult work deals with what Sartre calls "abandonment."

Tsanoff, Radoslav. *The Nature of Evil.* New York: Macmillan, 1931. Still worth looking at.

Whitely, C. H. *An Introduction to Metaphysics.* London: Methuen, 1950. Contains a forceful statement of the argument from evil.

CHAPTER FIVE

The thesis of determinism . . . is a plausible commonsensical belief for which there is reasonable evidence.
—*Kai Nielsen*

Man is condemned to be free.
—*Jean-Paul Sartre*

Free Will and Determinism

Is it right to punish people when they cannot help doing what they do? Is it right to praise them or reward them for doing good things when they cannot help doing good things? Most of us would be inclined to answer no to both of these questions. Punishments and rewards, we are inclined to say, should be deserved; they should be given for actions that people have some choice about. However, according to a philosophical doctrine known as *hard determinism* (this will be precisely defined later), no one has any choice about anything in a very fundamental and important sense, and therefore no one truly deserves any praise or blame. According to hard determinism, there is no free will, because everything in the universe has a cause or set of causes that have brought it into existence and have made it behave in the way that it does.

Most people, when they first learn about this doctrine, suppose that *somehow* it can be shown to be false. But to do so is not easy. An analysis of hard determinism requires an examination of the entire free will controversy.

In chapter 1 we said that philosophy differs from other disciplines because it asks more basic questions and even questions its own questions. Nowhere is this more apparent than in regard to the free will controversy. At the heart of it is the question:

> Do human beings have free will?

No one could begin to answer that question without first attempting to answer *this* question:

> In talking about free will what are we talking about? (That is, if free will exists what is it? If free will does not exist, what sort of thing are we saying does not exist?)

To this question, philosophers have given two quite different answers, each of which raises even further questions. Some philosophers say that free will is the following *(first definition)*:

> The ability to act upon one's desires

According to this definition, people do have free will because they are often able to do what they want to do. Sometimes they are prevented by some person or circumstance from doing what they want to do, but at other times they are not. People are not free all of the time, but they are free some of the time. For example, suppose that I would like to go on a hike sometime during the upcoming weekend. According to the above definition of free will, I am free to go on the hike (that is, I will exhibit free will in going on the hike) if no person or circumstance stops me. Someone who is in the hospital or is imprisoned or has broken a leg is not free to go on the hike. Circumstances prevent it. If a madman kidnaps me before the weekend, again I will not be free to go on the hike. In this case a person will prevent it. Moreover, if I am a compulsive individual who can never relax until all of my work is done, and if I have a lot of work that will not be finished before the weekend, I will not be free to go on the hike. In this case I will prevent myself from going (or, perhaps, the circumstance of my being compulsive will prevent me).

Is anything wrong with the above stated definition of free will? As a matter of fact, many philosophers would not accept it. Their view is that the concept of free will must be set in opposition to the concept of *causal determination*. Even if I decide to go on the hike and nothing prevents me, these philosophers would be interested in the question of whether I have been causally determined to go on the hike. We have said that I plan to go on the hike because I want to go. But it may make sense to say that I want to go on the hike because of the sort of person that I am and that heredity and environmental influences have made me that person. As a consequence, it may appear that I am not acting freely in going on the hike. It may appear that even though I *am* able to go on a hike this weekend, since circumstances allow me to go and no one will stop me, I *cannot help* but be the sort of person who takes advantage of opportunities to go hiking. It may appear that I am not free if free will means the following *(second definition)*:

> The human capacity to act in a way that is not causally determined by one's character (or personality) or circumstances

If this definition of free will is accepted, should we say that people ever have free will? Some philosophers would say yes, others would say no. By contrast, in terms of the first definition, *all* philosophers would say that there is free will, but some would also say that the first definition is not adequate, that it does not tell us what freedom of action really is. The second definition produces disagreements even among philosophers who accept it as the best. Some, but not all, would say that human actions can be free of causal determination.

Thus, philosophers divide themselves into three different groups on the question of whether there is free will:

1. *Soft determinists* believe that the first definition of free will is the best. They believe that people are free (i.e., exhibit free will in certain of their actions) whenever circumstances or persons, including themselves, do not prevent them from acting on their wants or their desires. In order to show that soft determinism is correct, its advocates must demonstrate primarily that the first definition of free will is indeed the best. They may also need to answer certain questions about what it means to say under various

circumstances that someone is prevented from doing what he or she wants to do.

2. *Libertarians* believe that the second definition of free will is the best and that free will does exist. When libertarians say that free will exists, however, they mean something quite different from what soft determinists mean. If libertarians are to show that their position is correct, they must demonstrate (a) that their definition of free will is best and (b) that people actually have the capacity to act in ways that are not causally determined by character or circumstances. In the course of doing this they must explain exactly what is meant by saying that an action is not causally determined.
3. *Hard determinists* agree with libertarians that the second definition of free will is best but, in contrast to libertarians, do not believe that free will exists. According to hard determinists everything in the world—including every human action—is subject to complete causal determination. Of the three groups of philosophers, only the hard determinists say that there is no free will. For them to defend their position, they must show (a) that the second definition of free will is best, and (b) that everything that people do is causally determined by character or circumstances.

Which of these philosophers has the right answer? Before that question can be decided, several further questions—some of them extremely difficult—must be answered. The two most important of these questions follow:

1. What does (or could) it mean to say that everything that people do is causally determined?
2. What does (or could) it mean to say that some things people do are not causally determined?

In answering the first question, some philosophers have said that everything that happens in the universe does so *by necessity*, and that the necessity lies in the connections between an event and its cause (or causes). For example, if I place a fragile china teacup on a table and strike it squarely with a heavy hammer, the cup, it is said, will shatter *necessarily*. The hammer blow *causes* it to break. The hammer blow *forces* the cup to shatter. Most hard determinists would say that everything that happens in the universe is like the breaking of the teacup. For every event there is some cause or set of causes that make it happen. Moreover, for every *cause* there is a further cause, and for that cause a still further cause, and for that cause a still further cause, and so on. Therefore, on this view everything that happens *now* is the necessary result of events that took place a hundred, a thousand, a million, or a billion years ago. The present is the inevitable unfolding of the past; the future will be the inevitable unfolding of the present. Hard determinists sometimes say that chains of causal necessity bind the future to the present and the present to the past.

Many philosophers are quite unhappy with this description of the universe. Libertarians, of course, reject it. Other philosophers also reject it because they have doubts about *causal necessity* as a clear concept. The philosophical issues that revolve around the concept of causality in general are among the most difficult in philosophy. One problem—often pointed out by soft determinists—is that we apparently never *observe* necessity in nature, let alone in human actions. We observe the cause of an event, then we observe the effect, but we do not observe the necessity that ties together cause and effect. Some soft determinists would go so far as to say that there is no necessity at all in nature. Everything *is* causally determined, they would say (and hence they reject the libertarian view of free will), but all that means is that everything that happens is *preceded* by its cause. It does not mean that a cause *necessitates* an effect. To say these things, of course, raises extremely difficult questions about the meaning of the word "cause" and about the basis in nature for making predictions about the future.

Equally difficult issues are raised by the second question. In fact, the concept of a human action that is not causally determined is perhaps the most controversial of all concepts in the free will controversy. Because it is probably easier to say what is not meant by this concept than to say what is meant, let us begin there. When libertarians say that some human actions are not causally determined, they do not mean that some human actions have no causes at all. Consider the following example. Many libertarians (but not all, for reasons that are too complex for us to go into here) would say that my choosing to buy the house I now live in was a free choice. I did not buy the house as the result of any inner compulsion. I was not forced by circumstances to buy it. But I did have what I thought were good reasons for buying it, and no one would deny that those reasons *in some sense* caused me to buy the house because without those reasons I would not have bought it. Determinists, whether hard or soft, would say that those reasons plus other relevant factors such as my personality were *sufficient* to get me to buy the house, that is, nothing else was needed, and, once all of the reasons and other relevant factors were in place, no other result was possible. Libertarians would deny that this is the case, arguing instead that I *could have chosen not to buy the house* even if all the reasons and other relevant factors such as my personality had been the same. According to libertarians, my reasons for buying the house together with the other relevant factors were *not sufficient* to get me to buy the house. Something else was needed, namely, my free choice.

Some libertarians would say that my reasons for buying the house plus other relevant factors were *partial* causes for my buying the house but were not sufficient causes. This raises the question of what is meant by talking about a partially determining cause. And how are we to understand the relation between a partially determining cause and whatever it is (this needs to be spelled out) that is contributed to human actions by the choice of a free will? Just as hard determinists must accept the burden of explaining causal necessity and soft determinists must accept the burden of explaining universal causality (even if it does not involve necessity), some libertarians must accept the burden of explaining *partial causality*. They also must accept the burden of explaining what an act of free choice is.

Not surprisingly then, the free will controversy has remained at center stage for a long time in the discussions of philosophers, and there certainly is no easy way to resolve it. The controversy has also retained its interest for philosophers and nonphilosophers alike because *both* determinism and libertarianism seem to have strong arguments in their favor. Brief summaries of these arguments follow.

- *Determinism* (let us leave unspecified which version) apparently has the strong support of science, which has been extremely successful in finding causes for events. Although causes for some phenomena, such as particularly troublesome diseases, have not yet been found, no one supposes that these diseases have no causes. Science appears to give us reason to believe that everything has a sufficient cause.
- *Libertarianism* appears to have the strong support of personal experience. When I bought my house, for example, I did not *feel* that I had to buy it, even given all the good reasons that I had for buying it plus the other relevant factors. I felt that I could have chosen to disregard all of these things. Many people would say that they have had many experiences of this kind. In other words, personal experience appears to give us strong reason to believe in free will as the libertarian defines it.

For very good reasons then, the free will controversy has not gone away. Moreover, much in our practical lives appears to be at stake in regard to its resolution. Libertarianism holds out a vision of human nature that is much more spontaneous and open to the future than the corresponding vision entailed by either version of determinism; determinism itself offers a picture of reality that appears to be much more stable and predictable.

As we mentioned at the beginning of this essay, many philosophers have argued that, if determinism is true, it is wrong to say that anyone deserves to be punished for misdeeds or praised for doing good. (Soft determinists, of course, would reject this claim.) At the extreme, it is said that we should correct criminals but not morally condemn them. The free will controversy embraces other real-life issues as well, some of which are discussed in the reading selections for this chapter.

The first of these selections, by Nicholas J. Dixon, presents an argument in defense of hard determinism. The second selection, from Jean-Paul Sartre, has become a classic. His position falls under the heading of libertarianism, although he does not refer to it in that way. Sartre's defense of human freedom grows out of the philosophy of *existentialism*, for which he is the best known exponent. In the selection reprinted here, Sartre discusses at some length two of the basic doctrines of existentialism, the doctrine of "subjectivism" and the doctrine that "existence (in regard to human beings) comes before essence." Fundamental to both doctrines is the idea that the important choices that people make in life are not determined by a human nature, or essence, that exists first, but rather that the contrary is the case—human nature is determined by choices. The choices come first. Human beings become what they choose to make of themselves. Therefore, according to existentialism, they are free.

The selection from Kai Nielsen is a general defense of soft determinism. Fred Alan Wolf discusses determinism in the light of contemporary science, in particular, the concept of discontinuous "quantum jumps" in subatomic physics and Werner Heisenberg's Principle of Indeterminacy. The final selection, from Susan Leigh Anderson, is a contemporary defense of libertarianism that is not based upon existentialism. It contains an extensive discussion of arguments both for and against libertarianism.

JEAN-PAUL SARTRE

Before there can be any truth whatever, . . . there must be an absolute truth, and there is such a truth which is simple, easily attained and within the reach of everybody: it consists in one's immediate sense of one's self."

—*Existentialism and Humanism*

If man, as the existentialist conceives him, is indefinable, it is because at first he is nothing. Only afterward will he be something, and he himself will have made what he will be.

We are all alone, with no excuses.

—*Existentialism*

It follows that my freedom is the unique foundation of values and that nothing, absolutely nothing, justifies me in adopting this or that particular value, this or that particular scale of values.

—*Being and Nothingness*

Jean-Paul Sartre (1905–1980) did what almost no one else has done; he made the name for his philosophy—existentialism—into practically a household word. Sartre was educated in Paris and taught in French secondary schools for several years until he took up writing full time. He fought in World War II, and was captured by the Germans, but he made his way back to Paris and fought in the Resistance. His philosophical novels, plays, and short stories have been read very widely. Many of the characters in Sartre's fictional works suffer because they are faced with agonizing choices. Some of his best known works are *Nausea, The Wall, No Exit*, and *Being and Nothingness*. In 1964 he refused the Nobel Prize for literature. Sartre's existentialism is a philosophy of freedom and also a moral philosophy—in which action is more important than moral deliberation and talk about what is good.

NICHOLAS J. DIXON

A "Slippery Slope" Argument in Defense of Hard Determinism

A schizophrenic in a mental hospital is hallucinating uncontrollably. A dose of lithium, or a similar drug, is administered, and within minutes the patient is back to normal, able to converse calmly, and amazed when told how she was behaving so recently. An epileptic flails his arms and legs around wildly during a seizure. We understand his behavior as uncontrollable reflex reactions due to a temporary brain disorder. When such stark *physiological* dysfunctions are cited as the cause of deviant behavior, we don't hesitate to excuse from responsibility. They "couldn't help" what they were doing.

Our attitude is similar toward those whose deviant actions have clear-cut *environmental* causes. It has been found that nearly all parents who sexually abuse their children were themselves sexually abused by their parents. Consider also a man in his mid-20's who is convicted of a series of assaults and violent robberies. After an investigation of his past, it is discovered that he was repeatedly beaten by his father, who was eventually jailed for assaulting his wife. The criminal and his nine siblings were raised by their mother, who encouraged them to shoplift in order to get enough food. In his early teens, he discovered that the easiest way to get money was to join the violent gangs to which many of his neighborhood friends belonged. He became more and more deeply involved in these gangs and their robberies until his conviction. The existence of such environmental causes is unlikely to exempt a malefactor from blame.[1] However, in proportion to the severity of the en-

1. It may be questioned whether these are genuine cases of causation. It is often pointed out, for example, that some victims of sexual abuse do *not* go on to abuse their children; and that some children with terribly violent home backgrounds "rise above" their origins and become respected professionals. Clearly such cases exist, and so having such a bad environment is at best a necessary condition for becoming a child molester or violent criminal. However, we do sometimes offer a necessary condition as a causal explanation, even if it only creates a low probability of the occurrence of the event it is cited to explain. For example, only 28 percent of those with untreated latent syphilis develop paresis or similar disorders, yet this does not prevent us from citing syphilis in our causal explanation of how they contracted paresis. This example is discussed by Wesley Salmon, in "Determinism and Indeterminism in Modern Science," in Joel Feinberg (ed.), *Reason and Responsibility* (4th edition, Dickinson, 1978), p. 340.

Nicholas J. Dixon teaches philosophy at Central Michigan University. His specialty is the philosophy of mind.

Used by permission of the author.

vironmental handicap suffered by the criminal, we are likely to *diminish* our blame. It seems perfectly appropriate for defense attorneys to bring such background information to light for the purposes of sentencing, if not for conviction itself. While such pleas for diminished responsibility may doubtless be abused, there seem to be clear cases in which they are appropriate.

A further kind of exculpating causation emerges in, for example, some murder trials. In the previous group of cases, the environmental influences were in the distant past, working on the criminal without her ever being aware of them. However, we sometimes consider the immediate "trigger" to action, of which the criminal is perfectly well aware, as a reason for leniency. Thus in most legal systems "crimes of passion" are distinguished from murder motivated by financial gain or other material goals. First degree murder is usually reserved for cold-blooded killing, and is less likely to be charged if the crime was committed in the heat of a rage. Murders committed out of anger, jealousy, frustration, rejection, humiliation, fear, feelings of inferiority and many other emotions are terrible crimes, and never to be condoned. However, it does seem appropriate that we regard them more leniently than callously planned murders done for profit only. A good example is the case of the Michigan woman, recently dramatized in the TV movie "The Burning Bed," who killed her husband after he had repeatedly beaten her for years. It is worth noting that the verdict of "not guilty by reason of insanity" is itself an example of legal and moral insanity. Given the woman's situation—her pleas to her husband, her courtroom battles to become separated, and his persistence in ignoring court orders, returning to live with her, and resuming his assaults on her—her decision to kill him was not at all irrational (though of course hardly commendable). It is precisely because her action was, to her mind, the only reasonable solution to a terrible situation, that we understand and tend to forgive her. Our leniency is based on the belief that her husband's cruel provocation *caused* her to kill him. So exculpating causation can operate *via* the malefactor's rationality, when she is reacting emotionally to events and situations of which she is perfectly well aware.[2]

Excuses based on the causation of our behavior are also common in everyday life. A good friend is unusually abrupt in greeting you one day, and treats you like a stranger. Your offense and resentment at her rudeness will be tempered if she later tells you that she was suffering from awful menstrual pains, or a splitting headache. And not only physical conditions provide excuses. You will be equally forgiving if you later discover that she had just been fired from her job, or learned that her mother had been diagnosed as having irreversible cancer. Causes of

2. Again, there is always the possibility that such excuses may be abused. In a recent case "pre-menstrual syndrome" (PMS) was admitted as a defense against murder charges. The attempt at such dubious excuses should not, however, blind us to clear cases where the excuse is valid.

behavior which stretch back into the past are also recognized in everyday life as excusing factors. During a classroom discussion of abortion, a student becomes uncharacteristically vehement and abusive in arguing against anti-abortionists. Your condemnation of her rudeness will diminish when you learn that as an 11-year-old, she was raped and had an abortion.

What is proven by all the examples so far discussed? It might well be insisted that these are all extreme cases in which causation does indeed diminish or negate responsibility, but that this is precisely because the cases are rare. Most of us, most of the time, are morally responsible for our actions. Most of us have indeed escaped the misfortunes described above: we were not sexually abused by our parents, we were not exposed to violent gangs in our youth, we suffer from no major chemical imbalance in our brains, we have never been exposed to provocation comparable to domestic violence, etc. However, we *are* all subject to causation.[3] We all had parents, who brought us up with varying degrees of loving care. We all suffered childhood traumas of varying severity, and were all exposed to role models of differing moral desirability among our peers and authority figures. We have all encountered occasional illnesses, anxieties, and provocations. These are the facts that threaten to send us uncontrollably down the "slippery slope" to moral exculpation for all actions. A "slippery slope" argument is analogous to the "domino theory" which often appears in political discussions. If a certain practice, which may in itself be unobjectionable, is allowed, it will inevitably lead to further practices which are definitely unacceptable. A familiar slippery slope argument is used in favor of a complete ban on mercy killing. While in many cases it may seem humane and desirable, it may be abused by greedy people eager to get rid of unwanted, elderly relatives. In the case under discussion, the slippery slope argument begins with the harmless-looking fact that we sometimes excuse people from responsibility. If causation negates responsibility in extreme cases, why does it not do so for our everyday actions, which are equally subject to causation?

The sciences of sociology and psychology are devoted to giving various kinds of causal explanation of our behavior. Provided that the causes involved are not the extreme ones already recognized as exculpating, it might be insisted, such explanations need not threaten our moral responsibility for everyday actions. We can, in other words, maintain a clear distinction between extreme cases where we are not to blame, and "business as usual," when we are responsible. Unfortunately, the everyday practice of modern psychiatry provides no basis for this distinction. Willard Gaylin describes two psychoanalytic principles that are almost universally accepted among psychiatrists, even those who reject Freudianism.

---

3. I am *not* here begging the question in favor of determinism. I am only making the modest claim, which even libertarians would surely accept, that at least some of our actions are subject to causation. This leaves open the possibility that we can transcend such causes by uncaused exercises of our will, of the kind described by the "agent causation" theory.

> The first axiom: Every individual act of behavior is the resultant of a multitude of emotional forces and counterforces; this is the "psychodynamic" principle. The second: These forces and counterforces are shaped by past experience; this is the principle of psychic causality.[4]

These principles require them to regard *all* actions, including those in which the standard excuses we have considered are absent, in the same, non-blaming light.

> The social view of behavior is essentially moralistic, an action is approved or disapproved, right or wrong, acceptable or non-acceptable. A person is guilty or innocent as more or less clearly defined in advance by law. But *psychiatrically speaking, nothing is wrong—only sick*. If an act is not a choice but merely the inevitable product of past experiences, a man can be no more guilty of a crime than he is guilty of an abscess.[5]

This attitude is not a mere quirk of the psychiatric profession: rather it seems essential to any scientific approach to human behavior. Any untoward behavior must be explained by the causal factors operating on the malefactor, whether they be physical brain events, provocations by other people, childhood experiences, or socio-economic background. Such explanations are the business of any of the social sciences. There are many minor transgressions—shoplifting, tax evasion, sexual unfaithfulness, parking offenses—for which we plainly expect people to take responsibility. However, a consistent application of the scientific view of human behavior would require us to search for the forces which led to these actions; and blame would have no place in this *scientific viewpoint*. In support of this viewpoint, new correlations are constantly being found between criminal behavior and both psychological and sociological background. In fact the same kind of correlation could be found between normal, healthy behavior and antecedent causal factors, though of course such correlations are of less interest to scientists, whose goal is to reduce deviant behavior. If the slippery slope argument is effective in ruling out moral blame for misdeeds, it should also exclude moral praise for our laudable actions. Both sides of the coin of responsibility are threatened by the scientific viewpoint.

Moreover, the slippery slope argument can also be formulated without reference to scientific practice. Even our everyday beliefs are susceptible to it. It has already been pointed out that in everyday life we forgive people for minor misdeeds when we discover their causes: illness, anxiety, emotional problems, etc. More generally, we tend to be more forgiving to a person's faults when we know her well. We "make allowances" for a person's character faults (within reason) and mitigate our blame: "Don't be too hard on her—she's just insecure/shy/impatient/hot headed, etc." On discovering that he was a murderer, how many parents would recommend that their son be executed? How many lovers would help to incriminate their loved ones? Very few, comes the obvious response, for the simple reason that these people are quite naturally biased. We need to consid-

4. Willard Gaylin, *The Killing of Bonnie Garland* (Penguin Books, 1983), p. 252.

5. Ibid., p. 253. (my emphasis)

er *why* they are biased. Isn't it likely that one of the reasons is that they know their son or lover intimately? They know just how their loved one was probably thinking, the stresses and provocations to which he was subject, at the time of the crime. The parent who vehemently calls for the execution of a mass murderer would most likely moderate her demands if she knew as much about the killer as she does about her own son [6] (even though this extra information is likely to make the murderer seem even more unpleasant). Parallel to the slippery slope argument which arose from our consideration of the social sciences, can we justify the difference in our attitude toward those whose character and history (i.e., causal influences) we know well, and those who are strangers? If the causation of people's actions drives out their responsibility, then shouldn't *all* misdeeds be forgiven? After all, a person's actions are none the less caused for the fact that, since we don't know her, we are unaware of the causes.

The "slippery slope" argument we have been drawn into may be summarized thus:

1. We are not responsible for actions caused in certain extreme "pathological" ways, e.g., chemical brain imbalances, extreme provocation.

2. No significant moral difference exists between so-called pathological, and so-called "normal" behavior, since they are equally subject to causation.

3. So we are never responsible for our actions.

The argument begins with uncontroversial cases, and shows how a consistent application of the scientific viewpoint, which is itself reflected in our everyday judgments, seems to require universal exculpation. What I consider to be the problem of free will is that this conclusion clashes with the widely held belief that we often *are* morally responsible for our actions (which I call the *moral viewpoint*). In other words, the problem is the apparent conflict between the *scientific* and *moral* viewpoints, both of which are deeply entrenched in our world view. Yet another formulation of the problem which captures my meaning is *the apparent conflict between causal explanations of human behavior and moral responsibility*. The advantage I claim for my slippery slope argument is that it brings out graphically the apparent conflict between these viewpoints. Moreover, it presents the free will problem as pressing, since the conflict is between beliefs which the ordinary person can easily be persuaded that she *already* holds.

6. On the other hand, a parent's intimate knowledge of her child's history and character does not lead her to mitigate her *praise* for the latter's good deeds. A parent would scarcely write off her son's achievements with the words, "Oh, it was nothing! Given his genetic make-up and home environment, he couldn't fail!" I will not attempt to justify this lack of symmetry, since my argument deals only with our attitudes towards *mis*deeds.

COMMENTS ■ QUESTIONS

1. The purpose of Dixon's paper is to present as strong an argument as possible in defense of hard determinism in order to show that the "free will problem" is truly pressing. The problem is pressing because almost no one (including Dixon himself) wants to give up the "moral viewpoint," which appears to conflict sharply with the "scientific viewpoint" that includes hard determinism. Do you agree with Dixon that the free will problem is pressing? If not, why not?
2. Dixon's presentation takes the form of a "slippery slope" argument. As its name suggests, this type of argument claims that once you get on the "slope" (in this case, admit we are not responsible in *some* cases) then you will slide all the way to the bottom (where you must admit that we are not responsible in *any* cases). Dixon's argument is intended as a challenge. Can a way be found to make the slope less slippery, that is, can a way be found to *show* a significant difference between instances when we are clearly *not* responsible and instances when we would like to believe that we *are* responsible? Do you believe that this challenge can be met? If so, what exactly are your grounds for rejecting the second premise of Dixon's argument?

JEAN-PAUL SARTRE

Existentialism and Freedom

What is meant by the term *existentialism?*

Most people who use the word would be rather embarrassed if they had to explain it, since, now that the word is all the rage, even the work of a musician or painter is being called existential-

A biographical sketch of Jean-Paul Sartre is to be found earlier in this chapter.

From *Existentialism* by Jean-Paul Sartre. Used by permission of Philosophical Library, Inc.

ist. . . . It seems that for want of an advance-guard doctrine analogous to surrealism, the kind of people who are eager for scandal and flurry turn to this philosophy which in other respects does not at all serve their purposes in this sphere.

Actually, it is the least scandalous, the most austere of doctrines. It is intended strictly for specialists and philosophers. Yet it can be defined easily. What complicates matters is that there are two kinds of existentialists; first, those who are Christian, among whom I include Jaspers and Gabriel Marcel, both Catholic; and on the other hand, the atheistic existentialists, among whom I class Heidegger, and then the French existentialists and myself. What they have in common is that they think that existence precedes essence, or, if you prefer, that subjectivity must be the starting point.

Just what does that mean? Let us consider some object that is manufactured, for example, a book or a paper-cutter: here is an object which has been made by an artisan whose inspiration came from a concept. He referred to the concept of what a paper-cutter is and likewise to a known method of production, which is part of the concept, something which is, by and large, a routine. Thus, the paper-cutter is at once an object produced in a certain way and, on the other hand, one having a specific use; and one cannot postulate a man who produces a paper-cutter but does not know what it is used for. Therefore, let us say that, for the paper-cutter, essence—that is, the ensemble of both the production routines and the properties which enable it to be both produced and defined—precedes existence. Thus, the presence of the paper-cutter or book in front of me is determined. Therefore, we have here a technical view of the world whereby it can be said that production precedes existence.

When we conceive God as the Creator, He is generally thought of as a superior sort of artisan. Whatever doctrine we may be considering, whether one like that of Descartes or that of Leibnitz, we always grant that will more or less follows understanding or, at the very least, accompanies it, and that when God creates He knows exactly what He is creating. Thus, the concept of man in the mind of God is comparable to the concept of paper-cutter in the mind of the manufacturer, and, following certain techniques and a conception, God produces man, just as the artisan, following a definition and a technique, makes a paper-cutter. Thus, the individual man is the realization of a certain concept in the divine intelligence.

In the eighteenth century, the atheism of the *philosophes* discarded the idea of God, but not so much for the notion that essence precedes existence. To a certain extent, this idea is found everywhere; we find it in Diderot, in Voltaire, and even in Kant. Man has a human nature; this human nature, which is the concept of the human, is found in all men, which means that each man is a particular example of a universal concept, man. In Kant, the result of this universality is that the wild-man, the natural man, as well as the bourgeois, are circumscribed by the same definition and have the same basic qualities. Thus, here too the essence of man precedes the historical existence that we find in nature.

Atheistic existentialism, which I represent, is more coherent. It states that if God does not exist, there is at least one being in whom existence precedes essence, a being who exists before he can be defined by any concept, and that this being is man, or, as Heidegger says, human reality. What is meant here by saying that existence precedes essence? It means that, first of all, man exists, turns up, appears on the scene, and, only afterwards, defines himself. If man, as the existentialist conceives him, is indefinable, it is because at first he is nothing. Only afterward will he be something, and he himself will have made what he will be. Thus, there is no human nature, since there is no God to conceive it. Not only is man what he conceives himself to be, but he is also only what he wills himself to be after this thrust toward existence.

Man is nothing else but what he makes of himself. Such is the first principle of existentialism. It is also what is called subjectivity, the name we are labeled with when charges are brought against us. But what do we mean by this, if not that man has a greater dignity than a stone or table? For we mean that man first exists, that is, that man first of all is the being in the future. Man is at the start a plan which is aware of itself, rather than a patch of moss, a piece of garbage, or a cauliflower; nothing exists prior to this plan; there is nothing in heaven; man will be what he will have planned to be. Not what he will want to be. Because by the word "will" we generally mean a conscious decision, which is subsequent to what we have already made of ourselves. I may want to belong to a political party, write a book, get married; but all that is only a manifestation of an earlier, more spontaneous choice that is called "will." But if existence really does precede essence, man is responsible for what he is. Thus, existentialism's first move is to make every man aware of what he is and to make the full responsibility of his existence rest on him. And when we say that a man is responsible for himself, we do not only mean that he is responsible for his own individuality, but that he is responsible for all men.

The word subjectivism has two meanings, and our opponents play on the two. Subjectivism means, on the one hand, that an individual chooses and makes himself; and, on the other, that it is impossible for man to transcend human subjectivity. The second of these is the essential meaning of existentialism. When we say that man chooses his own self, we mean that every one of us does likewise; but we also mean by that that in making this choice he also chooses all men. In fact, in creating the man that we want to be, there is not a single one of our acts which does not at the same time create an image of man as we think he ought to be. To choose to be this or that is to affirm at the same time the value of what we choose, because we can never choose evil. We always choose the good, and nothing can be good for us without being good for all.

If, on the other hand, existence precedes essence, and if we grant that we exist and fashion our image at one and the same time, the image is valid for everybody and for our whole age. Thus, our responsibility is much greater than we might have supposed, because it involves all mankind. If I am a workingman and choose to join a Christian trade-union rather than be a communist, and if by being a member I want to show that the best thing for man is resignation, that the kingdom of man is not of this world, I am not only involving my own case—I want to be resigned for everyone. As a result, my action has involved all humanity. To take a more individual matter, if I want to marry, to have children; even if this marriage depends solely on my own circumstances or passion or wish, I am involving all humanity in monogamy and not merely myself. Therefore, I am responsible for myself and for everyone else. I am creating a certain image of man of my own choosing. In choosing myself, I choose man.

This helps us understand what the actual content is of such rather grandiloquent words as anguish, forlornness, despair. As you will see, it's all quite simple.

First, what is meant by anguish? The existentialists say at once that man is anguish. What that means is this: the man who involves himself and who realizes that he is not only the person he chooses to be, but also a law-maker who is, at the same time, choosing all mankind as well as himself, cannot help escape the feeling of his total and deep responsibility. Of course, there are many people who are not anxious; but we claim that they are hiding their anxiety, that they are fleeing from it. Certainly, many people believe that when they do something, they themselves are the only ones involved, and when someone says to them, "What if everyone acted that way?" they shrug their shoulders and answer, "Everyone doesn't act that way." But really, one should always ask himself, "What would happen if everybody looked at things that way?" There is no escaping this disturbing thought except by a kind of double-dealing. A man who lies and makes excuses for himself by saying "not everybody does that," is someone with an uneasy conscience, because the act of lying implies that a universal value is conferred upon the lie.

Anguish is evident even when it conceals itself. This is the anguish that Kierkegaard called the anguish of Abraham. You know the story: an angel has ordered Abraham to sacrifice his son; if it really were an angel who has come and said, "You are Abraham, you shall sacrifice your son," everything would be all right. But everyone might first wonder, "Is it really an angel, and am I really Abraham? What proof do I have?" . . .

Now, I'm not being singled out as an Abraham, and yet at every moment I'm obliged to perform exemplary acts. For every man, everything happens as if all mankind had its eyes fixed on him and were guiding itself by what he does. And every man ought to say to himself, "Am I really the kind of man who has the right to act in such a way that humanity might guide itself by my actions?" And if he does not say that to himself, he is masking his anguish.

There is no question here of the kind of anguish which would lead to quietism, to inaction. It is a matter of a simple sort of anguish that anybody who has had responsibilities is familiar with. For example, when a military officer takes the responsibility for an attack and sends a certain number of men to death, he chooses to do so, and in the main he alone makes the choice. Doubtless, orders come from above, but they are too broad; he interprets them, and on this interpretation depend the lives of ten or fourteen or twenty men. In making a decision he cannot help having a certain anguish. All leaders know this anguish. That doesn't keep them from acting; on the contrary, it is the very condition of their action. For it implies that they envisage a number of possibilities, and when they choose one, they realize that it has value only because it is chosen. We shall see that this kind of anguish, which is the kind that existentialism describes, is explained, in addition, by a direct responsibility to the other men whom it involves. It is not a curtain separating us from action, but is part of action itself.

When we speak of forlornness, a term Heidegger was fond of, we mean only that God does not exist and that we have to face all the consequences of this. The existentialist is strongly opposed to a certain kind of secular ethics which would like to abolish God with the least possible expense. About 1880, some French teachers tried to set up a secular ethics which went something like this: God is a useless and costly hypothesis; we are discarding it; but meanwhile, in order for there to be an ethics, a society, a civilization, it is essential that certain values be taken seriously and that they be considered as having an *a priori* existence. It must be obligatory, *a priori*, to be honest, not to lie, not to beat your wife, to have children, etc., etc. So we're going to try a little device which will make it possible to show that values exist all the same, inscribed in a heaven of ideas, though otherwise God does not exist. In other words—and this, I believe, is the tendency of everything called reformism in France—nothing will be changed if God does not exist. We shall find ourselves with the same norms of honesty, progress, and humanism, and we shall have made of God an outdated hypothesis which will peacefully die off by itself.

The existentialist, on the contrary, thinks it very distressing that God does not exist, because all possibility of finding values in a heaven of ideas disappears along with Him; there can be no longer an *a priori* Good, since there is no infinite and perfect consciousness to think it. Nowhere is it written that the Good exists, that we must be honest, that we must not lie; because the fact is we are on a plane where there are only men. Dostoievsky said, "If God didn't exist, everything would be possible." That is the very starting point of existentialism. Indeed, everything is permissible if God does not exist, and as a result man is forlorn, because neither within him nor without does he find anything to cling to. He can't start making excuses for himself.

If existence really does precede essence, there is no explaining things away by reference to a fixed and given human nature. In other words, there is no determinism, man is free, man is freedom. On the other hand, if God does not exist, we find no values or commands to turn to which legitimize our conduct. So, in the bright realm of values, we have no excuse behind us, no justification before us. We are alone, with no excuses.

That is the idea I shall try to convey when I say that man is condemned to be free. Condemned, because he did not create himself, yet, in other respects is free; because, once thrown into the world, he is responsible for everything he does. The existentialist does not believe in the power of passion. He will never agree that a sweeping passion is a ravaging torrent which fatally leads a man to certain acts and is therefore an excuse. He thinks that man is responsible for his passion.

The existentialist does not think that man is going to help himself by finding in the world some omen by which to orient himself. Because he thinks that man will interpret the omen to suit himself. Therefore, he thinks that man, with no support and no aid, is condemned every moment to invent man. Ponge, in a very fine article, has said, "Man is the future of man." That's exactly it. But if it is taken to mean that this future is recorded in heaven, that God sees it, then it is false, because it would really no longer be a future. If it is taken to mean that, whatever a man may be, there is a future to be forged, a virgin future before him, then this remark is sound. But then we are forlorn.

To give you an example which will enable you to understand forlornness better, I shall cite the case of one of my students who came to see me under the following circumstances: his father was on bad terms with his mother, and, moreover, was inclined to be a collaborationist; his older brother had been killed in the German offensive of 1940, and the young man, with somewhat immature but generous feelings, wanted to avenge him. His mother lived alone with him, very much upset by the half-treason of her husband and the death of her older son; the boy was her only consolation.

The boy was faced with the choice of leaving for England and joining the Free French Forces—that is, leaving his mother behind—or remaining with his mother and helping her carry on. He was fully aware that the woman lived only for him and that his going-off—and perhaps his death—would plunge her into despair. He was also aware that every act that he did for his mother's sake was a sure thing, in the sense that it was helping her to carry on, whereas every effort he made toward going off and fighting was an uncertain move which might run aground and prove completely useless; for example, on his way to England he might, while passing through Spain, be detained indefinitely in a Spanish camp; he might reach England or Algiers and be stuck in an office at a desk job. As a result, he was faced with two very different kinds of action: one, concrete, immediate, but concerning only one individual; the other concerned an incomparably vaster group, a national collectivity, but for that very reason was dubious, and might be interrupted en route. And, at the same time, he was wavering between two kinds of ethics. On the one hand, an ethics of sympathy, of personal devotion; on the other, a broader ethics, but one whose efficacy was more dubious. He had to choose between the two.

Who could help him choose? Christian doctrine? No. Christian doctrine says, "Be charitable, love your neighbor, take the more rugged path, etc., etc." But which is the more rugged path? Whom should he love as a brother? The fighting man or his mother? Which does the greater good, the vague act of fighting in a group, or the concrete one of helping a particular human being to go on living? Who can decide *a priori*? Nobody. No book of ethics can tell him. The Kantian ethics says, "Never treat any person as a means, but as an end." Very well, if I stay with my mother, I'll treat her as an end and not as a means; but by virtue of this very fact, I'm running the risk of treating the people around me who are fighting, as means; and, conversely, if I go to join those who are fighting, I'll be treating them as an end, and, by doing that, I run the risk of treating my mother as a means.

If values are vague, and if they are always too broad for the concrete and specific case that we are considering, the only thing left for us is to trust our instincts. That's what this young man tried to do; and when I saw him, he said, "In the end, feeling is what counts. I ought to choose whichever pushes me in one direction. If I feel that I love my mother enough to sacrifice everything else for her—my desire for vengeance, for action, for adventure—then I'll stay with her. If, on the contrary, I feel that my love for my mother isn't enough, I'll leave.

But how is the value of a feeling determined. What gives his feeling for his mother value? Precisely the fact that he remained with her. I may say that I like so-and-so well enough to sacrifice a certain amount of money for him, but I may say so only if I've done it. I may say, "I love my mother well enough to remain with her" if I have remained with her. The only way to determine the value of this affection is, precisely, to perform an act which confirms and defines it. But, since I require this affection to justify my act, I find myself caught in a vicious circle. . . .

As for despair, the term has a very simple meaning. It means that we shall confine ourselves to reckoning only with what depends upon our will, or on the ensemble of probabilities which make our action possible. When we want something, we always have to reckon with probabilities. I may be counting on the arrival of a friend. The friend is coming by rail or street-car; this supposes that the train will arrive on schedule, or that the street-car will not jump the track. I am left in the realm of possibility; but possibilities are to be reckoned with only to the point where my action comports with the ensemble of these possibilities, and no further. The moment the possibilities I am considering are not rigorously involved by my action, I ought to disengage myself from them, because no God, no scheme, can adapt the world and its possibilities to my will. When Descartes said, "Conquer yourself rather than the world," he meant essentially the same thing.

The Marxists to whom I have spoken reply, "You can rely on the support of others in your action, which obviously has certain limits because you're not going to live forever. That means: rely on both what others are doing elsewhere to help you, in China, in Russia, and what they will do later on, after your death, to carry on the action and lead it to its fulfillment, which will be the revolution. You even *have* to rely upon that, otherwise you're immoral." I reply at once that I will always rely on fellow fighters insofar as these comrades are involved with me in a common struggle, in the unity of a party or a group in which I can more or less make my weight felt; that is, one whose ranks I am in as a fighter and whose movements I am aware of at every moment. In such a situation, relying on the unity and will of the party is exactly like counting on the fact that the train will arrive on time or that the car won't jump the track. But, given that man is free and that there is no human nature for me to depend on, I cannot count on men whom I do not know by relying on human goodness or man's concern for the good of society. I don't know what will become of the Russian revolution; I may make an example of it to the extent that at the present time it is apparent that the proletariat plays a part in Russia that it plays in no other nation. But I can't swear that this will inevitably lead to a triumph of the proletariat. I've got to limit myself to what I see.

Given that men are free, and that tomorrow they will freely decide what man will be, I cannot be sure that, after my death, fellow fighters will carry on my work to bring it to its maximum perfection. Tomorrow, after my death, some men may decide to set up Fascism, and the others may be cowardly and muddled enough to let them do it. Fascism will then be the human reality, so much the worse for us.

Actually, things will be as man will have decided they are to be. Does that mean that I should abandon myself to quietism? No. First, I should involve myself; then, act on the old saw, "Nothing ventured, nothing gained." Nor does it mean that I shouldn't belong to a party, but rather that I shall have no illusions and shall do what I can. For example, suppose I ask myself, "Will socialization, as such, ever come about?" I know nothing about it. All I know is that I'm going to do everything in my power to bring it about. Beyond that, I can't count on anything. Quietism is the attitude of people who say, "Let others do what I can't do." The doctrine I am presenting is the very opposite of quietism, since it declares, "There is no reality except in action." Moreover, it goes further, since it adds, "Man is nothing else than his plan; he exists only to the extent that he fulfills himself; he is, therefore, nothing else than the ensemble of his acts, nothing else than his life."

COMMENTS ■ QUESTIONS

1. Is Sartre's doctrine that "existence precedes essence" clear? Does it make sense to say of a human being that "at first he is nothing" and "only afterward will he be something"? Does Sartre's example of an object—a paper cutter—in which existence is said to come *after* essence make sense?
2. In saying "we always choose the good," Sartre means that in choosing *we determine* for ourselves and for others what the good will be. In a certain sense, according to Sartre, we create the good. This is part of what he means by the doctrine of "subjectivity." What arguments, if any, might be made against Sartre's position? (You may find that the discussion of "absolute values" in chapter 8 is relevant to answering this question.) Sartre states that his position is atheistic. Would you say that what he says about the good is *necessarily* atheistic? (See chapter 3 for a discussion of atheism.)
3. Is Sartre's version of libertarianism defensible? Through his doctrine of subjectivity and through his principle that existence precedes essence, has Sartre shown that human beings are free in the radical way that he says they are free?
4. For Sartre, something about freedom is undesirable. Does it make sense to say, as Sartre does, that human beings are "condemned to be free"?
5. Does Sartre give the correct account of the role that advice giving plays in decision making? (According to Sartre, we never make a decision solely on the basis of advice because we freely choose to seek and accept the advice in the first place.)
6. For Sartre, the existence of freedom in a strong sense entails that each of us has a high degree of responsibility in making choices. In choosing for ourselves, we are choosing for others. Is Sartre correct in assigning to human beings such a high degree of responsibility for their choices? How would you compare Sartre's view with the point of view that says, "to know all, is to forgive all"?

KAI NIELSEN

The Compatibility of Freedom and Determinism

I

I have argued that we do not know whether determinism is true or false, although we do have good grounds for believing that determinism is not an unfalsifiable, unprovable dogma. I have also argued that it is not equivalent to and does not even commit one to a belief in either fatalism or predestination. They are highly implausible notions, while the thesis of determinism, as I have characterized it, is a plausible commonsensical belief for which there is some reasonable evidence. I added "as I have characterized it," for there are mechanistic types of physical determinism that attempt to characterize human actions in terms of purely nonsymbolic, physical movements that will not, I believe, stand up to rational scrutiny. I have not tried to identify a human action as a species of physical event; instead, I have been content to state determinism as the claim that both events and actions always have sufficient conditions for their occurrence.

I shall not try here to give a fuller characterization of determinism or try further to show how we might establish or disestablish it. However, I would not like to lull you into complacency about this. My argument about the testability of determinism is controversial; many questions concerning the logical status of determinism remain. In some respects we have only scratched the surface, but I do hope that I have done enough to shake up the common view that determinism is an "unprovable dogma", "a metaphysical article of faith". And I hope I have done something to free determinism from some of its implausible metaphysical plumage and to make evident how deeply ingrained it is in reflective common sense.

What I now wish to consider is what I take to be the most significant question we can ask about de-

---

Kai Nielsen is Professor of Philosophy at the University of Calgary. He is past president of the Canadian Philosophical Association and is editor of the Canadian Journal of Philosophy. *He has written* Reason and Practice, Contemporary Critiques of Religion, Ethics Without God, Skepticism, An Introduction to the Philosophy of Religion, Equality and Liberty, Philosophy and Atheism, *and he will publish a new book in 1987 called* The Just Society *with Routledge & Kegan Paul.*

"The Compatibility of Freedom and Determinism" from *Reason and Practice* by Kai Nielsen. Copyright (c) 1971 by Kai Nielsen. Reprinted by permission of Harper & Row, Publishers.

terminism and human conduct: Is determinism compatible with our central beliefs concerning the freedom of conduct and moral responsibility? It was because they thought that such beliefs were plainly incompatible that Dostoevsky and James were so nagged by determinism. With such philosophers as Thomas Hobbes, David Hume, John Stuart Mill, Moritz Schlick, and A. J. Ayer—all staunch defenders of the compatibility thesis—there is a vast shift not only in argument but also in attitude. There is no *Angst* over the ubiquitousness of causal laws. There is no feeling that life would be meaningless and man would be a prisoner of his past if determinism were true. Holbach is wrong. Even if determinism is true, freedom is not an illusion. The belief that it is an illusion is a philosophical confusion resting on a failure to pay sufficiently close attention either to the actual role of our concept of freedom in our lives or to the actual nature of determinism. It is such a twin failure that generates the conflicts we have been investigating.

The crucial point to note initially is that Mill and Schlick, as much as Holbach and Darrow, are thoroughgoing determinists. But they are determinists who do not believe that freedom and determinism are incompatible. James dismissed this position contemptuously with the label "soft determinism". For him "soft determinism" had an emotive force similar to "soft on Communism". But while a summer bachelor is no bachelor at all, a soft determinist is just as much a determinist as a hard determinist. I shall continue to use the label "soft determinism"—although I shall not use it in any derogatory sense—to refer to the view that maintains that determinism and human freedom are logically compatible. (Sometimes in the literature they are called "compatibilists".) A view such as Holbach's or Darrow's, which Schlick says rests on "a whole series of confusions," I shall call "hard determinism". (Sometimes in the literature "hard determinists" are called "incompatibilists", for they believe freedom and determinism are incompatible.) But both hard and soft determinists agree that every event or state, including every human action or attitude, has a cause; that is, for anything whatsoever there are sufficient conditions for its occurrence.

The at least *prima facie* surprising thing is that these soft-determinists still believe in the freedom of conduct and believe that human beings are—at least sometimes, anyway—responsible moral agents capable of acting in specific situations in ways other than those in which they in fact acted. Let us see how the soft determinist argument unfolds.

II

Morality, soft determinists argue, has or should have no interest in the determinism/indeterminism controversy. Morality is indeed vitally interested in the freedom of conduct, for it only makes sense to say that men ought to do one thing rather than another on the assumption that sometimes they can do other than what they in fact do. If no man can do other than what he does in fact do, then all talk of what men ought to do or what is right and wrong is indeed senseless.[1] But to be interested in the freedom of conduct, as morality properly is, is not at all to be interested in some mysterious and no doubt illusory "freedom of the will". "Freedom" has its opposite, "compulsion" or "coercion". A man is free if he does not act under compulsion. He is free when he is able to do what he wants to do or when his acts and actions are in accordance with his own choices and decisions, and when what he wants to do or what he chooses is not determined by some person, force, or some disposition, such as kleptomania, which has gained ascendency over him. He is, by contrast, unfree to the extent that he is unable to achieve what he wants to achieve and to act in accordance with choices based on his own rational deliberation because of either outside influence or psychological malaise. "Freedom" does not mean some scarcely intelligible state of affairs, "exemption or partial exemption from causal law" or "breach of causal continuity". To be free is to have the ability and opportunity to do what one wants to do and to act in accordance with one's own rational deliberations, without constraint and compulsion. It is something which, of course, admits of degrees.

Mill, Schlick, and Ayer argue that an anthropomorphic view of our language tricks us into thinking that man cannot be free if determinism is true. People tend to think that if determinism is true, events are in the power of other events and a person's acts or actions cannot alter the course of events. What will happen in the future is already fixed by immutable causal laws. But such views rest on unrealistic, anthropomorphic thinking. They are scarcely a part of a tough-minded deterministic world perspective.

Similar anthropomorphic transformations are made with "necessity" and the little word "cause". And this, too, leads to needless befuddlement by causing us to misunderstand the actual workings of our language. It is, for example, terribly easy for the unwary to confuse causal and logical necessitation. But there is a very considerable difference in the meaning of "must" in "If you cut off his head, he must die" and "If it is a square, it must have four sides". In the latter case—an example of logical necessitation—"having four sides" follows by virtue of the meaning of the term "square". The "must" refers to this logical relationship. In the former case, it holds in virtue of something in the world. People also infer mistakenly that the event or effect is somehow contained in the cause. But this mystification is hardly intelligible.

There is also, as Schlick points out, a persistent confusion between laws of nature and legal laws.[2] The word "law" has very different meanings in such cases. Legal laws *prescribe* a certain course of action. Many of them are intended to constrain or coerce you into acting in a certain way. But laws of nature are not prescriptions to act in a certain

1. The point I make here is somewhat more controversial than my exposition would give one to understand. See here W. K. Frankena, "Obligation and Ability," in Max Black (ed.), *Philosophical Analysis* (Ithaca, N.Y.: 1950).

2. Moritz Schlick, *Problems of Ethics* (New York: 1939), pp. 146–148.

way. They do not constrain you; rather, they are statements of regularities, of *de facto* invariable sequences that are parts of the world. In talking of such natural laws we often bring in an uncritical use of "force", as if the earth were being pushed and pulled around by the sun. Putting the matter this way makes one feel as if one is always being compelled or constrained, when in reality one is not. Without the anthropomorphic embellishment, it becomes evident that a determinist commits himself, when he asserts that *A* causes *B*, to the view that *whenever* an event or act of type *A* occurs, an event or act of type *B* will occur. The part about compulsion or constraint is metaphorical. It is because of the metaphor, and not because of the fact, that we come to think that there is an antithesis between causality and freedom. It is the *manner* here and not the *matter* that causes the trouble.

Demythologized and correctly conceived, causal necessity as applied to human actions is, Mill argues, simply this: Given the motives that are present to an individual's mind, and given the character and disposition of the individual, the manner in which he will act can be "unerringly inferred." That is to say, if we knew the person thoroughly, and knew all the inducements acting upon him, we could predict or retrodict his conduct with as much certainty as we can predict any physical event. This, Mill argues, is a bit of common sense and is in reality not in conflict with our operative concept of human freedom, for even if we say that all human acts are in principle predictable, this is not to say that people are acting under compulsion or constraint, for to say that their actions are predictable is not to say or even to give one to understand that they are being manipulated by anything or anybody. Being under some sort of compulsion or constraint is what limits our freedom.

III

The natural reaction to such a belief is this: If "causal necessity" means anything, it means that no human being could, *categorically* could, do anything other in exactly similar circumstances than what he in fact does. If determinism is true, we must believe that for every event and for every action there are sufficient conditions, and when these conditions obtain, the action must occur. Since this is so, aren't all our actions in reality under constraint and thus, after all, not really free?

Soft determinists try to show that such an objection is a snarl of conceptual confusions, and that once we untangle them we will not take this incompatibilist line. A. J. Ayer makes one of the clearest and most forceful defenses of this view. His argument will be followed here, with a few supplementations from Mill.[3]

The conceptual facts we need to clarify are these: If the word "freedom" is to have a meaning, it must be contrasted with something, for otherwise it is quite unintelligible. If I tell you I have just bought a wok, but I cannot contrast a wok with any *conceivable* thing that I would *deny* is a wok or not assert is a wok, then I have not been able to convey to you

---

3. See A. J. Ayer, "Freedom and Necessity," in his *Philosophical Essays* (New York: 1963).

the meaning of "wok". In fact, if it is not so contrastable, it is indeed meaningless. The same thing obtains for any descriptive term. Thus, "freedom", if it is to be intelligible, must be contrastable with something. There must at least be some *conceivable* situations in which it is correct to use the word and some *conceivable* situations in which it would not be correct. Yet it is plainly not an unintelligible sound, but a word with a use in our discourse. So we must look for its nonvacuous contrast. It is here where the soft determinists' initial point is critical. "Freedom" is to be contrasted with "constraint" or "compulsion" rather than with "determinism", for if we try to contrast it with "determinism", it is far from clear that we get an intelligible contrast. It is not clear what sort of an action we would count as a "causeless action". But if we contrast "freedom" and "constraint", the contrast is clear. So we should say that a man's action is not free when it is constrained or when he is compelled to do what he does.

Suppose I say, "There is to be no smoking in the classroom." By this act I put the people in the room under constraint. I limit their freedom. But suppose Fearless Fosdick lights up anyway and I say, "Put it out, Mister, if you want to stay in the class." I in effect compel him, or at least attempt to compel him, to put it out. Being compelled or constrained to do something may very well entail that the act has a cause. But plainly the *converse* does not hold. As Ayer puts it, "From the fact that my action is causally determined it does not necessarily follow that I am constrained to do it." This is an important point to make, for to say this is in effect to claim that it does not necessarily follow from the fact that my actions are determined that I am not free. But, as I have said, if instead we take "freedom" and "being causally determined" as our contrastible terms, we get no clear contrast. On the other hand, even in a deterministic world we have with our above distinction between "freedom" and "compulsion" or "constraint" preserved the needed contrast.

In setting out this contrast between when a man is or is not free, it is important to ask in what circumstances I can legitimately be said to be constrained and so *not* to be free.

1. *When I am compelled by another person to do what he wants.* Such a compulsion need not altogether deprive me of my power of choice. The man who compels me in a certain way need not hypnotize me or make it physically impossible for me to go against his will. It is sufficient that he should induce me to do what he wants by making it plain to me that if I do not, he will bring about some situation that I regard as having even more undesirable consequences than the consequences of acting as he desires. In such a circumstance I am acting under constraint and involuntarily, although it is not true that my freedom to act here is utterly circumscribed.

2. *Where a man has attained a habitual ascendency over me.* Indeed, in such a circumstance I can come to want to do what Big Brother wishes. Nevertheless, I still do not act freely because I am in reality deprived of the power of choice. And in this context this means I have acquired so strong a habit of obedience that I no longer go through the process of

deciding whether or not to do what the other person wants. About other matters I may still deliberate, but as regards the fulfillment of this other person's desires, my own deliberations have ceased to be an effective causal factor in my behavior. For this reason I may properly be said to be constrained since I have lost my power of choice in these matters.

3. *In order for me to be unfree in certain respects, it need not be a man or group of men that have gained ascendency over me.* A kleptomaniac cannot correctly be said to be a free agent, in respect to his stealing, because even if he does go through what appears to be deliberations about whether to steal or not to steal, such deliberations are irrelevant to his actual behavior in the respect of whether he will or will not steal. Whatever he resolved to do, he would steal all the same.[4]

This case is important because it clearly shows the difference between the man—the kleptomaniac—who is not free with respect to his stealing and an ordinary thief who is. The ordinary thief goes through a process of deciding whether or not to steal, and his decision decisively effects his behavior. If he actually resolved to refrain from stealing, he could carry out his resolution. But this is not so with the kleptomaniac. Thus, this observable difference between the ordinary thief and the kleptomaniac, quite independently of the issue of determinism, enables us to ascertain that the former is freer than the latter.

Note that in both cases, if determinism is true, then what either individual decides to do is causally determined. When we reflect on this, we are inclined to say that although it may be true that, unlike the kleptomaniac, the ordinary thief could refrain from stealing *if he chose*, yet since there is a cause, or set of causes, which causally necessitates his choosing as he does, how can he properly be said to have the power of choice? He indeed may not *feel* compelled the way the kleptomaniac does, but neither in some circumstances does the person over whom someone else has gained an ascendency. But the chains of causation by which the thief is bound are no less effective or coercive for being invisible.

Cases are being run together in this last remark that ought not to be run together. If we keep them distinct, in each instance we have a clearer contrast between actions that are free and actions that are not free. There remains a crucial difference between the thief and the kleptomaniac, namely that *the thief can choose not to steal and his choice can be effective*. The kleptomaniac cannot do that. Again, even in a deterministic world, there is a difference between the neophyte over whom someone has gained ascendency and someone who is not afflicted with kleptomania. For the latter there is no one whose very word is law, that is, who compels action. The thief, but not the kleptomaniac, feels no overwhelming compulsion to steal; and

4. Some criminologists and psychologists have doubts about the viability of the very concept of kleptomania. And given the complexity of the phenomena referred to when we speak of "kleptomania", it might be alleged that we should probe deeper and use quite different arguments. This may very well be so. I have been content here to expound Ayer on this point and show that it is not unreasonable to give a soft-determinist account given such psychological phenomena.

the person who must do what Big Brother dictates will feel an irresistible compulsion to do what he dictates as soon as it goes against something he would *otherwise* very much want to do, or if his rationale for doing it is effectively challenged by someone else.

A simpler case will make even clearer how it is that the notions of compulsion and constraint give the necessary contrast with our concept of freedom and not the concept of determinism or causal necessitation. There is indeed a difference between the man who suffers from a compulsion neurosis to wash his hands and the man who gets up and washes his hands because they are in fact dirty. Both actions have causes, but not all causes are constraining or compelling causes—they are not like a compulsion to wash our hands—and it is only the latter sort of causes that makes men unfree.

IV

Yet, in spite of these evident contrasts, we are still haunted, when we are in the grip of a philosophical perplexity about freedom and determinism, by the question, or muddle felt as a question: Do not all causes equally necessitate? Is it not arbitrary "to say that a person is free when he is necessitated in one fashion but not when he is necessitated in another"?

Soft determinists reply that if "necessitate" merely means "cause", then of course "All causes equally necessitate" is equivalent to "All causes equally cause"—and that is hardly news. But "All causes equally constrain or compel" is not true. If one event is the cause of another, we are stating that the event said to be the effect would not have occurred if it had not been for the occurrence of the event said to be the cause. But this states nothing about compulsion or constraint. There is indeed an invariable concomitance between the two classes of events; but there is no compulsion in any but a metaphorical sense. Such invariable concomitance gives a necessary but not sufficient condition for causation. It is difficult and perhaps even impossible to say what constitutes a sufficient condition. But given the frequent situations in which we speak of one thing causing another without asserting or implying a compulsion or constraint, they plainly are not further necessary conditions. (When I watch a wren in the park my behavior has causes sufficient for its occurrence, but I was neither compelled, constrained, nor forced to watch the wren.) Whatever more we need beyond invariable concomitance for causation, compulsion isn't one of the elements.

Even in a deterministic world we can do other than what we in fact do, since all "cans" are constitutionally iffy.[5] That is to say, they are all hypothetical. This dark saying needs explanation. Consider what we actually mean by saying, "I could have done otherwise." It means, soft determinists argue, "I should have acted otherwise if I had chosen" or "I would have done otherwise if I had wanted to". And "I can do *X*" means "If I want to I shall do *X*" or

5. The phrase is J. L. Austin's, but he denies that all 'cans' are constitutionally iffy. See J. L. Austin, *Philosophical Papers* (Oxford: 1961), chapter 7.

"If I choose to do X I will do X".

In general, soft determinists argue, we say a man is free rather than unfree when the following conditions hold:

1. He could have done otherwise if he had chosen to.
2. His actions are voluntary in the sense that the kleptomaniac's stealing is not.
3. Nobody compelled him to choose as he did.

Now it should be noted that these conditions are frequently fulfilled or satisfied. Thus, "freedom" has a definite contrast and application. Basically it contrasts with constraint. Since this is so, we can say when it is true or probably true to assert that a man is free, and when it is false or probably false to say that he is free. Given the truth of this, it is evident that a man can act as a free and responsible moral agent even though his actions are determined. If we are not talking about some obscure notion of "free will" but about what Schlick calls the "freedom of conduct", freedom is after all compatible with determinism.

V

Hard determinists characteristically respond to such arguments by claiming that such an analysis does not dig deep enough. It neglects the fact that while we are frequently able to do what we will or choose, or to do what we want or dislike doing least, in no instance in our lives are we able to will other than what we will, choose other than what we choose, want other than what we in fact want, or dislike other than what we in fact dislike. This is what Holbach was driving at when he claimed that freedom is an illusion. We indeed may sometimes have freedom of *action*, but we do not have what is really crucial, namely freedom of *will* or freedom of *choice*. A man's choices and strivings characteristically flow from his character, but, as Mill puts the argument against his own position, "his character is formed *for* him, and not by him; therefore his wishing that it had been formed differently is of no use; he has no power to alter it." [6]

Mill's response here is very instructive. Because in the ultimate resort a man's character is formed for him, it does not follow that it cannot *in part* be formed by him. We may in fact desire in one way or another to alter our personalities. We indeed may not be satisfied with our lives. And sometimes when we feel this way we are in a position to alter in some measure the course of our lives. These things are sometimes in our power. Furthermore, no one willed us to be anything in particular. That we have a certain sort of character is not the result, in most instances at any rate, of a deliberate design on anyone's part. Moreover, "we are exactly as capable of making our character, if we will, as others are of making it for us." Our personalities are alterable and in fact do change in many instances. Although we have no control over the *initial formation* of our character, we, within limits, can alter it if we want to do so.

To this the hard determinist still

---

6. J. S. Mill, *System of Logic*, book IV, chapter 2. The relevant sections are reprinted in Paul Edwards and Arthur Pap (eds.), *A Modern Introduction to Philosophy* (New York: 1965), second edition.

replies that the rub is "*If* we will or *if* we want to". To admit this, he contends, is in effect to surrender the whole point, "since the will to alter our own character is given us, not by any efforts of ours, but by circumstances which we cannot help. . . . "

Mill agrees this is "most true," and if the hard determinist sticks here we cannot dislodge him. But, Mill goes on to say, "to think that we have no power of altering our character, and to think that we shall not use our power unless we desire to use it, are very different things, and have a very different effect on the mind." A person who does not wish to alter his character cannot *feel the depressing effect* of the hard-determinist doctrine. Mill then goes on to make the crucial observation that "a person feels morally free who feels that his habits or his temptations are not his masters but he theirs. . . . " And such a man, according to Mill, is a free agent even though he is a determined part in a deterministic universe.

I believe the general drift of Mill's remarks here are a step in the right direction, but they are not without their difficulties. And these difficulties are sufficient to require a modification of Mill's views. A man can certainly very well *feel* free and still not *be* free, *feel* that he is the master of his actions when he is not. Certain neurotic and psychotic types feel that certain things are in their power when in reality they are not. But it is here that the conditions I set forth earlier, largely following Ayer, are crucial. If a man is not being compelled or constrained by another person or institution or cataclysmic occurrence (for example, an earthquake or something of that order) and if no person, force, or disposition (for example, kleptomania) has gained ascendency over him so that he cannot think and act rationally, then when he *feels* his habits or temptations are not his masters but he theirs, in those circumstances he is indeed a free moral agent. If he is a rational agent he is responsible for what it is in his power to do; and to the degree that it is in his power to do one thing rather than another, he is correctly said to be free.

COMMENTS ■ QUESTIONS

1. Nielsen begins by remarking that the doctrine of determinism is not the same as either fatalism or predestination. Because he does not say what these doctrines are in the present selection, a brief description of each may be helpful. A good way to understand fatalism is to think of it as being a combination of determinism and the doctrine that human actions make no difference in regard to what is going to happen. In other words, fatalism is the doctrine that all events have causes, but human actions do not function effectively as such causes. Predestination is the view that God has

decreed "from eternity" how some, or all, events in the universe will work out. A good way to understand predestination is to think of it as a combination of determinism plus the belief that the determination of some or all events is brought about by a divine guiding force. Keep in mind that an objection to either fatalism or predestination need not be an objection to either hard or soft determinism.

2. Nielsen defends soft determinism. His basic strategy is to state, and then examine, possible ways to define "being free" and "being not free" in order to arrive at a definition of freedom that is compatible with determinism. His preferred definition of "being free" consists of the following conditions:
   a. The person could have done otherwise if he or she had chosen to.
   b. The person's actions are voluntary in the sense that the kleptomaniac's stealing is not.
   c. Nobody compelled the person to choose as he or she did.

Do you believe that this is an adequate definition?

FRED ALAN WOLF

Determinism, Indeterminism, and Science

The Nightmare of Determinism

Picture a quaint French drawing room, circa 1800. White wigged, white stockinged, drawing room society is enjoying an evening of folderol. The butler, or whatever he is called in such circles, announces the arrival of a famous philosopher and scientist, the Marquis de Laplace. Conversations hush and become murmurs. The Marquis enters. People move aside quietly as if to welcome a king into their ranks. Perhaps more to the occasion, we should view the

Fred Alan Wolf is a widely read science writer who formerly was a professor of physics at San Diego State University. In addition to Taking the Quantum Leap, *he has written* Space-Time and Beyond *and numerous articles.*

From *Taking the Quantum Leap* by Fred Alan Wolf. Copyright (c) 1981 by Youniverse Seminars, Inc., Reprinted by permission of Harper & Row, Publishers.

Marquis as a famous actor-artist. Chairs are drawn into semi-circular rows. The presentation was about to begin.

Pierre Simon Laplace, known as the Marquis, became the darling of Paris' early nineteenth-century drawing room crowd. He was known for his dramatic and eloquent presentations of that mysterious and quite abstract science known as *celestial mechanics*. He held his audiences completely suspended as he told of the worlds beyond, all of them caught in that action-at-a-distance force, which Newton called gravity. No cosmic strings, yet powerful was the influence of this never-observed, yet totally present, cause of acceleration.

The universe and all its worlds followed well-defined laws according to the same guiding principles. Everything was, and is, predictable. Only find the force, know the masses, positions, and velocities of the objects under study at one single time, and all is predictable. It matters not what the objects are. Planets, stars, and rolling cobblestones—all fall victim to the force.

The universe is a gigantic Newtonian clockwork. Cause and effect rule. Nothing is by chance; everything is ultimately accountable. Read Laplace's words (translated, of course):

> We ought then to regard the present state of the universe as the effect of its previous state and as the cause of the one which is to follow. Given for one instant a mind which could comprehend all the forces by which nature is animated and the respective situation of the beings who compose it—a mind sufficiently vast to submit these data to analysis—it would embrace in the same formula the movements of the greatest bodies of the universe and those of the lightest atom; for it, nothing would be uncertain and the future, as the past, would be present to its eyes.[1]

Perfect determinism, from a heartbreak to an empire's rise and fall, was no more than the inevitable workings of the Great Machine. The laws of physics are to be obeyed, because it is impossible to disobey them. The dream of an ultimate understanding of nature was the discovery of the hidden force that was the cause of the yet-to-be. Once this force was found, there would be no room for free will, salvation, and damnation, or for love and hate. Even the most trifling thought had been determined in a far-gone age.

Ethics, morality, pride, and prejudice were jokes. You may imagine that you are a free-thinking person, but even that imagination is nothing but the universal clockwork turning in some yet-to-be-discovered way. Discovery of how the whole universe works was still to be achieved, but nevertheless, in principle, this materialist philosophy was the basis for the universe.

The idea that free will had vanished was called the "nightmare of determinism." Even thinkers and philosophers of this period who were not disturbed by the "nightmare" felt the impact of Newtonian thinking. Because physics was able to explain a remarkably large number of physical phenomena, from the movements of planets

---

1. F. Rutherford, G. Holton, and F. G. Watson, dirs., *The Project Physics Course* (New York: Holt, Rinehart & Winston, 1970), unit 2, chap. 8, p. 120.

to the kinetic motions of the tiny particles within an enclosed volume of gas, with only a few principles, it became the model of human knowledge.[2]

Nineteenth-century thinkers sought to emulate the precision, universality, and orderly procedure of physics. They sought general laws to explain history and human behavior. Karl Marx, for example, suggested that matter is the only subject of change and that all change is the product of constant conflict between the opposing forces inherent in all things. When one force overcomes the other, change is produced. Thus, for Marx, a revolutionary movement can never be a cooperative venture between the ruling and working classes, for the force of one class must eventually overcome the opposing force of the other class. This theory, known as *dialectical materialism*, sounds very much like Newton's second law, which states that force is the cause of change in motion and matter is what force acts upon.

Even Clarence Darrow, the famous lawyer who defended the theory of evolution in the Scopes "monkey trial" of 1925, was influenced by Newton. In another of his well-known cases, the notorious Leopold and Loeb murder trial, Darrow defended his clients by pointing out that they were victims of heredity and environmental forces. Although Leopold and Loeb were clearly guilty, Darrow defended the two murderers on the grounds that they had no choice in their actions, that there was a lengthy series of causes leading inevitably to the eventual death of their victim. Even the environment in which the two murderers grew up was presented as a product of that long chain. Therefore, how could society presume to punish these two for a situation over which they had no control? They were as much victims of their crime as the individual they killed. All were powerless to stop the Newtonian clockwork.

It is understandable that Laplace, Marx, and Darrow should be so influenced by Newtonian machinery.[3] Certainly it is easier to imagine that the whole is simply a sum of its parts and that understanding the part will inevitably lead to understanding the whole than to consider a world in any other way. What other way could there be? Why, even mind itself must ultimately prove to be nothing more than an extremely complex mechanical device. Since mind must come from matter, what else could it be? Indeed, mind must show itself as a direct outcome of its material base. So thought Sigmund Freud.

Freud associated certain dream images with primitive ideas, myths, and rites.[4] He claimed that these dream images are "archaic remnants"—psychic elements that have survived in the brain from ages long ago. The subconscious mind is a trash heap. No wonder we suffer guilt, for we suffer not only for ourselves, but also for our ancestors who may have raped, murdered, and pillaged thousands of years ago.

Hugh Elliot (1881–1930), editor

2. R. March, *Physics for Poets*, p. 95.

3. Ibid.

4. C. G. Jung, ed., *Man and His Symbols* (New York: Dell Publishing Co., 1968), p. 9.

of England's Annual Register during the time of transition from classical physics to quantum physics, was a champion of mechanistic science and materialism.[5] He posited three principles: (1) the laws of the universe are uniform, and while the universe may appear disorderly, careful scrutiny by science reveals that these universal laws are to be obeyed; (2) teleology is a myth, for there is no such thing as a purpose to the universe and all events are due to the interaction of matter in motion; and (3) all forms of existence must have some kind of palpable material characteristics and qualities. Elliot wrote:

> It seems to the ordinary observer that nothing can be more remotely and widely separated than some so-called "act of consciousness" and a material object. An act of consciousness or mental process is a thing of which we are immediately and indubitably aware: so much I admit. But that it differs in any sort of way from a material process, that is to say, from the ordinary transformations of matter and energy, is a belief which I very strenuously deny.[6]

I enjoy quoting Elliot, because few individuals have expressed such confidence in the totality of a material universe as well as he did. He went on to say that "there exists no kind of spiritual substance or entity of a different nature from that of which matter is composed. . . . there are not two kinds of fundamental existences, material and spiritual, but one kind only. . . . "[7]

And thus is the stage set. We are, all of us, machines.

By the end of the nineteenth century, classical physics had become not only the model for the physical universe, but the model for human behavior as well. The wave of mechanical materialism, which began as a small ripple in the stream of seventeenth-century thought, had grown to tidal wave proportions, sweeping all Greek thinking aside. Physicists investigated dead things and physicians sought clockworks in living people.

* * * * *

The new atomic model was definitely planetary. The surprising thing of the planetary model was how small the nucleus appeared. If the golf ball-sized atom was once again inflated, this time to the size of a modern sports arena or football stadium, the nucleus of that atom would be the size of a grain of rice. Somehow the electrons whirled about, filling in the vast space within the tiny atomic world.

These experiments were carried out by Lord Ernest Rutherford and his assistant Ernest Marsden.[8] Rutherford was also given his own laboratory in the industrial Midlands of Manchester, England. With the success of what is now called the *Rutherford nuclear atom*, Lord Rutherford led his group of scientists in an attempt to picture how the electron "planets" were able to maintain themselves in orbit and yet radiate energy in the form of light waves. Rutherford's success was, I'm sure, not too palatable for his counterpart, Lord Thomson, down south.

Into this slight animosity a young

5. J. R. Burr and M. Goldinger, eds., *Philosophy and Contemporary Issues* (New York: The MacMillan Co., 1972), p. 254.

6. Ibid., p. 255.

7. Ibid., p. 259.

8. R. March, *Physics for Poets* (New York: McGraw-Hill Book Co., 1970), p. 194.

innocent was about to step. His name was Niels Bohr.

Bohr's Quantum Atom

Dr. Bohr had just completed his doctoral thesis in Copenhagen, Denmark, when he reported to work for J. J. Thomson at the "Cavendish." Lord Thomson, Bohr's first employer, probably felt less than enthusiastic over meeting the twenty-six-year-old Bohr. Besides possessing an incredible mind, Bohr was quite forthright and outspoken. Thomson's model for an electron had been the subject of Bohr's thesis, and Bohr immediately pointed out some mathematical errors in Thomson's earlier work.

By the autumn of 1911, Bohr found himself, much to Thomson's urging, on his way to Manchester to join Rutherford's group. He quickly joined in with this newly excited group of physicists and began his own search for the electrons within atoms.

The simplest and lightest-known atom in the universe was hydrogen. It contained, according to Rutherford, a tiny nucleus and a single electron orbiting that nucleus. It was hoped that, if a successful model of this atom could be made, all other atoms would fall into line and be explained. So Bohr attempted to make a model of the hydrogen atom.

There was, however, a severe stumbling block in the way of the planetary picture of an atom. The problem was how could the electron keep a stable orbit? If the atom was as big as it appeared to be, its electron would necessarily be whirling around inside it with greatly accelerated changes in speed and direction, filling out the space like the tip of a whirling propeller blade fills out a circle. The electron would have to do this and *not* emit any energy. Certainly, it could not emit its energy continuously. To do so would be a disaster for the model. The reason for this is that the planetary model predicts a spiraling motion of the planet into the sun for any planet that gives up energy continuously. That would mean the electron would crash into its nucleus every time it emitted its light energy. The whole atom would be suddenly deflated and all matter would undergo a rapid collapse. It is amazing to consider how tiny atoms would be if the atomic electrons were gobbled up by their nuclei. A football stadium would be shrunk to a grain of rice. The earth would be shrunk to the size of a football stadium! All matter would thus appear with enormous density. (Neutron stars do appear in our universe with these densities. The force of gravity crushes the atoms together.) And all matter would be dead and lifeless. The light would be gone.

But if the electron could not emit energy continuously, how was it to radiate any light? Light emission took energy. The electron would have to radiate energy sometime or no light would ever be seen. The question was how to make up a planetary model in which the electron would only radiate energy sporadically or in a discontinuous manner. Thus Bohr attempted to visualize under what circumstances the electron would be "allowed" to radiate energy and under what circumstances it would be "forbidden" to do so. This was not an easy decision to make. Bohr's model would have to show a reason for the discontinuity. How could Bohr explain it?

He explained it very simply. He postulated that an atom would only be allowed the privilege of emitting light when an electron jumped discontinuously from one orbit to another. It would be forbidden from doing so otherwise. Like Planck and Einstein before him, Bohr was setting out on a bold path. In fact he was encouraged by their example. He felt that somehow Planck's *h* factor had to be involved in the process. He knew that *h* had been used by both Planck and Einstein to point to the discontinuous movement of light energy in solid matter. Perhaps it could also be used inside of an atom. But how? Bohr found out.

This new secret was actually no mystery to anyone familiar with physics. It had to do with something that physicists call *units*. A unit is a measure of a physical quantity. Any unit can also be composed of other units. Take the common example of a monetary unit. An American dollar is a unit of money, and it is composed of other units as well. For example, a dollar is ten units called dimes, or one hundred units called pennies. Similarly, it is also one-tenth of a unit called a ten dollar bill.

Planck's constant *h* also was a unit. And it too could be made up of other units. It was a unit of energy-time, something that physicists call *action*, and it was a unit of momentum-distance, just as a dollar is also ten dime units. But Bohr had noticed that *h* could be viewed as a unit of angular momentum and that observation had a direct bearing on his atomic model.

Angular momentum is a familiar experience for children. It results whenever a moving object passes a fixed point in space. If the moving object joins or connects with the point it is moving past, the object begins to whirl in a circle. Angular momentum can be thought of as momentum moving in a circle. When children run towards a tether ball hanging from a pole, they often leap and swing in a circle about the pole. By hanging on to the tether the children exhibit their angular momentum "about" the pole. Angular momentum is the product of ordinary or linear momentum and the radius or distance from the object to the reference point. Since Bohr's electron was traveling in an orbit about the nucleus, it too was tethered, held to that nucleus by an invisible tether of electrical attraction between the electron and the atomic nucleus. Thus the electron had angular momentum. Could Planck's constant *h* be used as a unit of the electron's angular momentum?

To grasp the significance of this question, imagine that you have a ball attached to a string. Holding the loose end of the string in your hand, whirl the ball around over your head, cowboy style, as if you were about to rope a calf. The faster you whirl the ball, the greater the force you feel, holding on to the rope. When you whirl the ball faster, you increase its angular momentum.

Now picture an ice skater whirling in a spin. Notice that as the skater brings her arms toward her body, she whirls faster. Her arms are acting like balls attached to ropes. But, unlike the whirling balls, although she is spinning faster, her angular momentum remains the same. This is because the distance from her spin axis to her arms has decreased to compensate for her increased speed of rotation.

If you now picture the tiny electron whirling around in its orbit, you will realize that for a given force holding it to its circular path and for a given *fixed* amount of angular momentum, the speed of the electron is determined. The radius of the orbit is also determined. Everything depends on the delicate balance provided by the amount of angular momentum the electron is allowed to possess.

Bohr tried out a calculation imagining a circular orbit for the electron with one unit of angular momentum. He calculated the size of the orbit requiring that the electron have one unit of h. The orbit was the correct size; it filled out the atom. He then tried a new orbit with two units of h. It proved to be a new orbit with a larger diameter, four times the original orbit. When Bohr calculated an orbit for the electron with three units of h, the orbit grew in size to nine times the original orbit. Bohr had discovered a new model for the atom.

In this model there were only certain allowed orbits. By restricting the electron to these special or "quantized" orbits, as they were later called, Bohr successfully predicted the correct size for the atom. Each orbit grew in size as the electron increased its angular momentum. But the scale was correct.

This wasn't the only discovery. Bohr also discovered why the electron wasn't radiating as it whirled in its orbit. In other words he found a reason for the atom's stability. By allowing the electron to have only whole units of h and not any other amounts of angular momentum, Bohr discovered the rule that kept the electron in a stable orbit. Only electrons with whole amounts of angular momentum (i.e., integer multiples of Planck's constant: $1h$, $2h$, $3h$, etc.) would be allowed the privilege of orbiting peacefully inside of the atom. These quantized orbits were known as *Bohr orbits*. The integers of 1, 2, 3, and so forth were called the *quantum numbers* of the orbits. A quantum model of the atom had appeared.

The only thing still needed was the "rule" that allowed the electron to radiate light energy. Again, there was no physical reason for the quantization rule that held the electron in a stable orbit. Bohr had made it up. So Bohr again postulated that the electron would radiate light whenever it changed from one orbit to another. He calculated the energy of the electron in each of its possible orbits. By comparing the difference in energies between the orbits and using Planck's $E = hf$ formula, Bohr successfully predicted the frequencies of the light observed whenever an electron made an orbital "jump."

In January of 1913, a former classmate of Bohr's showed him a paper written by a Swiss schoolteacher named Johann Balmer. Balmer had observed light coming from hydrogen gas in 1880. Instead of a continuous spread of colors, the light from hydrogen showed missing colors when it was passed through a prism and analyzed. The spectrum it produced appeared as a horizontal strip containing several vertical lines, like teeth in a comb. Only some teeth were missing. Ordinarily, the light we see—for example, sunlight or light from an incandescent bulb—does not break down into such a spectrum. Instead, sunlight or light from any hot solid or liquid shows a continuous spread of colors like a rainbow. But Balmer's incomplete spectrum had been produced by hydrogen atoms in a gas. Bohr read Balmer's paper on atomic light and became very excited. Not only could he calculate the energy of the electron in each atomic orbit, but he could also calculate the energy that the electron radiated away when it changed orbits.

Balmer's hydrogen spectrum had missing "teeth" because the energy given out by the jumping electron was so well prescribed. Since there were only certain orbits for the electron, there had to be only certain frequencies for the light. The frequency of the light depended on the difference in energies of the electron involved in the quantum jump from one orbit to another. Balmer's atomic light was explained.

All well and good. However, Bohr's successful prediction was based on a very disturbing picture. The electron making the light was not oscillating or orbiting the nucleus to make the light. In fact, it wasn't doing anything that anyone could really imagine. To make the light it had to jump. It leaped like a desperate superman from one orbit to another inside the atom. It was not allowed to move in between orbits. Bohr tried to calculate that and failed. The best picture he could come up with was that of a quantum jump, a leap from one place to another without passing in between. As unreasonable as this picture was, it replaced any completely classical mechanical picture of that process.

* * * * *

Among the students who had gathered to hear Bohr was twenty-year-old Werner Heisenberg. This occasion would be the first of many meetings between Heisenberg and Bohr. Together these two would change the meaning of physics. Eager to rid physics of mechanical models, they would herald a new school, a school of discontinuists. Their interpretations would lead to a revolution of thought.

Heisenberg wrote of this first meeting with Bohr in his book, *Physics and Beyond*. After some remarks concerning Bohr's atomic theory, he wrote:

> Bohr must have gathered that my remarks sprang from profound interest in his atomic theory.... He replied hesitantly ... and asked me to join him that afternoon on a walk over the Hain Mountain.... This walk was to have profound repercussions on my scientific career, or perhaps it is more correct to say that my real scientific career only began that afternoon....Bohr's remark [that afternoon] reminded me that atoms were not things....[9]

But if atoms were not "things," then what were they? Heisenberg's answer was that all classical ideas about the world had to be abandoned. Motion could no longer be described in terms of the classical concept of a thing moving continuously from one place to another.

* * * * *

Heisenberg attempted to describe the method by which the position and momentum of an atom-sized object could be measured.

---

9. W. Heisenberg, *Physics and Beyond* (New York: Harper & Row, 1971), p. 38.

To see something, we must shine light on it. Determining the location of an electron would require our sense of sight. But for so tiny an object as an electron, Heisenberg knew a special kind of microscope would be needed. A microscope magnifies images by catching light rays, which were originally moving in different directions, and forcing them all to move in much the same direction toward the awaiting open eye. The larger the aperture or lens opening, the more rays of light there are to catch. In this way, a better image is obtained, but the viewer pays a price for that better image.

The price is that we don't know the precise path taken by the light ray after it leaves the object we were trying to view in the first place. Oh, we will see it all right—a fraction after its collision with the little light photon that was gathered up by the microscope. But was that photon heading north before it was corralled by the lens, was it heading south, or southwest? Once the photon is gathered in, that information gets lost.

But so what? We do get an exact measurement of the position of the electron. We can point out just where it was. Well, not exactly. We still must worry about the kind of light we use. Try to imagine painting a fine portrait the size of a Lincoln penny. What kind of brush would you use? The finer the hairs of your brush, the better your ability to create the miniature. If you were to reduce the size of the portrait even further, you would need an even finer brush.

Different kinds of light vary in their wavelengths in much the same way that brushes vary in the fineness of their hairs. To see something very tiny, you need to use light with a small wavelength. The smaller the object you are looking for, the tinier the wavelength you will need. Since an electron is very tiny, Heisenberg needed to use a kind of light that has a very small wavelength. This light is beyond our normal range of vision, though still detectable in a way similar to ordinary light. But according to de Broglie's formula, the smaller the wavelength of the light, the greater the momentum of the photon. Therefore, for Heisenberg to see the electron, the photon would have to hit it with a tremendous amount of momentum.

In Zen Buddhism, one speaks of using a thorn to remove a thorn as the process of finding out what is real. In Heisenberg's microscope, the tiny wavelengthed photon is as big a thorn as the electron it is inspecting. Thus, if we are able to catch the photon ray in the wide open lens of the microscope and if we are consequently able to "see" the position of the electron, we will have absolutely no idea of where the electron will be next. Our act of viewing the electron disrupts its motion. Though we learn the electron's position, we are left uncertain of its momentum; we simply do not know how fast or in what direction the electron was moving at the instant of impact.

We may attempt to remedy the situation by doing one of two things. First, we can use photons that do not give the electron so big a "kick." That is, we can use light that has a longer wavelength. But this remedy has a disadvantage: we lose information about the precise location of the electron. Like the painter with a brush of coarse hairs, we cannot manage the details of our electron portrait. Our second option is to make the lens opening, the aperture, smaller. For by taking in less light, we are able to determine more accurately the direction the photon takes after its collision with the electron. Unfortunately, this remedy also has a disadvantage. Light behaves very much like a wave with respect to the aperture. That means it bends or diffracts as it passes through the hole. The narrower the space offered to the light, the worse the bending. Consequently, narrowing the aperture brings us less information about the location of the electron, because the image we receive is distorted by the bent light rays.

If you have ever tried to convince someone to change his way of life, you may have noticed how he had some good reason why the change you suggested could never work. Even though the person sought your advice, he had a ready answer defeating your marvelous idea as soon as you offered it. Your stubborn friend, you probably realized, had simply made up his mind in advance. Similarly, Heisenberg had discovered nature's stubborn streak. Yet there seemed no way to catch her in her act. The more one knew of the position of the electron, the less one knew of its path to the future, its momentum. And the inverse was also true. But was nature just hiding from us? Heisenberg didn't think so.

Remember that we began this section with the premise that we can define only what we can measure. Since we cannot measure both the position and the momentum of any object in this universe with exact precision, the very concepts of "position" and "momentum" are in doubt. So how can these concepts be given any meaning? Heisenberg contended that although the notion of "path" implies clear knowledge of both "position" and "momentum" simultaneously, it could be retained in quantum physics. His rationale was extremely provocative. He said, "The path comes into existence only when we observe it." [10]

* * * * *

This uncertainty meant that no matter how accurately one tried to measure the classical quantities of position and momentum, there would always be an uncertainty in the measurement. Predicting or determining the future of atomic objects would be impossible under these circumstances. This was called the Heisenberg Principle of Uncertainty or the Principle of Indeterminacy. It had little relevance in the world of ordinary-sized objects. They were hardly bothered by disturbances produced through observation. But the uncertainty principle was serious business when it came to electrons. Indeed, it was so serious that it brought the very existence of electrons into question.

---

10. M. Jammer, *Conceptual Development*, p. 329.

COMMENTS ■ QUESTIONS

1. Wolf begins by discussing the views of Pierre Simon Laplace, a determinist, who believed that the present is the inevitable unfolding of the past, and that the future is the inevitable unfolding of the present. How would Laplace have accounted for the fact that so much in our lives seems to be unpredictable?
2. Laplace, like a great many other determinists, was also a materialist. But remember that a determinist is not logically committed to being a materialist. Do you believe that the materialistic version of determinism is the most plausible? (If determinism is true, is it a materialistic version of it that is true?)
3. Wolf discusses the work of two scientists that has appeared to be problematic for the defense of a deterministic view of matter. One of them, Niels Bohr, theorized that movement at the subatomic level was discontinuous: he postulated that sometimes an electron "jumps" from one orbit around an atomic nucleus to another orbit without traversing the intervening space. Several different questions might be asked about the concept of such a "quantum jump": Is the concept coherent, that is, does it make sense? If it does make sense, how does this affect the general concept of a "material particle"? If the concept of an electron that makes quantum jumps is coherent, what are the logical implications, if any, for determinism? (This is admittedly an unusually difficult question, but it is an important one.)
4. The second of the scientists whose work has appeared to be problematic for the defense of a deterministic view of matter is Werner Heisenberg, whose name is associated with the Principle of Indeterminacy. According to this principle, there will always be an uncertainty in attempts to measure both the position and momentum of a subatomic particle. This uncertainty results because attempts to measure the position and momentum of the particle require some form of interaction with the particle that can affect either its position or its momentum. An important question to be asked regarding the Principle of Indeterminacy is whether it makes the defense of a deterministic view of matter impossible. Is the lack of complete determination a consequence *only* of what happens in attempts to *measure* the position and momentum of a subatomic particle, or does the lack of complete determination belong to the particle "in itself"? (The general question of whether or not anything can be known "in itself" is discussed in chapter 10.)

S U S A N L E I G H A N D E R S O N

The Libertarian Conception of Freedom

There seem to be (at least) two distinct conceptions of freedom in the literature on the Free Will/Determinism issue, yet this point is seldom made clear in introductions to the topic. According to the first conception, a person is said to be free if he is not acting under compulsion, if he is able to translate his desires into action. In the words of David Hume,

> By liberty . . . we can only mean *a power of acting or not acting according to the determinations of the will*; that is, if we choose to remain at rest, we may; if we choose to move, we also may.[1]

This is the sense of freedom the "Soft" Determinist has in mind when he maintains that although Determinism [2] is the case, most of our actions are free.

The other conception of freedom is that which is associated with the position called Libertarianism. According to this conception, freedom can exist only if Determinism does not. To quote Henri Bergson:

> The argument of the [Determinists] implies that there is only one possible act corresponding to given antecedents; the believers in free will assume, on the other hand, that the same series could issue in several different acts, equally possible.[3]

Being able to perform alternative actions at a given moment in time, all antecedent conditions remaining the same, is not however a *sufficient* condition for saying that the act performed is free. It is also necessary that the agent be the *cause*—the *sole* cause—of the act. Thus C. A. Campbell, the primary spokesman for Libertarianism, states that "an act is a 'free' act . . . only if the agent (a) is

1. David Hume, *An Enquiry Concerning Human Understanding*, edited by L. A. Selby-Bigge (Oxford: Clarendon Press, 1894), Section 8, Part I, p. 95.
2. By "Determinism," I shall mean the view which holds that for every event that occurs there is some condition or set of conditions sufficient to bring about that event.
3. Henri Bergson, *Time and Free Will* (London: Allen & Unwin, 1910), pp. 174–75.

Susan Leigh Anderson, an associate professor of philosophy at the University of Connecticut, has had National Endowment for the Humanities Fellowships at Princeton and Brown universities and a Lilly Fellowship at Yale University. She has had several journal articles published on topics concerned with the self.

From "The Libertarian Conception of Freedom," *International Philosophical Quarterly*, volume 21, number 4 (1981). By permission of *International Philosophical Quarterly*.

the sole cause of the act; and (b) could exert his causality in alternative ways." [4] The Libertarian maintains that only if we are free in *this* sense, should we be held morally responsible for our actions. Thus Roderick M. Chisholm, who has recently tried to revive the libertarian notion of freedom, states:

> Let us consider some deed, or misdeed, that may be attributed to a responsible agent: one man, say, shot another. If the man *was* responsible for what he did, then, I would urge, what was to happen at the time of the shooting was something that was entirely up to the man himself. There was a moment at which it was true, both that he could have fired the shot and also that he could have refrained from firing it.[5]

It is this second conception of freedom that I am interested in examining. It is, I am convinced, the type of freedom the "common man" believes one must enjoy before one can rightfully be held responsible for one's actions; [6] yet most contemporary philosophers have found little difficulty in dismissing this notion of freedom. Why? In the first section of this paper, I would like to look at the case against Libertarianism which culminates in the charge that the position is unintelligible. In the second section, I would like to see if it is possible to defend Libertarianism against this ultimate attack. In the third, and final, section, I would like to consider a still further question: Assuming that the libertarian position can be made intelligible, how often are persons able to perform actions that are free in this second (libertarian) sense?

The Case Against Libertarianism

Most philosophers today accept the position of Determinism and, therefore, of necessity have had to hold that there can be no instances of actions which are free in the second (libertarian) sense. But this is not being fair to the Soft Determinist's position. From his basic conviction, the belief in Determinism, there have arisen a number of classic arguments to show that it must be the *first* conception of freedom, not the second, which we have in mind when we worry about the kind of freedom which is necessary in order to hold people responsible for their actions. Four of these arguments can be, and have been, easily attacked by the Libertarian:

(1) Moral appraisal does not impute freedom to the agent in the second sense; quite the contrary,

> When I pass a moral judgment on another, far from implying his free-will, I tacitly assume that my judgment of him, in so far as he takes cognizance of it, operates as a determining influence on his conduct. Thus moral criticism when interpreted naturalistically harmonizes with the theory of moral

4. C. A. Campbell, "In Defence of Free Will," in *In Defence of Free Will, with Other Philosophical Essays* (London: Allen and Unwin, 1967), p. 37.

5. Roderick M. Chisholm, "Freedom and Action," in *Freedom and Determinism*, edited by Keith Lehrer (Atlantic Highlands, N.J.: Humanities Press, 1976), p. 12.

6. Those who believe in the existence of God, for instance, must believe that we enjoy this type of freedom in order to absolve God from responsibility for our sins. Campbell agrees. See *On Selfhood and Godhood* (London: Allen & Unwin, 1957), pp. 171–72.

determinism.[7]

[The Libertarian replies: It may, indeed, be *effective* to pass a moral judgment on, punish, or reward a person under the theory of Determinism; but he doesn't *deserve* the judgment, punishment, or reward.]

(2) To hold a person morally responsible for an action it is necessary only that "he could have done otherwise if he had chosen to," which amounts to his having freedom in the *first* sense and is compatible with Determinism. [The Libertarian replies: But could he have *chosen* otherwise than he did? Only if he could have *chosen* otherwise—which implies that he has freedom in the *second* sense—should he be held morally responsible for his action.]

(3) If persons had the *second* kind of freedom, there would be no continuity of character, no basis for prediction of people's behavior. But it does seem that we are able to make such predictions. If we could not, social life would be reduced to complete chaos. [One Libertarian, Campbell, replies:

> The Libertarian view is perfectly compatible with prediction within certain limits. . . . (1) There is no question, on our view, of a free will that can will just anything at all. The range of possible choices is limited by the agent's character in every case . . . (2) There is *one* experiential situation, and *one only*, on our view, in which there is any possibility of the act of will not being in accordance with character . . . the situation of moral temptation. Now this is a situation of comparative rarity. . . . (3) Even within that one situation which is relevant to free will, our view can still recognize a certain basis for prediction. . . .[8]]

(4) There is also the argument, which is related to the third, that if persons were free in the Libertarian sense, then we would not be able to causally influence each other's behavior. But obviously we can affect others in this way, so Libertarianism must be false. [Chisholm's reply is that although certain actions are free, other people may exert a causal influence on these actions by *restricting* the agent's options or by *enabling* him to do what he otherwise could not have done.

> Thus if you provide me with the necessary *means* for getting to Boston, means without which I wouldn't have been able to get there, then, if I do go there, you can be said to have contributed causally to what I do even though my undertaking the trip had no sufficient causal conditions.[9]]

There is, however, a fifth argument which is generally thought to clinch the Soft Determinist's case. This argument appears to successfully reduce the libertarian position to absurdity.

> It is constantly objected against the Libertarian doctrine that it is fundamentally *unintelligible*. Libertarianism holds that [a free act] is the self's act, and yet insists at the same time that it is not influenced by any of those determinate features in the self's nature which go to constitute its "character." But, it is asked, do not these two propositions contradict one another?. . . If

---

7. Ledger Wood, "The Free-Will Controversy," *Philosophy*, 16 (1941), 392–93.

8. Campbell, "In Defence of Free Will," pp. 46–47.

9. Chisholm, "The Agent as Cause," in *Action Theory*, edited by M. Brand and D. Walton (Dordrecht: Reidel, 1976), p. 204.

> you really wish to maintain, it is urged, that the act of decision is not determined by the self's character, you ought to admit frankly that it is not determined by the *self* at all. But in that case, of course, you will not be advocating a freedom which lends any kind of support to moral responsibility; indeed very much the reverse.[10]

Can the Libertarian refute this argument? Surely he must be able to make his position intelligible or else he should give up his notion of freedom altogether.

Let us look first at Campbell's "official" reply to the objection that Libertarianism is unintelligible. He says that the objection is the product of

> the error of confining one's self to the categories of the external observer in dealing with the actions of human agents. . . .
>
> It is perfectly true that the standpoint of the external observer . . . does not furnish us with even a glimmering of a notion of what can be meant by an entity which acts causally and yet not through any of the determinate features of its character. . . . But then we are *not* obliged to confine ourselves to external observation in dealing with the human agent. . . . if we do adopt [an] inner standpoint . . . we find that we not merely can, but constantly do, attach meaning to a causation which is the self-causation but is yet not exercised by the self's character.[11]

This reply is not very satisfying. We are told that the idea of an act ensuing from the self, but not from the self's character, will be intelligible if we only look at it from an "inner" standpoint. But what if we try this perspective and still don't find the act intelligible? Or, even if we think we do, is it not possible that we are just deluding ourselves? We want some sort of explanation as to *how* this type of act is possible. Yet with this request Campbell becomes defensive. He suspects that what we mean by an "intelligible" act is "one whose occurrence is in principle capable of being inferred." But, of course, the Libertarian's free act will be unintelligible in this sense. This follows from the *definition* of a free act.

I think Campbell has a much better reply to give to the charge that the Libertarian's free act is unintelligible than the one he has given above.[12] It is suggested by many things he says, but it is never explicitly stated. Consider the following passages in which Campbell describes a free act:

> The agent distinguishes sharply between the self which makes the decision, and the self which, as formed character, determines not the decision but the situation within which the decision takes place.[13]
>
> The self which makes the decision must be something "beyond" its

---

10. Campbell, "In Defence of Free Will," pp. 47–48.

11. Ibid., p. 48.

12. The reply seems to be related to Kant's position that when a person is viewed as an *object* in the phenomenal world, his actions appear to be determined; but when a person views himself as an *agent*—an object in the noumenal world—he sees that he must be free. It also seems to be related to Sartre's view that human relationships are necessarily unhappy because each person attempts to reduce the other to an object—to define the other as a "fixed" entity—yet neither one believes *himself* to be a "fixed" entity.

13. Campbell, "In Defence of Free Will," p. 43.

> formed character.[14] Self-consciousness leads to the recognition of a . . . distinction within selfhood, the distinction of the self as it is from the self as it is capable of becoming.[15]

Campbell accepts a certain metaphysical view of the self which he is clearly employing in his descriptions of a free act. He is, of course, a dualist; but this is not what is important to the issue at hand. What is important is his view of the mind which is for him, as for all dualists, where the self is to be located. According to C. D. Broad, one may adopt either a Center-Theory or Non-Center Theory to account for the unity of the mind (and, as a result, the unity of the self). To quote his explanation of the difference between the two:

> By a centre-theory I mean a theory which ascribes the unity of the mind to the fact that there is a certain particular existent—a centre—which stands in a common asymmetrical relation to all the mental events which would be said to be states of a certain mind, and does not stand in this relation to any mental events which would not be said to be states of this mind. By a non-centre theory I mean one which denies the existence of any such particular centre and ascribes the unity of the mind to the fact that certain mental events are directly interrelated in certain characteristic ways and that other mental events are not related to these in the particular way in which these are related to each other.[16]

According to the Center-Theory, the self is not a logical construction out of mental experiences while the Non-Center Theory, usually known as the Bundle Theory, holds that it is.

There are, furthermore, two subdivisions within the Center-Theory according to what the center is thought to be. It might be:

> 1. a particular *substance* which owns, or has, mental experiences but is not itself a mental experience. This is the view which I shall call the *Substantive Center Theory*. It has been defended, historically, by such philosophers as Plato, Descartes, Locke, Reid, Kant and, more recently, by C. A. Campbell, H. J. Paton, H. D. Lewis and Roderick M. Chisholm.
>
> or
>
> 2. an *event*. Only William James seems to have espoused such a view.

How does Campbell's Substance Center Theory view of the mind help him to account for the intelligibility of the notion of an act which is caused by the self but which is not the result of the self's character being what it is? We may think of the self's character as having been formed by its past experiences. According to the Non-Center or Bundle Theory, the self at any given moment in time is simply the collection of mental experiences (related in a certain way) which the mind has had up to, and including, that moment. Philosophers holding this view of the self will tend to think of the self, then, as essentially its formed character. If, however, one thinks of the mind as containing, *in addition to* mental experiences (formed character), another entity

---

14. *On Selfhood and Godhood*, p. 152.
15. "Moral and Non-Moral Values," in *In Defence of Free Will, with Other Philosophical Essays*, p. 91.
16. C. D. Broad, *The Mind and Its Place in Nature* (Paterson, N.J.: Littlefield, Adams, 1960), p. 558.

(the substantive center) which properly speaking is the *self*, it does seem possible that *this* entity could initiate an action which is not in keeping with the self's formed character. The self which performs the free act is an entity which *has* mental experiences but is not to be identified with any particular set of such experiences. This notion of a substantive center need not, Campbell insists, be assimilated to either Locke's "unknowable substratum" or Kant's noumenal ego, both of which he thinks are too characterless and have been exposed over the years to many objections. Besides the possibility of using it to account for the intelligibility of the Libertarian's notion of a free act, are there any good reasons for supposing that there *is* a substantive center to the mind? I think there are,[17] but to discuss them here would take us too far from the topic at hand.

Perhaps, even now, the Libertarian should not feel assured that he is on the right road yet. There may still be a major obstacle to his giving a plausible description of a free act.

> How often . . . do we find the Determinist critic saying, in effect, "*Either* the act follows necessarily upon precedent states, *or* it is a mere matter of chance, and accordingly of no moral significance."[18]

Campbell and Chisholm believe that a false dilemma has been created. Let us refer to the denial of Determinism as Indeterminism. Indeterminism, then, is the view that for some events that occur (at least one) there is not some condition or set of conditions sufficient to bring them about. There is, in other words, a break in the causal chain of events. Indeterminism, Campbell and Chisholm would want to maintain, should be thought of as taking two possible forms:

Indeterminism

(There is a break in the causal chain of events)

(1) There is at least one action which is caused by the self but is not caused by any earlier event(s)/state(s) of affairs (the Libertarian's free act)

(2) There is at least one action for which there is no cause—"pure chance" operates

Most philosophers think that Libertarianism must eventually boil down to the second form—and the only intelligible one in their eyes—of Indeterminism, where supposed free acts are due to nothing but pure chance. The Libertarian, however, as we have seen, wants to maintain that it is possible that a decision to act *not* follow necessarily from antecedent events/states of affairs according to causal laws but still be *caused by something*, namely the *self*.

Many philosophers find it difficult to comprehend a notion of causation—*agent* or, as Chisholm calls it,

17. See, for example, Campbell, *On Selfhood and Godhood*, p. 71 and pp. 75–76; D. M. Armstrong, *A Materialist Theory of the Mind* (London: Routledge & Kegan Paul, 1968), pp. 22–23; Sidney Shoemaker, *Self-Knowledge and Self-Identity* (Ithaca, N.Y.: Cornell Univ. Press, 1963), p. 77; and Broad, *The Mind and Its Place in Nature*, p. 213 and pp. 584–85. I have discussed the case for and against the Substantive Center Theory in my article "The Substantive Center Theory Versus the Bundle Theory," *The Monist*, 61 (January, 1978).

18. Campbell, *On Selfhood and Godhood*, p. 177.

immanent causation—which cannot be reduced to causation by earlier events/states of affairs—*event* or *transeunt* causation. Either they claim that there is no such thing as *agent* causation or, like Alvin I. Goldman, they claim that it exists but can always be reduced to event causation:

> Whenever we say that an *object*, O, [and an agent is just a special type of object] is a cause of *x*, this presupposes that there is a *state of O* or an *event involving O* that caused, or was a partial cause of, *x* [19]

It would seem that the Libertarian, in order to satisfy both sorts of opponents, must show two things: (1) that there *is* such a thing as *agent* causation and (2) that it cannot be reduced to *event* causation. Concerning the first point, both Chisholm [20] and Richard Taylor [21] believe it is simply *obvious* that *agent* causation exists. "[A] perfectly natural way of expressing [the] notion of my activity is to say that, in acting, I make something happen, I cause it, or bring it about." [22] As a matter of fact, they both see this type of causation as more fundamental, as far as our understanding of causation is concerned, than *event* causation.

> The notion of immanent causation, or causation by an agent, is in fact more clear than that of transeunt causation, or causation by an event, . . . it is only by understanding our own causal efficacy, as agents, that we can grasp the concept of *cause* at all.[23]

Let us assume that there is such a thing as *agent* causation. It certainly seems natural to do so. The *real* issue appears to be: Can *agent* causation be reduced to *event* causation? Chisholm and Taylor both say "no" and essentially for the same reason. They believe that *agent* causation must be analyzed in terms of *intention* or *purpose*—the agent *undertaking x in order to bring about y*—and they don't think that this can be reduced to a relation between events or states of affairs.[24]

Jean-Paul Sartre, another Libertarian, characterizes voluntary actions in the following way: When a person acts he either continues to behave as he has in the past, presently *choosing* to maintain the *status quo*, which indicates that he approves of his present situation, or else he attempts to change his situation because he finds it unpleasant. In either case, the motivating factor is a *value judgement* [25] which the agent alone must, *at that moment*, make. The situation by itself is neither pleasant nor unpleasant and so cannot motivate the action ("No factual

---

19. Alvin I. Goldman, *A Theory of Human Action* (Englewood Cliffs, N.J.: Prentice-Hall, 1970), p. 81.

20. See Chisholm, "The Agent as Cause," p. 199.

21. See Richard Taylor, *Action and Purpose* (Englewood Cliffs, N.J.: Prentice-Hall, 1966), pp. 111–12, 261–64.

22. Ibid., p. 111.

23. Chisholm, "Freedom and Action," p. 22.

24. See Taylor, op. cit., p. 264; Chisholm, "The Agent as Cause," pp. 199–200.

25. How are these value judgments made? According to Sartre, the self must first imagine some ideal state of affairs and then either appreciate his own situation when he compares it favorably to this ideal or find his present situation intolerable when he compares it unfavorably to the ideal. The judgment the self makes about his present situation, the last step prior to action, then, presupposes two previous steps: (1) the imagining of some ideal state of affairs, and then (2) the comparing of one's present situation with the ideal.

state whatever it may be is capable by itself of motivating any act whatsoever." [26]). Even my past value judgements cannot determine my present and future actions because these value judgements are constantly open to reassessment. In a similar vein, Chisholm states that "no set of statements about a man's desires, beliefs, and stimulus situation at any time implies any statement, telling us what the man will try, set out, or undertake to do at that time." [27]

Still, Determinists maintain that there must be a reason why a person acts as he does; the action must be the result of antecedent conditions such as the person's desires, particular circumstances, etc. If correct, this would effectively reduce all cases of *agent* causation to instances of *event* causation. But it can only be done if one assumes the theory of Determinism to be true.

There is another reason why philosophers are generally reluctant to admit that there could be an action which is not caused by earlier events/states of affairs but is caused by the agent. Goldman wonders how, allowing such actions to exist, one could distinguish reflex actions from agent caused non-reflex actions and, more generally, uncaused actions from agent-caused actions.[28]

Chisholm considers how he would answer the question, "What is the difference between A's just happening and the agent's *causing* A to happen?" His reply is simple:

> The only answer, I think, can be this: that the difference between the man's causing A, on the one hand, and the event A just happening, on the other, lies in the fact that, in the first case but not the second, the event *A was* caused and was caused by the man.[29]

He admits that his answer may not seem entirely satisfactory. Someone way wonder what saying "the man *caused* A" amounts to, but Chisholm challenges the defender of *event* causation to spell out what "event B *caused* event A" amounts to. I think that Chisholm is right in maintaining that "the nature of transeunt causation is no more clear than is that of immanent causation." [30]

After eliminating this objection, it would seem that the belief that the Libertarian notion of freedom is unintelligible—that *agent* causation which cannot be reduced to *event* causation is unintelligible—just boils down to a firm conviction that Determinism must be the case. In the absence of any conclusive evidence for Determinism (and what kind of evidence would be conclusive?), however, this is just not a very good reason for dismissing the libertarian position as being unintelligible.

* * * * *

Conclusion

To conclude, I do not think that the libertarian notion of free will has been shown to be absolutely unintelligible. If one holds a view of the self like the Substantive Center Theory, one has a framework within which it is possible to claim that a

26. Jean-Paul Sartre, *Being and Nothingness*, trans. by Hazel Barnes (New York: Philosophical Library, 1956), p. 435.

27. Chisholm, "Freedom and Action," p. 24.

28. See Goldman, op. cit., p. 84.

29. Chisholm, "Freedom and Action," p. 21.

30. Ibid., p. 22.

free action can be the self's act yet not be the inevitable result of formed character. I do not believe, furthermore, that such actions have to be viewed as chance occurrences.

How often might an individual be free in the libertarian sense? I think it will vary from person to person. The important thing is that the agent sees that he/she has alternative courses of action open to him/her. Others will see to it that a person views himself/herself as having a choice *at least* in genuine moral temptation situations. There is a good reason, then, for Campbell's having focused on such situations. I believe, however, that these situations are even rarer than Campbell supposes because, once "desire" has been extended to include the urge one feels to do what one recognizes to be one's duty, there will be fewer occasions on which one desires to do the "wrong" action at least as much as the "right" one. Furthermore, I think (at least I hope) that this is not the *only* situation in which a person can be free in the libertarian sense, because otherwise two rather strange, related consequences result: *Naturally* good people (as opposed to people who repeatedly perform right actions even though it is difficult for them) will be less free than others; and to the extent that persons who begin asserting their freedom by doing morally correct actions in moral temptation situations start acquiring a *natural inclination* to do these actions, this will diminish the number of occasions in the future when they will be free.

I think it is likely that some people are capable of performing free actions in other situations as well. Those who have become accustomed, in some other specific situations or in general, to consider alternative ways of acting rather than simply following strongest desire will be free more often in the libertarian sense. The ability to envision different courses of action can, I think, be cultivated—remember that it is not necessary that the agent *invent* any of the choices. The behavior of individuals who have developed this ability will be less predictable than others, but that only makes them all the more interesting.

COMMENTS ■ QUESTIONS

1. In order for libertarianism to be defended, the libertarian must produce a clear (or relatively clear) concept of what libertarian free choice is. Has Anderson done this?
2. What would Jean-Paul Sartre say regarding Anderson's concept of free choice? What would Kai Nielsen say?
3. Anderson's method of presentation is to first state the case against libertarianism and then give reasons for rejecting that case—*and* in the course of doing these things to present a case *for* libertarianism. Has she done a fair job in presenting the case

against libertarianism? Is her response to it adequate?

4. Part of Anderson's defense of libertarianism is her statement and defense of the Center-Theory of the Self. Her remarks about the Center-Theory probably appear to be the most difficult part of her paper because they raise issues in the philosophy of mind, a topic that is not covered until chapter 6. Does the Center-Theory of the Self strike you as plausible? Why or why not?
5. Which of the papers in this chapter do you find the most convincing? Why?

READINGS

Besofsky, Bernard. *Free Will and Determinism.* New York: Harper & Row, 1966. This collection contains many widely referred to papers.

Brand, Myles, ed. *The Nature of Human Action.* Glenview, Ill.: Scott, Foresman & Co., 1970. An excellent anthology of work on the explanation of human actions.

Darrow, Clarence. *Attorney for the Damned.* Edited by Arthur Weinberg. New York: Simon & Schuster, 1957. Some speeches of this famous defense attorney defend a position close to hard determinism.

Gould, James A., and Willis H. Truitt, eds. *Existentialist Philosophy.* Belmont, Calif.: Wadsworth Publishing Co., 1973. A very good collection of excerpts and papers.

Hook, Sidney, ed. *Determinism and Freedom in the Age of Modern Science.* New York: Collier, 1961. One of the best known anthologies.

Hospers, John. *An Introduction to Philosophical Analysis.* Englewood Cliffs, N.J.: Prentice-Hall, 1967. Contains a chapter that is a particularly clear and comprehensive discussion of issues regarding free will and responsibility.

Melden, A. I. *Free Action.* London: Routledge & Kegan Paul, 1961. Presents arguments against some versions of determinism.

Morris, H. *Freedom and Responsibility.* Stanford, Calif.: Stanford University Press, 1966. Good collection that focuses on the free will issue in relation to responsibility and punishment.

Olafson, Frederick A. *Principles and Persons: An Ethical Interpretation of Existentialism.* Baltimore: Johns Hopkins University Press, 1967. Chapter 7 defends the existentialist theory of freedom.

Skinner, B. F. *Walden Two.* New York: Macmillan, 1960. A fictional account of a utopian society based on a deterministic view of human behavior.

Thomson, Judith Jarvis. *Acts and Other Events.* Ithaca, N.Y.: Cornell University Press, 1977. A contemporary treatment of action theory that addresses questions about the causal roles of motives and intentions in human actions.

CHAPTER SIX

The knower differs from the world he knows only in the greater complexity of his physical organization. Man is one with nature.
—*D. M. Armstrong*

Thought and choice are irreducible to the laws of physical nature.
—*James E. Royce*

The Philosophy of Mind

ore than any other field of study, philosophy by its very nature is interdisciplinary. Nowhere is this more apparent than in the philosophy of mind.

- What is the nature of the human mind?
- What is the nature of thought?
- What is consciousness?

As the above examples illustrate, the philosophical study of the human mind includes some very basic questions that are also questions in psychology.

- What is the relationship between thought and brain activity?

This is probably the single most important question being pursued in contemporary work in the philosophy of mind. But it is a question that also interests medical scientists doing research on the human nervous system.

- Can human consciousness or thought exist apart from the human body?

Throughout the history of philosophy, this question has probably been asked more often than any other in the philosophy of mind. It is also perhaps the most important question in any discussion of human nature from the point of view of religion. Moreover, it is one of the central questions asked by researchers in the area of parapsychology. (Parapsychology is a relatively new discipline whose academic respectability is a matter of considerable controversy, some of which is examined in chapter 13, "Science versus Pseudoscience".)

- Would it be possible to construct a machine that could think in all or most of the ways that human beings think?
- Would it be possible to construct a machine that was conscious or had feelings?

Contemporary philosophers have written about these questions extensively. They are also fundamental questions for scientists working in the areas of artificial intelligence and computer design.

Psychologists, anatomists, theologians, parapsychologists, and computer theoreticians ask the same questions about the human mind that philosophers do. The study of the human mind is also of great interest to novelists and playwrights, to psychiatrists, to sociologists and anthropologists, and to other writers and researchers. The fact that the philosophy of mind overlaps with all of these disciplines should not surprise us. The study of the human mind can readily be seen as the forerunner of all intellectual endeavors that human beings address to themselves.

- Who am I?
- What am I?
- What is the "real me" that underlies my changing moods, my memories, my hopes and fears, my beliefs and concerns?
- *Is* there a "real me" that underlies my memories, beliefs, hopes, and so on?
- What is my place in the world of things that are outside of me?

These would seem to be the most basic intellectual questions that we can ask about ourselves. The philosophy of mind tries to answer them, but they are too far-reaching to be encompassed by a single discipline—even by philosophy, which in a sense is the broadest discipline of all. Therefore, the philosophy of mind (and the same is true, but probably less so, of other areas in philosophy) continually makes reference to work undertaken by researchers who are not philosophers.

In the earlier history of philosophy, these references were most frequently made to religious writings of one kind or another (philosophy and religion have not always been clearly distinguished). As for contemporary philosophy of mind, references are probably most frequently made to work on the human nervous system by medical scientists and to work done by computer theoreticians. One reason for this is that medical researchers have had some success in finding correlations between thoughts, feelings, memories, and other states of consciousness on the one hand, and certain processes in the brain on the other hand. For example, some localized brain injuries cause memory loss, and other injuries impair the ability to use language, cause general mental confusion, or produce some other effect upon thoughts and feelings.

Along somewhat different lines, experiments have shown that weak electrical stimulation of a particular spot in the brain of a patient having brain surgery *brings back* certain memories. At the same time that medical research has been exploring links between thought and the brain, computer technology has been developing machines that have *some* of the capabilities of the human mind. Theoretical work on computers has suggested that many more (all?) of the mind's functions could in principle be duplicated by machines.

Medical research and computer work provide support for a *materialist* theory of the human mind that has been widely defended by contemporary philosophers (including D. M. Armstrong, who is represented in this chapter). Materialists believe that the human mind is *nothing but* the activity of the brain and nervous system. They believe that, if enough were known about the brain, we would be able to "match up" any thought, feeling, desire, memory, intention, and so on with some activity or state of the brain. Materialists readily acknowledge that relatively little actual progress has been made toward reaching this goal. But, they say, that is to be expected because (1) the brain is *extremely* complicated and (2) it is probably "soft-wired" to a certain degree. Soft-wired means, for example, that my thought of eating a piece of apple pie need not always be correlated with the very same location or activity in my brain, but can instead be correlated with a "network" of neurons in my brain. On different occasions or in the event of a brain injury, those neurons could take over the functions of others. Materialists also believe that, at least in principle (but perhaps never in the real world), computer-like machines could be built capable of thinking and feeling in exactly the same ways that human beings think and feel.

In chapter 1 we said that nothing in philosophy is as easy as it may seem. The materialist theory of the human mind is a good illustration of this. Not all philosophers accept it (more about that shortly), but even more to the point, some deep-rooted puzzles exist for both those who accept it and those who reject it in regard to how the materialist theory is to be stated. As we have noted, materialists would like to say that thoughts and feelings can be correlated or matched up with processes in the brain. They would also like to say that thoughts and feelings are *no more* than brain processes. But how can "two things" be matched up if they are one and the same thing? How can something be matched up with itself?

In an attempt to unravel some of the puzzles that lie behind these questions, contemporary materialists have distinguished between two different claims that they are committed to making.

1. According to contemporary materialists, the following statements are *false*:
   - When I have thoughts and feelings, it is true that certain things are happening in my brain, but it is also true that certain things are happening in a "spiritual" part of me that exists in addition to my brain.
   - When I die, my mind (or soul) will survive the disintegration of my body.
2. According to contemporary materialists, the following statements are *true*:
   - The language that we use in describing thoughts, feelings, and so on is very different from the language that we use in describing brain states and processes. Each of the two areas has very different concepts.
   - The experiences that we have of thoughts and feelings when they are ours—when we are actually experiencing them—are very different from the observations that a surgeon may have of a person's brain. My thoughts and feelings belong *within* my consciousness; a brain is something that must be examined as an *external* object.

Contemporary materialists maintain that thoughts and feelings can be matched up with brain processes at the level of scientific or philosophical explanation, but not at the level of ordinary language or personal experience. One contemporary version of materialism is called the *identity theory*. According to this theory even though thoughts and feelings are experienced differently from brain processes, and also are described and conceived of differently, they really are in the final analysis identical with brain processes.

The reading selection from Jerome Shaffer contains a statement of the identity theory and some objections to it.

Materialism is one of two major theories in the philosophy of mind. The other is *dualism*. The negative thesis of dualism is easily stated—that thoughts and feelings are *not* identical with brain processes. Not so easy to state is the positive thesis of dualism, because, first, not all dualists agree as to what dualism is. Second, there are inherent difficulties in stating each of the different versions of dualism.

The names of the most important versions of dualism can be arranged as follows:

- I. Substance dualism
    - A. The Cartesian theory
    - B. The "shadow-body" theory
- II. Nonsubstance dualism
    - A. The "stream of consciousness" theory
    - B. Epiphenomenalism

By the word "substance" philosophers mean something that, at least for the most part, is capable of existing by itself. Hence, according to substance dualism, the mind is capable of existing by itself and is therefore just as much a substance as the body. Substance dualists usually refer to the mind as the *spirit* or *soul* in order to draw attention to their belief that the mind is substantial. The concept of a human spirit or soul that can exist apart from the body is puzzling. Some of the puzzles revolve around the concept of personal identity:

- Does personal identity belong primarily to the body, to the mind (or soul), or to both together?
- If it belongs primarily to the mind or soul, then in what way? Apart from my body, how could *I* know that I am myself?
- Could other people identify me apart from my body? If so, how would they do it?

(The concept of personal identity is analyzed further in the following chapter, which is on the question of life after death.)

The Cartesian version of substance dualism is named for the seventeenth century French philosopher René Descartes, according to whom minds and bodies are radically different. Descartes' theory of the mind is difficult to understand; it states that the mind or soul *is* thought—it is not something other than thought that thinks. Descartes believed that his theory was the only one to make the mind a wholly independent substance. The essence of mind, he said, simply is thought.

He said that it makes no sense to ask what size a thought is, or how much space is occupied by a thought, and therefore it makes no sense to say that the mind has spatial extension. The essence of *body* or of anything material is spatial extension, Descartes said, while the mind is not *in any sense* a material thing.

This chapter contains two reading selections that defend Cartesian dualism. One is from Descartes himself, and one is from a contemporary philosopher, James E. Royce. Royce defends a theory that is close to that of Descartes but is also indebted to the work of the medieval philosopher Saint Thomas Aquinas. The selection from Gilbert Ryle that follows the one from Descartes is a criticism of Descartes' theory.

In contrast, according to the "shadow-body" theory, the human mind or soul *does* have spatial extension; it is *something like* the body, only much more ethereal. Perhaps the best way to think of the shadow-body theory of the mind is to think of Casper the Friendly Ghost from children's cartoons. Casper definitely takes up space, is sometimes visible in a translucent sort of way, and can pass through solid material objects. According to the shadow-body theory—but not the Cartesian theory—the mind or soul is something like Casper. It is a "quasi-material" object capable of having various sorts of mental states.

The shadow-body theory has found adherents primarily among researchers in parapsychology and in some Eastern philosophies (where the "shadow body" is sometimes referred to as the "astral body"). Almost no references are made to the shadow-body theory in the writings of Western philosophers. An exception is H. H. Price, whose paper "What Kind of Next World?" has been included among the readings for the following chapter on the question of life after death. (*All* of the readings in the next chapter are relevant to those in this chapter, and vice versa.)

The number one question that philosophers have asked about both versions of substance dualism is this:

- If minds are distinct substances from bodies, how can the two be joined together (in this life anyway) to form a person?

This question is particularly difficult for Cartesians to answer because they describe minds and bodies as being very different from each other. How can something that has no spatial extension (mind) causally act upon, or be acted upon by, body? For example, how can a thought or intention cause a person's arm to move? Likewise, how can an event in the body, such as the stimulation of the optic nerve, cause a person to have certain images in the mind?

The above questions are perhaps somewhat less difficult to answer by defenders of the shadow-body theory of the mind, but they are still exceedingly puzzling. Descartes claimed that mind and body interact at a single spot in the brain, the pineal gland, but it is not clear how he could justify saying that a wholly nonspatial mind could interact with the body at any spatial location in the body. For the shadow-body account, on the other hand, there would presumably be less of a problem in saying *where* the mind and body interact (presumably the shadow-body soul could contact the physical body in many different places), but there would still be formidable problems in spelling out the *mechanism* for interaction.

Would it be electrical? Chemical? And what might we suppose the shadow-body to be made of?

Let us turn now to the second type of dualism, nonsubstance dualism. The major feature of the first version of this theory is simply its rejection of the substance theory of mind. As William James puts it, there is no need to suppose that the mind is a substance because we can explain everything that needs to be explained about the mind by supposing that the mind is nothing more than a "stream of thoughts," or a stream of its conscious states. James says: "The unity, the identity, the individuality, and the immateriality that appear in the psychic life are thus accounted for as phenomenal and temporal facts exclusively, and with no need of reference to any more simple or substantial agent than the present thought or 'section' of the stream."

Epiphenomenalism, the second version of nonsubstance dualism, is like the first version in finding advocates among contemporary philosophers. It states that mental events are distinct in *some* way from purely bodily events, yet are not independent of the body. Some epiphenomenalists are very close to being materialists, others are not so close. The one thing they all agree on is that mind can have *no* causal effects upon body, while the body *can* causally act upon the mind. That is, events in the body, such as stimulation of nerves from the eyes, ears, taste buds, and so on, can bring about events in the mind, but not vice versa. Thus, epiphenomenalism need not explain how anything as ethereal as a shadow-body could bring about changes in the physical body, and it need not explain how anything as different from a material object as a Cartesian mind could bring about changes in a material object. However, epiphenomenalists still need to explain how the mind is different from the body and how it can be causally affected by the body.

A version of epiphenomenalism is defended by Keith Campbell. The last selection in this chapter, from Paul Ziff, is on the question of whether computers can have feelings.

RENÉ DESCARTES

It is now some years since I detected how many were the false beliefs that I had from my earliest youth admitted as true, and how doubtful was everything I had since constructed on this basis; and from that time I was convinced that I must for once and for all seriously undertake to rid myself of all the opinions which I had formerly accepted, and commence to build anew.

The first rule is to accept nothing as true which I do not clearly recognize to be so; that is to say, carefully to avoid precipitation and prejudice in my judgments, and to accept in them nothing more than what was presented to my mind so clearly and distinctly that I could have no occasion to doubt it.

Meditations

René Descartes (1596–1650), a French philosopher, is often called the "Founder of Modern Philosophy." From the age of eight until he was sixteen, Descartes was sent to a boarding school, the Jesuit College of La Fleche. Because his health was bad, he was allowed to lie in bed until late in the morning—where he pleasantly spent his time with his own thoughts. He learned to turn his thoughts inwardly upon themselves, a mental habit that is perhaps borne out in his mature philosophy, whose starting point is Descartes' famous maxim, *COGITO, ERGO SUM* (I think, therefore I exist). Descartes believed that everything apart from one's own existence could be doubted until a proof for it was constructed that was based upon thought reflecting back upon itself. His emphasis upon thought, or upon epistemology in contrast to metaphysics, as the starting point in philosophy marked the beginning of a new era.

Descartes regained his health in his late teens and in his early twenties became a gentleman-soldier. He traveled and became something of a man of the world—until three dreams convinced him that he should devote his life to philosophy. He then became a man with a mission, full of enthusiasm for his new approach to philosophy.

RENÉ DESCARTES

Meditations

* * * * *

Because I know with certitude that I exist, and because, in the meantime, I do not observe that aught necessarily belongs to my nature or essence beyond my being a thinking thing, I rightly conclude that my essence consists only in my being a thinking thing, [or a substance whose whole essence or nature is merely thinking]. And although I may, or rather, as I will shortly say, although I certainly do possess a body with which I am very closely conjoined; nevertheless, because, on the one hand, I have a clear and distinct idea of myself, in as far as I am only a thinking and unextended thing, and as, on the other hand, I possess a distinct idea of body, in as far as it is only an extended and unthinking thing, it is certain that I, [that is, my mind, by which I am what I am], is entirely and truly distinct from my body, and may exist without it.

Moreover, I find in myself diverse faculties of thinking that have each their special mode: for example, I find I possess the faculties of imagining and perceiving, without which I can indeed clearly and distinctly conceive myself as entire, but I cannot reciprocally conceive them without conceiving myself, that is to say, without an intelligent substance in which they reside, for [in the notion we have of them, or to use the terms of the schools] in their formal concept, they comprise some sort of intellection; whence I perceive that they are distinct from myself as modes are from things. I remark likewise certain other faculties, as the power of changing place, of assuming diverse figures, and the like, that cannot be conceived and cannot therefore exist, any more than the preceding, apart from a substance in which they inhere. It is very evident, however, that these faculties, if they really exist, must belong to some corporeal or extended substance, since in their clear and distinct concept there is contained some sort of extension, but no intellection at all.

* * * * *

But there is nothing which that nature teaches me more expressly [or more sensibly] than that I have a body which is ill affected when I feel pain, and stands in need of food and drink when I experience the sensations of hunger and thirst, etc. And therefore I ought not to doubt but that there is some truth in these informations.

A biographical sketch of René Descartes appears on the previous page.

From *The Meditations and Selections from the Principles of René Descartes*, translated by T. J. McCormack, 1901. *Meditations* was originally published in 1641.

Nature likewise teaches me by these sensations of pain, hunger, thirst, etc., that I am not only lodged in my body as a pilot in a vessel, but that I am besides so intimately conjoined, and as it were intermixed with it, that my mind and body compose a certain unity. For if this were not the case, I should not feel pain when my body is hurt, seeing I am merely a thinking thing, but should perceive the wound by the understanding alone, just as a pilot perceives by sight when any part of his vessel is damaged; and when my body has need of food or drink, I should have a clear knowledge of this, and not be made aware of it by the confused sensations of hunger and thirst: for, in truth, all these sensations of hunger, thirst, pain, etc., are nothing more than certain confused modes of thinking, arising from the union and apparent fusion of mind and body.

Besides this, nature teaches me that my own body is surrounded by many other bodies, some of which I have to seek after, and others to shun. And indeed, as I perceive different sorts of colours, sounds, odours, tastes, heat, hardness, etc., I safely conclude that there are in the bodies from which the diverse perceptions of the senses proceed, certain varieties corresponding to them, although, perhaps, not in reality like them; and since, among these diverse perceptions of the senses, some are agreeable, and others disagreeable, there can be no doubt that my body, or rather my entire self, in as far as I am composed of body and mind, may be variously affected, both beneficially and hurtfully, by surrounding bodies.

* * * * *

There is a vast difference between mind and body, in respect that body, from its nature, is always divisible, and that mind is entirely indivisible. For in truth, when I consider the mind, that is, when I consider myself in so far only as I am a thinking thing, I can distinguish in myself no parts, but I very clearly discern that I am somewhat absolutely one and entire; and although the whole mind seems to be united to the whole body, yet, when a foot, an arm, or any other part is cut off, I am conscious that nothing has been taken from my mind; nor can the faculties of willing, perceiving, conceiving, etc., properly be called its parts, for it is the same mind that is exercised [all entire] in willing, in perceiving, and in conceiving, etc. But quite the opposite holds in corporeal or extended things; for I cannot imagine any one of them [how small soever it may be], which I cannot easily sunder in thought, and which, therefore, I do not know to be divisible. This would be sufficient to teach me that the mind or soul of man is entirely different from the body, if I had not already been apprised of it on other grounds.

COMMENTS ■ QUESTIONS

1. For Descartes, the mind is something that is known directly from *within itself*, that is, from introspection, the act of looking into one's own mind. In contrast, the body is known from an *external* point of view, as an object to be observed. The introspective point of view tells us that mind is "altogether indivisible" and that, moreover, the essence of mind is thought itself. The external point of view tells us that body is something physical that can be divided up into spatial parts. The conclusion Descartes draws is that "the mind is entirely different from the body." How much of Descartes' basic philosophy of mind do you believe ought to be accepted? Would you agree, in the first place, with what Descartes says regarding the two points of view from which minds and bodies can be known? Would you agree, secondly, that mind and body are "entirely different"? If you disagree with Descartes, what is the basis for your disagreement?
2. According to Descartes, not only are mind and body "entirely different from each other," but they are also "intimately conjoined [so as to] form a unitary whole." Otherwise, says Descartes, a person's mind, or soul, would be lodged in his body the way that a pilot is lodged in a ship and would not experience hunger, pain, and other bodily sensations in the direct way that they are in fact experienced. In terms of your own perception of yourself, would you agree that your mind and body are intimately conjoined in the way described by Descartes? (Please observe that mind and body cannot be intimately conjoined, or conjoined in any way, unless they are, in themselves, distinct from each other. That is, it would not be correct to speak of them as conjoined if they were one and the same.)

GILBERT RYLE

Descartes' Myth

1. *The Official Doctrine*

There is a doctrine about the nature and place of minds which is so prevalent among theorists and even among laymen that it deserves to be described as the official theory. Most philosophers, psychologists and religious teachers subscribe, with minor reservations, to its main articles and, although they admit certain theoretical difficulties in it, they tend to assume that these can be overcome without serious modifications being made to the architecture of the theory. It will be argued here that the central principles of the doctrine are unsound and conflict with the whole body of what we know about minds when we are not speculating about them.

The official doctrine, which hails chiefly from Descartes, is something like this. With the doubtful exceptions of idiots and infants in arms every human being has both a body and a mind. Some would prefer to say that every human being is both a body and a mind. His body and his mind are ordinarily harnessed together, but after the death of the body his mind may continue to exist and function.

Human bodies are in space and are subject to the mechanical laws which govern all other bodies in space. Bodily processes and states can be inspected by external observers. So a man's bodily life is as much a public affair as are the lives of animals and reptiles and even as the careers of trees, crystals and planets.

But minds are not in space, nor are their operations subject to mechanical laws. The workings of one mind are not witnessable by other observers; its career is private. Only I can take direct cognisance of the states and processes of my own mind. A person therefore lives through two collateral histories, one consisting of what happens in and to his body, the other consisting of what happens in and to his mind. The first is public, the second private. The events in the first history are events in the physical world, those in the second are events in the mental world.

It has been disputed whether a person does or can directly monitor all or only some of the episodes of his own private history; but, according to the official doctrine, of at

---

Gilbert Ryle (1900–1978) was one of the most influential of the British analytical philosophers. For many years, he was editor of the prestigious philosophical journal Mind *and a professor at Oxford University. His book* The Concept of Mind *has become a classic.*

From Gilbert Ryle, *The Concept of Mind*, 1949. By permission of Century Hutchinson Limited.

least some of these episodes he has direct and unchallengeable cognisance. In consciousness, self-consciousness and introspection he is directly and authentically apprised of the present states and operations of his mind. He may have great or small uncertainties about concurrent and adjacent episodes in the physical world, but he can have none about at least part of what is momentarily occupying his mind.

It is customary to express this bifurcation of his two lives and of his two worlds by saying that the things and events which belong to the physical world, including his own body, are external, while the workings of his own mind are internal. This antithesis of outer and inner is of course meant to be construed as a metaphor, since minds, not being in space, could not be described as being spatially inside anything else, or as having things going on spatially inside themselves. But relapses from this good intention are common and theorists are found speculating how stimuli, the physical sources of which are yards or miles outside a person's skin, can generate mental responses inside his skull, or how decisions framed inside his cranium can set going movements of his extremities.

Even when "inner" and "outer" are construed as metaphors, the problem how a person's mind and body influence one another is notoriously charged with theoretical difficulties. What the mind wills, the legs, arms and the tongue execute; what affects the ear and the eye has something to do with what the mind perceives; grimaces and smiles betray the mind's moods and bodily castigations lead, it is hoped, to moral improvement. But the actual transactions between the episodes of the private history and those of the public history remain mysterious, since by definition they can belong to neither series. They could not be reported among the happenings described in a person's autobiography of his inner life, but nor could they be reported among those described in some one else's biography of that person's overt career. They can be inspected neither by introspection nor by laboratory experiment. They are theoretical shuttlecocks which are forever being bandied from the physiologist back to the psychologist and from the psychologist back to the physiologist.

Underlying this partly metaphorical representation of the bifurcation of a person's two lives there is a seemingly more profound and philosophical assumption. It is assumed that there are two different kinds of existence or status. What exists or happens may have the status of physical existence, or it may have the status of mental existence. Somewhat as the faces of coins are either heads or tails, or somewhat as living creatures are either male or female, so, it is supposed, some existing is physical existing, other existing is mental existing. It is a necessary feature of what has physical existence that it is in space and time; it is a necessary feature of what has mental existence that it is in time but not in space. What has physical existence is composed of matter, or else is a function of matter; what has mental existence consists of consciousness, or else is a function of consciousness.

There is thus a polar opposition between mind and matter, an opposition which is often brought out as follows. Material objects are situated in a common field, known as "space", and what happens to one body in one part of space is mechanically connected with what happens to other bodies in other parts of space. But mental happenings occur in insulated fields, known as "minds", and there is, apart maybe from telepathy, no direct causal connection between what happens in one mind and what happens in another. Only through the medium of the public physical world can the mind of one person make a difference to the mind of another. The mind is its own place and in his inner life each of us lives the life of a ghostly Robinson Crusoe. People can see, hear and jolt one another's bodies, but they are irremediably blind and deaf to the workings of one another's minds and inoperative upon them.

What sort of knowledge can be secured of the workings of a mind? On the one side, according to the official theory, a person has direct knowledge of the best imaginable kind of the workings of his own mind. Mental states and processes are (or are normally) conscious states and processes, and the consciousness which irradiates them can engender no illusions and leaves the door open for no doubts. A person's present thinkings, feelings and willings, his perceivings, rememberings and imaginings are intrinsically "phosphorescent"; their existence and their nature are inevitably betrayed to their owner. The inner life is a stream of consciousness of such a sort that it would be absurd to suggest that the mind whose life is that stream might be unaware of what is passing down it.

* * * * *

On the other side, one person has no direct access of any sort to the events of the inner life of another. He cannot do better than make problematic inferences from the observed behaviour of the other person's body to the states of mind which, by analogy from his own conduct, he supposes to be signalised by that behaviour. Direct access to the workings of a mind is the privilege of that mind itself; in default of such privileged access, the workings of one mind are inevitably occult to everyone else. For the supposed arguments from bodily movements similar to their own to mental workings similar to their own would lack any possibility of observational corroboration. Not unnaturally, therefore, an adherent of the official theory finds it difficult to resist this consequence of his premises, that he has no good reason to believe that there do exist minds other than his own. Even if he prefers to believe that to other human bodies there are harnessed minds not unlike his own, he cannot claim to be able to discover their individual characteristics, or the particular things that they undergo and do. Absolute solitude is on this showing the ineluctable destiny of the soul. Only our bodies can meet.

As a necessary corollary of this general scheme there is implicitly prescribed a special way of construing our ordinary concepts of mental powers and operations. The verbs, nouns and adjectives, with which in ordinary life we describe the wits, characters and higher-grade performances of the people with whom we have do, are required to be construed as signifying special episodes in their secret histories, or else as signifying tendencies for such episodes to occur. When someone is described as knowing, believing or guessing something, as hoping, dreading, intending or shirking something, as designing this or being amused at that, these verbs are supposed to denote the occurrence of specific modifications in his (to us) occult stream of consciousness. Only his own privileged access to this stream in direct awareness and introspection could provide authentic testimony that these mental-conduct verbs were correctly or incorrectly applied. The onlooker, be he teacher, critic, biographer or friend, can never assure himself that his comments have any vestige of truth. Yet it was just because we do in fact all know how to make such comments, make them with general correctness and correct them when they turn out to be confused or mistaken, that philosophers found it necessary to construct their theories of the nature and place of minds. Finding mental-conduct concepts being regularly and effectively used, they properly sought to fix their logical geography. But the logical geography officially recommended would entail that there could be no regular or effective use of these mental-conduct concepts in our descriptions of, and prescriptions for, other people's minds.

2. *The Absurdity of the Official Doctrine*

Such in outline is the official theory. I shall often speak of it, with deliberate abusiveness, as "the dogma of the Ghost in the Machine". I hope to prove that it is entirely false, and false not in detail but in principle. It is not merely an assemblage of particular mistakes. It is one big mistake and a mistake of a special kind. It is, namely, a category-mistake. It represents the facts of mental life as if they belonged to one logical type or category (or range of types or categories), when they actually belong to another. The dogma is therefore a philosopher's myth. In attempting to explode the myth I shall probably be taken to be denying well-known facts about the mental life of human beings, and my plea that I aim at doing nothing more than rectify the logic of mental-conduct concepts will probably be disallowed as mere subterfuge.

I must first indicate what is meant by the phrase "Category-mistake". This I do in a series of illustrations.

A foreigner visiting Oxford or Cambridge for the first time is shown a number of colleges, libraries, playing fields, museums, scientific departments and administrative offices. He then asks "But where is the University? I have seen where the members of the Colleges live, where the Registrar works, where the scientists experiment and the rest. But I have not yet seen the University in which reside and work the members of your University." It has then to be explained to him that the University is not another collateral institution, some ulterior counterpart to the colleges, laboratories and offices which he has seen. The University is just the way in which all that he has already seen is organized. When they are seen and when their co-ordination is understood, the University has been seen. His mistake lay in his innocent assumption that it was correct to speak of Christ Church, the Bodleian Library, the Ashmolean Museum *and* the University, to speak, that is, as if "the University" stood for an extra member of the class of which these other units are members. He was mistakenly allocating the University to the same category as that to which the other institutions belong.

The same mistake would be made by a child witnessing the march-past of a division, who, having had pointed out to him such and such battalions, batteries, squadrons, etc., asked when the division was going to appear. He would be supposing that a division was a counterpart to the units already seen, partly similar to them and partly unlike them. He would be shown his mistake by being told that in watching the battalions, batteries and squadrons marching past he had been watching the division marching past. The march-past was not a parade of battalions, batteries, squadrons *and* a division; it was a parade of the battalions, batteries and squadrons *of* a division.

One more illustration. A foreigner watching his first game of cricket learns what are the functions of the bowlers, the batsmen, the fielders, the umpires and the scorers. He then says "But there is no one left on the field to contribute the famous element of team-spirit. I see who does the bowling, the batting and the wicketkeeping; but I do not see whose role it is to exercise *esprit de corps*." Once more, it would have to be explained that he was looking for the wrong type of thing. Team-spirit is not another cricketing-operation supplementary to all of the other special tasks. It is, roughly, the keenness with which each of the special tasks is performed, and performing a task keenly is not performing two tasks. Certainly exhibiting team-spirit is not the same thing as bowling or catching, but nor is it a third thing such that we can say that the bowler first bowls *and* then exhibits team-spirit or that a fielder is at a given moment *either* catching *or* displaying *esprit de corps*.

These illustrations of category-mistakes have a common feature which must be noticed. The mistakes were made by people who did not know how to wield the concepts *University, division* and *team-spirit*. Their puzzles arose from inability to use certain items in the English vocabulary.

The theoretically interesting category-mistakes are those made by people who are perfectly competent to apply concepts, at least in the situations with which they are familiar, but are still liable in their abstract thinking to allocate those concepts to logical types to which they do not belong. An instance of a mistake of this sort would be the following story. A student of politics has learned the main differences between the British, the French and the American Constitutions, and has learned also the differences and connections between the Cabinet, Parliament, the various Ministries, the Judicature and the Church of England. But he still becomes embarrassed when asked questions about the connections between the Church of England, the Home Office and the British Constitution. For while the Church and the Home Office are institutions, the British Constitution is not another institution in the same sense of that noun. So inter-institutional relations which can be asserted or denied to hold between the

Church and the Home Office cannot be asserted or denied to hold between either of them and the British Constitution. "The British Constitution" is not a term of the same logical type as "the Home Office" and "the Church of England". In a partially similar way, John Doe may be a relative, a friend, an enemy or a stranger to Richard Roe; but he cannot be any of these things to the Average Taxpayer. He knows how to talk sense in certain sorts of discussions about the Average Taxpayer, but he is baffled to say why he could not come across him in the street as he can come across Richard Roe.

It is pertinent to our main subject to notice that, so long as the student of politics continues to think of the British Constitution as a counterpart to the other institutions, he will tend to describe it as a mysteriously occult institution; and so long as John Doe continues to think of the Average Taxpayer as a fellow-citizen, he will tend to think of him as an elusive insubstantial man, a ghost who is everywhere yet nowhere.

My destructive purpose is to show that a family of radical category-mistakes is the source of the double-life theory. The representation of a person as a ghost mysteriously ensconced in a machine derives from this argument. Because, as is true, a person's thinking, feeling and purposive doing cannot be described solely in the idioms of physics, chemistry and physiology, therefore they must be described in counterpart idioms. As the human body is a complex organized unit, so the human mind must be another complex organised unit, though one made of a different sort of stuff and with a different sort of structure. Or, again, as the human body, like any other parcel of matter, is a field of causes and effects, so the mind must be another field of causes and effects, though not (Heaven be praised) mechanical causes and effects.

* * * * *

When two terms belong to the same category, it is proper to construct conjunctive propositions embodying them. Thus a purchaser may say that he bought a left-hand glove and a right-hand glove, but not that he bought a left-hand glove, a right-hand glove and a pair of gloves. "She came home in a flood of tears and a sedan-chair" is a well-known joke based on the absurdity of conjoining terms of different types. It would have been equally ridiculous to construct the disjunction "She came home either in a flood of tears or else in a sedan-chair". Now the dogma of the Ghost in the Machine does just this. It maintains that there exist both bodies and minds; that there occur physical processes and mental processes; that there are mechanical causes of corporeal movements and mental causes of corporeal movements. I shall argue that these and other analogous conjunctions are absurd; but, it must be noticed, the argument will not show that either of the illegitimately conjoined propositions is absurd in itself. I am not, for example, denying that there occur mental processes. Doing long division is a mental process and so is making a joke. But I am saying that the phrase "there occur mental processes" does not mean the same sort of thing as "there occur physical processes", and, therefore, that it makes no sense to conjoin or disjoin the two.

If my argument is successful, there will follow some interesting consequences. First, the hallowed contrast between Mind and Matter will be dissipated, but dissipated not by either of the equally hallowed absorptions of Mind by Matter or of Matter by Mind, but in quite a different way. For the seeming contrast of the two will be shown to be as illegitimate as would be the contrast of "she came home in a flood of tears" and "she came home in a sedan-chair". The belief that there is a polar opposition between Mind and Matter is the belief that they are terms of the same logical type.

It will also follow that both Idealism and Materialism are answers to an improper question. The "reduction" of the material world to mental states and processes, as well as the "reduction" of mental states and processes to physical states and processes, presuppose the legitimacy of the disjunction "Either there exist minds or there exist bodies (but not both)". It would be like saying, "Either she bought a left-hand and a right-hand glove or she bought a pair of gloves (but not both)".

It is perfectly proper to say, in one logical tone of voice, that there exist minds and to say, in another logical tone of voice, that there exist bodies. But these expressions do not indicate two different species of existence, for "existence" is not a generic word like "coloured" or "sexed". They indicate two different senses of "exist", somewhat as "rising" has different senses in "the tide is rising", "hopes are rising", and "the average age of death is rising". A man would be thought to be making a poor joke who said that three things are now rising, namely the tide, hopes and the average age of death. It would be just as good or bad a joke to say that there exist prime numbers and Wednesdays and public opinions and navies; or that there exist both minds and bodies. In the succeeding chapters I try to prove that the official theory does rest on a batch of category-mistakes by showing that logically absurd corollaries follow from it. The exhibition of these absurdities will have the constructive effect of bringing out part of the correct logic of mental-conduct concepts.

COMMENTS ■ QUESTIONS

1. One reason philosophy is difficult for beginning students (and for everyone else) is evident in this selection from Ryle. Not only does Ryle wish to argue that Descartes' philosophy of mind is completely wrong, but he also wishes to defend a difficult philosophical concept—that of a "category-mistake"—as a tool to be used in arguing against Descartes. Philosophy, as we have said, is never a straightforward journey from point A to point B. The first question to ask yourself, then, regarding Ryle's discussion of Descartes is this: Is the concept of a category-mistake clear?

If you believe that it is, and that you understand how it can be applied in other contexts, you can then go on to ask whether Ryle has succeeded in showing that Descartes has made a category-mistake.

2. In calling the Cartesian mind a "Ghost in the Machine," Ryle means to say that human beings have no special "inner" perspective on the mind as a separate substance. Has Ryle given good reasons for believing that the mind as understood by Descartes is a Ghost in the Machine?

DAVID M. ARMSTRONG

Identification of the Mental With the Physical

* * * * *

But now we can ask "What objection is there to identifying mental states with physico-chemical states of the central nervous system?" It has been argued that mental states are states of the person defined solely in terms of causal relations, of a more or less complex sort, to the objects or situations that bring the mental states about and the physical behaviour that constitutes their "expression". In the same way, genes are defined solely in terms of their causal relations to hereditary characteristics. (These hereditary characteristics could be said to be the "expressions" of the genes.) There is good theoretical (as opposed to observational) scientific evidence to identify genes with the DNA molecule at the centre of living cells. *Assuming that our account of the concept of a mental occurrence is correct*, is there not almost equally good evidence to identify mental occurrences with physico-chemical states of the central nervous system?

Objections to the identification

David M. Armstrong is Challis Professor of Philosophy at the University of Sydney, Australia. In addition to A Materialist Theory of Mind, *he has written many other influential books. Among them are* Universals and Scientific Realism, Perception and the Physical World, *and* What Is a Law of Nature?

From D. M. Armstrong, *A Materialist Theory of the Mind*, Routledge and Kegan Paul, 1968. Reprinted by permission of Routledge and Kegan Paul and Humanities Press International, Inc., Atlantic Highlands, N.J.

may be classed under two heads. In the first place, the identification may be resisted because it is thought that physico-chemical processes in the central nervous system are not in fact adequate to explain the whole range of human behaviour. In the second place, it may be granted that physico-chemical processes are adequate to explain human behaviour, but the identification of mind and brain may still be resisted for other reasons. Objections of the first sort seem to be intellectually serious, those of the second sort intellectually frivolous. The reasons for making this distinction will emerge.

When considering the first sort of objections it is convenient to make a further distinction: between objections drawn from those manifestations of mind which everybody grants to exist, and objections drawn from those manifestations whose existence is a matter of dispute. The first class will include everything from "perceiving that there is an orange before us" and "adding five to seven" up to "writing the plays of Shakespeare" and "making the discoveries of Newton". The second class is the class of "paranormal" manifestations. It includes such alleged facts as the occurrence of telepathy and clairvoyance. Let us begin by considering the former or incontestable manifestations of mind.

We are now moving in the realm of science and empirical fact, not in the realm of logical possibility that is appropriate to conceptual analysis. It must therefore be accepted without dispute that physico-chemical processes in the central nervous system are one of the factors that determine the behaviour of men and the higher animals. All that may be questioned is whether such processes are *wholly* responsible for behaviour.

If we consider the known activities of man, it is clear that such things as intellectual discovery and artistic creation, and in particular such transcendent facts as the discoveries of Newton or the plays of Shakespeare are the facts that present Materialists with greatest difficulty. For intellectual discovery and artistic creation may be said to be "higher" activities of man in a perfectly objective sense: they are activities of greater complexity and sophistication than other human activities. It will be particularly hard to see how they can be products of a mere physical mechanism.

The anti-Materialist may here take his stand either on a stronger or on a weaker contention. In the first place, he may maintain that it is empirically impossible for *any* physical mechanism to produce such manifestations. In the second place, he may grant the possibility of a physical mechanism producing such manifestations, but may maintain that in fact man's body contains no mechanism that can undertake the task.

The first contention is being gradually undermined by the designing, and building, of machines that can duplicate an increasing range of human performances. It is true that no machine has yet been built which can be said to exhibit ingenuity or creativity in what it does. Present machines, for instance, can solve mathematical problems only if they are the sort of problem that can be answered by a set step-by-step procedure. But it is very unlikely that this represents the upper limit of the performances of machines, and suggestions already exist for the designing of a machine that will exhibit ingenuity. (Cf. J.J.C. Smart, *Philosophy and Scientific Realism*, Routledge, 1963, Ch. VI, Sect. 3, "Problem-solving ingenuity".) And if the 'ingenuity-barrier' is broken it will be very arbitrary still to maintain that there are other expressions of mind that are beyond the powers of a mechanism to produce.

However, an anti-Materialist who concedes that a machine which could duplicate the expression of the full range of human mental activity is physically possible may still maintain that mental states are not physical states of the central nervous system because in fact no mechanism that has this capacity can be found in the human body. In practice, however, this line of defence is seldom taken. Once the anti-Materialist has been convinced of the physical possibility of a mechanism that can produce a certain range of mind-like manifestations, he generally concedes that such a physical mechanism, or something not too dissimilar, will be found at work in the central nervous system. (Indeed, the construction or projection of mechanisms that produce mind-like manifestations has turned out to be one of the best sources of fruitful hypotheses about the workings of the central nervous system.)

Nevertheless, someone may argue that the anti-Materialist has let himself be satisfied so easily only because our knowledge of the central nervous system is as yet so slight. It may be that a really detailed knowledge of the workings of the brain would make it clear that it was inadequate for the discovery of the Law of Gravitation or the writing of *King Lear*.

The possibility may be freely admitted, and it may be freely admitted that it is more than a bare logical possibility. But what reasons are there to think that it is a possibility that has any great probability? I am not aware of any such reasons.

There is an interesting compromise possibility here which falls between a pure physico-chemical Materialism and an Attribute theory of the mind. It is possible to argue that the whole range of man's behaviour springs causally from physical processes in his central nervous system, but still to say that some at least of these physical processes are not the sort of thing that can be accounted for in terms of the laws of physics and chemistry. That is to say, one can hold that certain processes in the central nervous system operate according to *emergent* laws, laws that cannot be deduced, even in principle, from the laws of physics and chemistry. As a result, behaviour occurs that could not be produced by something working according to purely physico-chemical principles. Such a view would still be a Materialism, for it would not demand any emergent qualities, still less an emergent substance, but it would not be a *physico-chemical* Materialism.

The most natural hypothesis here would be that these emergent laws were something that developed in *all* physical systems that reached a certain degree of complex interrelation. In this way one would avoid the arbitrariness of associating the emergent laws with a high degree of complexity in *biological* systems only. One might expect a man-built machine of the requisite degree of complexity to operate according to the emergent laws just as much as the central nervous system did.

Again, if one did accept an hypothesis of this sort one would need to be more sympathetic to the idea of emergent laws generally. One would expect to find that *all* biological systems, which, after all, involve much more complex interrelations of components than ordinary physical systems, operate according to laws that transcend the principles of physics and chemistry. It would be a surprisingly arbitrary feature of the system of scientific laws if the physico-chemical laws applied to all ordinary collections of matter and there was just one point where a jump to emergent laws occurred: with the emergence of mind.

As I have said already, I know of no compelling scientific reason to make us think that even the discoveries of Newton or the art of Shakespeare require that we postulate emergent laws of operation in the central nervous system. Nevertheless, if such reasons exist, or are later discovered, then falling back upon this "Emergent-law" Materialism will be a quite natural and ontologically quite economical move.

(It may be remarked here, in passing, that a Parallelist of any sort must agree that the workings of the brain are by themselves sufficient to account for the whole range of human behaviour, although it is true that he may take an emergentist view of the laws according to which the brain works. For according to the Parallelist, mental states play no part in the causation of behaviour. If one wants to say that the brain is insufficient to account causally for the whole range of human behaviour one will have to be a Dualist and an Interactionist about the mind.)

It may be objected to "Emergent-law" Materialism that it could not be distinguished from Interactionist Dualism. Suppose that a physical event in the central nervous system is followed after a brief interval by another physical event, but the occurrence of the second event is inexplicable in physico-chemical terms. The "Emergent-law" Materialist postulates emergent laws of matter to explain the phenomenon. But a Dualist could explain what happened by saying that the first physical event brought about changes in a spiritual substance which in turn brought about the second physical event. How could we choose between the two hypotheses?

In answer to this objection it must be pointed out that the Dualist view can be developed in two different ways. If developed the first way, there would be no possible experimental decision between Dualism and "Emergent-law" Materialism. Considerations of economy, however, would favour the latter view. If developed in the second, more plausible, way, it would be possible in principle to decide the question empirically.

Suppose that the central nervous system is in a certain physical state. A physical event in the system brings about a spiritual event which brings about a further physical event. Is the causal efficacy of the spiritual substance on this occasion determined solely by the first physical event? Suppose firstly that it is. There are then laws to be discovered which permit us, given the current physical state of the central nervous system, to predict in principle the second physical event from the first physical event. Now how in this case do we decide that a spiritual event does play a part in the causal chain? How do we rule out the view that the first physical event gives rise to the second physical event directly, although according to "emergent" laws? We cannot. There is no possible observational difference between the theories as they are presented. However, every consideration of ontological economy tells against the Dualist view.

Suppose, more plausibly, that what happens in the spiritual substance, and the nature of the second physical event, is determined not simply by the first physical event *but also by what has happened to the spiritual substance in the past*. No straightforward prediction from the first physical event to the second event will then be possible. The impossibility of such a prediction would then be evidence for the truth of Interactionist Dualism. Of course, given that the genesis and subsequent history of the spiritual substance is determined solely by physical factors in the central nervous system, it would still be possible to argue that the second physical event followed on directly, by "emergent" laws, but without a spiritual event as intermediary, from the first physical event *in conjunction with other physical events in the past*. But the hypothesis would become so complicated that postulation of a spiritual substance that interacted with the brain would clearly be the better hypothesis. "Emergent-law" Materialism can therefore be distinguished from Interactionist Dualism.

The Materialist also has another line of retreat available in face of evidence that appears to contradict a materialist view of the mind, that may be even more congenial to him. It is conceivable that the whole range of human behaviour can be explained as an effect of the working of the brain, but that that working cannot be explained in terms of the physical principles that we *now* have. It might still be explained by a recasting of physics. Instead of admitting the existence of emergent laws we might discover a new basis for physics in terms of which the apparently special way of working of the brain becomes something derivable in principle from the basic laws of physics, applied to the particular physical structure of the brain.

If new basic principles for physics could explain, and could predict, ordinary (that is, non-mental) phenomena *at least* as well as those currently accepted, and if in addition they were able to predict the anomalous behaviour of the central nervous system, then we could switch to the new physics in the interest of a unified scheme of explanation. Of course, it is easy enough to talk airily of a new physics when one is not faced with the task of actually producing one. But it is one way that the Materialist could defend his monistic vision.

Nevertheless, it is conceivable that it should prove impossible to explain some human activities—presumably the "higher" activities—either in terms of emergent laws of working of the central nervous system or by recasting our physics. In that case Central-state Materialism would be false, although the *analysis* of the mental concepts put forward in Part Two—the Causal analysis—might still be true.

So much for those manifestations

of mind that everybody grants to have been manifested. We may now consider "paranormal" phenomena. These include telepathy, clairvoyance, precognition, psychokinesis (the direct action of mind on material objects) and disembodied existence.

The first great question that faces us here is whether these phenomena exist at all. If they do not, they constitute no objection to Central-state Materialism, for their mere logical possibility is no objection to a *contingent* identification of mind and brain. Now, not all those who have studied the subject closely are convinced of the occurrence of any of the alleged phenomena. (An article such as Michael Scriven's "New Frontiers of the Brain", *Journal of Parapsychology*, Vol. 25, 1961, pp. 305–18, gives a physicalist a great deal of comfort.)

In considering this question, it seems reasonable to let the matter turn on whether *experimentally reproducible* phenomena can be found. Admittedly this is a rigorous criterion, but, since it is almost a logical precondition of the scientific investigation of the phenomena, it is one that it seems methodologically correct to make.

Now the amount of suggestive experimental material is not very large, but there is a small body of results which are, at any rate, difficult to explain except by admitting that some paranormal faculty is being exercised. In particular, there is some experimental evidence for telepathy, and/or clairvoyance, and/or precognition. (I have put the conclusion in this ambiguous way because the evidence is regularly susceptible of different interpretations. To give an over-simple illustration. Suppose that a subject appears to have precognitive knowledge of what card in a pack will be turned up two times ahead. If we were dealing with a pack that was not shuffled between turns the fact could equally well be explained by postulating mere clairvoyant knowledge of the card that is now two from the top. Given this clairvoyant knowledge, a perfectly ordinary inference will suffice to yield the apparently "precognitive" knowledge.) And once it is allowed that the experimental material gives positive results, many of the alleged phenomena that did not occur under experimental conditions become plausible candidates for paranormal phenomena.

Suppose, then, that there are in fact paranormal phenomena. The question arises whether they stand in any necessary opposition to Central-state Materialism. Consider telepathy for instance. We might define telepathy as the gaining of non-inferential knowledge of what goes on in the mind of another. Or, to adopt a definition that is in better accord with the experimental facts, it is the making of guesses without evidence about what is currently going on in the mind of another, guesses that are significantly more successful than the results that could be attributed to mere chance. This phenomenon, if it exists, is "paranormal" because the only normal way to discover what is going on in the mind of another is to make an inference from what his body does. But why does this phenomenon contradict Central-state Materialism? Could there not be some as yet undiscovered physical processes (perhaps processes of a perfectly familiar kind in other contexts) which link one central nervous system with another, and so permit the transmission of information? And similar suggestions might be made about other paranormal phenomena.

Such suggestions may turn out to dissolve the problem posed by these phenomena without in any way disturbing Central-state Materialism. Nevertheless, if we consider the particular nature of the alleged phenomena, then, if they actually occur, it is not easy to find explanations within the framework of physics as we know it. For instance, it is an initially not unpromising suggestion that telepathic communication of information is mediated by some physical radiation emitted by one central nervous system and picked up by another. This hypothesis can be tested by conducting telepathic experiments with subjects isolated from each other by radiation-proof containers. Now such experiments have actually been carried out in the U.S.S.R., and it is claimed that guesses made about what was going on in the other minds in such conditions were still significantly better than chance expectation. (*Cf. Experiments in Mental Suggestion*, L. L. Vasiliev, English translation: Institute for the Study of Mental Images, 1963.) If the experiments can be repeated, an explanation of telepathy in terms of radiation will seem very implausible. But, given the careful design of modern experiments, what other channels of physical communication between subject and subject can be suggested? We could say that the radiation involved is quite unlike the physical radiation blocked by "radiation-proof" boxes. But then we are beginning to abandon the known structure of physics.

If precognition is a reality, it is still more difficult to explain. It is true that there is no particular difficulty in understanding the abstract possibility of non-inferential knowledge of the future. Suppose a system, S, is moving in a certain direction. Let us make the supposition that it is likely to be unimpeded, and that, if unimpeded, it will come to be in state S_1. It is easy to imagine that before the system comes to be in state S_1, a small portion of its energy "hives off" and acts upon a mind, producing in that mind non-inferential knowledge that S will shortly be in state S_1. Any warning-system, such as the oil-light in a car, works on similar principles, although it produces a less sophisticated result: the turning on of a light, not non-inferential knowledge. Indeed, it is possible that we sometimes acquire information of the sort like "I am going to be ill" not on the basis of any evidence, but simply as a result of the operation of such a mechanism producing in us non-inferential knowledge of our future bodily states.

But if we consider actual cases where precognitive ability is claimed, it is difficult to apply an explanation of this sort. For instance, suppose a subject guesses with better than chance results what sort of card will be turned up, but between each guess the pack is thoroughly shuffled by a random procedure. The physical causes that go to making a particular card turn up are incredibly many, and incredibly complexly interrelated. It then becomes almost impossible to see how "information" could be transmitted from that concatenation of causes which would be correlated in any degree with the result that the causes are about to bring into existence. So this sort of precognition, if it occurs, seems to defy all accepted patterns of explanation.

It is true that this is not the end of the argument. The Materialist might still take one of the two ways of escape discussed in connection with "normal" as opposed to "paranormal" phenomena. He might try to work out an emergent materialism, with special laws for the central nervous system not derivable, even in principle, from ordinary physics. Or he might seek for a new physics which, within a unified set of principles, would explain and predict not only the ordinary capacities of matter and of men, but also the paranormal skills of men. But if these ways of escape prove unsatisfactory, Central-state Materialism cannot be the whole truth about the mind.

I consider that the claims of psychical research are the small black cloud on the horizon of a Materialist theory of mind. If there were no questions about paranormal phenomena to consider, there would seem to be little serious obstacle to the *complete* identification of mental states with physico-chemical states of the central nervous system. (This, of course, is assuming that the *logical* objections can be met.) The identification would be as certain as the identification of the gene with the DNA molecule. The apparent existence of paranormal phenomena must leave a small doubt. The upholder of any scientific doctrine has an intellectual duty to consider very carefully the evidence that seems most likely to undermine his view. So the Central-state Materialist has an intellectual duty to consider very carefully the alleged results of psychical research.

Finally, we may briefly consider the position of those who grant that the physico-chemical processes in the central nervous system are adequate causes of the whole of human behaviour, but who nevertheless resist the identification of mental states with states of the brain. It is this position I described at the beginning of this chapter as intellectually frivolous.

It is important, once again, to re-emphasize that in this chapter I am assuming the general truth of the account of the mental concepts given in Part Two. We may therefore ignore here the position of those who argue, for instance, that it is evident to introspection that mental states are something different from, or are something more than, states of the person apt for the production of certain sorts of behaviour. Now if one accepts an account of mental states in terms of their causal relations to behaviour; and at the same time one agrees that physical operations of the brain are adequate to bring about all human behaviour; and yet one still wants to resist the identification of mental states and brain states; there seems to be only one position one can adopt. One must say that physical processes in the brain give rise to mental processes of a non-material sort which in turn give rise to behaviour. The mental processes must be inserted into the causal chain at some point, although the chain unfolds in exactly the same way that it would unfold if there was no such insertion. (*Cf.* the quarrel between an "Emergent-law" Materialism and a form of Interactionist Dualism where the interaction occurs in such a way that both theories yield exactly the same predictions.)

Now this is a logical possibility. It is logically compatible with the observed facts. But every principle of simplicity in science speaks against adopting the view. In order to see that this is so, consider another logical possibility. Perhaps it is the case that, at a certain point in the course of its operations, the DNA molecule brings into existence an immaterial principle. This immaterial principle in turn has further effects: the transmission of hereditary characteristics. The whole chain of causes operates exactly as if it were a physical chain, but in fact it contains this one immaterial link. One can see clearly that, although this hypothesis is a logically possible one, and logically compatible with the observed facts, it has nothing to recommend it. The same may be said of the parallel hypothesis about the mind.

This brings our long argument to an end. One of the great problems that must be solved in any attempt to work out a scientific world-view is that of bringing the being who puts forward the world-view *within* the world-view. By treating man, including his mental processes, as a purely physical object, operating according to exactly the same laws as all other physical things, this object is achieved with the greatest possible intellectual economy. The knower differs from the world he knows only in the greater complexity of his physical organization. Man is one with nature.

We must recognize, however, that even if the doctrine of mind put forward in this book is correct, a physicalist philosophy is not at the end, but rather at the beginning, of its problems. The clearing away of the problem of mind only brings us face to face with the deeper problems connected with matter. Such notions as substance, cause, law, space and time, remain in as much obscurity as ever when we have given an account of the local and temporary phenomenon of mind purely in terms of such concepts. A physicalist theory of mind is a mere prolegomenon to a physicalist metaphysics. Such a metaphysics, like the theory of mind, will no doubt be the joint product of scientific investigation and philosophical reflection.

COMMENTS ■ QUESTIONS

1. The selection reprinted here is the last chapter in Armstrong's book *A Materialist Theory of the Mind*. In the present selection, Armstrong focuses his attention on a single (but important) step in the materialist's argument: the claim by materialists that the entire range of human behavior can be explained in terms of the physicochemical processes of the central nervous system. In an earlier part of the book, Armstrong argues that the best way to talk about "inner" mental states is in terms of "outward" human behavior—that is, by reducing mentalistic concepts to behavioral concepts. This account of mentalistic concepts puts Armstrong in the tradition of Gilbert Ryle. In the present selection, Armstrong argues that, given a behavioral account of mental states, there is no good reason not to identify the mental with the physical. Is Armstrong correct about this? That is, does the identification of the mental with the physical follow from a behavioral account of mental states, or mental concepts?
2. According to Armstrong, the strongest objection to his position is the claim that intellectual discovery and artistic creation are types of human behavior that *cannot* be explained in terms of the physicochemical processes of the central nervous system. People claim that a machine (a "mere physical mechanism") could not have discovered the Law of Gravity or written *Hamlet*. Armstrong's response is that computers are being designed and built that can perform more and more of the mental operations of human beings; and, he says, there is no reason to believe that in principle, a machine could not duplicate all mental functions. In your opinion, is Armstrong correct about this? If he is not correct, how could it be shown that he is not correct? (The last selection in this chapter, by Paul Ziff, is relevant to answering this question.)
3. Another objection to Armstrong's materialist theory of the mind is the claim that, while the mental may be identical with the physical, the physical is more complex than Armstrong is willing to allow. Armstrong wants to reduce everything to the laws or principles of physics and chemistry; the objection is that certain biological processes can be explained only in terms of laws (called *emergent laws*) that cannot be reduced to the laws or principles of physics and chemistry. Armstrong does not believe that emergent laws are needed; but, he says, if it can be shown that they are needed, materialism can still be defended. Is this an adequate answer? (Armstrong's discussion of emergent laws is probably the most difficult part of the selection; the concept of an emergent law is worth getting clear about, however, because other writers quite

often appeal to it.)

4. Armstrong says that "the claims of psychical research [into the question of whether such phenomena as ESP or precognition exist] are the small black cloud on the horizon of a materialist theory of mind." The cloud is small, he says, because it may well be that no "paranormal" phenomena exist or, if they do, that a materialist explanation (that may or may not make use of emergent laws) could account for them. How small would you say that the "black cloud" is? (See chapter 13 for a discussion of related issues.)

WILLIAM JAMES

On the Theory of the Soul

* * * * *

The theory of the Soul is the theory of popular philosophy and of scholasticism, which is only popular philosophy made systematic. It declares that the principle of individuality within us must be *substantial*, for psychic phenomena are activities, and there can be no activity without a concrete agent. This substantial agent cannot be the brain but must be something *immaterial;* for its activity, thought, is both immaterial, and takes cognizance of immaterial things, and of material things in general and intelligible, as well as in particular and sensible ways,—all which powers are incompatible with the nature of matter, of which the brain is composed.

* * * * *

If we ask what a Substance is, the only answer is that it is a self-existent being, or one which needs no other subject in which to inhere. At bottom its only positive determination is Being, and this is something whose meaning we all realize even though we find it hard to explain. The Soul is moreover an *individual* being, and if we ask what that is, we are told to look in upon our Self, and we shall learn by direct intuition better than through any abstract reply.

* * * * *

This substantialist view of the soul was essentially the view of Plato and

---

A biographical sketch of William James is to be found in chapter 3.

From *Principles of Psychology*, 1890.

of Aristotle. It received its completely formal elaboration in the middle ages. It was believed in by Hobbes, Descartes, Locke, Leibnitz, Wolf, Berkeley, and is now defended by the entire modern dualistic or spiritualistic or common-sense school. Kant held to it while denying its fruitfulness as a premise for deducing consequences verifiable here below. Kant's successors, the absolute idealists, profess to have discarded it,—how that may be we shall inquire ere long. Let us make up our minds what to think of it ourselves.

It is at all events needless for expressing the actual subjective phenomena of consciousness as they appear. We have formulated them all without its aid, by the supposition of a stream of thoughts, each substantially different from the rest, but cognitive of the rest and "appropriative" of each other's content. At least, if I have not already succeeded in making this plausible to the reader, I am hopeless of convincing him by anything I could add now. The unity, the identity, the individuality, and the immateriality that appear in the psychic life are thus accounted for as phenomenal and temporal facts exclusively, and with no need of reference to any more simple or substantial agent than the present Thought or "section" of the stream. We have seen it to be single and unique in the sense of having no *separable* parts—perhaps that is the only kind of simplicity meant to be predicated of the soul. The present Thought also has being,—at least all believers in the Soul believe so—and if there be no other Being in which it "inheres," it ought itself to be a "substance." If *this* kind of simplicity and substantiality were all that is predicated of the Soul, then it might appear that we had been talking of the soul all along, without knowing it, when we treated the present Thought as an agent, an owner, and the like. But the Thought is a perishing and not an immortal or incorruptible thing. Its successors may continuously succeed to it, resemble it, and appropriate it, but they *are* not it, whereas the Soul-Substance is supposed to be a fixed unchanging thing. By the Soul is always meant something *behind* the present Thought, another kind of substance, existing on a non-phenomenal plane.

When we brought in the Soul . . . as an entity which the various brain-processes were supposed to affect simultaneously, and which responded to their combined influence by single pulses of its thought, it was to escape integrated mind-stuff on the one hand, and an improbable cerebral monad on the other. But when (as now, after all we have been through since that earlier passage) we take the two formulations, first of a brain to whose processes pulses of thought *simply* correspond, and second, of one to whose processes pulses of thought *in a Soul* correspond, and compare them together, we see that at bottom the second formulation is only a more roundabout way than the first, of expressing the same bald fact. That bald fact is that *when the brain acts, a thought occurs*. The spiritualistic formulation says that the brain-processes knock the thought, so to speak, out of a Soul which stands there to receive their influence. The simpler formulation says that the thought simply *comes*. But what positive meaning has the Soul, when scrutinized, but the *ground of possibility* of the thought? And what is the "knocking" but the *determining of the possibility to actuality?* And what is this after all but giving a sort of concreted form to one's belief that the coming of the thought, when the brain-processes occur, has *some* sort of ground in the nature of things? If the world Soul be understood merely to express that claim, it is a good word to use. But if it be held to do more, to gratify the claim,—for instance, to connect rationally the thought which comes, with the processes which occur, and to mediate intelligibly between their two disparate natures,—then it is an illusory term. It is, in fact, with the word Soul as with the word Substance in general. To say that phenomena inhere in a Substance is at bottom only to record one's protest against the notion that the bare existence of the phenomena is the total truth. A phenomenon would not itself be, we insist, unless there were something *more* than the phenomenon. To the more we give the provisional name of Substance. So, in the present instance, we ought certainly to admit that there is more than the bare fact of coexistence of a passing thought with a passing brain-state. But we do not answer the question "What is that more?" when we say that it is a "Soul" which the brain-state affects. This kind of more *explains* nothing; and when we are once trying metaphysical explanations we are foolish not to go as far as we can. For my own part I confess that the moment I become metaphysical and try to define the more, I find the notion of some sort of an *anima mundi* thinking in all of us to be a more promising hypothesis, in spite of all its difficulties, than that of a lot of absolutely individual souls. Meanwhile, as *psychologists*, we need not be metaphysical at all. The phenomena are enough, the passing Thought itself is the only *verifiable* thinker, and its empirical connection with the brain-process is the ultimate known law.

To the other arguments which would prove the need of a soul, we may also turn a deaf ear. The argument from free-will can convince only those who believe in free-will; and even they will have to admit that spontaneity is just as possible, to say the least, in a temporary spiritual agent like our "Thought" as in a permanent one like the supposed Soul. The same is true of the argument from the kinds of things cognized. Even if the brain could not cognize universals, immaterials, or its "Self," still the "Thought" which we have relied upon in our account *is* not the brain, closely as it seems connected with it; and after all, if the brain could cognize at all, one does not well see why it might not cognize one sort of thing as well as another. The great difficulty is in seeing how a thing can cognize *anything*. This difficulty is not in the least removed by giving to the thing that cognizes the name of Soul. The Spiritualists do not deduce any of the properties of the mental life from otherwise known properties of the soul. They simply find various characters ready-made in the mental life, and these they clap into the Soul, saying, "Lo! behold the source from whence they flow!" The merely verbal character of this "explanation" is obvious. The Soul invoked, far from making the phenomena more intelligible, can only be made intelligible itself by borrowing their form,—it must be represented, if at all, as a transcendent stream of consciousness duplicating the one we know.

Altogether, the Soul is an outbirth of that sort of philosophizing whose great maxim, according to Dr. Hodgson, is: "Whatever you are *totally* ignorant of, assert to be the explanation of everything else."

COMMENTS ■ QUESTIONS

1. James argues that the substantialist theory of the soul is unnecessary to give an account of the "actual subjective phenomena of consciousness as they appear." Therefore, he says, it should be rejected. James's reasoning appeals to a version of the principle known as "Occam's razor," according to which we should always choose the simpler explanation, or the explanation that entails a simpler view of the world. James is saying that the world is a simpler place if, other things being equal, it contains only the "subjective phenomena of consciousness," as opposed to containing these phenomena plus a substantial soul that underlies them. In your opinion, has James correctly applied Occam's razor in reaching this conclusion?
2. It may be argued that, if the "subjective phenomena of consciousness" do not belong to a substantial soul, they must belong to something else. According to James, they belong to the brain. Is his answer satisfactory?
3. James rejects the argument that the existence of free will requires the existence of a substantial soul. Do you agree?

JAMES E. ROYCE

Nature of the Human Soul

* * * * *

We have put the soul in the realm of substance. The nonphilosopher is inclined to think of substance as synonymous with material substance, as when he speaks of a very solid floor as substantial. But substance is opposed to accident, and means simply that which exists in itself and not in another by inherence. Substance can be either spiritual or material. God and angels (presuming they exist) are spiritual substances. They exist in themselves, not as accidents of something else.

Matter and form are called incomplete substances, because they require each other to form a complete nature. But no number of accidents would add up to a substance. Accidents may be material, like size, shape, and quantity. Or they may be spiritual, like ideas and volition. They can never exist by themselves; they are always the shape or idea of something. Since matter and form belong in the genus of substance rather than accident, we say that the soul is substantial even though not a complete substance. Powers, habits, and acts all require an ultimate subject in which they inhere. This is the material composite in the case of vegetative and sensory powers, but must be the soul alone for intellect and will.

The logical positivists who deny substance appear slightly less logical than positive at this point. These men are understandably reacting against the deductive essentialism of the rationalistic age which preceded them. Like some of the extreme semanticists, they seem inclined to say that because I cannot define "breakfast" to their satisfaction, they are justified in denying that I ate breakfast at all. But positivism is not the only alternative, as is clear even historically from the rise of existentialism and other realistic philosophies, and from the fact that several of the leaders of logical positivism in America have abandoned that position. Most of the difficulties of the positivists stem from a faulty concept

---

James E. Royce, S.J., is professor emeritus of psychology at Seattle University. With graduate degrees in psychology, philosophy, and theology, he has long had a special interest in the relations between the traditional philosophy of human nature and modern scientific psychology. He was co-founder of the American Psychological Association's division on philosophical psychology. He has also written on religion, psychology, and on alcoholism.

From James E. Royce, S.J., *Man and His Nature: A Philosophical Psychology*, 1961. By permission of the author.

of substance passed down from Locke and others, and the confusion of the proper realms of science and philosophy. Substance is not a static, unknowable substratum. It is existing reality, dynamic and changing, knowable by philosophical analysis which goes beyond the mere linking of words to individual sense experiences.

Soul Is Basis of Personal Identity. William James and others have proposed theories which would make the ultimate subject of our mental processes the stream of consciousness itself. In this hypothesis ideas would be accidents not inhering in any substance, thoughts without a thinker. This betrays a Cartesian concept of mind. It contradicts the very notion of an accident whose nature is to inhere in substance. And it fails to explain the enduring sense of personal identity we experience. They speak of a "brand" or "familiarity mark," but as James admits the crux of the whole explanation is a bald assumption: "the only point that is obscure is the act of appropriation itself." [1] If there is nothing to do the appropriating, nobody to recognize and claim the brand, I have no basis for asserting that these thoughts are all mine. The ultimate explanation of conscious identity throughout a stream of thoughts and memories is the fact that they are all acts of the same knower.

The metabolic cycle replaces all of the matter in our bodies regularly. Every seven years, it used to be said, but science and the monthly food bill tell us it is much sooner than that. Why am I still the same person? There must be some permanent element in man's nature which remains through all these changes. I am still responsible for acts committed when every molecule of matter was different. My lawyer could hardly get me off a murder charge on the grounds that I am not now the same person because my matter has been replaced since I committed the act. Chaucer or Dante might take twenty years to complete a masterwork; a scientist may pursue one line of research for even longer. The soul is what makes possible the continuity of their line of thought. We have seen in Chapter 15 that the abnormalities of amnesia and multiple personality do not invalidate this position, which is further confirmed by psychoanalytic and other studies of personality development from infancy through adulthood. Thanks to sodium pentothal and hypnosis, it now seems theoretically possible to recall any conscious experience we have ever had, given the right stimulus. If so, there must be an abiding substantial ego through all the interchanges of matter.

The Human Soul Is Simple

To be simple is to be undivided and indivisible, to lack parts. Since there are many different kinds of parts, there are many kinds of simplicity. *Spatial* parts are the result of extension. To have spatial parts is to be quantified. We can designate these parts in an extended being: this half, that third. Lack of spatial parts is called quantitative or integral simplicity. *Constituent* parts are the result of composition. To have constituent or entitative parts is to be com-

1. William James, *Principles of Psychology* (New York: Holt, 1896), I:340. He goes on to admit (p. 344) that he cannot prove it.

pounded in the order of essence or substance, e.g., by matter and form. Lack of such parts is called essential simplicity.

The human soul has integral and essential simplicity; i.e., it lacks spatial and constituent parts. We do not claim lack of the metaphysical "parts," essence and existence, which would be *absolute* simplicity and proper only to God. Nor do we claim that the soul lacks virtual or *operative* parts. The soul is complex, not simple, in so far as it has many different powers. But these "parts" do not destroy its entitative simplicity, since they do not indicate substantial composition as constituent elements and spatial extension do.

Proof. As usual, we argue from operations to nature. Any simple, inextended operation could only come from and reside in an inextended subject. Quantified being can only give rise to extended operations. Extension is an infallible sign of composition, for it shows potential multiplicity. But where there is no sign of composition, we can only conclude that the agent is simple. Now an idea, a judgment, an act of choice, perfect reflection, the permanent identity of the conscious ego, all show inextension. Matter excludes other matter from occupying the same space; these acts show a compenetration, a disregard for the limitations imposed by quantity, which can only be due to the fact that they are not spatial. My concept of a triangle cannot be measured. I can have larger and smaller images, but the idea of what a triangle is applies equally well to all triangles, large and small, which could not be possible if the idea had size itself. My idea of an elephant is no bigger than my idea of a flea, for neither is quantified. Ideas do not occupy space: not having parts, they cannot extend over quantified matter. Nor does a simple idea occupy many parts of the brain at once, for then we would have many ideas, not one, of any one thing. A judgment means recognition of identity or nonidentity of two concepts; but if one concept is in one space, and the other in another part, I could never get the two together in a judgment. The only conclusion is that the ultimate subject of such simple operations is itself simple.

The Human Soul Is Spiritual

The above argument may not strike one as overwhelmingly conclusive. This is partly because our imagination gets in the way. We cannot picture these concepts, so the reasoning is hard to make very graphic. Another reason is that the attribute of simplicity itself is not very impressive. Any form, even that of beings below man, is simple per se, extended only by reason of its varying relation to matter. Spirituality is much more important, and peculiar to man's soul alone. The argument may well be considered after spirituality has been discussed, to appreciate its full significance.

What does spirituality add to simplicity? Independence of matter. A mathematical point, say the mid-point of this wooden table, is simple. It is inextended, has no spatial or constituent parts. But it is not spiritual, for it is wholly dependent on the table for its existence. Burn the table, and the mid-point vanishes. We do not destroy it by breaking it up into pieces, for it has no actual or potential parts. But we destroy it by destroying that upon whose existence it totally depends.

The same applies to the substantial form or "soul" of the plant or brute animal, though here is positive perfection beyond that of the mathematical point. These forms are simple, and cannot be broken into parts. But since they are wholly dependent upon the material composite for their existence, when the plant or animal dies the form simply ceases. Ceases what? To coexist, since the only existence it has is coexistence with matter in the being of the composite. But in the case of the human soul, its intellectual and volitional acts indicate a different relation to matter. Matter is the principle of individuation. If ideas are universal, they are without individuation and therefore without matter.[2]

Spiritual in the strict sense means *intrinsically independent of matter*. This does not exclude extrinsic dependence on matter, as the rational intellect of man differs from the angelic and divine precisely by its dependence on sense organs and phantasms. But matter does not enter intrinsically into the very nature of thought. Matter is intrinsic to sense knowledge, only extrinsic to thought.

Proof. If the human soul is intrinsically independent of matter for at least some of its operations, then it must be intrinsically independent of matter in its being, for being is known by its operations. An effect cannot be above its cause; spiritual operations can never flow from a material principle. We have already established the strictly immaterial nature of thought and volition in earlier chapters. Now these operations cannot reside in a material being as their ultimate subject of inherence, for a spiritual accident cannot inhere in a material substance. Therefore the human soul is spiritual.

Spiritual does not mean supernatural, much less divine. We have insisted that the soul is a constituent of man's nature. But if it is the nature of man to think and choose, then an ultimate principle of such spiritual operations is natural to man. Immaterial does not mean unnatural, any more than metaphysical is the same as mystical or even mythical. Our thinking needs to be clear here, for not only do we naturally look for sensory images to accompany each concept; we also tend to think of real as synonymous with material.

The most powerful things in the world are things we cannot see or feel. Ideas start wars, and thinking can change a whole economy. Choices based on principle, or on love and hate, direct whatever is done by bulldozers or atom bombs. We yield to rights, or fight for them. None of these—idea, love, hate, principle, right—is something you can weigh or measure. The materialists themselves, by their elaborate hypotheses or appeals to unknown but discoverable factors, simply confirm the assertion that man can soar beyond the confines of sensory observation. If the facts argue that something is knowable in the realm of spirit, but unaccountable in material terms, logic demands that we accept the spiritual explanation rather than hold out blindly for a material one.

It is true that if you cut up a man,

---

2. St. Thomas Aquinas, *Summa Theologia*, Ia, 75, 2 and 3.

you will not find a soul. It is also true that if you cut into the man whose idea it is to deny the soul, you will not find an idea. Attempts to prove or disprove the soul by accurate weighing before and after death miss the point, as does photography at the moment of death. If the soul is spiritual, it can affect neither scale nor photographic plate. Discovery of more and more facts in physiology will never supplant the soul, for these facts will never explain spiritual operations. Biochemistry is continually revealing more marvels which call for soul as substantial form, but afford no explanation of universal ideas and lofty choices. If matter can think, you cannot explain why all material beings do not; if it cannot, then you cannot explain in material terms the beings that do. Thought and choice are irreducible to the laws of physical nature; above but not contrary to such laws, they remain within the metaphysical laws of being and causality.

Degree of Independence. We say that the soul is independent of matter "for at least some" of its operations, because we do not wish to imply for an instant that it is independent of matter for all. Distinct but not separate from soul, matter enters directly and necessarily into vegetative and sensory operations. For these the soul is *intrinsically dependent* on matter. Neither an angel nor a separated soul can digest or feel, because neither has bodily organs, which are essential for such processes. The subject of organic activity is the composite of which soul and matter are coordinate causes. St. Thomas acknowledged freely that fever, a blow on the head, or strong passion could diminish or even eliminate temporarily the exercise of free choice. He saw no contradiction between organic causation of mental disorder and the spirituality of the soul. The moderns have more in common with Aristotle and St. Thomas than they realize, and less with Plato and Descartes.

In contrast, soul alone is the principal cause of spiritual activities, with the organic (through sense) only a subordinate cause. Brain is only an extrinsic organ of the intellect. As seat of the internal senses, brain certainly has a relation to thought; but the relation is too indefinite and out of proportion for it to be intrinsic or essential. It is only extrinsic and instrumental.

COMMENTS ■ QUESTIONS

1. The selection from Royce is like the selection from Armstrong earlier in the chapter in that each presupposes claims about the nature of mental events that are argued for elsewhere in the books from which the selections are taken. Armstrong presupposes the view that mentalistic concepts can be reduced to behavioral concepts. Royce presupposes a contrary position—what he refers to as "the strictly immaterial nature of thought and volition." He means that thinking and making choices must be understood as being essentially different from any of the material processes of the body. In taking this position, Royce is in the tradition of Descartes. Which would you say is the sounder view of mentalistic concepts—that of Armstrong or that of Royce?
2. Royce rejects the position of William James, according to which an individual soul, or individual "self," is nothing more than "the stream of consciousness itself." According to Royce, if James were correct, then there would be thoughts without a thinker, and if that were correct, then there would be no basis for saying that all of one's thoughts were one's own. What response do you suppose James might have given in order to defend his position against Royce's objection to it? Do you believe that Royce is correct in saying that there must be a substantial soul because otherwise he would not be the same person that he was twenty years ago, a person whose particular thoughts and feelings and even whose cells have all or mostly changed during those years?
3. You must decide which of three different positions you believe is most defensible: (a) the position of materialists, who claim that *all* mental activities are dependent upon the material body; (b) the position of Royce (following Saint Thomas Aquinas), who says that only *some* mental activities, such as feelings, are dependent upon the body, while others, such as thinking, are not; or (c) the position of Descartes, who holds that *no* mental activities are dependent upon the body.

JEROME A. SHAFFER

The Identity Theory

* * * * *

The last version of materialism we shall consider, and currently the most seriously discussed, is known as the identity theory. It is the theory that thoughts, feelings, wishes, and the rest of so-called mental phenomena are identical with, one and the same thing as, states and processes of the *body* (and, perhaps, more specifically, states and processes of the nervous system, or even of the brain alone). Thus the having of a thought is identical with having such and such bodily cells in such and such states, other cells in other states.

* * * * *

The sense of "identity" relevant here is that in which we say, for example, that the morning star is "identical" with the evening star. It is not that the expression "morning star" means the same as the expression "evening star"; on the contrary, these expressions mean something different. But the object referred to by the two expressions is one and the same; there is just one heavenly body, namely, Venus, which when seen in the morning is called the morning star and when seen in the evening is called the evening star. The morning star is identical with the evening star; they are one and the same object.

Of course, the identity of the mental with the physical is not exactly of this sort, since it is held to be simultaneous identity rather than the identity of a thing at one time with the same thing at a later time. To take a closer example, one can say that lightning is a particularly massive electrical discharge from one cloud to another or to the earth. Not that the word "lightning" *means* "a particularly massive electrical discharge . . . "; when Benjamin Franklin discovered that lightning was electrical, he did not make a discovery about the meaning of words. Nor when it was discovered that water was H_2O was a discovery made about the meanings of words; yet water is identical with H_2O.

In a similar fashion, the identity theorist can hold that thoughts, feelings, wishes, and the like are identical with physical states. Not

Jerome A. Shaffer, professor and chairmen of the Philosophy Department at the University of Connecticut, has been a Fulbright Scholar, National Endowment for the Humanities Senior Fellow, and Fellow at the Center for Advanced Studies in the Behavioral Sciences. His major publications have been in the philosophy of mind.

From Jerome A. Shaffer, *Philosophy of Mind.* Copyright (c) 1968, pp. 42, 43–49. Reprinted by permission of Prentice-Hall, Inc., Englewood Cliffs, New Jersey.

"identical" in the sense that mentalistic terms are synonymous in meaning with physicalistic terms but "identical" in the sense that the actual events picked out by mentalistic terms are one and the same events as those picked out by physicalistic terms.

It is important to note that the identity theory does not have a chance of being true unless a particular sort of correspondence obtains between mental events and physical events, namely, that whenever a mental event occurs, a physical event of a particular sort (or at least one of a number of particular sorts) occurs, and vice versa. If it turned out to be the case that when a particular mental event occurred it seemed a matter of chance what physical events occurred or even whether any physical event at all occurred, or vice versa, then the identity theory would not be true. So far as our state of knowledge at the present time is concerned, it is still too early to say what the empirical facts are, although it must be said that many scientists do believe that there exists the kind of correspondences needed by identity theorists. But even if these correspondences turn out to exist, that does not mean that the identity theory will be true. For identity theorists do not hold merely that mental and physical events are correlated in a particular way but that they are one and the same events, i.e., not like lightning and thunder (which are correlated in lawful ways but not identical) but like lightning and electrical discharges (which always go together because they are one and the same).

What are the advantages of the identity theory? As a form of materialism, it does not have to cope with a world which has in it both mental phenomena and physical phenomena, and it does not have to ponder how they might be related. There exist only the physical phenomena, although there do exist two different ways of talking about such phenomena: physicalistic terminology and, in at least some situations, mentalistic terminology. We have here a dualism of language, but not a dualism of entities, events, or properties.

Some Difficulties in the Identity Theory

But do we have merely a dualism of languages and no other sort of dualism? In the case of Venus, we do indeed have only one object, but the expression "morning star" picks out one phase of that object's history, where it is in the mornings, and the expression "evening star" picks out another phase of that object's history, where it is in the evenings. If that object did not have these two distinct aspects, it would not have been a *discovery* that the morning star and the evening star were indeed one and the same body, and, further, there would be no point to the different ways of referring to it.

Now it would be admitted by identity theorists that physicalistic and mentalistic terms do not refer to different phases in the history of one and the same object. What sort of identity is intended? Let us turn to an allegedly closer analogy, that of the identity of lightning and a particular sort of electrical phenomenon. Yet here again we have two distinguishable aspects, the appearance to the naked eye on the one hand and the physical composition on the other. And this is also not the kind of identity which is plausible for mental and physical events. The appearance *to the naked eye* of a neurological event is utterly different from the experience of having a thought or a pain.

It is sometimes suggested that the physical aspect results from looking at a particular event "from the outside," whereas the mental results from looking at the same event "from the inside." When the brain surgeon observes my brain he is looking at it from the outside, whereas when I experience a mental event I am "looking" at my brain "from the inside."

Such an account gives us only a misleading analogy, rather than an accurate characterization of the relationship between the mental and the physical. The analogy suggests the difference between a man who knows his own house from the inside, in that he is free to move about within, seeing objects from different perspectives, touching them, etc., but can never get outside to see how it looks from there, and a man who cannot get inside and therefore knows only the outside appearance of the house, and perhaps what he can glimpse through the windows. But what does this have to do with the brain? Am I free to roam about inside my brain, observing what the brain surgeon may never see? Is not the "inner" aspect of my brain far more accessible to the brain surgeon than to me? He has the X rays, probes, electrodes, scalpels, and scissors for getting at the inside of my brain. If it is replied that this is only an analogy, not to be taken literally, then the question still remains how the mental and the physical are related.

Usually identity theorists at this point flee to even vaguer accounts of the relationship. They talk of different "levels of analysis," or of different "perspectives," or of different "conceptual schemes," or of different "language games." The point of such suggestions is that the difference between the mental and the physical is not a basic, fundamental, or intrinsic one, but rather a difference which is merely relative to different human purposes or standpoints. The difference is supposed to exist not in the thing itself but in the eye of the beholder.

But these are only hints. They do not tell us in precise and literal terms how the mental and the physical differ and are related. They only try to assure us that the difference does not matter to the real nature of things. But until we are given a theory to consider, we cannot accept the identity theorists' assurance that some theory will do only he does not know what it is.

One of the leading identity theorists, J. J. C. Smart, holds that mentalistic discourse is simply a vaguer, more indefinite way of talking about what could be talked about more precisely by using physiological terms. If I report a red afterimage, I mean (roughly) that something is going on which is like what goes on when I really see a red patch. I do not actually *mean* that a particular sort of brain process is occurring, but when I say something is going on I refer (very vaguely, to be sure) to just that brain process. Thus the thing referred to in my report of an afterimage is a brain process. Hence there is no need to bring in any nonphysical features.

Thus even the taint of dualism is avoided.

Does this ingenious attempt to evade dualistic implications stand up under philosophical scrutiny? I am inclined to think it will not. Let us return to the man reporting the red afterimage. He was aware of the occurrence of something or other, of some feature or other. Now it seems to me obvious that he was not necessarily aware of the state of his brain at that time (I doubt that most of us are ever aware of the state of our brain) nor, in general, necessarily aware of any physical features of his body at that time. He might, of course, have been incidentally aware of some physical feature but not insofar as he was aware of the red afterimage as such. Yet he was definitely aware of something, or else how could he have made that report? So he must have been aware of some nonphysical feature. That is the only way of explaining how he was aware of anything at all.

Of course, the thing that our reporter of the afterimage was aware of might well have had further features which he was *not* aware of, particularly, in this connection, physical features. I may be aware of certain features of an object without being aware of others. So it is not ruled out that the event our reporter is aware of might be an event with predominantly physical features—he just does not notice those. But he must be aware of some of its features, or else it would not be proper to say he was aware of *that* event. And if he is not aware of any physical features, he must be aware of something else. And that shows that we cannot get rid of those nonphysical features in the way that Smart suggests.

One would not wish to be dogmatic in saying that identity theorists will never work out this part of their theory. Much work is being done on this problem at the present time, for it arises in other areas of philosophy as well as in the philosophy of mind. In particular philosophers of science are concerned with the problem. We saw that the identity theory used such analogies as the identity of lightning with electrical phenomena and the identity of water with molecules consisting of hydrogen and oxygen. But the question to be raised is what kind of identity we are dealing with in such cases. Do we have mere duality of terms in these cases, duality of features, properties, or aspects, or even duality of substances? Very similar issues arise. So it is quite possible that further work on this problem of identity will be useful in clarifying the identity theory of the mental and the physical. But at the present the matter is by no means as clear as it should be.

Even if the identity theorist could clarify the sense of "identity" to be used in his theory, he would still face two other problems. These concern coexistence in time and space. Coexistence in time and space are conditions that must be met if there is to be identity. That is to say, for two apparently different things to turn out to be one and the same, they must exist at the same time and in the same location. If we could show that Mr. A existed at a time when Mr. B did not, or that Mr. A existed in a place where Mr. B did not, then this would show that Mr. A and Mr. B were different men. It is by virtue of these facts about identity that an alibi can exonerate a suspect: if Mr. A was not in Chicago at the time, then he could not be one and the same with the man who stole the diamonds in Chicago.

So if mental events are to be identical with physical events, then they must fulfill the conditions of coexistence in time and space. The question is, Do they?

So far as coexistence in time is concerned, very little is known. The most relevant work consists in direct stimulation of an exposed part of the brain during surgery. Since only a local anesthetic is necessary in many such cases the patient may well be fully conscious. Then, as the surgeon stimulates different parts of his brain, the patient may report the occurrence of mental events—memories, thoughts, sensations. Do the physical events in the brain and the mental events occur at precisely the same time? It is impossible to say. All that would be required is a very small time gap to prove that the physical events were not identical with the mental events. But it is very difficult to see how the existence of so small a time gap could be established. And even if it were, what would it prove? Only that the mental event was not identical with just that physical event; it would not prove it was nonidentical with any physical event. So it could well be that coexistence in time is present or is not. I do not think that we shall get much decisive information from empirical work of the sort here described. The identity theorist, then, does not have to fear refutation from this quarter, at least not for a long time.

How about coexistence in space? Do mental events occur in the same place the corresponding physical events occur? This is also a very difficult question to answer, for two reasons. First our present ignorance of neurophysiology, especially concerning the brain and how it functions, allows us to say very little about the location of the relevant physical events. This much does seem likely: they are located in the brain. Much more than that we do not at present know, although as the time passes, we should learn much more. The second reason for our difficulty in telling if there is coexistence in space has to do with the location of mental events. Where do thoughts, feelings, and wishes occur? Do they occur in the brain? Suppose you suddenly have the thought that it is almost suppertime; where does that occur? The most sensible answer would be that it occurs wherever you are when you have that thought. If you are in the library when you have that thought, then the thought occurs in the library. But it would be utterly unnatural to ask where inside your body the thought occurred; in your foot, or your liver, or your heart, or your head? It is not that any one of these places is more likely than another. They are all wrong. Not because thoughts occur somewhere *else* within your body than your foot, liver, heart, or head—but because it *makes no sense at all* to locate the occurrence of a thought at some place within your body. We would not understand someone who pointed to a place in his body and claimed that it was *there* that his entertaining of a thought was located. Certainly, if one *looked* at that place, one would not *see* anything resembling a thought. If it were replied to this that pains can be located in the body without being seen there, then it should be pointed out that one *feels* the pain there but one hardly feels a thought in the body.

The fact that it makes no sense at all to speak of mental events as occurring at some point within the body has the result that the identity theory cannot be true. This is because the corresponding physical events do occur at some point within the body, and if those physical events are identical with mental events, then those mental events must occur at the same point within the body. But those mental events do not occur at any point within the body, because any statement to the effect that they occurred here, or there, would be senseless. Hence the mental events cannot meet the condition of coexistence in space, and therefore cannot be identical with physical events.

Our inability to give the location within the body of mental events is different from our inability to give the location of the corresponding physical events within the body. In the latter case, it is that we do not know enough about the body, particularly the brain. Some day, presumably, we will know enough to pin down pretty exactly the location of the relevant physical events. But in the case of mental events it is not simply that at present we are ignorant but that someday we may well know. What would it be like to discover the location of a thought in the brain? What kind of information would we need to be able to say that the thought occurred exactly *here*? If by X rays or some other means we were able to see every event which occurred in the brain, we would never get a glimpse of a thought. If, to resort to fantasy, we could so enlarge a brain or so shrink ourselves that we could wander freely through the brain, we would still never observe a thought. All we could ever observe in the brain would be the *physical* events which occur in it. If mental events had location in the brain, there should be some means of detecting them there. But of course there is none. The very idea of it is senseless.

Some identity theorists believe this objection can be met. One approach is to reply that this objection begs the question: if the identity theory is true, and mental events are identical with brain events, then, paradoxical as it may sound, mental events do indeed have location, and are located precisely where the physical events are located. Another approach is to reply that the relevant physical events should be construed as events which happen to the body as a whole, and therefore occur where the body as a whole is located; then it is not so paradoxical to give location to the mental events, for they would be located where the body is located but would not be located in any particular part of the body.

We have carried our discussion of the identity theory to the very frontier of present philosophical thinking. We can only leave it to the reader to decide how well it can meet the objections which are raised to it.

COMMENTS ■ QUESTIONS

1. Shaffer first describes, and then argues against, the identity theory. Keeping in mind points made by Ryle and by Armstrong in earlier reading selections, would you say that Shaffer has presented the materialist theory of mind in the most defensible way? If not, how could it be made more defensible?
2. Are Shaffer's reasons for rejecting the identity theory sound? One of his claims is that when a person experiences a particular sort of mental event, such as a red afterimage, the person is not aware of any state of his brain but is, of course, aware of something. Therefore, says Shaffer, "he must have been aware of some nonphysical feature." Is this a good argument? Why or why not?
3. Another of Shaffer's arguments against the identity theory is the following: For two things to be identical, they must coexist in time and space. But it is impossible, for example, to say whether a particular thought that a person may have when his brain is stimulated during surgery occurs at exactly the same time as the brain process that is caused by the stimulation. Is this a good argument? Is Shaffer correct in saying that there is a similar problem regarding coexistence in space?

KEITH CAMPBELL

A New Epiphenomenalism

In chapter 5 [of *Body and Mind*] we argued that although mental states are indeed inner causes apt to produce behavior, this is not all they are. Mental states have also, among their mental properties, phenomenal properties; and it was urged that awareness by phenomenal properties is incompatible with a purely materialist doctrine of the inner, mental causes of behavior.

So the position we reach is this: some bodily states, namely some states of the brain, are mental states. That is to say, they are causes of particular forms of behavior. And provided that neurophysiology is in principle complete, the only properties of the brain relevant to their role in causing behavior will be physicochemical ones. But these brain states have a complexity beyond their physical complexity, for some of them are also awarenesses of phenomenal properties. The grasping of such phenomenal properties resists material reduction, even though the causal role of such states does not.

To have a painfully burned finger is not just to encode burned finger information, to initiate burn-soothing behavior, and to encode in an imperfect apprehension that both these processes have occurred. It is also to suffer a burning hurtfulness. To be so suffering is a property of the man not reducible to his physics. As it occurs only when he is in a particular brain-state, it is best to hold that suffering pain is in the first place a property of his brain-state, and hence secondarily of the man as a whole.

The account given of awareness by phenomenal properties is the only point where the new Epiphenomenalism diverges from Central-State Materialism. Perhaps the new Epiphenomenalism could be called Central-State Materialism Plus.

If the brain's activities of a physical kind all occur in accordance with physical laws, suffering a burn, tasting the sweetness of sugar, or smelling the piquancy of cloves are processes in which the experience of the quality in question is inoperative in behavior, even the behavior in which such experiences are described. It is other aspects of the to-

Keith Campbell, who has taught philosophy at the University of Sydney, Australia, since 1966 is a past president of the Australian Association of Philosophy. In addition to Body and Mind, *he has written* Metaphysics: An Introduction *and* A Stoic Philosphy of Life.

Excerpt from *Body and Mind* by Keith Campbell. Copyright (c) 1970 by Keith Campbell. Reprinted by permission of Doubleday and Company, Inc. and Macmillan, London and Basingstoke.

tal state which play the operative part in setting the tongue in motion. The new Epiphenomenalism is therefore rather paradoxical in its account of the causation of behavior. To preserve the completeness of the physical accounts of human action, it must hold that, contrary to common belief, it is not the hurtfulness of pain which causes me to shun it nor the sweet taste of sugar which drives me to seek it. Strictly, it must be physical features of the processes in which awareness by phenomenal property is involved which have any effect on what I do. Whether we suffer or enjoy can be a sign that a given state is aversive or attractive for us, but cannot be a cause of aversion or attraction. To insist that it is a cause, in the present context, is to deny that the nervous system operates by purely physical principles. It is to turn from Epiphenomenalism back to some form of Dualism.[1]

The enjoying or enduring of phenomenal properties are called *epiphenomenal* characteristics for two reasons. They furnish the intrinsic content of sensibility. And although produced by what produces brain-states, they stand outside the causal chains linking stimulus to response.

1. The Old and New Epiphenomenalisms

The doctrine labeled *Epiphenomenalism* which flourished in the nineteenth century also held that the causation of behavior was an entirely physical affair. But it denied the title *mental* to any state of the body, reserving that title for spiritual objects, experiences, which came into being when bodily conditions were suitable. These experiences had no effect on the course of a man's activity. This doctrine makes the mind an impotent side show to the serious business of real events in the physical world. It denies that mental events can be causes of behavior. It robs us of any satisfactory way of specifying different mental states, for this must be done through the links with behavior which the theory denies. It makes the Mind-Body problem wholly insoluble and makes it impossible to know if anyone, besides ourselves, has a mind at all.

So it is a most unattractive view, and was indeed only embraced because it alone seemed to allow for the completeness of physical explanations of what occurs in the physical world.

The new Epiphenomenalism, by contrast, holds that some bodily states are also mental states, and that the causal mental properties are physical properties of these bodily states. It insists only that the enjoying or enduring of phenomenal properties is not a physical affair. The new view allows, indeed requires, that mental states be causes, and allows, indeed requires, that different mental states be distinguished by reference to their differing links with behavior.

In contrast with the old, the new view denies that an epiphenomenal character is essential to the concept of a mind. On the new view, but not on the old, the inner states of the imitation man, which never have an epiphenomenal side, are never-

---

1. It may be a Dualism, not of things, body and mind, but of physical and mental properties of the same thing, the body. See, e.g., Ernest Nagel, "Are Naturalists Materialists?" in *Logic Without Metaphysics*, Glencoe, Ill., 1957.

theless states of mind.

2. Double Aspect

One common view of the mind is called the Theory of Double Aspect. This theory holds that mental states have an "outer" aspect, revealed to normal scientific investigation, under which mental states are states of the brain, and also a second, "inner" aspect, in which they are known to introspection or self-consciousness.

This theory is ambiguous. It might amount only to a doctrine that there are two ways of knowing about mental states, an outer way by perception and instruments, and an inner introspective way. This is perfectly true, but it is also perfectly compatible with Central-State Materialism, which maintains the same doctrine.

The Theory of Double Aspect on the other hand might mean that mental states have two sorts of properties, one physical sort accessible to perception and photography, and another sort, accessible only to an inner, introspecting, mental sort of eye. This is sometimes, but not always, the case. Take an example from bodily sense; knowing where my left foot is. This is a state of which "outer" investigation by, for example, electroencephalographs may one day tell us a good deal. And "inner" introspection can assure us that it is present. That is, we can just know, without research, that we know where our left foot is. But introspection yields us no knowledge of any property of the state *knowing where my left foot is* which is not just a causal property equally accessible, in principle, to outer investigation. Like our knowledge that we are awake, our knowledge of where our left foot is does not involve apprehension by a phenomenal property.

There is another alternative too. In recent years P. F. Strawson [2] has propounded a view of mankind which attempts to by-pass the traditional questions of the relations of mind to body. On his theory two different sorts of properties, one sort shared with inanimate objects, such as *having a certain weight,* and the other peculiar to objects with minds, such as *being depressed,* belong to the very same thing, a person. His account of the mental properties is not causal; the analysis they are given is typically in terms of behavioral dispositions plus conscious-experience. The mental properties involve their bodily expressions, but are not reducible to material properties in either the Behaviorist or the Materialist way. They are properties of the body, although since the body is not *just* a body, it is called a person. His view is thus one form of Double Aspect theory.

Strawson's doctrine is distinguished from other Double Aspect accounts insofar as he identifies the whole body, and not some special part of it, as the bearer of the irreducible mental characteristics. His view is a Double Aspect theory twice over; there are two sorts of properties which persons have, and the mental properties of persons have both a behavioral and an experiential aspect.

The Mind-Body problem certainly takes a different form when Dualism is abandoned, but Strawson has offered no opinion on the causal connections between material properties

---

2. Strawson, *Individuals,* chap. 3.

and those aspects of mental properties which are experiential rather than behavioral. So the introduction of the concept of a person will not by itself dissipate all problems of how the mental and the physical relate in men.

The phenomenal properties we do experience are not necessarily non-physical ones accessible only to introspection. They may be physical conditions imperfectly apprehended. We need a theory of Double Aspect only if the particular kind of imperfect introspection which occurs in real men is not describable in materialistic terms. The new Epiphenomenalism is therefore a theory of the Double Aspect of some mental processes. Those mental processes which involve awareness by way of a phenomenal property have a dual aspect; they have two sorts of property, material and non-material.

The duality is not fundamentally the duality of public and private, which is a duality concerned with how properties can be known. The fact that a non-material process is not publicly discernible is only accidental. If men were gifted with a suitable, wide-spread telepathetic power these processes would be public, yet they would still not be material. Conversely, it is possible to suppose a physical property which could be discerned by only one person who suffered a unique defect of color vision. This property would be private, yet material.

COMMENTS ■ QUESTIONS

1. In this selection from *Body and Mind*, Campbell makes use of the expression "phenomenal property," which he describes in an earlier chapter of the book in the following way: "Phenomenal properties are not . . . properties of things as they actually are. They are how certain inner properties, which are both material and mental, appear to him who has them." The following are some of Campbell's examples of phenomenal properties: "the burning, jabbing, throbbing, and aching sorts of pain, the salty, bitter, sweet, and avocado-like sorts of taste; the different experiences of seeing things as variously colored; the different feelings involved in different emotions." Is the concept of a phenomenal property clear?
2. Campbell defends a version of epiphenomenalism that is close to the identity theory. Its central feature is a theory of the "double aspect" of mental states. Is the concept of the double aspect clear? If not, could it be clarified? Can it be used, as Campbell wishes to use it, to show that certain properties of mental states cannot be reduced to physical properties?
3. Which of the reading selections in this chapter presents the most plausible account of the nature of the human mind?

PAUL ZIFF

The Feelings of Robots

Could a robot have feelings? Some say of course.[1] Some say of course not.[2]

1. I want the right sort of robots. They must be automata and without doubt machines.

I shall assume that they are essentially computing machines, having micro-elements and whatever micro-mechanisms may be necessary for the functioning of these engineering wonders. Furthermore, I shall assume that they are powered by micro-solar batteries: instead of having lunch they will have light.

And if it is clear that our robots are without doubt machines then in all other respects they may be as much like men as you like. They may be the size of men. When clothed and masked they may be virtually indistinguishable from men in practically all respects: in appearance, in movement, in the utterances they utter, and so forth. Thus except for the masks any ordinary man would take them to be ordinary men. Not suspecting they were robots nothing about them would make him suspect.

But unmasked the robots are to be seen in all their metallic lustre. What is in question here is not whether we can blur the line between a man and a machine and so attribute feelings to the machine. The question is whether we can attribute feelings to the machine and so blur the line between a man and a machine.

2. Could robots have feelings? Could they, say, feel tired, or bored?

Ex hypothesi robots are mechanisms, not organisms, not living creatures. There could be a broken-down robot but not a dead one. Only living creatures can literally have feelings.

If I say "She feels tired" one can generally infer that what is in question is (or was or will be in the case of talk about spirits [3]) a living crea-

1. Cf. D. M. MacKay, "The Epistemological Problem for Automata", in *Automata Studies* (Princeton: Princeton Univ. Press, 1956), 235–251.

2. Cf. M. Scriven, "The Mechanical Concept of Mind", *Mind LXII* 246 (1953), 230–240.

3. I shall henceforth omit the qualification.

Paul Ziff, professor of philosophy at the University of North Carolina at Chapel Hill, has written many books and articles in different areas in philosophy, including the philosophy of mind, language, aesthetics, and ethics.

From "The Feelings of Robots," *Analysis*, vol. 19 (1959). Reprinted by permission of Basil Blackwell and the author.

ture. More generally, the linguistic environment "... feels tired" is generally open only to expressions that refer to living creatures. Suppose you say "The robot feels tired". The phrase "the robot" refers to a mechanism. Then one can infer that what is in question is not a living creature. But from the utterance of the predicative expression "... feels tired" one can infer that what is in question is a living creature. So if you are speaking literally and you say "The robot feels tired" you imply a contradiction. Consequently one cannot literally predicate "... feels tired" of "the robot".

Or again: no robot will ever do everything a man can. And it doesn't matter how robots may be constructed or how complex and varied their movements and operations may be. Robots may calculate but they will not literally reason. Perhaps they will take things but they will not literally borrow them. They may kill but not literally murder. They may voice apologies but they will not literally make any. These are actions that only persons can perform: *ex hypothesi* robots are not persons.

3. "A dead robot" is a metaphor but "a dead battery" is a dead metaphor: if there were a robot around it would put its metaphor to death.

What I don't want to imply I need not imply. An implication can be weakened. The sense of a word can be widened or narrowed or shifted. If one wishes to be understood then one mustn't go too far: that is all. Pointing to one among many paintings, I say "Now *that* one is a *painting*". Do I mean the others are not? Of course not. Yet the stress on "that" is contrastive. So I say "The robot, that mechanism, not of course a living creature but a machine, it feels tired": you cannot infer that what is in question here is a living creature.

If I say of a person "He feels tired", do you think I am saying that he is a living creature and only that? If I say "The robot feels tired" I am not saying that what is in question is a living creature, but that doesn't mean that nothing is being said. If I say "The robot feels tired", the predicate "... feels tired" means whatever it usually means except that one cannot infer that what is in question is a living creature. That is the only difference.

And what has been said about "The robot feels tired" could be said equally well about "The robot is conscious", "The robot borrowed my cat", and so forth.

4. Could robots feel tired? Could a stone feel tired? Could the number 17 feel tired? It is clear that there is no reason to believe that 17 feels tired. But that doesn't prove anything. A man can feel tired and there may be nothing, there need be nothing at all, that shows it. And so with a robot or a stone or the number 17.

Even so, the number 17 could not feel tired. And I say this not because or not simply because there are no reasons to suppose that 17 does feel tired but because there are good reasons not to suppose that 17 feels tired and good reasons not to suppose that 17 ever feels anything at all. Consequently it is necessary to consider whether there are any reasons for supposing that robots feel tired and whether there are good reasons for not supposing that robots ever feel anything at all.

5. Knowing George and seeing the way he looks I say he feels tired. Knowing Josef and seeing the way he looks I don't say he feels tired. Yet if you don't know either of them then to you George and Josef may look alike.

In one sense they may look alike to me too, but not in another. For George but not Josef will look tired. If you ask me to point out the difference there may be nothing relevant, there need be nothing relevant, to point to. For the relevant difference may be like that between looking at an unframed picture and looking at it framed. Only the frame here is provided by what I know about them: you cannot see what I know.

(Speaking with the robots, one can say that the way things look to me, my present output, will not be the same as yours, the way things look to you, even though at present we may both receive the same input, the same stimuli, and this is because your mechanism was not in the same initial state as mine, owing either to a difference in structure or to a difference in previous inputs.)

If we say of a person that he feels tired, we generally do so not only on the basis of what we see then and there but on the basis of what we have seen elsewhere and on the basis of how what we have seen elsewhere ties in with what we see then and there. And this is only to say that in determining whether or not a person feels tired both observational and theoretic considerations are involved and, as everywhere, are inextricably interwoven.

6. Suppose you and I visit an actor at home. He is rehearsing the role of a grief-stricken man. He ignores our presence as a grief-stricken man might. His performance is impeccable. I know but you do not know that he is an actor and that he is rehearsing a role. You ask "Why is he so miserable?" and I reply "He isn't". "Surely," you say, "he is grief-stricken. Look at him! Show me what leads you to say otherwise!" and of course there may be nothing then and there to show.

So Turing [4] posed the question whether automata could think, be conscious, have feelings, etc., in the following naive way: what test would an automation fail to pass? MacKay [5] has pointed out that any test for mental or any other attributes to be satisfied by the observable activity of a human being can be passed by automata. And so one is invited to say what would be wrong with a robot's performance.

Nothing need be wrong with either the actor's or a robot's performance. What is wrong is that they are performances.

7. Suppose K is a robot. An ordinary man may see K and not knowing that K is a robot, the ordinary man may say "K feels tired". If I ask him what makes him think so, he may reply "K worked all day digging ditches. Anyway, just look at K: if he doesn't look tired, who does?"

So K looks tired to the ordinary man. That doesn't prove anything. If I know K is a robot, K may not look tired to me. It is not what I see

---

4. Cf. "Computing Machinery and Intelligence", *Mind LIX* 236 (1950), 433–466.

5. Cf. "Mentality in Machines", *Arist. Soc. Supp. XXVI* (1952), 61–86.

but what I know. Or it is not what I see then and there but what I have seen elsewhere. Where? In a robot psychology laboratory.

8. If I say "The robot feels tired", the predicate "... feels tired" means whatever it usually means except that one cannot infer that what is in question is a living creature. That is the only difference.

To speak of something living is to speak of an organism in an environment. The environment is that in which the behaviour of the organism takes place. Death is the dissolution of the relation between an organism and its environment. In death I am pluralized, converted from one to many. I become my remains. I merge with my environment.

If we think of robots being put together, we can think of them being taken apart. So in our laboratory we have taken robots apart, we have changed and exchanged their parts, we have changed and exchanged their programmes, we have started and stopped them, sometimes in one state, sometimes in another, we have taken away their memories, we have made them seem to remember things that were yet to come, and so on.

And what we find in our laboratory is this: no robot could sensibly be said to feel anything. Why not?

9. Because there are not psychological truths about robots but only about the human makers of robots. Because the way a robot acts (in a specified context) depends primarily on how we programmed it to act. Because we can programme a robot to act in any way we want it to act. Because a robot could be programmed to act like a tired man when it lifted a feather and not when it lifted a ton. Because a robot couldn't mean what it said any more than a phonograph record could mean what it said. Because we could make a robot say anything we want it to say. Because coveting thy neighbor's robot wife would be like coveting his car and not like coveting his wife. Because robots are replaceable. Because robots have no individuality. Because one can duplicate all the parts and have two virtually identical machines. Because one can exchange all the parts and still have the same machines. Because one can exchange the programmes of two machines having the same structure. Because....

Because no robot would act tired. Because a robot could only act like a robot programmed to act like a tired man. For suppose some robots are programmed to act like a tired man after lifting a feather while some are so programmed that they never act like a tired man. Shall we say "It is a queer thing but some robots feel tired almost at once while others never feel tired"? Or suppose some are programmed to act like a tired man after lifting something blue but not something green. Shall we say "Some robots feel tired when they lift blue things but not when they lift green things"? And shall we conclude "Some robots find blue things heavier than green things"? Hard work makes a man feel tired: what will make a robot act like a tired man? Perhaps hard work, or light work, or no work, or anything at all. For it will depend on the whims of the man who makes it (though these whims may be modified by whatever quirks may appear in the robot's electronic nerve network, and there may be unwanted and unforeseen consequences of an ill-conceived programme.) Shall we say "There's no telling what will make a robot feel tired"? And if a robot acts like a tired man then what? Some robots may be programmed to require a rest, others to require more work. Shall we say "This robot feels tired so put it back to work"?

What if all this were someday to be done with and to human beings? What if we were someday to break down the difference between a man and his environment? Then some day we would wake and find that we are robots. But we wouldn't wake to a mechanical paradise or even an automatic hell: for then it might not make sense to talk of human beings having feelings just as it now doesn't make sense to talk of robots having feelings.

A robot would behave like a robot.

COMMENTS ■ QUESTIONS

1. Whether you believe that robots have feelings may depend, at least in part, upon the basic view that you take of the nature of the human mind. What is your basic view? What bearing does it have on the question of whether robots have feelings?
2. Paul Ziff says: "If you are speaking literally and you say 'the robot feels tired' you imply a contradiction," because talk about feelings applies only to living creatures and robots are not living creatures. It might be objected that, once sophisticated robots have been produced, a new language will need to be developed that *will* allow us to say that robots have feelings in the most literal sense. Would you say that, as a consequence of the many recent science fiction movies and stories about robots, such a thing has begun to happen? Have the very popular science fiction movies and stories had any effect upon our language?
3. Ziff's major point is that robots cannot sensibly be said to feel anything simply because they are so different from flesh and blood people. For example, robots but not people are programmed to act as they do. Robots are replaceable. They have no individuality. Their parts are interchangeable. Would you say (a) that Ziff is correct in claiming that people are so different from robots and (b) that, if the differences are granted to exist, Ziff is correct in claiming that we should not say that robots have feelings?

R E A D I N G S

Anderson, Alan Ross, ed. *Minds and Machines*. Englewood Cliffs, N. J.: Prentice-Hall, 1964. Papers on whether or not computers can be said to think.

Boden, Margaret. *Artificial Intelligence and Natural Man.* New York: Basic Books, 1977. A very good and wide-ranging treatment.

Borst, Clive U., ed. *The Mind/ Brain Identity Theory.* New York: Macmillan, 1970. One of the best collections of critical essays.

Broad, C. D. *The Mind and Its Place in Nature.* London: Routledge & Kegan Paul, 1925. Contains one of the best known defenses of dualism.

Dennett, Daniel C., and Douglas R. Hofstadter, eds. *The Mind's I.* New York: Basic Books, 1981. A very intriguing collection of stories and papers on issues in the philosophy of mind. Particularly enjoyable to read.

Dreyfus, Hubert. *What Computers Can't Do: A Critique of Artificial Reason.* New York: Harper & Row, 1972. Title is very descriptive.

Flew, Anthony, ed. *Body, Mind, and Death.* New York: Macmillan, 1964. A very useful collection of classical and contemporary readings on the mind-body problem.

Fodor, Jerry. *The Language of Thought.* Cambridge: Harvard University Press, 1979. Argues against some of the views of Gilbert Ryle.

Gunderson, Keith. *Mentality and Machine.* Garden City, N.Y.: Doubleday, Anchor Books, 1971. Examines the possibility that machines could think or have feelings.

O'Connor, John, ed. *Modern Materialism: Reading on Mind-Body Identity.* New York: Harcourt Brace Jovanovich, 1969. A very useful anthology.

Penfield, Wilder. *The Mystery of the Mind.* Princeton: Princeton University Press, 1975. A famous anatomist and brain surgeon discusses research that is relevant to materialism.

Rhine, J. B. *New World of the Mind.* New York: Sloane, 1953. Argues that the data of psychical research support dualism.

Rosanthal, David M. *Materialism and the Mind-Body Problem.* Englewood Cliffs, N.J.: Prentice-Hall, 1971. A good contemporary anthology.

Strawson, P. F. *Individuals.* London: Methuen, 1959. Emphasizes the unity of mind and body. A difficult but very influential book.

CHAPTER SEVEN

In the afterlife, if there is one, telepathy might well be much more extensive and continuous than it is now.
—*H. H. Price*

It is not rational arguments but emotions that cause belief in a future life.
—*Bertrand Russell*

Life After Death

In order to make its subject matter easier to understand, this book follows the common practice of dividing philosophy into a number of distinct problems—the question of God's existence, free will versus determinism, the nature of the human mind, the nature of time, and so on. This approach is artificial, however, because, at a certain level, *all* philosophical problems are related to each other. Ultimately, none can be discussed apart from the others. A good illustration of this is found in the philosophical analysis of the question of life after death.

As an example, the question of life after death appears to have immediate implications in the area of values. How should I live my life? How should I prepare for death? How should I treat other people? What sorts of lives should I encourage other people to live? Answers to these questions seem to depend in some important respects on whether we believe in life after death. (However as you have learned by now, everything in philosophy is open to discussion, and this includes the question of whether a belief in life after death *should* make a difference to one's present life. Some philosophers argue that one should live exactly the same kind of life regardless of whether there is life after death.)

All philosophers agree that the question of survival after death is closely tied to the most important issues in the philosophy of mind. These in turn involve some of the most basic questions in metaphysics. Is the human mind an aspect of the human body and nothing more? Someone who takes a wholly materialistic position in metaphysics would say yes, and would, therefore, deny that there is life after death. If I am to survive the death of my body, the "inner me"—my mind (or some part of it), my personality (or some part of it), my sense of self (or some part of it, assuming that it can be thought of as having parts)—must in some way be capable of existing independently of my material body. How is it possible for the "inner me" to exist apart from my brain and nervous system?

The question of life after death involves some basic questions in epistemology. Assuming that "disembodied personalities" (or souls) exist, how could knowledge of them be acquired? Would this mean that human knowledge can be acquired in some way that is not dependent upon sensory experience? Could it make sense to say that "disembodied personalities" themselves perceive things?

The question of life after death is linked to the question of God's existence because, on most accounts, God is conceived to be a nonmaterial being. The existence of a supreme nonmaterial being seems to increase the likelihood that lesser nonmaterial beings, such as human souls, exist. (Please bear in mind, however, that not all philosophers who have believed in God's existence have also believed in life after death, nor have all those who believed in life after death believed in God's existence.)

If you have already read the chapter on evil, you have seen that for some philosophers the question of survival after death is closely linked to the problem of evil. John Hick, for example, argues that the problem of evil cannot be solved apart from belief in life after death.

In their discussions of the survival question, philosophers devote a large amount of time to an analysis of the concept of *personal identity*. They discuss the general question: What is personal identity? They also discuss the more specific question that we have already raised: Does it make sense, and if so how does it make sense, to say that the "inner me" could exist apart from my body? John Locke, in the selection reprinted here from his classic work *An Enquiry Concerning Human Understanding*, addresses the following question (among others): Would I still be me if I had a different body? Locke tells a story in which we are to imagine that one day a prince "awakens" in the body of a cobbler. In reading the story, you should ask yourself whether it makes sense. If it does make sense, what does this tell us about the concept of personal identity? If it does not make sense, what does this tell us?

The general position that Locke wishes to defend is that personal identity is determined by consciousness, or memory. Thus, according to Locke, because the prince who awakens in the cobbler's body remembers having been the prince—he remembers that "he" was the prince the day before, and he remembers many of the prince's experiences—it is correct to say that the prince/cobbler is the same person as the prince. As Locke says:

> For it being the same consciousness that makes a man be himself to himself, personal identity depends on that only, whether it be annexed only to one individual substance, or can be continued in a succession of several substances. For as far as any intelligent being can repeat the idea of any past action with the same consciousness it had of it at first, and with the same consciousness it has of any present action; so far it is the same personal self.

Some philosophers have objected to Locke's position on the ground that, if personal identity consists in consciousness or memory alone, then insofar as I forget a part of my past life, I cease to be identical with the person who lived during the forgotten period. This conclusion runs counter to the commonsensical belief that I am the same person now that I was at, say, three years of age, even though I have forgotten all, or most, of the events that took place in my life at that age. Joseph Butler, who lived in the early eighteenth century and who was very familiar with Locke's writings, put the objection in this way:

> Though consciousness of what is past does . . . ascertain our personal identity to ourselves, yet to say, that it makes personal identity, or is necessary to our being the same person, is to say, that a person has not existed a single moment, nor done one action, but what he can remember; indeed none but what he reflects upon. And one should really think it self evident, that consciousness of personal identity presupposes, and therefore cannot constitute, personal identity. *(The Analogy of Religion)*

Locke says repeatedly that personal identity consists *only* in memory. But in the prince and the cobbler story he says at one point that the prince's *soul* is in the cobbler's body. This seems to imply that personal identity consists in the identity of one's soul—a view that has been widely held. It raises the question: What might the sameness of one's soul consist in? What is meant by a human soul? Should the soul be conceived of as a Cartesian "thinking substance" (see the discussion of this concept in chapter 6) or as the very different sort of shadow body (also discussed in chapter 6 and in the present chapter in the selection from H. H. Price)?

On the Cartesian view, the soul is apparently "not made of anything" (at least, not anything having spatial extension), and as a consequence the Cartesian concept of the soul is particularly problematic. However, the concept of a shadow body is also problematic because it *is* supposed to be made of something "quasi-material," the nature of which would appear to be mysterious, to say the least.

There are two different sorts of puzzles regarding personal identity and the question of life after death. These puzzles are generated, respectively, by what can be referred to as the first person point of view and the third person point of view. On the one hand is the question that each of us can ask strictly for himself or herself: How would I know that *I* had survived the death of my body? That is, how, if I somehow found myself to be a conscious but "disembodied" being, would I know that I was the same person as I am now when I do have my body?

On the other hand is the question: How would I know that *someone else* had survived bodily death? How would I identify someone else as being the same person both before and after death? For this sort of identification to take place, would some version of the shadow-body theory need to be correct? It would seem that popular stories about ghostly apparitions do presuppose the shadow-body theory, because ghosts in stories are sometimes visible and also sometimes bear a resemblance to the deceased person. Ghost stories seem to provide a basis for conceiving what it could be like to identify someone after death as being the same person he or she was before death.

By contrast, in Locke's story of the prince and the cobbler, the prince/cobbler cannot be identified as the prince in terms of appearance because the prince looks different than he did the day before. As Locke sees it, this is sufficient reason for us to say that while the prince is the same *person* on the second day as he was the day before, he is not the same *man*. According to Locke, to be the same person, the prince needs only to have the same consciousness (and/or soul), but to be the same man he also needs the same body.

You may want to ask yourself what, if any, significance lies in the fact that the prince and the cobbler story makes more sense from a first person point of view than from a third person point of view. Suppose that the prince/cobbler was never able to convince anyone else that he was the same person—although not the same man—as the prince? Suppose, furthermore, that we were never able to arrive at a clear concept of what it would be like from a third person point of view to identify *any* "disembodied personality" as being the same person as someone who had died. What, if anything, might this tell us about the conceivability of life after death?

In the readings for this chapter, H. H. Price defends the view that life after death makes sense. Price discusses several different possible concepts of life after death. Bertrand Russell rejects belief in an afterlife, arguing that such belief is caused by emotional needs. Martin Ebon discusses sympathetically the work of Raymond Moody regarding "near death" experiences. James E. Alcock takes an opposing view, maintaining that "there is no doubt that ordinary hallucinations can contain virtually all of the elements described by Moody."

Paul and Linda Badham discuss the experiences of people who claim to "remember past lives," either through "hypnotic regression" or "spontaneously" without the use of hypnosis. The conceptual puzzles generated by claims to "remember past lives" are similar to those involved in the prince and the cobbler story. The Badhams focus their discussion on questions regarding the reliability of subjects, the historical accuracy of their alleged memories, and possible alternative explanations for their reports.

A final word: the reading selections in this chapter are a good illustration of a basic distinction between two different types of philosophical questions: (a) those having to do with *concepts* and (b) those having to do with *facts and evidence*. The selections from Locke and Price are addressed to the first type of question when they ask: What do we mean by personal identity? Does it make sense to suppose that one and the same person could exist in two different bodies? Does continued life apart from one's body make sense? What might *it* be like? Does it make sense to suppose that after death we have a different kind of body? What might it be like? Questions such as these are *logically prior* to the question of whether there is evidence for life after death, which is a question addressed in the selections from Russell, Ebon, Alcock, and the Badhams. One need not have an answer to the question of evidence in order to raise the conceptual questions about life after death. But if it turns out that the concept of life after death makes no sense, even asking whether there is evidence for life after death would be pointless. Put another way, philosophers must show that life after death is *conceptually possible* before asking whether there is evidence for its existence.

JOHN LOCKE

The same consciousness being preserved, whether in the same or different substances, personal identity is preserved.
—*Essay Concerning Human Understanding*

Men being, as has been said, by nature all free, equal, and independent, no one can be put out of this estate and subjected to the political power of another without his own consent.
—*Treatise on Civil Government*

John Locke (1632–1705) is generally regarded as one of the most influential philosophers of all time. He has been called the "philosopher of common sense" and also the founder of British empiricism. His *Essay Concerning Human Understanding* is the first comprehensive analysis of the origin and extent of human knowledge. His *Treatise on Civil Government* contains one of the first systematic statements of the principles of democratic government. The ideas contained in this book and in his Letters on Toleration, which advocate religious freedom, contributed significantly to the Declaration of Independence and the Constitution of the United States. For many years, Locke taught at Oxford University, where he also earned a medical degree. Later, because of his political views, he lived for several years in exile in Holland. The last years of his life were spent peacefully in England.

JOHN LOCKE

On Personal Identity

* * * * *

P*ersonal identity.*—This being premised, to find wherein personal identity consists, we must consider what "person" stands for; which, I think, is a thinking intelligent being, that has reason and reflection, and can consider itself as itself, the same thinking thing, in different times and places; which it does only by that consciousness which is inseparable from thinking, and it seems to me essential to it: it being impossible for any one to perceive, without perceiving that he does perceive. When we see, hear, smell, taste, feel, meditate, or will any thing, we know that we do so. Thus it is always as to our present sensations and perceptions: and by this every one is to himself that which he calls "self;" it not being considered, in this case, whether the same self be continued in the same or diverse substances. For since consciousness always accompanies thinking, and it is that that makes every one to be what he calls "self," and thereby distinguishes himself from all other thinking things; in this alone consists personal identity, *i.e.*, the sameness of a rational being: and as far as this consciousness can be extended backwards to any past action or thought, so far reaches the identity of that person; it is the same self now it was then; and it is by the same self with this present one that now reflects on it, that that action was done.

10. ***Consciousness makes personal identity.***—But it is farther inquired, whether it be the same identical substance? This, few would think they had reason to doubt of, if these perceptions, with their consciousness, always remained present in the mind, whereby the same thinking thing would be always consciously present, and, as would be thought, evidently the same to itself. But that which seems to make the difficulty is this, that this consciousness being interrupted always by forgetfulness, there being no moment of our lives wherein we have the whole train of all our past actions before our eyes in one view; but even the best memories losing the sight of one part whilst they are viewing another; and we sometimes, and that the greatest part of our lives, not reflecting on our past selves, being intent on our present thoughts, and, in sound sleep, having no thoughts at all, or, at least, none with that consciousness which remarks our waking thoughts: I say, in all these cases, our consciousness

A biographical sketch of John Locke appears on the previous page.

From *An Enquiry Concerning Human Understanding*, first published in 1690.

being interrupted, and we losing the sight of our past selves, doubts are raised whether we are the same thinking thing, *i.e.*, the same substance, or no? which, however reasonable or unreasonable, concerns not personal identity at all: the question being, what makes the same person? and not, whether it be the same identical substance which always thinks in the same person? which in this case matters not at all; different substances, by the same consciousness (where they do partake in it), being united into one person, as well as different bodies by the same life are united into one animal, whose identity is preserved, in that change of substances, by the unity of one continued life. For it being the same consciousness that makes a man be himself to himself, personal identity depends on that only, whether it be annexed only to one individual substance, or can be continued in a succession of several substances. For as far as any intelligent being can repeat the idea of any past action with the same consciousness it had of it at first, and with the same consciousness it has of any present action; so far it is the same personal self. For it is by the consciousness it has of its present thoughts and actions that it is self to itself now, and so will be the same self, as far as the same consciousness can extend to actions past or to come; and would be by distance of time, or change of substance, no more two persons than a man be two men, by wearing other clothes today than he did yesterday, with a long or short sleep between: the same consciousness uniting those distant actions into the same person, whatever substances contributed to their production.

11. ***Personal identity in change of substances.***—That this is so, we have some kind of evidence in our very bodies, all whose particles—whilst vitally united to this same thinking conscious self, so that we feel when they are touched, and are affected by and conscious of good or harm that happens to them—are a part of ourselves; *i.e.*, of our thinking conscious self. Thus the limbs of his body is to every one a part of himself: he sympathises and is concerned for them. Cut off an hand and thereby separate it from that consciousness he had of its heat, cold, and other affections, and it is then no longer a part of that which is himself, any more than the remotest part of matter. Thus we see the substance, whereof personal self consisted at one time, may be varied at another, without the change of personal identity; there being no question about the same person, though the limbs, which but now were a part of it, be cut off.

* * * * *

15. And thus we may be able, without any difficulty, to conceive the same person at the resurrection, though in a body not exactly in make or parts the same which he had here, the same consciousness going along with the soul that inhabits it. But yet the soul alone, in the change of bodies, would scarce to any one, but to him that makes the soul the man, be enough to make the same man. For, should the soul of a prince, carrying with it the consciousness of the prince's past life, enter and inform the body of a cobbler, as soon as deserted by his own soul, every one sees he would be the same person with the prince, ac-

countable only for the prince's actions: but who would say it was the same man? The body too goes to the making of the man, and would, I guess, to every body determine the man in this case, wherein the soul, with all its princely thoughts about it, would not make another man; but he would be the same cobbler to every one besides himself. I know that, in the ordinary way of speaking, the same person and the same man stand for one and the same thing. And, indeed, every one will always have a liberty to speak as he pleases, and to apply what articulate sounds to what ideas he thinks fit, and change them as often as he pleases. But yet, when we will inquire what makes the same spirit, man, or person, we must fix the ideas of spirit, man, or person in our minds; and having resolved with ourselves what we mean by them, it will not be hard to determine in either of them, or the like, when it is the same and when not.

16. **Consciousness makes the same person.**—But though the same immaterial substance or soul does not alone, wherever it be, and in whatsoever state, make the same man; yet it is plain, consciousness, as far as ever it can be extended, should it be to ages past, unites existences and actions, very remote in time, into the same person, as well as it does the existence and actions of the immediately preceding moment: so that whatever has the consciousness of present and past actions is the same person to whom they both belong. Had I the same consciousness that I saw the ark and Noah's flood, as that I saw an overflowing of the Thames last winter, or as that I write now, I could no more doubt that I who write this now, that saw the Thames overflowed last winter, and that viewed the flood at the general deluge, was the same self, place that self in what substance you please, than that I who write this am the same myself now whilst I write (whether I consist of all the same substance, material or immaterial, or no) that I was yesterday. For, as to this point of being the same self, it matters not whether this present self be made up of the same or other substances, I being as much concerned and as justly accountable for any action was done a thousand years since, appropriated to me now by this self-consciousness, as I am for what I did the last moment.

* * * * *

20. But yet possibly it will still be objected, "Suppose I wholly lose the memory of some parts of my life, beyond the possibility of retrieving them, so that perhaps I shall never be conscious of them again; yet am I not the same person that did those actions, had those thoughts, that I was once conscious of, though I have now forgot them?" To which I answer, That we must here take notice what the word "I" is applied to; which in this case, is the man only. And the same man being presumed to be the same person, "I" is easily here supposed to stand also for the same person. But if it be possible for the same man to have distinct incommunicable consciousnesses at different times, it is past doubt the same man would at different times make different persons; which, we see, is the sense of mankind in the solemnest declaration of their opinions, human laws not punishing the mad man for the sober man's actions, nor the sober

man for what the mad man did, thereby making them two persons; which is somewhat explained by our way of speaking in English, when we say, "Such an one is not himself, or is beside himself;" in which phrases it is insinuated as if those who now or, at least, first used them, thought that self was changed, the self-same person was no longer in that man.

COMMENTS ■ QUESTIONS

1. Locke identifies personal identity with consciousness, or memory. Can Locke's view be defended against the objections discussed in the opening essay for this chapter? Could additional objections be raised against it?
2. Does Locke's story about the prince and the cobbler make sense to you? Is his distinction between (1) *being the same person* and (2) *being the same man* a useful distinction?

H. H. PRICE

What Kind of "Next World"?

If we are to discuss the problem of survival intelligently, we must try to form some idea of what the life after death might conceivably be like. If we cannot form such an idea, however rough and provisional, it is pointless to discuss the factual evidence for or against the "survival hypothesis." A critic may object that there *is* no such hypothesis, on the ground that the phrase "survival of

H. H. Price, who taught for many years at Oxford University, was twice president of the Society for Psychical Research. He published many influential books and articles, including Perception, Thinking and Experience, *and* Belief.

This article first appeared in *Tomorrow*, Autumn 1956, published by Perennial Books, Bedfont, Middlesex, England. Reprinted by permission of the publisher.

human personality after death" has no intelligible meaning at all.

When we speak of the after-life or of life after death, the "life" we have in mind is not life in the physiological sense (by definition this ceases at death). "Life" here means consciousness or experience. And consciousness has to be consciousness *of* something. Experiences must have objects of some sort. In this way, the idea of life after death is closely bound up with the idea of "The Next World" or "The Other World." This Other World is what the surviving person is supposed to be conscious *of*. It provides the objects of his after-death experiences. The idea of life after death is indeed a completely empty one unless we can form at any rate some rough conceptions of what "The Other World" might be like.

On the face of it, there are two different ways of conceiving of the Next World. They correspond to two different conceptions of survival itself, and something must first be said about these. On the one hand, there is what I shall call the "embodied" conception of survival. On this view personality cannot exist at all without a body of some kind. At death one loses one's physical body. So after death one must have a body of another sort, an etheric body or an astral body, composed of a "higher" kind of matter. It is generally held, by those who accept this view, that each of us does in fact possess such a "higher" body even in this present life, and that this is the explanation of what are called "out of the body" experiences (experiences of being out of the *physical* body).

It is interesting to notice that this conception of survival is compatible with a new version of materialism. According to the classical, or ordinary version of the materialist theory, the one which philosophers call epiphenomenalism, consciousness is unilaterally dependent on processes in the physical body and could not continue once the physical body has disintegrated. But suppose it was suggested, instead, that consciousness is unilaterally dependent on processes in the "higher" body. This would be a new version of the materialist theory of human personality, and it would be compatible with survival, as the old version is not. Similarly there might be a new version of behaviorism. Instead of saying that consciousness is reducible in one way or another to the behavior of the physical organism (a view which excludes the possibility of survival) someone might suggest that it is reducible to the behavior of the "higher" organism. Perhaps some view of this kind—"higher body" materialism as one might call it—will be the prevailing one among the tough-minded naturalistic thinkers of the 21st century. Perhaps it is already the prevailing view among the tough-minded thinkers of the Next World, if there is one.

I turn now to the "disembodied" conception of survival. On this view what survives death is just the soul or spirit, and it is a wholly immaterial entity. Its essential attributes are consciousness, thought, memory, desire and the capacity of having emotions. In this present life the immaterial soul interacts continually with the physical organism, especially with the brain. At death, this interaction ceases; or rather death just *is* the permanent cessation of this interaction. And thereafter the immaterial soul continues to exist in a disembodied state. Most of the thinkers who have conceived of survival in this way, Plato and Descartes for instance, have also accepted the doctrine of a substantial soul. But the disembodied conception of survival is equally compatible with the "Serial Analysis" of personality advocated by Daniel Dunglas Home, the great physical medium, William James, the philosopher, and the Buddhists. We should merely have to say that the series of mental events which constitutes a person can be divided into two parts, an *ante mortem* part and a *post mortem* part; and that those in the first part are closely associated with physical events in a certain brain, whereas those in the second part are not associated with physical events of any kind. (This serial conception of personal identity is also, of course, compatible with the "embodied" conception of survival; and Buddhism, at least according to some Western interpretations of it, appears to accept both.)

The Next World—Two Views

Corresponding to these two different conceptions of survival, there are two different conceptions of the Next World; a quasiphysical conception of it on the one hand, and a psychological conception of it on the other.

If we accept the "embodied" conception of survival, we think of the Next World as a kind of material world. It would be the environment of the etheric or astral body, and composed of the same sort of "higher" matter. Presumably this body would have sense organs of some kind, though they might be very different from our present ones, and by means of them we should be aware of our after-death environment. In this way we should be provided with objects to be conscious of, and could have desires and emotions concerning them. Among such objects there would be the "higher" bodies of other surviving human beings; and possibly we might also encounter some personalities embodied in the same manner who had never had *physical* bodies at all.

The Other World, thus conceived, must of course be a spatial one. Both the "higher" body and the objects which constitute its environment would have to have properties which are at any rate analogous to shape, size, location and mobility as we know them in this present life. But if the Other World is a spatial one, *where* is it? Is it "above the bright blue sky" perhaps (that is, in or beyond the stratosphere)? Or is it somewhere in the bowels of the earth? Could we reach it by means of a rocket, or by digging a deep enough tunnel? Anyone who accepts this conception of the Other World must hold that such questions arise from a misconception. We have no *a priori* reason for assuming that the physical space with which we are now familiar is the only space there is. There might perfectly well be two worlds, both standing without spatial relation to the other, or indeed there might be more than two. Suppose that in the Next World there is a New Jerusalem, and that it is quite literally a spatial entity, with a shape and a size and complex spatial relations between its parts, as the traditional descriptions of it imply. It does not follow the New Jerusalem stands in any spatial relation at all to the old Jerusalem in Palestine. The Next World and all that is in it might just be in a space of its own, different from the space of the physical universe. Moreover, it might be a different *sort* of space as well. Its geometry need not be even approximately Euclidian. It might have more than three dimensions. When I say that the space of the Next World "might" have some queer features, I mean that its possession of them is compatible with the "embodied" conception of survival from which this whole line of thought starts. And similarly the causal laws which prevail in it might be very different from the laws of physics. Indeed they *must* differ to some extent from the laws of physics if such phrases as "higher" body and "higher kind of matter" are to have any meaning.

A Kind of Dream World

But now suppose we start from what I called the disembodied conception of survival. If the after-death personality is something wholly immaterial, can there be any sort of other world at all? It seems to me that there can. We could think of it as a kind of dream-world. To put it in another way, we could suppose that in the next life mental imagery will play the part which sense-perception plays in this one. People sometimes ask what is "the purpose" or "the point" of our present life in this world, or whether it has any. Perhaps this question is not so utterly senseless as most contemporary philosophers suppose. We might even be able to suggest an answer to it. The point of life in this present world, we might say, is to provide us with a stock of memories out of which an image world may be constructed when we are dead.

We are liable to think that there is something "unreal" about mental images in general and about dream-images in particular. This seems to me to be a confusion. Mental images are non-physical certainly, but they are as real as anything can be. They do actually exist or occur. Moreover some mental images (visual and tactual ones) are spatial entities, though they are not in physical space. But perhaps when people say that mental images are "unreal" they are using the word in a kind of evaluative sense. Perhaps they mean that mental images make no appeal to our feelings, that they are uninteresting or unexciting, that they "cut no ice" with us from the emotional point of view. But surely this is false, as anyone who has ever had a nightmare knows. Both for good and for ill our dream experiences may be as vividly felt as any of our waking ones, or more so. And for some people, indeed for many people on some occasions, the mental images they experience when awake are more interesting—more attention-absorbing—than the physical objects they perceive. Moreover, waking mental images may be interesting in an alarming or horrifying way, as dream images can. They may force themselves on our attention when we would much rather be without them.

It is worth while to emphasize these points because this way of conceiving life after death does enable us to answer a logically irrelevant but emotionally powerful objection to the whole idea of survival, the objection that it is "too good to be true." On the contrary, such a dream-like next world, composed of mental images, might be a very unpleasant world for some people and a rather unpleasant one for almost all of us some of the time.

It would of course be a psychological world and not a physical one. It might indeed *seem* to be physical to those who experience it. The image-objects which compose it might appear very like physical objects, as dream objects often do now; so much so that we might find it difficult at first to realize that we were dead (a point often mentioned in mediumistic communications). Nevertheless, the causal laws obeyed by these image-objects would not be the laws of physics, but something more like the laws of depth psychology which such investigators as Sigmund Freud and C. G. Jung began to explore. It is of course sometimes said that dreams are "incoherent," and this again may be part of what is meant by calling dream objects unreal. But dreams (or waking fantasies) are only incoherent if judged by the irrelevant standard of the laws of physics; and this is only another way of saying that dream objects are not physical objects, and that an image-world, as we are conceiving of it, would indeed be an "other" world, which is just what it ought to be.

To put it rather differently, the other world, according to this conception of it, would be the manifestation in image form of the memories and desires of its inhabitants, including their repressed or unconscious memories and desires. It might be every bit as detailed, as vivid and as complex as this present perceptible world which we experience now. We may note that it might well contain a vivid and persistent image of one's own body. The surviving personality, according to this conception of survival, is in actual fact an immaterial entity. But if one habitually *thinks* of oneself as embodied (as one well might, at least for a considerable time) an image of one's own body might be as it were the persistent center of one's image world, much as the perceived physical body is the persistent center of one's perceptible world in this present life.

It may be thought that such a Next World would be a purely private and subjective one, that each discarnate personality would experience a Next World of his own, with no access to anyone else's. But suppose we bring telepathy into the picture. It may well be that in this present life the physical brain inhibits the operation of our telepathic powers, or at any rate tends to prevent the results of their operations from reaching consciousness. In the after-life, if there is one, telepathy might well be much more extensive and continuous than it is now. If so, we might expect that A's images would manifest not only his own desires and memories, but also the desires and memories of other personalities B, C, D, etc. if these were sufficiently similar to his own. In this way, there might be a common image world for each group of sufficiently "like-minded" personalities, common to all the members of the group though private to the group as a whole. There would still be many Next Worlds and not one (a suggestion which most religious traditions would, I think, support) but none of them would be wholly private and subjective.

Physical and Psychological Conceptions

Let us now compare these two conceptions of the other world, the quasi-physical conception of it which goes with the "embodied" conception of survival, and the psychological conception of it which goes with the "disembodied" conception of survival. At first sight these two ways of thinking of the other world appear entirely different and indeed incompatible. If one is right, surely the other must be wrong? But perhaps they are not quite so different as they look. They do agree on several important points. In both, the Next World is a spatial one (I would remind the reader that visual and tactual images are spatial entities). In both, the space of the Next World is different from physical space. In both, the causal laws are other than the laws of physics. In the first, the discarnate personality has a body, but it is not an ordinary physical body. In the second he has a dream body or image body.

What we have really done in this discussion of the Other World is to start from two different analogies and work out their consequences. The first analogy which we considered was a physical one, suggested by our experience of the material world. The second was a psychological one, suggested by our experience of dreams and other forms of mental imagery. Some people will feel more at home with the physical analogy; others will be more attracted by the psychological one. But perhaps the choice between them is only a choice between starting points. Both analogies have to be stretched in one way or another if we are to achieve our aim, which is to give some intelligible content to the notion of the "next life" or the "next world."

It may well be that the two lines of thought, if pushed far enough, would meet in the middle. It is at any rate an attractive speculation that there may be realities in the universe which are intermediate between the physical and the psychological realms as these are ordinarily conceived. The contents of the other world, if there is one, may be in this intermediate position, more material than ordinary dream-images, more image-like or dream-like than ordinary material objects; like material objects in possessing spatial properties of some sort, and some degree at any rate of appearance; like mental images in that the causal laws they obey are the laws of psychology rather than the laws of physics.

COMMENTS ■ QUESTIONS

1. Price says that there are "two different ways of conceiving the Next World": (a) the "embodied" conception and (b) the "disembodied" conception. By the first he does not mean resurrection of the material body (which is actually a third way to conceive of survival), but instead the survival of a shadow body (which Price refers to as an "etheric" or "astral" body). By the second, he means either the survival of a kind of Cartesian soul or simply the survival of the "contents" of consciousness by themselves. (The concepts of shadow body, Cartesian soul, and the mind as no more than a stream of its contents—referred to as the "Serial Analysis" of personality by Price—are all discussed in chapter 6.) Would you say that these concepts are all sufficiently clear for Price to use in making his desired points? If not, what problems do you see?
2. In terms of the "embodied" conception of survival, the Next World is to be thought of as a kind of material world that is spatial in some way. Do you believe that Price's questions about such a world (Where is it? Could it be reached by a rocket?) could ever be answered satisfactorily?
3. "If the after-death personality is something wholly immaterial, can there be any sort of other world at all?" Price answers that it could be a world of dreamlike images. Does this make sense? If it does, would you say that this view of an afterlife is compatible with *both* the Cartesian theory of the soul and the "Serial Analysis" of personality, or is it compatible with only one (or none) of these views? Please explain.
4. Does it make sense, as Price says that it does, to suppose that in a "world" composed entirely of dreamlike images, one could imagine that one had a body even though, in fact, one did not?

BERTRAND RUSSELL

Do We Survive Death?

Before we can profitably discuss whether we shall continue to exist after death, it is well to be clear as to the sense in which a man is the same person as he was yesterday. Philosophers used to think that there were definite substances, the soul and the body, that each lasted on from day to day, that a soul, once created, continued to exist throughout all future time, whereas a body ceased temporarily from death till the resurrection of the body.

The part of this doctrine which concerns the present life is pretty certainly false. The matter of the body is continually changing by processes of nutriment and wastage. Even if it were not, atoms in physics are no longer supposed to have continuous existence; there is no sense in saying: this is the same atom as the one that existed a few minutes ago. The continuity of human body is a matter of appearance and behavior, not of substance.

The same thing applies to the mind. We think and feel and act, but there is not, in addition to thoughts and feelings and actions, a bare entity, the mind or the soul, which does or suffers these occurrences. The mental continuity of a person is a continuity of habit and memory: there was yesterday one person whose feelings I can remember, and that person I regard as myself of yesterday; but, in fact, myself of yesterday was only certain mental occurrences which are now remembered and are regarded as part of the person who now recollects them. All that constitutes a person is a series of experiences connected by memory and by certain similarities of the sort we call habit.

If, therefore, we are to believe that a person survives death, we must believe that the memories and habits which constitute the person will continue to be exhibited in a new set of occurrences.

No one can prove that this will not happen. But it is easy to see that it is very unlikely. Our memories and habits are bound up with the structure of the brain, in much the same way in which a river is connected with the riverbed. The water in the river is always changing, but it keeps to the same course because previous rains have worn a channel. In like manner, previous events have

A biographical sketch of Bertrand Russell is to be found in chapter 1.

From Bertrand Russell: "Do We Survive Death?" *Why I Am Not a Christian.* Copyright 1957, 1985 by George Allen and Unwin. Reprinted by permission of Simon and Schuster, Inc. and Allen & Unwin.

worn a channel in the brain, and our thoughts flow along this channel. This is the cause of memory and mental habits. But the brain, as a structure, is dissolved at death, and memory therefore may be expected to be also dissolved. There is no more reason to think otherwise than to expect a river to persist in its old course after an earthquake has raised a mountain where a valley used to be.

All memory, and therefore (one may say) all minds, depend upon a property which is very noticeable in certain kinds of material structures but exists little if at all in other kinds. This is the property of forming habits as a result of frequent similar occurrences. For example: a bright light makes the pupils of the eyes contract; and if you repeatedly flash a light in a man's eyes and beat a gong at the same time, the gong alone will, in the end, cause his pupils to contract. This is a fact about the brain and nervous system—that is to say, about a certain material structure. It will be found that exactly similar facts explain our response to language and our use of it, our memories and the emotions they arouse, our moral or immoral habits of behavior, and indeed everything that constitutes our mental personality, except the part determined by heredity. The part determined by heredity is handed on to our posterity but cannot, in the individual, survive the disintegration of the body. Thus both the hereditary and the acquired parts of a personality are, so far as our experience goes, bound up with the characteristics of certain bodily structures. We all know that memory may be obliterated by an injury to the brain, that a virtuous person may be rendered vicious by encephalitis lethargica, and that a clever child can be turned into an idiot by lack of iodine. In view of such familiar facts, it seems scarcely probable that the mind survives the total destruction of brain structure which occurs at death.

It is not rational arguments but emotions that cause belief in a future life.

The most important of these emotions is fear of death, which is instinctive and biologically useful. If we genuinely and wholeheartedly believed in the future life, we should cease completely to fear death. The effects would be curious, and probably such as most of us would deplore. But our human and subhuman ancestors have fought and exterminated their enemies throughout many geological ages and have profited by courage; it is therefore an advantage to the victors in the struggle for life to be able, on occasion, to overcome the natural fear of death. Among animals and savages, instinctive pugnacity suffices for this purpose; but at a certain stage of development, as the Mohammedans first proved, belief in Paradise has considerable military value as reinforcing natural pugnacity. We should therefore admit that militarists are wise in encouraging the belief in immortality, always supposing that this belief does not become so profound as to produce indifference to the affairs of the world.

Another emotion which encourages the belief in survival is admiration of the excellence of man. As the Bishop of Birmingham says, "His mind is a far finer instrument than anything that had appeared earlier—he knows right and wrong. He can build Westminster Abbey. He can make an airplane. He can calculate the distance of the sun.... Shall, then, man at death perish utterly? Does that incomparable instrument, his mind, vanish when life ceases?"

The Bishop proceeds to argue that "the universe has been shaped and is governed by an intelligent purpose," and that it would have been unintelligent, having made man, to let him perish.

To this argument there are many answers. In the first place, it has been found, in the scientific investigation of nature, that the intrusion of moral or aesthetic values has always been an obstacle to discovery. It used to be thought that the heavenly bodies must move in circles because the circle is the most perfect curve, that species must be immutable because God would only create what was perfect and what therefore stood in no need of improvement, that it was useless to combat epidemics except by repentance because they were sent as a punishment for sin, and so on. It has been found, however, that, so far as we can discover, nature is indifferent to our values and can only be understood by ignoring our notions of good and bad. The Universe may have a purpose, but nothing that we know suggests that, if so, this purpose has any similarity to ours.

Nor is there in this anything surprising. Dr. Barnes tells us that man "knows right and wrong." But, in fact, as anthropology shows, men's views of right and wrong have varied to such an extent that no single item has been permanent. We cannot say, therefore, that man knows right and wrong, but only that some men do. Which men? Nietzsche argued in favor of an ethic profoundly different from Christ's, and some powerful governments have accepted his teaching. If knowledge of right and wrong is to be an argument for immortality, we must first settle whether to believe Christ or Nietzsche, and then argue that Christians are immortal, but Hitler and Mussolini are not, or vice versa. The decision will obviously be made on the battlefield, not in the study. Those who have the best poison gas will have the ethic of the future and will therefore be the immortal ones.

Our feelings and beliefs on the subject of good and evil are, like everything else about us, natural facts, developed in the struggle for existence and not having any divine or supernatural origin. In one of Aesop's fables, a lion is shown pictures of huntsmen catching lions and remarks that, if he had painted them, they would have shown lions catching huntsmen. Man, says Dr. Barnes, is a fine fellow because he can make airplanes. A little while ago there was a popular song about the cleverness of flies in walking upside down on the ceiling, with the chorus: "Could Lloyd George do it? Could Mr. Baldwin do it? Could Ramsay Mac do it? Why, NO." On this basis a very telling argument could be constructed by a theologically-minded fly, which no doubt the other flies would find most convincing.

Moreover, it is only when we think abstractly that we have such a high opinion of man. Of men in the concrete, most of us think the vast majority very bad. Civilized states spend more than half their revenue on killing each other's citizens. Consider the long history of the activities inspired by moral fervor: human sacrifices, persecutions of heretics, witch-hunts, pogroms leading up to wholesale extermination by poison gases, which one at least of Dr. Barnes's episcopal colleagues must be supposed to favor, since he holds pacifism to be un-Christian. Are these abominations, and the ethical doctrines by which they are prompted, really evidence of an intelligent Creator? And can we really wish that the men who practiced them should live forever? The world in which we live can be understood as a result of muddle and accident; but if it is the outcome of deliberate purpose, the purpose must have been that of a fiend. For my part, I find accident a less painful and more plausible hypothesis.

COMMENTS ■ QUESTIONS

1. Russell rejects the substance theory of the self, or soul, that is defended by John Locke in this chapter and by James E. Royce in the preceding chapter. Is Russell correct to conclude that, once the substance theory of the soul is rejected, life after death becomes highly unlikely?
2. Russell argues that belief in a future life is not based upon rational arguments, but instead is caused by emotions. For this argument to be successful, human beings must be able to deceive themselves, (or in some cases to deceive others) to a very significant extent. Is such deception plausible?

MARTIN EBON

The Moody Phenomena

Ivor Potter's motorcycle had crashed, and he was taken, unconscious, to a nearby hospital: "I woke in the hospital to feel myself floating out of my body," he recalled later. "I was surrounded by a golden light." This is not the impression of a man easily given to spiritual fantasy: Potter, a telephone engineer, is as down-to-earth a person as you'd ever be likely to meet. He added, "I kept going upwards until I reached a beautiful garden in a peaceful land. There was a range of blue mountains in the distance."

These events took place when Potter was 26 years old. He now recalls his experience as "the most marvelous feeling," that he just "wanted to keep going." In this setting, away from his own unconscious body, Ivor Potter encountered his father—a man killed in a road accident, only two weeks earlier—who admonished him, "Go back; you have your mother and sister to care for."

Potter says he returned to his body reluctantly, but reconciled himself to this return when he found his mother and sister crying at his bedside. The physician in attendance, he recalls, "said I was almost a goner."

And what has this experience done to Potter, a man now 48 years old?

"I used to be scared of dying," he says. "Now the only thing that worries me is doing all the things I have to do while I'm alive."

Ivor Potter's story is the first one in this chapter, because it gives his full name, cites his profession, and tells where he lives: in Bude, Cornwall, England. Many accounts of such out-of-the-body experiences are published anonymously, presumably to protect those who tell them from embarrassment. At other times, they are simply broken down into categories and become dry statistics.

It was the work of a man who has collected some 150 such stories, Dr. Raymond Moody, which prompted people like Potter to come forward and tell their own experiences, and which almost precisely parallel those Moody accumulated. Potter, and dozens of others, reported their OBE's in a London newspaper, *The Sun*. The specific experiences and lasting impact of these near-death

---

Martin Ebon has written many widely read books and articles on topics related to parapsychology. He has served as Administrative Secretary of the Parapsychology Foundation and is a popular lecturer.

From *The Evidence for Life After Death* by Martin Ebon. Copyright (c) 1977 by Martin Ebon. Reprinted by arrangement with New American Library, NY, NY.

events are about as identical with the American cases that Moody collected, as anything like that can be. Floating experiences, encounters with departed relatives, and an end to fear of death are among the themes Moody encountered over and over again.

That Dr. Moody's collection should have such a swift transatlantic response is characteristic, I think, of the positive manner with which Moody lifted the dark veil of something heretofore as unspeakable as the death experience. Men and women, by the thousands, have lost their reluctance to tell of these striking impressions, no longer afraid they might be called peculiar of fanciful.

* * * * *

"I know I haven't really proven anything, scientifically," Moody says. "I have brought stories together, of people who have experienced clinical death, and of course the more I heard, the more they sounded like proof of life after death. They aren't, of course, and I am not presenting them as such. You must also keep in mind that I have my own bias: I like to believe that there is life after death, that there's life after life. And that affects my judgment, and it probably, or even certainly, affects my way of collecting these kinds of stories. I'd become known to friends and colleagues as someone who collects this kind of story, and so I probably got more than my share of the experience told to me."

When Moody spoke to the American Society for Psychical Research, his listeners included perhaps a dozen men and women who had spent much of their life studying the possible survival of the human personality after death. But Dr. Moody disarmed them, too. "I realize that I know very little about psychical research and parapsychology," he told them, "but I am now trying to catch up with all the valuable work that has gone before and that's now going on. As it happened, I just stumbled into this field, and I've been so busy with letters and talks that I've been very neglectful in catching up on these studies."

One of Moody's subjects, Danion Brinkley, told the *Washington Post* (March 27, 1977) that he had been struck by lightning eighteen months earlier, while talking on the telephone. Mr. Brinkley said, "I had to be resuscitated three times between the time my wife found me and they got me to the hospital. I was passing between this reality and that reality. It was excruciating pain because the lightning had fried my nervous system. I had been flung around the room and bounced off the ceiling, floor and wall when it happened."

Brinkley, then 27 years old and living in Aiken, South Carolina, reported: "Then I saw this 'being of light.' It was the purest light I've ever seen. It wasn't a physical being. I went to a place that was blue and gray, calm and peaceful. You simultaneously experienced every emotion you have ever had and your conscious mind puts it into words later."

Dr. Moody is fond of telling the story of one woman in the eighth month of pregnancy, who developed a toxic condition. Entering the hospital, labor was induced, severe bleeding began, and the attending staff was alarmed. Since the woman was herself a nurse, she knew she was in danger, and then lost consciousness.

The next thing she knew, she found herself on a ship sailing on a large body of water. "On the distant shore," she recalls, "I could see all my loved ones who had died—my mother, father, sister, and others. I could see their faces just as they were when I knew them on earth." As Moody tells the story, her family members waved to her to come to them, but she refused and said she was "not ready to go."

At the same time—and this is quite typical of this sort of out-of-the-body experience—the nurse could see the hospital staff bent over her unconscious body, lying prone, but she saw them as an onlooker, rather than as the center of the operation. Hovering about her own body, she tried to convey to the doctors that they need not worry, that she wasn't really going to die; but, of course, they couldn't hear her. And then, suddenly, her "outer" body or soul merged with the "unconscious" body on the operating table; she regained consciousness.

* * * * *

The statistically oriented scholars of modern parapsychology are unlikely to present the case of a woman who had suffered a heart attack and, in Moody's presentation, found herself first inside a black void and then moving toward a gray mist. As the British weekly, *Psychic News*, summarized this case, the woman was able to see through this mist and recognize "people she had known on earth." She "felt certain she was going through the mist," meeting those who had gone into an existence beyond death before her, and while this gave her "a wonderful, joyous feeling," she could not find words to describe it. This, too, is a common experience; Dr. Moody refers to it as the "ineffable" quality of the brink-of-death experience; for once, Moody yields to academic vernacular: he could have said, quite simply, that many people found it impossible to describe their experience properly, that it was "indescribable." This happens in much of psychical research, in transcendent or mystical religious experience, or even in the happily frequent experience of falling in love!

At any rate, the heart attack victim was unable to find words to describe the joy of meeting her family members in the mist beyond death, but "it wasn't her time to go through the mist." In front of her, a relative who had died several years before, her Uncle Carl, appeared as if to block her path; she remembered him as saying, "Your work on earth has not been completed; go back now."

She reentered her body, rather against her wish, but felt she had no choice. As soon as her disembodied soul was back inside the damaged body, she felt a terrible chest pain and heard her little boy crying, "God, bring my Mommy back to me."

* * * * *

COMMENTS ■ QUESTIONS

1. People who have had the kind of experiences described by Raymond Moody are much more likely than people who have not to believe that they provide good evidence for the existence of life after death. Is there, or could there be, a rational basis for this difference? If there is a rational basis, does it reflect the fact that we simply cannot trust other people in reporting their experiences the way that we can trust ourselves? If there is no rational basis, does this mean that people who have not had "out-of-body" experiences should take more seriously the reports of those who have had? Or does it mean that those who have had such experiences should take them *less* seriously?
2. Describing the stories about "out-of-body" experiences that he has collected, Moody says that they do not prove anything scientifically. Do you agree? Do you believe that Moody's stories help *at all* in providing evidence in support of life after death?

JAMES E. ALCOCK

Psychology and Near-Death Experiences

The Experience of Dying

According to Raymond Moody (1975, 1977), the experiences of patients who have survived "death" provide compelling evidence of the continued postmortem existence of the soul. People from widely divergent backgrounds and belief systems experience very similar events following their deaths, he says, and this communality of experience points to the *reality* of the experience. While there is considerable variation on the theme, the "theoretically complete model experience," according to Moody, is as follows: At the moment of greatest physical discomfort, the patient hears the physician pronounce him dead, and he hears an uncomfortably loud ringing or buzzing sound. He feels himself being drawn rapidly through a long tunnel. He notices that he has a new body with powers very different from the old one, and may even see his old body lying on the bed with the resuscitation team gathered around it; but his vantage point is outside and above his body. He catches sight of dead relatives and friends and encounters a "being" of very bright light, a "loving, warm spirit." This spirit helps him to panoramically review the events of his past life. He is overwhelmed by feelings of love, joy, and peace. He has a vision of all-encompassing knowledge, the wisdom of the ages. Finally, he comes to some kind of barrier, but is made to turn back and go, reluctantly, back into his body. Following his resuscitation, he is emotionally very moved and is no longer afraid of death.

Moody is a psychiatrist and is well aware that certain physiological conditions might bring on such experiences, but he takes great pains to argue that no physiological or psychological factors could account for all the data. However, he appears to ignore a great deal of the scientific literature dealing with hallucinatory experiences in general, just as he quickly glosses over the very real limitations of his research method. He argues that, since obvious possible causes of hallucinations can't account for his data (a conclusion he

James E. Alcock, an associate professor of psychology at York University in Toronto, is the author of Parapsychology: Science or Magic? *and other works in psychology and parapsychology. He is a founding member of the Committee for the Scientific Investigation of Claims of the Paranormal and serves on the editorial board of* The Skeptical Inquirer.

From "Psychology and Near-Death Experiences" in *Paranormal Borderlands of Science*, ed. K. Frazier, 1981. By permission of Prometheus Books.

draws more or less by fiat), therefore it must be a matter of genuine psychic experience. This argument is of the classic Abbott and Costello form, where one of them "proves" that the other person "isn't here":

> "Are you in London?"
> "No."
> "Are you in Paris?"
> "No."
> "Are you in Moscow?"
> "No."
> "Well, if you aren't in London, Paris, or Moscow, you must be somewhere else."
> "Yah, I guess so."
> "Well, if you're somewhere else, you can't be here."

If it's not due to psychological, neurological, or pharmacological factors (that can be identified), then it has no natural explanation. The explanation must lie somewhere else, beyond our "ordinary" world. This kind of reasoning is common in the survivalist literature.

We must wonder, too, about the reliability of the memories of Moody's respondents. They related their death experiences to him usually long after they occurred, and generally after having heard Moody speak on the subject. Even then, he finds a wide spectrum of experience, some people reporting only one or two of the key elements, others reporting most of them. Also, he says, many people report no experience at all. It is interesting to note (Moody, 1975, p. 26) that the respondents "uniformly characterize their experience as inexpressible," despite their ability to describe them in considerable detail. Moody admits that people have reported similar experiences in situations where no jeopardy to life was involved. Mystical and drug experiences can be quite similar, he admits. To account for this, Moody begs the question and speculates that during such non-death experiences, the mechanism that releases the soul at death may be prematurely triggered.

* * * * *

Hallucinations

While we often think of hallucinations (imagery so powerful that one is certain that it is real) as having an infinite variety of themes and contents, such is apparently not the case. As far back as 1926, Kluver (cited by Siegal, 1977), at the University of Chicago, found that mescaline-induced imagery was constructed around four constant form-types ("form constants"): (1) grating or lattice, (2) cobwebs, (3) tunnel/funnel, (4) spirals. These forms are characterized by vivid colors and intense brightness (perhaps brought about by the failure of inhibiting mechanisms in the visual system). Kluver discovered that these same form constants were typical of imagery brought about in a wide range of hallucinogenic conditions, from hypnagogic and hypnopompic sleep to delirium to dizziness to sensory deprivation. More recent experiments (Siegal, 1977) using cannabis found drug-induced imagery to have two stages. The first is characterized by Kluver's form constants, the second by more complex imagery that can incorporate the form constants but which can include memory images of familiar people and objects. One might again expect almost infinitely diverse images in the complex stages, but this wasn't the case. (Using LSD, 72 percent of subjects experienced the same form constants, and 79 percent experienced quite similar complex images. Seventy-two percent saw religious images and 49 percent saw human and animal images.) The typical imagery in the cannabis study was characterized by a bright light in the center of the field of vision: the location of the point of light created a *tunnel-like perspective* (a la Moody?). Subjects reported viewing much of their imagery in relation to the tunnel, and the other imagery seemed to move relative to the tunnel. (Subjects given placebos reported only black and white "random" form imagery.) Further studies showed that, whether the cannabis, mescaline, or LSD, after ninety minutes, most of the forms viewed were *tunnel-lattice* in nature. More complex imagery appeared usually only well after the shift to the tunnel-lattice. Common reported images involved childhood memories and scenes associated with strong emotional experiences that the person had undergone (similar to *panoramic review*?). They often reported an aerial perspective of themselves, and feelings of dissociation from the body. The imagery was also influenced by environmental stimuli. During the peak period, they asserted that the images were real.

Siegal concluded that "the experiments point to underlying mechanisms in the central nervous system as the source of a universal phenomenology of hallucinations" (p.132) and points to recent electrophysiological studies that "confirm that hallucinations are directly related to states of excitation and arousal of the central nervous system, which are coupled with a functional disorganization of the part of the brain that regulates memorizing stimuli."

It seems, then, that there is no doubt that ordinary hallucinations can contain virtually all of the elements described by Moody, and that preoccupation with dying is likely to make more likely the notion of the separation of the soul from the body and the meeting with loved ones who have died. Again it is surprising to see virtually no references to hallucination research (apart from cursory attempts to discredit the possibility that ordinary hallucinations are involved) in the life-after-life literature. Moody (1977) agrees that sensations of being drawn down a tunnel are often reported by persons being placed under anesthesia, especially when ether is used. But he argues that since very few of his subjects were under the influence of drugs, and since few had had any neurological problems, these experiences are not equivalent to drug-induced or other hallucinations. Again, he uses the Abbott-Costello logic—they hadn't had drugs, they had no neurological problems, therefore it was psychic. As mentioned earlier, Moody's trump card is to argue that, even if other types of hallucinations are similar to the death experiences, it is quite possible that the other hallucinations *themselves* are a manifestation of the premature release of the soul.

Hypnotic Regression

One more tool in the survivalist's armamentarium is hypnotic regression to lives past. Although you'd never know it on the basis of the literature in this area, there is considerable controversy in modern psychology about what ordinary hypnosis, not to mention regression, really does. Some argue that it puts the subject into a special state of consciousness; others argue that it leads only to a state of heightened suggestibility; where the subject and hypnotist tacitly ("unconsciously"?) collaborate to bring about the "experience" of hypnosis.

As for age-regression (even within the *current* lifetime!) there is mounting evidence that, while the subject may focus on long-dormant memories, no real "regression" (e.g., in cognitive function) actually occurs. While that is still the subject of some debate, the regression to memories of *past* lives is what's relevant for us at this point, and it goes without saying that past-life regression is not accepted as veridical by the vast majority of psychologists.

One of the most famous cases was the classic Bridey Murphy, the subject of the best-selling book *In Search of Bridey Murphy*. The story began in 1952, when a Colorado housewife by the name of Virginia Tighe (called Ruth Simmons in the book) was hypnotically "regressed" and began to describe her previous life as Bridey Murphy in Cork, Ireland. The fact that she spoke at this point in an uncharacteristic Irish brogue lent credence to her "experience." She told a very descriptive story about life and people in Ireland, even though investigators hired by the hypnotist-author, Morey Bernstein, could find no record in Ireland of a Bridey Murphy who lived in Cork (Gardner, 1957).

Dr. Ian Stevenson, a University of Virginia parapsychologist and a renowned "expert" and prolific writer on the subject, remains very impressed with the Bridey Murphy case. In fact, in an article (Stevenson, 1977) in the new *Handbook of Parapsychology*, he states that it still "has not been improved upon in the many books since written for the general public that have reported experiments with hypnotic regression" (p. 636). Yet, while Stevenson extols the merits of the Bridey Murphy case, he remains unimpressed by what others consider to be the undoing of Virginia Tighe (Gardner, 1957). In 1956, a *Chicago American* reporter visited Virginia's hometown and discovered that her background was far from being unrelated to her stories of Bridey Murphy. The reporter interviewed a Mrs. Anthony Corkell, who had lived across the street from Virginia for many years and whose Irish background and stories of Ireland apparently fascinated the young girl. Moreover, Virginia had been active in her high school drama program and had learned several Irish monologues, which she had delivered in what her former teacher referred to as a heavy Irish brogue. She even had an Irish aunt who had also entertained her with stories of Ireland. And, oh yes, about the lady across the street, Mrs. Corkell: her maiden name was Bridey Murphy! Despite this, and despite the assessment by Irish experts of her descriptions of Ireland as artificial and contrived, survivalist parapsychologists such as Stevenson reject this evidence and continue to consider this case to be a strong one, and the Bridey Murphy book is still undergoing regular reprintings.

In all likelihood, the material generated by the hypnotized subjects is a fictional blend of information and stories that they had once learned but had "forgotten." Stevenson and others naturally disagree with this interpretation. However, a study by

Zolik (1958) lends credence to this view. Zolik hypnotized subjects and "regressed" them to "past lives," and then induced posthypnotic amnesia; and at a later time rehypnotized them and questioned them about characters and events from their earlier "past-life" accounts. He found that subjects had constructed the past-life stories from events of their own lives combined with events and people from books and plays. Surely those who were not impressed by this would at least have used Zolik's approach to examine the reports of their subjects. But no. None of this has had any effect on the confirmed survivalist. For example, Dr. Wambach, the author of a recent book on past-life regression (Wambach, 1978), has admitted to me that the reports she has gathered from hypnotized subjects who had been "regressed" to past lives do not in any way differ from those of unhypnotized subjects. She interprets this as evidence that one can have access to past-life material *without* being hypnotized.

Assessment

Each and all of the various characteristics of the "death" experience have been found to occur, alone or in a combination, in various "normal," non-death circumstances, such as those associated with emotional or physical stress, sensory deprivation, hypnagogic sleep, drug-induced hallucination, and so on. We know that the nervous system can process these experiences, even if we can't always predict when the experiences will occur. The famous "tunnel," the very bright light, the visions of others, the sense of ineffability, the out-of-body experiences, and the subsequent loss of a fear of death, etc., are, at the very least, not *unique* to any postmortem existence. Thus, unless one accepts either that postmortem reality mimics these earthly experiences that some people have from time to time, or that, as Moody suggests, these experiences of the living are brought about by a premature and temporary release of the soul, the reports of people who have been near death pose no demand for metaphysical interpretation.

It is clear that the "scientific," "objective" evidence for life after death is very unimpressive indeed. However, survivalist researchers are undeterred by such criticisms of their work; and it is abundantly apparent that, evidence or no evidence, they are, most of them at least, thoroughly convinced of their own immortality. Moody admits this directly, as does Kubler-Ross (1977) when she describes death as the "peaceful transition into God's garden." I have no argument with people's theology or philosophy. What is bothersome, however, is the necessity these people feel to try to provide "objective" evidence to support their beliefs, and their attempts to fool the layman with their claims of scientific rigor and exactitude. Survival research is based on belief in search of data rather than observation in search of explanation. It is an extension of individual and collective anxiety about death. Already such research has yielded a palliative vision of death as a grand, beautiful transition to a newer and better life. Gone are the worries about hellfire and damnation of old.

If one were to believe Moody and others, why not abandon this often frustrating earthly existence and dispatch oneself forthwith to the wonderful world beyond? Even Moody doesn't want to encourage that, and he tells us that those who have survived death report that they had the "feeling" that those on the "other side" take a dim view of those here on earth who try to speed their admission to paradise. (The early Christians had a similar problem; for they too promised a wonderful life hereafter, and many of their converts, not too well taken care of in their earthly lives, chose to go directly to the next life without delay. It is hard to build a social movement if the recruits keep killing themselves, and so suicide quickly became a heinous sin for Christians.) Despite Moody's discouragements about suicide, there are bound to be those who are enthused enough by his reports to go ahead with it anyway. I have already heard of one woman whose child was killed and, having read a book like Moody's, attempted suicide in order to rejoin her child.

At any rate, we should not, in our irritation at both those who disseminate survivalist pseudoscience and those who so quickly swallow it whole, overlook the fact that some dying people do have "mystical" experiences just as some living people do. Remember that Mesmer was uniquely successful at treating hysteria; but when the scientists branded him a fraud because they were able to prove that magnets weren't essential to his treatment (contrary to his belief that they were), he was put out of business; and as a result there was no one around who could cure hysteria. We shouldn't overlook the phenomenon just because we reject the explanation. Even while seeing no reason to resort to metaphysics to explain it, we should nonetheless study it in its own right. A few medical researchers (e.g., Noyes, 1972; Noyes & Kletti, 1976) have gathered reports of near-death experiences that are quite similar to some of those described here but see no need to involve metaphysical explanations. We need more such research. It would be a pity to leave it all to the psychics.

References

Gardner, M. 1957. *Fads and Fallacies in the Name of Science.* New York: Dover.

Moody, R. 1977. *Reflections on Life After Life.* Atlanta: Mockingbird Books.

———. 1975. *Life After Life.* Atlanta: Mockingbird Books.

Noyes, R. 1972. "The Experience of Dying." *Psychiatry* 35: 174–183.

Noyes, R. and R. Kletti 1976. "Depersonalization in the Face of Life-Threatening Danger. *Psychiatry* 39: 19–27.

Siegal, R. K. 1977. "Hallucinations." *Scientific American* (October): 132–140.

Stevenson, I. 1977. "Reincarnation: Field Studies and Theoretical Issues." In *Handbook of Parapsychology*, ed. B. B. Wolman, pp. 631–663. New York: Van Nostrand.

Wambach, H. 1978. *Revisiting Past Lives.* New York: Harper & Row.

Zolik, E. S. 1958. "An Experimental Investigation of the Psychodynamic Implications of the Hypnotic 'Previous Existence' Fantasy." *Journal of Clinical Psychology* 14: 179–183.

COMMENTS ■ QUESTIONS

1. According to Alcock, those who claim that stories about near-death "out-of-body" experiences provide evidence in support of life after death make use of "Abbott-Costello logic," that is, they argue that the "out-of-body" experiences must have a paranormal cause because no psychological, neurological, or pharmacological causes are apparent. Alcock rejects this line of argument. Is he correct in doing so?
2. Near-death "out-of-body" experiences and certain experiences induced by drugs have reported similarities. Therefore, says Alcock, we have reason to believe that near-death experiences are hallucinations. In contrast, Raymond Moody (whose research is discussed by Martin Ebon in the preceding selection) argues that we should be open to the possibility that drugs may cause the soul to leave the body. What might be said in deciding which is the correct view?
3. Alcock discusses the phenomenon of "hypnotic past life regression." He concludes: "In all likelihood, the material generated by the hypnotized subjects is a fictional blend of information and stories that they had once learned but had forgotten." If you have had occasion to read a sampling of the stories told about "hypnotic past life regression" (some of which are cited in the bibliography at the end of the chapter), would you say that Alcock is correct?

PAUL AND LINDA BADHAM

Claimed Memories of Former Lives

Claimed memories of former lives seem to fall into two main categories. The first consists of spontaneous claims to "remember" a past life, made by the subject while awake and fully conscious. The second consists of apparent memories which emerge in dreams, or which are articulated in response to questions asked under hypnosis when a subject has been told to "go back in time".[1] Let us begin by looking at alleged cases of spontaneous waking memories of former lives.

There is clearly one name which stands above all others in this field of research: that of Ian Stevenson, whose university department has systematically investigated 1300 or so cases over two decades.[2] Professor Stevenson is especially noted for his caution in an area where accusations of fraud (whether conscious or unconscious, on the part of either experimenter or subjects) are so easily made.[3] Moreover, his attention to detail and the mass of evidence he accumulates so painstakingly and meticulously place his work on quite a distinct level. Consider the following which is a précis of one case from the study he published in 1966.[4]

At the age of 4½, a boy named Prakesh began to declare that his "real" name was Nirmal, and that

1. Cf. J. Iverson, *More Lives than One?* (Pan, 1977) p. 24.

2. I. Stevenson, *Cases of the Reincarnation Type*, vol. 1 *Ten Cases in India* (Univ. Press of Virginia, 1975) p. 1.

3. Dr. John Beloff, for example, describes Stevenson as "unquestionably one of the most intellectually distinguished persons at present working in the field of parapsychology. He is a person of unimpeachable integrity and judgment". JSPR (1967) p. 89.

4. I. Stevenson, *Twenty Cases Suggestive of Reincarnation* (ASPR 1966) pp. 20–33.

Paul Badham is chairman of Church History and Senior Lecturer in Theology and Religious Studies at Saint David's University College in the University of Wales. In addition to Immortality or Extinction? *he has written* Christian Beliefs about Life after Death *and is editor of* Religion State and Society in Modern Britain *and* The Value of Human Life. *Linda Badham, who has a doctorate in philosophy of science from the University of Wales, has published articles and coedited a book in the philosophy of religion. She is a sixth form tutor and teacher of mathematics at Aberaeron in West Wales.*

From *Immortality or Extinction?* by Paul and Linda Badham. Permission granted by Barnes and Noble Books, Totowa, N.J.

his "real" home was in Kosi Kalan. He named "his" father and sister, and talked of "his father's" shops in detail and longing, and the names of many neighbours. He insisted that he be called Nirmal, and night after night he tried to run off towards Kosi Kalan, "home". He went on and on until his parents beat him to stop his chatter. However, unknown to his parents, Prakesh's alleged memories exactly corresponded to the life situation of a boy named Nirmal who had died shortly before Prakesh's birth. This was not discovered until five years later when Nirmal's father happened to visit Prakesh's village. Prakesh immediately recognised "his" father and begged to be taken "home". This meeting led to further "reunions" and an eventual visit to Nirmal's former home. Prakesh recognised by name and with suitable emotional overtones all Nirmal's brothers, sisters, relatives and friends. He showed intimate knowledge of the house and all its fittings, save that his knowledge was geared to the situation of ten years previous so that he was puzzled by features that had been altered in the intervening decade. Stevenson came across this case three weeks after the first "reunion", and has set out in tabulated form 34 of Prakesh's claimed memories, the names of those who remembered him making each claimed memory prior to the "reunion", and the names of those in the other family who could verify the accuracy of each alleged memory as a fact pertaining to the actual life-situation of Nirmal. Moreover, every member of each family testified that before the "reunion", they had had no knowledge whatsoever of each other's families.[5]

The case is typical of those described by Stevenson in his books, except that Prakesh's exclusive identification of himself with his "former life" is unusual. Most children in such cases would say, "Now I'm called John, but I used to be called Fred when I was big, rather than saying, "I'm Fred, don't call me John".[6] But with this difference of emphasis, all the reported cases follow the same pattern. The case of a girl named Gnanatilleka is interesting, because her "reunion" with her alleged former family was arranged by an investigating committee under strict conditions.[7] Likewise the case of a girl named Swarnlata is interesting, in that her "former" family and home were traced for her by the parapsychology department at the University of Rajasthan on the basis of the description she gave them.[8] But the most impressive in this respect is the case of a Lebanese boy called Imad, for in this case, Stevenson arrived before anyone had tried to verify any of his alleged memories, and Stevenson was able to take down details of 47 supposed memories in writing before anyone had tried to find out to whose life-situation they might belong.[9] Further, the guesses made by Imad's parents about the possible identity of the former life were shown to be wrong,[10] so it is clear that there was no previous interaction between the two families. In spite of this, 44 out

5. Ibid., pp. 23–30.
6. Ibid., p. 320.
7. Ibid., p. 119.
8. Ibid., p. 64.
9. Ibid., pp. 257, 271.
10. Ibid., p. 290.

of the recorded 47 memories were found to be exactly right.[11] Moreover, as they journeyed to the home Imad claimed to remember, more memories came back to him, of which 7 included accurate knowledge about his supposed former self.[12]

Stevenson comments that far more important than the number of accurate memories is the fact that in all these cases the children's behaviour accords with the personalities of their supposed former selves. X not only claims to be Y in a new body, he also personates Y—he behaves as if he were Y being reunited to his old family. He weeps with joy to see his relatives again, he is upset and profoundly disturbed to hear of bad news affecting them; he is happier with those relatives to whom Y was particularly close than with others. His character, aptitudes, fears and pleasures are those of the person with whom he identifies. Stevenson writes, "The identification by these children with the previous personality seems to me one of the most important features of these cases. Such personation, with components of strongly emotional behaviour, transcends the simple recital by the child of information about another person who had lived before".[13]

Stevenson sums up the behavioural aspects of these cases thus:

"(a) Repeated statements by the subject of the identification;

(b) repeated presentation of information about the previous personality as coming to the subject in the form of memories of events experienced or of people already known;

(c) requests to go to the previous home either for a visit or permanently;

(d) familiar address and behaviour towards adults and children related to the previous personality according to the relationships and social customs which would be proper if the child really had had the relationships he claims to have had with these persons;

(e) emotional responses, e.g. of tears, joy, affection, fear or resentment appropriate for the relationships and attitudes shown by the previous personality toward other persons and objects; and

(f) mannerisms, habits, and skills which would be appropriate for the previous personality or which he was known to possess".[14]

One final interesting feature of these studies concerns the "fading" of general interest on the part of the subject in his former life, in his memories of it, and even of the distinctive behavioural traits (as in (f) above). For example in the case of Sunil Dutt Saxena who claimed to remember being a wealthy business man, Seth Sri Krishna, Stevenson reports: "In 1971 Sunil (who was then 12 years old) has almost completely forgotten about the previous life and had entirely lost the features of his behaviour which had set him apart from his siblings and which corresponded closely to similar traits re-

11. Ibid., pp. 257, 271.
12. Ibid., pp. 273–4.
13. Ibid., p. 5.
14. Ibid., p. 324.

ported for Seth Sri Krishna".[15] Although this is commonly the pattern, it is not invariably followed, and there are cases in which memories and some characteristic behavioural traits may linger on.[16]

Now whatever other interpretation we may choose to give to the data Stevenson has collected, one option seems not to be open. Fraud, whether intentional or unintentional, by Stevenson himself, his co-workers, or the subjects of their studies and their families and other witnesses, is not a plausible "explanation". The sheer thoroughness of Stevenson's methods precludes it for the cases he himself is prepared to endorse. Every witness was subjected to rigorous questioning, careful notes were taken of what was said and these were checked against a second inquiry some years later. Further, in some of these cases, Stevenson was able to compare his information with that acquired by other serious investigators.[17] The sheer numbers of witnesses involved would also make a conspiracy of fraud difficult, especially when sustained for several years. Further to these considerations we must add the difficulty of directing and staging the highly emotional scenes Stevenson observed. And in the case of Imad the hypothesis of fraud seems particularly to be ruled out by the fact that Stevenson conducted the full inquiry himself and learned that the preliminary hypothesis of Imad's parents was wholly false, and that therefore they could not have organised a fraud.

The only hypothesis which might enable one to discount the evidence is that of casting doubt on Stevenson's intellectual integrity. Unfortunately, some writers in this field are not always above twisting the data to fit their beliefs.[18] But it is just not plausible to write Stevenson off as being so keen to convince us of the truth of reincarnation that he misrepresents matters to fit his case. For he lists all the "wrong" memories as well as those which turned out to be correct; and he does not try to make weak cases appear stronger than the evidence warrants. Moreover, he gives careful consideration to various possible hypotheses (including cryptomnesia, i.e. the submerged memory of events forgotten by the conscious self) to account for the data, and even though he concludes that reincarnation is the most plausible, this is for him a bona fide conclusion and not a preconceived result he has set out to prove.

I shall take up this question of how such data are to be interpreted later. First, let us move on to review cases where the alleged memories only emerge in dreams, or when under hypnosis a person is asked to

---

15. Stevenson, *Cases of the Reincarnation Type*, p. 143.

16. Cf. the case of Jagdish Chandra, ibid., pp. 172–5.

17. Stevenson, *Twenty cases*, pp. 49 and viii.

18. It is not uncommon to find champions of reincarnation attributing falsely such beliefs to various of the early Christian Fathers, and even to philosophers like Hume and Kant. cf. discussion of this point in J. Hick, *Death and Eternal Life* (Collins, 1976) pp. 392 ff., notes 2 and 16 where Hick criticises Weatherhead. Note also the quotations from Hume and Kant cited by C. J. Ducasse, *The Belief in Life After Death* (Springfield, 1961) p. 216. A comparison with the original contexts shows the extent to which these quotations are misrepresentations of their authors' overall positions.

"remember" events of a previous life. Perhaps the best known case here is that of "Ruth Mill Simmons",[19] who under hypnosis apparently recalled vividly and accurately a previous life in nineteenth-century Ireland as Bridey Murphy. However, this case illustrates rather clearly the difficulty of establishing the evidential character of such information. For it has been claimed that subsequent research suggests that Ruth Simmons was recalling not "her own" memories of a former life, but rather she was bringing into consciousness and dramatising as her own experience, vivid stories about life in Ireland told to her in childhood by acquaintances of Irish extraction.

Yet there are cases of claimed memories that emerge under hypnosis or in dreams which do not seem so easily squeezed into this "reductive" explanatory mould. First there are cases which seem to supply accurate historical information transcending anything which might be considered readily available to non-experts. Secondly, and even more puzzling, are reported cases of responsive xenoglossy, i.e. where the subject under hypnosis is said to be able to converse in a language unknown to him otherwise, and which he seems not to have learned by any normal means.

Some of the most well-publicised cases in recent years of detailed historical memories belong to the Bloxham tape collection as researched by Jeffrey Iverson.[20] Of particular interest is the subject "Jane Evans" [21] who was regressed to seven quite different lives. Three of these lives particularly lend themselves to historical investigation. In these, Mrs Evans appears to relive, in the role of a minor character, situations whose features can be checked against documented historical facts. On the "plus" side for the reincarnationist there are four major considerations. First while under hypnosis subjects often identify completely with the person whose life they seem to be remembering. Indeed, they may show signs of suffering if they report "reliving" some nasty experience.[22] Moreover some stories, and in particular those of Mrs Evans, are not only detailed; they are also, by and large, consistent with what is known of the history of the relevant period. Thirdly, the perspectives from which the subjects tell their stories are in keeping with the characters they personate. For example, Mrs Evans often shows no knowledge of some of the best-known text-book facts about the situations she describes, where such facts would not have been available to the ordinary eye-witness who really was "there" at the time, and whose view of events would inevitably have been limited. Now if the subject has in fact read or heard stories about the events she relates, but has forgotten them in her conscious mind, it is surprising that she seems not to know some of the most commonly cited historical details. What is so hard to understand is the ap-

19. The pseudonym of Virginia Burns Tighe.

20. J. Iverson, *More Lives than One?*

21. Ibid.

22. Cf. ibid., pp. 24, 119; also Arthur Guirdham, *The Cathars and Reincarnation* (Neville Spearman, 1970) p. 89.

parent selection and arrangement of the material. Certainly, it would seem to be an extremely complicated process to sift through the data, extracting precisely that which is commensurate with the life-situation of a relatively insignificant individual while dispensing totally with the rest. Fourthly, it has been claimed, at least for Jane Evans, that she supplies historical details which were unknown to experts of the relevant period, but which were subsequently verified.[23]

But there are also many points on the "minus" side. First, we cannot take the indubitable reality of the experience for the subject as he "relives" some often extremely unpleasant experiences while under hypnosis or in dreams, to indicate anything more than that the subject is not pretending. Even if physical symptoms of disease, injury or extreme pain are manifested, this does not in itself suffice to show that the subject really once was the person with whom he identifies. As Stevenson has pointed out, mystics have also developed physical signs such as stigmata, by intense identification with the crucified Christ.[24] But we do not conclude that these individuals are reincarnations of Jesus.

Secondly, not all of the details given by the subjects are considered by experts to be right for an eye-witness in the situation as described.[25] Moreover, it strikes one immediately how much Mrs Evans' (who is Bloxham's "best" case) most impressive lives read like historical romances. So often, near-historical novels weave a plausible tale around some lesser (or even fictional) character through whose eyes we see a major historical drama unfold. Further the author of such a work may use it to air some pet theory on a subject for which the historical details are tantalisingly missing. Now Mrs Evans seems in many of her "lives" to re-enact the role of a minor figure in the history of some notable person or event. And in one case in particular, she "fills in" some highly plausible details about the lives of some of the best-known personalities in the Roman world.[26] Now I am not suggesting that what Mrs Evans is doing is a straightforward rehearsal of some elements in an historical novel which she has long-since consciously forgotten. But it does not seem entirely implausible that some combination of cryptomnesia involving the use of such material plus dramatisation might account for her

23. Cf. Iverson, *More Lives than One?* pp. 43–6, 83.

24. I. Stevenson, *The Evidence for Survival from Claimed Memories of Former Incarnations* (ASPR reprint, 1961) p. 40.

25. For example, at least two of Mrs Evans other "personnae" gave faulty information. Thus "Alison" seemed not to know that her master, Jacques Coeur, was married. (Iverson, *More Lives than One?*, pp. 68, 62 ff.) "Livonia" made reference to Roman ladies riding on horseback rather than in carriages. (Iverson, p. 58.) Again, Guirdham's subject reported being the mistress of a Cathar 'priest'. This seems intrinsically incredible, partly because Cathars rejected a set-apart priesthood, and also because their "parfaits" were those who had succeeded in "perfecting detachment from" the temptations of the flesh. Moreover they risked—and usually suffered—the unspeakable tortures of the inquisition in loyalty to their beliefs and ascetic practices. Why anyone should *pretend* to be a Cathar parfait at such an appalling risk beggars the imagination! (cf. Guirdham, *The Cathars and Reincarnation*, p. 92.)

26. Cf. Iverson, *More Lives than One?*, p. 47.

"memories".

There is one final enormous difficulty with taking these reports at their face value as evidential of genuine personal memories, namely that of language. Iverson does not feel that the failure of subjects like Jane Evans to speak the natural languages of their other personnae is necessarily a threat to their testimony. He writes: "No one is certain what areas [of the brain] are being activated under hypnosis. Memories, in any case, are frequently divorced from speech ... One of Bloxham's subjects told me being regressed was a mainly visual experience supplemented by 'words which just pop into your head' ".[27] He suggests that hypnotic regression may involve something similar to electrode stimulation of the brain during which patients vividly recall former experiences which they see, as if it were a film-strip running in their heads.[28] But even with these pleas in mitigation, the problem remains. For, it is no longer acceptable to think of language as just a means of naming private experiences. Rather, in the light of twentieth-century philosophy we have come to realise that what we see and experience is intimately linked with the language we use to report such experiences, whether to others or even to ourselves. It is thus highly implausible that so central a feature of someone's mental life as the language he spoke and in which he formulated his thoughts, should disappear completely in his "reincarnation".[29] In short, the absence of ability to speak the appropriate language counts strongly against any claim that the subject really once was the person whose life he or she seems to remember.

However, there have been some reported cases of responsive xenoglossy in which the subject under hypnosis was apparently able to converse in the language of the individual whose life he or she seemed to remember.[30] For example, Stevenson has mentioned the following two cases. One subject "assumed the personality of a Norseman of mediaeval times and conversed in the dialect [of early Norwegian] although still capable of understanding some English".[31] Another case involved an American woman, Lydia Johnson, who in earlier sessions of hypnosis spoke broken English punctuated with foreign words, but later spoke almost entirely in Swedish. She "became" a seventeenth-century Swedish farmer called Jansen Jacoby. But experiments were hastily wound up when Jacoby "reappeared" unbidden and without the prior hypnosis of the subject.[32] Similarly, Leslie Weatherhead cites the case of a Lancashire woman, Annie Baker, who, it was alleged, was able under hyp-

---

27. Ibid., p. 141.

28. Ibid., p. 142; cf. A. Spraggett, *The Case for Immortality* (Signet, 1975) p. 140.

29. I do not count "Livonia's" references to York as "Eboracum" and to Bath as "Aqua Sulis" as the ability to speak Latin. This is just the sort of minimal linguistic data which English language histories or novels might supply.

30. This is to be contrasted with recitative xenoglossy where the subject is able to reproduce only a limited number of phrases in the foreign language and cannot converse in it.

31. Stevenson, *The Evidence for Survival*, p. 42.

32. Cf. section on Stevenson in J. Head and S. L. Cranston, (compilers and editors), *Reincarnation: the Phoenix Fire Mystery* (Julian Press, 1966) pp. 437–9.

nosis (though not otherwise) to speak fluent French.[33] This lady apparently gave details of a former life during the French Revolution.

So what are we to make of these strange tales? The "normal" explanation, namely cryptomnesia, is supported by at least three psychological considerations. First, under hypnosis people are usually extremely suggestible and anxious to oblige; secondly hypnosis can enable them to recall long-forgotten information and past experiences; and thirdly, almost all of us have, according to Anthony Storr, a "B-movie" permanently running in our subconscious.[34] However, at first sight the cryptomnesia hypothesis might appear intrinsically implausible for cases where the subjects seem to supply impressively detailed information about history. For example, on reading the summary given in the secondary literature of a woman who "remembered" in dreams life during the Cathar persecution of the thirteenth century, one might well feel that here was a cast iron case of inexplicable historical knowledge.[35]

Turning to the original source material, however, it becomes apparent that the woman who possessed these "memories" had a singular capacity for unconscious memorising. For example, as a school girl, she had almost been expelled for cheating on the grounds that an examination script contained verbatim extracts from a commentary on poetry. She saved herself from the ignominy by reproducing under closer supervision the same passages.[36] Likewise in later life she burnt a novel she had written after she discovered that much of it was verbally very similar to an article which she could not recall having read. But having stumbled on this article, she called her own work "unconscious plagiarism".[37] For these reasons she herself refused to believe in her supposed "reincarnation"—a point insufficiently noted in the secondary literature.[38]

Moreover, concerning claimed historical memories which emerge under hypnotic regression, such as those in the Bloxham collection, there are two vexing omissions. First, it is a great pity that Bloxham seems not to have invited professional historians to supply questions whose answers might have provided a strong indication, one way or the other, as to the evidential quality of the subjects' "memories". Secondly, some experimenters like E. S. Zolick,[39] who have used hypnotic regression on patients, have in subsequent sessions asked the hypnotised subject what the source of his information was. Bloxham, however, does not seem to have tried this line of questioning. Now I am not suggesting that such tests could prove conclusively whether or not the knowledge hypnotised subjects seem to have is explicable by some purely "normal" hypothesis. But it would

33. L. Weatherhead, *The Christian Agnostic* (Hodder and Stoughton, 1967) pp. 248–9.

34. Iverson, *More Lives than One?*, p. 138.

35. Cf. Head and Cranston, *Reincarnation*, pp. 398–401; Christine Hartley, *A Case for Reincarnation* (Robert Hale, 1972) pp. 133 ff.

36. Guirdham, *The Cathars and Reincarnation*, p. 48.

37. Ibid., pp. 46, 135.

38. Ibid., p. 47.

39. E. S. Zolick, "An Experimental Investigation of the Psychodynamic Implications of the Hypnotic 'Previous Existence' Fantasy", *F. Clin. Psychol., 14*, (1958) pp. 179–183.

at least narrow the possibilities. In particular, when subjects seem to know some very obscure historical facts, it would be helpful if we could be sure about two points: (a) the veracity of the subjects' statements; and (b) that the previously "unknown" data they provide are really just that. This latter point is potentially highly significant. Much is made of subjects' apparent knowledge which is subsequently verified by "surprised" experts.[40] The problem is to assess the significance of such claims. Often, the cases involve trivial "facts" which might either be accidentally true (because they are not *prime facie* unlikely anyway), or they might be reasonable speculations on the part of the author of the (forgotten) source of the subject's information, or they might possibly be less "unknown" than proponents of reincarnation claim. The reincarnationist case would be more convincing if subjects were to supply answers to concrete questions concerning, for example, the exact whereabouts of a particular building which is known to have existed, but which has never been located in modern times.[41]

Even so, it has to be admitted that there are some puzzling aspects of cases where subjects have historically accurate, verifiable and detailed knowledge going far beyond anything found in the classic case which is usually cited as evidence for the cryptomnesia hypothesis, namely Zolick's work on "the previous existence fantasy",[42] or in the historical literature available to the non-expert. And in the absence of adequate substantiation either way, it remains at least possible that there may be some cases of hypnotically induced or dreamed "memories" of former lives which cannot be fully explained by the cryptomnesia hypothesis.

Moreover, responsive xenoglossy is particularly unsuited to this sort of reductive explanation. It may be that on occasion, someone unwittingly stores some foreign phrases in his unconscious memory, and that these phrases can be retrieved under hypnosis.[43] But it is less plausible to think that on the basis of, say, gazing absentmindedly at an old Swedish volume or perhaps seeing a film, a subject might glean enough information to infer correctly the rules and vocabulary of seventeenth century Swedish and apply them! Yet such is the "explanation" which a cryptomnesia hypothesis offers in the case of Lydia Johnson/Jansen Jacoby.

In sum, then, there seem to be a wide variety of cases brought together under hypnotic regression and dream experiences. Some may be little more than wish-fulfilment fantasies or the products of lively imaginations. Sometimes, such fantasies may be woven around ideas not consciously remembered in waking life, and may even involve strong identification by the subject with the character in his fantasy. Still others may owe a great deal to suggestions

40. Iverson, *More Lives than One?*, pp. 45–6; A. Guirdham, p. 92.

41. Cf. Iverson, *More Lives than One?*, p. 59.

42. Zolick, "*An Experimental Investigation*", p. 179.

43. Cf. Stevenson, *The Evidence for Survival*, p. 25, in which he cites Rosen's case of a young man who had unconsciously retained a few phrases of Oscan from a book which happened to be open on his table in a library.

implanted by the hypnotist. But when we have eliminated all these "normal" explanations, we seem to be left with a residuum of cases which are not so readily dismissed. Of these, providing we can eliminate the possibility of fraud or misrepresentation, instances of responsive xenoglossy must come at the top of the list. But it is just possible that there are some cases of historical "memories" which are so rich in obscure but potentially verifiable detail, that a "normal" explanation might not do them justice. Likewise, Stevenson's accounts of claimed waking memories are not satisfactorily explicable by a cryptomnesia hypothesis. The former lives which his subjects claim to remember are usually of very ordinary folk. Thus in most cases, the only possible "normal" source of the subjects' knowledge about the life of the deceased would be from living people. But how then could they spontaneously recognise people and places? Moreover, when we consider the relative isolation which village life and the caste system impose on many of Stevenson's respondents, and also the lengths to which Stevenson goes to establish that the families involved knew nothing of one another prior to the child's voicing his claimed memories, the cryptomnesia hypothesis must surely be discounted.[44]

Stevenson considers that in the absence of any satisfactory "normal" explanations for the data he has collected, we are obliged to take seriously the possibility of paranormal accounts. He reviews various possibilities like telepathy or other sorts of E.S.P. or communication with a surviving personality (or part-personality), and argues convincingly why none of these accounts does full justice to many of his cases.[45] He concludes that "for some of the cases all the facts are better accounted for by supposing a continuing influence of the previous personality after death".[46] Thus for Stevenson, the spontaneous waking "memories" his subjects have point towards either reincarnation or possession, cases falling "along a continuum in which the distinction between reincarnation and possession becomes blurred".[47] So too with cases of responsive xenoglossy, he comments "when we can exclude normal acquisition of knowledge of the foreign language by the subject, the explanatory hypotheses become helpfully reduced and almost restricted to possession and reincarnation".[48]

Stevenson presents a strong case therefore, for saying that at least some claimed "memories of a former life" appear to be evidential for and suggestive of some theory of reincarnation or possession. However, what significance such conclusions would have for belief in personal survival of bodily death, and how they might cohere with the other considerations we have discussed in earlier chapters are questions which we must now try to answer.

---

44. Stevenson also contrasts in some detail various cryptomnesia cases with subjects claiming verifiably correct spontaneous waking memories. cf. Stevenson, *Twenty cases*, pp. 293–304.

45. Cf. Stevenson, *The Evidence for Survival*, pp. 28 ff.; and Stevenson, *Twenty cases*, pp. 305 ff.

46. Stevenson, *Twenty cases*, pp. 339–40.

47. Ibid., p. 340.

48. Stevenson, *The Evidence for Survival*, p. 43.

COMMENTS ■ QUESTIONS

1. Does anything said in this selection pose any *conceptual* problems regarding life after death that have not already been touched upon in the earlier selections in this chapter? Does the idea of reincarnation help to *solve* any of the conceptual problems pertaining to the idea of survival in general?
2. In discussing the views of Ian Stevenson, the Badhams say this: "Stevenson comments that far more important than the number of accurate memories is the fact that in all these cases the children's behavior accords with the personalities of their supposed former selves. X not only claims to be Y in a new body, he also personates Y—he behaves as if he were Y being reunited to his old family." What is your reaction to Stevenson's claim?
3. Do you agree with Stevenson's view that the most plausible explanation for certain claims by children to have lived former lives is that the children have *actually lived* former lives? If you disagree with Stevenson, is this because (a) you find the idea of reincarnation to be unclear or incoherent; (b) you suspect fraud or misrepresentation in the reports of stories about children's "past life memories;" (c) you hold to the view that the hypothesis of reincarnation should not be taken seriously until more is known about the possible basis for reincarnation in human nature; (d) you suspect that alleged past life memories could all be explained in "normal" ways if enough were known about the individual cases; or (e) you have some other reason for rejecting Stevenson's conclusion?
4. In regard to supposed memories of past lives induced by hypnosis, the Badhams comment: "It strikes one immediately how much Mrs. Evans' (who is Bloxham's 'best' case) most impressive lives read like historical romances." The matter at issue here is whether or not the hypnotically induced stories "ring true." What is your feeling about this?

READINGS

Broad, C. D. *Lectures on Psychical Research.* New York: Humanities Press, 1962. A sympathetic treatment of psychical research as providing evidence for survival.

Ducasse, C. J. *A Critical Examination of the Belief in Life After Death.* Springfield Ill.: Charles C Thomas, 1961. Clearly presented arguments for the possibility of survival.

Flew, Anthony. *A New Approach to Psychical Research.* London: Watts, 1953. A critical view of the claim that psychical research supports survival.

Geach, Peter. *God and the Soul.* London: Routledge & Kegan Paul, 1969. Chapter 2 discusses the doctrine of the resurrection of the body.

Gurney, Edmund, F. W. H. Myers, and Frank Podmore. *Phantasms of the Living.* London: Trubner, 1886. The classical work on stories about the appearances of "ghosts."

Iverson, Jeffrey. *More Lives Than One?* New York: Warner, 1976. Perhaps the most engaging popular account of "hynotic past life regression."

Lamont, Corliss. *The Illusion of Immortality.* New York: G. P. Putnam's Sons, 1935. Presents the case against survival.

Lenz, Frederick. *Life Times: True Accounts of Reincarnation.* New York: Fawcett Crest, 1979. Popular, anecdotal accounts of "spontaneous memories of past lives."

Martin, C. B. *Religious Belief.* Ithaca, N.Y.: Cornell University Press, 1959. Chapter 6 discusses the claim that survival after death is not conceivable.

Monroe, Robert A. *Journeys Out of the Body.* Garden City, N.Y.: Doubleday, Anchor Books, 1971. Popular, anecdotal account of Monroe's claim that he has had "out-of-body" experiences.

Moody, Raymond. *Life After Life.* New York: Bantam Books, 1976. Contains a large number of stories about "near death" experiences.

Penelhum, T. *Survival and Disembodied Existence.* London: Routledge & Kegan Paul, 1970. Discusses the "shadow-body" theory of the soul (among other theories) in conjunction with an analysis of arguments for and against survival.

Stevenson, Ian. *Cases of the Reincarnation Type.* 3 Vols. Charlottesville, Va.: University of Virginia Press, 1980. The best known and most carefully researched study of children's "memories of past lives."

Wambach, Helen. *Reliving Past Lives: The Evidence Under Hypnosis.* New York: Bantam Books, 1978. A popular account of Wambach's experiences as a regression hypnotist.

C H A P T E R   E I G H T

By happiness is intended pleasure, and the absence of pain; by unhappiness, pain, and the privation of pleasure.

—*John Stuart Mill*

Goodness is not the same thing as being, but even beyond being, surpassing it in dignity and power.

—*Plato*

The Foundations of Morality

rom one perspective, the job of philosophy is to answer questions fundamental to our everyday lives. This description is especially appropriate to the subject matter of this chapter—moral values. Morality tells us how we ought to live; it tells us what is good and what is bad, what is right and what is wrong. Morality is part of the fabric of our lives.

To many people, the guidance that morality provides is not satisfactory unless there are at least implicit answers to a number of questions about the nature of moral values. Not everyone needs to study philosophy to learn the answers to these questions, and not all of the questions appear important to everyone. Yet, the more a person reflects upon life, the more he or she wants thoughtful answers to these questions before "plunging back into the stream of life" where moral choices must constantly be made.

The study of morality impinges upon life at many different points; as a consequence, the important questions about the nature of moral values are somewhat diverse. Some are clearly interrelated, while others appear to stand more by themselves. A brief introduction to the foundations of morality, such as that contained in the present chapter, cannot examine all of the interrelations among the questions. A good way to begin is, however, simply to list some of the questions and indicate which of the reading selections in the chapter deals with each:

1. Are moral judgments based upon feelings? If so, in what way? (Discussed by James, Russell, Ewing, and Emerson)
2. Can there be scientific knowledge of moral values? (Discussed by Russell and indirectly by Ewing)
3. Are moral values relative to different cultures? (Discussed by Rachels)
4. Are moral values relative to individuals? (Discussed by Russell and Ewing and indirectly by Plato)

5. Are moral values an essential part of the universe or are they merely "tacked on" at a superficial level? That is, how important are moral values in the overall scheme of things? (Discussed by James, Plato, and Emerson)
6. What *are* the basic moral values, or moral principles? (Discussed by Kant and Mill)

The readings address these questions from a wide diversity of viewpoints. You must carefully think through the material and compare and contrast the viewpoints. You should decide which are most important, which contain questions that need to be answered, which give additional support for ideas that you believe in, and which indicate new directions for your own thoughts.

In the first selection, William James describes the conditions he considers necessary for moral issues to arise at all, such as consciousness, feeling, desire, and the making of a claim by a concrete person. Put another way, James answers the following question: What conditions are necessary for the application of value terms?

The second reading, from the ancient Greek philosopher Plato, answers the above question in a very different way from James. Plato's selection is in the form of a dialogue between Socrates, who had been Plato's teacher, and Glaucon, who was Plato's brother. In the English translation from the Greek, the word "Good" is capitalized. This is done because the Good was a very special sort of reality for Plato. He believed in the existence of two worlds—the material world that is all around us and an immaterial or supernatural world that is more perfect than the material world. The second of these worlds is usually referred to as the "World of Platonic Forms." It cannot be seen or heard, said Plato, but instead can be known only by the use of reason or "pure thought" to contemplate the nature of reality.

As the central feature in Plato's philosophy, the theory of Forms has a major role in Plato's theory of knowledge, in his metaphysics, and in his value theory. Perhaps the best way to introduce Plato's theory of Forms briefly is to give his arguments for the existence of "geometrical Forms." Most philosophers would agree that they are the clearest examples of Platonic Forms.

Consider the nature of triangles. According to Plato, Triangularity, which is a Form, exists in addition to all triangles and also in addition even to thoughts about triangles. The existence of Triangularity can be proven, Plato believed, as follows. Suppose that all triangular objects were destroyed—all triangular structures torn down, all triangular figures made of any sort of material eliminated, all triangles drawn on blackboards erased, and so on. A plane figure with three straight sides would still have three interior angles and the sum of the angles would still be 180°. Moreover, this would be true even if no one was thinking about triangles. Triangularity, according to Plato, has a kind of "superreality" that serves as a *model* or *pattern* both for the existence of triangular objects and for the concept of a triangle. As a model or pattern, triangularity is more perfect than triangular objects because none of them, for example, has *exactly* straight sides. Even the most nearly perfect material object has imperfections at the microscopic level. Yet, said Plato, we can conceive what an ideal, perfect model for triangularity must be like, which again shows that triangularity is something different from actual triangles.

The Good, or the Form of the Good, according to Plato, is the most perfect and important of the Forms. Plato believed that moral goodness (the Good includes what we call moral goodness) is something quite exalted. It is, one could say, "better than the best" that any human being might accomplish. It transcends all examples of good deeds that anyone will ever do and good things that anyone will ever experience. The Good, in short, is a standard of perfection that is worth striving for more than anything else conceivable.

Plato, in his remarks about the Good (spoken by Socrates in the dialogue) says that a completely adequate description of the Good cannot be given. Therefore, instead of saying what the Good *is*, Plato says what the Good is *like*, namely, the sun, which is brightest and most glorious among all material things. (Christianized versions of Plato's philosophy developed early in the Christian era identified the Good with God or with an aspect of God.)

For Plato, moral philosophy takes us beyond ourselves. For Bertrand Russell, in the third reading selection, moral philosophy does not take us beyond ourselves at all. It does not take us beyond the material world or beyond human nature; it does not even take us individually beyond our individual selves. According to Russell, "when we assert that this or that has 'value,' we are giving expression to our emotions, not to a fact which would still be true if our personal feelings were different." It follows that, strictly speaking, matters of good and bad lie "outside the domain of knowledge," that is, outside the domain of scientific investigation of facts about the world or about human nature. Russell's view is that moral values are wholly subjective.

A greater contrast than that between the moral views of Plato and Russell would be difficult to imagine. For Plato, knowledge of the Good is the highest type of knowledge, and the Good is the loftiest of all realities. For Russell, there is no such thing as the Good and, moreover, a person's commitment to moral values is not a matter of knowledge at all.

Objections to the subjectivist position of Russell are given by A. C. Ewing. Ewing first states six different objections to a particular version of subjectivism. Second, he states the major arguments that have been made *in defense* of subjectivism and against objectivism. In the course of doing this he gives reasons for rejecting each of these arguments; that is, he defends objectivism, which, he says, "asserts of [moral judgments] a certain independence of the feelings or attitude of the person judging." Finally, Ewing examines an argument regarding the origin of moral beliefs.

James Rachels discusses the question of whether moral values are relative to different cultures. He examines a number of arguments, both pro and con, and concludes that some, but not all, of the claims associated with cultural relativism should be rejected.

The final two selections in this chapter, from the eighteenth century philosopher Immanuel Kant and the nineteenth century philosopher John Stuart Mill, mark a change in the direction of the chapter. The earlier readings are devoted primarily to what philosophers call *metaethics*, which is the study of questions about the nature of moral values and how they can be known. Metaethics stands in contrast to *normative ethics*, which is the study of actual values, or norms.

- Metaethics asks: What are moral values? (Are they objective or subjective, can they be discovered through the methods of science, and so on.)
- Normative ethics asks: What moral values are there? (Possible moral values include rights, duty, happiness, freedom, justice, equality, friendship, and the alleviation of suffering.)

Within the area of normative ethics, philosophers may focus their attention either on *normative theories* or on *answering specific moral questions*, such as those regarding capital punishment, euthanasia, affirmative action, welfare legislation, and so on. The readings from Kant and Mill are addressed to normative theories. The two basic types of normative theories are (1) those that emphasize the *consequences* of actions (called teleological moral theories) and (2) those that emphasize the *intrinsic nature* of actions (called deontological moral theories).

Among contemporary philosophers, *utilitarianism* has been the most influential teleological moral theory, and John Stuart Mill has been its best known advocate. The central idea in utilitarianism is usually referred to as the "Greatest Happiness Principle," that is, when we make an important moral choice, we should always attempt to do whatever will produce the greatest happiness for the human race as a whole.

The most influential deontological theory has been that of Immanuel Kant. The central idea in Kant's ethics is that of doing one's moral duty, where duty is determined by Kant's "Universalization Principle," which is also called the "Categorical Imperative." The gist of it is that people should not do things for themselves that they would not be willing to have done by everyone in similar circumstances.

IMMANUEL KANT

Nothing can possibly be conceived in the world, or even out of it, which can be called good, without qualification, except a Good Will.

Now I say: man and generally any rational being exists as an end in himself, not merely as a means to be arbitrarily used by this or that will.

—*Fundamental Principles of the Metaphysics of Morals*

[T]he understanding is the origin of the universal order of nature, in that it comprehends all appearances under its own laws.

—*Prolegomena to Any Future Metaphysics*

Immanuel Kant (1724–1804) is often regarded as the greatest philosopher since Plato and Aristotle. Kant devoted his entire life to the academic pursuit of philosophy. He did not marry (for many years he could not have afforded to), he took almost no part in political, social, or religious activities, he did not travel, he had little interest in works of art or musical performances, and his only hobby was watching birds in his garden. In his adult life he was a university student, a tutor, a poorly paid lecturer (for fifteen years), and finally a professor at the University of Königsberg in Germany (for thirty-four years). In contrast to other notable philosophers, such as Descartes, Leibniz, Locke, and Hume, Kant actually made his living as a philosopher. His daily life involved the same routine year after year—getting up early, preparing for his university lectures, having lunch with friends, having tea, taking a walk. In contrast to his daily activities, Kant's ideas were far from routine. It is fair to say that they have revolutionized Western civilization. Kant had very original things to say about metaphysics, epistemology, ethics, as well as religion and the philosophy of art. Kant himself described his own philosophy as bringing about a "Copernican revolution" in human thought.

WILLIAM JAMES

Conditions Required for the Application of Value Terms

* * * * *

First of all, it appears that such words [as "obligation," "good," and "ill"] can have no application or relevancy in a world in which no sentient life exists. Imagine an absolutely material world, containing only physical and chemical facts, and existing from eternity without a God, without even an interested spectator: would there be any sense in saying of that world that one of its states is better than another? Or if there were two such worlds possible, would there be any rhyme or reason in calling one good and the other bad,—good or bad positively, I mean, and apart from the fact that one might relate itself better than the other to the philosopher's private interests? But we must leave these private interests out of the account, for the philosopher is a mental fact, and we are asking whether goods and evils and obligations exist in physical facts *per se*. Surely there is no *status* for good and evil to exist in, in a purely insentient world. How can one physical fact, considered simply as a physical fact, be "better" than another? Betterness is not a physical relation. In its more material capacity, a thing can no more be good or bad than it can be pleasant or painful. Good for what? Good for the production of another physical fact, do you say? But what in a purely physical universe demands the production of that other fact? Physical facts simply *are* or are *not;* and neither when present or absent, can they be supposed to make demands. If they do, they can only do so by having desires; and then they have ceased to be purely physical facts, and have become facts of conscious sensibility. Goodness, badness, and obligation must be *realized* somewhere in order really to exist; and the first step in ethical philosophy is to see that no merely inorganic "nature of things" can realize them. Neither moral relations nor the moral law can swing *in vacuo*. Their only habitat can be a mind which feels them; and no world composed of merely physical facts can possibly be a world to which ethical propositions apply.

The moment one sentient being, however, is made a part of the universe, there is a chance for goods and evils really to exist. Moral relations now have their *status*, in that being's consciousness. So far as he feels anything to be good, he *makes* it good. It *is* good, for him; and be-

A biographical sketch of William James appears in chapter 3.

From "The Moral Philosopher and the Moral Life," an address to the Yale Philosophical Club, first published in 1891.

ing good for him, is absolutely good, for he is the sole creator of values in that universe, and outside of his opinion things have no moral character at all.

In such a universe as that it would of course be absurd to raise the question of whether the solitary thinker's judgments of good and ill are true or not. Truth supposes a standard outside of the thinker to which he must conform; but here the thinker is a sort of divinity, subject to no higher judge. Let us call the supposed universe which he inhabits a *moral solitude*. In such a moral solitude it is clear that there can be no outward obligation, and that the only trouble the god-like thinker is liable to have will be over the consistency of his own several ideals with one another. Some of these will no doubt be more pungent and appealing than the rest, their goodness will have a profounder, more penetrating taste; they will return to haunt him with more obstinate regrets if violated. So the thinker will have to order his life with them as its chief determinants, or else remain inwardly discordant and unhappy. Into whatever equilibrium he may settle, though, and however he may straighten out his system, it will be a right system; for beyond the facts of his own subjectivity there is nothing moral in the world.

If now we introduce a second thinker with his likes and dislikes into the universe, the ethical situation becomes much more complex, and several possibilities are immediately seen to obtain.

One of these is that the thinkers may ignore each other's attitude about good and evil altogether, and each continue to indulge his own preferences, indifferent to what the other may feel or do. In such a case we have a world with twice as much of the ethical quality in it as our moral solitude, only it is without ethical unity. The same object is good or bad there, according as you measure it by the view which this one or that one of the thinkers takes. Nor can you find any possible ground in such a world for saying that one thinker's opinion is more correct than the other's, or that either has the trurer moral sense. Such a world, in short, is not a moral universe but a moral dualism. Not only is there no single point of view within it from which the values of things can be unequivocally judged, but there is not even a demand for such a point of view, since the two thinkers are supposed to be indifferent to each other's thoughts and acts. Multiply the thinkers into a pluralism, and we find realized for us in the ethical sphere something like that world which the antique sceptics conceived of,—in which individual minds are the measures of all things, and in which no one "objective" truth, but only a multitude of "subjective" opinions, can be found.

But this is the kind of world with which the philosopher, so long as he holds to the hope of a philosophy, will not put up. Among the various ideals represented, there must be, he thinks, some which have the more truth or authority; and to these the others *ought* to yield, so that system and subordination may reign. Here in the word "ought" the notion of *obligation* comes emphatically into view, and the next thing in order must be to make its meaning clear.

* * * * *

The moment we take a steady

look at the question, *we see not only that without a claim actually made by some concrete person there can be no obligation, but that there is some obligation wherever there is a claim.* Claim and obligation are, in fact, coextensive terms; they cover each other exactly. Our ordinary attitude of regarding ourselves as subject to an overarching system of moral relations, true "in themselves," is therefore either an out-and-out superstition, or else it must be treated as a merely provisional abstraction from that real Thinker in whose actual demand upon us to think as he does our obligation must be ultimately based. In a theistic-ethical philosophy that thinker in question is, of course, the Deity to whom the existence of the universe is due.

I know well how hard it is for those who are accustomed to what I have called the superstitious view, to realize that every *de facto* claim creates in so far forth an obligation. We inveterately think that something which we call the "validity" of the claim is what gives to it its obligatory character, and that this validity is something outside of the claim's mere existence as a matter of fact. It rains down upon the claim, we think, from some sublime dimension of being, which the moral law inhabits, much as upon the steel of the compass-needle the influence of the Pole rains down from out of the starry heavens. But again, how can such an inorganic abstract character of imperativeness, additional to the imperativeness which is in the concrete claim itself, *exist?* Take any demand, however slight, which any creature, however weak, may make. Ought it not, for its own sole sake, to be satisfied? If not, prove why not. The only possible kind of proof you could adduce would be the exhibition of another creature who should make a demand that ran the other way. The only possible reason there can be why any phenomenon ought to exist is that such a phenomenon actually is desired. Any desire is imperative to the extent of its amount; it *makes* itself valid by the fact that it exists at all. Some desires, truly enough, are small desires; they are put forward by insignificant persons, and we customarily make light of the obligations which they bring. But the fact that such personal demands as these impose small obligations does not keep the largest obligations from being personal demands.

COMMENTS ■ QUESTIONS

1. According to James, neither goodness nor badness exists apart from consciousness. How should one go about deciding whether this is correct? Philosophers are fond of "armchair experiments," in which the plausibility of a particular theory is tested by imagining what the world would be like if the theory were true and what the world would be like if the theory were false. One such armchair experiment would have us imagine the existence of a garbage dump (or something else that we would say is ugly or unpleasant) in a universe that contains no conscious beings. The question is then asked: Would the garbage dump in such a universe be a bad thing or not? Can an armchair experiment of this sort help in deciding whether or not James's view is the correct one?
2. "Take any demand, however slight, which any creature, however weak, may make. Ought it not, for its own sake, to be satisfied? If not, prove why not." Are you willing to accept James' challenge to prove why not, or do you believe that James is correct? Because James is saying that the demand of a sentient creature should be satisfied "for its own sole sake," it does not follow that an actual moral obligation exists to fulfill that demand. James' discussion is intended to shed light on the more basic question of what conditions are necessary for there to be any values at all.

PLATO

The Good

* * * * *

But, Socrates, what is your own account of the Good? Is it knowledge, or pleasure, or something else? [1]

There you are! I exclaimed; I could see all along that you were not going to be content with what other people think.

Well, Socrates, it does not seem fair that you should be ready to repeat other people's opinions but not to state your own, when you have given so much thought to this subject.

And do you think it fair of anyone to speak as if he knew what he does not know?

No, not as if he knew, but he might give his opinion for what it is worth.

Why, have you never noticed that opinion without knowledge is always a shabby sort of thing? At the best it is blind. One who holds a true belief without intelligence is just like a blind man who happens to take the right road, isn't he? [2]

No doubt.

Well, then, do you want me to produce one of these poor blind cripples, when others could discourse to you with illuminating eloquence?

No, really, Socrates, said Glaucon, you must not give up within sight of the goal. We should be quite content with an account of the Good like the one you gave us of justice and temperance and the other virtues.

So should I be, my dear Glaucon, much more than content! But I am afraid it is beyond my powers; with the best will in the world I should only disgrace myself and be laughed at. No, for the moment let us leave the question of the real meaning of good; to arrive at what I at any rate believe it to be would call for an effort too ambitious for an inquiry like ours. However, I will tell you, though only if you wish it, what I picture to myself as the offspring of the Good and the thing most nearly resembling it.

Well, tell us about the offspring,

1. Here it begins to appear that the discussion is not confined to the "Human Good" but extends to the supreme Form, "Goodness itself."

2. At *Meno* 97 the man who has a correct belief at second-hand about the way from Athens to Larisa is contrasted with one who has certain knowledge of the road from having travelled by it himself.

A biographical sketch of Plato appears in chapter 2.

Reprinted from *The Republic of Plato,* translated by F. M. Cornford (1941). By permission of Oxford University Press.

and you shall remain in our debt for an account of the parent.

I only wish it were within my power to offer, and within yours to receive, a settlement of the whole account. But you must be content now with the interest only; [3] and you must see to it that, in describing this offspring of the Good, I do not inadvertently cheat you with false coin.

We will keep a good eye on you. Go on.

First we must come to an understanding. Let me remind you of the distinction we drew earlier and have often drawn on other occasions,[4] between the multiplicity of things that we call good or beautiful or whatever it may be and, on the other hand, Goodness itself or Beauty itself and so on. Corresponding to each of these sets of many things, we postulate a single Form or real essence, as we call it.

Yes, that is so.

Further, the many things, we say, can be seen, but are not objects of rational thought; whereas the Forms are objects of thought, but invisible.

Yes, certainly.

And we see things with our eyesight, just as we hear sounds with our ears and, to speak generally, perceive any sensible thing with our sense-faculties.

Of course.

Have you noticed, then, that the artificer who designed the senses has been exceptionally lavish of his materials in making the eyes able to see and their objects visible?

That never occurred to me.

Well, look at it in this way. Hearing and sound do not stand in need of any third thing, without which the ear will not hear nor sound be heard; [5] and I think the same is true of most, not to say all, of the other senses. Can you think of one that does require anything of the sort?

No, I cannot.

But there is this need in the case of sight and its objects. You may have the power of vision in your eyes and try to use it, and colour may be there in the objects; but sight will see nothing and the colours will remain invisible in the absence of a third thing peculiarly constituted to serve this very purpose.

By which you mean________?

Naturally I mean what you call light; and if light is a thing of value, the sense of sight and the power of being visible are linked together by a very precious bond, such as unites no other sense with its object.

No one could say that light is not a precious thing.

And of all the divinities in the skies [6] is there one whose light, above all the rest, is responsible for making our eyes see perfectly and making objects perfectly visible?

There can be no two opinions: of course you mean the Sun.

And how is sight related to this deity? Neither sight nor the eye

---

3. The Greek has a play on two meanings of the word *tokos*—"offspring" and "interest" on a loan, "a breed for barren metal."

4. Perhaps an allusion to the *Phaedo* (especially 78 E ff.), where the theory of Forms was first explicitly stated in similar terms. The earlier passage in the *Republic* is at 475 E ff., p. 183.

5. Plato held that the hearing of sound is caused by blows inflicted by the air (*Timaeus* 67 B, 80 A); but the air is hardly analogous to light.

6. Plato held that the heavenly bodies are immortal living creatures, i.e. gods.

which contains it is the Sun, but of all the sense-organs it is the most sun-like; and further, the power it possesses is dispensed by the Sun, like a stream flooding the eye.[7] And again, the Sun is not vision, but it is the cause of vision and also is seen by the vision it causes.

Yes.

It was the Sun, then, that I meant when I spoke of that offspring which the Good has created in the visible world, to stand there in the same relation to vision and visible things as that which the Good itself bears in the intelligible world to intelligence and to intelligible objects.

How is that? You must explain further.

You know what happens when the colours of things are no longer irradiated by the daylight, but only by the fainter luminaries of the night: when you look at them, the eyes are dim and seem almost blind, as if there were no unclouded vision in them. But when you look at things on which the Sun is shining, the same eyes see distinctly and it becomes evident that they do contain the power of vision.

Certainly.

Apply this comparison, then, to the soul. When its gaze is fixed upon an object irradiated by truth and reality, the soul gains understanding and knowledge and is manifestly in possession of intelligence. But when it looks towards that twilight world of things that come into existence and pass away, its sight is dim and it has only opinions and beliefs which shift to and fro, and now it seems like a thing that has no intelligence.

That is true.

This, then, which gives to the objects of knowledge their truth and to him who knows them his power of knowing, is the Form or essential nature of Goodness. It is the cause of knowledge and truth; and so, while you may think of it as an object of knowledge, you will do well to regard it as something beyond truth and knowledge and, precious as these both are, of still higher worth. And, just as in our analogy light and vision were to be thought of as like the Sun, but not identical with it, so here both knowledge and truth are to be regarded as like the Good, but to identify either with the Good is wrong. The Good must hold a yet higher place of honour.

You are giving it a position of extraordinary splendour, if it is the source of knowledge and truth and itself surpasses them in worth. You surely cannot mean that it is pleasure.

Heaven forbid, I exclaimed. But I want to follow up our analogy still further. You will agree that the Sun not only makes the things we see visible, but also brings them into existence and gives them growth and nourishment; yet he is not the same thing as existence.[8] And so with the

7. Plato's theory of vision involves three kinds of fire or light: (1) daylight, a body of pure fire diffused in the air by the Sun; (2) the visual current or "vision," a pure fire similar to daylight, contained in the eye-ball and capable of issuing out in a stream directed towards the object seen; (3) the colour of the external object, "a flame streaming off from every body, having particles proportioned to those of the visual current, so as to yield sensation" when the two streams meet and coalesce (*Timaeus*, 45 B, 67 C).

8. The ambiguity of *genesis* can hardly be reproduced. The Sun "gives things their *Genesis*" (generation, birth), but "is not itself *genesis*" (becoming, the existence in time of things which begin and cease to exist, as opposed to

objects of knowledge: these derive from the Good not only their power of being known, but their very being and reality; and Goodness is not the same thing as being, but even beyond being, surpassing it in dignity and power.

* * * * *

Next, said I, here is a parable to illustrate the degrees in which our nature may be enlightened or unenlightened. Imagine the condition of men living in a sort of cavernous chamber underground, with an entrance open to the light and a long passage all down the cave.[9] Here they have been from childhood, chained by the leg and also by the neck, so that they cannot move and can see only what is in front of them, because the chains will not let them turn their heads. At some distance higher up is the light of a fire burning behind them; and between the prisoners and the fire is a track [10] with a parapet built along it, like the screen at a puppet-show, which hides the performers while they show their puppets over the top.

I see, said he.

Now behind this parapet imagine persons carrying along various artificial objects, including figures of men and animals in wood or stone or other materials, which project above the parapet. Naturally, some of these persons will be talking, others silent.[11]

It is a strange picture, he said, and a strange sort of prisoners.

Like ourselves, I replied; for in the first place prisoners so confined would have seen nothing of themselves or of one another, except the shadows thrown by the fire-light on the wall of the Cave facing them, would they?

Not if all their lives they had been prevented from moving their heads.

And they would have seen as little of the objects carried past.

Of course.

Now, if they could talk to one another, would they not suppose that their words referred only to those passing shadows which they saw? [12]

Necessarily.

And suppose their prison had an echo from the wall facing them? When one of the people crossing behind them spoke, they could only suppose that the sound came from the shadow passing before their eyes.

No doubt.

---

the real being of eternal things in the intelligible world).

9. The length of the "way in" (eisodos) to the chamber where the prisoners sit is an essential feature, explaining why no daylight reaches them.

10. The track crosses the passage into the cave at right angles, and is *above* the parapet built along it.

11. A modern Plato would compare his Cave to an underground cinema, where the audience watch the play of shadows thrown by the film passing before a light at their backs. The film itself is only an image of "real" things and events in the world outside the cinema. For the film Plato has to substitute the clumsier apparatus of a procession of artificial objects carried on their heads by persons who are merely part of the machinery, providing for the movement of the objects and the sounds whose echo the prisoners hear. The parapet prevents these persons' shadows from being cast on the wall of the Cave.

12. Adam's text and interpretation. The prisoners, having seen nothing but shadows, cannot think their words refer to the objects carried past behind their backs. For them shadows (images) are the only realities.

In every way, then, such prisoners would recognize as reality nothing but the shadows of those artificial objects.

Inevitably.

Now consider what would happen if their release from the chains and the healing of their unwisdom should come about in this way. Suppose one of them set free and forced suddenly to stand up, turn his head, and walk with eyes lifted to the light; all these movements would be painful, and he would be too dazzled to make out the objects whose shadows he had been used to see. What do you think he would say, if someone told him that what he had formerly seen was meaningless illusion, but now, being somewhat nearer to reality and turned towards more real objects, he was getting a truer view? Suppose further that he were shown the various objects being carried by and were made to say, in reply to questions, what each of them was. Would he not be perplexed and believe the objects now shown him to be not so real as what he formerly saw? [13]

Yes, not nearly so real.

And if he were forced to look at the fire-light itself, would not his eyes ache, so that he would try to escape and turn back to the things which he could see distinctly, convinced that they really were clearer than these other objects now being shown to him?

Yes.

And suppose someone were to drag him away forcibly up the steep and rugged ascent and not let him go until he had hauled him out into the sunlight, would he not suffer pain and vexation at such treatment, and, when he had come out into the light, find his eyes so full of its radiance that he could not see a single one of the things that he was now told were real?

Certainly he would not see them all at once.

He would need, then, to grow accustomed before he could see things in that upper world.[14] At first it would be easiest to make out shadows, and then the images of men and things reflected in water, and later on the things themselves. After that, it would be easier to watch the heavenly bodies and the sky itself by night, looking at the light of the moon and stars rather than the Sun and the Sun's light in the day-time.

Yes, surely.

Last of all, he would be able to look at the Sun and contemplate its nature, not as it appears when reflected in water or any alien medium, but as it is in itself in its own domain.

No doubt.

And now he would begin to draw the conclusion that it is the Sun that produces the seasons and the course of the year and controls everything in the visible world, and moreover is in a way the cause of all that he and his companions used to see.

Clearly he would come at last to that conclusion.

Then if he called to mind his fellow prisoners and what passed for wisdom in his former dwelling-place,

13. The first effect of Socratic questioning is perplexity. Cf. p. 8.

14. Here is the moral—the need of habituation by mathematical study before discussing moral ideas and ascending through them to the Form of the Good.

he would surely think himself happy in the change and be sorry for them. They may have had a practice of honouring and commending one another, with prizes for the man who had the keenest eye for the passing shadows and the best memory for the order in which they followed or accompanied one another, so that he could make a good guess as to which was going to come next.[15] Would our released prisoner be likely to covet those prizes or to envy the men exalted to honour and power in the Cave? Would he not feel like Homer's Achilles, that he would far sooner "be on earth as a hired servant in the house of a landless man" [16] or endure anything rather than go back to his old beliefs and live in the old way?

Yes, he would prefer any fate to such a life.

Now imagine what would happen if he went down again to take his former seat in the Cave. Coming suddenly out of the sunlight, his eyes would be filled with darkness. He might be required once more to deliver his opinion on those shadows, in competition with the prisoners who had never been released, while his eyesight was still dim and unsteady; and it might take some time to become used to the darkness. They would laugh at him and say that he had gone up only to come back with his sight ruined; it was worth no one's while even to attempt the ascent. If they could lay hands on the man who was trying to set them free and lead them up, they would kill him.[17]

Yes, they would.

Every feature in this parable, my dear Glaucon, is meant to fit our earlier analysis. The prison dwelling corresponds to the region revealed to us through the sense of sight, and the fire-light within it to the power of the Sun. The ascent to see the things in the upper world you may take as standing for the upward journey of the soul into the region of the intelligible; then you will be in possession of what I surmise, since that is what you wish to be told. Heaven knows whether it is true; but this, at any rate, is how it appears to me. In the world of knowledge, the last thing to be perceived and only with great difficulty is the essential Form of Goodness. Once it is perceived, the conclusion must follow that, for all things, this is the cause of whatever is right and good; in the visible world it gives birth to light and to the lord of light, while it is itself sovereign in the intelligible world and the parent of intelligence and truth. Without having had a vision of this Form no one can act with wisdom, either in his own life or in matters of state.

---

15. The empirical politician, with no philosophic insight, but only a "knack of remembering what usually happens" (*Gorg.* 501 A). He has *eikasia* = conjecture as to what is likely (*eikos*).

16. This verse (already quoted at 386 c, p. 76), being spoken by the ghost of Achilles, suggests that the Cave is comparable with Hades.

17. An allusion to the fate of Socrates.

COMMENTS ■ QUESTIONS

1. Plato (speaking through Socrates) says that it is "beyond his powers" to say what the Good is, and that the best he can do is to describe "the offspring of the Good and the thing most nearly resembling it," namely, the sun. In your opinion, is Plato on the right track in taking this approach? Many people evaluate Plato's discussion of the Good in one of two ways: (1) as demonstrating a rare and an unusual wisdom or (2) as containing a "mystical mumbo-jumbo" of little value. Do you agree with either of these two extreme positions? Is there an intermediate position that you believe is more defensible?
2. Those who are sympathetic to Plato often believe that it is presumptuous to suppose that human knowledge can overcome all the deep mysteries about the world and human life. They believe that the most important concepts in life are tinged with mystery. They are sympathetic to the idea that the highest human ideals have to do with that which exceeds human understanding. Do you share any of these sympathies? If you do, how would you go about defending them to someone who does not? If you do not, how would you go about defending your views to those who *do* have the sympathies in question?
3. A basic parting of the ways is illustrated by Plato's philosophy of the Good. On the one hand are philosophers who believe that the most fundamental aspect of the world is the bare fact that it exists; for them, values are "added on" to reality at a more superficial level and do not belong to the most fundamental aspects of reality. On the other hand are philosophers who believe that the most fundamental aspect of the world *does* have to do with values; for them, values are not in any sense superficial or "added on" to a basically value-free ultimate reality. Defenders of materialism (chapter 6) belong to the first group of philsophers; Plato, along with such religious philosophers as Saint Anselm (chapter 3) and Saint Augustine (chapter 14), belongs to the second group. Which group would you put yourself into? Why?
4. Does the allegory of the Cave provide a good description of the "human condition"?

BERTRAND RUSSELL

Science and Ethics

* * * * *

Different philosophers have formed different conceptions of the Good. Some hold that it consists in the knowledge and love of God; others in universal love; others in the enjoyment of beauty; and yet others in pleasure. The Good once defined, the rest of ethics follows: we ought to act in the way we believe most likely to create as much good as possible, and as little as possible of its correlative evil. The framing of moral rules, so long as the ultimate Good is supposed known, is matter for science. For example: should capital punishment be inflicted for theft, or only for murder, or not at all? Jeremy Bentham [British philosopher, 1748–1832], who considered pleasure to be the Good, devoted himself to working out what criminal code would most promote pleasure, and concluded that it ought to be much less severe than that prevailing in his day. All this, except the proposition that pleasure is the Good, comes within the sphere of science.

But when we try to be definite as to what we mean when we say that this or that is "the Good," we find ourselves involved in very great difficulties. Bentham's creed that pleasure is the Good roused furious opposition, and was said to be a pig's philosophy. Neither he nor his opponents could advance any argument. In a scientific question, evidence can be adduced on both sides, and in the end one side is seen to have the better case—or, if this does not happen, the question is left undecided. But in a question as to whether this or that is the ultimate Good, there is no evidence either way; each disputant can only appeal to his own emotions, and employ such rhetorical devices as shall rouse similar emotions in others.

Take, for example, a question which has come to be important in practical politics. Bentham held that one man's pleasure has the same ethical importance as another man's, provided the quantities are equal; and on this ground he was led to advocate democracy. Nietzsche, on the contrary, held that only the great man can be regarded as important on his own account, and that the bulk of mankind are only means to his well-being. He viewed ordinary men as many people view animals: he thought it justifiable to make use of them, not for their own good, but for that of the superman, and this

A biographical sketch of Bertrand Russell is to be found in chapter 1.

Reprinted from *Religion and Science* by Bertrand Russell (1935) by permission of Oxford University Press.

view has since been adopted to justify the abandonment of democracy. We have here a sharp disagreement of great practical importance, but we have absolutely no means, of a scientific or intellectual kind, by which to persuade either party that the other is in the right. There are, it is true, ways of altering men's opinions on such subjects, but they are all emotional, not intellectual.

Questions as to "values"—that is to say, as to what is good or bad on its own account, independently of its effects—lie outside the domain of science, as the defenders of religion emphatically assert. I think that in this they are right, but I draw the further conclusion, which they do not draw, that questions as to "values" lie wholly outside the domain of knowledge. That is to say, when we assert that this or that has "value," we are giving expression to our own emotions, not to a fact which would still be true if our personal feelings were different. To make this clear, we must try to analyse the conception of the Good.

It is obvious, to begin with, that the whole idea of good and bad has some connection with *desire. Prima facie*, anything that we all desire is "good," and anything that we all dread is "bad." If we all agreed in our desires, the matter could be left there, but unfortunately our desires conflict. If I say "what I want is good," my neighbour will say "No, what *I* want." Ethics is an attempt—though not, I think, a successful one—to escape from this subjectivity. I shall naturally try to show, in my dispute with my neighbour, that my desires have some quality which makes them more worthy of respect than his. If I want to preserve a right of way, I shall appeal to the landless inhabitants of the district; but he, on his side, will appeal to the landowners. I shall say: "What use is the beauty of the countryside if no one sees it?" He will retort: "What beauty will be left if trippers are allowed to spread devastation?" Each tries to enlist allies by showing that his own desires harmonize with those of other people. When this is obviously impossible, as in the case of a burglar, the man is condemned by public opinion, and his ethical status is that of a sinner.

Ethics is thus closely related to politics: it is an attempt to bring the collective desires of a group to bear upon individuals; or, conversely, it is an attempt by an individual to cause his desires to become those of his group. This latter is, of course, only possible if his desires are not too obviously opposed to the general interest: the burglar will hardly attempt to persuade people that he is doing them good, though plutocrats make similar attempts, and often succeed. When our desires are for things which all can enjoy in common, it seems not unreasonable to hope that others may concur; thus the philosopher who values Truth, Goodness and Beauty seems, to himself, to be not merely expressing his own desires, but pointing the way to the welfare of all mankind. Unlike the burglar, he is able to believe that his desires are for something that has value in an impersonal sense.

Ethics is an attempt to give universal, and not merely personal, importance to certain of our desires. I say "certain" of our desires, because in regard to some of them this is obviously impossible, as we saw in the case of the burglar. The man who makes money on the Stock Exchange by means of some secret knowledge does not wish others to be equally well informed: Truth (in so far as he values it) is for him a private possession, not the general human good that it is for the philosopher. The philosopher may, it is true, sink to the level of the stock-jobber, as when he claims priority for a discovery. But this is a lapse: in his purely philosophic capacity, he wants only to enjoy the contemplation of Truth, in doing which he in no way interferes with others who wish to do likewise.

To seem to give universal importance to our desires—which is the business of ethics—may be attempted from two points of view, that of the legislator, and that of the preacher. Let us take the legislator first.

I will assume, for the sake of argument, that the legislator is personally disinterested. That is to say, when he recognizes one of his desires as being concerned only with his own welfare, he does not let it influence him in framing the laws; for example, his code is not designed to increase his personal fortune. But he has other desires which seem to him impersonal. He may believe in an ordered hierarchy from king to peasant, or from mine-owner to black indentured labourer. He may believe that women should be submissive to men. He may hold that the spread of knowledge in the lower classes is dangerous. And so on and so on. He will then, if he can, so construct his code that conduct promoting the ends which he values shall, as far as possible, be in accordance with individual self-interest; and he will establish a system of moral instruction which will, where it succeeds, make men feel wicked if they pursue other purposes than his.[1] Thus "virtue" will come to be in fact, though not in subjective estimation, subservience to the desires of the legislator, in so far as he himself considers these desires worthy to be universalized.

The standpoint and method of the preacher are necessarily somewhat different, because he does not control the machinery of the State, and therefore cannot produce an artificial harmony between his desires and those of others. His only method is to try to rouse in others the same desires that he feels himself, and for this purpose his appeal must be to the emotions. Thus Ruskin caused people to like Gothic architecture, not by argument, but by the moving effect of rhythmical prose. *Uncle Tom's Cabin* helped to make people think slavery an evil by causing them to imagine themselves as slaves. Every attempt to persuade people that something is good (or bad) in itself, and not merely in its effects, depends upon the art of rousing feelings, not upon an appeal to evidence. In every case the preacher's skill consists in creating in others emotions similar to his own—or dissimilar, if he is a hypocrite. I am not saying this as a criticism of

---

1. Compare the following advice by a contemporary of Aristotle (Chinese, not Greek): "A ruler should not listen to those who believe in people having opinions of their own and in the importance of the individual. Such teachings cause men to withdraw to quiet places and hide away in caves or on mountains, there to rail at the prevailing government, sneer at those in authority, belittle the importance of rank and emoluments, and despise all who hold official posts." Waley, *The Way and its Power*, p. 37.

the preacher, but as an analysis of the essential character of his activity.

When a man says "this is good in itself," he *seems* to be making a statement, just as much as if he said "this is square" or "this is sweet." I believe this to be a mistake. I think that what the man really means is: "I wish everybody to desire this," or rather "Would that everybody desired this." If what he says is interpreted as a statement, it is merely an affirmation of his own personal wish; if, on the other hand, it is interpreted in a general way, it states nothing, but merely desires something. The wish, as an occurrence, is personal, but what it desires is universal. It is, I think, this curious interlocking of the particular and the universal which has caused so much confusion in ethics.

The matter may perhaps become clearer by contrasting an ethical sentence with one which makes a statement. If I say "all Chinese are Buddhists," I can be refuted by the production of a Chinese Christian or Mohammedan. If I say "I believe that all Chinese are Buddhists," I cannot be refuted by any evidence from China, but only by evidence that I do not believe what I say; for what I am asserting is only something about my own state of mind. If, now, a philosopher says "Beauty is good," I may interpret him as meaning either "Would that everybody loved the beautiful" (which corresponds to "all Chinese are Buddhists") or "I wish that everybody loved the beautiful" (which corresponds to "I believe that all Chinese are Buddhists"). The first of these makes no assertion, but expresses a wish; since it affirms nothing, it is logically impossible that there should be evidence for or against it, or for it to possess either truth or falsehood. The second sentence, instead of being merely optative, does make a statement, but it is one about the philosopher's state of mind, and it could only be refuted by evidence that he does not have the wish that he says he has. This second sentence does not belong to ethics, but to psychology or biography. The first sentence, which does belong to ethics, expresses a desire for something, but asserts nothing.

Ethics, if the above analysis is correct, contains no statements, whether true or false, but consists of desires of a certain general kind, namely such as are concerned with the desires of mankind in general—and of gods, angels, and devils, if they exist. Science can discuss the causes of desires, and the means for realizing them, but it cannot contain any genuinely ethical sentences, because it is concerned with what is true or false.

The theory which I have been advocating is a form of the doctrine which is called the "subjectivity" of values. This doctrine consists in maintaining that, if two men differ about values, there is not a disagreement as to any kind of truth, but a difference of taste. If one man says "oysters are good" and another says "*I* think they are bad," we recognize that there is nothing to argue about. The theory in question holds that all differences as to values are of this sort, although we do not naturally think them so when we are dealing with matters that seem to us more exalted than oysters. The chief ground for adopting this view is the complete impossibility of finding any arguments to prove that this or that has intrinsic value. If we all agreed, we might hold that we know values by intuition. We cannot *prove*, to a colour-blind man, that grass is green and not red. But there are various ways of proving to him that he lacks a power of discrimination which most men possess, whereas in the case of values there are no such ways, and disagreements are much more frequent than in the case of colours. Since no way can be even imagined for deciding a difference as to values, the conclusion is forced upon us that the difference is one of tastes, not one as to any objective truth.

The consequences of this doctrine are considerable. In the first place, there can be no such thing as "sin" in any absolute sense; what one man calls "sin" another may call "virtue," and though they may dislike each other on account of this difference, neither can convict the other of intellectual error. Punishment cannot be justified on the ground that the criminal is "wicked," but only on the ground that he has behaved in a way which others wish to discourage. Hell, as a place of punishment for sinners, becomes quite irrational.

In the second place, it is impossible to uphold the way of speaking about values which is common among those who believe in Cosmic Purpose. Their argument is that certain things which have been evolved are "good," and therefore the world must have had a purpose which was ethically admirable. In the language of subjective values, this argument becomes: "Some things in the world are to our liking, and therefore they must have been created by a Being with our tastes, Whom, therefore, we also like, and Who, consequently, is good." Now it seems fairly evident that, if creatures having likes and dislikes were to exist at all, they were pretty sure to like *some* things in their environment, since otherwise they would find life intolerable. Our values have been evolved along with the rest of our constitution, and nothing as to any original purpose can be inferred from the fact that they are what they are.

Those who believe in "objective" values often contend that the view which I have been advocating has immoral consequences. This seems to me to be due to faulty reasoning. There are, as has already been said, certain ethical consequences of the doctrine of subjective values, of which the most important is the rejection of vindictive punishment and the notion of "sin." But the more general consequences which are feared, such as the decay of all sense of moral obligation, are not to be logically deduced. Moral obligation, if it is to influence conduct, must consist not merely of a belief, but of a desire. The desire, I may be told, is the desire to be "good" in a sense which I no longer allow. But when we analyse the desire to be "good" it generally resolves itself into a desire to be approved, or, alternatively, to act so as to bring about certain general consequences which we desire. We have wishes which are not purely personal, and, if we had not, no amount of ethical teaching would influence our conduct except through fear of disapproval. The sort of life that most of us admire is one which is guided by large impersonal desires; now such desires can, no doubt, be encouraged by example, education, and knowledge, but they can hardly be created by the mere abstract belief that they are good, nor discouraged by an analysis of what is meant by the word "good."

When we contemplate the human race, we may desire that it should be happy, or healthy, or intelligent, or warlike, and so on. Any one of these desires, if it is strong, will produce its own morality; but if we have no such general desires, our conduct, whatever our ethic may be, will only serve social purposes in so far as self-interest and the interests of society are in harmony. It is the business of wise institutions to create such harmony as far as possible, and for the rest, whatever may be our theoretical definition of value, we must depend upon the existence of impersonal desires. When you meet a man with whom you have a fundamental ethical disagreement—for example, if you think that all men count equally, while he selects a class as alone important—you will find yourself no better able to cope with him if you believe in objective values than if you do not. In either case, you can only influence his conduct through influencing his desires: if you succeed in that, his ethic will change, and if not, not.

Some people feel that if a general desire, say for the happiness of mankind, has not the sanction of absolute good, it is in some way irrational. This is due to a lingering belief in objective values. A desire cannot, in itself, be either rational or irrational. It may conflict with other desires, and therefore lead to unhappiness; it may rouse opposition in others, and therefore be incapable of gratification. But it cannot be considered "irrational" merely because no reason can be given for feeling it. We may desire A because it is a means to B, but in the end, when we have done with mere means, we must come to something which we desire for no reason, but not on that account "irrationally." All systems of ethics embody the desires of those who advocate them, but this fact is concealed in a mist of words. Our desires are, in fact, more general and less purely selfish than many moralists imagine; if it were not so, no theory of ethics would make moral improvement possible. It is, in fact, not by ethical theory, but by the cultivation of large and generous desires through intelligence, happiness, and freedom from fear, that men can be brought to act more than they do at present in a manner that is consistent with the general happiness of mankind. Whatever our definition of the "Good," and whether we believe it to be subjective or objective, those who do not desire the happiness of mankind will not endeavour to further it, while those who do desire it will do what they can to bring it about.

I conclude that, while it is true that science cannot decide questions of value, that is because they cannot be intellectually decided at all, and lie outside the realm of truth and falsehood. Whatever knowledge is attainable, must be attained by scientific methods; and what science cannot discover, mankind cannot know.

COMMENTS ■ QUESTIONS

1. Russell's argument uses an important distinction in ethics, the distinction between (a) instrumental goods, that is, things that are good, not in themselves, but because they lead to something else that *is* good (an example would be unpleasant work that pays well) and (b) intrinsic goods, or things that *are* good in themselves. According to Russell, intrinsic goods belong outside the realm of science or knowledge because no evidence can be found for or against them. Do you believe that this is true? Do you believe that even the most basic facts about human life or about the world can play no role in supporting claims as to what is or is not intrinsically good?
2. According to Russell, "ethics is an attempt to give universal, and not merely personal, importance to certain of our desires." To what extent would Plato have agreed or disagreed?

A. C. EWING

The Objectivity of Moral Judgements

* * * * *

The simplest form of the subjectivist view is that according to which ethical judgements, though genuine judgements, assert only that the person who makes the judgement has or tends to have certain feelings. "This is good" or "right" on such a view becomes "I have [or tend to have] an emotion of approval on considering this." A number of incredibly paradoxical consequences would follow from the adoption of this view. Firstly, the judgements could not be false unless the person judging had made a mistake about his own psychology. Secondly, two different people would never mean the same thing when they made such a judgement, since each would mean "This is approved by *me*." Indeed the same person would never mean the same by it on two different occasions, because each time he would mean "I *now* feel [or tend to feel] approval of this."

Thirdly, if I judge something to be good and you judge it to be bad, our judgements would never be logically incompatible with each other. It is not a sufficient reply to point out that they can still be incompatible with each other in some different sense, for example in the sense that they express attitudes which are in conflict with each other or lead to incompatible policies. For we do not see merely that A's judgement "This is good" and B's judgement "This is bad" (in the corresponding sense of the word) lead to or express incompatible policies like A's judgement "I desire to further X" and B's judgement "I desire to oppose X." We see that the two judgements logically contradict each other so that it is logically impossible that they could both be true. No doubt, since "good" and "bad" can each be used in different senses, "this is bad" may not always contradict "this is good," because, for example, "good" may mean "instrumentally good" and "bad" may mean "intrinsically bad"; but at any rate they sometimes do so, and on the view under discussion they could, when asserted by different people, never do so. Fourthly,

---

A. C. Ewing, who died in 1973, taught philosophy for many years at Cambridge University and had many visiting appointments in the United States. He was one of the most influential defenders of Rationalism. His books include The Morality of Punishment, The Individual, The State and World Government, The Definition of Good, The Fundamental Questions of Philosophy, *and* Non-Linguistic Philosophy.

From A. C. Ewing, *The Definition of Good*, Macmillan, 1947. Reprinted by permission of Routledge and Kegan Paul.

no argument or rational discussion, nor indeed any citation of empirical facts, could be in any degree relevant to supporting or casting doubt on any ethical judgement unless it could be directed to showing that the person who makes the judgement has made a mistake about his own feelings or tendencies to have feelings. It is true that argument or fresh knowledge about the circumstances and likely consequences of an act might lead me to have different feelings about it and so judge it right while I had judged it wrong before, or vice versa; but it would not in any way indicate that my previous judgement was false.[1] The judgements would be different; but since they referred only to my feelings at different times they would not contradict each other any more than "I was ill on January 1" contradicts "I was well on February 1." Yet it is clear that argument can really cast doubt on propositions in ethics.

Fifthly, I could not, while asserting an ethical belief, conceive that I might possibly be wrong in this belief and yet be certain that I now feel (or tend to feel) disapproval. Since it is quite clear that I can conceive this in some cases at least, this argument provides another *reductio ad absurdum* of the theory. To think that an ethical belief now expressed by me may possibly be wrong is not the same as thinking that I may come in the future to have different feelings, for I think that the present judgement may be wrong and not a future one. To put the objection in another way, it would follow from the theory that to say "If I feel approval of A, A is always right [good]" is to utter a tautology. But it is not, it is a piece of gross conceit, if made in any ordinary context. Even if it were true that, if I feel approval of A, I shall always at the time judge A to be right (good), this is quite a different statement. I need not always be certain that my judgements are correct (unless judgement is so defined as to cover only cases of *knowledge*).

Sixthly, it would follow from the theory under discussion that, when I judge that Hitler was bad or acted wrongly, I am not really talking about Hitler at all but about my own psychology.

To me the consequences that I have mentioned are all quite incredible and constitute a fully sufficient *reductio ad absurdum* of the theory from which they are deduced. They hold whether it is applied both to "good" and to "right" or only to one of them.

* * * * *

Let us now examine the case against the objectivity of ethical judgements. If it is conclusive we shall have to be subjectivists in the sense that we shall have to admit the impossibility of making any true or at least any justified ethical judgements, even if we do not admit that ethical judgements are of such a nature that they could not conceivably be true at all or true of anything but

1. I am therefore quite unmoved by the elaborate discussion by C. L. Stevenson in *Ethics and Language* as to how argument can be relevant to ethical disagreements on a subjectivist view. It does not show it to be relevant in the sense in which we really see it to be relevant, but in some other sense. The book is no doubt a very able exposition of subjectivism for those who are already convinced, but it does not, as far as I can see, bring any real argument for it or avoid any of the objections that I have mentioned against it.

the mental state or dispositions of the speaker.

One argument is based on the striking differences in ethical views between different people. But the differences between the views of savages and those of modern scientists about eclipses, or between the views of different politicians as to the causes and likely effects of contemporary events, are as great as the differences between the views of savages and of Christians, or the views of democrats and of Nazis, as to ethics. Are we to conclude from this that the scientists are no more right than the savages or that the political events about which the disputes turn have not objectively any causes or effects? If we do not draw this conclusion here, why draw the corresponding conclusion about ethics? There are also various ways of explaining the differences of view that exist without casting doubt on the objectivity of ethics. In the first place, acts which bear the same name may be very different acts in different states of society, because the circumstances and the psychology of the people concerned are very different. So it might be the case that, for example, slavery or polygamy was right, as the course which involved least evil, in certain more primitive societies and wrong in ours. This is quite compatible with the objectivity of ethical judgements. The proposition that slavery was right in ancient Egypt would not contradict the proposition that it was wrong in the United States in 1850 A.D. Both we and the ancient Egyptians may be right in our ethical judgements. Let us, however, take cases where one party is wrong. Now it is important to note that differences in ethical beliefs are often due to differences of opinion as to matters of fact. If A and B differ as to the likely consequences of an action, they may well differ as to whether the action is right or wrong, and this is perhaps the most fertile source of disputes as to what is right. But it is not an ethical difference at all; it is a difference such as arises between rival scientific predictions based on inductive evidence. Differences or apparent differences of opinion of these two kinds obviously constitute no possible argument against the objectivity of ethics.

But there are also genuine ethical differences—that is, differences as to our judgements not of fact but of value. These may sometimes be explained by differences in people's experience of life. If I never experience A, I cannot realize the intrinsic goodness of A and may therefore wrongly subordinate it to something less good. And we must remember that what is intrinsically good is not a physical thing or a physical act, but the experience or state of mind associated with it. Even a long study of philosophical books would not qualify a person to pass a judgement on the intrinsic value of philosophy if he were hopelessly bad at the subject, because then, however many books he read, he would not have a genuinely philosophical experience. Two persons who differ as to the aesthetic value of a picture may really be judging about different things, their several experiences of it. Or at least their judgements will be based on different data. Other differences of view may be due to the misapplication of principles previously accepted, or to genuine intellectual confusions such as the philosopher or even the man of common sense who is not a philosopher could remove. For instance a man may confuse badness and wrongness and conclude or assume, for example, that, because he really sees lying to be always bad (an evil), he sees it to be always wrong, while it may be a case of choosing the lesser evil rather than the greater. Often a man will think that he knows intuitively P to be R when he really only sees it to be Q but confuses Q with R.

Or the judgement that something is good or bad on the whole may have been due to concentrating attention on one side of it while ignoring or underestimating the other sides, as, for instance, militarists concentrate their attention on the unselfish heroism which war brings out in men and forget or underestimate war's evils. Lesser degrees of such onesidedness it is impossible to avoid, and yet they may detrimentally influence ethical judgements. To decide what is right in a particular case is often a difficult matter of balancing the good or evil likely to be produced by one proposed act against that likely to be produced by others. For, even if we do not hold the view that the rightness of an act depends solely on its consequences, we cannot in any case deny that such balancing of the consequences should play the predominant part in at least many ethical decisions. Perhaps, if we foresaw all the consequences clearly as they would be in their factual character and could keep our attention fixed equally on them all, we should always be in agreement as to the degree in which they were good or evil as compared with the consequences of other possible acts. But, apart from the difficulty of estimating what the consequences of an act will be, it is practically impossible in cases which are at all complex to keep our attention sufficiently fixed at the same time on all the foreseeable consequences likely to be seriously relevant for good or evil, and so we are likely through lack of attention to underestimate the value or disvalue of some as compared to that of others.

The lack of attention I have mentioned is in some degree inevitable, but it is greatly enhanced by the influence of desire and prejudice. It is a commonplace that ethical mistakes are often due to non-intellectual factors. Whether these act only through affecting the attention or whether they can lead to mistaken valuations even in the presence of full attention to the object valued we need not discuss. Their influence is certainly not confined to ethical mistakes; we may note the different conclusions as to the factual consequences of a policy which members of different political parties may draw from the same evidence. There is in any case a large class of errors for which some form of "psychoanalysis" (I do not say necessarily the Freudian) is required rather than argument, and another (probably much larger) of which it can be said only that the person in question fell into error because he did not steadfastly will to seek the truth and therefore did not fix his attention on points which displeased him. The convictions of some people as to the objectivity of ethics appear to have been shaken by the fact that enthusiastic Nazis seem to have believed that it was their duty to do things which we are convinced are completely wrong, such as ill-treating the Jews; but is there any reason to think that these Nazis really wanted to arrive at the truth regarding the question whether it was right or wrong to send Jews to concentration camps? If not, we need not be so surprised that they did not attain the truth which they did not seek.

So it may well be the case that all differences in people's judgements whether certain actions are right or wrong or certain things good or bad are due to factors other than an irreducible difference in ethical intuition. But, even if they should not be, we must remember that ethical intuition, like our other capacities, is presumably a developing factor and therefore may be capable of error. But in any case we have said enough to show that great differences of opinion as to ethics are quite compatible with the objectivity of ethical judgements.

Differences between philosophers about the general theory of ethics are remarkably great; but experience shows that very wide philosophical differences are quite compatible with striking agreement as regards the kind of action judged right or wrong, just as radical differences between philosophers in their theory of perception and of physical objects are quite compatible with complete agreement in ordinary life as to what particular physical objects are in a particular place at a particular time. The differences between philosophers are differences not mainly as to their ethical judgements in concrete ethical situations, but as to the general theory explaining these. We may add that the differences between different peoples and different civilisations as to concrete ethical judgements are commonly exaggerated. David Livingstone says that nowhere had he need to teach the African savages at any rate the ethical, as opposed to the religious, portion of the Decalogue. But there is of course a great inconsistency (not only among savages) in confining to a limited group rules which demand universal extension.

Another argument is that ethical beliefs can be explained psychologically as having originated from non-ethical factors such as fear of punishment. Now there must be a psychological history of the origin of any beliefs, and there must have been a time when no ethical ideas or beliefs yet existed, both in the history of the individual and in the history of the race. But this does not prove that ethical beliefs originated solely from the pre-existing ideas through a sort of confusion and were not due to a genuine cognition of properties really present. There was also a time when there were no logical or mathematical ideas, but nobody would entertain a similar argument against logic or mathematics.

Further, to be sceptical about ethics on the strength of a theory as to the origin of ethical ideas would be to give up the more for the far less certain, indeed the extremely uncertain. For such a sceptical theory would rest on the psychology of children if applied to individual development, and the psychology of savages if applied to the evolutionary development of the race. But, owing to the impossibility of obtaining reliable introspective evidence, the psychology of children and savages, at least when we consider their higher mental processes or the beginnings of such, is speculative in the extreme. To quote from Broad, "Of all branches of empirical psychology that which is concerned with what goes on in the minds of babies must, from the nature of the case, be one of the most precarious. Babies, whilst they remain such, cannot tell us what their experiences are; and all statements made by grown persons about their own infantile experiences on the basis of ostensible memory are certainly inadequate and probably distorted. The whole of this part of psychology therefore is, and will always remain, a mere mass of speculations about infantile mental processes, put forward to explain certain features in the lives of grown persons and incapable in principle of any independent check or verification. Such speculations are of the weakest kind known to science." [2] The psychology of primitive savages is in an equally or almost equally weak position. Some of our ethical judgments, on the other hand, I should insist, are quite or almost as certain as any judgement, and, even if the reader is not prepared to go so far, he must admit that they are at any rate far more certain than could be any theory founded on the psychology of children and savages which explained them away. The same uncertainty must attach to any theory of ethics or analysis of ethical terms based on the way in which children learn the use of the terms. Such a theory is irrelevant unless it is based on a study of what children exactly have in mind and what their mental processes are when they use the words, and how can we possibly have a well founded idea of that when they cannot introspect or adequately report introspections?

* * * * *

2. *Mind*, Vol. LIII, No. 212, p. 354.

Probably the principal reason which makes people inclined to deny the objectivity of ethics is the fact that in ethical argument we are very soon brought to a point where we have to fall back on intuition, so that disputants are placed in a situation where there are just two conflicting intuitions between which there seem to be no means of deciding. However, it is not only ethics but all reasoning which presupposes intuition. I cannot argue A, ∴ B, ∴ C without seeing that A entails B and B entails C, and this must either be seen immediately or require a further argument. If it is seen immediately, it is a case of intuition; [3] if it has to be established by a further argument, this means that another term, D, must be interpolated between A and B such that A entails D and D entails B, and similarly with B and C, but then the same question arises about A entailing D, so that sooner or later we must come to something which we see intuitively to be true, as the process of interpolation cannot go on *ad infinitum*. We cannot therefore, whatever we do, get rid of intuition if we are to have any valid inference at all. It may, however, be said that in subjects other than ethics people at any rate agree in their intuitions. But outside mathematics or formal logic this is by no means universally true. There is frequent disagreement about matters of fact as to what has happened or will happen or concerning the causes of something, and when we have exhausted the argu-

3. This proposition is not convertible: I include under "intuition" cases where some mediation is required but insight goes beyond anything that could be strictly proved by the mediation.

ments on a given point in these matters there still remains a difference between the ways in which these arguments are regarded by the disputants. In any science where you cannot prove your conclusions but only make them more or less probable there will be different estimates as to the balance of probability. As in ethics you have to balance different values against each other in order to decide what you ought to do, so here you have to balance different probable arguments, and in order to do this you must rely at some point or other on an estimate of their strength which cannot itself be further justified by mediate reasoning. Yet, when everything has been said in the way of argument, people may not all agree. Some will attribute more weight to one consideration, others to another, as they do in ethical questions about what is the right action in a given case. Our decision as to which of two probable arguments is the stronger may be influenced by other arguments in turn; but in order to deal with the situation rationally we must also estimate the weight of these other arguments, so that in the last resort it is a matter of insight into their nature which cannot be settled by other arguments *ad infinitum*. Just as in a demonstrative argument you must see intuitively how each step follows from the preceding one, so in the case of a probable argument you must rely on estimates of the degree of probability given by the argument as compared to that given by arguments on the other side, and these estimates, unless the degree of probability can be mathematically calculated, must either be themselves intuitive or be deduced from other estimates which are intuitive. I do not wish to maintain that reasoning in these matters is altogether analogous to that which occurs in dealing with ethical questions, but at any rate it is the case here that, as in ethics, we are often confronted with a situation in which we either see or do not see, and cannot logically prove, that what we seem to see is true. Yet we cannot surely therefore conclude that the scientific or historical propositions under discussion are really only propositions about the state of mind of the people who assert them, or that they are neither true nor false, or that we have no justification whatever for believing any of them!

We must therefore have intuition, and in a subject where infallibility is not attainable intuitions will sometimes disagree. Some philosophers indeed prefer not to call them intuitions when they are wrong, but then the problem will be to distinguish real from ostensible intuitions, since people certainly sometimes think they see intuitively what is not true. Now Earl Russell says: "Since no way can be even imagined for deciding a difference as to values, the conclusion is forced upon us that the difference is one of tastes, not one as to any objective truth"; [4] but what I have said shows that we can imagine plenty of ways. I have indicated that errors as to judgements of value may arise (a) from lack of the requisite experience, (b) from intellectual confusions of some sort, (c) from failure to attend adequately to certain aspects of the situation or of the consequences, or (d) from psychological causes such as those with

4. *Religion and Science*, p. 250.

which the psychoanalyst deals. Therefore to remove errors we may (a) supply the lacking experience, or failing this, if possible, describe it in a way which will make its nature clear to the other party; we may (b) dispel intellectual confusions by making adequate distinctions or exposing actual fallacies such as make a person think he has seen that A is C when he has really only seen that A is B and mistakenly identified B with C; we may (c) suggest the direction of attention to the neglected points, or we may (d) use psychological methods. And we shall, if we are wise, also look out to see whether we ourselves have tripped up in any of these ways. Further, even when inference cannot completely prove or disprove, we may use it to confirm or cast doubt on ostensible intuition. The large class of errors which result mainly from an unwillingness really to seek for the truth can hardly be used as an argument against objectivity, since they are due to the moral fault of the persons who are in error and could have been removed if the latter had tried. In these cases the trouble is not that there are no means of deciding but that the means are not used.

The methods I have suggested will not always be successful, but then is there any sphere in which human efforts always do succeed? Even the methodology of physical science cannot lay down rules which will guarantee that any scientist can make discoveries or show him in detail in advance how to prove to others the truth of the discoveries when made. I am not claiming that it is possible in practice to remove all ethical differences, but how do we know that it could not be done if there were a will on each side to listen to what the other had to say and an intelligence to discern the best methods to adopt in order to facilitate a decision? A person cannot be brought into agreement even with the established truths of science if he will not listen to what the scientist says, and there is no reason to think even with ethical intuition that there are not describable processes by which any cause of error can on principle be removed. I insert the words "on principle" simply because it will still often be the case that none of the disputants thinks of the right way of removing the error or that the person in error will not or cannot take it, as also occurs in disputes about questions of fact outside ethics.

Where the intuitive belief is due to non-intellectual factors of a kind which vitiate it, there seem to be two possibilities of cure. First, the person concerned may lose all tendency to hold the intuitive conviction when its alleged cause is clearly pointed out to him. The alleged cause is then in his case probably at least an essential part of the real cause. If, on the other hand, the intuitive belief remains unimpaired, and the man does not react to the causal explanation in a way which suggests that it has really touched a sore point, this is presumptive evidence that the explanation is mistaken. But, secondly, the cure from a false belief due to non-intellectual factors is more likely to arise because the man has been induced to approach the subject in a new spirit than merely because the true causation of the belief has been suggested to him. After all it is impossible to prove even to an unprejudiced person that such a causal theory as to the origin of a person's belief is really correct. How to induce a person to make such a new approach is a question not of logical argument but of practical psychology.

We must not think of intuition as something quite by itself, uninfluenced by inference; it is helped by inference but sees beyond what could be proved by inference. And, when intuitive ethical views differ, use may be made of inference to support one or other of the clashing views, especially by showing that it fits well into a coherent ethical system. This will not settle the question absolutely conclusively, but it can help toward settlement. Perhaps as the result of the inference one of the parties to the dispute may realize that he does not see by intuition what he claimed to see, but something rather different. It would thus be a great mistake to say that, when two men disagree on an ethical question, there is nothing to be done about it or that there is no scope in ethics for inference. No argument is available which could prove the subjectivity or fallaciousness of all ethics without establishing a similar conclusion about all other branches of study except mathematics and formal logic.

COMMENTS ■ QUESTIONS

1. Ewing begins by discussing what he calls the simplest version of moral subjectivism. This position, against which Ewing presents six different arguments, should not be confused with the rather different subjectivist position of Russell, against which Ewing also presents arguments. Has Ewing shown that the simplest version of subjectivism is unsound? Has Ewing adquately responded to the position of Russell? Specifically, in arguing against the position of Russell, has Ewing shown "plenty of ways" to rationally settle differences of opinion in regard to values?
2. Ewing's primary aim is to show that judgments about intrinsic moral values are not essentially different from other sorts of basic judgments. Subjectivists such as Russell say that basic moral disagreements reduce to what Ewing refers to as *intuitions*: I see things one way, you see things another way. But, says Ewing, judgments in other areas make use of intuition in the same way as in ethics, that is, we look to see whether the person making a judgment based on intuition has the requisite experience, is not confused, has properly examined various aspects of the situation, and does not have any serious psychological problems. Is Ewing's account of intuition—intended to apply both to judgments regarding moral values and to judgments in other areas—clear and plausible? Are there any counterexamples?

JAMES RACHELS

The Challenge of Cultural Relativism

1. How Different Cultures Have Different Moral Codes

Darius, a king of ancient Persia, was intrigued by the variety of cultures he encountered in his travels. He had found, for example, that the Callatians (a tribe of Indians) customarily ate the bodies of their dead fathers. The Greeks, of course, did not do that—the Greeks practiced cremation and regarded the funeral pyre as the natural and fitting way to dispose of the dead. Darius thought that a sophisticated understanding of the world must include an appreciation of such differences between cultures. One day, to teach this lesson, he summoned some Greeks who happened to be present at his court and asked them what they would take to eat the bodies of their dead fathers. They were shocked, as Darius knew they would be, and replied that no amount of money could persuade them to do such a thing. Then Darius called in some Callatians, and while the Greeks listened asked them what they would take to burn their dead fathers' bodies. The Callatians were horrified and told Darius not even to mention such a dreadful thing.

This story, recounted by Herodotus in his *History*, illustrates a recurring theme in the literature of social science: different cultures have different moral codes. What is thought right within one group may be utterly abhorrent to the members of another group, and vice versa. Should we eat the bodies of the dead or burn them? If you were a Greek, one answer would seem obviously correct; but if you were a Callatian, the opposite would seem equally certain.

It is easy to give additional examples of the same kind. Consider the Eskimos. They are a remote and inaccessible people. Numbering only about 25,000, they live in small, isolated settlements scattered mostly along the northern fringes of North America and Greenland. Until the beginning of this century, the outside world knew little about them. Then explorers began to bring back strange tales.

Eskimo customs turned out to be very different from our own. The

James Rachels is university professor at the University of Alabama at Birmingham, where previously he was dean of the School of Humanities. He is the author of The Elements of Moral Philosophy, The End of Life: Euthanasia and Morality, *and other works in moral philosophy.*

From The *Elements of Moral Philosophy,* by James Rachels. Copyright (c) 1986 by Random House, Inc. Reprinted by permission of the publisher.

men often had more than one wife, and they would share their wives with guests, lending them for the night as a sign of hospitality. Moreover, within a community, a dominant male might demand—and get—regular sexual access to other men's wives. The women, however, were free to break these arrangements simply by leaving their husbands and taking up with new partners—free, that is, so long as their former husbands chose not to make trouble. All in all, the Eskimo practice was a volatile scheme that bore little resemblance to what we call marriage.

But it was not only their marriage and sexual practices that were different. The Eskimos also seemed to have less regard for human life. Infanticide, for example, was common. Knud Rasmussen, one of the most famous early explorers, reported that he met one woman who had borne twenty children but had killed ten of them at birth. Female babies, he found, were especially liable to be destroyed, and this was permitted simply at the parents' discretion, with no social stigma attached to it. Old people also, when they became too feeble to contribute to the family, were left out in the snow to die. So there seemed to be, in this society, remarkably little respect for life.

To the general public, these were disturbing revelations. Our own way of living seems so natural and right that for many of us it is hard to conceive of others living so differently. And when we do hear of such things, we tend immediately to categorize those other peoples as "backward" or "primitive." But to anthropologists and sociologists, there was nothing particularly surprising about the Eskimos. Since the time of Herodotus, enlightened observers have been accustomed to the idea that conceptions of right and wrong differ from culture to culture. If we assume that *our* ideas of right and wrong will be shared by all peoples at all times, we are merely naive.

2. Cultural Relativism

To many thinkers, this observation—"Different cultures have different moral codes"—has seemed to be the key to understanding morality. The idea of universal truth in ethics, they say, is a myth. The customs of different societies are all that exist. These customs cannot be said to be "correct" or "incorrect," for that implies we have an independent standard of right and wrong by which they may be judged. But there is no such independent standard; every standard is culture-bound. The great pioneering sociologist William Graham Sumner, writing in 1906, put the point like this:

> The "right" way is the way which the ancestors used and which has been handed down. The tradition is its own warrant. It is not held subject to verification by experience. The notion of right is in the folkways. It is not outside of them, of independent origin, and brought to test them. In the folkways, whatever is, is right. This is because they are traditional, and therefore contain in themselves the authority of the ancestral ghosts. When we come to the folkways we are at the end of our analysis.

This line of thought has probably persuaded more people to be skeptical about ethics than any other single thing. *Cultural Relativism*, as it has been called, challenges our ordinary belief in the objectivity and universality of moral truth. It says, in effect, that there is no such thing as universal truth in ethics; there are only the various cultural codes, and nothing more. Moreover, our own code has no special status; it is merely one among many.

As we shall see, this basic idea is really a compound of several different thoughts. It is important to separate the various elements of the theory because, on analysis, some parts of the theory turn out to be correct, whereas others seem to be mistaken. As a beginning, we may distinguish the following claims, all of which have been made by cultural relativists:

1. Different societies have different moral codes.

2. There is no objective standard that can be used to judge one societal code better than another.

3. The moral code of our own society has no special status; it is merely one among many.

4. There is no "universal truth" in ethics—that is, there are no moral truths that hold for all peoples at all times.

5. The moral code of a society determines what is right within that society; that is, if the moral code of a society says that a certain action is right, then that action *is* right, at least within that society.

6. It is mere arrogance for us to try to judge the conduct of other peoples. We should adopt an attitude of tolerance toward the practices of other cultures.

Although it may seem that these six propositions go naturally together, they are independent of one another, in the sense that some of them might be true even if others are false. In what follows, we will try to identify what is correct in Cultural Relativism, but we will also be concerned to expose what is mistaken about it.

3. *The Cultural Differences Argument*

Cultural Relativism is a theory about the nature of morality. At first blush it seems quite plausible. However, like all such theories, it may be evaluated by subjecting it to rational analysis; and when we analyze Cultural Relativism we find that it is not so plausible as it first appears to be.

The first thing we need to notice is that at the heart of Cultural Relativism there is a certain *form of argument*. The strategy used by cultural relativists is to argue from facts about the differences between cultural outlooks to a conclusion about the status of morality. Thus we are invited to accept this reasoning:

1. The Greeks believed it was wrong to eat the dead, whereas the Callatians believed it was right to eat the dead.

2. Therefore, eating the dead is neither objectively right nor objectively wrong. It is merely a matter of opinion, which varies from culture to culture.

Or, alternatively:

1. The Eskimos see nothing wrong with infanticide, whereas Americans believe infanticide is immoral.

2. Therefore, infanticide is neither objectively right nor objectively wrong. It is merely a matter of opinion, which varies from cul-

ture to culture.

Clearly, these arguments are variations of one fundamental idea. They are both special cases of a more general argument, which says:

1. Different cultures have different moral codes.

2. Therefore, there is no objective "truth" in morality. Right and wrong are only matters of opinion, and opinions vary from culture to culture.

We may call this the *Cultural Differences Argument*. To many people, it is very persuasive. But from a logical point of view, is it a *sound* argument?

It is not sound. The trouble is that the conclusion does not really follow from the premise—that is, even if the premise is true, the conclusion still might be false. The premise concerns what people *believe:* in some societies, people believe one thing; in other societies, people believe differently. The conclusion, however, concerns *what really is the case*. The trouble is that this sort of conclusion does not follow logically from this sort of premise.

Consider again the example of the Greeks and Callatians. The Greeks believed it was wrong to eat the dead; the Callatians believed it was right. Does it follow, *from the mere fact that they disagreed*, that there is no objective truth in the matter? No, it does not follow; for it *could* be that the practice was objectively right (or wrong) and that one or the other of them was simply mistaken.

To make the point clearer, consider a very different matter. In some societies, people believe the earth is flat. In other societies, such as our own, people believe the earth is (roughly) spherical. Does it follow, *from the mere fact that they disagree*, that there is no "objective truth" in geography? Of course not; we would never draw such a conclusion because we realize that, in their beliefs about the world, the members of some societies might simply be wrong. There is no reason to think that if the world is round everyone must know it. Similarly, there is no reason to think that if there is moral truth everyone must know it. The fundamental mistake in the Cultural Differences Argument is that it attempts to derive a substantive conclusion about a subject (morality) from the mere fact that people disagree about it.

It is important to understand the nature of the point that is being made here. We are *not* saying (not yet, anyway) that the conclusion of the argument is false. Insofar as anything being said here is concerned, it is still an open question whether the conclusion is true. We *are* making a purely logical point and saying that the conclusion does not *follow from* the premise. This is important, because in order to determine whether the conclusion is true, we need arguments in its support. Cultural Relativism proposes this argument, but unforunately the argument turns out to be fallacious. So it proves nothing.

4. The Consequences of Taking Cultural Relativism Seriously

Even if the Cultural Differences Argument is invalid, Cultural Relativism might still be true. What would it be like if it were true?

In the passage quoted above, William Graham Sumner summarizes the essence of Cultural Relativism. He says that there is no measure of right and wrong other than the standards of one's society: "The notion of right is in the folkways. It is not outside of them, of independent origin, and brought to test them. In the folkways, whatever is, is right."

Suppose we took this seriously. What would be some of the consequences?

1. *We could no longer say that the customs of other societies are morally inferior to our own.* This, of course, is one of the main points stressed by Cultural Relativism. We would have to stop condemning other societies merely because they are "different." So long as we concentrate on certain examples, such as the funerary practices of the Greeks and Callatians, this may seem to be a sophisticated, enlightened attitude.

However, we would also be stopped from criticizing other, less benign practices. Suppose a society wages war on its neighbors for the purpose of taking slaves. Or suppose a society was violently anti-Semitic and its leaders set out to destroy the Jews. Cultural Relativism would preclude us from saying that either of these practices was wrong. We would not even be able to say that a society tolerant of Jews is *better* than the anti-Semitic society, for that would imply some sort of transcultural standard of comparison. The failure to condemn *these* practices does not seem "enlightened"; on the contrary, slavery and anti-Semitism seem wrong *wherever* they occur. Nevertheless, if we took Cultural Relativism seriously, we would have to admit that these social practices also are immune from criticism.

2. *We could decide whether actions are right or wrong just by consulting the standards of our society.* Cultural Relativism suggests a simple test for determining what is right and what is wrong: all one has to do is ask whether the action is in accordance with the code of one's society. Suppose a resident of South Africa is wondering whether his country's policy of *apartheid*—rigid racial segregation—is morally correct. All he has to do is ask whether this policy conforms to his society's moral code. If it does, there is nothing to worry about, at least from a moral point of view.

This implication of Cultural Relativism is disturbing because few of us think that our society's code is perfect—we can think of ways it might be improved. Yet Cultural Relativism would not only forbid us from criticizing the codes of *other* societies; it would stop us from criticizing our *own*. After all, if right and wrong are relative to culture, this must be true for our own culture just as much as for others.

3. *The idea of moral progress is called into doubt.* Usually, we think that at least some changes in our society have been for the better. (Some, of course, may have been changes for the worse.) Consider this example: Throughout most of Western history the place of women in society was very narrowly circumscribed. They could not own property; they could not vote or hold political office; with a few exceptions, they were not permitted to have paying jobs; and generally they were under the almost absolute control of their husbands. Recently

much of this has changed, and most people think of it as progress.

If Cultural Relativism is correct, can we legitimately think of this as progress? Progress means replacing a way of doing things with a *better* way. But by what standard do we judge the new ways as better? If the old ways were in accordance with the social standards of their time, then Cultural Relativism would say it is a mistake to judge them by the standards of a different time. Eighteenth-century society was, in effect, a different society from the one we have now. To say that we have made progress implies a judgment that present-day society is better, and that is just the sort of transcultural judgment that, according to Cultural Relativism, is impermissible.

Our idea of social *reform* will also have to be reconsidered. A reformer such as Martin Luther King, Jr., seeks to change his society for the better. Within the constraints imposed by Cultural Relativism, there is one way this might be done. If a society is not living up to its own ideals, the reformer may be regarded as acting for the best: the ideals of the society are the standard by which we judge his or her proposals as worthwhile. But the "reformer" may not challenge the ideals themselves, for those ideals are by definition correct. According to Cultural Relativism, then, the idea of social reform makes sense only in this very limited way.

These three consequences of Cultural Relativism have led many thinkers to reject it as implausible on its face. It does make sense, they say, to condemn some practices, such as slavery and anti-Semitism, wherever they occur. It makes sense to think that our own society has made some moral progress, while admitting that it is still imperfect and in need of reform. Because Cultural Relativism says that these judgments make no sense, the argument goes, it cannot be right.

5. *Why There Is Less Disagreement than It Seems*

The original impetus for Cultural Relativism comes from the observation that cultures differ dramatically in their views of right and wrong. But just how much do they differ? It is true that there are differences. However, it is easy to overestimate the extent of those differences. Often, when we examine what *seems* to be a dramatic difference, we find that the cultures do not differ nearly as much as it appears.

Consider a culture in which people believe it is wrong to eat cows. This may even be a poor culture, in which there is not enough food; still, the cows are not to be touched. Such a society would *appear* to have values very different from our own. But does it? We have not yet asked why these people will not eat cows. Suppose it is because they believe that after death the souls of humans inhabit the bodies of animals, especially cows, so that a cow may be someone's grandmother. Now do we want to say that their values are different from ours? No; the difference lies elsewhere. The difference is in our belief systems, not in our values. We agree that we shouldn't eat Grandma; we simply disagree about whether the cow *is* (or could be) Grandma.

The general point is this. Many factors work together to produce the customs of a society. The society's values are only one of them. Other matters, such as the religious and factual beliefs held by its members and the physical circumstances in which they must live, are also important. We cannot conclude, then, merely because customs differ, that there is a disagreement about *values*. The difference in customs may be attributable to some other aspect of social life. Thus there may be less disagreement about values than there appears to be.

Consider the Eskimos again. They often kill perfectly normal infants, especially girls. We do not approve of this at all; a parent who did this in our society would be locked up. Thus there appears to be a great difference in the values of our two cultures. But suppose we ask *why* the Eskimos do this. The explanation is not that they have less affection for their children or less respect for human life. An Eskimo family will always protect its babies if conditions permit. But they live in a harsh environment, where food is often in short supply. A fundamental postulate of Eskimo though is: "Life is hard, and the margin of safety small." A family may want to nourish its babies but be unable to do so.

As in many "primitive" societies, Eskimo mothers will nurse their infants over a much longer period of time than mothers in our culture. The child will take nourishment from its mother's breast for four years, perhaps even longer. So even in the best of times there are limits to the number of infants that one mother can sustain. Moreover, the Eskimos are a nomadic people—unable to farm, they must move about in search of food. Infants must be carried, and a mother can carry only one baby in her parka as she travels and goes about her outdoor work. Other family members can help, but this is not always possible.

Infant girls are more readily disposed of because, first, in this society the males are the primary food providers—they are the hunters, according to the traditional division of labor—and it is obviously important to maintain a sufficient number of food gatherers. But there is an important second reason as well. Because the hunters suffer a high casualty rate, the adult men who die prematurely far outnumber the women who die early. Thus if male and female infants survived in equal numbers, the female adult population would greatly outnumber the male adult population. Examining the available statistics, one writer concluded that "were it not for female infanticide ... there would be approximately one-and-a-half times as many females in the average Eskimo local group as there are food-producing males."

So among the Eskimos, infanticide does not signal a fundamentally different attitude toward children. Instead, it is a recognition that drastic measures are sometimes needed to ensure the family's survival. Even then, however, killing the baby is not the first option considered. Adoption is common; childless couples are especially happy to take a more fertile couple's "surplus." Killing is only the last resort. I emphasize this in order to show that the raw data of the anthropologists can be misleading; it can make the differences in values between cultures appear greater than they are. The Eskimos' values are not all that different from our values. It is only that life forces upon them choices that we do not have to make.

6. *How All Cultures Have Some Values in Common*

It should not be surprising that, despite appearances, the Eskimos are protective of their children. How could it be otherwise? How could a group survive that did *not* value its young? This suggests a certain argument, one which shows that all cultural groups must be protective of their infants:

1. Human infants are helpless and cannot survive if they are not given extensive care for a period of years.

2. Therefore, if a group did not care for its young, the young would not survive, and the older members of the group would not be replaced. After a while the group would die out.

3. Therefore, any cultural group that continues to exist must care for its young. Infants that are *not* cared for must be the exception rather than the rule.

Similar reasoning shows that other values must be more or less universal. Imagine what it would be like for a society to place no value at all on truth telling. When one person spoke to another, there would be no presumption at all that he was telling the truth—for he could just as easily be speaking falsely. Within that society, there would be no reason to pay attention to what anyone says. (I ask you what time it is, and you say "Four o'clock." But there is no presumption that you are speaking truly; you could just as easily have said the first thing that came into your head. So I have no reason to pay attention to your answer—in fact, there was no point in my asking you in the first place!) Communication would then be extremely difficult, if not impossible. And because complex societies cannot exist without regular communication among their members, society would become impossible. It follows that in any complex society there *must* be a presumption in favor of truthfulness. There may of course be exceptions to this rule: there may be situations in which it is thought to be permissible to lie. Nevertheless, these will be exceptions to a rule that *is* in force in the society.

Let me give one further example of the same type. Could a society exist in which there was no prohibition on murder? What would this be like? Suppose people were free to kill other people at will, and no one thought there was anything wrong with it. In such a "society," no one could feel secure. Everyone would have to be constantly on guard. People who wanted to survive would have to avoid other people as much as possible. This would inevitably result in individuals trying to become as self-sufficient as possible—after all, associating with others would be dangerous. Society on any large scale would collapse. Of course, people might band together in smaller groups with others that they *could* trust not to harm them. But notice what this means: they would be forming smaller societies that *did* acknowledge a rule against murder. The prohibition of murder, then, is a necessary feature of all societies.

There is a general theoretical point here, namely, that *there are some moral rules that all societies will have in common, because those rules are necessary for society to exist.* The rules against lying and murder are two examples. And in fact, we do find these rules in force in all viable cultures. Cultures may differ in what they regard as legitimate exceptions to the rules, but this disagreement exists against a background of agreement on the larger issues. Therefore, it is a mistake to overestimate the amount of difference between cultures. Not *every* moral rule can vary from society to society.

7. *What Can Be Learned from Cultural Relativism*

At the outset, I said that we were going to identify both what is right and what is wrong in Cultural Relativism. Thus far I have mentioned only its mistakes: I have said that it rests on an invalid argument, that it has consequences that make it implausible on its face, and that the extent of cultural disagreement is far less than it implies. This all adds up to a pretty thorough repudiation of the theory. Nevertheless, it is still a very appealing idea, and the reader may have the feeling that all this is a little unfair. The theory *must* have something going for it, or else why has it been so influential? In fact, I think there *is* something right about Cultural Relativism, and now I want to say what that is. There are two lessons we should learn from the theory, even if we ultimately reject it.

1. Cultural Relativism warns us, quite rightly, about the danger of assuming that all our preferences are based on some absolute rational standard. They are not. Many (but not all) of our practices are merely peculiar to our society, and it is easy to lose sight of that fact. In reminding us of it, the theory does a service.

Funerary practices are one example. The Callatians, according to Herodotus, were "men who eat their fathers"—a shocking idea, to us at least. But eating the flesh of the dead could be understood as a sign of respect. It could be taken as a symbolic act that says: We wish this person's spirit to dwell within us. Perhaps this was the understanding of the Callatians. On such a way of thinking, burying the dead could be seen as an act of rejection, and burning the corpse as positively scornful. If this is hard to imagine, then we may need to have our imaginations stretched. Of course we may feel a visceral repugnance at the idea of eating human flesh in any circumstances. But what of it? This repugnance may be, as the relativists say, only a matter of what is customary in our particular society.

There are many other matters that we tend to think of in terms of objective right and wrong, but that are really nothing more than social conventions. Should women cover their breasts? A publicly exposed breast is scandalous in our society, whereas in other cultures it is unremarkable. Objectively speaking, it is neither right nor wrong—there is no objective reason why either custom is better. Cultural Relativism begins with the valuable insight that many of our practices are like this—they are only cultural products. Then it goes wrong by concluding that, because *some* practices are like this, *all* must be.

2. The second lesson has to do

with keeping an open mind. In the course of growing up, each of us has acquired some strong feelings: we have learned to think of some types of conduct as acceptable, and others we have learned to regard as simply unacceptable. Occasionally, we may find those feelings challenged. We may encounter someone who claims that our feelings are mistaken. For example, we may have been taught that homosexuality is immoral, and we may feel quite uncomfortable around gay people and see them as alien and "different." Now someone suggests that this may be a mere prejudice; that there is nothing evil about homosexuality; that gay people are just people, like anyone else, who happen, through no choice of their own, to be attracted to others of the same sex. But because we feel so strongly about the matter, we may find it hard to take this seriously. Even after we listen to the arguments, we may still have the unshakable feeling that homosexuals *must*, somehow, be an unsavory lot.

Cultural Relativism, by stressing that our moral views can reflect the prejudices of our society, provides an antidote for this kind of dogmatism. When he tells the story of the Greeks and Callatians, Herodotus adds:

> For if anyone, no matter who, were given the opportunity of choosing from amongst all the nations of the world the set of beliefs which he thought best, he would inevitably, after careful consideration of their relative merits, choose that of his own country. Everyone without exception believes his own native customs, and the religion he was brought up in, to be the best.

Realizing this can result in our having more open minds. We can come to understand that our feelings are not necessarily perceptions of the truth—they may be nothing more than the result of cultural conditioning. Thus when we hear it suggested that some element of our social code is *not* really the best and we find ourselves instinctively resisting the suggestion, we might stop and remember this. Then we may be more open to discovering the truth, whatever that might be.

We can understand the appeal of Cultural Relativism, then, even though the theory has serious shortcomings. It is an attractive theory because it is based on a genuine insight—that many of the practices and attitudes we think so natural are really only cultural products. Moreover, keeping this insight firmly in view is important if we want to avoid arrogance and have open minds. These are important points, not to be taken lightly. But we can accept these points without going on to accept the whole theory.

COMMENTS ■ QUESTIONS

1. Cultural relativism is one type of *ethical* relativism. (The other type is *individual relativism*, according to which, moral values are relative to individuals.) The opposite of ethical relativism is *ethical absolutism*. You should note that Rachels does more to argue *against* cultural relativism than he does to argue *for* ethical absolutism. He argues, in the first place, that the extent of cultural disagreement is much less than it may seem. That this is so restricts the possible scope of cultural relativism, but does not in itself show that the theory is false. Rachels also argues that cultural relativism rests on an invalid argument; but this does not show that cultural relativism is false, only that it has not been proven true. Lastly, Rachels argues that cultural relativism has implausible consequences (such as that ruling out the possibility of moral progress makes it impossible to judge that one culture is morally inferior to another). This *does* imply the truth of ethical absolutism. Drawing upon the views of the other authors in this chapter, what additional points (if any) could be made in defense of ethical absolutism?
2. If cultural relativism can be shown to be false (not just not shown to be true), then ethical absolutism has to be true. If this is so, then what would you say are the most important moral values or principles that hold for all cultures?
3. Do you agree with Rachels in regard to specific moral practices (such as not burying the dead, requiring women to cover their breasts, making homosexuality a crime) that he says, or implies, are not morally right or wrong absolutely but only seem that way to people living in certain cultures?
4. On which points would Rachels and Bertrand Russell agree? On which points would they disagree?

IMMANUEL KANT

The Categorical Imperative and the Practical Imperative

Nothing can possibly be conceived in the world, or even out of it, which can be called good without qualification, except a Good Will. Intelligence, wit, judgment, and the other *talents* of the mind, however they may be named, or courage, resolution, perseverance, as qualities of temperament, are undoubtedly good and desirable in many respects; but these gifts of nature may also become extremely bad and mischievous if the will which is to make use of them, and which, therefore, constitutes what is called *character*, is not good. It is the same with the *gifts of fortune*. Power, riches, honour, even health, and the general well-being and contentment with one's condition which is called *happiness*, inspire pride, and often presumption, if there is not a good will to correct the influence of these on the mind, and with this also to rectify the whole principle of acting, and adapt it to its end. The sight of a being who is not adorned with a single feature of a pure and good will, enjoying unbroken prosperity, can never give pleasure to an impartial rational spectator. Thus a good will appears to constitute the indispensable condition even of being worthy of happiness.

There are even some qualities which are of service to this good will itself, and may facilitate its action, yet which have no intrinsic unconditional value, but always presuppose a good will, and this qualifies the esteem that we justly have for them, and does not permit us to regard them as absolutely good. Moderation in the affections and passions, self-control and calm deliberation are not only good in many respects, but even seem to constitute part of the intrinsic worth of the person; but they are far from deserving to be called good without qualification, although they have been so unconditionally praised by the ancients. For without the principles of a good will, they may become extremely bad, and the coolness of a villain not only makes him far more dangerous, but also directly makes him more abominable in our eyes than he would have been without it.

A good will is good not because of what it performs or effects, not by its aptness for the attainment of some proposed end, but simply by virtue of the volition, that is, it is good in itself, and considered by itself is to be esteemed much higher

A biographical sketch of Immanuel Kant appears earlier in this chapter.

From *Fundamental Principles of the Metaphysics of Morals*, translated by T. K. Abbott, 1898. First published in 1785.

than all that can be brought about by it in favour of any inclination, nay, even of the sum total of all inclinations. Even if it should happen that, owing to special disfavour of fortune, or the niggardly provision of a step-motherly nature, this will should wholly lack power to accomplish its purpose, if with its greatest efforts it should yet achieve nothing, and there should remain only the good will (not, to be sure, a mere wish, but the summoning of all means in our power), then, like a jewel, it would still shine by its own light, as a thing which has its whole value in itself.

* * * * *

Thus the moral worth of an action does not lie in the effect expected from it, nor in any principle of action which requires to borrow its motive from this expected effect. For all these effects—agreeableness of one's condition, and even the promotion of the happiness of others—could have been also brought about by other causes, so that for this there would have been no need of the will of a rational being; whereas it is in this alone that the supreme and unconditional good can be found. The pre-eminent good which we call moral can therefore consist in nothing else than *the conception of law* in itself, *which certainly is only possible in a rational being*, in so far as this conception, and not the expected effect, determines the will. This is a good which is already present in the person who acts accordingly, and we have not to wait for it to appear first in the result.

But what sort of law can that be, the conception of which must determine the will, even without paying any regard to the effect expected from it, in order that this will may be called good absolutely and without qualification? As I have deprived the will of every impulse which could arise to it from obedience to any law, there remains nothing but the universal conformity of its actions to law in general, which alone is to serve the will as a principle, *i.e.* I am never to act otherwise than so *that I could also will that my maxim should become a universal law*. Here now, it is the simple conformity to law in general, without assuming any particular law applicable to certain actions, that serves the will as its principle, and must so serve it, if duty is not to be a vain delusion and a chimerical notion. The common reason of men in its practical judgments perfectly coincides with this, and always has in view the principle here suggested. Let the question be, for example: May I when in distress make a promise with the intention not to keep it? I readily distinguish here between the two significations which the question may have: Whether it is prudent, or whether it is right, to make a false promise. The former may undoubtedly often be the case. I see clearly indeed that it is not enough to extricate myself from a present difficulty by means of this subterfuge, but it must be well considered whether there may not hereafter spring from this lie much greater inconvenience than that from which I now free myself, and as, with all my supposed *cunning*, the consequences cannot be so easily foreseen but that credit once lost may be much more injurious to me than any mischief which I seek to avoid at present, it should be considered whether it would not be more *prudent* to act herein according to a universal maxim, and to make it a habit to promise nothing except with the intention of keeping it. But it is soon clear to me that such a maxim will still only be based on the fear of consequences. Now it is a wholly different thing to be truthful from duty, and to be so from apprehension of injurious consequences. In the first case, the very notion of the action already implies a law for me; in the second case, I must first look about elsewhere to see what results may be combined with it which would affect myself. For to deviate from the principle of duty is beyond all doubt wicked; but to be unfaithful to my maxim of prudence may often be very advantageous to me, although to abide by it is certainly safer. The shortest way, however, and an unerring one, to discover the answer to this question whether a lying promise is consistent with duty, is to ask myself, Should I be content that my maxim (to extricate myself from difficulty by a false promise) should hold good as a universal law, for myself as well as for others? and should I be able to say to myself, "Every one may make a deceitful promise when he finds himself in a difficulty from which he cannot otherwise extricate himself"? Then I presently become aware that while I can will the lie, I can by no means will that lying should be a universal law. For with such a law there would be no promises at all, since it would be in vain to allege my intention in regard to my future actions to those who would not believe this allegation, or if they over-hastily did so would pay me back in my own coin. Hence my maxim, as soon as it should be made a universal law, would necessarily destroy itself.

I do not, therefore, need any far-reaching penetration to discern what I have to do in order that my will may be morally good. Inexperienced in the course of the world, incapable of being prepared for all its contingencies, I only ask myself: Canst thou also will that thy maxim should be a universal law? If not, then it must be rejected, and that not because of a disadvantage accruing from it to myself or even to others, but because it cannot enter as a principle into a possible universal legislation, and reason extorts from me immediate respect for such legislation. I do not indeed as yet *discern* on what this respect is based (this the philosopher may inquire), but at least I understand this, that it is an estimation of the worth which far outweighs all worth of what is recommended by inclination, and that the necessity of acting from *pure* respect for the practical law is what constitutes duty, to which every other motive must give place, because it is the condition of a will being good *in itself*, and the worth of such a will is above everything.

* * * * *

The conception of an objective principle, in so far as it is obligatory for a will, is called a command (of reason), and the formula of the command is called an Imperative.

All imperatives are expressed by the word *ought* [or *shall*], and thereby indicate the relation of an objective law of reason to a will.

* * * * *

Now all *imperatives* command either *hypothetically* or *categorically*. The former represent the practical necessity of a possible action as means to something else that is willed (or at least which one might possibly will).

The categorical imperative would be that which represented an action as necessary of itself without reference to another end, *i.e.* as objectively necessary.

Since every practical law represents a possible action as good, and on this account, for a subject who is practically determinable by reason, necessary, all imperatives are formulæ determining an action which is necessary according to the principle of a will good in some respects. If now the action is good only as a means *to something else*, then the imperative is *hypothetical*; if it is conceived as good *in itself* and consequently as being necessarily the principle of a will which of itself conforms to reason, then it is *categorical*.

* * * * *

When I conceive a categorical imperative I know at once what it contains. For as the imperative contains besides the law only the necessity that the maxims shall conform to this law, while the law contains no conditions restricting it, there remains nothing but the general statement that the maxim of the action should conform to a universal law, and it is this conformity alone that the imperative properly represents as necessary.

There is therefore but one categorical imperative, namely this: *Act only on that maxim whereby thou canst at the same time will that it should become a universal law.*

Now if all imperatives of duty can be deduced from this one imperative as from their principle, then, although it should remain undecided whether what is called duty is not merely a vain notion, yet at least we shall be able to show what we understand by it and what this notion means.

Since the universality of the law according to which effects are produced constitutes what is properly called *nature* in the most general sense (as to form), that is, the existence of things so far as it is determined by general laws, the imperative of duty may be expressed thus: *Act as if the maxim of thy action were to become by thy will a Universal Law of Nature.*

We will now enumerate a few duties, adopting the usual division of them into duties to ourselves and to others, and into perfect and imperfect duties:

1. A man reduced to despair by a series of misfortunes feels wearied of life, but is still so far in possession of his reason that he can ask himself whether it would not be contrary to his duty to himself to take his own life. Now he inquires whether the maxim of his action could become a universal law of nature. His maxim is: From self-love I adopt it as a principle to shorten my life when its longer duration is likely to bring more evil than satisfaction. It is asked then simply whether this principle founded on self-love can become a universal law of nature. Now we see at once that a system of nature of which it should be a law to destroy life by means of the very feeling whose special nature it is to impel to the improvement of life would contradict itself, and therefore could not exist as a system of nature; hence that maxim cannot possibly exist as a universal law of nature, and consequently would be wholly inconsistent with the supreme principle of all duty.

2. Another finds himself forced

by necessity to borrow money. He knows that he will not be able to repay it, but sees also that nothing will be lent to him, unless he promises stoutly to repay it in a definite time. He desires to make this promise, but he has still so much conscience as to ask himself: Is it not unlawful and inconsistent with duty to get out of a difficulty in this way? Suppose however that he resolves to do so, then the maxim of his action would be expressed thus: When I think myself in want of money, I will borrow money and promise to repay it, although I know that I never can do so. Now this principle of self-love or of one's own advantage may perhaps be consistent with my whole future welfare; but the question now is, is it right? I change then the suggestion of self-love into a universal law, and state the question thus: How would it be if my maxim were a universal law? Then I see at once that it could never hold as a universal law of nature but would necessarily contradict itself. For supposing it to be a universal law that everyone when he thinks himself in a difficulty should be able to promise whatever he pleases, with the purpose of not keeping his promise, the promise itself would become impossible, as well as the end that one might have in view in it, since no one would consider that anything was promised to him, but would ridicule all such statements as vain pretences.

3. A third finds in himself a talent which with the help of some culture might make him a useful man in many respects. But he finds himself in comfortable circumstances, and prefers to indulge in pleasure rather than to take pains in enlarging and improving his happy natural capacities. He asks, however, whether his maxim of neglect of his natural gifts, besides agreeing with his inclination to indulgence, agrees also with what is called duty. He sees then that a system of nature could indeed subsist with such a universal law although men (like the South Sea islanders) should let their talents rust, and resolve to devote their lives merely to idleness, amusement, and propagation of their species—in a word, to enjoyment; but he cannot possibly *will* that this should be a universal law of nature, or be implanted in us as such by a natural instinct. For, as a rational being, he necessarily wills that his faculties be developed, since they serve him, and have been given him, for all sorts of possible purposes.

4. A fourth, who is in prosperity, while he sees that others have to contend with great wretchedness and that he could help them, thinks: What concern is it of mine? Let everyone be as happy as heaven pleases, or as he can make himself; I will take nothing from him nor even envy him, only I do not wish to contribute anything to his welfare or to his assistance in distress! Now no doubt if such a mode of thinking were a universal law, the human race might very well subsist, and doubtless even better than in a state in which every one talks of sympathy and good-will, or even takes care occasionally to put it into practice, but on the other side, also cheats when he can, betrays the rights of men, or otherwise violates them. But although it is possible that a universal law of nature might exist in accordance with that maxim, it is impossible to *will* that such a principle should have the universal validi-

ty of a law of nature. For a will which resolved this would contradict itself, inasmuch as many cases might occur in which one would have need of the love and sympathy of others, and in which, by such a law of nature, sprung from his own will, he would deprive himself of all hope of the aid he desires.

These are a few of the many actual duties, or at least what we regard as such, which obviously fall into two classes on the one principle that we have laid down. We must be *able to will* that a maxim of our action should be a universal law. This is the canon of the moral appreciation of the action generally. Some actions are of such a character that their maxim cannot without contradiction be even *conceived* as a universal law of nature, far from it being possible that we should *will* that it *should* be so. In others this intrinsic impossibility is not found, but still it is impossible to *will* that their maxim should be raised to the universality of a law of nature, since such a will would contradict itself.

* * * * *

Now I say: man and generally any rational being *exists* as an end in himself, *not merely as a means* to be arbitrarily used by this or that will, but in all his actions, whether they concern himself or other rational beings, must be always regarded at the same time as as end. All objects of the inclinations have only a conditional worth, for if the inclinations and the wants founded on them did not exist, then their object would be without value. But the inclinations themselves being sources of want, are so far from having an absolute worth for which they should be desired, that on the contrary it must be the universal wish of every rational being to be wholly free from them. Thus the worth of any object which is *to be acquired* by our action is always conditional. Beings whose existence depends not on our will but on nature's, have nevertheless, if they are irrational beings, only a relative value as means, and are therefore called *things*; rational beings, on the contrary, are called *persons*, because their very nature points them out as ends in themselves, that is as something which must not be used merely as means, and so far therefore restricts freedom of action (and is an object of respect). These, therefore, are not merely subjective ends whose existence has a worth *for us* as an effect of our action, but *objective ends*, that is things whose existence is an end in itself: an end moreover for which no other can be substituted, which they should subserve *merely* as means, for otherwise nothing whatever would possess *absolute worth*; but if all worth were conditioned and therefore contingent, then there would be no supreme practical principle of reason whatever.

If then there is a supreme practical principle or, in respect of the human will, a categorical imperative, it must be one which, being drawn from the conception of that which is necessarily an end for every one because it is *an end in itself*, constitutes an *objective* principle of will, and can therefore serve as a universal practical law. The foundation of this principle is: *rational nature exists as an end in itself.* Man necessarily conceives his own existence as being so: so far then this is a *subjective* principle of human actions. But every other rational being regards its existence similarly, just on the same rational principle that holds for me: so that it is at the same time an objective principle, from which as a supreme practical law all laws of the will must be capable of being deduced. Accordingly the practical imperative will be as follows: *So act as to treat humanity, whether in thine own person or in that of any other, in every case as an end withal, never as means only.*

* * * * *

The conception of every rational being as one which must consider itself as giving in all the maxims of its will universal laws, so as to judge itself and its actions from this point of view—this conception leads to another which depends on it and is very fruitful, namely, that of *a kingdom of ends*.

By a *kingdom* I understand the union of different rational beings in a system by common laws. Now since it is by laws that ends are determined as regards their universal validity, hence, if we abstract from the personal differences of rational beings, and likewise from all the content of their private ends, we shall be able to conceive all ends combined in a systematic whole (including both rational beings as ends in themselves, and also the special ends which each may propose to himself), that is to say, we can conceive a kingdom of ends, which on the preceding principles is possible.

For all rational beings come under the *law* that each of them must treat itself and all others *never merely as means*, but in every case *at the same time an ends in themselves*. Hence results a systematic union of rational beings by common objective laws, *i.e.*, a kingdom which may be called a kingdom of ends.

COMMENTS ■ QUESTIONS

1. Suppose that three different people perform the same act of giving to charity. The first does it because he is a benevolent sort of person who likes other human beings a lot and wants to make those who receive the charity feel better. The second does it as part of a sales campaign for a successful company of which she is president; she wants to improve her company's self-image so as to be able to sell more of the product that her company manufactures (which, by the way, is a very worthwhile product that is sold at a reasonable price). The third does it simply because she feels it is the right thing to do. She feels it is her duty to give to charity. According to Kant, which of these people is acting morally? How would Kant defend his choice or choices?
2. Kant's Categorical Imperative is stated as follows: "I am never to act otherwise than so that I could also will that my maxim should become a universal law." By "my maxim" Kant means roughly a description of what I may tell myself to do. For example, in order to save money, I may tell myself to put cheaper leaded gasoline in

a car that is supposed to take only unleaded gasoline. In applying the Categorical Imperative, I must ask myself whether I could will that everyone do likewise (which would significantly increase air pollution). Can you think of any cases in which applying the Categorical Imperative would appear *not* to produce an acceptable universal principle? What would you say about the case of a person who loves trumpet music so much that he would gladly will that everyone practice the trumpet much of the time? What do you suppose Kant would say about such a case?

3. Kant's Practical Imperative is stated as follows: "So act as to treat humanity, whether in thine own person or in that of any other, in every case as an end withal, never as a means only." In light of this imperative, Kant would no doubt approve of the contemporary saying that it is wrong to "use other people." Can you think of a case in which it *would* appear to be morally justifiable to use someone else, or to treat them as a means and not as an end? Some philosophers have said that Kant's Practical Imperative is the most important of all moral principles. Do you agree? Why or why not?

4. According to Kant, the Practical Imperative does not apply to animals because they are not rational agents; animals are not ends in themselves and therefore do not have moral rights. Do you believe that Kant is correct about this?

JOHN STUART MILL

Utilitarianism

The creed which accepts as the foundation of morals, Utility, or the Greatest Happiness Principle, holds that actions are right in proportion as they tend to promote happiness, wrong as they tend to produce the reverse of happiness. By happiness is intended pleasure, and the absence of pain; by unhappiness, pain, and the privation of pleasure. To give a clear view of the moral standard set up by the the-

A biographical sketch of John Stuart Mill appears in chapter 12.

From *Utilitarianism*, first published in 1863.

ory, much more requires to be said; in particular, what things it includes in the ideas of pain and pleasure; and to what extent this is left an open question. But these supplementary explanations do not affect the theory of life on which this theory of morality is grounded—namely, that pleasure, and freedom from pain, are the only things desirable as ends; and that all desirable things (which are as numerous in the utilitarian as in any other scheme) are desirable either for the pleasure inherent in themselves, or as means to the promotion of pleasure and the prevention of pain.

Now, such a theory of life excites in many minds, and among them in some of the most estimable in feeling and purpose, inveterate dislike. To suppose that life has (as they express it) no higher end than pleasure—no better and nobler object of desire and pursuit—they designate as utterly mean and grovelling; as a doctrine worthy only of swine, to whom the followers of Epicurus were, at a very early period, contemptuously likened; and modern holders of the doctrine are occasionally made the subject of equally polite comparisons by its German, French, and English assailants.

When thus attacked, the Epicureans have always answered, that it is not they, but their accusers, who represent human nature in a degrading light; since the accusation supposes human beings to be capable of no pleasures except those of which swine are capable. If this supposition were true, the charge could not be gainsaid, but would then be no longer an imputation; for if the sources of pleasure were precisely the same to human beings and to swine, the rule of life which is good enough for the one would be good enough for the other. The comparison of the Epicurean life to that of beasts is felt as degrading, precisely because a beast's pleasures do not satisfy a human being's conceptions of happiness. Human beings have faculties more elevated than the animal appetites, and when once made conscious of them, do not regard anything as happiness which does not include their gratification. I do not, indeed, consider the Epicureans to have been by any means faultless in drawing out their scheme of consequences from the utilitarian principle. To do this in any sufficient manner, many Stoic, as well as Christian elements require to be included. But there is no known Epicurean theory of life which does not assign to the pleasures of the intellect, of the feelings and imagination, and of the moral sentiments, a much higher value as pleasures than to those of mere sensation. It must be admitted, however, that utilitarian writers in general have placed the superiority of mental over bodily pleasures chiefly in the greater permanency, safety, uncostliness, etc., of the former—that is, in their circumstantial advantages rather than in their intrinsic nature. And on all these points utilitarians have fully proved their case; but they might have taken the other, and, as it may be called, higher ground, with entire consistency. It is quite compatible with the principle of utility to recognise the fact, that some *kinds* of pleasure are more desirable and more valuable than others. It would be absurd that while, in estimating all other things, quality is considered as well as quantity, the estimation of pleasures should be supposed to depend on quantity alone.

If I am asked, what I mean by difference of quality in pleasures, or what makes one pleasure more valuable than another, merely as a pleasure, except its being greater in amount, there is but one possible answer. Of two pleasures, if there be one to which all or almost all who have experience of both give a decided preference, irrespective of any feeling of moral obligation to prefer it, that is the more desirable pleasure. If one of the two is, by those who are competently acquainted with both, placed so far above the other that they prefer it, even though knowing it to be attended with a greater amount of discontent, and would not resign it for any quantity of the other pleasure which their nature is capable of, we are justified in ascribing to the preferred enjoyment a superiority in quality, so far outweighing quantity as to render it, in comparison, of small account.

Now it is an unquestionable fact that those who are equally acquainted with, and equally capable of appreciating and enjoying, both, do give a most marked preference to the manner of existence which employs their higher faculties. Few human creatures would consent to be changed into any of the lower animals, for a promise of the fullest allowance of a beast's pleasures; no intelligent human being would consent to be a fool, no instructed person would be an ignoramus, no person of feeling and conscience would be selfish and base, even though they should be persuaded that the fool, the dunce, or the rascal is better satisfied with his lot than they are with theirs. They would not resign what they possess more than he for the most complete satisfaction of all the desires which they have in common with him. If they ever fancy they would, it is only in cases of unhappiness so extreme, that to escape from it they would exchange their lot for almost any other, however undesirable in their own eyes. A being of higher faculties requires more to make him happy, is capable probably of more acute suffering, and certainly accessible to it at more points, than one of an inferior type; but in spite of these liabilities, he can never really wish to sink into what he feels to be a lower grade of existence. We may give what explanation we please of this unwillingness; we may attribute it to pride, a name which is given indiscriminately to some of the most and to some of the least estimable feelings of which mankind are capable: we may refer it to the love of liberty and personal independence, an appeal to which was with the Stoics one of the most effective means for the inculcation of it; to the love of power, or to the love of excitement, both of which do really enter into and contribute to it: but its most appropriate appellation is a sense of dignity, which all human beings possess in one form or other, and in some, though by no means in exact, proportion to their higher faculties, and which is so essential a part of the happiness of those in whom it is strong, that nothing which conflicts with it could be, otherwise than momentarily, an object of desire to them. Whoever supposes that this preference takes place at a sacrifice of happiness—that the superior being, in anything like equal circumstances, is not happier than the inferior—confounds the two very different ideas, of happiness, and content. It is undisputable that the being whose capacities of enjoyment are low, has the greatest chance of having them fully satisfied; and a highly endowed being will always feel that any happiness which he can look for, as the world is constituted, is imperfect. But he can learn to bear its imperfections, if they are at all bearable; and they will not make him envy the being who is indeed unconscious of the imperfections, but only because he feels not at all the good which those imperfections qualify. It is better to be a human being dissatisfied than a pig satisfied; better to be Socrates dissatisfied than a fool satisfied. And if the fool, or the pig, are of a different opinion, it is because they only know their own side of the question. The other party to the comparison knows both sides.

It may be objected, that many who are capable of the higher pleasures, occasionally, under the influence of temptation, postpone them to the lower. But this is quite compatible with a full appreciation of the intrinsic superiority of the higher. Men often, from infirmity of character, make their election for the nearer good, though they know it to be the less valuable; and this no less when the choice is between two bodily pleasures, than when it is between bodily and mental. They pursue sensual indulgences to the injury of health, though perfectly aware that health is the greater good. It may be further objected, that many who begin with youthful enthusiasm for everything noble, as they advance in years sink into indolence and selfishness. But I do not believe that those who undergo this very common change, voluntarily choose the lower description of pleasures in preference to the higher. I believe that before they devote themselves exclusively to the one, they have already become incapable of the other. Capacity for the nobler feelings is in most natures a very tender plant, easily killed, not only by hostile influences, but by mere want of sustenance; and in the majority of young persons it speedily dies away if the occupation to which their position in life has devoted them, and the society into which it has thrown them, are not favourable to keeping that higher capacity in exercise. Men lose their high aspirations as they lose their intellectual tastes, because they have not time or opportunity for indulging them; and they addict themselves to inferior pleasures, not because they deliberately prefer them, but because they are either the only ones to which they have access, or the only ones which they are any longer capable of enjoying. It may be questioned whether any one who has remained equally susceptible to both classes of pleasures, ever knowingly and calmly preferred the lower; though many, in all ages, have broken down in an ineffectual attempt to combine both.

From this verdict of the only competent judges, I apprehend there can be no appeal. On a question which is the best worth having of two pleasures, or which of two modes of existence is the most grateful to the feelings, apart from its moral attributes and from its consequences, the judgment of those who are qualified by knowledge of both, or, if they differ, that of the majority among them, must be admitted as final. And there needs be the less hesitation to accept this judgment respecting the quality of pleasures, since there is no other tribunal to be referred to even on the question of quantity. What means are there of determining which is the acutest of two pains, or the intensest of two pleasurable sensations, except the general suffrage of those who are familiar with both? Neither pains nor pleasures are homogeneous, and pain is always heterogeneous with pleasure. What is there to decide whether a particular pleasure is worth purchasing at the cost of a particular pain, except the feelings and judgment of the experienced? When, therefore, those feelings and judgment declare the pleasures derived from the higher faculties to be preferable *in kind*, apart from the question of intensity, to those of which the animal nature, disjoined from the higher faculties, is susceptible, they are entitled on this subject to the same regard.

I have dwelt on this point, as being a necessary part of a perfectly just conception of Utility or Happiness, considered as the directive rule of human conduct. But it is by no means an indispensable condition to the acceptance of the utilitarian standard; for that standard is not the agent's own greatest happiness, but the greatest amount of happiness altogether; and if it may possibly be doubted whether a noble character is always the happier for its nobleness, there can be no doubt that it makes other people happier, and that the world in general is immensely a gainer by it. Utilitarianism, therefore, could only attain its end by the general cultivation of nobleness of character, even if each individual were only benefited by the nobleness of others, and his own, so far as happiness is concerned, were a sheer deduction from the benefit. But the bare enunciation of such an absurdity as this last, renders refutation superfluous.

According to the Greatest Happiness Principle, as above explained, the ultimate end, with reference to and for the sake of which all other things are desirable (whether we are considering our own good or that of other people), is an existence exempt as far as possible from pain, and as rich as possible in enjoyments, both in point of quantity and quality; the test of quality, and the rule for measuring it against quantity, being the preference felt by those who in their opportunities of experience, to which must be added their habits of self-consciousness and self-observation, are best furnished with the means of comparison. This, being, according to the utilitarian opinion, the end of human action, is necessarily also the standard of morality; which may accordingly be defined, the rules and precepts for human conduct, by the observance of which an existence such as has been described might be, to the greatest extent possible, secured to all mankind; and not to them only, but, so far as the nature of things admits, to the whole sentient creation.

* * * * *

The happiness which forms the utilitarian standard of what is right in conduct, is not the agent's own happiness, but that of all concerned. As between his own happiness and that of others, utilitarianism requires him to be as strictly impartial as a disinterested and benevolent spectator. In the golden rule of Jesus of Nazareth, we read the complete spirit of the ethics of utility. To do as you would be done by, and to love your neighbour as yourself, constitute the ideal perfection of utilitarian morality.

COMMENTS ■ QUESTIONS

1. Mill's utilitarianism is a version of *ethical hedonism*, which is the doctrine that all morally right actions ought to aim at increasing pleasure and decreasing pain. Do you believe that increasing pleasure and decreasing pain are the only moral goods? Does the following argument demonstrate that ethical hedonism ought to be rejected? Suppose that a device existed that could be called a Pleasure Machine. Its electrodes could be implanted in a person's head to contact the "pleasure centers" in the brain. The electrodes would be connected to a computer that could be programmed to produce all possible pleasurable sensations. A person hooked up to the Pleasure Machine could experience any pleasure he or she might desire (along with no pain at all), but none of the other elements in experience. Would a life lived in response to the Pleasure Machine be lacking in anything that was morally good? If it would be, does this show that ethical hedonism is false?
2. Mill's utilitarianism can be thought of as consisting of ethical hedonism combined with a version of altruism. According to Mill, the morally right choice is always the one that increases pleasure and decreases pain as much as possible for *the greatest number of people*, not just for oneself. The contrasting position is *egoistic* hedonism. Do you agree that morality should be essentially altruistic? (For a more complete treatment of egoism and altruism, see chapter 9.)
3. Do you accept the distinction drawn by Mill between higher and lower pleasures? If so, do you believe that Mill's examples of higher and lower pleasures are acceptable? If not, why not?
4. Can you think of any occasions when doing what will produce the greatest happiness for the greatest number (where happiness is defined either as Mill defines it or in any other way that you may find more acceptable) would be morally wrong? What would Kant say about Mill's Greatest Happiness Principle?
5. Which of the two philosophers, Kant or Mill, do you believe gives the best account of basic moral principles? What are your reasons for making the choice that you have?

READINGS

Aristotle. *Nicomachean Ethics.* Translated by Sir David Ross. London: Oxford University Press, 1969. The classic, but difficult, discussion of moral virtue.

Baier, Kurt. *The Moral Point of View.* Ithaca, N.Y.: Cornell University Press, 1965. Widely read discussion of the necessary conditions for a position to count as ethical.

Bayles, Michael, ed. *Contemporary Utilitarianism.* Garden City, N.Y.: Doubleday, Anchor Books, 1968. An excellent anthology of recent work.

Feinberg, Joel, and Henry West, eds. *Moral Philosophy: Classic Texts and Contemporary Problems.* Belmont, Calif.: Wadsworth, 1977. A very useful collection.

Foot, Phillippa, ed. *Theories of Ethics.* Oxford: Oxford University Press, 1967. Excellent contemporary collection that contains, among other notable papers, John Rawls's "Two Concept of Rules," which defends a version of utilitarianism.

Gifford, N. *When in Rome.* Albany: State University of New York Press, 1981. A good introductory treatment of relativism.

Glickman, Jack, ed. *Moral Philosophy: An Introduction.* New York: St. Martin's Press, 1976. Well-chosen excerpts from the ethical writings of Plato, Hume, Kant, Mill along with critiques by contemporary philosophers.

Helm, P., ed. *Divine Commands and Morality.* New York: Oxford University Press, 1981. A collection of papers on the question of whether morality is based upon divine commands.

Hospers, John. *Human Conduct.* New York: Harcourt Brace Jovanovich, 1972. A comprehensive and clear discussion of most of the important ethical theories.

Johnson, Oliver A. *Ethics: Selections from Classical and Contemporary Writers.* 5th ed. New York: Holt, Rinehart and Winston, 1984. A very useful collection of excerpts and papers covering the major ethical theories.

Krausz, M., and J. Meiland, eds. *Relativism: Cognitive and Moral.* Notre Dame: University of Notre Dame Press, 1982. Important but often difficult contemporary essays.

Ladd, John, ed. *Ethical Relativism.* Belmont, Calif.: Wadsworth, 1973. A good anthology.

CHAPTER NINE

All good . . . is relative. Nothing can be good at all unless it is good for at least some one individual. The good for him is always what he needs and what satisfies him.
—*Gardner Williams*

Genuine egoists, people who really don't care at all about anyone other than themselves, are rare.
—*James Rachels*

Egoism and Altruism

One lesson that can be learned from the writings of philosophers, regardless of the area, is that philosophical disagreements are never simple or straightforward. A good illustration of this is the longstanding controversy between egoists and altruists. Their disagreement may *appear* simple and straightforward—egoists believe in selfishness while altruists do not—but in reality the dispute may be addressed to any one, or all three, of the following areas.

1. *Questions regarding human psychology, particularly questions about motivation.* Some philosophers believe that, given the psychological nature of human beings, everyone acts for the sake of basically selfish reasons. This position is known as *psychological egoism.* It has been held by some notable figures in the history of philosophy, such as Thomas Hobbes in the seventeenth century, and many people who are not philosophers find it to be intuitively plausible. Almost no philosophers at the present time, however, would accept it. Arguments against it are to be found in this chapter's selection from James Rachels. Some of the questions that would arise in a thoroughgoing analysis of psychological egoism follow (Rachels addresses most, but not all, of these questions).

- Do people always act to derive some pleasure or satisfaction for themselves, or at least to avoid some pain for themselves?
- If people always act to either gain satisfaction or avoid pain for themselves, does this mean that all human actions are selfish? If so, is this the case regardless of whether a person is doing something that benefits others?
- What role does one's conscience play in human motivation? What is the basis for one's conscience? Does everyone have a conscience?

2. *Questions regarding moral obligations. Altruists* believe that one should not, overall in one's life, put concern for oneself above concern for others. *Ethical egoists*, on the other hand, believe that everyone should always, or usually, act for the sake of self-interest, regardless of the needs or supposed rights of others.

According to ethical egoism, a person should take into account the rights and needs of others only when it is in the person's self-interest to do so.

There are, then, two quite distinct theories, both of which may be referred to as egoism: psychological egoism and ethical egoism. The latter is called *ethical* egoism because, in contrast to psychological egoism, it concerns ethical values, not because it is "ethical" in the sense of being morally correct. Its defenders would say that it is morally correct, but many philosophers argue against this view. Rachels presents arguments against *both* psychological and ethical egoism. Another reading selection for this chapter, the Sermon on the Mount from the New Testament, contains the most famous statement of Christian altruism. The selection from Gardner Williams defends one version of ethical egoism.

The views of ethical egoists differ among themselves and are best thought of as falling on a continuum. At one extreme is what could be called *cutthroat egoism*, which is the view that in the pursuit of self-interest a person should pay no attention whatsoever to what may be helpful or harmful to others. Its defenders would give the following moral advice (at least to themselves!):

> To get the things in life that you value for yourself do whatever you need to do—including murder, theft, and betrayal—as long as you can be reasonably sure that you will not be caught and punished.

Needless to say, cutthroat egoism is the sort of position that philosophers discuss only to dismiss or to refer to for the sake of clarifying other positions; no one defends it.

In contrast is the version of ethical egoism that stands at the opposite extreme. Usually called *rational egoism*, it has had quite a few important defenders, including the ancient Greek philosopher Aristotle. Rational egoists would give the following advice:

> To get the things in life that are valuable for yourself, pay close attention to the wants and needs of others because very often you can bring benefits to yourself by helping others.

The rational egoist believes that friendship, family life, a stable government, cooperation and trust in the world of business, and so on are important, or even essential, if a person is to have the best sort of life. For the rational egoist, *I* cannot be happy unless, to quite a considerable degree, I do things to help *you*. In the present chapter, Gardner Williams defends a version of rational egoism:

> An individual always has a duty, from his own point of view, to attain as nearly as possible his highest good. . . . An individual has a duty to help others if, when, and because he needs to help them. Helping them is an individual moral imperative of his whenever it will satisfy him most deeply in the long run.

3. *Questions regarding what kind of person one ought to be, or specifically, the question of whether, or to what degree, a person ought to be selfish.* From one point of view, the question of whether we ought to be selfish is not very different from the question discussed above of whether we ought to *do* selfish things. We expect a person who *is* selfish to *act* selfishly. A person who *acts* selfishly may rightly be judged to *be* a selfish person.

But from another point of view, the two kinds of questions are very different. We take up this point of view when we ask what it *means* to be selfish or not to be selfish. It may appear easy enough to give an answer: selfish people are those who put their own self-interest first, helping others only when doing so is conducive to their own self-interest. This sort of answer however, only puts off the really interesting question, namely, *what we ought to conceive our self-interest to be*. Specifically, to what extent and in what ways should we suppose that our own self-interest is bound up with the interests of others? Different people will give different answers to this question. The contrast between the cutthroat egoist and the rational egoist should illustrate the truth of this dramatically, since, in the pursuit of self-interest, each will live a kind of life very different from the other.

At this point in the discussion, matters become rather complicated. The first thing we must do is ask about the *kind* of basic dispute that divides cutthroat egoists from rational egoists. Is it a dispute about values, that is, about *how* people ought to live? Or is it a dispute about what the facts *are*. It may seem that it is a factual dispute because cutthroat egoists simply seem to be wrong in their beliefs about human nature. The dispute between them and rational egoists may seem to be the same kind as that between the defenders of psychological egoism and those who reject it. Those who accept psychological egoism, as we said, believe that all people are basically selfish. Those who reject psychological egoism take a different view of human nature. Neither side makes a value claim regarding egoism because neither side says that we should or should not be selfish. Likewise, rational egoists may argue that cutthroat egoists have gotten their facts wrong—that friendship, trust, and cooperation *are* essential ingredients in the pursuit of self-interest. They are essential as *means* to achieving a selfish *end*.

But is this really the best way to look at the matter? Could it really be shown that, as a matter of fact, everyone or nearly everyone would be happier pursuing the life of a rational egoist as opposed to the life of a cutthroat egoist? (Let us assume for the sake of the argument that these are the only two choices.) Is it not true instead that some people are, or tend to be, selfish in a very narrow way and consequently cannot be expected to derive much happiness from friendship or cooperation? Is it not true that people do differ a great deal from each other and therefore can be expected to find satisfaction in many diverse ways? Is it not true also that people can do things to bring about changes in themselves and in the sorts of lives that they find satisfying?

Philosophers who would answer yes to the last three questions would typically subscribe to what is called *virtue-based ethics*. This is the view that the most basic moral questions need to be asked about human nature, for example: Of all the different kinds of people that there are or that there could be, which should we be or, at least, *try* to become?

According to the approach taken in virtue-based ethics, what people do or intend to do *is* important (for example, whether we help or intend to help others); at the same time, it is believed that what we do or intend to do is largely determined by what we *are* and what we believe other people ought to be. The following are some of the major characteristics, or virtues, that defenders of virtue-based ethics have said that people should have:

- Compassion or sympathy for others
- A well-developed ability to apply one's understanding to moral questions—to be able to think carefully about moral values and all relevant matters of fact
- Self-control and moderation in one's appetites and desires
- Strength of will, or strength of character, that is needed to carry through on one's moral decisions

With the concept of virtue-based ethics in mind, let us return to an examination of the basic differences between altruists and ethical egoists. From this new perspective, the distinction between altruism and ethical egoism is no longer very clear-cut. The concept of altruism is probably the easier of the two to analyze, however, so let us begin there. From the perspective of virtue-based ethics, altruism is the view that a person ought to have the virtues given above, especially compassion. It follows that an altruist will advocate a reform of character in people who do not have enough compassion or are deficient in other important virtues. The reading selection from Josiah Royce discusses what Royce believed to be the most important aspect of an altruistic character—the capacity to view others in the same way that we view ourselves.

How should we describe an ethical egoist in terms of virtue-based ethics? Suppose we say that the ethical egoist cares nothing about acquiring or strengthening his or her virtues, but instead does whatever *happens* to be conducive to self-interest as it is perceived at the time. It will follow that it is okay for self-destructive people to go ahead and do self-destructive things. But if ethical egoism does entail this, no thinking person would ever take it seriously.

If we say that the ethical egoist does pay attention to the virtues, then to which ones? One possible answer would distinguish between "self-regarding" virtues and "other-regarding" virtues. With this view, an ethical egoist is someone who believes in developing the virtues of self-control and the capacity to reason out solutions to problems but not in developing such virtues as compassion. With this view, an ethical egoist *is* easily distinguished from an ethical altruist.

This version of ethical egoism, however, may seem unsatisfactory to those who believe that a person who *has* the virtue of compassion (and consequently spends a great deal of time helping others) will in either the short or the long run find the most personal satisfaction in life. If this view is adopted, is there any longer a clear difference between ethical egoists and altruists in terms of a virtue-based ethics? Both would favor the same, or nearly the same, set of virtues. A paper of my own, entitled "The Concept of Altruism," which I have included in the present chapter, attempts to explore this common ground where ethical egoism and altruism may appear to coincide. The selection by Bernard Mayo is a more general discussion of virtue-based ethical systems.

JOSIAH ROYCE

The spiritual world that Kant bade us build is the modern world; and Kant is the true hero of all modern thought. If in one sense it is only by transcending him and even by forgetting some of his limitations that we are to triumph, he is none the less forever our guide.

—*The Spirit of Modern Philosophy*

And in the eternal world there are therefore moral personalities—individuals, who are yet one in God. The only immortality that I pretend to know about is precisely the presence of these individuals in the eternal world.

—*The Conception of God*

We have no habits of self-consciousness which are not derived from social habits, counterparts thereof. Where the analogy of our relations to our fellows ceases, reflection ceases also.

—*Studies in Good and Evil*

Josiah Royce (1855–1916) was the most influential American defender of philosophical idealism. Born in a mining camp in California, he attended the recently founded University of California, then studied in Germany at Leipzig and Gottingen where he read widely in German idealist philosophy. After receiving a Ph. D. from Johns Hopkins, he was a professor at Harvard during most of his career. A very prolific writer, he was the author of a novel and a history of California in addition to many books and articles in philosophy. While still a young man, he visited Australia and published an account of his travels. Among his best known books are *The Religious Aspect of Philosophy, The Spirit of Modern Philosophy, The World and the Individual*, and *The Conception of Immortality*.

GARDNER WILLIAMS

Individual, Social, and Universal Ethics

I shall define and recommend an ethical or axiological terminology which has seemed to me adequate for the expression of all of the valid principles of man's moral experience.[1] I shall try to show, by the use of this terminology, (1) that there is a sense in which ethics is purely individualistic, (2) that there is another sense in which it is social, and (3) that there are three other senses in which it is universal. I shall also try to show that all social ethics is derived from individual ethics, and that all universal ethics is a dialectical elucidation of individualistic ethical principles. In other words, individualism is axiologically basic.

We should indicate the proposed meanings of good, value, right, and duty. The good is the satisfactory. The satisfactory is anything which causes a feeling of satisfaction, or any experience which contains this feeling. The good also is equivalently defined as anything which is *needed*. Everyone needs what is satisfactory simply because it is satisfactory. The good is the same as the valuable. It is anything that has value. There are two kinds of good, intrinsic and extrinsic, and two corresponding kinds of value. Intrinsic good has intrinsic or primary value, and extrinsic good has extrinsic or secondary value.

Primary value is the feeling of satisfaction. It is the felt intrinsic satisfactoriness which any experience may have or contain. It, and its opposite, dissatisfaction or intrinsic disvalue, are probably produced by neural processes in the central nervous system. These feelings are not sensations or desires or ideas. They are called, respectively, positive and negative feeling-tone, or positive and negative affects, or pleasure-pain. I do not think that they can be analyzed into simpler experiential elements. Like any ultimate qualities of experience they can be referred to or pointed at. They can not be described. No one could understand what was meant by the words "satisfaction" and "dissatisfaction" if he had never experienced the kinds of consciousness to which these words

1. This paper was read at the Tenth International Congress of Philosophy, Amsterdam, August, 1948.

Gardner Williams, who died in 1972, was a professor of philosophy for many years at Toledo University. He wrote many articles and books, among them The Human Perspective *and* Humanistic Ethics.

From "Individual, Social and Universal Ethics" by Gardner Williams in *The Journal of Philosophy*, volume XLV, number 24 (1948). By permission of *The Journal of Philosophy*.

refer. But everybody has experienced such consciousness. All experience is immediately felt as being either satisfactory or unsatisfactory, and probably almost all is simultaneously felt as being both, in varying proportions. Possibly some experience is absolutely pure joy, and possibly some is pure anguish, but probably very little is pure in either of these senses.

From this meaning of primary value it will follow that our theory may properly be called an *affective axiology*. Feeling tone or affect is the *axiological absolute*. This feeling is basic in determining all good and evil, though of course it depends for its existence upon the life processes of a biological organism. It is axiologically primary and ultimate, but it is ontologically and metaphysically secondary, dependent, peripheral, and ephemeral.

An *intrinsic good*, we have indicated, is an experience that has primary value. It is any total happy experience as of any given moment. It will be a complex *gestalt* including, in many cases, sensation, imagination, desire, perhaps a rational concept, retrospection, anticipation, and feeling-tone. The *primary value* or feeling-tone is, like each of the other elements, a quality or abstract aspect of the complex total.

An *extrinsic good* is an instrumental good. It has secondary value. It is a cause of intrinsic good. The *secondary value* which it has, and which makes it instrumentally good, is its causal relation to intrinsic good.

This terminology, combined with some sound psychological principles, commits us to a radical individualism. Our theory may properly be called an *affective axiological individualism*. For all intrinsic goods are individual, since they are total complexes of consciousness or experience, which is always individual. The individuality of all experience may be disputed, and it can not be proved beyond peradventure, but it is indicated by the truth that only a biological organism can be conscious. This too may be disputed. Disembodied spirits, or portions of spirits, might exist. But scientific psychology indicates pretty clearly that all consciousness depends for its existence upon the neurones of a biological organism.[2] Then since such organisms are individual, that is, since they are spatially distinct from each other, so are people's consciousnesses, perhaps with the exception of any Siamese twins who might have parts of their central nervous systems in common. Barring such abnormalities, consciousness is in every case tied down to the neurones of an individual, separate, and distinct biological organism. Minds never merge or overlap if persons are not Siamese twins, and they seldom or never do even in these linked organisms. Ideas never fly through the air from one mind to another. The group mind is a fiction, unless it is just the interactions or inter-communication of a number of individual minds. Communication occurs, but it is never a direct contact of mind with mind. It is never intuitive. It is always effected through some physical medium. We must reject the theory of mental telepathy, which is that one mind can apprehend directly the thoughts in other minds. Supposed telepathy is

2. See R. M. Brickner, "Man and His Values Considered Neurologically," this Journal, Vol. XLI (1944), pp. 225–243.

either an unintentional error, or a fraud, or else it is signalling from a distance, through physical media which are not now understood, and which stimulate sense organs which have not yet been located. We must also reject the theory of Platonic universals, the view that one identical universal concept can exist simultaneously or successively in several minds which are located in distinct bodies spatially separated from each other.

If, then, all experience is absolutely individual in its existence, all intrinsic good must be individual, for intrinsic good is experience. Moreover, every primary value must be individual, for it will in every case belong to an individual intrinsic good. Also all instrumental goods are purely individual in the sense that they are good only because of their causal relations to individual intrinsic goods. And secondary values are individual in the sense that they are always causal relations between some instrumental good and an individual intrinsic good.

This value theory is also in some sense relativistic. Its full name is *affective axiological individualistic relativism*. Instrumental goods are relative by definition. They are things causally *related* to some intrinsic goods and values. Secondary value is relative in the sense that it *is* this causal relation. Even intrinsic good is in a sense relative. This may seem like a contradiction in terms, but at least we must recognize that the terminology of relativism applies properly to it, for an intrinsic good is intrinsically good only in and to itself. It has its primary value inside itself. This value may be known and appreciated by others, but the only value that an intrinsic good can actually have to others is an instrumental value. Anything that can be a cause can have instrumental value. An intrinsic good which causes another intrinsic good to exist will have both its own primary value within itself and a secondary value, which is its causal relation to the other intrinsic good. It will be simultaneously both an intrinsic good in itself, and an instrumental good to all individuals in whom it causes satisfaction. It will cause this in the souls of all who sympathize with and love the person that contains it, and in all who are made happy by the knowledge that this person has intrinsic value and is happy. Its ultimate justification or value, from their points of view, depends upon the satisfaction which they feel as a result of it.

All good, then, is relative. Nothing can be good at all unless it is good for at least some one individual. The good, for him, is always what he needs and what satisfies him. This is always determined by his actual individual character or nature. What is good for a canary bird is determined by the nature of the canary bird, and what is good for a man is determined by the nature of the man. Moreover, when something is in fact good for him, there is no logical necessity that it should be good for anybody else. Others may not need it. It may not satisfy them. Their natures may be different from his, by biological inheritance or by training. His good often *is* good for others, but that is because their natures are similar to his, or because they love him, or because his well-being enables him to help them.

This relativistic theory does not mean that there is nothing either good or bad but *thinking* makes it so. Rather the principle is that there is nothing either good or bad but *feeling* makes it so. Feeling, the axiological absolute, however, is not the goal of all desire. Nor ought it to be. The egoistic hedonists were wrong in thinking that it should be. But they were right in thinking that it is the ultimate value and justification of whatever is morally justified and worthy. This affective axiology reiterates what is true in their ancient, oft libelled, and seldom understood doctrine.

This axiological theory is also in the tradition of the interest theory of value, the essential truth of which is that the intrinsic good of any individual is the satisfactions involved in, and resulting from, the fulfillment of his major interests or desires such as love, ambition, and the desires for truth, for beauty, and for sensuous enjoyment.[3]

We now come to the definitions of right and duty. These are equivalent terms. One always has a duty to do what is right, and it is always right for one to do his duty. The meaning of these terms is to be derived from the meanings which we have already found for good and value. An individual always has a duty, from his own point of view, to attain as nearly as possible his highest good. His highest good is that which is most deeply satisfactory to him in the long run. An equivalent statement of this principle of obligation is that he always ought to do what he needs the most. His duty to attain this objective as nearly as possible is a *categorical imperative*. It is unconditionally binding upon him, from his own point of view. Such an imperative is binding, without exception, upon every individual that is capable of experiencing satisfaction or dissatisfaction. This principle of duty is universal and absolute. It is a definition. I think that we ought to adopt this definition because it is the one which will help us the most in understanding man's moral experience.

This theory indicates that there is a plurality of ultimate moral standards, one for each conscious organism, each standard being determined by the individual nature of its organism. What is a duty for one, from his point of view, may be contrary to the duty of another, from the other's point of view; and there is no standard by which either of these duties may be validly proclaimed absolutely right apart from all points of view, or right from every point of view, or right from one absolute point of view. How, then, shall we discover, and how shall we validate, social obligations? I shall maintain that social ethics exists, that it is valid, and that its validity is derived from individual moral imperatives which are ultimate.

An individual has a duty to help others if, when, and because he needs to help them. Helping them is an individual moral imperative of his whenever it will satisfy him most deeply in the long run. In his helpfulness he will be, in part, selfish in the ordinary sense. He will help others as a means to getting help from them in return. This is ethical. No moral taint attaches when he pays his debts and respects his neighbors' rights in order to secure services and consideration for himself. Should he omit to give what society demands of him he will be

3. See D. H. Parker, *Human Values*, New York (1931), pp. 21, 46 ff.

made to suffer. Society can inflict terrible punishments upon almost anybody. Also it can bestow valuable rewards upon those who coöperate. It is constantly rewarding those who have not broken the law, by letting them circulate about freely and say pretty much what they think. It gives thrilling honors and distinctions to those who are thought to have made outstanding contributions. Each individual ought to try to coöperate and to make a creative contribution, partly because he needs to avoid social penalties and to enjoy great social distinctions. He needs these rewards because he will be dissatisfied if he does not get them, and because he will be deeply satisfied if he does get them.

Man's duty to help others is, then, based partly on ordinary selfishness. It is also based partly on ordinary unselfishness, benevolence, or love. Love aims ultimately at the welfare of others. When love is combined with the sensuous desires of sex it is called romantic love. But it may exist independently of sex, as in mother-love or in the brotherly love which has always been the leading principle of Christian ethical teaching. *A*'s love for *B* is a desire, located in *A*'s soul, whose objective is *B*'s welfare, considered not as a means to any further end, but as a final goal. *A*'s desire, so to speak, terminates upon its object *B*. *A*'s love is satisfied when *A* can help *B* to be happy and when *A* knows that *B* is happy. Successful love always satisfies the lover. A mother enjoys caring for her children and knowing that they are well-off. She does not aim at this enjoyment. She aims at the children's enjoyment. But the joy or satisfaction which she feels is the intrinsic value of her love to her. From her point of view she ought to lavish her loving care upon her children because *she* enjoys having them happy. The "cause" involved in this "because" is not Aristotle's final cause; it is his formal cause. Her own joy is not her goal. But by definition it characterizes what she ought to do.

The primary value or satisfaction which she experiences is purely selfish in the sense that it is part of herself. Her love too is purely selfish in the sense that it is part of herself, and that its expression is her self-expression. But this is not the ordinary meaning of selfishness. This is a Pickwickian selfishness which consists in being and in expressing one's own individual self. Ordinary selfishness, on the other hand, consists in pursuing one's own future welfare and self-expression as a final objective. This Pickwickian individualistic selfishness is absolutely inescapable as long as one lives. No man can desire or enjoy anything unless it is his individual self that desires and enjoys it. And clearly no moral taint is necessarily involved in this.

In caring for others by reason of selfish prudence one is selfish both in the ordinary and in the Pickwickian senses. In caring for others by reason of one's love, one is selfish only in the Pickwickian sense.

Let us reformulate the ultimate principle of duty so as to include the compelling social obligations which are binding upon each person because of the needs of his own nature. Every individual has a duty, from his own point of view, to attain as nearly as possible (1) his own maximum satisfaction in the long run, (2) that of those whom he loves, to the extent that he loves them, (3) that of those who will help him, to the extent that they will help, and (4) that of those who will coöperate with his institutions, so far as they will coöperate. But clearly his duties, from his own point of view, to attain the second, third, and fourth items, are all due to the fact that these things will be satisfactory to him. They are all obligatory, from his point of view, because of the first item. All duty to others is ultimately analyzable into an individual duty to maximize individual satisfaction.

We must in no way belittle the importance of society in this individualistic theory. When an individual confronts society he should realize that all of the people who make it up generate just as completely autonomous authorities as he does, and he ought to know that the social value of his behavior depends upon their intrinsic satisfactions. Social value, however, *is* always secondary value. The social value of his love for his children is its causal relations to all of the satisfactions which it produces, directly or indirectly, in other people. If his loving care helps to make his children happy, it has a certain social value to them. If it helps to make them useful citizens, it has added social values to many other people who are helped by his children, and whose happiness thus results, indirectly, from his love for his children.

Society is also very important because of the imperious demands which it makes upon every individual member, and because of the tremendous power which it exercises over individual satisfactions, to back up these demands. Society requires that each individual make certain contributions, and that he conform to laws, mores, and folkways. We have already referred to the fact that it often makes individuals happy who contribute and conform, and it often makes individuals miserable who do not. But axiological individualism is not impugned by these facts. Society's demands are only the demands of individuals seeking what will satisfy them. A social demand is, more accurately, just a lot of individual demands. Each of the citizens requires that an individual contribute and conform, largely so that each of the citizens' lives may be safe, prosperous, and happy. And an individual ought in most cases to contribute and conform largely because that will tend to make his own life safe, prosperous, and happy.

Although society is very powerful, still its might does not essentially or necessarily make right. Society's power to punish an individual and to make him miserable does not necessarily make his misery good for him. A man's misery is good for him only if it causes him to be more deeply satisfied later on. Sometimes it does this. It may strengthen his character and discipline his spirit and thus help him eventually to triumph over the obstacles which once blocked his path. This is the redemptive power of suffering. But the fact that the force of society imposes the suffering does not guarantee this blessed eventuality. Force may, of course, make the right exist or cause it to prevail. A social order, which is right for those who benefit from it, is caused to exist by force. It would be destroyed by its enemies if force were not used for its protection. But force will sometimes make the wrong prevail. Not force, but long-range individual satisfaction is the only essential characteristic which necessarily and universally makes a thing right.

The tremendous power which society wields is exerted in the endeavor to bring each individual's right into conformity with society's demands. When it rewards a man for doing what it approves, it makes his doing this very satisfactory to him, and thus in most cases it tends to harmonize his highest good with the highest goods of its other members. When it punishes him for doing what is a wrong to it, it makes this wrong also wrong to him, for his act thus brings suffering to himself. But there are exceptions to this. Sometimes it fails to reward its friends and to punish its enemies. And even when it succeeds, by rewards and punishments, in making social coöperation right for any individual, still this is only Aristotle's efficient making or causing, not his formal or essential making or causing.

Moreover, when society thus succeeds, its success is directly attributable to the natures of the individuals involved. Society can not reward an individual unless he needs what it can give. It could not reward a man who found no joy in honor or status or wealth or security or love. It could not punish an individual who was indifferent to any attempted punishment it might seek to inflict. It could not torture him unless he was an organism capable of experiencing either mental anguish or sensory pain. It can execute him, but if that is just what he desires most, his death will, from his point of view, be a reward and not a punishment.

The worst of all social conflicts, war, can be properly evaluated only from individual points of view. A successful war might be a benefit to most of the people of a nation. It would be, so far as it saved them from slavery or gave them prosperity and freedom. For them it would be good. The same war would be evil to its victims, and possibly to nearly everyone in the defeated country, if, as sometimes happens, most of these folk were enslaved, impoverished, or killed. Then the freedom and prosperity which the victorious power achieved might help to launch it on a career of aggression which might end in disaster for itself three generations hence. Then its original victory will have been good for most of its citizens who were there at the time, but bad for most of their descendants in the third generation. What is good for the individuals of one generation may be bad for those of a later one in the same country, or anywhere else. However, so far as people are not satisfied with a system which protects them but threatens disaster to their descendants, that system is bad for them.

It should be clear that a federal world government ought to be set up. Probably most people now and in the future would live more satisfactory lives if this were done, with representative democracy and with safeguards to individual freedom. Then from these people's points of view, such a state ought to be created. This state would work hardships on some who have vested interests in nationalistic separatism and aggression. For them, the added satisfactions, if any, from world peace would not compensate for the frustrations. From their points of view a world state would be evil. Then it is our duty, from our points of view, to inflict this evil upon them, and to crush their opposition, by force, if we must, and if we can, because to do so would be more deeply satisfactory to us in the long run.

The clash of autonomous individual axiological standards comes out very clearly in crime. Consider a dangerous felon who has been properly sentenced to life imprisonment for murder. Here the highest good of most of the law-abiding citizens demands his incarceration. He must not be allowed to get away with murder. His punishment is required in order to help protect their lives and property. But it might be better for him, from his point of view, to escape. He might be better satisfied. On the other hand, in some cases he would not be better satisfied. Worry and a bad conscience might make such an individual more dissatisfied than if he had stayed in jail. But I think that there are cases where escape would be more satisfactory in the long run for such a felon. A life lived in the open might be happier. If so, to escape would be his duty,—from his own point of view. If maximum individual long-range satisfaction makes duty for decent people it does so for rascals also. It does so for all conscious organisms. The principle is universal.

There are three senses in which genuine universality appears in ethical theory.[4]

First off, as we have already seen, the ultimate principle of individualistic relativism is itself universal by definition.

In a second form, universality is present in ethics, in that, from the point of view of any conscious individual, all things in the universe without exception ought to help him because he needs their help. All of his needs for satisfactory living ought, from his point of view, to be met. From a citizen's point of view a felon ought not to escape, and everything in the universe ought to conspire to prevent him from escaping. But from the culprit's point of view everything and everybody ought to help him escape, if that would be more deeply satisfactory to him in the long run.

Of course a normal citizen will repudiate this latter obligation because it is not imposed upon him by his own point of view. He knows that, as St. Thomas said, he must be true to his *own* highest good, which is God. Also the criminal will repudiate the duty created by the citizen's need. In this ultimate conflict of categorical individual duties, involving, obviously, war in heaven, force determines what is done on earth. The power of organized society will have to be exerted in order to inflict the legal penalty upon the culprit. Force, we have seen, does not determine essentially what ought to be done. The battles of the gods, that is, the final conflicts of human ideals, are not settled by force. They are not settled. The ultimate brittle good of one individual contestant may be in grim, tight-lipped, and unyielding conflict with the ultimate brittle good of another individual contestant.

Men often grasp vaguely the truth that from their own points of view the whole universe ought to help

4. See my paper, this Journal, "Universality and Individuality in Ethics," Vol. XL (1943), pp. 348–356.

them and ought to further what they are interested in; and then they unwarrantably infer that *apart from any point of view*, that is, objectively, it ought to do so. They have not yet fully grasped that the highest good of one individual may be contrary to the highest good of another. Their thinking is still on the level of the sort of objective ethics which denies axiological individualism. To free oneself from the belief in this kind of objectivity is an indispensable step in ethical enlightenment.

Universality is present in ethics in a third form, in that the truth about every particular good and value is, like all truth, absolutely universal. This will be seen if we compare two propositions:

1. Criminal *A* says truly, "It is false that (*X*) this punishment of *A* is good for me."

2. Citizen *B* says truly, "It is true that (*Y*) this punishment of *A* is good for me."

It may seem as if sentences *X* and *Y* were one proposition and that this proposition is true for citizen *B* and false for criminal *A*. But nothing that is true for one can be false for another, or *vice versa*. Sentences *X* and *Y* express different propositions because "me" has a different meaning in each. It means criminal *A* in *X* and citizen *B* in *Y*. Assuming that criminal *A* would be better satisfied if he escaped, proposition *X* is universally false in the sense that whenever anyone asserts exactly that subjective meaning or proposition, namely, that "the punishment of criminal *A* is good for *A*," it is false no matter who says it, and no matter what words are used. And proposition *Y* is universally true in the sense that whenever anyone asserts exactly that meaning, that "the punishment of criminal *A* is good for citizen *B*," it is true no matter who says it, and no matter what words are used.

Thus in three senses value, good, and duty are universal; and at the same time, in another sense, without contradiction, they are all purely individual, relative, and thus obviously subjective.

However they are also genuinely objective in another sense, namely, that they are real independently of anyone's cognitive ideas about them. What actually satisfies individual need is good no matter whether anybody knows that it does so or not. The good is the satisfactory and some things really are satisfactory. This doctrine is not nihilism. It shows the invalidity, not of morals, but of prevalent alternative theories about morals. It does this because it reveals the actual ground and nature of all genuine moral obligation.

COMMENTS ■ QUESTIONS

1. All of the arguments in this paper are based upon Williams' theory of *primary value*, according to which happy, or satisfactory, experiences are the only things that are intrinsically good, or good in themselves (in contrast to things that are extrinsically good, or good for the sake of something else). Williams calls his position *affective* (pertaining to feelings) *axiological* (pertaining to values) *individualism* (because experiences, and hence intrinsic goods, belong to individuals). Does this appear to be a satisfactory foundation for one's ethical philosophy? (Questions about the foundations of morality are pursued further in chapter 8.)
2. "All good, then, is relative. Nothing can be good at all unless it is good for at least some one individual. The good, for him, is always what he needs and what satisfies him." In saying these things, has Williams paid enough attention to the possibility that a person may fail to develop the proper perception of his or her needs? Has Williams ignored the apparent fact that some (many?) people find satisfaction in doing things they clearly ought not do?
3. "An individual always has a duty, from his own point of view, to attain as nearly as possible his highest good. Many philosophers would disagree with this, believing instead that we have a duty to achieve the highest good, period, even if it is not our *own* highest good. What reply might Williams make to such an objection? Which of the two basic positions do you believe is most defensible?
4. Williams' own position is completely opposed to any ethical philosophy based upon the concept of self-sacrifice. Is Williams' rejection of self-sacrifice defensible? Are there any reasons to believe that Williams is wrong, and that self-sacrifice *is* one of the central moral concepts?
5. According to Williams, a dangerous murderer who has been sentenced to life imprisonment but who would be happier if he escaped from prison has a duty, from his own point of view, to attempt to escape. Do you agree? Or is this view intolerably paradoxical, as some philosophers would maintain?
6. Many writers have said that the ultimate condition of human beings is war. Williams seems to agree: "The battles of the gods, that is, the final conflicts of human ideals, are not settled by force. They are not settled. The ultimate brittle good of one individual contestant may be in grim, tight-lipped, and unyielding conflict with the ultimate brittle good of another individual contestant." Should the fact that we now live in an age of nuclear weapons make a difference in regard to whether one agrees with the view expressed in this quotation?

JAMES RACHELS

Egoism and Moral Scepticism

Our ordinary thinking about morality is full of assumptions that we almost never question. We assume, for example, that we have an obligation to consider the welfare of other people when we decide what actions to perform or what rules to obey; we think that we must refrain from acting in ways harmful to others, and that we must respect their rights and interests as well as our own. We also assume that people are in fact capable of being motivated by such considerations, that is, that people are not wholly selfish and that they do sometimes act in the interests of others.

Both of these assumptions have come under attack by moral sceptics, as long ago as by Glaucon in Book II of Plato's *Republic*. Glaucon recalls the legend of Gyges, a shepherd who was said to have found a magic ring in a fissure opened by an earthquake. The ring would make its wearer invisible and thus would enable him to go anywhere and do anything undetected. Gyges used the power of the ring to gain entry to the Royal Palace where he seduced the Queen, murdered the King, and subsequently seized the throne. Now Glaucon asks us to determine that there are two such rings, one given to a man of virtue and one given to a rogue. The rogue, of course, will use his ring unscrupulously and do anything necessary to increase his own wealth and power. He will recognize no moral constraints on his conduct, and, since the cloak of invisibility will protect him from discovery, he can do anything he pleases without fear of reprisal. So, there will be no end to the mischief he will do. But how will the so-called virtuous man behave? Glaucon suggests that he will behave no better than the rogue: "No one, it is commonly believed, would have such iron strength of mind as to stand fast in doing right or keep his hands off other men's goods, when he could go to the market-place and fearlessly help himself to anything he wanted, enter houses and sleep with any woman he chose, set prisoners free and kill men at his pleasure, and in a word go about among men with the powers of a god. He

James Rachels is university professor at the University of Alabama at Birmingham, where previously he was dean of the School of Humanities. He is the author of The Elements of Moral Philosophy, The End of Life: Euthanasia and Morality, *and other works in moral philosophy.*

Reprinted from *A New Introduction To Philosophy* (New York: Harper and Row, 1971), by permission of the editor, Steven M. Cahn.

would behave no better than the other; both would take the same course."[1] Moreover, why shouldn't he? Once he is freed from the fear of reprisal, why shouldn't a man simply do what he pleases, or what he thinks is best for himself? What reason is there for him to continue being "moral" when it is clearly not to his own advantage to do so?

These sceptical views suggested by Glaucon have come to be known as *psychological egoism* and *ethical egoism* respectively. Psychological egoism is the view that all men are selfish in everything that they do, that is, that the only motive from which anyone ever acts is self-interest. On this view, even when men are acting in ways apparently calculated to benefit others, they are actually motivated by the belief that acting in this way is to their own advantage, and if they did not believe this, they would not be doing that action. Ethical egoism is, by contrast, a normative view about how men *ought* to act. It is the view that, regardless of how men do in fact behave, they have no obligation to do anything except what is in their own interests. According to the ethical egoist, a person is always justified in doing whatever is in his own interests, regardless of the effect on others.

Clearly, if either of these views is correct, then "the moral institution of life" (to use Butler's well-turned phrase) is very different than what we normally think. The majority of mankind is grossly deceived about what is, or ought to be, the case, where morals are concerned.

1. *The Republic of Plato*, translated by F. M. Cornford (Oxford, 1941), p. 45.

2. Psychological egoism seems to fly in the face of the facts. We are tempted to say: "Of course people act unselfishly all the time. For example, Smith gives up a trip to the country, which he would have enjoyed very much, in order to stay behind and help a friend with his studies, which is a miserable way to pass the time. This is a perfectly clear case of unselfish behavior, and if the psychological egoist thinks that such cases do not occur, then he is just mistaken." Given such obvious instances of "unselfish behavior," what reply can the egoist make? There are two general arguments by which he might try to show that all actions, including those such as the one just outlined, are in fact motivated by self-interest. Let us examine these in turn:

A. The first argument goes as follows. If we describe one person's action as selfish, and another person's action as unselfish, we are overlooking the crucial fact that in both cases, assuming that the action is done voluntarily, *the agent is merely doing what he most wants to do*. If Smith stays behind to help his friend, that only shows that he wanted to help his friend more than he wanted to go to the country. And why should he be praised for his "unselfishness" when he is only doing what he most wants to do? So, since Smith is only doing what he wants to do, he cannot be said to be acting unselfishly.

This argument is so bad that it would not deserve to be taken seriously except for the fact that so many otherwise intelligent people have been taken in by it. First, the argument rests on the premise that people never voluntarily do anything except what they want to do. But this is patently false; there are at least two classes of actions that are exceptions to this generalization. One is the set of actions which we may not want to do, but which we do anyway as a means to an end which we want to achieve; for example, going to the dentist in order to stop a toothache, or going to work every day in order to be able to draw our pay at the end of the month. These cases may be regarded as consistent with the spirit of the egoist argument, however, since the ends mentioned are wanted by the agent. But the other set of actions are those which we do, not because we want to, nor even because there is an end which we want to achieve, but because we feel ourselves *under an obligation* to do them. For example, someone may do something because he has promised to do it, and thus feels obligated, even though he does not want to do it. It is sometimes suggested that in such cases we do the action because, after all, we want to keep our promises; so, even here, we are doing what we want. However, this dodge will not work: if I have promised to do something, and if I do not want to do it, then it is simply false to say that I want to keep my promise. In such cases we feel a conflict precisely because we do *not* want to do what we feel obligated to do. It is reasonable to think that Smith's action falls roughly into this second category: he might stay behind, not because he wants to, but because he feels that his friend needs help.

But suppose we were to concede, for the sake of the argument, that all voluntary action is motivated by the agent's wants, or at least that Smith is so motivated. Even if this were granted, it would not follow that Smith is acting selfishly or from self-interest. For if Smith wants to do something that will help his friend, even when it means forgoing his own enjoyments, that is precisely what makes him unselfish. What else could unselfishness be, if not wanting to help others? Another way to put the same point is to say that it is the *object* of a want that determines whether it is selfish or not. The mere fact that I am acting on *my* wants does not mean that I am acting selfishly; that depends on *what it is* that I want. If I want only my own good, and care nothing for others, then I am selfish; but if I also want other people to be well-off and happy, and if I act on *that* desire, then my action is not selfish. So much for this argument.

B. The second argument for psychological egoism is this. Since so-called unselfish actions always produce a sense of self-satisfaction in the agent,[2] and since this sense of satisfaction is a pleasant state of consciousness, it follows that the point of the action is really to achieve a pleasant state of consciousness, rather than to bring about any good for others. Therefore, the action is "unselfish" only at a superficial level of analysis. Smith will feel much better with himself for having stayed to help his friend—if he had gone to the country, he would have felt terrible about it—and that is the real point of the action. According to a well-known story, this argument was

2. Or, as it is sometimes said, "It gives him a clear conscience," or "He couldn't sleep at night if he had done otherwise," or "He would have been ashamed of himself for not doing it," and so on.

once expressed by Abraham Lincoln:

> Mr. Lincoln once remarked to a fellow-passenger on an old-time mud-coach that all men were prompted by selfishness in doing good. His fellow-passenger was antagonizing this position when they were passing over a corduroy bridge that spanned a slough. As they crossed this bridge they espied an old razor-backed sow on the bank making a terrible noise because her pigs had got into the slough and were in danger of drowning. As the old coach began to climb the hill, Mr. Lincoln called out, "Driver, can't you stop just a moment?" Then Mr. Lincoln jumped out, ran back, and lifted the little pigs out of the mud and water and placed them on the bank. When he returned, his companion remarked: "Now, Abe, where does selfishness come in on this little episode?" "Why, bless your soul, Ed, that was the very essence of selfishness. I should have had no peace of mind all day had I gone on and left that suffering old sow worrying over those pigs. I did it to get peace of mind, don't you see?" [3]

This argument suffers from defects similar to the previous one. Why should we think that merely because someone derives satisfaction from helping others this makes him selfish? Isn't the unselfish man precisely the one who *does* derive satisfaction from helping others, while the selfish man does not? If Lincoln "got peace of mind" from rescuing the piglets, does this show him to be selfish, or, on the contrary, doesn't it show him to be compassionate and good-hearted? (If a man were truly selfish, why should it bother his conscience that *others* suffer—much less pigs?) Similarly, it is nothing more than shabby sophistry to say, because Smith takes satisfaction in helping his friend, that he is behaving selfishly. If we say this rapidly, while thinking about something else, perhaps it will sound all right; but if we speak slowly, and pay attention to what we are saying, it sounds plain silly.

Moreover, suppose we ask *why* Smith derives satisfaction from helping his friend. The answer will be, it is because Smith cares for him and wants him to succeed. If Smith did not have these concerns, then he would take no pleasure in assisting him; and these concerns, as we have already seen, are the marks of unselfishness, not selfishness. To put the point more generally: if we have a positive attitude toward the attainment of some goal, then we may derive satisfaction from attaining that goal. But the *object* of our attitude is *the attainment of that goal;* and we must want to attain the goal *before* we can find any satisfaction in it. We do not, in other words, desire some sort of "pleasurable consciousness" and then try to figure out how to achieve it; rather, we desire all sorts of different things—money, a new fishing-boat, to be a better chess-player, to get a promotion in our work, etc.—and because we desire these things, we derive satisfaction from attaining them. And so, if someone desires the welfare and happiness of another person, he will derive satisfaction from that; but this does not mean that this satisfaction is the object of his desire, or that he is in any way selfish on account of it.

It is a measure of the weakness of psychological egoism that these in-

3. Frank C. Sharp, *Ethics* (New York, 1928), pp. 74–75. Quoted from the Springfield (Ill.) *Monitor* in the *Outlook*, vol. 56, p. 1059.

supportable arguments are the ones most often advanced in its favor. Why, then, should anyone ever have thought it a true view? Perhaps because of a desire for theoretical simplicity: In thinking about human conduct, it would be nice if there were some simple formula that would unite the diverse phenomena of human behavior under a single explanatory principle, just as simple formulae in physics bring together a great many apparently different phenomena. And since it is obvious that self-regard is an overwhelmingly important factor in motivation, it is only natural to wonder whether all motivation might not be explained in these terms. But the answer is clearly No; while a great many human actions are motivated entirely or in part by self-interest, only by a deliberate distortion of the facts can we say that all conduct is so motivated. This will be clear, I think, if we correct three confusions which are commonplace. The exposure of these confusions will remove the last traces of plausibility from the psychological egoist thesis.

The first is the confusion of selfishness with self-interest. The two are clearly not the same. If I see a physician when I am feeling poorly, I am acting in my own interest but no one would think of calling me "selfish" on account of it. Similarly, brushing my teeth, working hard at my job, and obeying the law are all in my self-interest but none of these are examples of selfish conduct. This is because selfish behavior is behavior that ignores the interests of others, in circumstances in which their interests ought not to be ignored. This concept has a definite evaluative flavor; to call someone "selfish" is not just to describe his action but to condemn it. Thus, you would not call me selfish for eating a normal meal in normal circumstances (although it may surely be in my self-interest); but you would call me selfish for hoarding food while others about are starving.

The second confusion is the assumption that every action is done *either* from self-interest or from other-regarding motives. Thus, the egoist concludes that if there is no such thing as genuine altruism then all actions must be done from self-interest. But this is certainly a false dichotomy. The man who continues to smoke cigarettes, even after learning about the connection between smoking and cancer, is surely not acting from self-interest, not even by his own standards—self-interest would dictate that he quit smoking at once—and he is not acting altruistically either. He *is*, no doubt, smoking for the pleasure of it, but all that this shows is that undisciplined pleasure-seeking and acting from self-interest are very different. This is what led Butler to remark that "The thing to be lamented is, not that men have so great regard to their own good or interest in the present world, for they have not enough." [4]

The last two paragraphs show (*a*) that it is false that all actions are selfish, and (*b*) that it is false that all actions are done out of self-interest. And it should be noted that these two points can be made, and were,

4. *The Works of Joseph Butler*, edited by W. E. Gladstone (Oxford, 1896), vol. II, p. 26. It should be noted that most of the points I am making against psychological egoism were first made by Butler. Butler made all the important points; all that is left for us is to remember them.

without any appeal to putative examples of altruism.

The third confusion is the common but false assumption that a concern for one's own welfare is incompatible with any genuine concern for the welfare of others. Thus, since it is obvious that everyone (or very nearly everyone) does desire his own well-being, it might be thought that no one can really be concerned with others. But again, this is false. There is no inconsistency in desiring that everyone, including oneself *and* others, be well-off and happy. To be sure, it may happen on occasion that our own interests conflict with the interests of others, and in these cases we will have to make hard choices. But even in these cases we might sometimes opt for the interests of others, especially when the others involved are our family or friends. But more importantly, not all cases are like this: sometimes we are able to promote the welfare of others when our own interests are not involved at all. In these cases not even the strongest self-regard need prevent us from acting considerately toward others.

Once these confusions are cleared away, it seems to me obvious enough that there is no reason whatever to accept psychological egoism. On the contrary, if we simply observe people's behavior with an open mind, we may find that a great deal of it is motivated by self-regard, but by no means all of it; and that there is no reason to deny that "the moral institution of life" can include a place for the virtue of beneficence.[5]

3. The ethical egoist would say at this point, "Of course it is possible for people to act altruistically, and perhaps many people do act that way—but there is no reason why they *should* do so. A person is under no obligation to do anything except what is in his own interests." [6] This is really quite a radical doctrine. Suppose I have an urge to set fire to some public building (say, a department store) just for the fascination of watching the spectacular blaze: according to this view, the fact that several people might be burned to death provides no reason whatever why I should not do it. After all, this only concerns *their* welfare, not my own, and according to the ethical egoist the only person I need think of is myself.

Some might deny that ethical egoism has any such monstrous consequences. They would point out that it is really to my own advantage not to set the fire—for, if I do that I may be caught and put into prison (unlike Gyges, I have no magic ring for protection). Moreover, even if I could avoid being caught it is still to my advantage to respect the rights and interests of others, for it is to my advantage to live in a society in which people's rights and interests are respected. Only in such a society can I live a happy and secure life; so, in acting kindly toward others, I

---

5. The capacity for altruistic behavior is not unique to human beings. Some interesting experiments with rhesus monkeys have shown that these animals will refrain from operating a device for securing food if this causes other animals to suffer pain. See Masserman, Wechkin, and Terris, " 'Altruistic' Behavior in Rhesus Monkeys," *The American Journal of Psychiatry*, vol. 121 (1964), 584–585.

6. I take this to be the view of Ayn Rand, in so far as I understand her confusing doctrine.

would merely be doing my part to create and maintain the sort of society which it is to my advantage to have.[7] Therefore, it is said, the egoist would not be such a bad man; he would be as kindly and considerate as anyone else, because he would see that it is to his own advantage to be kindly and considerate.

This is a seductive line of thought, but it seems to me mistaken. Certainly it is to everyone's advantage (including the egoist's) to preserve a stable society where people's interests are generally protected. But there is no reason for the egoist to think that merely because *he* will not honor the rules of the social game, decent society will collapse. For the vast majority of people are not egoists, and there is no reason to think that they will be converted by his example—especially if he is discreet and does not unduly flaunt his style of life. What this line of reasoning shows is not that the egoist himself must act benevolently, but that he must encourage *others* to do so. He must take care to conceal from public view his own self-centered method of decision-making, and urge others to act on precepts very different from those on which he is willing to act.

The rational egoist, then, cannot advocate that egoism be universally adopted by everyone. For he wants a world in which his own interests are maximized; and if other people adopted the egoistic policy of pursuing their own interests to the exclusion of his interests, as he pursues his interests to the exclusion of theirs, then such a world would be impossible. So he himself will be an egoist, but he will want others to be altruists.

This brings us to what is perhaps the most popular "refutation" of ethical egoism current among philosophical writers—the argument that ethical egoism is at bottom inconsistent because it cannot be universalized.[8] The argument goes like this:

To say that any action or policy of action is *right* (or that it *ought* to be adopted) entails that it is right for *anyone* in the same sort of circumstances. I cannot, for example, say that it is right for me to lie to you, and yet object when you lie to me (provided, of course, that the circumstances are the same). I cannot hold that it is all right for me to drink your beer and then complain when you drink mine. This is just the requirement that we be consistent in our evaluations; it is a requirement of logic. Now it is said that ethical egoism cannot meet this requirement because, as we have already seen, the egoist would not want others to act in the same way that he acts. Moreover, suppose he *did* advocate the universal adoption of egoistic policies: he would be saying to Peter, "You ought to pursue your own interests even if it means destroying Paul"; and he would be saying to Paul, "You ought to pursue your own interests even if it means destroying Peter." The attitudes expressed in these two recommendations seem clearly inconsistent—he is urging the ad-

7. Cf. Thomas Hobbes, *Leviathan* (London, 1651), chap. 17.

8. See, for example, Brian Medlin, "Ultimate Principles and Ethical Egoism," *Australasian Journal of Philosophy*, vol. 35 (1957), 111–118; and D. H. Monro, *Empiricism and Ethics* (Cambridge, 1967), chap. 16.

vancement of Peter's interest at one moment, and countenancing their defeat at the next. Therefore, the argument goes, there is no way to maintain the doctrine of ethical egoism as a consistent view about how we ought to act. We will fall into inconsistency whenever we try.

What are we to make of this argument? Are we to conclude that ethical egoism has been refuted? Such a conclusion, I think, would be unwarranted; for I think that we can show, contrary to this argument, how ethical egoism can be maintained consistently. We need only to interpret the egoist's position in a sympathetic way: we should say that he has in mind a certain kind of world which he would prefer over all others; it would be a world in which his own interests were maximized, regardless of the effects on other people. The egoist's primary policy of action, then, would be to act in such a way as to bring about, as nearly as possible, this sort of world. Regardless of however morally reprehensible we might find it, there is nothing *inconsistent* in someone's adopting this as his ideal and acting in a way calculated to bring it about. And if someone did adopt this as his ideal, then he would not advocate universal egoism; as we have already seen, he would want other people to be altruists. So, if he advocates any principles of conduct for the general public, they will be altruistic principles. This would not be inconsistent; on the contrary, it would be perfectly consistent with his goal of creating a world in which his own interests are maximized. To be sure, he would have to be deceitful; in order to secure the good will of others, and a favorable hearing for his exhortations to altruism, he would have to pretend that he was himself prepared to accept altruistic principles. But again, that would be all right; from the egoist's point of view, this would merely be a matter of adopting the necessary means to the achievement of his goal—and while we might not approve of this, there is nothing inconsistent about it. Again, it might be said: "He advocates one thing, but does another. Surely *that's* inconsistent." But it is not; for what he advocates and what he does are both calculated as means to an end (the *same* end, we might note); and as such, he is doing what is rationally required in each case. Therefore, contrary to the previous argument, there is nothing inconsistent in the ethical egoist's view. He cannot be refuted by the claim that he contradicts himself.

Is there, then, no way to refute the ethical egoist? If by "refute" we mean show that he has made some *logical* error, the answer is that there is not. However, there is something more that can be said. The egoist challenge to our ordinary moral convictions amounts to a demand for an explanation of why we should adopt certain policies of action, namely policies in which the good of others is given importance. We can give an answer to this demand, albeit an indirect one. The reason one ought not to do actions that would hurt other people is: other people would be hurt. The reason one ought to do actions that would benefit other people is: other people would be benefited. This may at first seem like a piece of philosophical sleight-of-hand, but it is not. The point is that the welfare of human beings is something that most of us value *for its own sake*, and not merely for the sake of something else. Therefore, when *further* reasons are demanded for valuing the welfare of human beings, we cannot point to anything further to satisfy this demand. It is not that we have no reason for pursuing these policies, but that our reason *is* that these policies are for the good of human beings.

So: if we are asked "Why shouldn't I set fire to this department store?" one answer would be "Because if you do, people may be burned to death." This is a complete, sufficient reason which does not require qualification or supplementation of any sort. If someone seriously wants to know why this action shouldn't be done, that's the reason. If we are pressed further and asked the sceptical question "But why shouldn't I do actions that will harm others?" we may not know what to say—but this is because the questioner has included in his question the very answer we would like to give: "Why shouldn't you do actions that will harm others? Because, doing those actions would harm others."

The egoist, no doubt, will not be happy with this. He will protest that *we* may accept this as a reason, but *he* does not. And here the argument stops: there are limits to what can be accomplished by argument, and if the egoist really doesn't care about other people—if he honestly doesn't care whether they are helped or hurt by his actions—then we have reached those limits. If we want to persuade him to act decently toward his fellow humans, we will have to make our appeal to such other attitudes as he does possess, by threats, bribes, or other cajolery. That is all that we can do.

Though some may find this situation distressing (we would like to be able to show that the egoist is just *wrong*), it holds no embarrassment for common morality. What we have come up against is simply a fundamental requirement of rational action, namely, that the existence of reasons for action always depends on the prior existence of certain attitudes in the agent. For example, the fact that a certain course of action would make the agent a lot of money is a reason for doing it only if the agent wants to make money; the fact that practicing at chess makes one a better player is a reason for practicing only if one wants to be a better player; and so on. Similarly, the fact that a certain action would help the agent is a reason for doing the action only if the agent cares about his own welfare, and the fact that an action would help others is a reason for doing it only if the agent cares about others. In this respect ethical egoism and what we might call ethical altruism are in exactly the same fix: both require that the agent *care* about himself, or about other people, before they can get started.

So a nonegoist will accept "It would harm another person" as a reason not to do an action simply because he cares about what happens to that other person. When the egoist says that he does *not* accept that as a reason, he is saying something quite extraordinary. He is saying that he has no affection for friends or family, that he never feels pity or compassion, that he is the sort of person who can look on scenes of human misery with complete indifference, so long as he is not the one suffering. Genuine egoists, people who really don't care at all about anyone other than themselves, are rare. It is important to keep this in mind when thinking about ethical egoism; it is easy to forget just how fundamental to human psychological makeup the feeling of sympathy is. Indeed, a man without any sympathy at all would scarcely be recognizable as a man; and that is what makes ethical egoism such a disturbing doctrine in the first place.

4. There are, of course, many different ways in which the sceptic might challenge the assumptions underlying our moral practice. In this essay I have discussed only two of them, the two put forward by Glaucon in the passage that I cited from Plato's *Republic*. It is important that the assumptions underlying our moral practice should not be confused with particular judgments made within that practice. To defend one is not to defend the other. We may assume—quite properly, if my analysis has been correct—that the virtue of beneficence does, and indeed should, occupy an important place in "the moral institution of life"; and yet we may make constant and miserable errors when it comes to judging when and in what ways this virtue is to be exercised. Even worse, we may often be able to make accurate moral judgments, and know what we ought to do, but not do it. For these ills, philosophy alone is not the cure.

COMMENTS ■ QUESTIONS

1. In discussing and rejecting psychological egoism, Rachels tells a story about Abraham Lincoln helping some baby pigs out of a muddy stream. The point of the story is to suggest that Lincoln believed in psychological egoism. Do you find this to be a surprising fact (if it is a fact) about Lincoln? Would his own life not appear to have exemplified unselfishness? Can the story be explained in any way other than that suggested by Rachels?

2. Rachels describes the ethical egoist as follows: "He has in mind a certain kind of world which he would prefer over all others; it would be a world in which his own interests were maximized, regardless of the effects on other people." Would Gardner Williams agree with this? Recall that according to Williams a person has a duty to help those he loves to the extent that he loves them.

3. According to Rachels, arguments that do not appeal to the ethical egoist's self-interest cannot reasonably be expected to have any persuasive force against the egoist. "There are limits to what can be accomplished by argument, and if the egoist really doesn't care about other people. . . then we have reached those limits." Is Rachels correct about this? Why could the following sort of argument not be expected to carry some weight against certain ego-

ists: "You [the egoist] ought to become the sort of person who cares more about others and who sometimes puts their well-being ahead of your own, since if you did become this sort of person, you would then be glad you had made the change. You would be happy about your own moral development." Does Rachels perhaps exaggerate the difficulties to be found when an altruist confronts an egoist?

4. Is Rachels correct when he says that genuine ethical egoists—people who care only for themselves—are rare? What would Gardner Williams' view be?

SAINT MATTHEW

The Sermon on the Mount

And seeing the multitudes,
he went up into a moun-
tain: and when he was set,
his disciples came unto him:
2 And he opened his mouth,
and taught them, saying,
3 Blessed *are* the poor in spirit:
for theirs is the kingdom of heaven.
4 Blessed *are* they that mourn:
for they shall be comforted.
5 Blessed *are* the meek: for they
shall inherit the earth.
6 Blessed *are* they which do
hunger and thirst after righteousness: for they shall be filled.
7 Blessed *are* the merciful: for
they shall obtain mercy.
8 Blessed *are* the pure in heart:
for they shall see God.
9 Blessed *are* the peacemakers:
for they shall be called the children
of God.
10 Blessed *are* they which are
persecuted for righteousness' sake:
for theirs is the kingdom of heaven.
11 Blessed are ye, when *men*
shall revile you, and persecute *you*,
and shall say all manner of evil
against you falsely, for my sake.
12 Rejoice, and be exceeding
glad: for great *is* your reward in
heaven: for so persecuted they the
prophets which were before you.
13 Ye are the salt of the earth:
but if the salt have lost his savour,
wherewith shall it be salted? it is
thenceforth good for nothing, but to
be cast out, and to be trodden under
foot of men.
14 Ye are the light of the

From *Matthew* 5–7 in the New Testament of the King James Version of the *Holy Bible*, first published in 1611.

world. A city that is set on an hill
cannot be hid.
15 Neither do men light a can-
dle, and put it under a bushel, but
on a candlestick; and it giveth light
unto all that are in the house.
16 Let your light so shine
before men, that they may see your
good works, and glorify your Father
which is in heaven.
17 Think not that I am come to
destroy the law, or the prophets: I
am not come to destroy, but to
fulfil.
18 For verily I say unto you,
Till heaven and earth pass, one jot
or one tittle shall in no wise pass
from the law, till all be fulfilled.
19 Whosoever therefore shall
break one of these least command-
ments, and shall teach men so, he
shall be called the least in the kingdom of heaven: but whosoever shall
do and teach *them*, the same shall be
called great in the kingdom of
heaven.
20 For I say unto you, That except your righteousness shall exceed
the righteousness of the scribes and
Pharisees, ye shall in no case enter
into the kingdom of heaven.
21 Ye have heard that it was
said by them of old time, Thou shalt
not kill; and whosoever shall kill
shall be in danger of the judgment:
22 But I say unto you, That
whosoever is angry with his brother
without a cause shall be in danger of
the judgment: and whosoever shall
say to his brother, Raca, shall be in
danger of the council: but whosoever shall say, Thou fool, shall be in
danger of hell fire.
23 Therefore if thou bring thy
gift to the altar, and there
rememberest that thy brother hath
ought against thee;
24 Leave there thy gift before
the altar, and go thy way; first be
reconciled to thy brother, and then
come and offer thy gift.
25 Agree with thine adversary
quickly, whiles thou art in the way
with him; lest at any time the adversary deliver thee to the judge, and
the judge deliver thee to the officer,
and thou be cast into prison.
26 Verily I say unto thee, Thou
shalt by no means come out thence,
till thou hast paid the uttermost
farthing.
27 Ye have heard that it was
said by them of old time, Thou shalt
not commit adultery:
28 But I say unto you, That
whosoever looketh on a woman to
lust after her hath committed adultery with her already in his heart.
29 And if thy right eye offend
thee, pluck it out, and cast *it* from
thee: for it is profitable for thee that
one of thy members should perish,
and not *that* thy whole body should
be cast into hell.
30 And if thy right hand offend
thee, cut it off, and cast *it* from thee:
for it is profitable for thee that one
of thy members should perish, and
not *that* thy whole body should be
cast into hell.
31 It hath been said, Whosoever
shall put away his wife, let him give
her a writing of divorcement:
32 But I say unto you, That
whosoever shall put away his wife,
saving for the cause of fornication,
causeth her to commit adultery: and
whosoever shall marry her that is divorced committeth adultery.
33 Again, ye have heard that it
hath been said by them of old time,
Thou shalt not forswear thyself, but
shalt perform unto the Lord thine
oaths:

34 But I say unto you, Swear not at all; neither by heaven; for it is God's throne:

35 Nor by the earth; for it is his footstool: neither by Jerusalem; for it is the city of the great King.

36 Neither shalt thou swear by thy head, because thou canst not make one hair white or black.

37 But let your communication be, Yea, yea; Nay, nay: for whatsoever is more than these cometh of evil.

38 Ye have heard that it hath been said, An eye for an eye, and a tooth for a tooth:

39 But I say unto you, That ye resist not evil: but whosoever shall smite thee on thy right cheek, turn to him the other also.

40 And if any man will sue thee at the law, and take away thy coat, let him have *thy* cloak also.

41 And whosoever shall compel thee to go a mile, go with him twain.

42 Give to him that asketh thee, and from him that would borrow of thee turn not thou away.

43 Ye have heard that it hath been said, Thou shalt love thy neighbour, and hate thine enemy.

44 But I say unto you, Love your enemies, bless them that curse you, do good to them that hate you, and pray for them which despitefully use you, and persecute you;

45 That ye may be the children of your Father which is in heaven: for he maketh his sun to rise on the evil and on the good, and sendeth rain on the just and on the unjust.

46 For if ye love them which love you, what reward have ye? do not even the publicans the same?

47 And if ye salute your brethren only, what do ye more *than others?* do not even the publicans so?

48 Be ye therefore perfect, even as your Father which is in heaven is perfect.

Chapter 6

Take heed that ye do not your alms before men, to be seen of them: otherwise ye have no reward of your Father which is in heaven.

2 Therefore when thou doest *thine* alms, do not sound a trumpet before thee, as the hypocrites do in the synagogues and in the streets, that they may have glory of men. Verily I say unto you, They have their reward.

3 But when thou doest alms, let not thy left hand know what thy right hand doeth:

4 That thine alms may be in secret: and thy Father which seeth in secret himself shall reward thee openly.

5 And when thou prayest, thou shalt not be as the hypocrites *are:* for they love to pray standing in the synagogues and in the corners of the streets, that they may be seen of men. Verily I say unto you, They have their reward.

6 But thou, when thou prayest, enter into thy closet, and when thou hast shut thy door, pray to thy Father which is in secret; and thy Father which seeth in secret shall reward thee openly.

7 But when ye pray, use not vain repetitions, as the heathen *do:* for they think that they shall be heard for their much speaking.

8 Be not ye therefore like unto them: for your Father knoweth what things ye have need of, before ye ask him.

9 After this manner therefore

pray ye: Our Father which art in
heaven, Hallowed be thy name.
10 Thy kingdom come. Thy will
be done in earth, as *it is* in heaven.
11 Give us this day our daily
bread.
12 And forgive us our debts, as
we forgive our debtors.
13 And lead us not into temptation, but deliver us from evil: For
thine is the kingdom, and the power, and the glory, for ever. Amen.
14 For if ye forgive men their
trespasses, your heavenly Father will
also forgive you:
15 But if ye forgive not men
their trespasses, neither will your Father forgive your trespasses.
16 Moreover when ye fast, be
not, as the hypocrites, of a sad coun-
tenance: for they disfigure their
faces, that they may appear unto
men to fast. Verily I say unto you,
They have their reward.
17 But thou, when thou fastest,
anoint thine head, and wash thy
face;
18 That thou appear not unto
men to fast, but unto thy Father
which is in secret: and thy Father,
which seeth in secret, shall reward
thee openly.
19 Lay not up for yourselves
treasures upon earth, where moth
and rust doth corrupt, and where
thieves break through and steal:
20 But lay up for yourselves
treasures in heaven, where neither
moth nor rust doth corrupt, and
where thieves do not break through
nor steal:
21 For where your treasure is,
there will your heart be also.
22 The light of the body is the
eye: if therefore thine eye be single,
thy whole body shall be full of light.
23 But if thine eye be evil, thy
whole body shall be full of darkness.
If therefore the light that is in thee
be darkness, how great *is* that
darkness!
24 No man can serve two masters: for either he will hate the one,
and love the other; or else he will
hold to the one, and despise the other. Ye cannot serve God and
mammon.
25 Therefore I say unto you,
Take no thought for your life, what
ye shall eat, or what ye shall drink;
nor yet for your body, what ye shall
put on. Is not the life more than
meat, and the body than raiment?
26 Behold the fowls of the air:
for they sow not, neither do they
reap, nor gather into barns; yet your
heavenly Father feedeth them. Are
ye not much better than they?
27 Which of you by taking
thought can add one cubit unto his
stature?
28 And why take ye thought for
raiment? Consider the lilies of the
field, how they grow; they toil not,
neither do they spin:
29 And yet I say unto you, That
even Solomon in all his glory was
not arrayed like one of these.
30 Wherefore, if God so clothe
the grass of the field, which to day
is, and to morrow is cast into the ov-
en, *shall he* not much more *clothe*
you, O ye of little faith?
31 Therefore take no thought,
saying, What shall we eat? or, What
shall we drink? or, Wherewithal
shall we be clothed?
32 (For after all these things do
the Gentiles seek:) for your heavenly Father knoweth that ye have need
of all these things.
33 But seek ye first the kingdom of God, and his righteousness;
and all these things shall be added

unto you.
34 Take therefore no thought
for the morrow: for the morrow
shall take thought for the things of
itself. Sufficient unto the day *is* the
evil thereof.

Chapter 7

Judge not, that ye be not judged.
2 For with what judgment ye
judge, ye shall be judged: and with
what measure ye mete, it shall be
measured to you again.
3 And why beholdest thou the
mote that is in thy brother's eye, but
considerest not the beam that is in
thine own eye?
4 Or how wilt thou say to thy
brother, Let me pull out the mote
out of thine eye; and, behold, a
beam *is* in thine own eye?
5 Thou hypocrite, first cast out
the beam out of thine own eye; and
then shalt thou see clearly to cast
out the mote out of thy brother's
eye.
6 Give not that which is holy
unto the dogs, neither cast ye your
pearls before swine, lest they tram-
ple them under their feet, and turn
again and rend you.
7 Ask, and it shall be given you;
seek, and ye shall find; knock, and it
shall be opened unto you:
8 For every one that asketh
receiveth; and he that seeketh
findeth; and to him that knocketh it
shall be opened.
9 Or what man is there of you,
whom if his son ask bread, will he
give him a stone?
10 Or if he ask a fish, will he
give him a serpent?
11 If ye then, being evil, know
how to give good gifts unto your
children, how much more shall your
Father which is in heaven give good
things to them that ask him?
12 Therefore all things whatsoever ye would that men should do
to you, do ye even so to them: for
this is the law and the prophets.
13 Enter ye in at the strait gate:
for wide *is* the gate, and broad *is* the
way, that leadeth to destruction, and
many there be which go in thereat:
14 Because strait *is* the gate,
and narrow *is* the way, which
leadeth unto life, and few there be
that find it.
15 Beware of false prophets,
which come to you in sheep's cloth-
ing, but inwardly they are ravening
wolves.
16 Ye shall know them by their
fruits. Do men gather grapes of
thorns, or figs of thistles?
17 Even so every good tree
bringeth forth good fruit; but a corrupt tree bringeth forth evil fruit.
18 A good tree cannot bring
forth evil fruit, neither *can* a corrupt
tree bring forth good fruit.
19 Every tree that bringeth not
forth good fruit is hewn down, and
cast into the fire.
20 Wherefore by their fruits ye
shall know them.
21 Not every one that saith unto me, Lord, Lord, shall enter into
the kingdom of heaven; but he that
doeth the will of my Father which is
in heaven.
22 Many will say to me in that
day, Lord, Lord, have we not
prophesied in thy name? and in thy
name have cast out devils? and in
thy name done many wonderful
works?
23 And then will I profess unto
them, I never knew you: depart
from me, ye that work iniquity.
24 Therefore whosoever

heareth these sayings of mine, and
doeth them, I will liken him unto a
wise man, which built his house upon a rock:
25 And the rain descended, and
the floods came, and the winds
blew, and beat upon that house; and
it fell not: for it was founded upon a
rock.
26 And every one that heareth
these sayings of mine, and doeth
them not, shall be likened unto a
foolish man, which built his house
upon the sand:
27 And the rain descended, and
the floods came, and the winds
blew, and beat upon that house; and
it fell: and great was the fall of it.
28 And it came to pass, when
Jesus had ended these sayings, the
people were astonished at his
doctrine:
29 For he taught them as *one*
having authority, and not as the
scribes.

COMMENTS ■ QUESTIONS

1. Few moral statements in the history of Western civilization have been discussed more than the Sermon on the Mount. But few people follow it exactly, especially its advice regarding wrongdoers: "Do not set yourself against the man who wrongs you. If someone slaps you on the right cheek, turn and offer him your left. If a man wants to sue you for your shirt, let him have your coat as well." In your opinion, why do people not follow this advice? Because it simply is not good advice? Because it *is* good advice, but people are too weak, or too far from moral perfection, to follow it? Because it really was never intended to be followed exactly, but rather was presented in an exaggerated way in order to combat the moral outlook of the time? Is there another explanation?
2. In rejecting the moral principle of "an eye for an eye, a tooth for a tooth," Jesus is rejecting what is called the retributive theory of punishment (punishment should equal the crime just because the crime was committed and equal punishment is deserved). An altruist cares for others. Should altruists care as much for wrongdoers as for anyone else? If so, should altruists reject the retributive theory of punishment?
3. "Pass no judgment, and you will not be judged." Is this good advice? Is it consistent with a strong love for the good and hatred for the bad? Is it good advice for everyone or only for those who are excessively or hypocritically judgmental of others?

JOSIAH ROYCE

The Moral Insight

* * * * *

What follows is an account of the process that, in some form, must come to every one under the proper conditions. In this process we see the beginning of the real knowledge of duty to others. The process is one that any child can and does, under proper guidance, occasionally accomplish. It is the process by which we all are accustomed to try to teach humane behavior in concrete cases. We try to get people to realize what they are doing when they injure others. But to distinguish this process from the mere tender emotion of sympathy, with all its illusions, is what moralists have not carefully enough done. Our exposition has tried to take this universally recognized process, to distinguish it from sympathy as such, and to set it up before the gates of ethical doctrine as the great producer of insight.

But when we say that to this insight common sense must come, under the given conditions, we do not mean to say: "So the man, once having attained insight, must act thenceforth." The realization of one's neighbor, in the full sense of the word realization, is indeed the resolution to treat him as if he were real, that is, to treat him unselfishly. But this resolution expresses and belongs to the moment of insight. Passion may cloud the insight in the very next moment. It always does cloud the insight after no very long time. It is as impossible for us to avoid the illusion of selfishness in our daily lives, as to escape seeing through the illusion at the moment of insight. We see the reality of our neighbor, that is, we determine to treat him as we do ourselves. But then we go back to daily action, and we feel the heat of hereditary passions, and we straightway forget what we have seen. Our neighbor becomes obscured. He is once more a foreign power. He is unreal. We are again deluded and selfish. This conflict goes on and will go on as long as we live after the manner of men. Moments of insight, with their accompanying resolutions; long stretches of delusion and selfishness: That is our life.

To bring home this view in yet another way to the reader, we ask him to consider very carefully just what experience he has when he tries to realize his neighbor in the full sense that we have insisted upon. Not pity as such is what we desire him to feel. For whether or no pity happens to work in him as self-

---

A biographical sketch of Josiah Royce appears earlier in this chapter.

From *The Religious Aspect of Philosophy*, first published in 1885.

ishly and blindly as we have found that it often does work, still not the emotion, but its consequences, must in the most favorable case give us what we seek. All the forms of sympathy are mere impulses. It is the insight to which they bring us that has moral value. And again, the realization of our neighbor's existence is not at all the discovery that he is more or less useful to us personally. All that would contribute to selfishness. In an entirely different way we must realize his existence, if we are to be really altruistic. What then is our neighbor?

We find that out by treating him in thought just as we do ourselves. What art thou? Thou art now just a present state, with its experiences, thoughts, and desires. But what is thy future Self? Simply future states, future experiences, future thoughts and desires, that, although not now existing for thee, are postulated by thee as certain to come, and as in some real relation to thy present Self. What then is thy neighbor? He too is a mass of states, of experiences, thoughts, and desires, just as real as thou art, no more but yet no less present to thy experience now than is thy future Self. He is not that face that frowns or smiles at thee, although often thou thinkest of him as only that. He is not the arm that strikes or defends thee, not the voice that speaks to thee, not that machine that gives thee what thou desirest when thou movest it with the offer of money. To be sure, thou dost often think of him as if he were that automaton yonder, that answers thee when thou speakest to it. But no, thy neighbor is as actual, as concrete, as thou art. Just as thy future is real, though not now thine, so thy neighbor is real, though his thoughts never are thy thoughts. Dost thou believe this? Art thou sure what it means? This is for thee the turning-point of thy whole conduct towards him. What we now ask of thee is no sentiment, no gush of pity, no tremulous weakness of sympathy, but a calm, clear insight.

But one says: "All this have I done from my youth up. Surely I hold and always have held my neighbor to be real and no automaton. Surely I have feared his reproof, have been angry at his ill-will, have rejoiced in his sympathy, have been influenced by his opinions, all my life. And yet I have remained selfish." Nay, but just at the moment when thou hadst to act towards him so or so, thou wert no longer quick to realize him. Then it was that thy passion made him for thee a shadow. Thou couldst not love him, because thou didst forget who he was. Thou didst believe in him enough to fear him, to hate him, to fight with him, to revenge thyself upon him, to use his wit as thy took, but not enough to treat him as real, even as thou thyself art real. He seems to thee a little less living than thou. His life is dim, it is cold, it is a pale fire beside thy own burning desires. He is a symbol of passion to thee, and imperfectly, coldly, with dull assent, without full meaning to thy words, thou dost indeed say, when asked, that the symbol stands for something real, as real as thyself. But what those words mean,—hast thou realized it, as, through selfish feeling, thou dost realize thy equally external future Self?

If he is real like thee, then is his life as bright a light, as warm a fire, to him, as thine to thee; his will is as full of struggling desires, of hard problems, of fateful decisions; his pains are as hateful, his joys as dear. Take whatever thou knowest of desire and of striving, of burning love and of fierce hatred, realize as fully as thou canst what that means, and then with clear certainty add: *Such as that is for me, so is it for him, nothing less.* If thou dost that, can he remain to thee what he has been, a picture, a plaything, a comedy, or a tragedy, in brief a mere Show? Behind all that show thou hast indeed dimly felt that there is something. Know that truth thoroughly. Thou hast regarded his thought, his feeling, as somehow different in sort from thine. Thou hast said: "A pain in him is not like a pain in me, but something far easier to bear." Thou hast made of him a ghost, as the imprudent man makes of his future self a ghost. Even when thou hast feared his scorn, his hate, his contempt, thou hast not fully made him for thee as real as thyself. His laughter at thee has made thy face feel hot, his frowns and clenched fists have cowed thee, his sneers have made thy throat feel choked. But that was only the social instinct in thee. It was not a full sense of his reality. Even so the little baby smiles back at one that smiles at it, but not because it realizes the approving joy of the other, only because it by instinct enjoys a smiling face; and even so the baby is frightened at harsh speech, but not because it realizes the other's anger. So, dimly and by instinct, thou has lived with thy neighbor, and hast known him not, being blind. Thou hast even desired his pain, but thou hast not fully realized the pain that thou gavest. It has been to thee, not pain in itself, but the sight of his submission, of his tears, or of his pale terror. Of thy neighbor thou hast made a thing, no Self at all.

When thou hast loved, hast pitied, or hast reverenced thy neighbor, then thy feeling has possibly raised for a moment the veil of illusion. Then thou hast known what he truly is, a Self like thy present Self. But thy selfish feeling is too strong for thee. Thou hast forgotten soon again what thou hadst seen, and hast made even of thy beloved one only the instrument of thy own pleasure. Even out of thy power to pity thou hast made an object of thy vainglory. Thy reverence has turned again to pride. Thou hast accepted the illusion once more. No wonder that in this darkness thou findest selfishness the only rule of any meaning for thy conduct. Thou forgottest that without realization of thy future and as yet unreal self, even selfishness means nothing. Thou forgottest that if thou gavest thy present thought even so to the task of realizing thy neighbor's life, selfishness would seem no more plain to thee than the love of thy neighbor.

Have done then with this illusion that thy Self is all in all. Intuition tells thee no more about thy future Self than it tells thee about thy neighbors. Desire, bred in thee by generations of struggle for existence, emphasizes the expectation of thy own bodily future, the love for thy own bodily welfare, and makes thy body's life seem alone real. But simply try to know the truth. The truth is that all this world of life about thee is as real as thou art. All conscious life is conscious in its own measure. Pain is pain, joy is joy, everywhere even as in thee. The result of thy insight will be inevitable. The illusion vanishing, the glorious prospect opens before thy vision. Seeing the oneness of this life everywhere, the equal reality of all its moments, thou wilt be ready to treat it all with the reverence that prudence would have thee show to thy own little bit of future life. What prudence in its narrow respectability counseled, thou wilt be ready to do universally. As the prudent man, seeing the reality of his future self, inevitably works for it; so the enlightened man, seeing the reality of all conscious life, realizing that it is no shadow, but fact, at once and inevitably desires, if only for that one moment of insight, to enter into the service of the whole of it.

COMMENTS ■ QUESTIONS

1. According to Royce, "moral insight" is a necessary condition for altruism. It consists of "realizing the existence" of our neighbor by "treating him in thought just as we do ourselves." It means recognizing that "his pains are as hateful, his joys as dear" as our own. Do you agree with Royce that the moral insight he describes lies at the heart of altruistic ethics?
2. What would Gardner Williams say about Royce's moral insight? Would Williams necessarily disagree with all of the major points that Royce makes? What points could Williams agree with?
3. Compare Royce's moral insight with the Golden Rule. Does the Golden rule (or, to the extent that they may be different, does Royce's moral insight) take sufficient account of the significant differences among people? (Perhaps others do not want you to do unto them exactly what you want them to do unto you!) Does the Golden Rule provide an ideal way to overcome differences among people?
4. A certain sort of egoist would ask of Royce: Why should I realize my neighbor's existence? Why, to use Royce's phrase, should I not treat him as a ghost? To altruists who accept what Royce has to say about altruism, this question will be seen as equivalent to the troubling question, why be moral? What response might Royce give? What response would Rachels give? What response do you believe should be given?

BERNARD MAYO

Doing and Being

* * * * *

Attention to the novelists can be a welcome correction to a tendency of philosophical ethics of the last generation or two to lose contact with the ordinary life of man which is just what the novelists, in their own way, are concerned with. Of course there are writers who can be called in to illustrate problems about Duty (Graham Greene is a good example). But there are more who perhaps never mention the words duty, obligation or principle. Yet they are all concerned—Jane Austen, for instance, entirely and absolutely—with the moral qualities or defects of their heroes and heroines and other characters. This points to a radical one-sidedness in the philosophers' account of morality in terms of principles: it takes little or no account of qualities, of what people *are*. It is just here that the old-fashioned word Virtue used to have a place; and it is just here that the work of Plato and Aristotle can be instructive. Justice, for Plato, though it is closely connected with acting according to law, does not *mean* acting according to law: it is a quality of character, and a just action is one such as a just man would do. Telling the truth, for Aristotle, is not, as it was for Kant, fulfilling an obligation; again it is a quality of character, or, rather, a whole range of qualities of character, some of which may actually be defects, such as tactlessness, boastfulness, and so on—a point which can be brought out, in terms of principles, only with the greatest complexity and artificiality, but quite simply and naturally in terms of character.

If we wish to enquire about Aristotle's moral views, it is no use looking for a set of principles. Of course we can find *some* principles to which he must have subscribed—for instance, that one ought not to commit adultery. But what we find much more prominently is a set of character-traits, a list of certain types of person—the courageous man, the niggardly man, the boaster, the lavish spender and so on. The basic moral question, for Aristotle, is not, What shall I do? but, What shall I be?

Bernard Mayo is Professor Emeritus of Moral Philosophy at St. Andrews University. He has published three books and some 50 journal articles, and in addition is the former editor of both Analysis *and* Philosophical Quarterly. *His most recent book is* The Philosophy of Right and Wrong.

From *Ethics and the Moral Life*, 1958, by Bernard Mayo by permission of Macmillan, London and Basingstoke.

These contrasts between doing and being, negative and positive, and modern as against Greek morality were noted by John Stuart Mill; I quote from the *Essay on Liberty*:

> Christian morality (so-called) has all the characters of a reaction; it is, in great part, a protest against Paganism. Its ideal is negative rather than positive; passive rather than active; Innocence rather than Nobleness; Abstinence from Evil, rather than energetic Pursuit of the Good; in its precepts (as has been well said) "Thou shalt not" predominates unduly over "Thou shalt". . . . Whatever exists of magnanimity, highmindedness, personal dignity, even the sense of honour, is derived from the purely human, not the religious part of our education, and never could have grown out of a standard of ethics in which the only worth, professedly recognised, is that of obedience.

Of course, there are connections between being and doing. It is obvious that a man cannot just *be*; he can only be what he is by doing what he does; his moral qualities are ascribed to him because of his actions, which are said to manifest those qualities. But the point is that an ethics of Being must include this obvious fact, that Being involves Doing; whereas an ethics of Doing, such as I have been examining, may easily overlook it. As I have suggested, a morality of principles is concerned only with what people do or fail to do, since that is what rules are for. And as far as this sort of ethics goes, people might well have no moral qualities at all except the possession of principles and the will (and capacity) to act accordingly.

Principles and Ideals

When we speak of a moral quality such as courage, and say that a certain action was courageous, we are not merely saying something about the action. We are referring, not so much to what is done, as to the kind of person by whom we take it to have been done. We connect, by means of imputed motives and intentions, with the character of the agent as courageous. This explains, incidentally, why both Kantians and Utilitarians encounter, in their different ways, such difficulties in dealing with motives, which their principles, on the face of it, have no room for. A Utilitarian, for example, can only praise a courageous action in some such way as this: the action is of a sort such as a person of courage is likely to perform, and courage is a quality of character the cultivation of which is likely to increase rather than diminish the sum total of human happiness. But Aristotelians have no need of such circumlocution. For them a courageous action just is one which proceeds from and manifests a certain type of character, and is praised because such a character-trait is good, or better than others, or is a virtue. An evaluative criterion is sufficient: there is no need to look for an imperative criterion as well, or rather instead, according to which it is not the character which is good, but the cultivation of the character which is right.

Dispositions of the special sort applicable to human beings are, as we saw [earlier] in an important sense "elastic"; that is, from the information that someone is timid we cannot rigorously deduce that he will be frightened on a given occasion, as we can rigorously deduce from the solubility of sugar that it will dissolve when immersed in water. Timid people sometimes act courageously, that is, as courageous people behave; in general, people can act "out of character". Acting out of character is interestingly different from breaking a principle. There are no degrees about rule-breaking: the rule is either kept or broken. In terms of rules, all we are entitled to consider is the relation between an action (the subject of judgment) and a rule (the criterion of judgment), and the verdict is either Right or Wrong. But in considering action by an agent, we have to take into account as well a whole range of other actions by the agent, on the basis of which we form a judgment of character. Actions are "in character" or "out of character" in varying degrees, and, further, we can never state precisely what a person's character is. Instead of the extreme simplicity of the moral judgment based on a moral principle and an instance of conduct which either does or does not conform to that principle, we have a double complexity. Corresponding to the moral principle (which represents the conduct of an ideally righteous man) we have, instead, the idea of a virtue (which represents the conduct and conduct-tendency of an ideally good man). But whereas a man's action can be compared directly with the principle and only two possible verdicts result (or three, if we include "indifferent"), it cannot be compared in this way with the standard of virtue. For we cannot say exactly either how far the action is "in character" for the man, nor how far the character of the man matches or fails to match the ideal. It is not surprising that moral principles, with their superior logical manageability, have proved more attractive than moral ideals as material for ethical theory.

No doubt the fundamental moral question is just "What ought I to do?" And according to the philosophy of moral principles, the answer (which must be an imperative "Do this") must be derived from a conjunction of premisses consisting (in the simplest case) firstly of a rule, or universal imperative, enjoining (or forbidding) all actions of a certain type in situations of a certain type, and, secondly, a statement to the effect that this is a situation of that type, falling under that rule. In practice the emphasis may be on supplying only one of these premisses, the other being assumed or taken for granted: one may answer the question "What ought I to do?" either by quoting a rule which I am to adopt, or by showing that my case is legislated for by a rule which I do adopt. To take a previous example of moral perplexity, if I am in doubt whether to tell the truth about his condition to a dying man, my doubt may be resolved by showing that the case comes under a rule about the avoidance of unnecessary suffering, which I am assumed to accept. But if the case is without precedent in my moral career, my problem may be soluble only by adopting a new principle about what I am to do now and in the future about cases of this kind.

This second possibility offers a connection with moral ideals. Suppose my perplexity is not merely an unprecedented situation which I could cope with by adopting a new rule. Suppose the new rule is thoroughly inconsistent with my existing moral code. This may happen, for instance, if the moral code is one to which I only pay lip-service; if (in the language [introduced earlier]) its authority is not yet internalised, or if it has ceased to be so; it is ready for rejection, but its final rejection awaits a moral crisis such as we are assuming to occur. What I now need is not a rule for deciding how to act in this situation and others of its kind. I need a whole set of rules, a complete morality, new principles to live by.

Now according to the philosophy of moral character, there is another way of answering the fundamental question "What ought I to do?" Instead of quoting a rule, we quote a quality of character, a virtue: we say "Be brave", or "Be patient" or "Be lenient". We may even say "Be a man": if I am in doubt, say, whether to take a risk, and someone says "Be a man", meaning a morally sound man, in this case a man of sufficient courage. (Compare the very different ideal invoked in "Be a gentleman". I shall not discuss whether this is a *moral* ideal.) Here, too, we have the extreme cases, where a man's moral perplexity extends not merely to a particular situation but to his whole way of living. And now the question "What ought I to do?" turns into the question "What ought I to be?"—as, indeed, it was treated in the first place. ("Be brave.") It is answered, not by quoting a rule or a set of rules, but by describing a quality of character or a type of person. And here the ethics of character gains a practical simplicity which offsets the greater logical simplicity of the ethics of principles. We do not have to give a list of characteristics or virtues, as we might list a set of principles. We can give a unity to our answer.

Of course we can in theory give a unity to our principles: this is implied by speaking of a *set* of principles. But if such a set is to be a system and not a mere aggregate, the unity we are looking for is a logical one, namely the possibility that some principles are deducible from others, and ultimately from one. But the attempt to construct a deductive moral system is notoriously difficult, and in any case ill-founded. Why should we expect that all rules of conduct should be ultimately reducible to a few?

Saints and Heroes

But when we are asked "What shall I be?" we can readily give a unity to our answer, though not a logical unity. It is the unity of character. A person's character is not merely a list of dispositions; it has the organic unity of something that is more than the sum of its parts. And we can say, in answer to our morally perplexed questioner, not only "Be this" and "Be that", but also "Be like So-and-So"—where So-and-So is either an ideal type of character, or else an actual person taken as representative of the ideal, an exemplar. Examples of the first are Plato's "just man" in the Republic; Aristotle's man of practical wisdom, in the Nicomachean Ethics; Augustine's citizen of the City of God; the good Communist; the American way of life (which is a collective expression for a type of character). Examples of the second kind, the exemplar, are Socrates, Christ, Buddha, St. Francis, the heroes of epic writers and of novelists. Indeed the idea of the Hero, as well as the idea of the Saint, are very much the expression of this attitude to morality. Heroes and saints are not merely people who did things. They are people whom we are expected, and expect ourselves, to imitate. And imitating them means not merely doing what they did; it means being like them. Their status is not in the least like that of legislators whose laws we admire; for the character of a legislator is irrelevant to our judgment about his legislation. The heroes and saints did not merely give us principles to live by (though some of them did that as well): they gave us examples to follow.

Kant, as we should expect, emphatically rejects this attitude as "fatal to morality" . . . . According to him, examples serve only to render *visible* an instance of the moral principle, and thereby to demonstrate its practical feasibility. But every exemplar, such as Christ himself, must be judged by the independent criterion of the moral law, before we are entitled to recognize him as worthy of imitation. I am not suggesting that the subordination of exemplars to principles is incorrect, but that it is one-sided and fails to do justice to a large area of moral experience.

Imitation can be more or less successful. And this suggests another defect of the ethics of principles. It has no room for ideals, except the ideal of a perfect set of principles (which, as a matter of fact, is intelligible only in terms of an ideal character or way of life), and the ideal of perfect conscientiousness (which is itself a character-trait). This results, of course, from the "black-or-white" nature of moral verdicts based on rules. There are no degrees of rule-keeping and rule-breaking. But there certainly are degrees by which we approach or recede from the attainment of a certain quality or virtue; if there were not, the word "ideal" would have no meaning. Heroes and saints are not people whom we try to be *just* like, since we know that is impossible. It is precisely because it is impossible for ordinary human beings to achieve the same qualities as the saints, and in the same degree, that we do set them apart from the rest of humanity. It is enough if we try to be a little like them.

COMMENTS ■ QUESTIONS

1. According to Mayo, the question "What ought I to do?" (which reflects an ethics of principles) should be replaced with the question "What ought I to be?" (which reflects a virtue-based ethics). What is the relevance of this shift for an evaluation of arguments for or against psychological egoism? What is the relevance to an evaluation of arguments for or against ethical egoism?
2. What answer do you suppose Josiah Royce would give to the question "What ought I to be?" What answer would Jesus have given? What answer would Williams give?
3. What sorts of arguments might one advance in defense of the cultivation of such "altruistic" virtues as companionship and gratitude? What arguments might one advance in defense of the "egoistic" virtues of pride and self-control?

RALPH W. CLARK

The Concept of Altruism

A dialogue such as the following is familiar to many teachers of philosophy:

Professor: Psychological egoism is false because there are many people who behave unselfishly.
Student: These people are not behaving unselfishly. They help others in order to get into heaven and to avoid hell, which means that they don't really care for other people, but only for themselves.
Professor: Let us then consider examples of atheists who help others. They provide us with unproblematic counterexamples to psychological egoism.

The purpose of this paper is to show that the student's objection is unfounded, and that therefore counterexamples to psychological egoism can be found among religious people. More broadly, I want to show that a person can be unselfish,

Reprinted from *Faith and Philosophy*, volume II, number 2 (April, 1985) pages 158–167, by permission of the editors of *Faith and Philosophy*.

or altruistic, in offering help to others even if he believes that it is in his own best interest to offer the help in question. He may believe this on religious grounds, which is the case with the person who is afraid that he will not go to heaven when he dies unless he helps others, or he may base his belief upon nonreligious grounds, which is the case with someone who believes simply that a life devoted to helping others is the best sort of life he can live.

The concept of altruism is usually understood by philosophers to be tied essentially to the concept of self-sacrifice. Nicholas Rescher's definition is typical:

> A person is *altruistic* (rather than *egoistic*) if he gives such weight to the welfare of others that he is prepared in principle to subordinate his own welfare to that of others, setting his own welfare aside in the interest of theirs in certain circumstances.[1]

According to this definition, the kind of person I have described in the previous paragraph is not altruistic. In order for him to be prepared to subordinate his own welfare to that of others, he would need to believe that helping others (in any of the ways that he ever intends to help others) could in some cases hurt him. But the kind of person I am describing does not believe this.

If he is religious, he probably believes that the most important thing in his present life and his life to come is God's approval of his actions, which he can receive only through caring for and helping others. Mother Teresa, who was written about a lot in recent years for her work in India and elsewhere, seems to be an example of this kind of person. There are also nonreligious examples, although they are harder to find. They may be people who believe that friendship is very important in their lives, and that friendship requires sincerity in caring for others. This means that they must want to help others gladly and cheerfully, and not begrudgingly, since otherwise they could not claim to really care for their friends.

The sort of person I am describing may go so far as to believe that it would be *impossible* for her to sacrifice her own interests by helping other people, or she may believe simply that she *never will* sacrifice her own interests in looking out for the interests of others. Such a person may believe that her short term interests sometimes need to be sacrificed when she helps others; but she will not believe that her long term interests are sacrificed when she helps others.

We could say that the kind of person described above is not altruistic. But that seems to me to be the wrong thing to do since there is no reason to doubt that the sort of person I am describing is sincerely concerned for other people's welfare. Such a person can be counted on to do all of the things that would normally be expected of someone who "really cares for" someone else: expending large amounts of time, money, or emotional energy, and enduring pain and deprivation.

What I have described are people who do not meet Rescher's criterion for being altruistic, but who nevertheless should, it seems, be called altruistic. There is another sort of

1. Nicholas Rescher, *Unselfishness* (Pittsburgh, University of Pittsburgh Press, 1975), p. 9.

person who *does* meet Rescher's criterion, but who, it seems, should *not* be called altruistic. Such a person *is* prepared to subordinate his own welfare to that of others. The problem is that he is completely self-centered in his perception of his own interests and the interests of others. He is someone who believes that he has the complete and final answers to all questions about human welfare. As a consequence, he totally disregards the beliefs and aspirations of the people whom he intends to help, and runs roughshod over the protestations of those who want no part of the "help" which is being forced upon them. Fortunately, people such as this are rare, but some do exist.

A defender of Rescher's definition of the word "altruistic" could say that such people *are* altruists, only very misguided ones. However, I believe that it is best to say that they are not altruists since they do not appear to care for others *as autonomous agents* who are capable of giving some direction to their own lives. Such a person as I am describing appears to view only himself as autonomous; and thus, since to be human in the full sense is to be autonomous, it would appear that such a person is capable of caring only for himself as a human being in the full sense. That is a sufficient reason for calling him selfish. Probably what he really wants in life—though he may not admit this even to himself—is to control other people, rather than to promote their welfare.

II

If Rescher's definition of "altruistic" is rejected, then what should we put in its place? Should we say that an altruistic person is, essentially, someone who is made happy by the happiness of others and unhappy by their unhappiness? This definition would rule out the fanatic who disregards the beliefs and desires of other people in his zeal to impose upon them his own ideas about happiness. He is someone who is not moved at all by the actual happiness or unhappiness of the people he is trying to help. This definition also may seem to encompass the first class of counterexamples to Rescher's definition of "altruistic." Religious, "saintly" people and those who believe very strongly in the value of sincere friendship appear to be people who are made happy by the happiness of others and sad by their sadness.

The drawback is that this need not be so. There may not be many actual examples, but surely a person can be an altruist even if he himself has little or no capacity for happiness in his own life. And temporarily many people are incapable of happiness—as a consequence of any number of different kinds of personal problems and pressures upon them. But this does not prevent them from performing altruistic acts. Hence, we must look for another definition of "altruistic."

In order to formulate a new definition, which is what I propose to do, we need first to decide what the basic altruistic category is. It is not actions since a *person* can be altruistic even though his actions are blocked by illness or other circumstances. The basic category cannot be persons since someone who is not an altruistic person can do something which is altruistic. He would be someone who is acting out of character. The basic category cannot be reasons for acting since people don't always have reasons for performing altruistic acts (or, equally, for performing nonaltruistic acts). They can be done on impulse or simply because the person feels that he ought to do them—in which case his "reason" for acting would simply be his desire or inclination to act, and would not be that for the sake of which, or on account of which, he was acting.

It may be argued that the basic altruistic category is intentions. A person can have an altruistic intention even if he does not act upon it and even if he is not an altruistic person. The problem with this answer is that what makes a person's intention to act altruistic is the reason which he has for acting. An intention understood in terms of a description of the kind of act intended (for example if I were to say, "his intention is to buy his aunt a birthday present") would be neither altruistic nor nonaltruistic. We need to know *why*, in the example, the person intends to buy his aunt a birthday present. ("His intention is to make his aunt happy.") However, as has already been pointed out, people don't always have reasons for altruistic acts.

What is left, as I see it, is the general category of *motivations* for acting. I shall defend the position that the basic altruistic category is that of wants or desires. Without question, wants or desires are the most common motivations for acting. Whether or not they are the only basic motivations is controversial and is a question which I shall leave open. What I wish to argue for is the claim that every altruistic act must be motivated by a certain kind of desire which in itself is altruistic. The desire is altruistic even if no act results from it, and, when an act does result from it, it is the desire which makes the act altruistic. The possession of a sufficient quantity of such desires in sufficient strength is what makes a *person* altruistic.

Human desires can be divided into two basic classes, which I shall call first order desires and second order desires. A person has a second order desire when he desires that the desire of someone else be fulfilled. Every other desire that anyone may have is a first order desire. To illustrate: my desire to own a larger house is a first order desire; my desire that a friend's desire to own a larger house be fulfilled is a second order desire.

Altruistic desires are always second order desires. However, not all second order desires are altruistic since the objects of some of them are desired only as a means to fulfill a person's own first order desires. If I desire that my friend get the house which he wants solely because this will then make it possible for me to fulfill my desire to visit him often, then my desire is not altruistic. My desire is altruistic when I desire that the desires of others be satisfied and when my desire that this be so is not solely for the sake of my own first order desires, but at least in part is desired for itself.

It seems to me that most people have a great many such desires. If you doubt that this is so, then perhaps you do not see that the claim I am making is rather modest. First, I am not saying that most people are altruistic. (Later on in the paper I will discuss conditions requisite for a person to be altruistic.) Second, I am not saying that most people perform a great many altruistic acts. (I will discuss the issue of what makes an act altruistic later also.) A person can have an altruistic desire even if he never does anything which is altruistic. He may have nonaltruistic desires which are stronger and which always outweigh the altruistic desire. It seems to me that most people have a great many altruistic desires because it seems to me that I myself have a great many such desires, and I have no reason to believe that I am unique in this respect.

As an example, over the years I have received many solicitations from the March of Dimes. Sometimes but not always I have given them a small donation. But even on those occasions when I have not given a donation I have had altruistic desires regarding the crippled children who are helped by the March of Dimes. I have wanted them to have the kinds of lives which they themselves would like to have—lives which are free of the pain and deprivations caused by being crippled. Moreover, my desire for the improved well-being of these children is independent of all of my other desires, such as my desire to feel a sense of satisfaction when I make a donation. If I could receive the same feeling of satisfaction by doing something else which would cost me nothing, I would still want the crippled children to be better off. My desire for this is independent of my desire for any "reward" I might get from donating to the March of Dimes. If I could be convinced that people would think just as well of me even if I never gave to charity, I would still want the crippled children to be better off. If I could be convinced even that the most appealing description of heaven were true, and that I did not need to give to charity in order to go there for eternity, I would still want the crippled children to be helped. I am not saying that my desire that they be helped is very strong, but only that it is an altruistic desire. It seems to me that desires such as mine are commonplace.

Now, a person's motivation for acting is often a complex matter. Hence, we cannot say that an act is altruistic if it is motivated by an altruistic desire, but otherwise is not altruistic. Most often, the things people do are motivated by a combination of altruistic and nonaltruistic desires. Let us say that an act is altruistic if it is motivated by an altruistic desire or, when it is motivated by more than one desire, by a predominance of altruistic over nonaltruistic desires. If I loan my friend money in order to help him buy a house, then my act is altruistic if my desire that he get for himself the house he wants is stronger than my desire to be able to visit him often once he has bought the house.

It may be that I would loan the money even if I were to learn that I would not be able to visit my friend at all in his new house. Without question, my act would be altruistic. There is another sort of case that is not as clear. It may be that, although my altruistic desire in the matter outweighs my nonaltruistic desire, I would not loan my friend any money to buy a house unless I were to anticipate visiting him once he buys the house. We may be tempted to say that, assuming this to be the case, my lending the money is not altruistic since it is not something I am prepared to do as the consequence of an altruistic desire alone. I believe that we probably should resist the temptation to say this since it would reduce very dramatically the number of acts that we could properly call altruistic. Many helpful things that people do they would perhaps not do if they did not, in doing them, receive some satisfaction of first order desires.

To consider an example that parents are familiar with, it is much easier for an adult to help a child to do something which the child wants to do if the child shows just a little bit of gratitude—a smile, a thank you, an increased disposition to be cheerful and enjoyable company. This satisfaction of an adult's first order desire can often make the difference as to whether or not he provides the help in question. I think that we would want to say that the help which the adult gives in such a case is altruistic as long as the altruistic desire motivating it is stronger than any other desires motivating it.

Let us consider next what makes a *person* altruistic. There are many sorts of troublesome borderline cases which I want to sidestep in this paper for the sake of brevity. Generally, what I want to say is that a person is altruistic if his altruistic desires outweigh his nonaltruistic desires. He need not have only altruistic desires. The possession of altruistic desires exclusively cannot be defended even as part of a moral ideal since second order desires could not exist unless there were first order desires. Someone must have first order desires if someone else is to have second order desires. Indeed, there is something *prima facie* blameworthy in the behavior of a person who deliberately attempts to reduce his own first order desires to a minimum since he thereby makes it much more difficult for others to have second order desires in regard to him. If it is a good thing to have second order desires, then it is a good thing to do whatever can be done to make it easier for people to have second order desires, unless doing so has some greater consequence that is objectionable.

III

The way in which I have defined the word "altruistic" is, I believe, in accord with our intuitions regarding its usage. Moreover, it is not open to the objections which I have raised against the other two definitions of "altruistic." These are Rescher's definition, which is in terms of the subordination of one person's welfare to that of another person, and the definition of "altruistic" in terms of happiness. Regarding the latter, I am not claiming that a person must be made happy by the happiness of others in order to be altruistic. All that is required is that, to a sufficient degree, he desires for its own sake that other people get what they desire. Whether or not any actions which are motivated by his desire make him or anyone else happy is left an open question.

My definition of "altruistic" is not open to the two objections which I raised against Rescher's definition. Let us consider the second of them first. It has to do with the example of a person who intends to subordinate his own welfare to that of others, but who pays no attention to what other people actually want. Given my definition of "altruistic," a person who is altruistic must pay a great deal of attention to what other people want.

Let us now consider the first objection which I raised against Rescher's definition—having to do with a certain class of religious and nonreligious people who do not meet Rescher's criterion for being altruists. They are people who help others a great deal but who believe that they will never sacrifice their own welfare to the welfare of others in giving to them any of the kinds of help which they intend to give to them. In terms of my definition of "altruistic," a religious, "saintly" person, such as I am supposing Mother Teresa as an example to be, can be called altruistic. It is safe to assume that in devoting her life to helping others her altruistic desires have predominated over her nonaltruistic desires. It is of course possible for this not to be so; but from what has been written about Mother Teresa there is no reason for us to believe that it is not so.

In particular, the fact that a person is religious and believes that helping others is a necessary condition for getting into heaven is not a sufficient ground for saying that the person is not altruistic. Given my definition of the term "altruistic," there would be no point at all in arguing that a "saintly" religious person cannot be altruistic just because that person believes that he will provide for his own long-term welfare best through wanting to help other people.

IV

I will now discuss possible objections:

(1) A desire can be altruistic even when its object is *not* the satisfaction of someone else's desire; all that is needed is that the desire have as its object the welfare of someone else.

My response is that it would not be possible for me to desire what I believe will promote your welfare as an autonomous individual unless I desire the satisfaction of desires which you now have or which I believe you *are likely to have in the future*. For purposes of simplicity earlier in the paper I have been referring only to the desires of other people which they have at present. But all of the points made above can equally well be made in terms of expected future desires. Parents and teachers are sometimes good examples of altruists who want primarily to satisfy the expected future desires of children when they grow up, while clergymen sometimes are altruists who want primarily to satisfy expected desires of people in the next life.

In the preceding paragraph I am supposing that there is an essential tie at some point in the conscious existence of a person between the person's welfare and the satisfaction of the person's desires. My reason for supposing this is that it seems to me that a person could not truly be concerned about the welfare of another person (P) as an autonomous individual if (a) he believed that P would absolutely never—in this life or the next—desire X; and (b) he set out to do X and only X on behalf of P. But what should we say if it is the case that X really is good and if it is also the case that X stands in the way of all the things P wants or ever will want? Then, it seems to me that the conclusion to be drawn is not that it is possible for me to desire the welfare of P even when I entirely ignore P's own desires, but rather that P's welfare as an autonomous individual is simply not compatible with the good.

(Needless to say, that would be a very unfortunate state of affairs for P. It may be that it never occurs. In certain theological traditions it would be both necessary and sufficient to justify eternal damnation for P. According to Dante, for example, from a certain point of view those in hell really want to be there.)

(2) This objection is the other side of the coin from the first objection. It may be argued that altruism should not be defined in terms of second order desires just because the other person's desire could be evil, and that it is wrong to desire that an evil desire be fulfilled.

A possible response would be to say that altruism is not always good. However, it seems to me that, as I have defined it, altruism always *is good* since it seems to me that altruistic desires are always a good thing to have and that this is so even in cases where the other person's desire is evil. Of course, in such cases it would be wrong to act upon the desire that the other person's evil desire be fulfilled. Also, it goes without saying that it is bad for someone to have an evil desire; and therefore it would be wrong for me to desire that someone else have an evil desire. Furthermore, it would be a bad thing if I desired that the other person's evil desire be fulfilled for its own sake and also did not have a *stronger* desire that it not be fulfilled for its own sake since in such a case I would in effect share the other person's evil outlook on life. But it is possible both to have a desire that X obtain and to have a desire that X not obtain.

The reason that it is a good thing for me to desire that someone else's desire be fulfilled for its own sake—regardless of the content of the desire—is that my having such a desire is a way for me to be *sympathetic* toward the other person, and sympathy is a good thing. Suppose that the other person suffers from severe psychological and spiritual limitations (whether or not these are his own fault we may leave an open question), and consequently is capable of having only evil desires. Suppose further that there is no reason to believe that the person will ever change. Then the only way that I could have sympathy for that person *as the person that he is*, an autonomous human being, would be to have the desire that some of the person's evil desires be fulfilled for their own sake—that is, be fulfilled just because the person in question wants them to be fulfilled and would derive some happiness from their fulfillment. It seems to me that I can have such sympathy while at the same time be strongly repulsed by the kind of life the person wants for himself, and in addition do everything in my power to ensure that none of the person's desires will ever be fulfilled.

It seems to me that people do, at least in a modest way, quite often have the sort of second order desire which is discussed in the last two paragraphs. An example would be the parent who wishes that *somehow* it could be morally permissible for his wayward child to be allowed the satisfaction he gets from, say, teasing his playmates in a mildly malicious way. Of course, the parent does not really, on balance, want his child to enjoy himself in this way.

(3) It may be argued that, given my definition of "altruistic," a "saintly" person such as Mother Teresa *could be* altruistic, but still is likely not to be. In support of this objection, it may be argued that a person is never, or just about never, born "saintly." Rather, she is converted to her strong religious convictions at some point in her life, prior to which she may have lived an ordinary life or even a very immoral life. (I do not mean to suggest that this was the case with Mother Teresa, whose early biography I know little about.) Isn't it reasonable to suppose, then, that the person changed her attitudes and life style because she was afraid that otherwise she would suffer in hell, or at least be denied some of the blessings of heaven? Doesn't this tell us that her nonaltruistic desires outweigh her altruistic desires?

The above objection presupposes that the question of what caused a person to have second order desires is relevant to the question of whether or not those desires are altruistic. However, as I am using the term "altruistic," that is not the case at all. As long as a person genuinely desires for its own sake that the desire of someone else be fulfilled, that person's desire is altruistic; and the person is then altruistic if she has a predominance of such desires. She may have had selfish reasons for becoming altruistic; but if she really has become altruistic, why should that matter? She has, so to speak, left her selfish reasons behind.

At the risk of belaboring the point at issue, let me distinguish explicitly between the following two kinds of cases:

> (1) The kind of case where a person helps others only as (he believes) a means to get into heaven. He is a person who would not help others if there were some other way to get into heaven. He is, of course, not an altruist. (And, incidentally, in terms of traditional Christian views he will not succeed in getting into heaven.)
> (2) The kind of case where a person *has acquired* the desire to help others for its own sake from his fear that unless he were to want to help others he would not get into heaven. He is a person who, at some earlier time in his life, would not have helped others if there had been some other way for him to get into heaven; but now that he has acquired the second order desire to help others for its own sake, he *would* still want to help them even if he believed that he could get into heaven by some other means. He is an altruist if his altruistic desires are sufficiently strong.

An objection similar to the one I have been discussing might be raised against the purported nonreligious altruist who believes that a sincere desire to help others is requisite for his living the kind of life he believes is best. It could be argued that he desires to help others because he wants to be admired, or to ease his conscience, and so on. Again, two kinds of possible cases would need to be distinguished: In the first, the person is not an altruist at all because the objects of his second order desires are seen by him to be means only to satisfying first order desires. In the second, the person *is* an altruist since he does to a sufficient degree desire for its own sake that the desires of others be satisfied.

COMMENTS ■ QUESTIONS

1. Are the arguments given in this paper sufficient to show that Rescher's definition of "altruism" should be rejected?
2. The major purpose of this paper is to show that, in a certain sense, behaving altruistically can be in a person's own interest. Do you believe that this is so? What would Williams say about it? What would Rachels say? What would Josiah Royce say?
3. Is the distinction between first order desires and second order desires clear? If not, what is unclear about it?

SUSAN WOLF

Moral Saints

I don't know whether there are any moral saints. But if there are, I am glad that neither I nor those about whom I care most are among them. By *moral saint* I mean a person whose every action is as morally good as possible, a person, that is, who is as morally worthy as can be. Though I shall in a moment acknowledge the variety of types of person that might be thought to satisfy this description, it seems to me that none of these types serve as unequivocally compelling personal ideals. In other words, I believe that moral perfection, in the sense of moral saintliness, does not constitute a model of personal well-being toward which it would be particularly rational or good or desirable for a human being to strive.[1]

Outside the context of moral dis-

1. I have benefited from the comments of many people who have heard or read an earlier draft of this paper. I wish particularly to thank Douglas MacLean, Robert Nozick, Martha Nussbaum, and the Society for Ethics and Legal Philosophy.

Susan Wolf is an Associate Professor of Philosophy at the John Hopkins University. She is the author of numerous articles in ethics and the philosophy of mind.

From "Moral Saints" by Susan Wolf in *The Journal of Philosophy*, volume *LXXIX*, No. 8 (1982). By permission of *The Journal of Philosophy*.

cussion, this will strike many as an obvious point. But, within that context, the point, if it be granted, will be granted with some discomfort. For within that context it is generally assumed that one ought to be as morally good as possible and that what limits there are to morality's hold on us are set by features of human nature of which we ought not to be proud. If, as I believe, the ideals that are derivable from common sense and philosophically popular moral theories do not support these assumptions, then something has to change. Either we must change our moral theories in ways that will make them yield more palatable ideals, or, as I shall argue, we must change our conception of what is involved in affirming a moral theory.

In this paper, I wish to examine the notion of a moral saint, first, to understand what a moral saint would be like and why such a being would be unattractive, and, second, to raise some questions about the significance of this paradoxical figure for moral philosophy. I shall look first at the model(s) of moral sainthood that might be extrapolated from the morality or moralities of common sense. Then I shall consider what relations these have to conclusions that can be drawn from utilitarian and Kantian moral theories. Finally, I shall speculate on the implications of these considerations for moral philosophy.

Moral Saints and Common Sense

Consider first what, pretheoretically, would count for us—contemporary members of Western culture—as a moral saint. A necessary condition of moral sainthood would be that one's life be dominated by a commitment to improving the welfare of others or of society as a whole. As to what role this commitment must play in the individual's motivational system, two contrasting accounts suggest themselves to me which might equally be thought to qualify a person for moral sainthood.

First, a moral saint might be someone whose concern for others plays the role that is played in most of our lives by more selfish, or, at any rate, less morally worthy concerns. For the moral saint, the promotion of the welfare of others might play the role that is played for most of us by the enjoyment of material comforts, the opportunity to engage in the intellectual and physical activities of our choice, and the love, respect, and companionship of people whom we love, respect, and enjoy. The happiness of the moral saint, then, would truly lie in the happiness of others, and so he would devote himself to others gladly, and with a whole and open heart.

On the other hand, a moral saint might be someone for whom the basic ingredients of happiness are not unlike those of most of the rest of us. What makes him a moral saint is rather that he pays little or no attention to his own happiness in light of the overriding importance he gives to the wider concerns of morality. In other words, this person sacrifices his own interests to the interests of others, and feels the sacrifice as such.

Roughly, these two models may be distinguished according to whether one thinks of the moral saint as being a saint out of love or one thinks of the moral saint as being a saint out of duty (or some other intellectual appreciation and recognition of moral principles). We may refer to the first model as the model of the Loving Saint; to the second, as the model of the Rational Saint.

The two models differ considerably with respect to the qualities of the motives of the individuals who conform to them. But this difference would have limited effect on the saints' respective public personalities. The shared content of what these individuals are motivated to be—namely, as morally good as possible—would play the dominant role in the determination of their characters. Of course, just as a variety of large-scale projects, from tending the sick to political campaigning, may be equally and maximally morally worthy, so a variety of characters are compatible with the ideal of moral sainthood. One moral saint may be more or less jovial, more or less garrulous, more or less athletic than another. But, above all, a moral saint must have and cultivate those qualities which are apt to allow him to treat others as justly and kindly as possible. He will have the standard moral virtues to a nonstandard degree. He will be patient, considerate, even-tempered, hospitable, charitable in thought as well as in deed. He will be very reluctant to make negative judgments of other people. He will be careful not to favor some people over others on the basis of properties they could not help but have.

Perhaps what I have already said is enough to make some people begin to regard the absence of moral saints in their lives as a blessing. For there comes a point in the listing of virtues that a moral saint is likely to have where one might naturally begin to wonder whether the moral saint isn't, after all, too good—if not too good for his own good, at least too good for his own well-being. For the moral virtues, given that they are, by hypothesis, *all* present in the same individual, and to an extreme degree, are apt to crowd out the nonmoral virtues, as well as many of the interests and personal characteristics that we generally think contribute to a healthy, well-rounded, richly developed character.

In other words, if the moral saint is devoting all his time to feeding the hungry or healing the sick or raising money for Oxfam, then necessarily he is not reading Victorian novels, playing the oboe, or improving his backhand. Although no one of the interests or tastes in the category containing these latter activities could be claimed to be a necessary element in a life well lived, a life in which *none* of these possible aspects of character are developed may seem to be a life strangely barren.

The reasons why a moral saint cannot, in general, encourage the discovery and development of significant nonmoral interests and skills are not logical but practical reasons. There are, in addition, a class of nonmoral characteristics that a moral saint cannot encourage in himself for reasons that are not just practical. There is a more substantial tension between having any of these qualities unashamedly and being a moral saint. These qualities might be described as going against the moral grain. For example, a cynical or sarcastic wit, or a sense of humor that appreciates this kind of wit in others, requires that one take an attitude of resignation and pessimism toward the flaws and vices to be found in the world. A moral saint, on the other hand, has reason to take an attitude in opposition to this—he should try to look for the best in people, give them the benefit of the doubt as long as possible, try to improve regrettable situations as long as there is any hope of success. This suggests that, although a moral saint might well enjoy a good episode of *Father Knows Best*, he may not in good conscience be able to laugh at a Marx Brothers movie or enjoy a play by George Bernard Shaw.

An interest in something like gourmet cooking will be, for different reasons, difficult for a moral saint to rest easy with. For it seems to me that no plausible argument can justify the use of human resources involved in producing a *paté de canard en croute* against possible alternative beneficent ends to which these resources might be put. If there is a justification for the institution of haute cuisine, it is one which rests on the decision *not* to justify every activity against morally beneficial alternatives, and this is a decision a moral saint will never make. Presumably, an interest in high fashion or interior design will fare much the same, as will, very possibly, a cultivation of the finer arts as well.

A moral saint will have to be very, very nice. It is important that he not be offensive. The worry is that, as a result, he will have to be dull-witted or humorless or bland.

This worry is confirmed when we consider what sorts of characters, taken and refined both from life and from fiction, typically form our ideals. One would hope they would be figures who are morally good—and by this I mean more than just not morally bad—but one would hope, too, that they are not *just* morally good, but talented or accomplished or attractive in nonmoral ways as well. We may make ideals out of athletes, scholars, artists—more frivolously, out of cowboys, private eyes, and rock stars. We may strive for Katharine Hepburn's grace, Paul Newman's "cool"; we are attracted to the high-spirited passionate nature of Natasha Rostov; we admire the keen perceptiveness of Lambert Strether. Though there is certainly nothing immoral about the ideal characters or traits I have in mind, they cannot be superimposed upon the ideal of a moral saint. For although it is a part of many of these ideals that the characters set high, and not merely acceptable, moral standards for themselves, it is also essential to their power and attractiveness that the moral strengths go, so to speak, alongside of specific, independently admirable, nonmoral ground projects and dominant personal traits.

When one does finally turn one's eyes toward lives that are dominated by explicitly moral commitments, moreover, one finds oneself relieved at the discovery of idiosyncrasies or eccentricities not quite in line with the picture of moral perfection. One prefers the blunt, tactless, and opinionated Betsy Trotwood to the unfailingly kind and patient Agnes Copperfield; one prefers the mischievousness and the sense of irony in Chesterton's Father Brown to the innocence and undiscriminating love of St. Francis.

It seems that, as we look in our ideals for people who achieve nonmoral varieties of personal excellence in conjunction with or colored by some version of high moral tone, we look in our paragons of moral excellence for people whose moral achievements occur in conjunction with or colored by some interests or traits that have low moral tone. In other words, there seems to be a limit to how much morality we can stand.

One might suspect that the essence of the problem is simply that there is a limit to how much of *any* single value, or any single type of value, we can stand. Our objection then would not be specific to a life in which one's dominant concern is morality, but would apply to any life that can be so completely characterized by an extraordinarily dominant concern. The objection in that case would reduce to the recognition that such a life is incompatible with well-roundedness. If that were the objection, one could fairly reply that well-roundedness is no more supreme a virtue than the totality of moral virtues embodied by the ideal it is being used to criticize. But I think this misidentifies the objection. For the way in which a concern for morality may dominate a life, or, more to the point, the way in which it may dominate an ideal of life, is not easily imagined by analogy to the dominance an aspiration to become an Olympic swimmer or a concert pianist might have.

A person who is passionately committed to one of these latter concerns might decide that her attachment to it is strong enough to be worth the sacrifice of her ability to maintain and pursue a significant portion of what else life might offer which a proper devotion to her dominant passion would require. But a desire to be as morally good as possible is not likely to take the form of one desire among others which, because of its peculiar psychological strength, requires one to forego the pursuit of other weaker and separately less demanding desires. Rather, the desire to be as morally good as possible is apt to have the character not just of a stronger, but of a higher desire, which does not merely successfully compete with one's other desires but which rather subsumes or demotes them. The sacrifice of other interests for the interest in morality, then, will have the character, not of a choice, but of an imperative.

Moreover, there is something odd about the idea of morality itself, or moral goodness, serving as the object of a dominant passion in the way that a more concrete and specific vision of a goal (even a concrete *moral* goal) might be imagined to serve. Morality itself does not seem to be a suitable object of passion. Thus, when one reflects, for example, on the Loving Saint easily and gladly giving up his fishing trip or his stereo or his hot fudge sundae at the drop of the moral hat, one is apt to wonder not at how much he loves morality, but at how little he loves these other things. One thinks that, if he can give these up so easily, he does not know what it *is* to truly love them. There seems, in other words, to be a kind of joy which the Loving Saint, either by nature or by practice, is incapable of experiencing. The Rational Saint, on the other hand, might retain strong nonmoral and concrete desires—he simply denies himself the opportunity to act on them. But this is no less troubling. The Loving Saint one might suspect of missing a piece of perceptual machinery, of being blind to some of what the world has to offer. The Rational Saint, who sees it but foregoes it, one suspects of having a different problem—a pathological fear of damnation, perhaps, or an extreme form of self-hatred that interferes with his ability to enjoy the enjoyable in life.

In other words, the ideal of a life of moral sainthood disturbs not simply because it is an ideal of a life in which morality unduly dominates. The normal person's direct and specific desires for objects, activities, and events that conflict with the attainment of moral perfection are not simply sacrificed but removed, suppressed, or subsumed. The way in which morality, unlike other possible goals, is apt to dominate is particularly disturbing, for it seems to require either the lack or the denial of the existence of an identifiable, personal self.

This distinctively troubling feature is not, I think, absolutely unique to the ideal of the moral saint, as I have been using that phrase. It is shared by the conception of the pure aesthete, by a certain kind of religious ideal, and, somewhat paradoxically, by the model of the thorough-going, self-conscious egoist. It is not a coincidence that the ways of comprehending the world of which these ideals are the extreme embodiments are sometimes described as "moralities" themselves. At any rate, they compete with what we ordinarily mean by 'morality'. Nor is it a coincidence that these ideals are naturally described as fanatical. But it is easy to see that these other types of perfection cannot serve as satisfactory personal ideals; for the realization of these ideals would be straightforwardly immoral. It may come as a surprise to some that there may in addition be such a thing as a *moral* fanatic.

Some will object that I am being unfair to "common-sense morality"—that it does not really require a moral saint to be either a disgusting goody-goody or an obsessive ascetic. Admittedly, there is no logical inconsistency between having any of the personal characteristics I have mentioned and being a moral saint. It is not morally wrong to notice the faults and shortcomings of others or to recognize and appreciate nonmoral talents and skills. Nor is it immoral to be an avid Celtics fan or to have a passion for caviar or to be an excellent cellist. With enough imagination, we can always contrive a suitable history and set of circumstances that will embrace such characteristics in one or another specific fictional story of a perfect moral saint.

If one turned onto the path of moral sainthood relatively late in life, one may have already developed interests that can be turned to moral purposes. It may be that a good golf game is just what is needed to secure that big donation to Oxfam. Perhaps the cultivation of one's exceptional artistic talent will turn out to be the way one can make one's greatest contribution to society. Furthermore, one might stumble upon joys and skills in the very service of morality. If, because the children are short a ninth player for the team, one's generous offer to serve reveals a natural fielding arm or if one's part in the campaign against nuclear power requires accepting a lobbyist's invitation to lunch at Le Lion d'Or, there is no moral gain in denying the satisfaction one gets from these activities. The moral saint, then, may, by happy accident, find himself with nonmoral virtues on which he can capitalize morally or which make psychological demands to which he has no choice but to attend. The point is that, for a moral saint, the existence of these interests and skills can be given at best the status of happy accidents—they cannot be encouraged for their own sakes as distinct, independent aspects of the realization of human good.

It must be remembered that from the fact that there is a tension between having any of these qualities and being a moral saint it does not follow that having any of these qualities is immoral. For it is not part of common-sense morality that one ought to be a moral saint. Still, if someone just happened to want to be a moral saint, he or she would not have or encourage these qualities, and, on the basis of our common-sense values, this counts as a reason *not* to want to be a moral saint.

One might still wonder what kind of reason this is, and what kind of conclusion this properly allows us to draw. For the fact that the models of moral saints are unattractive does not necessarily mean that they are unsuitable ideals. Perhaps they are unattractive because they make us feel uncomfortable—they highlight our own weaknesses, vices, and flaws. If so, the fault lies not in the characters of the saints, but in those of our unsaintly selves.

To be sure, some of the reasons behind the disaffection we feel for the model of moral sainthood have to do with a reluctance to criticize ourselves and a reluctance to committing ourselves to trying to give up activities and interests that we heartily enjoy. These considerations might provide an *excuse* for the fact that we are not moral saints, but they do not provide a basis for criticizing sainthood as a possible ideal. Since these considerations rely on an appeal to the egoistic, hedonistic side of our natures, to use them as a basis for criticizing the ideal of the moral saint would be at best to beg the question and at worst to glorify features of ourselves that ought to be condemned.

The fact that the moral saint would be without qualities which we have and which, indeed, we like to have, does not in itself provide reason to condemn the ideal of the moral saint. The fact that some of these qualities are good qualities, however, and that they are qualities we *ought* to like, does provide reason to discourage this ideal and to offer other ideals in its place. In other words, some of the qualities the moral saint necessarily lacks are virtues, albeit nonmoral virtues, in the unsaintly characters who have them. The feats of Groucho Marx, Reggie Jackson, and the head chef at Lutèce are impressive accomplishments that it is not only permissible but positively appropriate to recognize as such. In general, the admiration of and striving toward achieving any of a great variety of forms of personal excellence are character traits it is valuable and desirable for people to have. In advocating the development of these varieties of excellence, we advocate nonmoral reasons for acting, and in thinking that it is good for a person to strive for an ideal that gives a substantial role to the interests and values that correspond to these virtues, we implicitly acknowledge the goodness of ideals incompatible with that of the moral saint. Finally, if we think that it is *as* good, or even better for a person to strive for one of these ideals than it is for him or her to strive for and realize the ideal of the moral saint, we express a conviction that it is good not to be a moral saint.

C O M M E N T S ■ Q U E S T I O N S

1. Wolf says, "I believe that moral perfection, in the sense of moral saintliness, does not constitute a model of personal well-being toward which it would be particularly rational or good or desirable for a human being to strive." What (aside from possible relief that it may be so!) is your response to this? Has Wolf given good reasons for rejecting the more commonsensical view that everyone ought to try to be as morally good as they possibly can be?
2. You may find some value in comparing what Wolf says about the "Loving Saint" with what is said about "second order desires" in the preceding reading selection. Note that being an altruist, as defined in terms of the concept of second order desires, does not at all entail being a moral saint, as this is understood by Wolf. Would you want to say (in agreement first with Wolf) that it is not desirable to be a moral saint and also (in agreement with the preceding reading selection) that being altruistic *is* desirable?

READINGS

Brandt, Richard C. *Ethical Theory.* Englewood Cliffs, N.J.: Prentice-Hall, 1959. Chapter 14 is a very helpful discussion of ethical egoism.

Duncan-Jones, Austin. *Butler's Moral Philosophy.* Baltimore: Penguin Books, 1952. Chapter 4 presents Butler's classical arguments against psychologist egoism.

Gauthier, D. P., ed. *Morality and Rational Self-Interest.* Englewood Cliffs, N.J.: Prentice-Hall, 1970. A very good collection.

Hospers, John. *Human Conduct.* New York: Harcourt, Brace World, 1961. Chapter 4 contains a very helpful discussion of the question: Why should I be moral? (Why should I help others?)

MacIntyre, Alasdair. *After Virtue.* Notre Dame: Notre Dame University Press, 1984. A widely cited recent treatment of virtue-based ethics that contains an excellent discussion of the history of ethics.

Milo, Ronald D., ed. *Egoism and Altruism.* Belmont, Calif.: Wadsworth, 1973. A very useful anthology.

Prichard, H. A. *Duty and Interest.* Oxford: Clarendon Press, 1928. Discusses and defends a version of altruism.

Rand, Ayn. *The Virtue of Selfishness.* New York: New American Library, 1964. One of the most consistent and most uncompromising defenses of ethical egoism that is available.

Rescher, Nicholas. *Unselfishness.* Pittsburgh: University of Pittsburgh Press, 1975. One of the best discussions of altruism.

Sommers, Christina Hoff, ed. *Vice and Virtue in Everyday Life.* New York: Harcourt, Brace Jovanovich, 1985. An excellent collection of readings, both classical and contemporary, on virtue-based ethics.

White, Nicholas P. *A Companion to Plato's Republic.* Indianapolis: Hackett, 1979. Contains a good discussion of Plato's altruistic ethical theory.

CHAPTER TEN

Let not the eyes see light or colors; nor the ears hear sounds; let the palate not taste, nor the nose smell, and all colors, tastes, odors and sounds . . .vanish and cease.

—John Locke

Arithmetic must be true of whatever can be numbered at all.

—A. C. Ewing

Knowledge and Perception

Does philosophy have a common theme that unites all of its branches? Is there a single, general sort of answer that philosophy seeks for all of the diverse questions that it raises? The answer is probably yes. A grand theme does underlie much of philosophy. A certain amount of controversy attaches to this theme, but a great many philosophers have been, and continue to be, guided by it in one way or another. It is *to seek the reality that lies behind appearances*. From the time when our most primitive ancestor first touched a glowing coal because it looked pretty, human beings have been aware that things are not what they seem to be. Attractive-looking fruit may be poisonous. An apparently hostile stranger may turn out to be a friend. A quiet and peaceful evening may hide the coming storm.

Philosophy seeks the reality beneath appearances at the deepest possible level. Consider: A piece of fruit may look attractive but taste bitter when we eat it; or it may taste sweet when eaten but later on make us ill; or it may appear to nourish us as part of our diet, but lack some essential nutrients, which we discover only at a much later time. As we look more and more deeply into the composition of the fruit, we uncover more and more completely its true effects *upon us*. Philosophy is interested in seeking reality in a different way. Philosophers do want to know the true effects of things upon human beings, but more importantly, they want to know what things are like "in themselves," apart from human beings. Actually, philosophers want to know, first of all, whether it even makes sense to ask what things are like in themselves. Then, if it turns out that it does make sense to ask this question, philosophers want to answer it.

This chapter is an introduction to some issues in epistemology, or the theory of knowledge. The focal point for the chapter is the philosophy of perception. Issues raised by the conflict between appearance and reality are nowhere more puzzling than in the study of perception. By perception is meant at least the experiences of the five "external" senses plus the "internal" kinesthetic sense that tells me, for example, where my leg is without my looking at it or touching it. Philosophical discussions of perception usually concentrate on the experiences of seeing, hearing, and, to a lesser extent, the sense of touch, because these senses contribute the most to what we believe is our knowledge of the world. To begin, let us restrict our discussion to the sense of sight.

Epistemological puzzles regarding vision arise immediately in the act of seeing: seeing something seems to be *both* essentially objective (we seem to see what is "out there" *apart from us*) and essentially subjective (the way we see things seems to *depend upon us*—on how sharp our vision is, for example, or on whether we are color blind).[1] I have just said that vision *seems* to be both objective and subjective. Not all philosophers would agree that it *is* both.

Idealists such as George Berkeley, who is represented in this chapter, emphasize the "subjective" element in perception to the virtual exclusion of the objective element. According to Berkeley, *to be is to be perceived*—that is, nothing exists at all apart from experience of it. Berkeley's position in its turn generates many puzzles. At the same time, it has at least one important virtue—it avoids having to say that something exists "out there in the world," apart from us, while still being subject somehow to conditions *in us* who are perceiving it.

At the other extreme from the idealists are the philosophers who want to deemphasize the subjective element in sense experience as much as possible. No philosopher completely ignores the subjective element. You may at some point come across the expression "naive realist" used to describe philosophers who allegedly believe that "the world really is in itself just the way we normally perceive it to be." But, of course, no one refers to himself or herself as a naive realist! Moreover, the meaning of the expression "naive realist" is not entirely clear. If there were naive realists, perhaps they would believe that the sense of sight is like a clear mirror, reflecting things "just as they are." Many objections can be raised regarding the adequacy of this analogy.

What usually happens when philosophers stress the objective character of perception is that they draw an important distinction between *sense experience* and *thought*. There is, they say, a world out there "in itself," independent of us, and we are able to see such a world; *but we do not see it wholly as it is in itself*. Rather, what we see is partly the world in itself and partly our "contributions" to the appearance of the world as we see it. When we *think* about what we see, we can separate the two aspects. We can, according to some philosophers, extract from visual images of things an objective *conception* of the world.

Philosophers who pursue this line of reasoning are moving from a theory strictly about perception to a general theory about the world, or in other words a metaphysics. (Berkeley in his own way also makes this move, but his idealistic metaphysics makes the world itself dependent upon the mind.) In separating the objective from the subjective elements in perception, philosophers most often appeal to a distinction between *primary qualities* and *secondary qualities*. The former are said to belong to things in themselves, while the latter are said to depend upon the perceiving subject.

John Locke, who is represented in this chapter, is well known for defending the distinction between primary and secondary qualities. According to Locke, primary qualities include shape, spatial extension, weight, and movement or rest. Secondary qualities include colors, sounds, "felt textures," tastes, and smells. If Locke is correct, the world "in itself" is filled with spatially extended objects in motion or at rest that are colorless, soundless, tasteless, and so on, because secondary qualities depend for their existence upon the perceiving subject. According to Locke, a tree that falls in the forest when no one is around makes no sound!

Such a view of reality may remind us of contemporary physics, which says that everything in the universe is composed of particles (belonging to atoms and electromagnetic radiation) in motion within empty space—or more accurately, within various fields of force. Neither atomic particles nor fields of force can be assigned colors or other secondary qualities. Needless to say, the atomic theory raises many questions, one of which is the following:

> Do atomic particles (plus force fields and any other components of the worldview of physics) *constitute the entire sum of reality* or, instead, are they the *foundation for a reality that transcends them?*

The selection from Frank Jackson defends Locke's position from the perspective of contemporary philosophy and contemporary science. Jackson's presentation has the virtue of being focused on a single argument, with all of Jackson's comments serving as support either for his claim that the premises of the argument are true or his claim that the argument is valid.

Eugene Valberg's paper illustrates a move commonly made by philosophers who believe that no progress has been made toward answering a long-standing philosophical question. They ask: Does the question itself make sense? Is it a question that really can be answered? Both Locke and Jackson wish to defend a negative answer to the question: Do material things in themselves have secondary qualities, such as colors? Valberg argues that, for this question to make sense, a meaningful distinction must be drawn between saying that color is in objects and saying that color is somewhere else, such as in the mind. Valberg's view is that this distinction is very problematic, and the question stated above is therefore not one that can really be answered. Thus he attempts not to solve the "problem of secondary qualities," but to *dissolve* it.

John Stuart Mill holds that both of the following statements are true:

1. The material world exists independently of us.
2. We cannot think what the material world is like apart from the ways that we perceive it.

To resolve the appearance of conflict between these two statements, Mill defines "material substance" as a "permanent possibility of sensation".

Thus far, we have been discussing the philosophy of perception and the primary/secondary quality distinction that belongs within it. A more inclusive study of human knowledge will take us beyond the philosophy of perception to an examination of answers to the following question: What role does perception play in human knowledge? Two quite different kinds of answers have been given by philosophers to this question. On the one hand have been the *empiricists*, who have said that knowledge is closely tied to perception, that is, to the experiences of the senses. On the other hand have been the *rationalists*, who have said that knowledge is not so closely tied to sensory experience. There have been many different versions of both empiricism and rationalism. In this chapter, the empiricist position is represented by a selection from David Hume, who is generally regarded as the most influential empiricist. The rationalist position is represented by a selection from A. C. Ewing. His version of rationalism, or something close to it, has received the widest support in recent years from philosophers sympathetic to rationalism.

Hume's empiricist theory of knowledge is centered around a distinction he draws that is probably the most significant to be found in the history of philosophy over the last three centuries. It is the distinction between "relations of ideas" and "matters of fact." Hume discusses this distinction at some length, and it is also briefly summarized in the "Comments and Questions" that follow his selection.

The upshot of Hume's distinction, in conjunction with some other claims that he makes about perception, is that human knowledge is very limited. First, according to Hume, statements that can be known with certainty ("relations of ideas"), such as that 2 + 2 = 4, inform us only about ourselves, that is, about our ideas and the operations of our minds. They do not inform us about the world as it may exist apart from our minds. Second, according to Hume, statements that *do* inform us about the world ("matters of fact") cannot be known with certainty and, indeed, cannot be supported in any way by human reason. We come to *believe*, says Hume, that certain matters of fact will continue to be as they have been. For example, we believe that the sun will rise tomorrow; but we have no *reason* to believe that this is so. Our expectation that the sun will rise tomorrow becomes a habit, but that is the sole basis for our belief that the expectation will continue to be fulfilled.

If knowledge is understood to be *true belief supported by good reasons* (a definition of knowledge that is accepted by a great many philosophers, but one that also has generated a lot of controversy), then according to Hume we do not have knowledge of matters of fact. Thus, Hume is a *skeptic*. You must carefully read what he has to say to reconstruct all of the steps in his skeptical argument.

The skeptical views of David Hume are widely regarded as having been very forcefully presented. Many contemporary philosophers reject Hume's basic skeptical position (quite a few accept it as well, or accept significant portions of it), but acknowledge that "answering David Hume" is difficult. The selection in this chapter from A. C. Ewing is a partial response to Hume. A more complete response would be too lengthy for the present chapter. Ewing attacks Hume's skeptical position by arguing that some statements can *both* be known with certainty and be about the world, not just about our minds or thoughts. Ewing refers to such statements as being *synthetic a priori*. Ewing's philosophical analyses and arguments, like Hume's, are complex and need to be read carefully.

Note

1. Many philosophical terms are used with different meanings by different philosophers. The meanings given here "objective" ("belonging to objects apart from experience") and "subjective" ("dependent in some way upon the nature of the experiencing subject") are not the only meanings that you will encounter).

DAVID HUME

In vain do you pretend to have learned the nature of bodies from your past experience. Their secret nature, and consequently all their effects and influence, may change, without any change in their sensible qualities.

—*Treatise of Human Nature*

Truth is disputable, not taste.... Propositions in geometry may be proved, systems in physics may be controverted, but the harmony of verse, the tenderness of passion, the brilliancy of wit must give immediate pleasure.

—*Inquiry Concerning the Principles of Morals*

David Hume (1711–1776) was born in Scotland, where except for visits to London and Paris, he spent most of his life. At age 25, Hume completed his most famous book, *Treatise of Human Nature*. The skeptical ideas and arguments in this book have earned him recognition as the greatest British philosopher. Hume argued so forcefully against the views of his predecessors that even today philosophers are still trying to "answer David Hume". His philosophical fierceness was in sharp contrast to his thoroughgoing good nature as a person.

In the spirit of Descartes, Hume's philosophy begins with an analysis of the contents of the mind—ideas. How can we show, Hume wanted to know, that our ideas really match up with a world "out there"? How can we show that the way things appear to be now is the way they will appear to be in the future? How can we show that anything will necessarily lead to anything else? Said Hume: We cannot prove any of these things, or even show that there is a likelihood that they are true. Nevertheless, we must live our lives *as though* we did have knowledge of the external world, of the future, and of causality.

JOHN LOCKE

The Distinction Between Primary and Secondary Qualities

* * * * *

To discover the nature of our *ideas* the better, and to discourse of them intelligibly, it will be convenient to distinguish them as they are ideas or perceptions in our minds, and as they are modifications of matter in the bodies that cause such perceptions in us: that so we may not think (as perhaps usually is done) that they are exactly the images and resemblances of something inherent in the subject; most of those of sensation being in the mind no more the likeness of something existing without us, than the names that stand for them are the likeness of our ideas, which yet upon hearing they are apt to excite in us.

8. Whatsoever the mind perceives *in itself*, or is the immediate object of perception, thought, or understanding, that I call *idea*; and the power to produce any idea in our mind, I call *quality* of the subject wherein that power is. Thus a snowball having the power to produce in us the ideas of white, cold, and round, the power to produce those ideas in us, as they are in the snowball, I call qualities; and as they are sensations or perceptions in our understandings, I call them ideas; which *ideas*, if I speak of sometimes as in the things themselves, I would be understood to mean those qualities in the objects which produce them in us.

9. Qualities thus considered in bodies are:

First, such as are utterly inseparable from the body, in what state soever it be; and such as in all the alterations and changes it suffers, all the force can be used upon it, it constantly keeps; and such as sense constantly finds in every particle of matter which has bulk enough to be perceived; and the mind finds inseparable from every particle of matter, though less than to make itself singly be perceived by our senses: e.g. take a grain of wheat, divide it into two parts; each part has still solidity, extension, figure, and mobility: divide it again, and it retains still the same qualities; and so divide it on, till the parts become insensible; they must retain still each of them all those qualities. For division can never take away either solidity, extension, figure, or mobility from any body, but only makes two or more distinct separate masses of matter, of that which was but one before; all which distinct masses, reckoned as so many distinct bodies, after division, make a certain number. These I call *origi-*

A biographical sketch of John Locke appears in chapter 7.

From *An Enquiry Concerning Human Understanding*, first published in 1690.

nal or *primary qualities* of body, which I think we may observe to produce simple ideas in us, viz. solidity, extension, figure, motion or rest, and number.

10. Secondly, such qualities which in truth are nothing in the objects themselves but powers to produce various sensations in us by their primary qualities, i.e. by the bulk, figure, texture, and motion of their insensible parts, as colours, sounds, tastes, etc. These I call *secondary qualities*. To these might be added a *third* sort, which are allowed to be barely powers; though they are as much real qualities in the subject as those which I, to comply with the common way of speaking, call qualities, but for distinction, secondary qualities. For the power in fire to produce a new colour, or consistency, in *wax* or *clay*, by its primary qualities, is as much a quality in fire, as the power it has to produce in *me* a new idea or sensation of warmth or burning, which I felt not before, by the same primary qualities, viz. the bulk, texture, and motion of its insensible parts.

11. The next thing to be considered is, how bodies produce ideas in us; and that is manifestly by impulse, the only way which we can conceive bodies to operate in.

12. If then external objects be not united to our minds when they produce ideas therein; and yet we perceive these *original* qualities in such of them as singly fall under our senses, it is evident that some motion must be thence continued by our nerves, or animal spirits, by some parts of our bodies, to the brains or the seat of sensation, there to produce in our minds the particular ideas we have of them. And since the extension, figure, number, and motion of bodies of an observable bigness, may be perceived at a distance by the sight, it is evident some singly imperceptible bodies must come from them to the eyes, and thereby convey to the brain some motion; which produces these ideas which we have of them in us.

13. After the same manner that the ideas of these original qualities are produced in us, we may conceive that the ideas of *secondary* qualities are also produced, viz. by the operation of insensible particles on our senses. For, it being manifest that there are bodies and good store of bodies, each whereof are so small, that we cannot by any of our senses discover either their bulk, figure, or motion—as is evident in the particles of the air and water, and others extremely smaller than those; perhaps as much smaller than the particles of air and water, as the particles of air and water are smaller than peas or hail-stones—let us suppose at present that the different motions and figures, bulk and number, of such particles, affecting the several organs of our senses, produce in us those different sensations which we have from the colours and smells of bodies; v.g. that a violet, by the impulse of such insensible particles of matter, of peculiar figures and bulks, and in different degrees and modifications of their motions, causes the ideas of the blue colour and sweet scent of that flower to be produced in our minds. It being no more impossible to conceive that God should annex such ideas to such motions, with which they have no similitude, than that he should annex the idea of pain to the motion of a piece of steel dividing our flesh, with which

that idea hath no resemblance.

14. What I have said concerning colours and smells may be understood also of tastes and sounds, and other the like sensible qualities; which, whatever reality we by mistake attribute to them, are in truth nothing in the objects themselves, but powers to produce various sensations in us; and depend on those primary qualities, viz. bulk, figure, texture, and motion of parts.

15. From whence I think it easy to draw this observation—that the ideas of primary qualities of bodies are resemblances of them, and their patterns do really exist in the bodies themselves, but the ideas produced in us by these secondary qualities have no resemblance of them at all. There is nothing like our ideas, existing in the bodies themselves. They are, in the bodies we denominate from them, only a power to produce those sensations in us: and what is sweet, blue, or warm in idea, is but the certain bulk, figure, and motion of the insensible parts, in the bodies themselves, which we call so.

16. Flame is denominated hot and light; snow, white and cold; and manna, white and sweet, from the ideas they produce in us. Which qualities are commonly thought to be the same in those bodies that those ideas are in us, the one the perfect resemblance of the other, as they are in a mirror, and it would by most men be judged very extravagant if one should say otherwise. And yet he that will consider that the same fire that at one distance produces in us the sensation of warmth does, at a nearer approach, produce in us the far different sensation of pain, ought to bethink himself what reason he has to say—that this idea of warmth, which was produced in him by the fire, is *actually in the fire*; and his idea of pain, which the same fire produced in him the same way, is *not* in the fire. Why are whiteness and coldness in snow, and pain not, when it produces the one and the other idea in us; and can do neither, but by the bulk, figure, number, and motion of its solid parts?

17. The particular bulk, number, figure, and motion of the parts of fire or snow are really in them, whether any one's senses perceive them or no: and therefore they may be called *real* qualities, because they really exist in those bodies. But light, heat, whiteness, or coldness, are no more really in them than sickness or pain is in manna. Take away the sensation of them; let not the eyes see light or colours, nor the ears hear sounds; let the palate not taste, nor the nose smell, and all colours, tastes, odours, and sounds, as they are such particular ideas, vanish and cease, and are reduced to their causes, i.e. bulk, figure, and motion of parts.

18. A piece of manna of a sensible bulk is able to produce in us the idea of a round or square figure; and by being removed from one place to another, the idea of motion. This idea of motion represents it as it really is in manna moving: a circle or square are the same, whether in idea or existence, in the mind or in the manna. And this, both motion and figure, are really in the manna, whether we take notice of them or no: this everybody is ready to agree to. Besides, manna, by the bulk, figure, texture, and motion of its parts, has a power to produce the sensations of sickness, and sometimes of

acute pains or gripings in us. That these ideas of sickness and pain are *not* in the manna, but effects of its operations on us, and are nowhere when we feel them not; this also every one readily agrees to. And yet men are hardly to be brought to think that sweetness and whiteness are not really in manna; which are but the effects of the operations of manna, by the motion, size, and figure of its particles, on the eyes and palate: as the pain and sickness caused by manna are confessedly nothing but the effects of its operations on the stomach and guts, by the size, motion, and figure of its insensible parts.

19. Let us consider the red and white colours in porphyry. Hinder light from striking on it, and its colours vanish; it no longer produces any such ideas in us: upon the return of light it produces these appearances on us again. Can any one think any real alterations are made in the porphyry by the presence or absence of light; and that those ideas of whiteness and redness are really in porphyry in the light, when it is plain *it has no colour in the dark*? It has, indeed, such a configuration of particles, both night and day, as are apt, by the rays of light rebounding from some parts of that hard stone, to produce in us the idea of redness, and from others the idea of whiteness; but whiteness or redness are not in it at any time, but such a texture that hath the power to produce such a sensation in us.

20. Pound an almond, and the clear white colour will be altered into a dirty one, and the sweet taste into an oily one. What real alteration can the beating of the pestle make in any body, but an alteration of the texture of it?

21. Ideas being thus distinguished and understood, we may be able to give an account how the same water, at the same time, may produce the idea of cold by one hand and of heat by the other, which yet *figure* never does, that never producing the idea of a square by one hand which has produced the idea of a globe by another. But if the sensation of heat and cold be nothing but the increase or diminution of the motion of the minute parts of our bodies, caused by the corpuscles of any other body, it is easy to be understood, that if that motion be greater in one hand than in the other; if a body be applied to the two hands, which has in its minute particles a greater motion than in those of one of the hands, and a less than in those of the other, it will increase the motion of the one hand and lessen it in the other; and so cause the different sensations of heat and cold that depend thereon.

22. I have in what just goes before been engaged in physical inquiries a little further than perhaps I intended. But, it being necessary to make the nature of sensation a little understood; and to make the *difference between the qualities in bodies, and the ideas produced by them in the mind*, to be distinctly conceived, without which it were impossible to discourse intelligibly of them; I hope I shall be pardoned this little excursion into natural philosophy; it being necessary in our present inquiry to distinguish the *primary* and *real* qualities of bodies, which are always in them (viz. solidity, extension, figure, number, and motion, or rest, and are sometimes perceived by us, viz. when the bodies they are in are big

enough singly to be discerned), from those *secondary* and *imputed* qualities, which are but the powers of several combinations of those primary ones, when they operate without being distinctly discerned; whereby we may also come to know what ideas are, and what are not, resemblances of something really existing in the bodies we denominate from them.

23. The qualities, then, that are in bodies, rightly considered, are of three sorts:

First, The bulk, figure, number, situation, and motion or rest of their solid parts. Those are in them, whether we perceive them or not; and when they are of that size that we can discover them, we have by these an idea of the thing as it is in itself; as is plain in artificial things. These I call *primary qualities*.

Secondly, The power that is in any body, by reason of its insensible primary qualities, to operate after a peculiar manner on any of our senses, and thereby produce in *us* the different ideas of several colours, sounds, smells, tastes, etc. These are usually called *sensible qualities*.

Thirdly, The power that is in any body, by reason of the particular constitution of its primary qualities, to make such a change in the bulk, figure, texture, and motion of *another body*, as to make it operate on our senses differently from what it did before. Thus the sun has a power to make wax white, and fire to make lead fluid. These are usually called *powers*.

The first of these, as has been said, I think may be properly called real, original, or primary qualities; because they are in the things themselves, whether they are perceived or not: and upon their different modifications it is that the secondary qualities depend.

The other two are only powers to act differently upon other things: which powers result from the different modifications of those primary qualities.

* * * * *

25. In the operations of bodies changing the qualities one of another, we plainly discover that the quality produced hath commonly no resemblance with anything in the thing producing it; wherefore we look on it as a bare effect of power. For, through receiving the idea of heat or light from the sun, we are apt to think *it* is a perception and resemblance of such a quality in the sun; yet when we see wax, or a fair face, receive change of colour from the sun, we cannot imagine *that* to be the reception or resemblance of anything in the sun, because we find not those different colours in the sun itself. For, our senses being able to observe a likeness or unlikeness of sensible qualities in two different external objects, we forwardly enough conclude the production of any sensible quality in any subject to be an effect of bare power, and not the communication of any quality which was really in the efficient, when we find no such sensible quality in the thing that produced it. But our senses not being able to discover any unlikeness between the idea produced in us and the quality of the object producing it, we are apt to imagine that our ideas are resemblances of something in the objects, and not the effects of certain powers placed in the modification of their primary qualities, with which primary qualities the ideas produced in us

have no resemblance.

26. To conclude. Beside those before-mentioned primary qualities in bodies, viz. bulk, figure, extension, number, and motion of their solid parts; all the rest, whereby we take notice of bodies, and distinguish them one from another, are nothing else but several powers in them, depending on those primary qualities; whereby they are fitted, either by immediately operating on our bodies to produce several different ideas in us; or else, by operating on other bodies, so to change their primary qualities as to render them capable of producing ideas in us different from what before they did. The former of these, I think, may be called secondary qualities *immediately perceivable*: the latter secondary qualities, *mediately perceivable*.

COMMENTS ■ QUESTIONS

1. Locke defines *quality in general* as the "power" in things to "produce any idea in our mind." According to Locke, there are two kinds of ideas, simple and complex. Examples of simple ideas are white, cold, round, solidity, extension. Complex ideas are made up of simple ideas, an example being the idea of a snowball—something that is white, round, and cold. Two different kinds of qualities correspond to simple ideas: (1) *primary qualities* that *resemble* the ideas that they produce in our minds and (2) *secondary qualities* that do not in any way resemble the ideas that they produce. Thus, solidity and extension, which are primary qualities, really do belong to things, while whiteness and coldness, which are secondary qualities, do not. Put another way, if the sensations of secondary qualities were taken away, then according to Locke the qualities themselves would disappear, while primary qualities, by contrast, are "utterly inseparable from the body [that is perceived], in what state soever it be." At what point, or points, (if any) would you object to Locke's theory of primary and secondary qualities? Why?
2. Clearly, Locke's position does not agree in all respects with common sense. We would ordinarily be inclined to say that, for example, the whiteness of snow belongs to snow in itself. What about such secondary qualities as sweetness or the smell of roses? In regard to them, does common sense give any support to Locke? Overall, what degree of support would you say is given by common sense or ordinary experience to Locke's primary/secondary quality distinction?
3. Locke gives the following reasons for his claim that primary qualities do belong to things in themselves:

a. The mind cannot conceive any particle of matter that does not have solidity, figure, extension, and other primary qualities.
b. Regardless of how finely a particle of matter may be dividend—even if it becomes so small that it cannot be perceived—it cannot lose its primary qualities. (In contrast, it appears to make no sense to say that something too small to be seen has a color or some other secondary quality.)
c. Primary qualities in things constitute the powers that the things have to produce secondary qualities in our minds.

Do the above reasons each provide support for Locke's position?

4. Locke does not use the expressions "*subjective*" and "*objective*" in describing primary and secondary qualities. These expressions are often used by other writers, however, and therefore it is important to distinguish between two different senses of the word "subjective" that are relevant to Locke's theory: (a) belonging to the perceiving subject, as opposed to the object perceived, and (b) varying from one person to another. Secondary qualities are subjective in the first sense, but not in the second, that is, they do not belong to the object perceived. At the same time, it is not up to each individual to specify for himself or herself whether or not an object is white, cold, and so on. If a person does not perceive snow to be white, we say that the person fails to meet the requirements for being a *normal observer*; snow, we say, simply is white even though certain people cannot perceive it to be white. Does the application of the two senses of the word "subjective" that have just been described help to support Locke's theory of primary and secondary qualities? Or instead help to show that the theory is not plausible?

GEORGE BERKELEY

To Be Is to Be Perceived

* * * * *

It is evident to anyone who takes a survey of the *objects* of human knowledge that they are either ideas actually imprinted on the senses, or else such as are perceived by attending to the passions and operations of the mind, or lastly, ideas formed by help of memory and imagination—either compounding, dividing, or barely representing those originally perceived in the aforesaid ways. By sight I have the ideas of light and colors, with their several degrees and variations. By touch I perceive, for example, hard and soft, heat and cold, motion and resistance, and of all these more and less either as to quantity or degree. Smelling furnishes me with odors, the palate with tastes, and hearing conveys sounds to the mind in all their variety of tone and composition. And as several of these are observed to accompany each other, they come to be marked by one name, and so to be reputed as one thing. Thus, for example, a certain color, taste, smell, figure, and consistence having been observed to go together, are accounted one distinct thing signified by the name "*apple*"; other collections of ideas constitute a stone, a tree, a book, and the like sensible things—which as they are pleasing or disagreeable excite the passions of love, hatred, joy, grief, and so forth.

2. But, besides all that endless variety of ideas or objects of knowledge, there is likewise something which knows or perceives them and exercises divers operations, as willing, imagining, remembering, about them. This perceiving, active being is what I call *mind, spirit, soul*, or *myself*. By which words I do not denote any one of my ideas, but a thing entirely distinct from them, wherein they exist or, which is the same thing, whereby they are perceived—for the existence of an idea consists in being perceived.

3. That neither our thoughts, nor passions, nor ideas formed by the imagination exist without the mind is what everybody will allow. And it seems no less evident that the various sensations or ideas imprinted on the sense, however blended or

---

George Berkeley (1685–1753) was born in Ireland and educated at Trinity College, Dublin. His most important philosophical works were all written while he was still a young man: Essay Towards a New Theory of Vision, The Principles of Human Knowledge, and Three Dialogues Between Hylas and Philonus. *Berkeley was a bishop in the Church of England for nearly twenty years.*

From *Treatise Concerning the Principles of Knowledge*, first published in 1710.

combined together (that is, whatever objects they compose), cannot exist otherwise than in a mind perceiving them.—I think an intuitive knowledge may be obtained of this by anyone that shall attend to what is meant by the term *exist* when applied to sensible things. The table I write on I say exists, that is, I see and feel it; and if I were out of my study I should say it existed—meaning thereby that if I was in my study I might perceive it, or that some other spirit actually does perceive it. There was an odor, that is, it was smelled, there was a sound, that is to say, it was heard; a color or figure, and it was perceived by sight or touch. This is all that I can understand by these and the like expressions. For as to what is said of the absolute existence of unthinking things without any relation to their being perceived, that seems perfectly unintelligible. Their *esse* is *percipi*, nor is it possible they should have any existence out of the minds or thinking things which perceive them.

4. It is indeed an opinion strangely prevailing amongst men that houses, mountains, rivers, and, in a word, all sensible objects have an existence, natural or real, distinct from their being perceived by the understanding. But with how great an assurance and acquiescence soever this principle may be entertained in the world, yet whoever shall find in his heart to call it in question may, if I mistake not, perceive it to involve a manifest contradiction. For what are the forementioned objects but the things we perceive by sense? And what do we perceive besides our own ideas or sensations? And is it not plainly repugnant that any one of these, or any combination of them, should exist unperceived?

5. If we thoroughly examine this tenet it will, perhaps, be found at bottom to depend on the doctrine of *abstract ideas*. For can there be a nicer strain of abstraction than to distinguish the existence of sensible objects from their being perceived, so as to conceive them existing unperceived? Light and colors, heat and cold, extension and figures—in a word, the things we see and feel—what are they but so many sensations, notions, ideas, or impressions on the sense? And is it possible to separate, even in thought, any of these from perception? For my part, I might as easily divide a thing from itself. I may, indeed, divide in my thoughts, or conceive apart from each other, those things which, perhaps, I never perceived by sense so divided. Thus I imagine the trunk of a human body without the limbs, or conceive the smell of a rose without thinking on the rose itself. So far, I will not deny, I can abstract—if that may properly be called *abstraction* which extends only to the conceiving separately such objects as it is possible may really exist or be actually perceived asunder. But my conceiving or imagining power does not extend beyond the possibility of real existence or perception. Hence, as it is impossible for me to see or feel anything without an actual sensation of that thing, so is it impossible for me to conceive in my thoughts any sensible thing or object distinct from the sensation or perception of it.

6. Some truths there are so near and obvious to the mind that a man need only open his eyes to see them. Such I take this important one to be, to wit, that all the choir of heaven and furniture of the earth, in a word,

all those bodies which compose the mighty frame of the world, have not any subsistence without a mind—that their *being* is to be perceived or known, that, consequently, so long as they are not actually perceived by me or do not exist in my mind or that of any other created spirit, they must either have no existence at all or else subsist in the mind of some eternal spirit—it being perfectly unintelligible, and involving all the absurdity of abstraction, to attribute to any single part of them an existence independent of a spirit. To be convinced of which, the reader need only reflect, and try to separate in his own thoughts, the *being* of a sensible thing from its *being perceived*.

7. From what has been said it follows there is not any other substance than *Spirit*, or that which perceives. But, for the fuller proof of this point, let it be considered the sensible qualities are color, figure, motion, smell, taste, and such like—that is, the ideas perceived by sense. Now, for an idea to exist in an unperceiving thing is a manifest contradiction, for to have an idea is all one as to perceive; that, therefore, wherein color, figure, and the like qualities exist must perceive them; hence it is clear there can be no unthinking substance or *substratum* of those ideas.

8. But, say you, though the ideas themselves do not exist without the mind, yet there may be things like them, whereof they are copies or resemblances, which things exist without the mind in an unthinking substance. I answer, an idea can be like nothing but an idea; a color or figure can be like nothing but another color or figure. If we look but ever so little into our thoughts, we shall find it impossible for us to conceive a likeness except only between our ideas. Again, I ask whether those supposed originals or external things, of which our ideas are the pictures or representations, be themselves perceivable or no? If they are, then they are ideas and we have gained our point; but if you say they are not, I appeal to anyone whether it be sense to assert a color is like something which is invisible; hard or soft, like something which is intangible; and so of the rest.

9. Some there are who make a distinction betwixt *primary* and *secondary* qualities. By the former they mean extension, figure, motion, rest, solidity or impenetrability, and number; by the latter they denote all other sensible qualities, as colors, sounds, tastes, and so forth. The ideas we have of these they acknowledge not to be the resemblances of anything existing without the mind, or unperceived, but they will have our ideas of the primary qualities to be patterns or images of things which exist without the mind, in an unthinking substance which they call "matter." By "matter," therefore, we are to understand an inert, senseless substance, in which extension, figure, and motion do actually subsist. But it is evident from what we have already shown that extension, figure, and motion are only ideas existing in the mind, and that an idea can be like nothing but another idea, and that consequently neither they nor their archetypes can exist in an unperceiving substance. Hence it is plain that the very notion of what is called *matter* or *corporeal substance* involves a contradiction in it.

10. They who assert that figure, motion, and the rest of the primary

or original qualities do exist without the mind in unthinking substances do at the same time acknowledge that colors, sounds, heat, cold, and suchlike secondary qualities do not—which they tell us are sensations existing in the mind alone, that depend on and are occasioned by the different size, texture, and motion of the minute particles of matter. This they take for an undoubted truth which they can demonstrate beyond all exception. Now, if it be certain that those original qualities are inseparably united with the other sensible qualities, and not, even in thought, capable of being abstracted from them, it plainly follows that they exist only in the mind. But I desire anyone to reflect and try whether he can, by any abstraction of thought, conceive the extension and motion of a body without all other sensible qualities. For my own part, I see evidently that it is not in my power to frame an idea of a body extended and moved, but I must withal give it some color or other sensible quality which is acknowledged to exist only in the mind. In short, extension, figure, and motion, abstracted from all other qualities, are inconceivable. Where therefore the other sensible qualities are, there must these be also, to wit, in the mind and nowhere else.

11. Again, *great* and *small, swift* and *slow* are allowed to exist nowhere without the mind, being entirely relative, and changing as the frame or position of the organs of sense varies. The extension, therefore, which exists without the mind is neither great nor small, the motion neither swift nor slow; that is, they are nothing at all. But, say you, they are extension in general, and motion in general: thus we see how much the tenet of extended movable substances existing without the mind depends on that strange doctrine of *abstract ideas*. And here I cannot but remark how nearly the vague and indeterminate description of matter or corporeal substance, which the modern philosophers are run into by their own principles, resembles that antiquated and so much ridiculed notion of *materia prima*, to be met with in Aristotle and his followers. Without extension, solidity cannot be conceived; since, therefore, it has been shown that extension exists not in an unthinking substance, the same must also be true of solidity.

12. That number is entirely the creature of the mind, even though the other qualities be allowed to exist without, will be evident to whoever considers that the same thing bears a different denomination of number as the mind views it with different respects. Thus the same extension is one, or three, or thirty-six, according as the mind considers it with reference to a yard, a foot, or an inch. Number is so visibly relative and dependent on men's understanding that it is strange to think how anyone should give it an absolute existence without the mind. We say one book, one page, one line; all these are equally units, though some contain several of the others. And in each instance it is plain the unit relates to some particular combination of ideas arbitrarily put together by the mind.

13. Unity I know some will have to be a simple or uncompounded idea accompanying all other ideas into the mind. That I have any such idea answering the word *unity* I do not find; and if I had, me-

thinks I could not miss finding it; on the contrary, it should be the most familiar to my understanding, since it is said to accompany all other ideas and to be perceived by all the ways of sensation and reflection. To say no more, it is an *abstract idea*.

14. I shall further add that, after the same manner as modern philosophers prove certain sensible qualities to have no existence in matter, or without the mind, the same thing may be likewise proved of all other sensible qualities whatsoever. Thus, for instance, it is said that heat and cold are affections only of the mind, and not at all patterns of real beings existing in the corporeal substances which excite them, for that the same body which appears cold to one hand seems warm to another. Now, why may we not as well argue that figure and extension are not patterns or resemblances of qualities existing in matter, because to the same eye at different stations, or eyes of a different texture at the same station, they appear various and cannot, therefore, be the images of anything settled and determinate without the mind? Again, it is proved that sweetness is not really in the sapid thing, because, the thing remaining unaltered, the sweetness is changed into bitter, as in case of a fever or otherwise vitiated palate. Is it not as reasonable to say that motion is not without the mind, since if the succession of ideas in the mind become swifter, the motion, it is acknowledged, shall appear slower without any alteration in any external object?

15. In short, let anyone consider those arguments which are thought manifestly to prove that colors and taste exist only in the mind, and he shall find they may with equal force be brought to prove the same thing of extension, figure, and motion. Though it must be confessed this method of arguing does not so much prove that there is no extension or color in an outward object as that we do not know by sense which is the true extension or color of the object. But the arguments foregoing plainly show it to be impossible that any color or extension at all, or other sensible quality whatsoever, should exist in an unthinking subject without the mind, or, in truth, that there should be any such thing as an outward object.

* * * * *

28. I find I can excite ideas in my mind at pleasure, and vary and shift the scene as oft as I think fit. It is no more than willing, and straightway this or that idea arises in my fancy; and by the same power it is obliterated and makes way for another. This making and unmaking of ideas does very properly denominate the mind active. Thus much is certain and grounded on experience; but when we talk of unthinking agents or of exciting ideas exclusive of volition, we only amuse ourselves with words.

29. But, whatever power I may have over my own thoughts, I find the ideas actually perceived by sense have not a like dependence on my will. When in broad daylight I open my eyes, it is not in my power to choose whether I shall see or no, or to determine what particular objects shall present themselves to my view; and so likewise as to the hearing and other senses; the ideas imprinted on them are not creatures of my will. There is therefore some *other* will or spirit that produces them.

30. The ideas of sense are more

strong, lively, and distinct than those of the imagination; they have likewise a steadiness, order, and coherence, and are not excited at random, as those which are the effects of human wills often are, but in a regular train or series, the admirable connection whereof sufficiently testifies the wisdom and benevolence of its Author. Now the set rules or established methods wherein the mind we depend on excites in us the ideas of sense are called the *laws of nature*; and these we learn by experience, which teaches us that such and such ideas are attended with such and such other ideas in the ordinary course of things.

31. This gives us a sort of foresight which enables us to regulate our actions for the benefit of life. And without this we should be eternally at a loss; we could not know how to act anything that might procure us the least pleasure or remove the least pain of sense. That food nourishes, sleep refreshes, and fire warms us; that to sow in the seedtime is the way to reap in the harvest; and in general that to obtain such or such ends, such or such means are conducive—all this we know, not by discovering any necessary connection between our ideas, but only by the observation of the settled laws of nature, without which we should be all in uncertainty and confusion, and a grown man no more know how to manage himself in the affairs of life than an infant just born.

32. And yet this consistent, uniform working which so evidently displays the goodness and wisdom of that Governing Spirit whose Will constitutes the laws of nature, is so far from leading our thoughts to Him that it rather sends them awandering after second causes. For when we perceive certain ideas of sense constantly followed by other ideas, and we know this is not of our own doing, we forthwith attribute power and agency to the ideas themselves and make one the cause of another, than which nothing can be more absurd and unintelligible. Thus, for example, having observed that when we perceive by sight a certain round, luminous figure, we at the same time perceive by touch the idea or sensation called heat, we do from thence conclude the sun to be the cause of heat. And in like manner perceiving the motion and collision of bodies to be attended with sound, we are inclined to think the latter an effect of the former.

33. The ideas imprinted on the senses by the Author of Nature are called *real things;* and those excited in the imagination, being less regular, vivid, and constant, are more properly termed *ideas* or *images of things* which they copy and represent. But then our sensations, be they never so vivid and distinct, are nevertheless ideas, that is, they exist in the mind, or are perceived by it, as truly as the ideas of its own framing. The ideas of sense are allowed to have more reality in them, that is, to be more strong, orderly, and coherent than the creatures of the mind; but this is no argument that they exist without the mind. They are also less dependent on the spirit, or thinking substance which perceives them, in that they are excited by the will of another and more powerful spirit; yet still they are *ideas;* and certainly no idea, whether faint or strong, can exist otherwise than in a mind perceiving it.

COMMENTS ■ QUESTIONS

1. Berkeley begins his discussion by presenting an account of the nature of ideas that is similar to the view of John Locke. Some ideas, says Berkeley, are "actually imprinted on the senses" (colors, sounds, textures, hot and cold, and so on); some ideas are produced by the imagination as combinations of other ideas (an example is the idea of a unicorn); some ideas are perceived when the mind examines its own operations (examples are the ideas of love and hatred, grief and joy). Berkeley then says that it is "perfectly unintelligible to suppose that something exists that does not think or have ideas of its own or that is not perceived by a thinking being." We know what the various sorts of ideas are, says Berkeley, and we also understand what a mind or soul that has ideas is. But we have no understanding of anything that has no relation to ideas or to minds. In other words, says Berkeley, to be is to be perceived (*esse est percipi*) or to be a perceiving subject. Thus, Berkeley is an idealist, a philosopher who says that all of reality is dependent upon mind. What would Locke say about Berkeley's idealism? In what way would Locke make use of the primary/secondary quality distinction to argue against the position of Berkeley?
2. As part of the defense for his position, Berkeley argues that primary qualities depend upon the mind in just the same sorts of ways that secondary qualities do. What would Locke say in response to what Berkeley says about various examples of primary qualities? Which of the two philosophers do you believe has the stronger position? What is it that makes his position stronger?
3. One of Berkeley's arguments regarding the mind dependence of primary qualities turns upon the concept of an *abstract idea*, by which is meant, roughly, an idea that can be separated from other ideas and considered entirely by itself. Berkeley argues that there are no abstract ideas. Therefore, he says, it is not possible to think of primary qualities abstractly apart from secondary qualities. It is not possible, for example, to think of spatial extension apart from the perceptions of extended things that are colored, are hot or cold, and so on. But, if secondary qualities are mind-dependent (he agrees with Locke on this point), and if primary qualities are not independent of secondary qualities, then it follows that primary qualities also are mind-dependent. What response would Locke make to this line of reasoning? Is Berkeley correct in what he says about abstract ideas? (This is a difficult but important question.)

JOHN STUART MILL

The Permanent Possibility of Sensation

* * * * *

I see a piece of white paper on a table. I go into another room. If the phænomenon always followed me, or if, when it did not follow me, I believed it to disappear . . . I should not believe it to be an external object. I should consider it as a phantom—a mere affection of my senses: I should not believe that there had been any Body there. But, though I have ceased to see it, I am persuaded that the paper is still there. I no longer have the sensations which it gave me; but I believe that when I again place myself in the circumstances in which I had those sensations, that is, when I go again into the room, I shall again have them; and further, that there has been no intervening moment at which this would not have been the case. Owing to this property of my mind, my conception of the world at any given instant consists, in only a small proportion, of present sensations. Of these I may at the time have none at all, and they are in any case a most insignificant portion of the whole which I apprehend. The conception I form of the world existing at any moment, comprises, along with the sensations I am feeling, a countless variety of possibilities of sensation: namely, the whole of those which past observation tells me that I could, under any supposable circumstances, experience at this moment, together with an indefinite and illimitable multitude of others which though I do not know that I could, yet it is possible that I might, experience in circumstances not known to me. These various possibilities are the important thing to me in the world. My present sensations are generally of little importance, and are moreover fugitive: the possibilities, on the contrary, are permanent, which is the character that mainly distinguishes our idea of Substance or Matter from our notion of sensation. These possibilities, which are conditional certainties, need a special name to distinguish them from mere vague possibilities, which experience gives no warrant for reckoning upon. Now, as soon as a distinguishing name is given, though it be only to the same thing regarded in a different aspect, one of the most familiar experiences of our mental nature teaches us, that the different name comes to be considered as the name of a different thing.

There is another important peculiarity of these certified or guaranteed possibilities of sensation; namely,

A biographical sketch of John Stuart Mill appears in chapter 12.

From *An Examination of Sir William Hamilton's Philosophy*, first published in 1865.

that they have reference, not to single sensations, but to sensations joined together in groups. When we think of anything as a material substance, or body, we either have had, or we think that on some given supposition we should have, not some *one* sensation, but a great and even an indefinite number and variety of sensations, generally belonging to different senses, but so linked together, that the presence of one announces the possible presence at the very same instant of any or all of the rest. In our mind, therefore, not only is this particular Possibility of sensation invested with the quality of permanence when we are not actually feeling any of the sensations at all; but when we are feeling some of them, the remaining sensations of the group are conceived by us in the form of Present Possibilities, which might be realized at the very moment. And as this happens in turn to all of them, the group as a whole presents itself to the mind as permanent, in contrast not solely with the temporariness of my bodily presence, but also with the temporary character of each of the sensations composing the group; in other words, as a kind of permanent substratum, under a set of passing experiences or manifestations: which is another leading character of our idea of substance or matter, as distinguished from sensation.

Let us now take into consideration another of the general characters of our experience, namely, that in addition to fixed groups, we also recognise a fixed Order in our sensations; an Order of succession, which, when ascertained by observation, gives rise to the ideas of Cause and Effect, according to what I hold to be the true theory of that relation, and is on any theory the source of all our knowledge what causes produce what effects. Now, of what nature is this fixed order among our sensations? It is a constancy of antecedence and sequence. But the constant antecedence and sequence do not generally exist between one actual sensation and another. Very few such sequences are presented to us by experience. In almost all the constant sequences which occur in Nature, the antecedence and consequence do not obtain between sensations, but between the groups we have been speaking about, of which a very small portion is actual sensation, the greater part being permanent possibilities of sensation, evidenced to us by a small and variable number of sensations actually present. Hence, our ideas of causation, power, and activity, do not become connected in thought with our sensations as *actual* at all, save in the few physiological cases where these figure by themselves as the antecedents in some uniform sequence. Those ideas become connected, not with sensations, but with groups of possibilities of sensation. The sensations conceived do not, to our habitual thoughts, present themselves as sensations actually experienced, inasmuch as not only any one or any number of them may be supposed absent, but none of them need be present. We find that the modifications which are taking place more or less regularly in our possibilities of sensation, are mostly quite independent of our consciousness, and of our presence or absence. Whether we are asleep or awake the fire goes out, and puts an end to one particular possibility of warmth and light.

Whether we are present or absent the corn ripens, and brings a new possibility of food. Hence we speedily learn to think of Nature as made up solely of these groups of possibilities, and the active force in Nature as manifested in the modification of some of these by others. The sensations, though the original foundation of the whole, come to be looked upon as a sort of accident depending on us, and the possibilities as much more real than the actual sensations, nay, as the very realities of which these are only the representations, appearances, or effects. When this state of mind has been arrived at, then, and from that time forward, we are never conscious of a present sensation without instantaneously referring it to some one of the groups of possibilities into which a sensation of that particular description enters; and if we do not yet know to what group to refer it, we at least feel an irresistible conviction that it must belong to some group or other; *i.e.* that its presence proves the existence, here and now, of a great number and variety of possibilities of sensation, without which it would not have been. The whole set of sensations as possible, form a permanent background to any one or more of them that are, at a given moment, actual; and the possibilities are conceived as standing to the actual sensations in the relation of a cause to its effects, or of canvas to the figures painted on it, or of a root to the trunk, leaves, and flowers, or of a substratum to that which is spread over it, or, in transcendental language, of Matter to Form.

When this point has been reached, the Permanent Possibilities in question have assumed such unlikeness of aspect, and such difference of apparent relation to us, from any sensations, that it would be contrary to all we know of the constitution of human nature that they should not be conceived as, and believed to be, at least as different from sensations as sensations are from one another. Their groundwork in sensation is forgotten, and they are supposed to be something intrinsically distinct from it. We can withdraw ourselves from any of our (external) sensations, or we can be withdrawn from them by some other agency. But though the sensations cease, the possibilities remain in existence; they are independent of our will, our presence, and everything which belongs to us. We find, too, that they belong as much to other human or sentient beings as to ourselves. We find other people grounding their expectations and conduct upon the same permanent possibilities on which we ground ours. But we do not find them experiencing the same actual sensations. Other people do not have our sensations exactly when and as we have them: but they have our possibilities of sensation; whatever indicates a present possibility of sensations to ourselves, indicates a present possibility of similar sensations to them, except so far as their organs of sensation may vary from the type of ours. This puts the final seal to our conception of the groups of possibilities as the fundamental reality in Nature. The permanent possibilities are common to us and to our fellow-creatures; the actual sensations are not. That which other people become aware of when, and on the same grounds, as I do, seems more real to me than that which they do not know of unless I tell them. The world of Possible Sensations succeeding one another according to laws, is as much in other beings as it is in me; it has therefore an existence outside me; it is an External World.

If this explanation of the origin and growth of the idea of Matter, or External Nature, contains nothing at variance with natural laws, it is at least an admissible supposition, that the element of Non-ego which Sir W. Hamilton regards as an original datum of consciousness, and which we certainly do find in what we now call our consciousness, may not be one of its primitive elements—may not have existed at all in its first manifestations. But if this supposition be admissible, it ought, on Sir W. Hamilton's principles, to be received as true. The first of the laws laid down by him for the interpretation of Consciousness, the law (as he terms it) of Parcimony, forbids to suppose an original principle of our nature in order to account for phænomena which admit of possible explanation from known causes. If the supposed ingredient of consciousness be one which might grow up (though we cannot prove that it did grow up) through later experience; and if, when it had so grown up, it would, by known laws of our nature, appear as completely intuitive as our sensations themselves; we are bound, according to Sir W. Hamilton's and all sound philosophy, to assign to it that origin. Where there is a known cause adequate to account for a phænomenon, there is no justification for ascribing it to an unknown one. And what evidence does Consciousness furnish of the intuitiveness of an impression, except instantaneousness, apparent simplicity, and unconsciousness on our part of how the impression came into our minds? These features can only prove the impression to be intuitive, on the hypothesis that there are no means of accounting for them otherwise. If they not only might, but naturally would, exist, even on the supposition that it is not intuitive, we must accept the conclusion to which we are led by the Psychological Method, and which the Introspective Method furnishes absolutely nothing to contradict.

Matter, then, may be defined, a Permanent Possibility of Sensation. If I am asked, whether I believe in matter, I ask whether the questioner accepts this definition of it. If he does, I believe in matter: and so do all Berkeleians. In any other sense than this, I do not. But I affirm with confidence, that this conception of Matter includes the whole meaning attached to it by the common world, apart from philosophical, and sometimes from theological, theories. The reliance of mankind on the real existence of visible and tangible objects, means reliance on the reality and permanence of Possibilities of visual and tactual sensations, when no such sensations are actually experienced. We are warranted in believing that this is the meaning of Matter in the minds of many of its most esteemed metaphysical champions, though they themselves would not admit as much: for example, of Reid, Stewart, and Brown. For these three philosophers alleged that all mankind, including Berkeley and Hume, really believed in Matter, inasmuch as unless they did, they would not have turned aside to save themselves from running against a post. Now all which this manœuvre really proved is, that they believed in Permanent Possibilities of Sensation. We have therefore the unintentional sanction of these three eminent defenders of the existence of matter, for affirming, that to believe in Permanent Possibilities of Sensation is believing in Matter. It is hardly necessary, after such authorities, to mention Dr. Johnson, or any one else who resorts to the *argumentum baculinum* of knocking a stick against the ground.

* * * * *

Whatever relation we find to exist between any one of our sensations and something different from *it*, that same relation we have no difficulty in conceiving to exist between the sum of all our sensations and something different from *them*. The differences which our consciousness recognises between one sensation and another, give us the general notion of difference, and inseparably associate with every sensation we have, the feeling of its being different from other things: and when once this association has been formed, we can no longer conceive anything, without being able, and even being compelled, to form also the conception of something different from it. This familiarity with the idea of something different from *each* thing we know, makes it natural and easy to form the notion of something different from *all* things that we know, collectively as well as individually. It is true we can form no conception of what such a thing can be; our notion of it is merely negative; but the idea of a substance, apart from its relation to the impressions which we conceive it as making on our senses, *is* a merely negative one. There is thus no psychological obstacle to our forming the notion of a something which is neither a sensation nor a possibility of sensation, even if our consciousness does not testify to it; and nothing is more likely than that the Permanent Possibilities of sensation, to which our consciousness does testify, should be confounded in our minds with this imaginary conception. All experience attests the strength of the tendency to mistake mental abstractions, even negative ones, for substantive realities; and the Permanent Possibilities of sensation which experience guarantees, are so extremely unlike in many of their properties to actual sensations, that since we are capable of imagining something which transcends sensation, there is a great natural probability that we should suppose these to be it.

COMMENTS ■ QUESTIONS

1. It may be helpful to think of Mill's position as constituting a sort of compromise between the positions of Locke and Berkeley. Locke says that objects having primary qualities exist apart from perception. Berkeley says that nothing exists apart from perception or perceiving subjects. Mill says that when we think of objects in the world there is a *reference* to perception. According to Mill, when we think of an object, we think of the *Permanent Possibility of Sensation* that exists apart from us. We mean by an object that which, though it need not be perceived to exist, *can* be perceived by us and, moreover, can be perceived by us in many different ways. Which, if any, of the claims that Mill has made regarding the concept of a "permanent possibility of sensation" would Locke object to? Which would Berkeley object to?
2. Mill refers to the *argumentum baculinum* of Dr. Samuel Johnson, the eighteenth century British writer. What Johnson did, in one version of the story, was to proclaim that he had refuted Berkeley's idealism by kicking a stone across the road! What do you think of Johnson's "refutation"?
3. The material world, says Mill, really is nothing more than a Permanent Possibility of Sensation. Yet many philosophers and most nonphilosophers believe that the world is more than this. How, it may be asked, could they have gotten the *idea* of something more than a Permanent Possibility of Sensation unless there really were something more? Mill answers that from thinking what it is like for one thing to be different from something else, people have formed the idea of "something different from all things that we know" and different even from sensation or the possibility of sensation. Is Mill's explanation inconsistent with what Berkeley has said about abstraction? If so, does this show that Mill's explanation is wrong or that Berkeley's account of abstraction is wrong?

FRANK JACKSON

Color and Science

It is a commonplace that there is an apparent clash between the picture Science gives of the world around us and the picture our senses give us. We *sense* the world as made up of colored, materially continuous, macroscopic, stable objects; Science and, in particular, Physics, tells us that the material world is constituted of clouds of minute, colorless, highly-mobile particles.

The precise relationship between these two pictures has been a matter of considerable debate, and we will at the end of this chapter be able to give a simple and intuitively plausible account of it (namely, what I take to be Locke's account); but what I want to focus on to begin with is just one aspect of the question, namely, the implications of what Science says about the world for whether or not material things have the property of being colored. Does Science imply, contrary to what we seem to see, that the pen I am now writing with does not have the property of being blue? I will argue that it does, that Science forces us to acknowledge that physical or material things are not colored (which, as we will see, is not at all the same as saying that Science shows that every statement like "My pen is blue" is false).

* * * * *

2. My argument for the conclusion that material things are not colored derives from science in general rather than from Modern Physics in particular. Whether or not Modern Physics gives us an acceptable picture of the ultimate nature of the material world, it is clear that scientific inquiry (in all the sciences) has made enormous progress in providing causal explanations of what goes on in the world around us. The Molecular theory of gases and the laws associated with it really do explain why gases diffuse, why increase in pressure leads to decrease in volume, why increasing the temperature of a fixed volume of gas increases its pressure, and so on; the Oxidation theory of combustion really does explain (as the Phlogisten theory does not) what happens when something burns; the Newtonian theory of gravitation really does explain aspects of planetary motion;

Frank Jackson, a professor of philosophy at the Australian National University, has written many journal articles on topics in epistemology, metaphysics, and logic, and two books: Perception *and* Conditionals *(forthcoming from Basil Blackwell).*

From *Perception: A Representative Theory* by Frank Jackson, copyright (c) 1977 by Cambridge University Press. By permission of Cambridge University Press.

and so on and so forth.

These various causal explanations differ in respect of how fundamental they are; and, perhaps, as physicalists claim, the most fundamental explanations are those offered in Physics, and all the others can in principle be reduced to those offered in Physics. But all I need for my argument is the truth of certain scientific causal explanations, and, in particular, the truth of certain accounts of how the material things around us cause changes in our brains. We need not enquire into which, if any, are the most fundamental.

I will start by arguing for the intermediate conclusion that either color is a scientific property or it is not a property of material things.

3. First we need an account of what a scientific property is. A scientific property is a property appealed to by current science in explaining the causal effect of one material thing on another material thing, or a logical consequence of such a property or properties. Thus having mass and charge are scientific properties, and so is having a property in common with something, for the latter is a logical consequence of having the same mass as that thing. This definition explicitly ties being a scientific property to current explanations of causal interactions; having a certain amount of calorific fluid is thus not a scientific property, nor are any new properties which may be invoked by scientists in the future. This definition is sketchy, but sufficient for our needs.

Now consider the following argument:

pr. 1. Our reason for believing that material things are colored is (certain of) the perceptual experiences we have.[2]

pr. 2. When material things cause perceptual experiences in us, the immediate causes of these experiences are certain events in our brains.

pr. 3. The causal effect a material thing has on our brain is, as far as it is concerned, a function solely of its scientific properties.

pr. 4. If premises 2 and 3 are true, then our perceptual experiences provide no reason for believing that material things have non-scientific properties.

∴ Either color is a scientific property, or we have no reason to believe that material things are colored.

The argument is valid. Premises 2, 3 and 4 together entail the consequent of premise 4—that our perceptual experiences provide no reason for believing that material things have non-scientific properties; and this with premise 1 entails that only if color were a scientific property would we have reason to believe that material things were colored, and so, entails the conclusion. Further, the conclusion makes it totally reasonable to assert that either color is a scientific property or it is not a property of material things. For though the precise status of Occam's razor is a matter of dispute, it seems clear enough here that properties we have no reason to believe are possessed by material things are properties we ought not

---

2. This is to be understood as equivalent to "What, if anything, makes it rational to believe that material things are colored is (certain of) the perceptual experiences we have".

ascribe to them. I claim that premises 1 and 4 are true on essentially conceptual or philosophical grounds, and that premises 2 and 3 are empirically well-supported. I will consider the premises in turn.

4. (i) Premise 1 is clearly true. The reason we have for believing that material things are colored is certain of the experiences we have, in particular, the kind most people have when their eyes are open and suitably illuminated objects are before them. In short, we believe material things are colored because they *look* colored. By contrast, we believe things are shaped because, in addition to looking so, they *feel* so and behave so; and we believe some things have magnetic fields because this supposition *explains* observed phenomena; but with color it is essentially the look of things and nothing more. This is why there would be no reason to believe that things are colored in "the country of the blind".

Some behaviorists may object that our reason for believing that material things are colored is the sorting behaviour of human beings in daylight.[3] However, human beings do not believe that things are colored because they sort things in certain ways; they sort them in certain ways because they believe them to be (differently) colored. Indeed, in cases where the objects have all properties other than color in common, the only way they can sort them is on the basis of color. Moreover, we have already looked askance at Behaviorism, and surely Behaviorism applied to color is one of the least plausible manifestations of that doctrine. . . . .

(ii) Premise 2 employs the notion of an immediate cause, which may be defined in the usual way via the notion of a mediate (remote) cause. A is a *mediate* case of B if A caused B, and there is a C such that A caused C and C caused B; A is an *immediate* cause of B if it is a cause, but not a mediate one, of B. A familiar example of mediate causation is the movement of a train causing the brake van to move. The engine causes the van to move by causing the intermediate carriages to move, and the movement of those carriages then causes the van to move. In the same way, premise 2 asserts that when material objects cause perceptual experiences in humans, they do so by causing certain events in the brain which then cause the experiences. (Obviously, premise 2 presupposes the falsity of Parallelism.)

This account of how to construe premise 2 makes it clear how we show that it is true. With the train we show that the movement of the carriage next to the brake van (or, more precisely, the movement of the connecting coupling) is the immediate cause, rather than the engine's movement, by showing that (*a*) if the engine moves, but for some reason the relevant carriage does not, the van does not move, and that, (*b*) if the relevant carriage does move, although the engine does not, the van moves. In the same way, showing premise 2 true is a matter of showing that, (*a*), if the appropriate brain events occur, the experiences occur, regardless of changes in material things around us, and that, (*b*), if the brain events do not occur, neither do the experiences, regard-

3. Cf., J. J. C. Smart, "Colours", and *Philosophy and Scientific Realism*, ch. 4.

less of changes in the world around us. All neuro-physiologists accept both contentions, and they are in the best position to judge. Everything we know about how the objects around us cause sense experiences in us points to the causal chain going through the brain and central nervous system. The hypothesis that physical things act *directly* in causing sense-experiences may once have been plausible, but it is no longer.

(iii) Premise 3 asserts that the effect of the action of a material object on our brains is, as far as the object is concerned, just a (causal) function of certain of its scientific properties. What this means is that, whether or not objects have non-scientific properties, the effect they have on human brains (via light rays, contact, or whatever) depends, as far as they are concerned, solely on certain of their scientific properties. A simplified illustration of this kind of situation is when a piece of litmus paper is inserted in a liquid. Whether or not it turns red is solely a function of whether the liquid is acid or not: the density of the liquid, its temperature, and so on are all irrelevant. The property of the liquid relevant to whether the paper turns red is its degree of acidity. Likewise, according to premise 3, the properties of material objects relevant to the kind of brain event their action produces are all scientific.

Now it is known in broad outline how a material thing causes the brain events relevant to sensory experience. For those experiences particularly relevant to our perception of color, the process involves the action of light reflected from the object into the eye. And the role of the object is essentially that of modifying the wave-length composition of the light, and the properties of the object which effect this modification are scientific ones like the texture and the molecular structure of its surface.[4] The details of this account will, of course, be modified by future research on the sense organs and how they are affected by external objects, but the present approach gives every indication of being along the right lines. There is, in particular, no reason to expect that future research will uncover the need to add a brand new property to the stock of scientific properties in order to effect a satisfactory explanation of just what happens when external objects cause changes in our brains and central nervous system. In other words, we do not yet know the (operative) necessary and sufficient conditions in full detail, but we are far enough along the road to knowing them to be able to predict with fair confidence that they will not require us to invoke properties over and above those countenanced by current science.

It might reasonably be urged that premise 3 goes too far in that it supposes we have, at the present stage of scientific knowledge, sufficient reason to reject certain forms of dualist attribute theories of the person. If persons are merely their material bodies plus appropriate, *causally efficacious*, irreducibly psychological properties, it may be that certain material bodies—those belonging to sentient creatures—sometimes affect human brains in ways not fully explicable without attributing non-scien-

4. For something more than this schematic outline see, Wyburn, Pickford, and Hirst, *Human Senses and Perception*, part 1.

tific properties to these bodies. But we can admit this possibility by restricting premise 3 in a way which does not impair our argument.

If we take premise 3 to apply just to *inanimate* material things, and make the corresponding changes throughout the argument, we will end up with the conclusion that color is not a property of *inanimate* material things. But no one thinks that the bodies of persons are colored in a different sense to that in which, for example, flowers are; so that we will still be able to draw the conclusion that color is not a property of material things in general. (Alternatively, premise 3 could be restricted to those causal effects of material things on our brains *relevant to judging that they are colored*.)

(iv) The case for premise 4 is that if premises 2 and 3 are true, then the occurrence of (perceptual) experiences, any experiences at all, will be irrelevant to whether or not material things possess non-scientific properties. Because if our experiences are immediately dependent on certain of our brain events and if the only properties of material things relevant to their effect on our brains are scientific, then our experiences would be exactly the same regardless of whether or not material things had non-scientific properties in addition to their scientific ones.

The point is that, if premises 2 and 3 are true, it is unnecessary to suppose that material things have non-scientific properties in order to explain the occurrence of the relevant perceptual experiences. Indeed, the supposition that material things have non-scientific properties will not only be unnecessary, it will be quite useless. Premise 2 asserts that, when material things produce perceptual experiences in us, it is the nature of certain brain events which determines the kind of experiences produced, because these brain events are the immediate cause. And premise 2 asserts that the properties of material things relevant to the nature of the brain events they may cause, are all scientific. Therefore, if premises 2 and 3 are true, the non-scientific properties of material things, supposing there are such for the purposes of argument, have no causal role to play in the production of experiences. And so, our perceptual experiences cannot be any sort of evidence for material things having non-scientific properties. These experiences cannot be regarded as *reflecting* or *registering* the instantiation of any non-scientific properties, for they would be just the same whether or not material things had such properties.

In order to make the reasoning being advanced in support of premise 4 clearer, let us apply it in a different case.[5] Suppose I have a barometer which is normally a good indicator of approaching rain. When the reading drops sharply, it nearly always rains soon after. Now suppose the reading drops sharply on some particular occasion, but that I happen to know that the cause of this drop is a mechanical failure. Surely it is clear that, despite the past correlation between the reading dropping sharply and subsequent rain, I have no evidence whatever on this occasion for impending rain. And the reason is that, because the

5. A similar example is used to different purpose by B. Skyrms, "The Explication of '*X* knows that p' ".

drop is caused by a mechanical failure and not a drop in atmospheric pressure, it would have occurred whether or not the pressure had dropped, and so, whether or not rain were in the offing.

Thus it appears a valid epistemological principle that if I know that *p* would obtain whether or not *q* were the case, I cannot regard *p* as evidence for *q*. This is just the principle which lies behind premise 4.

This completes my argument for the conclusion that either color is a scientific property or it is not a property of material things. It is not intended to be apodeictic. Premises 2 and 3 might conceivably turn out to be false. Future research might show that material things act directly to produce perceptual experiences, or that we need to add some radically new properties to the present stock of scientific properties to explain certain interactions between material things. Either is possible, but neither is likely. And, moreover, we must believe at *t* the best theories available at *t*; and the best theories presently available favor both premises. If we do not like the conclusion, we may *hope* future research shows one or both premises are false, but we have, I think, no choice at the present time but to accept them both.

5. The final step from the intermediate conclusion that either color is a scientific property or it is not a property of material things to the desired conclusion that color is not a property of material things, is via Disjunctive Syllogism [an argument having the form a or b; not a; therefore b]: for color is not a scientific property.

The color of things does not appear in any currently accepted (or even recent) scientific causal explanations of the interactions between objects. A chemist may remark that acids turn litmus paper red, but his *explanation* of this will not mention color at all. It will be in terms of free hydrogen ions combining with certain chemicals in the paper to form new compounds with different responses to incident light waves etc., etc. There is not one causal law in which "is red", "is blue", and so on appear.

COMMENTS ■ QUESTIONS

1. Jackson presents an argument with four premises whose conclusion is, "Either color is a scientific property, or we have no reason to believe that material things are colored." He claims that the argument is valid, that is, that its conclusion follows from it premises. Do you agree? Jackson Claims, moreover, that the argument is sound (that is, is valid and also has true premises). Do you agree? If you do not agree, but believe that the argument is valid, which of the premises do you believe not to be true?
2. In essence, Jackson is defending

the primary/secondary quality distinction of John Locke. Does Jackson present a more, or a less, persuasive case than Locke? Are there any objections to the way that Locke presents *his* case that are not applicable to the way that Jackson presents *his* case?

3. One of the most important steps in Jackson's argument is the observation that no scientific explanations make reference to colors. Some critics might argue that no scientific explanations make reference to the existence of God, but that this does not show that God does not exist. In your opinion, does this response carry any weight against Jackson's position? If not, why not?

EUGENE VALBERG

A Theory of Secondary Qualities

1. One idea that has been around for a long time is that "secondary" qualities—colour, sound, temperature, taste and smell—are not really "in objects" but only "in our minds". If, however, one tries, without assuming any philosophical concepts, to argue for this view, he is likely to find it more difficult than he might have thought.

A cursory reading of Locke and Berkeley, for instance, shows that they argue that these qualities are not in objects only after having introduced their concept of "ideas". Locke: "Whatever the mind perceives in itself, or is the immediate object of perception, thought, or understanding, that I call idea; and the power to produce any idea in our mind, I call quality of the subject wherein that power is".[1] And *then* he goes on to state his view—which at that point somehow seems hardly to need arguing—that certain ideas "resemble" qualities "in" the object (size, shape, motion) and others do not (colour, taste, etc.). Similarly, Berkeley begins by introducing the notion of "sensible things" ("ideas")

1. *Essay Concerning Human Understanding*, Book II, Chapter xxiii.

Eugene Valberg teaches philosophy at the University of Nairobi, Kenya.

From Eugene Valberg, "A Theory of Secondary Qualities," *Philosophy*, vol. 55 (1980), copyright (c) by Cambridge University Press. By permission of Cambridge University Press.

as "those only which can be perceived immediately by sense",[2] and only then presents the thesis that secondary qualities are not really in objects; and once this notion is accepted, the view about secondary qualities follows rather easily.

But how could one try to establish this view without already having this notion of ideas? Well, one could as well as anything simply state it: "Do you know that things aren't really coloured in themselves or that sugar is not really sweet in itself? All that is in the object itself are molecules (etc.) moving in certain ways, causing light to be reflected towards our eyes or causing chemical events on our tongues, which in turn cause us to have a sensation of seeing blue, tasting a sweet taste, etc. But the molecules themselves aren't coloured or sweet . . . ", proceeding then to round out the picture by showing how neatly everything can be accounted for; e.g. when you have a cold, sugar might not taste sweet since your tongue may be in a different condition, and with different conditions a different sensation results, etc.

Something closer to an argument would begin by asking about the colour of such things as the sky. "Is the sky in itself really blue?" Well, everyone knows it is not, because if you go "where" the sky is you will not find anything that is blue, neither a surface nor particles, etc. What then is it that is blue, or, where is the blue colour?

The most natural response is to say that it is "not really in" the sky but is produced by various conditions in the atmosphere (light refraction, etc.) as a result of which we "see" a blue colour. But if we persist and ask, "That may tell us what *causes* us to see blue colour, but precisely *what is it* that is coloured, if it is neither a surface nor particles?", we are liable to be told it is the light. But the same problem will arise, viz. do you mean that if we could look at light rays we would find that they are themselves "literally" coloured, that they contain coloured specks or fluid? Of course not; light is no more made up of tiny coloured particles than the sky is. We are thus "driven back" to the suggestion, e.g. that the colour is in our eyes. (Only someone who has yet to succumb to philosophical reasoning would make such a suggestion, for it is not yet really a "philosophical" position but rather his original point of view—that "things are coloured in themselves"—being "shoved" from one thing (the sky, the light) to another (the eye). The peculiarly philosophical move has yet to be made, but will be shortly.) But of course this can be attacked in the same manner, viz. do you really think that if you could look into someone's eye when he is looking at the sky you would find something that is blue—that part of the eye turns blue? One final step may be attempted—to the brain—and will obviously be dealt with in a similar fashion.

At this point the non-philosopher, quite perplexed, will either suggest or at least be ripe for the *philosophical* move: well, maybe the blue colour is just "in our minds" (and therefore not "in the object" at all). All of these other things—the moisture in the atmosphere, the light, the

2. *Three Dialogues Concerning Hylas and Philonous* (First Dialogue).

events in our eyes and brain—are the *causes* of our having the sensation of blue, but the sensation and hence the blue colour itself are only in our minds.

Essentially the same reasoning constitutes Berkeley's microscope argument: ". . . is it not evident . . . that, upon the use of microscopes, . . . the colours of any object are either changed or totally disappear?"[3] In other words, the minute particles of a leaf are not themselves green—i.e. when we look at them under a microscope (which of course is the only way we can look at them) they do not look green.

Now it is an assumption shared by Locke and Berkeley that if the parts of a thing do not have colour "in" them then neither can the whole. But why? Well, what are the alternatives? If we are to say that the minute parts of a thing are not coloured but that the whole is, the "stuff" of the object must somehow "acquire" the colour when the parts come together. Perhaps the parts, when (originally) apart, do not have colour, but when (put) together they (and therefore the whole) do, whether or not they retain their colour if (again) separated. In the present case, however, this possibility is not open to us, for the parts are not separated; they are merely being looked at separately—and they can be seen to have no colour.

But the only other possibility would seem to be that a whole (or a sufficiently large part of it) has a colour while its minute parts do not, in the sense that we can only *see* the colour when we look at the whole; i.e. the leaf has the colour in it all right—it is just that you can only *see* it if you look at a sufficiently large part of it. The problem, of course, is that this is indistinguishable from what Berkeley would say, for to say that the colour of the leaf can only be seen from a distance that allows you to see a sufficient portion of it seems tantamount to saying that it is merely "apparent" in the same way as the colour of the sky. In other words, the reasoning concerning the sky can be applied to all objects, viewing things with the naked eye being parallel to seeing the sky from a distance, and seeing them through a microscope being parallel to getting "closer" to the sky.

Berkeley's main argument regarding taste is simply to point to the fact of "perceptual relativity": what ordinarily tastes sweet may taste bitter to someone with a "distempered palate", so that what we actually taste depends (in part) on the condition of our tongues. Therefore, the sweetness that we taste cannot itself be in the sugar; only the cause of it is. If we try to say that the sweetness is on the tongue, the reply is: do you think that when someone tastes something sweet part of his tongue becomes itself sweet—i.e. would taste sweet? Obviously not. Neither is there something sweet in the brain, etc. The taste of sweetness may be caused by the chemical properties of the sugar, the things that happen on our tongues and in the brain, etc., but the sweet taste itself is only in the mind.

With temperature there is a readily available instance of such relativity: if we put one hot and one cold hand in lukewarm water, it will feel cool to one and warm to the other. Therefore the temperature *that we*

3. Op. cit., First Dialogue.

feel cannot be "in the water". But the temperature we feel always depends as much on our bodies as on the things we feel. All that is really in the object are certain causes, certain motions of the minute particles, which produce various sensations in us. But, we can ask, do you think that these particles are themselves hot? Of course not. Then is their motion itself hot? That makes no sense at all. Well then, what can you say except that these particles moving in certain ways cause us to have the experience of feeling heat. And again, you certainly don't think that when something feels hot your nerve endings or part of your brain becomes hot. The heat itself, then, must only be in your mind.

2. Now while I do not think these arguments establish the doctrine of secondary qualities, they can get us to accept a certain picture of things which directly leads to it, viz. external objects affecting our sense organs and thereby producing ideas in our minds. Consider, for example, the argument used by both Locke and Berkeley which consists in effect of drawing a parallel between fire causing pain and feeling hot: just as we do not think the pain is in the fire so neither should we think the heat is. The real point of this is simply to reinforce this model of perception.

The end result is the doctrine of secondary qualities. It is important to understand that this is seen as a *revelation* or discovery in the sense of showing us something we did not previously know, viz. that colour, tastes, etc., are not "inherent in" objects. It is assumed that we ordinarily think they are, and hence that this refutes something we previously thought was true. Thus we should be able to state the following two straightforward propositions.

A. Colours (etc.) are (really) in objects

B. Colours (etc.) are not (really) in objects

such that B is the contradictory of A and says simply that A is false. Common sense is assumed to think that A is true and so would presumably reject B, whereas the doctrine of secondary qualities rejects A and asserts B.

Now obviously if B is to make sense, so must A, since B consists simply in denying A. And since B is the heart of the doctrine of secondary qualities we must, if we are to understand that doctrine, know what B—and hence A—mean. I suggest that we begin by asking the following seemingly simple question of one who holds this doctrine: "You say that colour is not in objects but only in our minds. Let us suppose you are right. Only tell me: what *would it be like* for colour to *be* in objects? I ask this because you seem to be denying that something is the case (that colour is in objects) and I simply want to know precisely *what it is* that you are denying. How would things, in any way you choose to imagine, be different if colour *was* in objects, as you say it is not?"

It may seem that in asking this I am in effect assuming some kind of verification principle. If so, then the fact that this is such a natural, reasonable and appropriate question to ask here would by itself seem to be an argument for some kind of verification principle. Certainly one answer that is not acceptable is, "Well, for a thing to be really coloured would be for the colour to be in the thing itself and not merely in our minds".

Now most persons who would accept this doctrine would not think our question particularly difficult. If the colour really was in the leaf, they might say, then when you look at it with a microscope it would still look green. And in general, those facts which lead us to say that colour is not in objects would no longer hold.

If taken to its inevitable limit, however, this will lead to something that is patently absurd. Is it being said that the molecules look green and the atoms and electrons too? And that no matter how powerful the microscope, and whatever the conditions, it will still look green? This seems so bizarre as really to need no arguing. Clearly the colour must "arise" in the sense that there is a certain structural level at which it looks green and "below" which it does not.

But even if we supposed that no matter how small the part, it still looked green, that would not prove, or even be evidence, that the colour was "inherent" in the leaf; for we would not have found that it has the colour "in" it, but only that it *looks* green under *all* conditions, whereas before it did so only to the naked eye. In other words, even if the facts which apparently lead to the doctrine of secondary qualities were not the case, and the colour of a thing did not disappear when looked at through a microscope, etc., that would not provide us with circumstances which in any clear way would define what is meant by the colour being *in the leaf itself* as opposed to being in the mind. Rather, we would have the odd (if not impossible) situation of a thing's *always looking the same colour* no matter how you looked at it. Someone who held that colour was not "in" objects could simply say, "Well, that would be very odd, but it would just mean that a molecule causes us to have a sensation of green, whereas now only a larger portion does".

One might then be tempted to say, "Well, for the colour to be really *in* the leaf would be for there to be some 'green stuff' in it". But even if we could make sense out of this "stuff", we are going to run into the same problem in explaining what it means to say that the colour "inheres" in it—that since it is indivisible and hence has no parts, no matter how you look at it (with any microscope) it looks green? Still, what does it mean to say that the colour "inheres" in it other than that it always looks green? And once it is understood that that is all you *can* say, the "stuff" becomes superfluous and we might just as well say that the molecules (etc.) are really green—i.e. always looks green.

In short, I am saying, it is impossible to give *any* meaning to the (philosophical) idea that colour is "in" the object *as opposed to* somewhere else ("in the mind"), for there is no *conceivable* observation that would constitute evidence for such an "hypothesis". In trying to say what would, we are led to such absurdities as electrons looking green, etc., and in any case are unable to say anything more than that a thing *looks* a certain colour.

From this I conclude that the *philosophical* idea of colour "inhering in an object" is unintelligible; but then so is the idea that it is *not* in objects, for obviously the latter can make sense only if the former does. And hence the (philosophical) idea of colour being "in the mind" is also without meaning, since to say that it is (only) "in our minds" is in part to say that it is not "in objects".

My assumption that for "not p" to make sense "p" must also, can be challenged by the following sort of counter-example: "Valberg's nose is President of Nigeria" is absurd and hence (in some sense) meaningless, yet "Valberg's nose is *not* President of Nigeria" is meaningful and true.[4] Correct; but notice that "Valberg's nose is not President of Nigeria" is a conceptual—and hence necessary—truth. Hence, in so far as this type of counter-example is well-taken, it implies that "colour is not in objects" is also a necessary truth. And that is in fact a philosophically important consequence, for the doctrine of secondary qualities is ordinarily taken as some kind of factual claim. Hence we could qualify our assumption to read, "For the denial of a *factual* claim to be meaningful, the claim denied must be meaningful", and at the same time accept the implication that the doctrine of secondary qualities is a necessary truth, i.e. that colour does not just happen not to be in objects, but *could* not be. But then that is essentially my thesis, since it is to say that the concept of colour being *in* objects is a logical impossibility, which, for our purposes, amounts to saying that it is "meaningless". Hence, to accept the doctrine of secondary qualities as a necessary truth is in effect to accept my thesis, for what I deny is that the concept of colour not being in objects has meaning *in opposition to* its being *in* objects. And whatever "colour is not in objects", understood as a necessary truth, means (see part III, below), it is clearly not what the doctrine of secondary qualities is ordinarily meant to assert.

Hence, the (philosophical) dichotomy between colour being in objects and its not being in objects (but only in our minds) is entirely bogus and meaningless. Yet it is just this dichotomy which underlies virtually all traditional thinking about secondary qualities. Someone who does not accept the arguments for the doctrine of secondary qualities and who thinks that colour *is* in objects is equally assuming its meaningfulness. But if in fact it has no meaning, then any discussion which presupposes that it does is fundamentally misguided.

Notice, of course, that there is an "ordinary" distinction to be made here. A white building bathed in red light would not have the red colour "on" it, and if you take a drug and "see" colours on a (white) wall, they would be "in your mind". But these ideas have meaning precisely because they have intelligible contrasts, i.e. because we know what it would be like for the colour to *be* on the building or the wall (etc.); and it is just this which is lacking in the "philosophical" use.[5]

Consider temperature. The doctrine of secondary qualities claims to have shown that heat is not really

4. Suggested by my colleague H. Odera Oruka.

5. I thank Professor Kwasi Wiredu, of the University of Ghana, for calling my attention to the usefulness of making this point, as well as for several other helpful comments on an earlier draft of this paper.

"in" what we call "hot things". But now what would it be like if it were? That a molecule, atom or electron, taken from hot water, should be hot—i.e. feel hot? Hopefully not. Then what? That no matter what the conditions of our bodies, and for all persons under all circumstances, hot water should feel hot and warm water warm, etc.? Well, aside from the near insanity of this, what would it prove? Only that our perceptual apparatus (temperature-wise) was wildly different than it is now and that certain things always feel hot. But again, this presents us with nothing more than a rather bizarre—*and, knowledge-wise, useless*—set of conditions about how and when certain things feel certain temperatures. We are no closer to the idea of things having heat "really in them", and we will never get closer, because the idea is without meaning. But then of course so is the idea that heat is *not* in objects but only "in our minds", since this derives its meaning from a denial that heat *is* "in things". But the dichotomy is without meaning and we are left with a similar conclusion—that all we can say about the temperature of things is that they feel hot or cold under such and such conditions.

3. Let us take another look at some of our earlier arguments. The microscope argument says that when you look at the minute particles of a leaf they are seen not to be green, and if the parts are not green then the colour is not "really in the leaf". In other words, since the parts are *colourless*, so is the leaf. But there appear to be two different senses of "colourless" (and "having colour") operating here, what we might call the "ordinary" and the "philosophical". Examples of the former are that fire engines are red, grass is green, and a drop of water colourless; the latter, whatever it is, is apparently different, since on it, all are equally colourless. Now in which sense are the molecules of the leaf supposed to be colourless? Well, the argument says that if you look at them (through a microscope) they will not look any colour; and if that is true then I think it is correct to say that they are colourless. So this is clearly the "ordinary" sense. But if the criterion one uses for the colour of a thing is how it looks, one cannot then turn around and say that the leaf is also colourless, since it plainly looks green and therefore, in the "ordinary" sense, is green.

In other words, there is a "shift" involved in going from the colour of the minute particles to the colour of the leaf itself. The only sense in which it is true that the molecules are colourless, and the only sense in which this is understood by anyone, is the perfectly ordinary sense of their not looking any (particular) colour. The argument gets us to admit that they are (thus) colourless and then moves to the conclusion that the leaf is colourless. But if the criterion that is in fact being used for the particles is used for the leaf, it clearly is coloured, for the same reasons and in the same way that the particles are colourless.

The fact is, there is only one kind of concept involved in all of these arguments, viz., how things look, feel, taste (etc.). When we ask the rhetorical question, do you really think that light consists of tiny coloured particles?, what we are in fact asking is, do you really think that if you could look at the particles of green light they would *look green*? We assume they would not. But more important, we are, without realizing it, using the criterion of how things look for determining their colour. Similarly, when we ask, do you really think that part of the retina (or brain) is green? we mean, do you think that if you look at it it would look green?, etc.

What I mean to point out here is threefold. (1) The typical arguments for the doctrine of secondary qualities involve a confusion between an "ordinary" (or "straightforward") sense of secondary quality predication and an apparent "philosophical" sense; they shift from saying that something is without colour in a straightforward sense to saying that it is without colour in a completely general sense, since, of course, absolutely everything turns out to be "colourless". (2) The only kinds of facts involved in all of these arguments are facts about how things look, feel, taste, etc. And (3), the fact that these arguments can be passed off so easily and convincingly is an indication that looking a certain colour (or no colour) is *in fact* accepted as (roughly) equivalent to being that colour (or colourless) and hence that the ultimately correct analysis of a thing's having colour (etc.) may be in terms of its looking that colour—which is what I will now argue.

COMMENTS ■ QUESTIONS

1. Valberg attacks the arguments both for and against the primary/secondary quality distinction by raising questions about *meaning*. Locke, Berkeley, Jackson, and many other philosophers have argued that colors are not really in objects. Valberg asks: what would it mean to say that colors *were* in objects? We need to know what this would mean, he says, because otherwise we will not know *what is being denied* by Locke and other defenders of the primary/secondary quality distinction. (Consider: Someone says, "The earth is not a cube." Unless I know what it would be like for the earth *to be* a cube, I will not understand the force of what is being said in denying that this is so.) Valberg answers the above question by saying that there is *no way* to say what it would mean for colors to be in objects as opposed to being somewhere else, such as in the mind. Do you agree with Valberg? What do you suppose Locke would say in response? What would Berkeley say? What would Jackson say?
2. One of the arguments against Valberg's position is to attack the claim stated in question 1 that for the denial of a statement to make sense the statement itself must make sense (that is, to deny that for "not p"

to make sense, "p" must make sense). Valberg's reply to this argument makes use of the important philosophical distinction between *conceptual truth and falsity*, on the one hand, and *factual truth and falsity*, on the other hand. The first of these has to do with an analysis of concepts and meaning, while the second has to do with judgments about the way the world is. Valberg's point is that in regard to conceptual truth and falsity the principle that "p" must make sense if "not p" is to make sense can be ignored; but it cannot be ignored regarding factual truths. Then he says that the claim that color is not in objects is ordinarily taken to be a factual claim; therefore, after all, to say that color is not in objects requires that we know what it would mean for color *to be* in objects as opposed to somewhere else. Now, one of the questions that needs to be asked is precisely whether the claim that color is not in objects *is* a factual truth. Frank Jackson, for one, does appear to say that it is a factual claim. Does this signal a weakness in Jackson's account, or does the weakness lie instead in Valberg's paper?

3. "If the criterion one uses for the color of a thing is how it looks, one cannot then turn around and say that the leaf is . . . colorless." What would Locke's response to this be? Jackson's response?

DAVID HUME

The Limitations of Experience

All the objects of human reason or enquiry may naturally be divided into two kinds, to wit, *Relations of Ideas*, and *Matters of Fact*. Of the first kind are the sciences of Geometry, Algebra, and Arithmetic; and in short, every affirmation which is either intuitively or demonstratively certain. *That the square of the hypothenuse is equal to the squares of the two sides*, is a proposition which expresses a relation between these figures. *That three times five is equal to the half of*

A biographical sketch of David Hume is to be found earlier in this chapter.

From *An Inquiry Concerning Human Understanding*. First published in 1748.

thirty, expresses a relation between these numbers. Propositions of this kind are discoverable by the mere operation of thought, without dependence on what is anywhere existent in the universe. Though there never were a circle or triangle in nature, the truths demonstrated by Euclid would for ever retain their certainty and evidence.

Matters of fact, which are the second objects of human reason, are not ascertained in the same manner; nor is our evidence of their truth, however great, of a like nature with the foregoing. The contrary of every matter of fact is still possible; because it can never imply a contradiction, and is conceived by the mind with the same facility and distinctness, as if ever so conformable to reality. *That the sun will not rise to-morrow* is no less intelligible a proposition, and implies no more contradiction than the affirmation, *that it will rise*. We should in vain, therefore, attempt to demonstrate its falsehood. Were it demonstratively false, it would imply a contradiction, and could never be distinctly conceived by the mind.

It may, therefore, be a subject worthy of curiosity, to enquire what is the nature of that evidence which assures us of any real existence and matter of fact, beyond the present testimony of our senses, or the records of our memory. This part of philosophy, it is observable, has been little cultivated, either by the ancients or moderns; and therefore our doubts and errors, in the prosecution of so important an enquiry, may be the more excusable; while we march through such difficult paths without any guide or direction. They may even prove useful, by exciting curiosity, and destroying that implicit faith and security, which is the bane of all reasoning and free enquiry. The discovery of defects in the common philosophy, if any such there be, will not, I presume, be a discouragement, but rather an incitement, as is usual, to attempt something more full and satisfactory than has yet been proposed to the public.

All reasonings concerning matter of fact seem to be founded on the relation of *Cause and Effect*. By means of that relation alone we can go beyond the evidence of our memory and senses. If you were to ask a man, why he believes any matter of fact, which is absent; for instance, that his friend is in the country, or in France; he would give you a reason; and this reason would be some other fact; as a letter received from him, or the knowledge of his former resolutions and promises. A man finding a watch or any other machine in a desert island, would conclude that there had once been men in that island. All our reasonings concerning fact are of the same nature. And here it is constantly supposed that there is a connexion between the present fact and that which is inferred from it. Were there nothing to bind them together, the inference would be entirely precarious. The hearing of an articulate voice and rational discourse in the dark assures us of the presence of some person: Why? because these are the effects of the human make and fabric, and closely connected with it. If we anatomize all the other reasonings of this nature, we shall find that they are founded on the relation of cause and effect, and that this relation is either near or remote, direct or collateral. Heat and light are collateral effects of fire, and the one effect may justly be inferred from the other.

If we would satisfy ourselves, therefore, concerning the nature of that evidence, which assures us of matters of fact, we must enquire how we arrive at the knowledge of cause and effect.

I shall venture to affirm, as a general proposition, which admits of no exception, that the knowledge of this relation is not, in any instance, attained by reasonings *a priori;* but arises entirely from experience, when we find that any particular objects are constantly conjoined with each other.

* * * * *

To convince us that all the laws of nature, and all the operations of bodies without exception, are known only by experience, the following reflections may, perhaps, suffice. Were any object presented to us, and were we required to pronounce concerning the effect, which will result from it, without consulting past observation; after what manner, I beseech you, must the mind proceed in this operation? It must invent or imagine some event, which it ascribes to the object as its effect; and it is plain that this invention must be entirely arbitrary. The mind can never possibly find the effect in the supposed cause, by the most accurate scrutiny and examination. For the effect is totally different from the cause, and consequently can never be discovered in it. Motion in the second Billiard-ball is a quite distinct event from motion in the first: nor is there anything in the one to suggest the smallest hint of the other. A stone or piece of metal raised into the air, and left without any support, immediately falls; but to consider the matter *a priori*, is there anything we discover in this situation which can beget the idea of a downward, rather than an upward, or any other motion, in the stone or metal?

And as the first imagination or invention of a particular effect, in all natural operations, is arbitrary, where we consult not experience; so must we also esteem the supposed tie or connexion between the cause and effect, which binds them together, and renders it impossible that any other effect could result from the operation of that cause. When I see, for instance, a Billiard-ball moving in a straight line towards another; even suppose motion in the second ball should by accident be suggested to me, as the result of their contact or impulse; may I not conceive, that a hundred different events might as well follow from that cause? May not both these balls remain at absolute rest? May not the first ball return in a straight line, or leap off from the second in any line or direction? All these suppositions are consistent and conceivable. Why then should we give the preference to one, which is no more consistent or conceivable than the rest?

* * * * *

But we have not yet attained any tolerable satisfaction with regard to the question first proposed. Each solution still gives rise to a new question as difficult as the foregoing, and leads us on to farther enquiries. When it is asked, *What is the nature of all our reasonings concerning matter of fact?* the proper answer seems to be, that they are founded on the relation of cause and effect. When again it is asked, *What is the foundation of all our reasonings and conclu-*

sions concerning that relation? it may be replied in one word, Experience. But if we still carry on our sifting humour, and ask, *What is the foundation of all conclusions from experience?* this implies a new question, which may be of more difficult solution and explication. Philosophers, that give themselves airs of superior wisdom and sufficiency, have a hard task when they encounter persons of inquisitive dispositions, who push them from every corner to which they retreat, and who are sure at last to bring them to some dangerous dilemma. The best expedient to prevent this confusion, is to be modest in our pretensions; and even to discover the difficulty ourselves before it is objected to us. By this means, we may make a kind of merit of our very ignorance.

I shall content myself, in this section, with an easy task, and shall pretend only to give a negative answer to the question here proposed. I say then, that, even after we have experience of the operations of cause and effect, our conclusions from that experience are *not* founded on reasoning, or any process of the understanding. This answer we must endeavour both to explain and to defend.

It must certainly be allowed, that nature has kept us at a great distance from all her secrets, and has afforded us only the knowledge of a few superficial qualities of objects; while she conceals from us those powers and principles on which the influence of those objects entirely depends. Our senses inform us of the colour, weight, and consistence of bread; but neither sense nor reason can ever inform us of those qualities which fit it for the nourishment and support of a human body. Sight or feeling conveys an idea of the actual motion of bodies; but as to that wonderful force or power, which would carry on a moving body for ever in a continued change of place, and which bodies never lose but by communicating it to others; of this we cannot form the most distant conception. But notwithstanding this ignorance of natural powers [1] and principles, we always presume, when we see like sensible qualities, that they have like secret powers, and expect that effects, similar to those which we have experienced, will follow from them. If a body of like colour and consistence with that bread, which we have formerly eat, be presented to us, we make no scruple of repeating the experiment, and foresee, with certainty, like nourishment and support. Now this is a process of the mind or thought, of which I would willingly know the foundation. It is allowed on all hands that there is no known connexion between the sensible qualities and the secret powers; and consequently, that the mind is not led to form such a conclusion concerning their constant and regular conjunction, by anything which it knows of their nature. As to past *Experience*, it can be allowed to give *direct* and *certain* information of those precise objects only, and that precise period of time, which fell under its cognizance: but why this experience should be extended to future times, and to other objects, which, for aught we know, may be only in ap-

1. The word, Power, is here used in a loose and popular sense. The more accurate explication of it would give additional evidence to this argument.

pearance similar; this is the main question on which I would insist. The bread, which I formerly eat, nourished me; that is, a body of such sensible qualities was, at that time, endued with such secret powers: but does it follow, that other bread must also nourish me at another time, and that like sensible qualities must always be attended with like secret powers? The consequence seems nowise necessary. At least, it must be acknowledged that there is here a consequence drawn by the mind; that there is a certain step taken; a process of thought, and an inference, which wants to be explained. These two propositions are far from being the same, *I have found that such an object has always been attended with such an effect*, and *I foresee, that other objects, which are, in appearance, similar, will be attended with similar effects*. I shall allow, if you please, that the one proposition may justly be inferred from the other; I know, in fact, that it always is inferred. But if you insist that the inference is made by a chain of reasoning, I desire you to produce that reasoning. The connexion between these propositions is not intuitive. There is required a medium, which may enable the mind to draw such an inference, if indeed it be drawn by reasoning and argument. What that medium is, I must confess, passes my comprehension; and it is incumbent on those to produce it, who assert that it really exists, and is the origin of all our conclusions concerning matter of fact.

This negative argument must certainly, in process of time, become altogether convincing, if many penetrating and able philosophers shall turn their enquiries this way and no one be ever able to discover any connecting proposition or intermediate step, which supports the understanding in this conclusion. But as the question is yet new, every reader may not trust so far to his own penetration, as to conclude, because an argument escapes his enquiry, that therefore it does not really exist. For this reason it may be requisite to venture upon a more difficult task; and enumerating all the branches of human knowledge, endeavour to show that none of them can afford such an argument.

All reasonings may be divided into two kinds, namely demonstrative reasoning, or that concerning relations of ideas, and moral reasoning, or that concerning matter of fact and existence. That there are no demonstrative arguments in the case seems evident; since it implies no contradiction that the course of nature may change, and that an object, seemingly like those which we have experienced, may be attended with different or contrary effects. May I not clearly and distinctly conceive that a body, falling from the clouds, and which, in all other respects, resembles snow, has yet the taste of salt or feeling of fire? Is there any more intelligible proposition than to affirm, that all the trees will flourish in December and January, and decay in May and June? Now whatever is intelligible, and can be distinctly conceived, implies no contradiction, and can never be proved false by any demonstrative argument or abstract reasoning *a priori*.

If we be, therefore, engaged by arguments to put trust in past experience, and make it the standard of our future judgment, these arguments must be probable only, or such as regard matter of fact and real existence, according to the division above mentioned. But that there is no argument of this kind, must appear, if our explication of that species of reasoning be admitted as solid and satisfactory. We have said that all arguments concerning existence are founded on the relation of cause and effect; that our knowledge of that relation is derived entirely from experience; and that all our experimental conclusions proceed upon the supposition that the future will be conformable to the past. To endeavour, therefore, the proof of this last supposition by probable arguments, or arguments regarding existence, must be evidently going in a circle, and taking that for granted, which is the very point in question.

In reality, all arguments from experience are founded on the similarity which we discover among natural objects, and by which we are induced to expect effects similar to those which we have found to follow from such objects. And though none but a fool or madman will ever pretend to dispute the authority of experience, or to reject that great guide of human life, it may surely be allowed a philosopher to have so much curiosity at least as to examine the principle of human nature, which gives this mighty authority to experience, and makes us draw advantage from that similarity which nature has placed among different objects. From causes which appear *similar* we expect similar effects. This is the sum of all our experimental conclusions. Now it seems evident that, if this conclusion were formed by reason, it would be as perfect at first, and upon one instance, as after ever so long a course of experience. But the case is far otherwise. Nothing so like as eggs; yet no one, on account of this appearing similarity, expects the same taste and relish in all of them. It is only after a long course of uniform experiments in any kind, that we attain a firm reliance and security with regard to a particular event. Now where is that process of reasoning which, from one instance, draws a conclusion, so different from that which it infers from a hundred instances that are nowise different from that single one? This question I propose as much for the sake of information, as with an intention of raising difficulties. I cannot find, I cannot imagine any such reasoning. But I keep my mind still open to instruction, if any one will vouchsafe to bestow it on me.

Should it be said that, from a number of uniform experiments, we *infer* a connexion between the sensible qualities and the secret powers; this, I must confess, seems the same difficulty, couched in different terms. The question still recurs, on what process of argument this *inference* is founded? Where is the medium, the interposing ideas, which join propositions so very wide of each other? It is confessed that the colour, consistence, and other sensible qualities of bread appear not, of themselves, to have any connexion with the secret powers of nourishment and support. For otherwise we could infer these secret powers from the first appearance of these sensible qualities, without the aid of experience; contrary to the sentiment of all philosophers, and contrary to plain matter of fact. Here, then, is our natural state of ignorance with regard to the powers and influence of all objects. How is this remedied by experience? It only shows us a number of uniform effects, resulting from certain objects, and teaches us that those particular objects, at that particular time, were endowed with such powers and forces. When a new object, endowed with similar sensible qualities, is produced, we expect similar powers and forces, and look for a like effect. From a body of like colour and consistence with bread we expect like nourishment and support. But this surely is a step or progress of the mind, which wants to be explained. When a man says, *I have found, in all past instances, such sensible qualities conjoined with such secret powers*: And when he says, *Similar sensible qualities will always be conjoined with similar secret powers,* he is not guilty of a tautology, nor are these propositions in any respect the same. You say that the one proposition is an inference from the other. But you must confess that the inference is not intuitive; neither is it demonstrative: Of what nature is it, then? To say it is experimental, is begging the question. For all inferences from experience suppose, as their foundation, that the future will resemble the past, and that similar powers will be conjoined with similar sensible qualities. If there be any suspicion that the course of nature may change, and that the past may be no rule for the future, all experience becomes useless, and can give rise to no inference or conclusion. It is impossible, therefore, that any arguments from experience can prove this resemblance of the past to the future; since all these arguments are founded on the supposition of that resemblance. Let the course of things be allowed hitherto ever so regular; that alone, without some new argument or inference, proves not that, for the future, it will continue so. In vain do you pretend to have learned the nature of bodies from your past experience. Their secret nature, and consequently all their effects and influence, may change, without any change in their sensible qualities. This happens sometimes, and with regard to some objects: Why may it not happen always, and with regard to all objects? What logic, what process of argument secures you against this supposition? My practice, you say, refutes my doubts. But you mistake the purport of my question. As an agent, I am quite satisfied in the point; but as a philosopher, who has some share of curiosity, I will not say scepticism, I want to learn the foundation of this inference. No reading, no enquiry has yet been able to remove my difficulty, or give me satisfaction in a matter of such importance. Can I do better than propose the difficulty to the public, even though, perhaps, I have small hopes of obtaining a solution? We shall, at least, by this means, be sensible of our ignorance, if we do not augment our knowledge.

COMMENTS ■ QUESTIONS

1. According to David Hume, the "basic building blocks" of knowledge are ideas, and all ideas come from experience of the senses. "A blind man can form no notion of colors, a deaf man of sounds." Is there any reason to doubt the correctness of Hume's position on this matter? That is, assuming that it makes sense to talk about the "basic building blocks" of knowledge, is there any reason to doubt that they all come from experience of the senses?
2. According to Hume, knowledge consists of more than its basic building blocks, or ideas; it also consists of *relations* among these basic building blocks. These relations are of two different kinds and as a consequence, according to Hume, objects of knowledge are of two different kinds. (Objects of knowledge are usually referred to by contemporary philosophers as statements or propositions; Hume calls them "objects of human reason or inquiry.") Hume insists, moreover, that there are *only* two kinds of objects of knowledge: (a) "relations of ideas" and (b) "matters of fact." By the first he means what we might want to call *mere* relations of ideas, because he maintains that their truth is dependent *solely* upon the ideas themselves ("the mere operation of thought") and not upon the world. An example is "three times five is equal to the half of thirty." The second kind of statement, or object of knowledge, does *not* derive its truth from ideas themselves, or from the "mere operation of thought." An example is "the sum will rise tomorrow." You will want to ask yourself the following questions regarding Hume's distinction between relations of ideas and matters of fact: Is there a third kind of statement that Hume has failed to mention? Does the truth of Hume's examples of relations of ideas depend *solely* upon ideas, or the operation of thought, or does it depend also upon the way the world is apart from thought? Does the truth of Hume's example of matters of fact depend *not at all* upon ideas, or the operation of thought?
3. According to Hume, the second kind of statement, or object of knowledge (what he calls "matters of fact"), depends for its truth upon what we understand to be cause and effect relationships in the world, for example, that fire is the cause of heat and light. But, says Hume, we never have any sensory experience of a causal relationship. All we experience is that certain things go together over and over again. We experience only the "repeated conjunction of events." Therefore, we do not *really know* that any cause will continue to produce what we believe to be its effect. Hume's position can be summarized as follows: All of our ideas come from experience; we

have no experience of any idea of *casual necessity* that ties together cause and effect; "relations among ideas" are not the basis for a knowledge of causal necessity; "matters of fact" are dependent upon the causal relation; therefore, there is *no knowledge* of matters of fact. We have *beliefs*, but no good reason to suppose that they are true. Such is Hume's skepticism regarding knowledge of the material world. Is his skeptical argument sound? If you believe that it is not, at what point, or points, would you say that it fails?

A. C. EWING

The "A Priori" and the Empirical

Meaning of the Distinction; "A Priori" Character of Mathematics

In the theory of knowledge, the first point that confronts us is the sharp distinction between two kinds of knowledge which have been called respectively *a priori* and empirical. Most of our knowledge we obtain by observation of the external world (sense-perception) and of ourselves (introspection). This is called empirical knowledge. But some knowledge we can obtain by simply thinking. That kind of knowledge is called *a priori*. Its chief exemplifications are to be found in logic and mathematics. In order to see that 5 + 7 = 12 we do not need to take five things and seven things, put them together, and then count the total number. We can know what the total number will be simply by thinking.

Another important difference between *a priori* and empirical knowl-

A. C. Ewing, who died in 1973, taught philosophy for many years at Cambridge University and had many visiting appointments in the United States. He was one of the most influential defenders of Rationalism. His books include The Morality of Punishment; The Individual, The State and World Government; The Definition of Good; The Fundamental Questions of Philosophy; and Non-Linguistic Philosophy.

From *The Fundamental Problems of Philosophy*, Macmillan, 1951. Reprinted by permission of Routledge and Kegan Paul.

edge is that in the case of the former we do not see merely that something, S, is in fact P, but that it must be P and why it is P. I can discover that a flower is yellow (or at least produces sensations of yellow) by looking at it, but I cannot thereby see why it is yellow or that it must be yellow. For anything I can tell it might equally well have been a red flower. But with a truth such as that 5 + 7 = 12 I do not see merely that it is a fact but that it must be a fact. It would be quite absurd to suppose that 5 + 7 might have been equal to 11 and just happened to be equal to 12, and I can see that the nature of 5 and 7 constitutes a fully adequate and intelligible reason why their sum should be 12 and not some other number. It is indeed conceivable that some of the things which make the two groups of 5 and 7 might, when they were put together, fuse like drops of water, or even vanish, so that there were no longer 12 things; but what is inconceivable is that there could *at the same time* be 5 + 7 things of a certain kind at once in a certain place and yet less than 12 things of that kind in that place. Before some of the things fused or vanished they would be 5 + 7 in number and also 12 in number, and after the fusion or disappearance they would be neither 5 + 7 nor 12. When I say in this connection that something is inconceivable, I do not mean merely or primarily that we cannot conceive it—this is not a case of a mere psychological inability like the inability to understand higher mathematics. It is a positive insight: we definitely see it to be impossible that certain things could happen. This we do not see in the case of empirical propositions which are false: they are not true but might for anything we know have been true. It is even conceivable, so far as we can see, that the fundamental laws of motion might have been quite different from what they are, but we can see that there could not have been a world which contradicted the laws of arithmetic. This is expressed by saying that empirical propositions are *contingent*, but true *a priori* propositions *necessary*. What we see to be necessary is not indeed that arithmetic should apply to the universe. It is conceivable that the universe might have been constituted entirely of a homogeneous fluid, and then, since there would have been no distinction between different things, it is difficult to see how arithmetic could have applied to it. What we do see is that arithmetic must be true of whatever can be numbered at all.

We must not be misled here by the fact that in order to come to understand arithmetic we originally required examples. Once we have learnt the beginnings of arithmetic in the kindergarten with the help of examples, we do not need examples any more to grasp it, and we can see the truth of many arithmetical propositions, e.g. that 3112 + 2467 = 5579, of which we have never had examples. We have probably never taken 3112 things and 2467 things, put them together and counted the resulting set, but we still know that this is what the result of the counting would be. If it were empirical knowledge, we could not know it without counting. The examples are needed, not to prove anything, but only in order to enable us to come to understand in the first instance what is meant by number.

In geometry we indeed stand more in need of examples than in arithmetic, though I think this is only a psychological matter. In arithmetic we only need examples at the most elementary stage, but in geometry most people need a drawn figure, or at least an image of one in their minds, to see the validity of most proofs. But we must distinguish between an illustration and the basis of a proof. If the particular figure were not merely an illustration but the basis of the theorem, the latter would have to be proved by measuring it, but a measurement with a ruler or protractor never figures in Euclid's proofs. That the proof is not really based on the figure drawn is shown by the fact that we can still follow a proof concerning the properties of right-angled triangles even if the figure used to illustrate it is so badly drawn that it is obviously not a right-angled triangle at all. Again, if geometry were empirical, it would be a very hazardous speculation from the single example before us on the blackboard to conclude that all triangles had a property. It might be an individual idiosyncracy of some triangles and not others. These considerations should be conclusive of themselves, but we might add that recent developments in geometry have had the effect of much loosening the connection between geometrical proofs and the empirical figure. It is possible to work out non-Euclidean geometries where we cannot depend on figures.

The "A Priori" in Logic

Another important field for *a priori* knowledge is logic. The laws of logic must be known *a priori* or not at all. They certainly are not a matter for empirical observation, and the function of logical argument is just to give us conclusions which we have not discovered by observation. The argument would be superfluous if we had observed them already. We are able to make inferences because there is sometimes a logical connection between one or more propositions (the premise or premises) and another proposition, the conclusion, such that the latter must be true if the former is. Then, if we know the former, we can assert the latter on the strength of it, thus anticipating any experience. To take an example, there is a story that Mr. X., a man of high reputation and great social standing, had been asked to preside at a big social function. He was late in coming, and so a Roman Catholic priest was asked to make a speech to pass the time till his arrival. The priest told various anecdotes, including one which recorded his embarrassment when as confessor he had to deal with his first penitent and the latter confessed to a particularly atrocious murder. Shortly afterwards Mr. X. arrived, and in his own speech he said: "I see Father ______ is here. Now, though he may not recognize me, he is an old friend of mine, in fact I was his first penitent." It is plain that such an episode would enable one to infer that Mr. X. had committed a murder without having observed the crime. The form of inference involved: The first penitent was a murderer, Mr. X. was the first penitent, therefore Mr. X. was a murderer—is of the famous kind to which logicians have given the name of *syllogism*. The importance of syllogisms has often been exaggerated, but they are as important as any kind of inference, and we cannot deny that in many cases a syllogism has given people information of which they were not in any ordinary sense aware before they used the syllogism and which they did not acquire by observation. Inference is only possible because there are special connections between the propositions involved such that one necessarily follows from others. It is a chief function of logic to study these connections, of which that expressed in the syllogism is by no means the only one.

(A *syllogism* consists of three propositions, two forming the *premises* and the other the *conclusion*. Each proposition can be expressed by a subject and predicate connected by the verb "to be," the *copula*, and if we call everything which stands as either subject or predicate a *term*, there must be three and only three terms in the syllogism. The one common to the two premises is called the *middle term*, and it is on this common element that the inference depends. The other two, having been connected by means of it, occur without it in the conclusion. Thus in the usual example of the syllogism—All men are mortal, Socrates is a man, ∴Socrates is mortal—"man" is the middle term connecting Socrates with mortality so that we could, even if he had not already died, know that he was mortal.)

Other Cases of the "A Priori"

A priori knowledge, while most prominent in mathematics and logic, is not limited to these subjects. For instance, we can see *a priori* that the same surface cannot have two different colours all over at the same time, or that a thought cannot have a shape. Philosphers have been divided into *rationalists* and *empiricists* according to whether they stressed the *a priori* or the empirical element more. The possibility of metaphysics depends on *a priori* knowledge, for our experience is quite inadequate to enable us to make on merely empirical grounds any sweeping generalizations of the kind the metaphysician desires. The term *a priori* covers both self-evident propositions, i.e. those which are seen to be true in their own right, and those which are derived by inference from propositions themselves self-evident.

The Linguistic Theory of the "A Priori" and the Denial That "A Priori" Propositions or Inferences Can Give New Knowledge

At the present time even empiricist philosophers recognize the impossibility of explaining away *a priori* propositions as merely empirical generalizations, but they are inclined to the view that *a priori* propositions and *a priori* reasoning are merely concerned with language, and so cannot tell us anything new about the real world. Thus it is said that, when we make an inference, the conclusion is just part of the premises expressed in different language.[1] If so, inference would be of use merely for clarifying our language and would involve no real advance in knowledge. Some inferences are of this type, e.g. A is a father, there-

1. This theory is not applied to *inductive* inference.

fore A is male. But are they all? That would be hard indeed to square with the *prima facie* novelty of many conclusions. Take, for instance, the proposition that the square on the hypotenuse of a right-angled triangle is equal to the sum of the squares on the other two sides. Such a proposition can be inferred from the axioms and postulates of Euclid, but it certainly does not seem to be included in their meaning.[2] Otherwise we should know it as soon as we understood the axioms and postulates. The example I gave of the murder discovered by a logical argument seems to be another case of a fact not known at all beforehand by the reasoner which is discovered by his reasoning. Extreme empiricist philosophers contend that this appearance of novelty is really illusory, and that in some sense we knew the conclusion all along; but they have never succeeded in making clear in what sense we did so. It is not enough to say that the conclusion is implicit in the premises. "Implicit" means "implied by," and of course a conclusion is implied by its premises, if the inference is correct at all.[3] But this admission leaves quite open the question whether or not a proposition can follow from a different one which does not contain it as part of itself; and since we obviously can by deductive inference come to know things which we did not know before in any ordinary sense of "know," we must treat the empiricist's claim as unjustified till he has produced a clearly defined sense of "implicit in" or "contained in" which leaves room for that novelty in inference which we all cannot help really admitting. In any ordinary sense of "know" the conclusion is not in the cases I have mentioned known prior to the inference, and since the premises are and indeed must be known before we know the conclusion, it is therefore in no ordinary sense of "part" part of the premises.

It is indeed sometimes said that the premises include the conclusion in a confused form, but it is obvious that the beginner in geometry cannot be said to be aware of Pythagoras's theorem even in a confused form though he may know all the premises from which it can be deduced. Nor does awareness of the propositions that A was B's first penitent and that B's first penitent was a murderer include even confusedly the awareness that A was a murderer as long as the premises are not combined. When they are combined therefore something new appears that was not present to consciousness before in any way; there is a new discovery. We can also show by definite logical argument that the interpretation we are discussing does not enable one to avoid the admission of novelty in inference. For, what is it to know something in a confused

2. It is no objection to this illustration that Euclidean geometry has not been proved true of the physical world, for the proposition in question undoubtedly follows from the premises of Euclid and therefore should on the theory we are discussing be included as part of them. What is denied by modern scientists is not that the conclusion follows from the premises, but that the premises and what follows from them are true of the world.

3. Similarly, the phrase "is contained in" is sometimes used just to mean "follows from" or "is implied by" and need not connote that the conclusion is actually part of the premises, as would be the case on the literal meaning of "contained."

form? It is surely to know some general attributes present in a whole but not others. To be aware of *p* even confusedly must involve discriminating some general attributes in *p*, and those are given in the premises, which are admittedly understood in some degree. If we do not discriminate any attributes, the confusion is too great for argument to be possible at all. Now it is admitted that, when we reach the conclusion, we do discriminate attributes which we did not discriminate before, even if they are alleged to have been contained in the confused whole which was present to our minds before we started inferring. It is further admitted that the conclusion follows necessarily from the premises. Therefore the general attributes which we discriminated at the time when we knew only the premises and not the conclusion must be linked with the attributes we discriminate afterwards in such a way that the latter follow necessarily from the former. So we still have to admit that sheer *a priori* inference can enable us to discover new attributes. In some cases it may take a good while to draw the inference, in other cases it may be practically instantaneous as soon as the premises are known and combined, but whether it takes a long or a short time to draw the inference cannot be relevant to the principle.

Nevertheless, the view that inference cannot yield new conclusions dies hard, and so it will not be superfluous to bring further arguments. (1) "This has shape" admittedly follows logically from "this has size" and vice versa. If the view I am criticizing were true, "this has size" would, therefore, have to include in its meaning "this has shape," and "this has shape" would also have to include in its meaning "this has size." But this would only be possible if the two sentences meant exactly the same thing, which they obviously do not. (2) Take an argument such as—Montreal is to the north of New York, New York is to the north of Washington, therefore Montreal is to the north of Washington. If the view I am discussing is true, the conclusion is part of the premises. But it is not part of either premise by itself, otherwise both premises would not be needed. So the only way in which it could be part of both together would be if it were divisible into two propositions one of which was part of the first and the other part of the second. I defy anybody to divide it in this way. (3) The proposition "Socrates was a philosopher" certainly entails the proposition "if Socrates had measles some philosophers have had measles," but it cannot be that the second proposition is included in the first. For the first proposition certainly does not include the notion of measles.

What is really the same view is often expressed by saying that all *a priori* propositions are "analytic." A distinction has commonly been drawn between *analytic* propositions, in which the predicate is in the notion of the subject already formed before the proposition is asserted, so that the proposition gives no new information, and *synthetic* propositions in which the predicate is not so contained and which are thus capable of giving new information.[4] Analytic

4. This definition would have to be amended slightly to suit modern logicians

propositions are essentially verbal, being all true by definition, e.g. all fathers are male. As an example of a synthetic proposition we could take any proposition established by experience such as "I am cold" or "It is snowing," but empiricists often assert that there are no synthetic *a priori* propositions. That this view cannot be justified may be shown at once. The proposition that there are no synthetic *a priori* propositions, since it cannot be established by empirical observations, would be, if justified, itself a synthetic *a priori* proposition, and we cannot affirm it as a synthetic *a priori* proposition that there are no synthetic *a priori* propositions. We may therefore dismiss off-hand any arguments for the theory. Such arguments, whatever they were, would have to involve synthetic *a priori* propositions. Further, the view must be false if it is ever true that the conclusion of an inference is not part of its premises. For, if the proposition—S is Q—ever follows validly from—S is P, the proposition—all that is SP is SQ, must be true *a priori*. But, unless the concept Q is part of the concept SP, the proposition—all that is SP is SQ—cannot be analytic. Therefore our arguments against the view that in all valid inferences the conclusion is part of the premises expressed in different language are also arguments against the view that all *a priori* propositions are analytic.

The analytic view seems plausible when we are concerned with the simplest propositions of logic and arithmetic, but we must not assume that a proposition is analytic because it is obvious. Though it may be very difficult to determine precisely where analytic propositions end and synthetic propositions begin, we cannot use this as a ground for denying the latter. It is very difficult to say precisely where blue ends and green begins, since the different shades run into each other imperceptibly, but we cannot therefore argue that all blue is really green. Taking arithmetic, even if there is a good deal of plausibility in saying that $2 + 2$ is included in the meaning of "4," there is none in saying $95 - 91$ or $\frac{216}{2} - \frac{287 + 25}{3}$ are so included. Yet, if the analytic view were true, all the infinite numerical combinations which could be seen *a priori* to be equal to 4 would have to be included in the meaning of "4."

Some empiricists, without committing themselves to the view that all *a priori* propositions are analytic, still say these are a matter of arbitrary choice or verbal convention. They are influenced here by a modern development in the view of geometry. It used to be held that the axioms of Euclid expressed a direct insight into the nature of physical space, but this is denied by modern scientists, and the view is taken that they are arbitrary postulates which geometricians make because they are interested in what would follow *if* they were true. Whether they are true or not is then a matter of empirical fact to be decided by science. But, even if this suggests that the premises of our *a priori* arguments may be arbitrary postulates, this does not make the subsequent steps arbitrary. From the postulates of Euclid

---

who (I think, rightly) deny that all propositions are of the subject-predicate form, but this would not alter the principle though importing a complication of detail with which we need not deal here.

it follows that the three angles of a triangle are equal to two right angles. If the original postulates are arbitrary, it is not certain that the conclusion is true of the real world; but it is still not an arbitrary matter that it follows from the postulates. The postulates may well be false, but there can be no doubt that *if* they were true the conclusions must be so, and it is in this hypothetical working out of the consequences of postulates which may not be true that pure geometry consists. The *a priori* necessity of pure geometry is not therefore in the least invalidated by modern developments. What is *a priori* is that the conclusions follow from the axioms and postulates, and this is not at all affected by the (empirical) discovery that not all the axioms and postulates exactly apply to the physical world. (Applied Euclidean geometry is possible in practice because it is an empirical fact that they approximately apply. The divergencies only show themselves when we consider unusually great velocities or distances.)

If not only the postulates but the successive stages in the inference were themselves arbitrary, we might just as well infer from the same premises that the angles of a triangle were equal to a million right angles or to none at all. All point in inference would be lost. Dictators may do a great deal, but they cannot alter the laws of logic and mathematics; these laws would not change even if by a system of intensive totalitarian education every human being were persuaded to fall in with a world dictator's whim in the matter and believe they were different from what they are. Nor can they change with alterations in language, though they may be expressed differently. That the truth of *a priori* propositions does not just depend on the nature of language can be easily seen when we consider that, even if we do not know any Fijian or Hottentot, we can know that also in these languages and not only in the languages we know the propositions $5 + 7 = 12$ must be true. It is of course true that by altering the meaning of the words we could make the proposition we expressed by "$5 + 7 = 12$" false, e.g. if I used "12" in a new sense to mean what other people mean by "11," but then it would be a different proposition. I could play the same trick with empirical propositions and say truly, e.g., that "fire does not burn" or "there is an elephant in this room" if I used "burn" to mean "drown" or "elephant" to mean "table." This does not in the least impair the obviousness of the contrary propositions established by experience. Finally, as we argued above that the proposition that there can be no synthetic *a priori* propositions would itself, if justified, have to be a synthetic *a priori* proposition, so we may argue that the proposition that all *a priori* propositions are a matter of arbitrary linguistic convention would, if true, have to be itself a matter of arbitrary linguistic convention. It therefore could not be vindicated by any argument and would be merely a matter of a new usage of words arbitrarily established by the persons who assert it, since it certainly does not express the usual meaning of "*a priori* propositions." So we must reject any attempt to explain away the *a priori* as a genuine source of new knowledge. If the attempt had succeeded, we should have had to admit that philosophy in anything like its old sense was impossible, for philosophy clearly cannot be based merely on observation.

The views we have been criticizing contain the following elements of truth. (1) *A priori* propositions can be seen to be true and the conclusions of an inference seem to follow from their premises without any further observation, provided we understand the meaning of the words used. But to say that q follows from p once we understand the meaning of the words is not to say that q is part of the meaning of the words used to express p. "Follow from" and "be part of" are not synonyms. (2) If q follows from p you cannot assert p and deny q without contradicting yourself, but this is only to say that in that case the denial of q implies the denial of p. It is not to say that q is part of what you assert when you assert p, unless we already assume that what is implied is always part of what implies it, i.e. beg the question at issue. (3) An *a priori* proposition cannot be fully understood without being seen to be true. It may be impossible to understand something fully without understanding something else not included in it at all, so it may still be synthetic.

People have been inclined to deny synthetic *a priori* propositions because they could not see how one characteristic could necessarily involve another, but that this could not happen would be itself a synthetic *a priori* metaphysical proposition. People have also thought that it was necessary to give some sort of explanation of *a priori* knowledge, and could not see how this could be done except in terms of language. To this I should reply that there is no reason to suppose that *a priori* knowledge requires some special explanation any more than does our ability to attain knowledge empirically by observation. Why not take it as an ultimate fact? Human beings certainly cannot explain everything, whether there is ultimately an explanation for it or not.

COMMENTS ■ QUESTIONS

1. The distinction that A. C. Ewing draws between *a priori knowledge* and *empirical knowledge* is in some important respects similar to the distinction that David Hume, in the preceding reading selection, draws between "relations of ideas" and "matters of fact." In what ways are the two distinctions *different?*
2. The claim that all a priori statements, or propositions, are analytic is approximately equivalent to Hume's claim that only "relations of ideas" are "intuitively or demonstrably certain," and that the truth of "relations of ideas" depends solely upon ideas and the operations of thought, and not at all upon the world apart from thought. Against this position, Ewing argues that some a priori propositions are "synthetic," not analytic. Has Ewing successfully

shown that this is the case, and that the position of David Hume is not correct? Or is Hume's position the correct one?

3. In discussing the statement that 5 plus 7 equals 12, Ewing says the following: "When I say in this connection that something is inconceivable, I do not mean merely or primarily that we cannot conceive it . . . . It is a positive insight: we definitely see it to be impossible that certain things could happen." Comment on this quotation. What would David Hume's response to it be?

READINGS

Ammerman, Robert A., and Marcus G. Singer, eds. *Belief, Knowledge, and Truth.* New York: Scribner's, 1970. Very useful readings on the major problems in epistemology.

Armstrong, D. M., and C. B. Martin, eds. *Locke and Berkeley: A Collection of Essays.* Notre Dame: University of Notre Dame Press, 1968. Contains many excellent papers on Locke and Berkeley.

Arner, Douglas G., ed. *Perception, Reason, and Knowledge.* Glenview, Ill.: Scott, Foresman, 1972. A very useable collection of excerpts from Hume, Locke, Berkeley, Descartes, Kant, and others.

Ayer, A. J. *Language, Truth, and Logic.* New York: Dover, 1946. Defends the view that all a priori propositions are analytic.

Ayer, A. J. *The Problem of Knowledge.* New York: St. Martin's Press, 1956. A very good general introduction.

Blanshard, Brand. *Reason and Analysis.* LaSalle, Ill.: Open Court. Contains forceful arguments against many of the empiricist claims of David Hume and his followers.

Chisholm, Roderick M., and Robert J. Swartz, eds. *Empirical Knowledge: Readings from Contemporary Sources.* Englewood Cliffs, N.J.: Prentice-Hall, 1973. A very useful collection.

Cormman, James, and Keith Lehrer, *Philosophical Problems and Arguments: An Introduction.* New York: Macmillan, 1968. Contains a very clear and comprehensive introduction to the philosophy of perception.

Gregory, R. L. *Eye and Brain.* New York: McGraw-Hill, 1973. A good introduction to the psychology of perception.

Hamlyn, D. W. *The Theory of Knowledge.* New York: Doubleday, Anchor Books, 1970. A particularly good discussion of issues in epistemology, clear and comprehensive.

Nagel, E., and R. Brandt, eds. *Meaning and Knowledge.* New York: Harcourt Brace Jovanovich, 1965. An excellent, comprehensive anthology.

Pappas, George S., ed. *Justification and Knowledge: New Studies* in *Empistemology*. Dortrecht, Holland: D. Reidel, 1980. One of the best and most up-to-date anthologies.

Pitcher, George. *A Theory of Perception.* Princeton: Princeton University Press, 1971. Defends a nonrepresentational, causal theory of perception—a version of "direct realism."

Russell, Bertrand. *Problems of Philosophy.* London: Oxford University Press, 1912. An excellent and widely read introduction to epistemology and some other issues in philosophy.

Sumer, L. W. and John Woods, eds. *Necessary Truth.* New York: Random House, 1970. A collection of papers that have been widely referred to.

Swartz, Robert J., eds. *Perceiving, Sensing, Knowing.* New York: Doubleday, Anchor Books, 1965. A good collection of modern studies.

Unger, Peter. *Ignorance.* London: Oxford University Press, 1975. A contemporary defense of skepticism.

Vesey, Godfrey, *Perception*. Garden City, N.Y.: Doubleday, 1971. Criticizes causal theories of perception.

CHAPTER ELEVEN

We are at a crossroads in human history. Never before has there been a moment so simultaneously perilous and promising.

—*Carl Sagan*

The advantages of hindsight show how easy it might have been to avoid the tragedy of Hiroshima and Nagasaki.

—*Peter Pringle and James Spigelman*

Technology and Values

This chapter is the last of three whose primary subject matter is the study of values. It differs from the others in several important ways. First, chapter 8, "The Foundations of Morality," and chapter 9, "Egoism and Altruism," have to do with the "timeless" questions that people most often think of as belonging to philosophy. Philosophers have been discussing the foundations of morality and the issue of egoism versus altruism for at least 2500 years. In contrast, the philosophical discussion of technology in relation to values goes back only about 150 years, to the time when the Industrial Revolution first made a dramatic impact upon civilization. Some of the more specific issues covered in this chapter, such as the morality of genetic engineering, date back no more than one or two decades. It is not true that philosophy addresses only the so-called "timeless" questions.

As a related point of contrast, this chapter is unlike chapters 8 and 9 in its concern with specific normative questions, that is, questions about specific values as opposed to the broad metaethical and theoretical questions that are addressed in the earlier chapters. The following are examples of the normative questions raised by the readings for the present chapter:

- To what extent is civilization threatened by the existence of nuclear weapons? What is the best way to respond to the threat?
- To what extent should wilderness areas be protected against the encroachments of civilization? What human purposes should wilderness serve?
- What can be done about the "diseases of civilization" that are caused by pollution, psychological stress, and other changes in the quality of life?
- In what ways should genetic engineering be controlled? In what ways can genetic engineering improve the quality of life?

Questions such as these presuppose answers to the broader questions of chapters 8 and 9. For example, the question about pollution presupposes a broad view of each person's moral responsibilities to other people. At the same time, an examination of the impact of technological civilization may cause us to reassess our answers to some of the broader questions in ethics. Hence, this chapter should be thought of as both applying and possibly amplifying the lessons to be learned from the earlier chapters.

A third difference between this chapter and chapters 8 and 9 is that its subject matter is much more urgent than that of the earlier chapters. One incontrovertible fact regarding the impact of technology is that, after many thousands of years of history and prehistory, human beings can now hurt themselves in the most profound ways imaginable. As everyone is aware, present-day technological civilization contains dangers that were unimaginable only a few years ago, ranging from the threat of nuclear war to the threat of producing new and deadly disease organisms and the threat of poisoning the atmosphere. This need not mean that technological civilization is a bad thing. Without question, it *does* mean that the human race has finally grown up. Human beings are now adults, no longer playing with the relatively innocuous toys of earlier times. Until the dawn of the nuclear age, while it was true that human beings could kill each other (admittedly in increasingly more effective ways), they could not possibly destroy the human race. We now live in a time when questions of practical morality have taken on an entirely new kind of urgency.

As a consequence, the role of philosophy has changed. In today's world philosophy cannot be thought of as a mere luxury, not that it ever was viewed as such by serious-minded people. One testament to this is the great increase over the past two decades in the emphasis that professional philosophers place on *applied philosophy*, which is the concern of the present chapter.

Now, it will readily be seen that the study of technology and values is broader in scope than what is indicated by the readings for this chapter. With this point in mind, it may be helpful to list all of the most important and morally significant ways that technology has affected our lives.

1. Technology has enabled a great many more people to exist. In terms of the basic utilitarian moral principle (referred to in chapter 8), according to which human actions should always aim to bring about the greatest good for the greatest number of people, the increase in the world's population is perhaps the most important benefit of technology. On the negative side, the world's population is increasing at such a high rate that it threatens to exhaust many essential resources. For people living in the most crowded countries, high population levels have very much hurt the overall quality of life.

2. Technology has enabled human beings to help each other on a grand scale. Because people cannot give what they do not have, in earlier times the realities of the world severely restricted the humanitarian spirit. Now a great many more people have the means to be generous, and governments have a much greater tax base to support programs that help the needy. The other side of the coin is the phenomenon of "welfare dependency," which occurs when people are given more material help than they are able to benefit from.

3. Technology has made books, high quality works of art, sophisticated music, and so on available to almost everyone in advanced countries. By contrast, before industrialization, even in the richest and freest countries only a tiny fraction of the population had ready access to these things. The dark side of the

picture is that mass production has often fostered the distribution of books, art, and so on embodying standards that appeal to the lowest common denominator in popular taste.

4. By decreasing drastically the number of mothers who die in childbirth and the number of children who die before growing up, technology has removed what was perhaps the most heartbreaking aspect of life for people in earlier times—the great likelihood that loved ones would die young. The negative concomitant of this is that technology has produced some entirely new circumstances in which young people may die. Auto accidents are probably the best example.

5. The pace and quality of life have been changed by technology. On the positive side, labor-saving machinery has liberated the population at large from what someone has referred to as the "unmechanized horrors" of preindustrial times. This liberating effect has been felt by even the richest and most fortunate human beings; it has changed the lives of almost everyone else in the most revolutionary way. On the negative side, industrial squalor and the frantic, stressful pace of many present-day jobs have taken their toll on human happiness.

6. The technological development of civilization has, on the whole, given people more leisure time to enjoy themselves. A possible drawback is that, once people are freed from the grim task of working simply to survive, they may wonder what the purpose of life is. They may find a new emptiness in their lives that needs to be filled.

7. Technology has multiplied manyfold the creative opportunities of human beings, as for example, in architecture and the interior design and decoration of homes and offices; in music, motion pictures, and television; in the creation of new vehicles, including space vehicles; in unifying and ordering vast complexities through the use of computers; in inventing all manner of new machines; and in finding new solutions to old problems of disease, hunger, earthquakes, floods, and storms. The negative side of all this is that people can be creative not only in constructive ways but also in destructive ways.

The first reading selection for this chapter begins with a description of the atomic test in 1945 that inaugurated the nuclear age. It also describes events following the test that led to President Truman's decision to drop atom bombs on Hiroshima and Nagasaki. The man referred to as Groves near the beginning of the selection was General Leslie Groves, head of the Manhattan Project, begun in 1942 for the purpose of producing an atom bomb. Robert Oppenheimer was the physicist chosen by Groves to direct the facility at Los Alamos where the first atom bomb was designed and assembled. The Manhattan Project was not restricted to Los Alamos, but involved many factories around the country that produced components—most importantly, uranium 235 and the plutonium used in the 1945 test—for the first atom bombs.

The man referred to as Szilard was Leo Szilard, who apparently was the first physicist who took seriously the possibility of producing an atom bomb. A Hungarian who emigrated to Great Britain in 1935, he soon obtained two British patents for possible ways to make an atom bomb. He urged first Great Britain and then the United States to develop atomic weapons. At Szilard's request Albert Einstein wrote to President Roosevelt to argue in favor of atomic weapons.

Szilard, Einstein, and others believed that the Allies should work on the bomb in self-defense, against the possibility that Germany would build it first. However, as the reading selection indicates, Szilard and other physicists opposed Truman's decision to drop the first bombs on Japan.

The second selection is on a very different topic, the question of what value wilderness areas have. William Godfrey-Smith discusses two possible sorts of justification for the preservation of wilderness: (1) the "instrumental justification," according to which wilderness should be preserved for its beneficial effects (in Godfrey-Smith's words, because it may serve as a cathedral, a laboratory, a silo, or a gymnasium), and (2) the "wholistic view of nature," according to which human beings and nature should be thought of as forming a moral community.

The paper by René Dubos is on the subject of human ecology, which Dubos defines as "a consideration of the adaptive responses of man to the demands of his environment as an expression of his place on a health-disease continuum." Dubos' focus is on the ways that contemporary industrial environments contribute to ill health.

In the future, one of the possible ways to combat the "diseases of civilization" discussed by Dubos, and other problems as well, will be through the application of genetic engineering to human beings, plants, and animals. The article by Stephen P. Stich is addressed to moral issues in genetic engineering.

The last reading, from a book by Carl Sagan, presents an engaging overview—more optimistic than pessimistic—of the good and bad aspects of technology.

One reading for the next chapter, by Po-Keung Ip, is directly relevant to this chapter. Ip argues that some concepts from Chinese Taoism can effectively be appealed to in establishing the foundations for environmental ethics.

RENÉ DUBOS

Scientific research, properly focused, [can] usefully complement the traditional humanistic approach to the study of human life.

—*So Human An Animal*

Fitness achieved through constant medical care has distressing social and economic implications for the future.

—*Man, Medicine, and Environment*

All sensible persons know that the best experiences of life are free and depend wholly upon our direct perception of the world—as when we feel glad to be alive, to be the kind of person we are, to be amidst unspoiled scenery, to be doing what we like to do.

—*Celebrations of Life*

René Dubos (1901–1982), a noted microbiologist and environmentalist, became well known both for his work as an experimental scientist and for his popular writings. He wrote more than twenty books, receiving a Pulitzer Prize in 1969 for *So Human An Animal*. Born in France, Dubos emigrated to America at the age of twenty-four. During most of his career he was at Rockefeller University, where his interests ranged from the study of disease-causing bacteria to the effects of nutrition and sanitation upon animal life and the effects of the environment upon human health and happiness. Among his best known books are *Man, Medicine, and Environment; The Bacterial Cell in Its Relation to Problems of Virulence; Celebrations of Life; A God Within*; and *The Dreams of Reason: Science and Utopias*.

PETER PRINGLE AND JAMES SPIGELMAN

The Beginnings of the Nuclear Age

* * * * *

The morning of July 16, 1945, began with steady rain over the Journado del Muerto, a desert area on part of the Alamogordo bombing range in New Mexico. Atop a one-hundred-foot metal tower sat the plutonium bomb. At three points ten thousand yards (nearly six miles) from the tower, observation dugouts were filled with nervous scientists and military men. Groves had given the order for the test to go ahead at 5:30 A.M. At 5:29:45 precisely, a pinprick of searing white light pierced the desert darkness from the top of the tower. Within a fraction of a second a terrifying fireball had vaporized the tower, turned the desert sand into glass, and was climbing into the dawn sky. The temperature at the fireball's center was four times that at the center of the sun and more than ten thousand times that at the sun's surface.

Oppenheimer's face, tense and drawn over the final hours, at last appeared relaxed. His thoughts, he said later, turned to the sacred Hindu epic, the Bhagavad Gita:

> if the radiance of a thousand suns
> were to burst at once into the sky,
> that would be like the splendor of the mighty one ...
> I am become death,
> the shatterer of worlds.

Groves, sitting on the ground in a dugout between Bush and Conant, shook hands with them in silence. His more pedestrian mind could only summon up the image of Blondin's successful crossing of Niagara Falls on his tightrope. "Only this tightrope had lasted three years," he observed.

As the shock wave reached the observation dugouts, Enrico Fermi let fall a few pieces of paper he had kept in his pocket for the occasion.

Peter Pringle, who was educated at Oxford, is a journalist whose employers have included the London *Sunday Times and the* London *Observer. He has covered Washington, the Middle East, Africa, Europe, and Latin American. In addition to* The Nuclear Barons, *he is author of* Insight on the Middle East War *and* Insight on Portugal. *James Spigelman has held several positions in the Australian government, including Senior Advisor and Principle Private Secretary to the Prime Minister. His other publications include* Secrecy: Political Censorship in Australia.

From *The Nuclear Barons* by Peter Pringle and James Spigelman. Copyright (c) 1981 by Peter Pringle and James Spigelman. Reprinted by permission of Henry Holt and Company.

Watching and measuring how far they were blown by the shock wave, he pulled out his slide rule and made a rapid calculation. The paper had sailed two and a half yards away. "That corresponds to a blast produced by ten thousand tons of TNT," Fermi announced.

Groves turned to his aides. "We must keep this thing quiet," he ordered. "Sir," said an aide, "I think they have heard the noise in five states."

Indeed, some alarmed citizens had actually witnessed the flash of light from as far away as 150 miles. It was like the sun coming up and going down again, one woman observed. For quizzical citizens, the army had concocted a story about an explosion at an ammunition dump. It produced such a brilliant flash, they said, because the dump had contained a mixture of high explosives and pyrotechnics. Groves had prepared an excuse that would both explain and forewarn should the radioactive fallout from the bomb become hazardous enough to force evacuation of the locals; weather conditions affecting the content of some gas shells that had been exploded by the blast might blow poison gases over populated areas. As the radioactive cloud drifted north from the test site, however, Groves determined that no evacuation was necessary, and therefore no one had cause to ask why the army had been so idiotic as to store poison gas shells near an ammunition dump—or, indeed, what they were doing with the poison gas.

Several months before the Alamogordo test, the defeat of Nazi Germany had become a reality, and some of the Manhattan Project scientists, particularly the immigrant physicists from Europe like Szilard and Wigner, lost their original motivation to make a bomb. Moreover, at Chicago, where Szilard worked, the scientists had completed their part of the project earlier than most and had had time to reflect on their achievement. Groves, sensing their growing frustration at having little to do and wary of their developing sudden moral qualms about their work, wanted Arthur Compton to cut back the size of his staff. But Compton resisted such a change and managed to keep the team together with research on new types of reactors. What Groves had feared soon became a reality: Chicago emerged as the center of opposition to America's use of the bomb against Japan.

As before, Szilard sounded the first warning. His objections to the use of the bomb were based on moral grounds, but he also believed—and in this he was not alone—that its use would lead to an awesome postwar arms race. Accordingly, he prepared a document outlining his case to Roosevelt, but the President died on April 12 before the appeal could reach him. Szilard then tried to see Truman, but Truman declined. He got Einstein to write a letter, as before, to the new President, but even that did not open the door to the Oval Office. Szilard presented his case to James Byrnes, soon to become Truman's Secretary of State, but once again had no luck. Byrnes, an astute politician, had already warned the White House, before Roosevelt's death, of the congressional repercussions if the $2 billion Manhattan Project failed. He was not open to arguments about the immorality of using the bomb.

Groves, on learning of Szilard's attempt, was furious. How dare this Hungarian upstart meddle in affairs of state without his permission? Seeing Byrnes was a grave breach of security, apart from anything else.

Meanwhile, a presidential committee was appointed at the beginning of May to advise on a future policy for atomic energy. Secretary of War Henry L. Stimson called it the "Interim Committee" because he thought Congress probably would wish to appoint a permanent commission at a later date to supervise, regulate, and control the future development of atomic energy. This interim body was to advise only on the bomb, but it never had in its terms of reference the key question: Should the bomb be dropped? Only the scientists at Chicago had confronted the issue.

When the committee met in Washington at the end of May, Compton, a member of the committee's scientific panel and fully conscious of what his scientists back in Chicago were thinking, asked the committee's chairman, Stimson, if it would be possible to arrange something less than a surprise atomic attack. Perhaps a bomb could be exploded out at sea or on an island, something that would give the Japanese an example of the power of the new weapon.

No record exists of what precisely followed from Compton's suggestion, because the discussion took place over lunch. But there are minutes of what followed that afternoon. Considering that this was the only time an alternative to dropping the bomb was seriously discussed by the presidential committee, the minutes are perfunctory and, indeed, stunning in their callous disregard. The discussion is recorded under paragraph eight of the minutes, entitled, "Effect of the bombing on the Japanese and their will to fight."

> After much discussion concerning various types of targets and the effects to be produced, Secretary Stimson expressed the conclusion, on which there was general agreement, that we could not give the Japanese any warning; that we could not concentrate on a civilian area; but that we should seek to make a profound psychological impression on as many of the inhabitants as possible. At the suggestion of Dr. Conant the Secretary agreed that the most desirable target would be a vital war plant employing a large number of workers and closely surrounded by workers' houses.

Both at lunch and afterward, the scientific advisers, including Compton, Fermi, Lawrence, and Oppenheimer, had failed to come up with a suitable way of demonstrating the bomb without actually dropping it on people. For his part, Groves, also a member of the committee, was irked that scientists, rather than military men, should be discussing what sort of target to select. He had already chosen Hiroshima, and Hiroshima it would be.

To underline his annoyance, Groves entered a strong objection into the minutes under what was called: "Handling of undesirable scientists." The Manhattan Project, Groves said, had been "plagued since its inception by the presence of certain scientists of doubtful discretion and uncertain loyalty." Groves was referring specifically to Szilard and the Chicago physicists. His attack on the scientists was more than the bloodlust of a general with victory in sight, wanting to give the enemy one last decisive blow. There was a serious prospect that the war might end before the bomb was ready to be dropped. Groves's sense of urgency is well illustrated by the orders he sent out on the eve of Germany's surrender in May 1945. The Manhattan Project, he said, "will continue and increase after VE Day with Japan as the objective. It is suggested that pre-educational programs for project employees be considered at this time. These should stress the *continuing urgency* of the work and *increasing tempo* after VE Day, focusing attention on Japan as our ultimate objective . . . the avoidance of lost time on riotous celebration on VE Day itself should also be stressed if deemed necessary."

In June, the Chicago scientists responded. A group of six scientists, calling themselves the Committee on Political and Social Problems and led by the Nobel laureate James Frank, who had fled Germany in 1933, issued their report. In it, they again argued the case for a demonstration of the bomb in an uninhabited place, a place where the Japanese could appreciate its terrifying force without experiencing it directly. The report stressed that killing thousands of civilians with the new weapon would prejudice America's postwar image and undermine any effort to reach an agreement on international control of the atom. Such a momentous decision should not be left to military tacticians alone, the scientists concluded. The document was rushed to Washington for the final meeting of the Scientific Panel of the Interim Committee. The Chicago scientists had not mentioned the key problem of their recommendation: that it would prolong the war. Other points had to be considered, too. There was a fear, for example, that if a technical demonstration was announced, the Japanese would move American P.O.W.s to any island marked for the demonstration. In the end, persuaded, above all, by their obligation to save American lives, the Scientific Panel saw no acceptable alternative to direct military use. Their advice was passed on to Truman. It included a suggestion that the United States approach its principal allies before using the new weapon and ask them for plans for postwar control. What was to happen afterward was a strictly political question, however, and it was not part of the discussions at presidential level that led up to America's use of the bomb.

Once Truman inherited the scattered strands of partial information about Roosevelt's deferred decisions on the issue, he had never been in any doubt about one thing: if the bomb could be built, it would be used. Until he became President, he had known nothing about the bomb; he had never been briefed on it as a senior congressman, or as Vice-President. When finally told, he reacted with enthusiasm. It seemed a total confirmation of all his basic faith in the American system: it was the ultimate better mousetrap.

It also presented him with a momentous decision, and that was the job of the President of the United States: to make decisions. It was how Harry Truman explained his first day in office to his mother. Later, he would title the first volume of his memoirs *The Year of Decision*. That revealing sign THE BUCK STOPS HERE had not yet appeared on the presidential desk, but the concept was already firmly in place. Conscious of nothing more than his sense of inadequacy and sharing the belief in the inevitably invidious comparison with his predecessor, Truman was determined to rise to the challenge that fate had placed before him. He would make decisions—as firmly and as clearly as possible. That was his job. Not so much his constitutional prerogative as his constitutional duty. Harry Truman had a strong sense of duty.

Acutely aware, more so than any President before or since, of the distinction between himself as President and the institution of The Presidency, he was determined that his unsought occupancy of the position would do nothing to diminish the stature of the office. Whatever doubts and fears he might have himself, he would at least give the appearance of decisiveness. He had no doubts about the bomb. He dutifully signed the crucial piece of paper. "This is the greatest thing in history," he declared when he heard the news of Hiroshima on his way back from the Potsdam Conference. It would definitively shorten the war and save American lives. He believed this passionately, as did every person who had an opportunity to advise him about the use of the bomb. This was the dominant overriding consideration for all the key actors in this decision-making process. The bomb was a weapon of war to be used in war. The sense of moral outrage that had existed in 1939 about the bombing of civilian centers had all but disappeared in the moral numbness of holy war. Truman's "decision" was not based on the "mature consideration" Roosevelt and Churchill had regarded as necessary in September 1944, when the two leaders had signed a memorandum—not shown to Truman—that treated the decision to drop the bomb as open. The question had long since become not "Why?" but "Why not?" No one ever gave Truman a good reason why not.

In retrospect, the scientists who had argued against its use in political terms, in particular in terms of the postwar atom race, had failed to build a case on their own particular competence. The one thing they knew, which in their naïveté never struck them as *politically* relevant, could have been a key factor: the effects of radioactivity from the bomb were known to be delayed. Many people died from the blast and immediate radiation effects of the explosion, but the scientists knew that many more would die from delayed effects in the years ahead.

No one had told any of the political decision-makers this basic fact. Among the thousands who would die immediately and the millions who would be threatened by an arms race, the later injuries did not seem significant at the time, yet they were to prove decisive. It is why Hiroshima and Nagasaki are remembered whereas the much deadlier conventional attacks of World War II, such as Tokyo and Dresden, are all but forgotten. Good politicians like Byrnes and Truman could have understood the difference. If people were still to be dying from the effects of the bomb a decade or more later, politically it had to be treated in different terms than any other means of ending the war. We will never know whether this would have been a determining factor.

The advantages of hindsight show how easy it might have been to avoid the tragedy of Hiroshima and Nagasaki. Intercepted cable traffic was already showing the desire of senior administrators in Japan to end the war through Russian mediation. The psychological effect of the secretly planned Russian declaration of war, which came the day after Hiroshima, was expected to be profound. So, too, was the impact the Russians would have on the one surviving significant Japanese military force, the Manchurian Army. Senior American military commanders still reaffirmed their faith in the ability of their own commands to win the war: the air force believed conventional strategic bombardment would do it and the admirals believed the naval blockade would do it. Even the option everyone was trying to avoid, direct military invasion, was not planned to begin for almost two months. All of these factors might have been given more prominence, or at least given cause for delay, if the political leadership of the U.S. government had had the long-term effects of radiation put to them as a reason to avoid dropping the bomb. The question was not presented in those terms.

Throughout the world, except possibly in the Soviet Union, the atomic bomb was seen as the definite final act that won the war: an act that brought to an end years of misery and death and the most stunning manifestation of man's control over nature that anyone had ever experienced. An entire generation would marvel at the ingenuity of the achievement. The rhetoric of the atomic age began on August 6, 1945, at Hiroshima. It gave rise to wonder and enthusiasm. It would be a decade before the aftereffects of that day, the insidious, invisible consequences of radioactivity, began to balance exhilaration with fear. It would be two decades before the powerful image of the mushroom cloud, representative of man's Promethean urge to control nature, would need to adjust to an equally powerful image: the first picture of spaceship earth taken from outer space, which so dramatically stressed the limits of man's environment. And the scientific and technological control of the energy in the atom would never be separated from the impact of the decision to drop the bomb.

COMMENTS ■ QUESTIONS

1. "Byrnes, an astute politician, had already warned the White House, before Roosevelt's death, of the congressional repercussions if the $2 billion Manhattan Project failed. He was not open to arguments about the immorality of using the bomb." What is your reaction to this?
2. What do you believe are the major lessons that can be learned from studying the historical development of nuclear weapons?

WILLIAM GODFREY-SMITH

The Value of Wilderness

The framework which I examine is the framework of *Western* attitudes toward our natural environment, and wilderness in particular. The philosophical task to which I shall address myself is an exploration of attitudes toward wilderness, expecially the sorts of justification to which we might legitimately appeal for the preservation of wilderness: what grounds can we advance in support of the claim that wilderness is something which we should *value*?

There are two different ways of appraising something as valuable. It may be that the thing in question is good or valuable *for the sake* of something which we hold to be valuable. In this case the thing is not considered to be good in itself; value in this sense is ascribed in virtue of the thing's being a *means* to some valued end, and not as an *end*

William Godfrey-Smith [Grey] has taught philosophy at the Australian National University, Canberra, and Temple University, Philadelphia. His major philosophical interests include environmental philosophy and metaphysics. He is at present working in the Department of Science in Canberra.

From *Environmental Ethics*, vol. 1 (1979). Reprinted by permission of *Environmental Ethics* and the author.

in itself. Such values are standardly designated *instrumental* values. Not everything which we hold to be good or valuable can be good for the sake of something else: our values must ultimately be *grounded* in something which is held to be good or valuable in itself. Such things are said to be *intrinsically* valuable. As a matter of historical fact, those things which have been held to be intrinsically valuable, within our Western traditions of thought, have nearly always been taken to be states or conditions of *persons*, e.g., happiness, pleasure, knowledge, or self-realization, to name but a few.

It follows from this that a very central assumption of Western moral thought is that value can be ascribed to the nonhuman world only insofar as it is good for the sake of the well-being of human beings.[2] Our entire attitude toward the natural environment, therefore, has a decidedly anthropocentric bias, and this fact is reflected in the sorts of justification which are standardly provided for the preservation of the natural environment.

A number of thinkers, however, are becoming increasingly persuaded that our anthropocentric morality is in fact inadequate to provide a satisfactory basis for a moral philosophy of ecological obligation. It is for this reason that we hear not infrequently the claim that we need a "new morality." A new moral framework—that is, a network of recognized obligations and duties—is not, however, something that can be casually conjured up in order to satisfy some vaguely felt need. The task of developing a sound biologically based moral philosophy, a philosophy which is not anthropocentrically based, and which provides a satisfactory justification for ecological obligation and concern, is, I think, one of the most urgent tasks confronting moral philosophers at the present. It will entail a radical reworking of accepted attitudes—attitudes which we currently accept as "self-evident"—and this is not something which can emerge suddenly. Indeed, I think the seminal work remains largely to be done, though I suggest below the broad outline which an environmentally sound moral philosophy is likely to take.

In the absence of a comprehensive and convincing ecologically based morality we naturally fall back on *instrumental* justifications for concern for our natural surroundings, and for preserving wilderness areas and animal species. We can, I think, detect at least four main lines of instrumental justification for the preservation of wilderness. By *wilderness* I understand any reasonably large tract of the Earth, together with its plant and animal communities, which is substantially unmodified by humans and in particular by human technology. The natural contrast to *wilderness* and *nature* is an *artificial* or *domesticated* environment. The fact that there are borderline cases which are difficult to classify does not, of

2. Other cultures have certainly included the idea that nature should be valued for its own sake in their moral codes, e.g., the American Indians (cf. Chief Seattle's letter to President Franklin Pierce of 1854, reprinted in *The Canberra Times*, 5 July 1966, p. 9), the Chinese (cf. Joseph Needham, "History and Human Values," in H. and S. Rose, eds. *The Radicalisation of Science* [London: Macmillan, 1976], pp. 90–117), and the Australian Aborigines (cf. W. E. H. Stanner, *Aboriginal Man in Australia* [Sydney: Angus and Robertson, 1965], pp. 207–237).

course, vitiate this distinction.

The first attitude toward wilderness espoused by conservationists to which I wish to draw attention is what I shall call the "cathedral" view. This is the view that wilderness areas provide a vital opportunity for spiritual revival, moral regeneration, and aesthetic delight. The enjoyment of wilderness is often compared in this respect with religious or mystical experience. Preservation of magnificent wilderness areas for those who subscribe to this view is essential for human well-being, and its destruction is conceived as something akin to an act of vandalism, perhaps comparable to—some may regard it as more serious than [3]—the destruction of a magnificent and moving human edifice, such as the Parthenon, the Taj Mahal, or the Palace of Versailles.

Insofar as the "cathedral" view holds that value derives solely from human satisfactions gained from its contemplation it is clearly an instrumentalist attitude. It does, however, frequently approach an *intrinsic value* attitude, insofar as the feeling arises that there is importance in the fact that it is there to be contemplated, whether or not anyone actually takes advantage of this fact. Suppose for example, that some wilderness was so precariously balanced that *any* human intervention or contact would inevitably bring about its destruction. Those who maintained that the area should, nevertheless, be preserved, unexperienced and unenjoyed, would certainly be ascribing to it an intrinsic value.

The "cathedral" view with respect to wilderness in fact is a fairly recent innovation in Western thought. The predominant Graeco-Christian attitude, which generally speaking was the predominant Western attitude prior to eighteenth- and nineteenth-century romanticism, had been to view wilderness as threatening or alarming, an attitude still reflected in the figurative uses of the expression *wilderness*, clearly connoting a degenerate state to be avoided. Christianity, in general, has enjoined "the transformation of wilderness, those dreaded haunts of demons, the ancient nature-gods, into farm and pasture," [4] that is, to a domesticated environment.

The second instrumental justification of the value of wilderness is what we might call the "laboratory" argument. This is the argument that wilderness areas provide vital subject matter for scientific inquiry which provides us with an understanding of the intricate interdependencies of biological systems, their modes of change and development, their energy cycles, and the source of their stabilities. If we are to understand our own biological dependencies, we require natural systems as a norm, to inform us of the biological laws which we transgress at our peril.

The third instrumentalist justification is the "silo" argument which points out that one excellent reason for preserving reasonable areas of the natural environment intact is that

3. We can after all *replace* human artifacts such as buildings with something closely similar, but the destruction of a wilderness or a biological species is irreversible.

4. John Passmore, *Man's Responsibility for Nature* (London: Duckworth, 1974; New York: Charles Scribner's Sons, 1974), p. 17; cf. chap. 5.

we thereby preserve a stockpile of genetic diversity, which it is certainly prudent to maintain as a backup in case something should suddenly go wrong with the simplified biological systems which, in general, constitute agriculture. Further, there is the related point that there is no way of anticipating our future needs, or the undiscovered applications of apparently useless plants, which might turn out to be, for example, the source of some pharmacologically valuable drug—a cure, say, for leukemia. This might be called, perhaps, the "rare herb" argument, and it provides another persuasive instrumental justification for the preservation of wilderness.

The final instrumental justification which I think should be mentioned is the "gymnasium" argument, which regards the preservation of wilderness as important for athletic or recreational activities.

An obvious problem which arises from these instrumental arguments is that the various activities which they seek to justify are not always possible to reconcile with one another. The interests of the wilderness lover who subscribes to the "cathedral" view are not always reconcilable with those of the ordinary vacationist. Still more obvious is the conflict between the recreational use of wilderness and the interests of the miner, the farmer, and the timber merchant.

The conflict of interest which we encounter here is one which it is natural to try and settle through the economic calculus of cost-benefit considerations. So long as the worth of natural systems is believed to depend entirely on instrumental values, it is natural to suppose that we can sort out the conflict of interests within an objective frame of reference, by estimating the human satisfactions to be gained from the preservation of wilderness, and by weighing these against the satisfactions which are to be gained from those activities which may lead to its substantial modification, domestication, and possibly even, destruction.

Many thinkers are liable to encounter here a feeling of resistance to the suggestion that we can apply purely economic considerations to settle such conflicts of interest. The assumption behind economic patterns of thought, which underlie policy formulation and planning, is that the values which we attach to natural systems and to productive activities are commensurable; and this is an assumption which may be called into question. It is not simply a question of the difficulty of quantifying what value should be attached to the preservation of the natural environment. The feeling is more that economic considerations are simply out of place. This feeling is one which is often too lightly dismissed by tough-minded economists as being obscurely mystical or superstitious; but it is a view worth examining. What it amounts to, I suggest, is the belief that there is something *morally* objectionable in the destruction of natural systems, or at least in their wholesale elimination, and this is precisely the belief that natural systems, or economically "useless" species do possess an *intrinsic* value. That is, it is an attempt to articulate the rejection of the anthropocentric view that all value, ultimately, resides in *human* interests and concerns. But it is a difficult matter to try and provide justification for such attitudes, and this is, for reasons which are deeply bound up with the problems of resolving basic value conflict, a problem which I have discussed elsewhere.[5]

The belief that all values are commensurable, so that there is no problem *in principle* in providing a satisfactory resolution of value conflict, involves the assumption that the quantitative social sciences, in particular economics, can provide an *objective* frame of reference within which all conflicts of interest can be satisfactorily resolved. We should, however, note that in the application of cost-benefit analyses there is an inevitable bias in the sorts of values that figure in the calculation, viz., a bias toward those considerations which are readily quantifiable, and toward those interests which will be staunchly defended. This is a fairly trivial point, but it is one which has substantial consequences, for there are at least three categories of values and interests which are liable to be inadequately considered, or discounted altogether.[6] First, there are the interests of those who are too widely distributed spatially, or too incrementally affected over time, to be strongly supported by any single advocate. Second, there are the interests of persons not yet existing, viz., future generations, who are clearly liable to be affected by present policy, but who are clearly not in a position to press any claims. Third, there are interests not associated with humans at all, such as the "rights" of wild animals.[7]

This last consideration, in particular, is apt to impress many as ludicrous, as quite simply "unthinkable." It is an unquestioned axiom of our present code of ethics that the class of individuals to which we have obligations is the class of humans. The whole apparatus of rights and duties is in fact based on an ideal of reciprocal contractual obligations, and in terms of this model the class of individuals to whom we may stand in moral relations—i.e., those with whom we recognize a network of rights, duties, and obligations—is the class of humans. A major aspect of a satisfactory ethic of ecological obligation and concern will be to challenge this central anthropocentric assumption. I return to this point below.

Even restricting our attention to the class of human preference havers, however, we should be wary of dismissing as simply inadmissable the interests of future generations. The claims of posterity tend to be excluded from our policy deliberations not, I suspect, because we believe that future generations will be unaffected by our policies, but because

5. In "The Rights of Non-humans and Intrinsic Values," in M. A. McRobbie, D. Mannison, and R. Routley, eds. *Environmental Philosophy* (Canberra: Australian National University Research School of Social Sciences, forthcoming).

6. Cf. Laurence H. Tribe, "Policy Science: Analysis or Ideology?" *Philosophy and Public Affairs* 2 (1972–3): 66–110.

7. I should mention that I am a skeptic about "rights": it seems to me that talk about rights is always eliminable in favor of talk about legitimate claims for considerations, and obligations to respect those claims. Rights-talk does, however, have useful rhetorical effect in exhorting people to recognize claims. The reason for this is that claims pressed in these terms perform the crucial trick of shifting the onus of proof. This is accomplished by the fact that a *denial* of a right appears to be a more positive and deliberate act than merely refusing to acknowledge an obligation.

we lack any clear idea as to how to set about attaching weight to their interests. This is an instance of the familiar problem of "the dwarfing of soft variables." In settling conflicts of interest, any consideration which cannot be precisely quantified tends to be given little weight, or more likely, left out of the equation altogether: "If you can't measure it, it doesn't exist." [8] The result of ignoring soft variables is a spurious appearance of completeness and precision, but in eliminating all soft variables from our cost-benefit calculations, the conclusion is decidedly biased. If, as seems plausible, it is *in principle* impossible to do justice to soft variables, such as the interests of posterity, it may be that we have to abandon the idea that the economic models employed in cost-benefit calculations are universally applicable for sorting out all conflicts of interest. It may be necessary to abandon the economic calculus as the universal model for rational deliberation.[9]

Another category of soft variable which tends to be discounted from policy deliberations is that which concerns economically unimportant species of animals or plants. A familiar subterfuge which we frequently encounter is the attempt to invest such species with spurious economic value, as illustrated in the rare herb argument. A typical example of this, cited by Leopold, is the reaction of ornithologists to the threatened disappearance of certain species of songbirds: they at once came forward with some distinctly shaky evidence that they played an essential role in the control of insects.[10] The dominance of economic modes of thinking is again obvious: the evidence has to be economic in order to be acceptable. This exemplifies the way in which we turn to instrumentalist justifications for the maintenance of biotic diversity.

The alternative to such instrumentalist justifications, the alternative which Leopold advocated with great insight and eloquence, is to widen the boundary of the moral community to include animals, plants, the soil, or collectively *the land*.[11] This involves a radical shift in our conception of nature, so that land is recognized not simply as property, to be dealt with or disposed of as a matter of expediency: land in Leopold's view is not a commodity which belongs to us, but a community to which we belong. This change in conception is far-reaching and profound. It involves a shift in our metaphysical conception of nature—that is, a change in what sort of thing we take our natural surroundings to *be*. This is a point which I would like to elaborate, albeit sketchily.

The predominant Western conception of nature is exemplified in—and to no small extent is a conse-

8. Laurence H. Tribe, "Trial by Mathematics: Precision and Ritual in Legal Process," *Harvard Law Review* 84 (1971):1361.

9. Of course, in practice cost-benefit considerations *do* operate within deontic constraints, and we do *not* accept economics unrestrictedly as providing the model for rational deliberation. We would not accept exploitative child labor, for example, as a legitimate mode of production, no matter how favorable the economics. This is not just because we attach too high a cost to this form of labor: it is just unthinkable.

10. Aldo Leopold, "The Land Ethic," in *Sand County Almanac*, p. 210.

11. Cf. Aldo Leopold, "The Conservation Ethic," *Journal of Forestry* 31 (1933):634–43, and "The Land Ethic," *Sand County Almanac*.

quence of—the philosophy of Descartes, in which nature is viewed as something separate and apart, to be transformed and controlled at will. Descartes divided the world into conscious thinking substances—minds—and extended, mechanically arranged substances—the rest of nature. It is true that we find in Western thought alternatives to the Cartesian metaphysical conception of nature—the views of Spinoza and Hegel might be mentioned in particular [12]—but the predominant spirit, especially among scientists, has been Cartesian. These metaphysical views have become deeply embedded in Western thought, which has induced us to view the world through Cartesian spectacles. One of the triumphs of Descartes' mechanistic view of nature has been the elimination of occult qualities and forces from the explanation of natural events. The natural world is to be understood, in the Cartesian model, in purely mechanistic terms. An unfortunate consequence of the triumph, nevertheless, has been a persistent fear among some thinkers that the rejection of Cartesian metaphysics may lead to the reinstatement of occult and mystical views of nature.

An important result of Descartes' sharp ontological division of the world into active mental substances and inert material substances, has been the alienation of man from the natural world. Although protests have been raised against Cartesian metaphysics ever since its inception, it has exercised a deep influence on our attitudes toward nature.

12. Cf. John Passmore, "Attitudes to Nature," in R. S. Peters, ed. *Nature and Conduct* (London: Macmillan, 1975), pp. 251–64.

Descartes' mechanistic conception of nature naturally leads to the view that it is possible in principle to obtain complete mastery and technical control over the natural world. It is significant to recall that for Descartes the paradigm instance of a natural object was a lump of wax, the perfect exemplification of malleability. This conception of natural objects as wholly pliable and passive is clearly one which leaves no room for anything like a network of obligations.

A natural corollary of the mechanistic conception of nature, and integral to the Cartesian method of inquiry, is the role played by reductive thinking. In order to understand a complex system one should, on this view, break it into its component parts and examine them. The Cartesian method of inquiry is a natural correlate of Cartesian metaphysics, and is a *leitmotif* of our science-based technology.

It should be stressed that a rejection of the Cartesian attitude and its method of inquiry need *not* involve a regression to occult and mystical views about the "sacredness" of the natural world, and the abandoning of systematic rational inquiry. It must be conceded, however, that the rejection of the view that nature is an exploitable commodity has, unfortunately, frequently taken this form. This sort of romantic nature mysticism *does* provide a powerful exhortation for exercising restraint in our behavior to the natural world, but it carries with it a very clear danger. This is that while prohibiting destructive acts toward the natural world, it equally prohibits constructive acts: we surely cannot rationally adopt a complete "hands off" policy with respect to nature, on the basis of what looks like the extremely implausible—and highly cynical—*a priori* assumption that *any* attempt to modify our surroundings is bound to be for the worse.

It may, however, be that advocates of the "sacredness" of nature are attempting to do no more than articulate the idea that natural systems have their own intrinsic value, and adopt this manner of speaking as a convenient way of rejecting the dominant anthropocentric morality. If *this* is all that is being claimed, then I have no quarrel with it. And it may be inevitable that this mode of expression is adopted in the absence of a developed ecologically sound alternative morality. But I think we should be wary of this style of justification; what is needed, as Passmore has nicely expressed it, is not the spiritualizing of nature, but the naturalizing of man.[13] This involves a shift from the piecemeal reductive conception of natural items to a *holistic* or systemic view in which we come to appreciate the symbiotic interdependencies of the natural world. On the holistic or total-field view, organisms—including man—are conceived as nodes in a biotic web of intrinsically related parts.[14] That is, our understanding of biological organisms requires more than just an understanding of their structure and properties; we also have to attend seriously to their interrelations. Holistic or systemic thinking does not deny that organisms are complex physicochemical systems, but it affirms that the methods employed in establishing the high-level functional relationships expressed by physical laws are often of very limited importance in understanding the nature of biological systems. We may now be facing, in the terminology of Thomas Kuhn,[15] a shift from a physical to a biological paradigm in our understanding of nature. This seems to me to be an important aspect of the rejection of Cartesian metaphysics.

The limitations of the physical paradigm have long been accepted in the study of human society, but the tendency has been to treat social behavior and human action as quite distinct from the operations of our natural surroundings. The inappropriateness of the physical paradigm for understanding *human* society seems to me to be quite correct; what is comparatively new is the post-Cartesian realization that the physical paradigm is of more limited application for our understanding of *nature* than was previously supposed.

The holistic conception of the natural world contains, in my view, the possibility of extending the idea of community beyond human society. And in this way biological wisdom does, I think, carry implications for ethics. Just as Copernicus showed us that man does not occupy the physical center of the universe, Darwin and his successors have shown us that man occupies no *biologically* privileged position. We still have to assimilate the implications which this biological knowledge has for morality.

13. Ibid., p. 260.

14. Cf. Arne Naess, "The Shallow and the Deep, Long-Range Ecology Movement," *Inquiry* 16 (1973):95–100.

15. T. S. Kuhn, *The Structure of Scientific Revolutions* (Chicago: University of Chicago Press, 1962).

Can we regard man and the natural environment as constituting a community in any morally significant sense? Passmore, in particular, has claimed that this extended sense of community is entirely spurious.[16] Leopold, on the other hand, found the biological extension of community entirely natural.[17] If we regard a community as a collection of individuals who engage in cooperative behavior, Leopold's extension seems to me entirely legitimate. An ethic is no more than a code of conduct designed to ensure cooperative behavior among the members of a community. Such cooperative behavior is required to underpin the health of the community, in this biologically extended sense, *health* being understood as the biological capacity for self-renewal,[18] and *ill-health* as the degeneration or loss of this capacity.

Man, of course, cannot be placed on "all fours" with his biologically fellow creatures in all respects. In particular, man is the only creature who can act as a full-fledged moral agent, i.e., an individual capable of exercising reflective rational choice on the basis of principles. What distinguishes man from his fellow creatures is not the capacity to *act*, but the fact that his actions are, to a great extent, free from programming. This capacity to modify our own behavior is closely bound up with the capacity to acquire knowledge of the natural world, a capacity which has enabled us, to an unprecedented extent, to manipulate the environment, and—especially in the recent past—to alter it rapidly, violently, and globally. Our hope must be that the capacity for knowledge, which has made ecologically hazardous activities possible, will lead to a more profound understanding of the delicate biological interdependencies which some of these actions now threaten, and thereby generate the wisdom for restraint.

To those who are skeptical of the possibility of extending moral principles, in the manner of Leopold, to include items treated heretofore as matters of expediency, it can be pointed out that extensions have, to a limited extent, already taken place. One clear—if partial—instance, is in the treatment of animals. It is now generally accepted, and this is a comparatively recent innovation,[19] that we have at least a *prima facie* obligation not to treat animals cruelly or sadistically. And this certainly constitutes a shift in moral attitudes. If—as seems to be the case—cruelty to animals is accepted as intrinsically wrong, then there *is* at least one instance in which it is *not* a matter of moral indifference how we behave toward the nonhuman world.

More familiar perhaps are the moral revolutions which have occurred within the specific domain of human society—witness the progressive elimination of the "right" to racial, class, and sex exploitation. Each of these shifts involves the acceptance, on the part of some individuals, of new obligations, rights, and values which, to a previous generation, would have been considered

16. Passmore, *Man's Responsibility for Nature*, chap. 6; "Attitudes to Nature," p. 262.

17. Leopold, "The Land Ethic."

18. Ibid., p. 221.

19. Cf. Passmore, "The Treatment of Animals," *Journal of the History of Ideas* 36 (1975): 195–218.

unthinkable.[20] The essential step in recognizing an enlarged community involves coming to see, feel, and understand what was previously perceived as alien and apart: it is the evolution of the capacity of *empathy*.

I have digressed a little into the history of ideas, stressing in particular the importance of the influence of Descartes.[21] My justification for this excursion is that our present attitudes toward nature, and toward wilderness, are very largely the result of Descartes' metaphysical conception of what nature is, and the concomitant conception which man has of himself. Our metaphysical assumptions are frequently extremely influential invisible persuaders: they determine the boundaries of what is thinkable. In rejecting the Cartesian conception the following related shifts in attitudes can, I think, be discerned.

1. A change from reductive convergent patterns of thought to divergent holistic patterns.

2. A shift from man's conception of himself as the center of the biological world, to one in which he is conceived of as a component in a network of biological relations, a shift comparable to the Copernican discovery that man does not occupy the *physical* center of the universe.

3. An appreciation of the fact that in modifying biological systems we do not simply modify the properties of a substance, but alter a network of relations. This rejection of the Cartesian conception of nature as a collection of independent physical parts is summed up in the popular ecological maxim "it is impossible to do only one thing."

4. A recognition that the processes of nature are independent and indifferent to human interests and concerns.

5. A recognition that biological systems are items which possess intrinsic value, in Kant's terminology, that they are "ends in themselves."

We can, however, provide—and it is important that we can provide—an answer to the question: "What is the *use* of wilderness?" We certainly ought to preserve and protect wilderness areas as gymnasiums, as laboratories, as stockpiles of genetic diversity, and as cathedrals. Each of these reasons provides a powerful and sufficient instrumental justification for their preservation. But note how the very posing of this question about the *utility* of wilderness reflects an anthropocentric system of values. From a genuinely ecocentric point of view the question "What is the *use* of wilderness?" would be as absurd as the question "What is the *use* of happiness?"

The philosophical task is to try to provide adequate justification, or at least clear the way for a scheme of values according to which concern and sympathy for our environment is immediate and natural, and the desirability of protecting and preserving wilderness self-evident. When once controversial propositions become platitudes, the philosophical

20. Cf. Christopher D. Stone, "Should Trees Have Standing? Toward Legal Rights for Natural Objects," *Southern California Law Review* 45 (1972): 450–501.

21. Here I differ from the well-known claim of Lynn White ("The Historical Roots of Our Ecological Crisis," *Science* 155 [1967]:1203–7) that the Judeo-Christian tradition is predominantly responsible for the development of Western attitudes toward nature.

task will have been successful.

I will conclude, nevertheless, on a deflationary note. It seems to me (at least much of the time) that the shift in attitudes which I think is required for promoting genuinely harmonious relations with nature is too drastic, too "unthinkable," to be very persuasive for most people. If this is so, then it will be more expedient to justify the preservation of wilderness in terms of instrumentalist considerations; and I have argued that there *are* powerful arguments for preservation which can be derived from the purely anthropocentric considerations of human self-interest. I hope, however, that there will be some who feel that such anthropocentric considerations are not wholly satisfying, i.e., that they do not really do justice to our intuitions. But at a time when *human* rights are being treated in some quarters with a great deal of skepticism it is perhaps unrealistic to expect the rights of nonhumans to receive sympathetic attention. Perhaps, though, we should not be too abashed by this: extensions in ethics have seldom followed the path of political expediency.

COMMENTS ■ QUESTIONS

1. Godfrey-Smith begins by observing that in Western philosophy intrinsic value is almost always ascribed to "conditions or states of persons." (Certainly Bertrand Russell and William James in chapter 8 have a view of intrinsic value that could be described in this way.) Godfrey-Smith suggests that a "new morality" is needed that would present a different view of intrinsic value. Do you agree? Why or why not?
2. Godfrey-Smith presents four possible *instrumentalist* justifications for the preservation of wilderness—the "cathedral" view, the "laboratory" view, the "silo" view, and the "gymnasium" view. Do you agree with what he says about each? Which do you believe is the most important instrumentalist justification? Can you think of any additional instrumentalist justifications?
3. Godfrey-Smith associates instrumentalist justifications with economic ones, in which monetary value becomes the common denominator for all values. This is objectionable, says Godfrey-Smith, because, for one thing, it is thoroughly anthropocentric—it ties all values to human interests and concerns. Thus, for example, it allows no place for the rights of animals. Do you believe that animals should be assigned "rights" apart from human interests and concerns? Moreover, do you believe that there is any value concept analogous to that of rights that might be assigned to plants or even to inorganic objects?
4. Godfrey-Smith describes what he calls the "Cartesian mechanistic

view of nature." This view must be distinguished from the sort of materialism that in chapter 6 was *contrasted* with the view of Descartes. In chapter 6 materialism was contrasted with Cartesian "dualism" pertaining to *human beings*. Materialists believe that human beings, along with the rest of the world, are nothing more than material systems. Descartes held that human beings are both material and spiritual, but that *the rest of nature is purely material and mechanistic*. In this way, Descartes wished to emphasize what he took to be crucial differences between human beings and nature. Godfrey-Smith's intention is to *soften* the contrast between human beings and nature, and this is the basis for his rejection of Cartesian mechanism. Do you believe that he is on the right track in this regard? Explain.

RENÉ DUBOS

The Crisis of Man in His Environment

For most laymen and not a few scientists, the work environment evokes nightmares—the toxic effects of chemical pollution, the behavioral disturbances caused by crowding or automated work, the pathologic consequences of exposure to intense and unnatural stimuli, the thousand devils of the ecologic crisis.

Physicians have long known, furthermore, that sudden changes in the ways of life and in the surroundings are likely to have damaging effects on biological and mental health. In brief, the modern environment is dangerous on two accounts: It contains elements that are outright noxious; it changes so rapidly that man cannot make fast enough the proper adaptive responses to it.

The general worry about the environment has resulted in a distortion of the meaning conveyed by the phrase "human ecology." At present, this phrase is exclusively identified with the social and biological dangers that man faces in the modern world. But there is more to human ecology than this one-sided

A biographical sketch of René Dubos appears earlier in this chapter.

From *Proceedings of Symposium on Human Ecology*. Published by the U.S. Department of Health, Education, and Welfare, 1968.

view of man's relation to his environment. In the long run, the most important aspect of human ecology is that all environmental factors exert a direct effect on the development of human characteristics, in health as well as in disease. In fact, it can be said that the body and the mind are *shaped* by the adaptive responses that man makes to the physiochemical, social, behavioral, and even historical stimuli that impinge on him from the time of conception to the time of death. Genetically and phenotypically, man is being constantly transformed by the environment in which he lives.

Human ecology therefore involves both the pathological and the formative effects of the total environment. I shall first illustrate by a few examples these two aspects of the problem, then attempt to formulate a general approach to the study of the interplay between man and environmental forces.

The general state of public health has greatly improved during the past century, but therapeutic procedures have played a relatively small role in this achievement. Advances in health and in the expectancy of life have come chiefly from higher standards of living, and from the application of natural sciences to the *prevention* of infectious and nutritional diseases.

Although the early sanitarians did not use the phrase "human ecology" their slogan "pure air, pure water, pure food" implied sound ecological concepts. Their awareness of the effects that environmental factors exert on biological health was furthermore supplemented by a shrewd understanding of man's emotional needs. For example, they advocated that urban areas be ornamented with trees and flowers and that city dwellers be given ready access to country lanes.

Thanks to their efforts, we have gone far toward solving the problems of infectious and nutritional disease generated by the first industrial revolution. Unfortunately, the new revolution in the ways of life and in the environment that is now occurring in technological societies is bringing about profound changes in the pattern of diseases, causing in particular alarming increases in various types of chronic and degenerative disorders.

Whereas the 19th century was concerned with malnutrition, overwork, filth, and microbial contamination, the diseases most characteristic of our times result in large part from economic affluence, chemical pollution, and high-population densities. The medical problems are still largely environmental in origin, but they have different ecologic determinants.

The average expectancy of life has increased all over the world and especially in prosperous countries as a result of the prevention of early deaths that used to be caused by acute infections and malnutrition. But, contrary to general belief, life expectancy past the age of 45 has not increased significantly anywhere in the world, not even in the social groups that can afford the most elaborate medical care. It is no longer permissible to take comfort in the belief that various types of vascular diseases, of cancers, of chronic ailments of the respiratory tract, have become more prevalent simply because people live longer in affluent societies. The increase in chronic and degenerative diseases is due in part at least, and probably in a very large part, to the environmental and behavioral changes that have resulted from industrialization and urbanization.

The so-called diseases of civilization are certainly the results of man's failure to respond successfully to the stresses of the modern environment. But, there is as yet no convincing knowledge of the mechanisms relating the environment and the ways of life to the increased incidence of chronic and degenerative diseases among adults. Granted the deficiences in etiological understanding, it is obvious nevertheless that man feels threatened and is threatened by the constant and unavoidable exposure to the stimuli of urban and industrial civilization; by the varied aspects of environmental pollution; by the physiological disturbances associated with sudden changes in the ways of life; by his estrangement from the conditions and natural cycles under which human evolution took place; by the emotional trauma and the paradoxical solitude in congested cities; by the monotony, the boredom, indeed the compulsory leisure ensuing from automated work. These are the very influences which are now at the origin of most medical problems in affluent societies. They affect all human beings, irrespective of genetic constitution. They are not inherent in man's nature but the products of the interplay between his genetic environment and the new world created by social and technological innovations. To a very large extent the disorders of the body and mind are but the expression of inadequate adaptive responses to environmental influences which differ drastically from the conditions under which man evolved.

As already mentioned, hardly anything is known concerning the natural history of the diseases characteristic of modern civilization—let alone concerning methods for their treatment. It is urgent therefore to develop a new science of human ecology focused on the conditions prevailing in the technological environment.

One can take it for granted that medical science will continue to develop useful techniques for treating cancers, vascular diseases, and other degenerative disorders; methods for organ transplants and for the use of artificial prostheses will certainly be improved during the forthcoming decades. But most of the conditions that will thus be treated need not have occurred in the first place. Greater knowledge of the environmental determinants of disease would certainly constitute the most important factor in helping biomedical sciences to improve human health. Prevention is always better than cure, and also much less expensive.

As presently managed, the technological urban civilization subjects all human beings to endless and dangerous stresses. Yet men of all ethnic groups elect to live in huge megalopolis, and indeed manage to function effectively in this traumatic environment. Most of them seem to develop tolerance to environmental pollutants, intense stimuli, and high-population density, just as they develop herd immunity to microbial pathogens that are ubiquitous.

The acquisition of tolerance, however, is not an unmixed blessing. Air pollution provides tragic evidence of the fact that many of the physiological, mental, and social processes which make it possible to live in a hostile environment commonly express themselves at a later date in overt disease and in economic loss. During the past two centuries, for instance, the inhabitants of the industrial areas of northern Europe have been exposed to large concentrations of many types of air pollutants produced by incomplete combustion of coal, and released in the fumes from chemical plants. Such exposure is rendered even more objectionable by the inclemency of the Atlantic climate. However, long experience with pollution and with bad weather results in the development of physiological reactions and living habits that obviously have adaptive value, since northern Europeans seem to accept almost cheerfully conditions which appear unbearable to a non-experienced person.

Unfortunately, adaptation to the stresses of the present often has to be paid in the form of physiological misery at some future date. Even among persons who seem to be unaware of the smogs surrounding them, the respiratory tract registers the insult of the various air pollutants. Eventually, the cumulative effects of irritation result in chronic bronchitis and other forms of irreversible pulmonary disease. Generally, however, this does not happen until several years later.

Chronic pulmonary disease now constitutes the greatest single medical problem in northern Europe, as well as the most costly. It is increasing in prevalence at an alarming rate also in North America and it will undoubtedly spread to all areas undergoing industrialization. There is good evidence, furthermore, that air pollution contributes to the incidence of various cancers—not only pulmonary carcinoma. It also increases the number of fatalities among persons suffering from vascular disorders. The delayed effects of air pollutants thus constitute a model for the kind of medical problems likely to arise in the future from the various forms of environmental pollution.

Noise levels that are accepted almost as a matter of course bring about a progressive impairment of hearing; pathogens that do not cause destructive epidemics because they are ubiquitous and have therefore elicited herd immunity can generate endogenous infections when resistance to them is decreased by physiological or mental stress; crowding, regimentation, or intense stimuli that become acceptable through habituation indirectly elicit physiological or behavioral disorders. In brief, most adaptive adjustments to deleterious influences are achieved at the price of bodily or mental disturbances later in life. Some at least of these disturbances contribute to the diseases of civilization.

From the point of view of the general biologist, an environment is suitable if it enables the species to reproduce itself and increase its population; but this concept is not applicable to man. An environment allowing man to produce a family and to be economically effective during his adult years should be regarded as unacceptable if it generates disease later in life. This of course is the case for many modern technological and urban environments, which rarely destroy human life but frequently spoil its later years.

Human ecology thus differs from orthodox biomedical sciences in the much greater emphasis that it should put on the indirect and delayed effects of environmental forces, even when these do not appear to cause significant damage at the time of exposure.

Man's responses to the environmental forces that impinge on him determine to a very large extent how his genetic potentialities are converted into existential, phenotypic reality.

Contrary to what is commonly assumed, genes do not determine the traits by which we know a person; they only govern the responses he makes to environmental stimuli. Such responses become incorporated, usually in an irreversible manner in the person's whole being and thus mold his individuality. This is true not only for emotional characteristics, but also for most other physical, physiological, and mental characteristics. Man makes himself in the very act of responding to his environment through an uninterrupted series of feedback processes. Since each person continues to respond to environmental stimuli throughout his life and to be lastingly modified by such responses, individuality can be defined as the continuously evolving phenotype.

Many of the most striking differences in size, shape, attitudes, and mental abilities between ethnic groups are not innate; they are the expressions of environmental influences. In other words, men are as much the products of their environment as of their genetic endowment. This is what Winston Churchill had in mind when he asserted "We shape our buildings, and afterwards our buildings shape us."

The influences experienced very early in life during the formative phases of development deserve special emphasis, because they exert profound and lasting effects on the anatomical, physiological, and behavioral characteristics of the adult. Experimentation in animals and observations in man have revealed that the fetus and the newborn can be so profoundly affected by environmental conditions acting indirectly through the mother, or directly after birth, that the adult reflects throughout his life the consequences of this early experience. Early influences are of particular importance because man's body and brain are incompletely developed at the time of birth. Hence, the need for precise observations and searching experimental studies concerning the conditions of prenatal and early postnatal life.

Biological and social deprivation are well known to have deleterious effects on development. For example, there is now overwhelming evidence that various types of deprivation early in life exert irreversible damage on learning ability—a fact of obvious importance in all underprivileged populations. On the other hand, it is also possible that some of the conditions prevailing in affluent societies have undesirable consequences.

It is known that injection into newborn mice of particulate materials separated from urban air greatly increases the frequency of various types of tumors during the adult life of these animals. If this observation can be extrapolated to human beings, the worst effects of environmental pollution are yet to come, since it is only during the past decade that large numbers of babies have been exposed to high levels of pollutants in urban areas.

It is known also that animals offered a rich and abundant regimen early in life thereby become conditioned to large nutritional demands as adults and tend to become obese. This may explain why the bigger baby does not necessarily become a healthy adult.

By acting on the child during his formative stages, the environment thus shapes him physically and mentally, thereby influencing what he will become and how he will function as an adult. For this reason, environmental planning plays a key role in enabling human beings to actualize their potentialities.

Children who are denied the opportunity to experience early in life the kind of stimuli required for mental development, do not acquire the mental resources that would be necessary for the full utilization of their free will. It is not right to say that lack of culture is responsible for the behavior of slum children or for their failure to be successful in our society. The more painful truth is that these children acquire early in life a slum culture from which escape is almost impossible. Their early surroundings and ways of life at a critical period of their development limit the range of manifestations of their innate endowment and thus destroy much of their potential freedom.

It would be unethical and in any case futile to try creating one particular type of environment optimum for all of mankind. Such a course would impose a common pattern of development on all human beings and thus would be tantamount to suppressing their freedom. Society should instead provide as wide a range of environmental conditions as practically and safely possible so that each human being can select the experiences most suitable to the development of his attributes and to the prosecution of his goals.

Human potentialities, whether physical or mental, can be realized only to the extent that circumstances are favorable to their existential manifestation. For this reason, diversity within a given society is an essential component of true functionalism; the latent potentialities of human beings have a better chance to emerge when the social environment is sufficiently diversified to provide a variety of stimulating experiences, especially for the young. As more and more persons find it possible to express their biologic endowments under a variety of conditions, society becomes richer and civilizations continue to unfold. In contrast, if the surroundings and ways of life are highly stereotyped, the only components of man's nature that flourish are those adapted to the narrow range of prevailing conditions.

Thus, one of the most important problems of human ecology is to study the effects of environmental forces not only in the here and now, but also with regard to their future consequences.

As seen from the preceding sections, the problems of ecology are conceptually very different from those of the orthodox biomedical sciences. The latter are primarily concerned with the structures and functions of the body and of the mind in their universal and essentially unchangeable aspects. This kind of knowledge is just as valid for stone age man as for the Beatles; it applies equally well to the man living in the jungles of New Guinea or in a New York City penthouse. Human ecology, in contrast, is concerned with the problems emerging from the interplay between man and the various forces of the environment in which he develops and lives. Human ecology deals not with man in the abstract, but with particular men at a particular time in one particular place. The interplay between man's nature and his total environment is governed of course by general laws, but their manifestations differ greatly according to circumstances.

Human ecology involves not only the immediate and direct effects of environmental forces, but also their indirect and long-range consequences. Such knowledge cannot be obtained from the study of oversimplified biological systems. It requires the analysis of actual human situations and the use of experimental models reproducing some selected aspects of these situations. Fortunately, experience has shown that for almost all human problems, there exists in the animal kingdom several species suitable for the development of useful models; there is no doubt therefore that human ecology could be readily developed into a flourishing experimental science.

The following are a few examples of problems in human ecology that can be studied through the use of experimental models with animals:

1. Indirect and delayed effects of biologically active substances, such as drugs and environmental pollutants.

2. The effect of sensory stimuli—or lack of—and of other environmental conditions, on the development of sense organs and on physiological processes.

3. The effects of relative degrees of isolation or crowding on hormonal activities and behavioral patterns.

4. The acquisition of tolerance to injurious agents and situations; its distant consequences.

5. Enduring effects of perinatal influences; i.e., of the factors (nutritional, infectious, toxic, behavioral, etc.) that impinge on the organism during critical periods of its development (prenatal and early postnatal).

6. The conditioning of the response to any particular insult (of physiochemical, infectious, or behavioral origin) by the effects of the total environment on the host; i.e., the role of nonspecific etiological factors in epidemiology.

7. The necessity to keep social and technological innovations within a framework determined by the biological limitations of man.

8. The adaptive potentialities of the human organism at various stages of its development.

The phrase "adaptive potentialities" has been introduced above to emphasize once more that the environmental study of human life should not be limited to a consideration of pathological phenomena. Each person has a wide range of physical and mental potentialities that remain untapped. These become expressed phenotypically only to the extent that the person is given a chance to respond adaptively to the proper stimuli under the proper circumstances.

The problems of human ecology necessarily deal with complex situations in which several interrelated systems function in an integrated manner. Multifactorial investigations will demand new conceptual and experimental methods, very different from those involving only one variable, which have been the stock in trade of orthodox biology. They will require also research facilities which hardly exist at the present time. Almost any kind of animal or plant tissue will do for electron microscopy of cellular elements, or for analysis of intermediate metabolism. But the experimental study of responses and adaptation to environmental insults and stimuli is far more demanding. It will require the observation of human beings under a wide range of conditions. It will also demand new kinds of research facilities.

The following items immediately come to mind:

a. Experimental animals of known genetic structure and of controlled experimental past.

b. Quarters for maintaining animals under a wide range of conditions throughout their whole lifespan and indeed for several generations.

c. Large enclosures for maintaining animal populations of various sizes and densities, exposed to different types of stimuli.

d. Equipment (using telemetry) for observing and measuring responses without disturbing the experimental system.

e. Equipment for recording, retrieving, and analyzing the complex data to be derived from the study of large populations and multifactorial systems.

The mere listing of these facilities points to the need for new types of institutions with a special organization of highly integrated personnel. What is required is nothing less than a bold imaginative departure to create a new science of environmental biomedicine.

Needless to say, there does exist now a definite body of knowledge concerning man's interplay with his environment. But it is a highly episodic kind of knowledge, derived from attempts to solve a few practical problems. For example, research in human ecology has been stimulated by the training of combat forces for operation in the tropics or in the Arctic, by preparation for space travel, or by concern with brainwashing and the effects of solitary confinement. Useful as it is, the knowledge thus obtained is piecemeal and does not go far toward creating a systematic science of man in his environment.

In theory, this science could be and should be developed within the university. In practice, however, this will not be readily achieved. Universities are the reservoirs of classical knowledge, and still constitute the most important source of new knowledge. But their administrative structure—in addition to their educational responsibilities—make it difficult for them to develop the facilities and highly technical information required for solving the problems of rapidly changing societies.

Furthermore, the academic investigator insists, as he should, on his right to follow the internal logic of his intellectual interests. He is "discipline" oriented rather than "mission" oriented. Since human ecology derives its importance from social concerns rather than from its relation to orthodox biological disciplines, there is reason to fear that it will be given a low priority in the academic scale of values. The requirements of human ecology for new kinds of research facilities and for a change in intellectual approach will provide a ready excuse for neglect. In my opinion, this science will develop only if society recognizes that ecological knowledge is essential to its welfare, and if facilities for the procurement of this knowledge are provided either outside the university complex, or in new academic institutions not yet committed to the orthodox fields of science.

On several occasions in the past new fields of science have been developed outside the university in response to social needs.

For example: Agricultural experiment stations, supported by theoretical laboratories, were established throughout the United States in the late 19th century, because farming practices introduced from Europe were not suited to the natural conditions and social structures prevailing in most parts of the American continent.

Independent institutes of microbiology also were created all over the world at the end of the 19th century, because infectious processes were then the most important causes of death and disease. Medical schools did not undertake microbiological research until this science had been established in the new institutes.

Institutions devoted to aeronautics, space sciences, communication theory have recently been established outside universities (often by large industrial firms) to deal more rapidly with these new aspects of theoretical and practical knowledge. Several research institutes concerned with the nutritional problems peculiar to underdeveloped countries are now being sponsored by international organizations.

Thus, new research institutes commonly emerge in response to social demands. These institutes in turn affect the development of theoretical science by shifting the areas of emphasis—then they may or may not become incorporated in the university structure.

A last historical example will serve to illustrate how certain scientific fields must be nurtured outside the university system before they are accepted in the academic establishment.

At the beginning of this century, many physicians and laymen realized that medicine could not progress without more knowledge of the physiochemical bases of bodily functions. Medical schools, however, did not find it possible or even advisable to involve themselves in such a paramedical field. Fortunately, the founders of the Rockefeller Institute for Medical Research decided to take the responsibility for this task; they devoted large resources to the support of a kind of biomedical research that was then foreign to American medical schools. The prosecution of the physicochemical basis of medicine at the Rockefeller Institute gave intellectual recognition and glamor to this field in the United States. Within less than a quarter of a century, every important medical school tried to develop on its campus research facilities similar to those of the Rockefeller Institute.

The social need for human ecology is even more acute today than was the demand for a physicochemical basis of medicine at the turn of the century. For this reason it is essential to create new kinds of institutions to study the interplay between human life, technology, urbanization, and natural resources. One can expect that if investigators are given a chance to demonstrate the usefulness of human ecology, many medical schools and biological research institutes will consider as a legitimate aspect of their programs the interplay between man and his total environment. Historians of medical science will then discover that Hippocrates' treatise on "Airs, Waters, and Places" is a classical expression of what we now call "Human Ecology."

COMMENTS ■ QUESTIONS

1. Since the time that Dubos' paper was published in 1968, much has been done, particularly in Western countries, to combat water and air pollution and to reduce stresses in the work environment. At the same time, technological disasters have affected, or threatened to affect, human ecology, for example, at Three Mile Island in the United States, Bhopal in India, and Chernobyl in the USSR. In terms of a worldwide ecological perspective, would you say that things have gotten better or worse since 1968?
2. Says Dubos: "The modern environment is dangerous on two accounts: It contains elements that are outright noxious; it changes so rapidly that man cannot make fast enough the proper adaptive responses to it." Which of these two do you believe is the greater danger?
3. In what way or ways (if any) could the preservation of wilderness (discussed in the preceding article by William Godfrey-Smith) play a role in combating the "diseases of civilization"?
4. One condition cited by Dubos as contributing to the diseases of civilization is "the compulsory leisure ensuing from automated work." How might the increased leisure that is characteristic of life in advanced countries be put to better use? What role could, or should, the discipline of philosophy play in this?
5. Dubos discusses possible uses of experimental animals in solving problems in human ecology. Are there any ethical conflicts between these uses of animals and the view of Godfrey-Smith that animals should be thought of as having intrinsic value?
6. Do you believe that an "ethics of altruism" is needed to solve present-day ecological problems, or is an "ethics of enlightened self-interest" preferable, or at least adequate?

STEPHEN P. STICH

The Recombinant DNA Debate

The debate over recombinant DNA research is a unique event, perhaps a turning point, in the history of science. For the first time in modern history there has been widespread public discussion about whether and how a promising though potentially dangerous line of research shall be pursued. At root the debate is a moral debate and, like most such debates, requires proper assessment of the facts at crucial stages in the argument. A good deal of the controversy over recombinant DNA research arises because some of the facts simply are not yet known. There are many empirical questions we would like to have answered before coming to a decision—questions about the reliability of proposed containment facilities, about the viability of enfeebled strains of *E. coli*, about the ways in which pathogenic organisms do their unwelcome work, and much more. But all decisions cannot wait until the facts are available; some must be made now. It is to be expected that people with different hunches about what the facts will turn out to be will urge different decisions on how recombinant DNA research should be regulated. However, differing expectations about the facts have not been the only fuel for controversy. A significant part of the current debate can be traced to differences over moral principles. Also, unfortunately, there has been much unnecessary debate generated by careless moral reasoning and a failure to attend to the logical structure of some of the moral arguments that have been advanced.

In order to help sharpen our perception of the moral issues underlying the controversy over recombinant DNA research, I shall start by clearing away some frivolous arguments that have deflected attention from more serious issues. We may then examine the problems involved in deciding whether the potential benefits of recombinant DNA research justify pursuing it despite the risks that it poses.

I Three Bad Arguments

My focus in this section will be on three untenable arguments, each of

Stephen P. Stich, a professor of philosophy at the University of California at San Diego, is the author of From Folk Psychology to Cognitive Science *and many articles in the areas of the philosophy of psychology and public policy.*

From Stephen P. Stich, "The Recombinant DNA Debate," *Philosophy & Public Affairs* 7, no. 3 (Spring 1978). Copyright (c) 1978 by Princeton University Press. Reprinted by permission of Princeton University Press.

which has surfaced with considerable frequency in the public debate over recombinant DNA research.

The first argument on my list concludes that recombinant DNA research should not be controlled or restricted. The central premise of the argument is that scientists should have full and unqualified freedom to pursue whatever inquiries they may choose to pursue. This claim was stated repeatedly in petitions and letters to the editor during the height of the public debate over recombinant DNA research in the University of Michigan community.[1] The general moral principle which is the central premise of the argument plainly does entail that investigators using recombinant DNA technology should be allowed to pursue their research as they see fit. However, we need only consider a few examples to see that the principle invoked in this "freedom of inquiry" argument is utterly indefensible. No matter how sincere a researcher's interest may be in investigating the conjugal behavior of American university professors, few would be willing to grant him the right to pursue his research in my bedroom without my consent. No matter how interested a researcher may be in investigating the effects of massive doses of bomb-grade plutonium on preschool children, it is hard to imagine that anyone thinks he should be allowed to do so. Yet the "free inquiry" principle, if accepted, would allow both of these projects and countless other Dr. Strangelove projects as well. So plainly the simplistic "free inquiry" principle is indefensible. It would, however, be a mistake to conclude that freedom of inquiry ought not to be protected. A better conclusion is that the right of free inquiry is a qualified right and must sometimes yield to conflicting rights and to the demands of conflicting moral principles. Articulating an explicit and properly qualified principle of free inquiry is a task of no small difficulty. We will touch on this topic again toward the end of Section II.

The second argument I want to examine aims at establishing just the opposite conclusion from the first. The particular moral judgment being defended is that there should be a total ban on recombinant DNA research. The argument begins with the observation that even in so-called low-risk recombinant DNA experiments there is at least a possibility of catastrophic consequences. We are, after all, dealing with a relatively new and unexplored technolo-

1. For example, from a widely circulated petition signed by both faculty and community people: "The most important challenge may be a confrontation with one of our ancient assumptions—that there must be an absolute and unqualified freedom to pursue scientific inquiries. We will soon begin to wonder what meaning this freedom has if it leads to the destruction or demoralization of human beings, the only life forms able to exercise it." And from a letter to the editor written by a Professor of Engineering Humanities: "Is science beyond social and human controls, so that freedom of inquiry implies the absence of usual social restrictions which we all, as citizens, obey, respecting the social contract?"

It is interesting to note that the "freedom of inquiry" argument is rarely proposed by defenders of recombinant DNA research. Rather, it is proposed, then attacked, by those who are opposed to research involving recombinant molecules. Their motivation, it would seem, is to discredit the proponents of recombinant DNA research by attributing a foolish argument to them, then demonstrating that it is indeed a foolish argument.

gy. Thus it is at least possible that a bacterial culture whose genetic makeup has been altered in the course of a recombinant DNA experiment may exhibit completely unexpected pathogenic characteristics. Indeed, it is not impossible that we could find ourselves confronted with a killer strain of, say, *E. coli* and, worse, a strain against which humans can marshal no natural defense. Now if this is possible—if we cannot say with assurance that the probability of it happening is zero—then, the argument continues, all recombinant DNA research should be halted. For the negative utility of the imagined catastrophe is so enormous, resulting as it would in the destruction of our society and perhaps even of our species, that no work which could possibly lead to this result would be worth the risk.

The argument just sketched, which might be called the "doomsday scenario" argument, begins with a premise which no informed person would be inclined to deny. It is indeed *possible* that even a low-risk recombinant DNA experiment might lead to totally catastrophic results. No ironclad guarantee can be offered that this will not happen. And while the probability of such an unanticipated catastrophe is surely not large, there is no serious argument that the probability is zero. Still, I think the argument is a sophistry. To go from the undeniable premise that recombinant DNA research might possibly result in unthinkable catastrophe to the conclusion that such research should be banned requires a moral principle stating that *all* endeavors that might possibly result in such a catastrophe should be prohibited. Once the principle has been stated, it is hard to believe that anyone would take it at all seriously. For the principle entails that, along with recombinant DNA research, almost all scientific research and many other commonplace activities having little to do with science should be prohibited. It is, after all, at least logically possible that the next new compound synthesized in an ongoing chemical research program will turn out to be an uncontainable carcinogen many orders of magnitude more dangerous than aerosol plutonium. And, to vary the example, there is a non-zero probability that experiments in artificial pollination will produce a weed that will, a decade from now, ruin the world's food grain harvest.[2]

I cannot resist noting that the principle invoked in the doomsday scenario argument is not new. Pascal used an entirely parallel argument to show that it is in our own best interests to believe in God. For though the probability of God's existence may be very low, if He nonetheless should happen to exist, the disutility that would accrue to the disbeliever would be catastrophic—an eternity in hell. But, as introductory philosophy students should all know, Pascal's argument only looks persuasive if we take our options to be just

---

2. Unfortunately, the doomsday scenario argument is *not* a straw man conjured only by those who would refute it. Consider, for example, the remarks of Anthony Mazzocchi, spokesman for the Oil, Chemical and Atomic Workers International Union, reported in *Science News*, 19 March 1977, p. 181: "When scientists argue over safe or unsafe, we ought to be very prudent. . . . If critics are correct and the Andromeda scenario has *even the smallest possibility of* occurring, we must assume it will occur on the basis of our experience" (emphasis added).

two: Christianity or atheism. A third possibility is belief in a jealous non-Christian God who will see to our damnation if and only if we *are* Christians. The probability of such a deity existing is again very small, but non-zero. So Pascal's argument is of no help in deciding whether or not to accept Christianity. For we may be damned if we do and damned if we don't.

I mention Pascal's difficulty because there is a direct parallel in the doomsday scenario argument against recombinant DNA research. Just as there is a non-zero probability that unforeseen consequences of recombinant DNA research will lead to disaster, so there is a non-zero probability that unforeseen consequences of *failing* to pursue the research will lead to disaster. There may, for example, come a time when, because of natural or man-induced climatic change, the capacity to alter quickly the genetic constitution of agricultural plants will be necessary to forestall catastrophic famine. And if we fail to pursue recombinant DNA research now, our lack of knowledge in the future may have consequences as dire as any foreseen in the doomsday scenario argument.

The third argument I want to consider provides a striking illustration of how important it is, in normative thinking, to make clear the moral *principles* being invoked. The argument I have in mind begins with a factual claim about recombinant DNA research and concludes that stringent restrictions, perhaps even a moratorium, should be imposed. However, advocates of the argument are generally silent on the normative principle(s) linking premise and conclusion. The gap thus created can be filled in a variety of ways, resulting in very different arguments. The empirical observation that begins the argument is that recombinant DNA methods enable scientists to move genes back and forth across natural barriers, "particularly the most fundamental such barrier, that which divides prokaryotes from eukaryotes. The results will be essentially new organisms, self-perpetuating and hence permanent."[3] Because of this, it is concluded that severe restrictions are in order. Plainly this argument is an enthymeme; a central premise has been left unstated. What sort of moral principle is being tacitly assumed?

The principle that comes first to mind is simply that natural barriers should not be breached, or perhaps that "essentially new organisms" should not be created. The principle has an almost theological ring to it, and perhaps there are some people who would be prepared to defend it on theological grounds. But short of a theological argument, it is hard to see why anyone would hold the view that breaching natural barriers or creating new organisms is *intrinsically* wrong. For if a person were to advocate such a principle, he would have to condemn the creation of new bacterial strains capable of, say, synthesizing human clotting factor or insulin, *even if* creating the new organism generated *no unwelcome side effects*.

---

3. The quotation is from George Wald, "The Case Against Genetic Engineering," *The Sciences*, September/October 1976; to be reprinted in David A. Jackson and Stephen P. Stich, eds., *The Recombinant DNA Debate*, forthcoming.

There is quite a different way of unraveling the "natural barriers" argument which avoids appeal to the dubious principles just discussed. As an alternative, this second reading of the argument ties premise to conclusion with a second factual claim and a quite different normative premise. The added factual claim is that at present our knowledge of the consequences of creating new forms of life is severely limited; thus we cannot know with any assurance that the probability of disastrous consequences is very low. The moral principle needed to mesh with the two factual premises would be something such as the following:

> If we do not know with considerable assurance that the probability of an activity leading to disastrous consequences is very low, then we should not allow the activity to continue.

Now this principle, unlike those marshaled in the first interpretation of the natural barriers argument, is not lightly dismissed. It is, to be sure, a conservative principle, and it has the odd feature of focusing entirely on the dangers an activity poses while ignoring its potential benefits.[4] Still, the principle may have a certain attraction in light of recent history, which has increasingly been marked by catastrophes attributable to technology's unanticipated side effects. I will not attempt a full scale evaluation of this principle just now. For the principle raises, albeit in a rather extreme way, the question of how risks and benefits are to be weighed against each other. In my opinion, that is the really crucial moral question raised by recombinant DNA research. It is a question which bristles with problems. In Section II I shall take a look at some of these problems and make a few tentative steps toward some solutions. While picking our way through the problems we will have another opportunity to examine the principle just cited.

II Risks and Benefits

At first glance it might be thought that the issue of risks and benefits is quite straightforward, at least in principle. What we want to know is whether the potential benefits of recombinant DNA research justify the risks involved. To find out we need only determine the probabilities of the various dangers and benefits. And while some of the empirical facts—the probabilities—may require considerable ingenuity and effort to uncover, the assessment poses no particularly difficult normative or conceptual problems. Unfortunately, this sanguine view does not survive much more than a first glance. A closer look at the task of balancing the risks and benefits of recombinant DNA research reveals a quagmire of sticky conceptual problems and simmering moral disputes. In the next few pages I will try to catalogue and comment on some of these moral disputes. I wish I could also promise solutions to all of them, but to do so would be false advertising.

---

4. It is important to note, however, that the principle is considerably less conservative, and correspondingly more plausible, than the principle invoked in the doomsday scenario argument. That latter principle would have us enjoin an activity if the probability of the activity leading to catastrophe is anything other than zero.

Problems about Probabilities

In trying to assess costs and benefits, a familiar first step is to set down a list of possible actions and possible outcomes. Next, we assign some measure of desirability to each possible outcome, and for each action we estimate the conditional probability of each outcome given that the action is performed. In attempting to apply this decision-making strategy to the case of recombinant DNA research, the assignment of probabilities poses some perplexing problems. Some of the outcomes whose probabilities we want to know can be approached using standard empirical techniques. Thus, for example, we may want to know what the probability is of a specific enfeebled host *E. coli* strain surviving passage through the human intestinal system, should it be accidentally ingested. Or we may want to know what the probability is that a host organism will escape from a P-4 laboratory. In such cases, while there may be technical difficulties to be overcome, we have a reasonably clear idea of the sort of data needed to estimate the required probabilities. But there are other possible outcomes whose probabilities cannot be determined by experiment. It is important, for example, to know what the probability is of recombinant DNA research leading to a method for developing nitrogen-fixing strains of corn and wheat. And it is important to know how likely it is that recombinant DNA research will lead to techniques for effectively treating or preventing various types of cancer. Yet there is no experiment we can perform nor any data we can gather that will enable us to *empirically* estimate these probabilities. Nor are these the most problematic probabilities we may want to know. A possibility that weighs heavily on the minds of many who are worried about recombinant DNA research is that this research may lead to negative consequences for human health or for the environment *which have not yet even been thought of*. The history of technology during the last half-century surely demonstrates that this is not a quixotic concern. Yet here again there would appear to be no data we can gather that would help much in estimating the probability of such potential outcomes.

It should be stressed that the problems just sketched are not to be traced simply to a paucity of data. Rather, they are conceptual problems; it is doubtful whether there is *any clear empirical sense* to be made of objective probability assignments to contingencies like those we are considering.

Theorists in the Bayesian tradition may be unmoved by the difficulties we have noted. On their view all probability claims are reports of subjective probabilities.[5] And, a Bayesian might quite properly note, there is no special problem about assigning *subjective* probabilities to outcomes such as those that worried us. But even for the radical Bayesian, there remains the problem of *whose* subjective probabilities ought to be employed in making a *social* or *political* decision. The problem is a press-

---

5. For an elaboration of the Bayesian position, see Leonard J. Savage, *The Foundations of Statistics* (New York: John Wiley & Sons, 1954); also cf. Leonard J. Savage, "The Shifting Foundations of Statistics," in Robert G. Colodny, ed., *Logic, Laws and Life* (Pittsburgh: University of Pittsburgh Press, 1977).

ing one since the subjective probabilities assigned to potential dangers and benefits of recombinant DNA research would appear to vary considerably even among reasonably well informed members of the scientific community.

The difficulties we have been surveying are serious ones. Some might feel they are so serious that they render rational assessment of the risks and benefits of recombinant DNA research all but impossible. I am inclined to be rather more optimistic, however. Almost all of the perils posed by recombinant DNA research require the occurrence of a sequence of separate events. For a chimerical bacterial strain created in a recombinant DNA experiment to cause a serious epidemic, for example, at least the following events must occur:

1. a pathogenic bacterium must be synthesized
2. the chimerical bacteria must escape from the laboratory
3. the strain must be viable in nature
4. the strain must compete successfully with other micro-organisms which are themselves the product of intense natural selection.[6]

Since *all* of these must occur, the probability of the potential epidemic is the product of the probabilities of each individual contingency. And there are at least two items on the list, namely (2) and (3), whose probabilities are amenable to reasonably straightforward empirical assessment. Thus the product of these two individual probabilities places an upper limit on the probability of the epidemic. For the remaining two probabilities, we must rely on subjective probability assessments of informed scientists. No doubt there will be considerable variability. Yet even here the variability will be limited. In the case of 4., as an example, the available knowledge about microbial natural selection provides no precise way of estimating the probability that a chimerical strain of enfeebled *E. coli* will compete successfully outside the laboratory. But no serious scientist would urge that the probability is *high*. We can then use the highest responsible subjective estimate of the probabilities of (1) and (4) in calculating the "worst case" estimate of the risk of epidemic. If in using this highest "worst case" estimate, our assessment yields the result that benefits outweigh risks, then lower estimates of the same probabilities will, of course, yield the same conclusion. Thus it may well be the case that the problems about probabilities we have reviewed will not pose insuperable obstacles to a rational assessment of risks and benefits.

Weighing Harms and Benefits

A second cluster of problems that confronts us in assessing the risks and benefits of recombinant DNA research turns on the assignment of a measure of desirability to the various possible outcomes. Suppose that we have a list of the various harms and benefits that might possibly result from pursuing recombinant DNA research. The list will include such "benefits" as development of an inexpensive way to synthesize hu-

6. For an elaboration of this point, see Bernard D. Davis, "Evolution, Epidemiology, and Recombinant DNA," *The Recombinant DNA Debate*, forthcoming.

man clotting factor and development of a strain of nitrogen-fixing wheat; and such "harms" as release of a new antibiotic-resistant strain of pathogenic bacteria and release of a strain of *E. coli* carrying tumor viruses capable of causing cancer in man.

Plainly, it is possible that pursuing a given policy will result in more than one benefit and in more than one harm. Now if we are to assess the potential impact of various policies or courses of action, we must assign some index of desirability to the possible *total outcomes* of each policy, outcomes which may well include a mix of benefits and harms. To do this we must confront a tangle of normative problems that are as vexing and difficult as any we are likely to face. We must *compare* the moral desirabilities of various harms and benefits. The task is particularly troublesome when the harms and benefits to be compared are of different kinds. Thus, for example, some of the attractive potential benefits of recombinant DNA research are economic: we may learn to recover small amounts of valuable metals in an economically feasible way, or we may be able to synthesize insulin and other drugs inexpensively. By contrast, many of the risks of recombinant DNA research are risks to human life or health. So if we are to take the idea of cost-benefit analysis seriously, we must at some point decide how human lives are to be weighed against economic benefits.

There are those who contend that the need to make such decisions indicates the moral bankruptcy of attempting to employ risk-benefit analyses when human lives are at stake. On the critics' view, we cannot reckon the possible loss of a human life as just another negative outcome, albeit a grave and heavily weighted one. To do so, it is urged, is morally repugnant and reflects a callous lack of respect for the sacredness of human life.

On my view, this sort of critique of the very idea of using risk-benefit analyses is ultimately untenable. It is simply a fact about the human condition, lamentable as it is inescapable, that in many human activities we run the risk of inadvertently causing the death of a human being. We run such a risk each time we drive a car, allow a dam to be built, or allow a plane to take off. Moreover, in making social and individual decisions, we cannot escape weighing economic consequences against the risk to human life. A building code in the Midwest will typically mandate fewer precautions against earthquakes than a building code in certain parts of California. Yet earthquakes are not impossible in the Midwest. If we elect not to require precautions, then surely a major reason must be that it would simply be too expensive. In this judgment, as in countless others, there is no escaping the need to balance economic costs against possible loss of life. To deny that we must and do balance economic costs against risks to human life is to assume the posture of a moral ostrich.

I have been urging the point that it is not *morally objectionable* to try to balance economic concerns against risks to human life. But if such judgments are unobjectionable, indeed necessary, they also surely are among the most difficult any of us has to face. It is hard to imagine a morally sensitive person not feeling extremely uncomfortable when confronted with the need to put a dollar value on human lives. It might be thought that the moral dilemmas engendered by the need to balance such radically different costs and benefits pose insuperable practical obstacles for a rational resolution of the recombinant DNA debate. But here, as in the case of problems with probabilities, I am more sanguine. For while some of the risks and potential benefits of recombinant DNA research are all but morally incommensurable, the most salient risks and benefits are easier to compare. The major risks, as we have noted, are to human life and health. However, the major potential benefits are *also* to human life and health. The potential economic benefits of recombinant DNA research pale in significance when set against the potential for major breakthroughs in our understanding and ability to treat a broad range of conditions, from birth defects to cancer. Those of us, and I confess I am among them, who despair of deciding how lives and economic benefits are to be compared can nonetheless hope to settle our views about recombinant DNA research by comparing the potential risks to life and health with the potential benefits to life and health. Here we are comparing plainly commensurable outcomes. If the balance turns out to be favorable, then we need not worry about factoring in potential economic benefits.

There is a certain irony in the fact that we may well be able to ignore economic factors entirely in coming to a decision about recombinant DNA research. For I suspect that a good deal of the apprehension about recombinant DNA research on the part of the public at large is rooted in the fear that (once again) economic benefits will be weighed much too heavily and potential damage to health and the environment will be weighed much too lightly. The fear is hardly an irrational one. In case after well-publicized case, we have seen the squalid consequences of decisions in which private or corporate gain took precedence over clear and serious threats to health and to the environment. It is the profit motive that led a giant chemical firm to conceal the deadly consequences of the chemical which now threatens to poison the James River and perhaps all of Chesapeake Bay. For the same reason, the citizens of Duluth drank water laced with a known carcinogen. And the ozone layer that protects us all was eroded while regulatory agencies and legislators fussed over the loss of profits in the spray deodorant industry. Yet while public opinion about recombinant DNA research is colored by a growing awareness of these incidents and dozens of others, the case of recombinant DNA is fundamentally different in a crucial respect. The important projected benefits which must be set against the risks of recombinant DNA research are not economic at all, they are medical and environmental.

COMMENTS ■ QUESTIONS

1. Three arguments regarding recombinant DNA research are bad arguments, says Stich. Do you agree that all three are bad arguments?
2. Stich defends the application of cost-benefit analysis to recombinant DNA research. Is his defense successful? Is cost-benefit analysis appropriate in this case?
3. Does Stich place sufficient weight on the possibility that DNA research may lead to "negative consequences for human health or for the environment *which have not yet even been thought of*?" Put another way, is Stich cautious enough? Or is he too cautious?

CARL SAGAN

In Praise of Science and Technology

In the middle of the nineteenth century, the largely self-educated British physicist Michael Faraday was visited by his monarch, Queen Victoria. Among Faraday's many celebrated discoveries, some of obvious and immediate practical benefit, were more arcane findings in electricity and magnetism, then little more than laboratory curiosities. In the traditional dialogue between heads of state and heads of laboratories, the Queen asked Faraday of what use such studies were, to which he is said to have replied, "Madam, of what use is a baby?" Faraday had an idea that there might someday be something practical in electricity and magnetism.

In the same period the Scottish physicist James Clerk Maxwell set down four mathematical equations,

Carl Sagan, who is David Duncan Professor of Astronomy and Space Sciences and Director of the Laboratory for Planetary Studies at Cornell University, is well known for his many popular and scientific books and articles, which include Dragons of Eden *and* Cosmos.

From *Broca's Brain,* by Carl Sagan. Copyright (c) 1979 by Carl Sagan. Reprinted by permission of Random House, Inc.

based on the work of Faraday and his experimental predecessors, relating electrical charges and currents with electric and magnetic fields. The equations exhibited a curious lack of symmetry, and this bothered Maxwell. There was something unaesthetic about the equations as then known, and to improve the symmetry Maxwell proposed that one of the equations should have an additional term, which he called the displacement current. His argument was fundamentally intuitive; there was certainly no experimental evidence for such a current. Maxwell's proposal had astonishing consequences. The corrected Maxwell equations implied the existence of electromagnetic radiation, encompassing gamma rays, X-rays, ultraviolet light, visible light, infrared and radio. They stimulated Einstein to discover Special Relativity. Faraday and Maxwell's laboratory and theoretical work together have led, one century later, to a technical revolution on the planet Earth. Electric lights, telephones, phonographs, radio, television, refrigerated trains making fresh produce available far from the farm, cardiac pacemakers, hydroelectric power plants, automatic fire alarms and sprinkler systems, electric trolleys and subways, and the electronic computer are a few devices in the direct evolutionary line from the arcane laboratory puttering of Faraday and the aesthetic dissatisfaction of Maxwell, staring at some mathematical squiggles on a piece of paper. Many of the most practical applications of science have been made in this serendipitous and unpredictable way. No amount of money would have sufficed in Victoria's day for the leading scientists in Britain to have simply sat down and invented, let us say, television. Few would argue that the net effect of these inventions was other than positive. I notice that even many young people who are profoundly disenchanted with Western technological civilization, often for good reason, still retain a passionate fondness for certain aspects of high technology—for example, high-fidelity electronic music systems.

Some of these inventions have fundamentally changed the character of our global society. Ease of communication has deprovincialized many parts of the world, but cultural diversity has been likewise diminished. The practical advantages of these inventions are recognized in virtually all human societies; it is remarkable how infrequently emerging nations are concerned with the negative effects of high technology (environmental pollution, for example); they have clearly decided that the benefits outweigh the risks. One of Lenin's aphorisms was that socialism plus electrification equals communism. But there has been no more vigorous or inventive pursuit of high technology than in the West. The resulting rate of change has been so rapid that many of us find it difficult to keep up. There are many people alive today who were born before the first airplane and have lived to see Viking land on Mars, and Pioneer 10, the first interstellar spacecraft, be ejected from the solar system, or who were raised in a sexual code of Victorian severity and now find themselves immersed in substantial sexual freedom, brought about by the widespread availability of effective contraceptives. The rate of change has been disorienting for many, and it is easy to understand the nostalgic appeal of a return to an earlier and simpler existence.

But the standard of living and conditions of work for the great bulk of the population in, say, Victorian England, were degrading and demoralizing compared to industrial societies today, and the life-expectancy and infant-mortality statistics were appalling. Science and technology may be in part responsible for many of the problems that face us today—but largely because public understanding of them is desperately inadequate (technology is a tool, not a panacea), and because insufficient effort has been made to accommodate our society to the new technologies. Considering these facts, I find it remarkable that we have done as well as we have. Luddite alternatives can solve nothing. More than one billion people alive today owe the margin between barely adequate nutrition and starvation to high agricultural technology. Probably an equal number have survived, or avoided disfiguring, crippling or killing diseases because of high medical technology. Were high technology to be abandoned, these people would also be abandoned. Science and technology may be the cause of some of our problems, but they are certainly an essential element in any foreseeable solution to those same problems—both nationally and planetwide.

I do not think that science and technology have been pursued as effectively, with as much attention to their ultimate humane objectives and with as adequate a public understanding as, with a little greater effort, could have been accomplished. It has, for example, gradually dawned on us that human activities can have an adverse effect on not only the local but also the global environment. By accident a few research groups in atmospheric photochemistry discovered that halocarbon propellants from aerosol spray cans will reside for very long periods in the atmosphere, circulate to the stratosphere, partially destroy the ozone there, and let ultraviolet light from the sun leak down to the Earth's surface. Increased skin cancer for whites was the most widely advertised consequence (blacks are neatly adapted to increased ultraviolet flux). But very little public attention has been given to the much more serious possibility that microorganisms, occupying the base of an elaborate food pyramid at the top of which is *Homo sapiens*, might also be destroyed by the increased ultraviolet light. Steps have finally, although reluctantly, been taken to ban halocarbons from spray cans (although no one seems to be worrying about the same molecules used in refrigerators) and as a result the immediate dangers are probably slight. What I find most worrisome about this incident is how accidental was the discovery that the problem existed at all. One group approached this problem because it had written the appropriate computer programs, but in quite a different context: they were concerned with the chemistry of the atmosphere of the planet Venus, which contains hydrochloric and hydrofluoric acids. The need for a broad and diverse set of research teams, working on a great variety of problems in pure science, is clearly required for our continued survival. But what other problems, even more severe, exist which we do not know about because no research group happens as yet to have stumbled on them? For each problem we have uncovered, such as the effect of halocarbons on the ozonosphere, might there not be another dozen lurking around the corner? It is therefore an astonishing fact that nowhere in the federal government, major universities or private research institutes is there a single highly competent, broadly empowered and adequately funded research group whose function it is to seek out and defuse future catastrophes resulting from the development of new technologies.

The establishment of such research and environmental assessment organizations will require substantial political courage if they are to be effective at all. Technological societies have a tightly knit industrial ecology, an interwoven network of economic assumptions. It is very difficult to challenge one thread in the network without causing tremors in all. Any judgment that a technological development will have adverse human consequences implies a loss of profit for someone. The DuPont Company, the principal manufacturers of halocarbon propellants, for example, took the curious position in public debates that all conclusions about halocarbons destroying the ozonosphere were "theoretical." They seemed to be implying that they would be prepared to stop halocarbon manufacture only after the conclusions were tested experimentally—that is, when the ozonosphere was destroyed. There are some problems where inferential evidence is all that we will have; where once the catastrophe arrives it is too late to deal with it.

Similarly, the new Department of Energy can be effective only if it can maintain a distance from vested commercial interests, if it is free to pursue new options even if such options imply loss of profits for selected industries. The same is clearly true in pharmaceutical research, in the pursuit of alternatives to the internal-combustion engine, and in many other technological frontiers. I do not think that the development of new technologies should be placed in the control of old technologies; the temptation to suppress the competition is too great. If we Americans live in a free-enterprise society, let us see substantial independent enterprise in all of the technologies upon which our future may depend. If organizations devoted to technological innovation and its boundaries of acceptability are not challenging (and perhaps even offending) at least *some* powerful groups, they are not accomplishing their purpose.

There are many practical technological developments that are not being pursued for lack of government support. For example, as agonizing a disease as cancer is, I do not think it can be said that our civilization is threatened by it. Were cancer to be cured completely, the average life expectancy would be extended by only a few years, until some other disease—which does not now have its chance at cancer victims—takes over. But a very plausible case can be made that our civilization is fundamentally threatened by the lack of adequate fertility control. Exponential increases of population will dominate any arithmetic increases, even those brought about by heroic technological initiatives, in the availability of food and resources, as Malthus long ago realized. While some industrial nations have approached zero population growth, this is not the case for the world as a whole.

Minor climatic fluctuations can destroy entire populations with marginal economies. In many societies where the technology is meager and reaching adulthood an uncertain prospect, having many children is the only possible hedge against a desperate and uncertain future. Such a society, in the grip of a consuming famine, for example, has little to lose. At a time when nuclear weapons are proliferating unconscionably, when an atomic device is almost a home handicraft industry, widespread famine and steep gradients in affluence pose serious dangers to both the developed and the underdeveloped worlds. The solution to such problems certainly requires better education, at least a degree of technological self-sufficiency, and, especially, fair distribution of the world's resources. But it also cries out for entirely adequate contraception—long-term, safe birth-control pills, available for men as well as for women, perhaps to be taken once a month or over even longer intervals. Such a development would be very useful not just abroad but also here at home, where considerable concern is being expressed about the side effects of the conventional estrogen oral contraceptives. Why is there no major effort for such a development?

Many other technological initiatives are being proposed and ought to be examined very seriously. They range from the very cheap to the extremely expensive. At one end is soft technology—for example, the development of closed ecological systems involving algae, shrimp and fish which could be maintained in rural ponds and provide a highly nutritious and extremely low-cost dietary supplement. At the other is the proposal of Gerard O'Neill of Princeton University to construct large orbital cities that would, using lunar and asteroidal materials, be self-propagating—one city being able to construct another from extraterrestrial resources. Such cities in Earth orbit might be used in converting sunlight into microwave energy and beaming power down to Earth. The idea of independent cities in space—each perhaps built on differing social, economic or political assumptions, or having different ethnic antecedents—is appealing, an opportunity for those deeply disenchanted with terrestrial civilizations to strike out on their own somewhere else. In its earlier history, America provided such an opportunity for the restless, ambitious and adventurous. Space cities would be a kind of America in the skies. They also would greatly enhance the survival potential of the human species. But the project is extremely expensive, costing at minimum about the same as one Vietnam war (in resources, not in lives). In addition, the idea has the worrisome overtone of abandoning the problems on the Earth—where, after all, self-contained pioneering communities can be established at much less cost.

Clearly, there are more technological projects now possible than we can afford. Some of them may be extremely cost-effective but may have such large start-up costs as to remain impractical. Others may require a daring initial investment of resources, which will work a benevolent revolution in our society. Such options have to be considered extremely carefully. The most prudent strategy calls for combining low-risk/moderate-yield and moderate-risk/high-yield endeavors.

For such technological initiatives to be understood and supported, significant improvements in public understanding of science and technology are essential. We are thinking beings. Our minds are our distinguishing characteristic as a species. We are not stronger or swifter than many other animals that share this planet with us. We are only smarter. In addition to the immense practical benefit of having a scientifically literate public, the contemplation of science and technology permits us to exercise our intellectual faculties to the limits of our capabilities. Science is an exploration of the intricate, subtle and awesome universe we inhabit. Those who practice it know, at least on occasion, a rare kind of exhilaration that Socrates said was the greatest of human pleasures. It is a communicable pleasure. To facilitate informed public participation in technological decision making, to decrease the alienation too many citizens feel from our technological society, and for the sheer joy that comes from knowing a deep thing well, we need better science education, a superior communication of its powers and delights. A simple place to start is to undo the self-destructive decline in federal scholarships and fellowships for science researchers and science teachers at the college, graduate and post-doctoral levels.

The most effective agents to communicate science to the public are television, motion pictures and newspapers—where the science offerings are often dreary, inaccurate, ponderous, grossly caricatured or (as with much Saturday-morning commercial television programing for children) hostile to science. There have been astonishing recent findings on the exploration of the planets, the role of small brain proteins in affecting our emotional lives, the collisions of continents, the evolution of the human species (and the extent to which our past prefigures our future), the ultimate structure of matter (and the question of whether there are elementary particles or an infinite regress of them), the attempt to communicate with civilizations on planets of other stars, the nature of the genetic code (which determines our heredity and makes us cousins to all the other plants and animals on our planet), and the ultimate questions of the origin, nature and fate of life, worlds and the universe as a whole. Recent findings on these questions can be understood by any intelligent person. Why are they so rarely discussed in the media, in schools, in everyday conversation?

Civilizations can be characterized by how they approach such questions, how they nourish the mind as well as the body. The modern scientific pursuit of these questions represents an attempt to acquire a generally accepted view of our place in the cosmos; it requires open-minded creativity, tough-minded skepticism and a fresh sense of wonder. These questions are different from the practical issues I discussed earlier, but they are connected with such issues and—as in the example of Faraday and Maxwell—the encouragement of pure research may be the most reliable guarantee available that we will have the intellectual and technical wherewithal to deal with the practical problems facing us.

Only a small fraction of the most able youngsters enter scientific careers. I am often amazed at how much more capability and enthusiasm for science there is among elementary school youngsters than among college students. Something happens in the school years to discourage their interest (and it is not mainly puberty); we must understand and circumvent this dangerous discouragement. No one can predict where the future leaders of science will come from. It is clear that Albert Einstein became a scientist in spite of, not because of, his schooling. In his *Autobiography*, Malcolm X describes a numbers runner who never wrote down a bet but carried a lifetime of transactions perfectly in his head. What contributions to society, Malcolm asked, would such a person have made with adequate education and encouragement? The most brilliant youngsters are a national and a global resource. They require special care and feeding.

Many of the problems facing us may be soluble, but only if we are willing to embrace brilliant, daring and complex solutions. Such solutions require brilliant, daring and complex people. I believe that there are many more of them around—in every nation, ethnic group and degree of affluence—than we realize. The training of such youngsters must not, of course, be restricted to science and technology; indeed, the compassionate application of new technology to human problems requires a deep understanding of human nature and human culture, a general education in the broadest sense.

We are at a crossroads in human history. Never before has there been a moment so simultaneously perilous and promising. We are the first species to have taken our evolution into our own hands. For the first time we possess the means for intentional or inadvertent self-destruction. We also have, I believe, the means for passing through this stage of technological adolescence into a long-lived, rich and fulfilling maturity for all the members of our species. But there is not much time to determine to which fork of the road we are committing our children and our future.

COMMENTS ■ QUESTIONS

1. It is apparently inescapable that in solving old problems technology creates new ones. Very often, as Sagan points out, the new problems are discovered only by chance. Sagan proposes that research groups be established whose exclusive "function it is to seek out and defuse future catastrophes resulting from the development of new technologies." Can you think of any reason why this proposal should not be carried out? How high a priority do you believe should be assigned to it?
2. According to Sagan, overpopulation is a much greater threat to civilization than cancer. Do you agree?
3. Sagan discusses the possibility of establishing independent and self-sufficient cities in space. One of the benefits of having them, he says, would be to "greatly enhance the survival potential of the human species." Considering both the positive and the negative aspects of technology at the present time, would you say that, overall, technology has increased the survival potential of the human race or decreased it?

READINGS

Buckley, John J., ed. *Genetics Now: Ethical Issues in Genetic Research.* Washington: University Press of America, 1978. A good anthology.

Caldicott, Helen. *Nuclear Madness.* New York: Bantam Books, 1978. Argues against all uses of nuclear energy.

Cherfas, Jeremy. *Man-Made Life.* New York: Pantheon Books, 1982. A very good account of recent developments in genetic engineering.

Clark, Ralph W., ed. *Introduction to Moral Reasoning: Applying Basic Moral Principles to Selected Readings.* St. Paul: West, 1986. Chapter 10 contains readings on the morality of war and nuclear deterrence.

Dubos, René. *A God Within.* New York: Charles Scribner's Sons, 1972. Develops some of Dubos' ideas on ecology that are presented in this chapter.

Leopold, Aldo. *A Sand County Almanac.* New York: Oxford University Press, 1966. Defends the view that value belongs primarily to nature (or to the "biosphere") as a whole.

Rand, Ayn. *Capitalism: The Unknown Ideal.* New York: New American Library, 1965. Praises free enterprise and industrial development.

Schell, Jonathan. *The Fate of the Earth.* New York: Avon Books, 1982. Contains a vivid description of the possible effects of nuclear war.

Snow, C. P. *The Two Cultures and the Scientific Revolution.* New York: Cambridge University Press, 1959.

Discusses the impact of science upon culture and the reaction to science by nonscientists.

Sterba, James P., ed. *The Ethics of War and Nuclear Deterrence.* Belmont, Calif.: Wadsworth, 1985. A very useful collection of recent articles.

Toffler, Alvin. *Future Shock.* New York: Bantam Books, 1970. Discusses the effects of rapid change upon people's lives.

CHAPTER TWELVE

[It is] natural to the human mind, even in a high state of culture, to be incapable of conceiving and on that ground to believe impossible what is afterward not only found to be conceivable but proved to be true.
—*John Stuart Mill*

Not only can we come to know other "conceptual frameworks," but we see evidence in our own culture of being able to create *such frameworks beyond the limitations of our ordinary, everyday language.*
— *N. L. Gifford*

Cross-Cultural Understanding

In chapter 2 we quoted with approval the famous line from John Stuart Mill: "He who knows only his own side of the case knows little of that." The present chapter has two basic goals, both of which can be thought of as responses to the quote from Mill. First, consider the question of how best to ensure that you will, in fact, know more than your own side of the case. Exactly what investigative obligations do you have?

Chapter 2 focused on the obligation to seek out the writings of philosophers and others who have argued against your position. One goal of the present chapter is to suggest that, while doing this is clearly necessary, it may not be sufficient. The people who argue explicitly against a particular philosophical doctrine may be committed to a certain way of describing the oppositions among competing doctrines that itself should be scrutinized. Consider, for example, the free will question.

The major purpose of the opening essay for chapter 5, "Free Will and Determinism," is to summarize the most important points of view on the free will question. But it may be that the three positions discussed there—soft determinism, hard determinism, and libertarianism—are not the most important alternatives. I believe that they *are* the most important alternatives. It may be, however, that they appear to be the most important alternatives only to those who have been trained in one of the philosophical traditions of contemporary Western philosophy. What about the traditions of Eastern philosophies? What about schools of thought, such as mysticism, that contain philosophical ideas, but which in themselves are more religious than philosophical? What about viewpoints that have not yet solidified into anything that is close to the sort of "academic philosophy" that we normally have in mind when we talk about philosophy (e.g., the world views of certain primitive peoples)?

We have an ultimate investigative responsibility to seek opposing viewpoints that are outside of our own traditions. We have an obligation to seek philosophical understanding that cuts across the boundaries separating cultures. We have an ultimate obligation to read the works of writers who do not argue explicitly against the beliefs that we have because they see the basic oppositions among competing positions differently from the way that we see them—that is, we have an obligation not only to seek viewpoints that oppose our own on *our* terms, but also to seek viewpoints that are in opposition even to our ways of setting up a particular philosophical question in the first place.

I must hasten to add that this book, because of its length, does little to fulfill the investigative responsibilities that have just been described. The most it can do is to point you toward certain doors that you may at some time want to open (and that some of you may already have opened).

At the beginning of this essay I said that the present chapter has two basic goals. The first is to present samples of readings that may help us fulfill the investigative obligation to examine viewpoints that differ basically from our own. The selections from Ahmed M. Abou-Zeid and Po-keung Ip are intended, in a very limited way of course, to serve this purpose. (The selection from Abou-Zeid, on the peasant concept of time, can also profitably be read in conjunction with chapter 14, while the article by Ip can profitably be read in conjunction with chapter 11.)

The second goal is to raise questions about the conceptual framework underlying the first goal. Why is it desirable to seek out points of view that differ from our own? The answer may seem obvious—we want to get at the truth. We want to compare *all* of the important competing points of view, see what can be said for or against each, and then pick the one with the strongest support. Doing this, we believe, will make it most likely that the beliefs we adopt will be true and the beliefs we reject will be false.

Now, we must ask what we mean when we say that we want to pick the position most likely to be true. More specifically, what is meant by saying that we search for the truth among points of view that compete in the very fundamental way that points of view from different cultures may compete? Are we to suppose that there is a single "reality in itself" that each of the opposing viewpoints does a better or worse job of presenting? Or is it instead the case that the concept of a "single reality" that lies behind all possible opposing points of view is not clear? The question regarding which of these alternatives is most defensible is a matter of deep philosophical controversy.

Some philosophers who deny that there is a single "reality in itself" lying behind all opposing viewpoints do so by claiming that, in the most fundamental sense, our views of reality are relative to cultures, by which they mean to include shared ways of living and thinking and a shared language. Such a view is defended in the reading selection by Henry L. Ruf. As you read it, remember that Ruf is defending a more radical view than the type of cultural relativism described in chapter 8, "The Foundations of Morality," which has to do only with values. Ruf's position, which he calls "cultural pluralism," embraces metaphysics and epistemology as well as questions about values. A view that stands in partial opposition to that of Ruf is presented in the selection from a recent book by N. L. Gifford.

The brief selection from John Stuart Mill contains an argument against what is sometimes called "the inconceivability test for necessary truth." According to this test, if we cannot conceive what it would be like for a statement to be false, the statement is *necessarily* true. But if a statement is necessarily true, it would seem that its truth cannot be relative to a particular culture. Thus, the inconceivability test, if it is acceptable, would seem to provide a way to overcome cultural relativity in the domain of knowledge. Consequently, even through Mill does not mention cultural relativism, in arguing against the inconceivability test he is, if he is successful, providing some ammunition that could be used by the defenders of cultural relativism, or cultural pluralism.

If you have already read chapter 10, you may recall that A. C. Ewing, *defends* the inconceivability test. Ewing can thus be seen as providing a response to Mill. You must decide which has the stronger claim.

In recent years a new discipline has developed that, in the debate between relativists and nonrelativists, takes the side of the nonrelativists. The discipline is called *sociobiology*. Its thesis is that biology is a much stronger determinant of human behavior, beliefs, and social structures than culture. The selection from Roger Trigg examines and criticizes the sociobiological position.

In reading the material for this chapter, remember that philosophers traditionally have distinguished among three different theories regarding the nature of truth. The first is the Correspondence Theory of Truth. It maintains that a judgment or a statement (or possibly a sentence—philosophers disagree as to what the "bearers" of truth are) will be true if it represents, or in some way corresponds to, the way the world is in itself. The second is the Coherence Theory of Truth. It maintains that a statement will be true if it "fits in" with, or coheres with, other statements. While the Correspondence Theory focuses on the relationship between statements and the world, the Coherence Theory focuses on the relationships among statements themselves, ascribing truth to an overall system of statements that is internally coherent. The Pragmatic Theory of Truth is the third of the three theories of truth. According to this theory, statements, or systems of statements, have the best claim to being considered true if they "work," that is lead to success in our dealings with the world.

The present book does not contain readings on the three theories of truth. Before drawing your own final conclusions about the readings for this chapter and others, you may want to look at some readings on theories of truth (sources are listed at the end of this chapter) or you may want to read the articles on truth in the *Encyclopedia of Philosophy*.

JOHN STUART MILL

The despotism of custom is everywhere the standing hindrance to human advancement, being in unceasing antagonism to that disposition to aim at something better than customary.

The individual is not accountable to society for his actions, in so far as these concern the interests of no person but himself.
—*On Liberty*

It is evident that the only government which can fully satisfy all the exigencies of the social state is one in which the whole people participate.
—*Representative Government*

John Stuart Mill (1806–1873) was the most influential British philosopher in the nineteenth century. As an advocate of the moral philosophy of utilitarianism, he was a very effective social reformer. He was one of the first advocates of birth control and fought for the humane treatment of prisoners. Mill served for a short time as a member of the House of Commons. During a large part of his adult life he worked for the East India Company, in a position that gave him leisure time to write philosophy.

Mill was a child prodigy whose education in philosophy and the classics was directed by his father, James Mill, also a defender of utilitarianism. The major works of John Stuart Mill are *Utilitarianism, A System of Logic, Examination of Sir William Hamilton's Philosophy, Principles of Political Economy, On Liberty*, and *Representative Government*.

N. L. GIFFORD

Relativism and Knowledge

* * * * *

The nonrelativist wants to show that no matter who comes into my office—a student, a Hopi visitor, a Martian—"This is a chair" remains a true claim. This presumes, as we have seen, that my diverse visitors share the concepts of "physical object" and "chair," for example, or concepts which are substantially equivalent. Or, in the case of the Martian, we may have to pantomime the function of a chair. But we expect that an embodied Martian can sit in the chair and can learn the concept enabling him/her/it to recognize other chairs, not just this one in my office.

So what we need confirmation and explanation to do is to show that our experience (sitting in the chair), the uniformities observed in the world (that chairs stay where they are placed under normal circumstances) do in fact inform us of things and uniformities in the world. How do the notions of confirmation and explanation provide such "proof"?

Confirmation is a procedure in which we assume the truth of a statement, hypothesis, or general law and make very specific predictions about what will happen on the basis of the statement, hypothesis, or general law. If these predictions are successful—if they are realized—we take this success to "confirm" to some degree the reliability of the original statement, hypothesis or law. A simple example can represent the method used. Assume the truth of "Here is a chair." Now, let's make some predictions: if I rest my hand here, I will encounter resistance; if I seat myself, I won't fall on the floor. Then I put my hand here and encounter resistance. I seat myself and I don't fall on the floor. This little test, which shows my predictions to be accurate, is not foolproof in showing there to be a chair here, i.e., the success of my predictions cannot *guarantee* my belief that there is a chair here (for there may be other statements which can yield the same predictions). However, the success of my predictions does give me some assurance that my belief is sufficiently sound to act on. I can feel reasonably safe seating myself on objects of this sort and will not have to repeat, each time, my little confirmation test.

Even if my culture chose to insist

N. L. Gifford teaches in the philosophy department at the State University of New York at Stony Brook.

Reprinted from *When In Rome* by N. L. Gifford, 1983, by permission of the State University of New York Press.

that I would fall on the floor when I sat down, I wouldn't. Even if my culture, for whatever reason, insisted that my feeling resistance when I put my hand here is fantasy, I would still feel resistance and so would *anybody else*. In using these examples I do not intend to be obtuse (and refuse to see the point of relativism) nor do I intend to say that Cultural Relativism would make any such claim as "You'll fall on the floor if you attempt to seat yourself on a chair." I do intend, however, to overstate the case in these fanciful examples to make the point very clear.

So long as Cultural Relativism stops the investigation of knowledge with intersubjectivity—agreement within a community—and claims, as well, that this agreement is *idiosyncratic to this culture or that, all scientific claims* (in whatever culture) *become indistinguishable from perceptual claims, mythical beliefs or dogmatic claims*. In abandoning the inquiry into the "nature of" the world beyond convention and culture, we accept (whether we want to or intend to) prejudice, ill-founded generalizations and transistory fads on a par with carefully investigated claims and well-argued conclusions. This is an exceptionally strong charge I am leveling against popular Cultural Relativism but recall the relativist's claims . . . : (1) Cultural belief is so integrated into our thinking and is so deeply enforced in our daily lives that investigation "outside" of cultural influence is impossible. (Even the work of Benedict and Marx . . . seems to support this claim.) (2) Any demonstration of knowledge must arrive at intersubjectivity. Such agreement is a product of human communities, human "choice." Given the diversity of belief across cultures, there is no reason to assume that agreement "originates" from a world independent of culture.

(1) and (2) are themselves strong statements from the relativist, and do sound plausible if we don't think of what they commit us to. Hence, my fanciful examples on the previous page are intended to be extreme, showing that if we apply (1) and (2) to all knowledge claims, we arrive at a very peculiar position. Its very oddity, I hope, will cause us to stop and think more carefully about what Cultural Relativism would have us give up.

One thing we must give up if we adopt relativism is the use of confirmation as an "independent" means of gathering evidence for our knowledge claims. When truth and "reality" are made relative to a culture, the best that confirmation can show is that the predictions are *consistent* with other cultural belief and, if successful, the predictions can only "confirm" this consistency. For example, the relativist would say that the fact that I don't fall on the floor when I seat myself can only show that the prediction "I won't fall on the floor" is consistent and compatible with other beliefs of my culture, e.g., the belief that there are distinct, rigid physical objects that support weight. Under relativism, any belief (such as the belief that there are physical objects) is accepted, thought true, if it is consistent with the existing body of beliefs in a given culture. It will not be accepted or rejected on the grounds that, in this case, there are (or are not) such objects in the world.

My objection to this trivialization

(by the relativist) of the use of confirmation is even more clear when we consider what happens to the use of explanation, our nonrelativist's second tool of evidence. Thus far, confirmation has given us a means of predicting events: "Where there's lightning, there's thunder" enables us to [successfully] predict hearing a clap of thunder after we've seen a flash of lightning. And, sure enough, during the next storm claps of thunder follow flashes of lightning with unceasing regularity.

However, confirmation can't account for these successes: why does thunder always follow lightning? We look now for an *explanation*. In this case we turn to an expert who tells us that lightning and thunder actually occur simultaneously. But sound waves don't travel as rapidly as light waves so we will see the lightning before we hear the thunder. The lapse of time between the two can, additionally, tell us how far away the lightning is from us. (And our expert may continue by showing us how to compute this distance.)

Explanation, then, gives us reasons why, for example, thunder is seen as following lightning. The explanation offers us a clue to the relationship between the perceived phenomena, and may formulate a general law which might account for the relationship. If we were to be very curious about thunder and lightning, having just heard that they occur simultaneously, we might want to find out what atmospheric conditions will produce thunder and lightning. (Notice that this increase in knowledge increased our capacity for prediction, for now we can predict when lightning might occur as well.) We might also investigate wave theory, learning how to compute the speed of light waves and sound waves as well as discovering additional explanations as to why wave theory explains more about our world than other theories.

You can see even in this brief example that confirmation and explanation create an intricate, complex network of ideas, concepts, hypotheses, predictions and built-in checks on the worth of these ideas, concepts and hypotheses. But something else appears as well. Notice as I make predictions successfully, my curiosity about the world is piqued. That is, I am not satisfied just to be "right" about what will happen. I want to know why I am right. So I was prompted to seek an explanation of why my prediction was right. Once I got a reasonable explanation, my interest did not cease: (a) now I am becoming acquainted with previously unknown (to me) areas of the world, (b) thus my curiosity is aroused about these particular areas, and (c) the explanation itself suggests, implicitly, ways of continuing my investigation and increasing my knowledge of the world. In other words, no matter how satisfying an explanation is, a good explanation will prompt further interest and be able to stimulate further investigation.

Let's consider, now, a radically different explanation that is popular in culture X. Culture X is diametrically opposed to ours in describing natural events in terms of the attributes and behavior of God instead of in terms of the laws of science: "Whenever lightning flashes, God is rudely awakened, and the thunder you hear is the roar of His disapproval." For Smithe, a member of culture X, this is a plausible-sounding explanation since there have been times when she herself has roared with disapproval upon being rudely awakened.

Given the presuppositions of culture X, will the notions of confirmation and explanation provide the same benefits for Smithe as they do for Smith in our culture? Smithe is certainly able to make successful predictions, for she does hear thunder after seeing a flash of lightning. Hence the explanation that God is roaring His disapproval seems to be confirmed by her continued successful predictions.

However, Smithe may not find her interest aroused or further investigation encouraged: (a) she doesn't feel new areas of the world are opened up—she's heard the list of God's attributes and behaviors for as long as she can recall; (b) her curiosity, rather than being stimulated, begins to wane, as a result; but (c) being adventurous she decides she does want to pursue this explanation further. Where, then, shall she turn to investigate? She might read more theology, she might critically assess the value of arguments in favor of God's existence and attributes, or she might simply seek to renew her faith, confusing curiosity with heretical doubt.

Our Cultural Relativist, at this point, must be nodding his/her head in approval. Yes, this is the extent of what we can claim for confirmation and explanation. Confirmation shows a statement/prediction/hypothesis to be consistent with other beliefs in the culture. Explanation provides the best account *within* the scope of cultural belief. How on earth is Smithe going to conceive of explanations utilizing concepts she doesn't even possess? Our supposed "benefits," the relativist would say, would be meaningless to Smithe.

But, of course, I want to object to this pessimistic view of human ability. I want to argue, as well, that we give up far too much in thinking confirmation and explanation are solely manifestations of culture. I believe we should allow the two explanations to compete, vie for the status of which is the most adequate or best. I do not want to agree here with the relativist who is bound to say they are *both* right, *both* adequate for their respective cultures. Nor do I want to insist that the first explanation from our Western scientific community is *necessarily* the best explanation, that our beliefs and practices are *always* preferable to those of another culture. I don't think they always are. (And I also think Benedict and Marx showed that without a doubt ethnocentrism is groundless and inhibits the pursuit of knowledge.)

Hence, for any comparison to take place (following Benedict and Marx), we must avoid *prima facie* judgments about the ultimate worth of each explanation, such as "Well it's just silly to think that God roars, so whatever explanation is left must be right." *First*, if you recall, we need to make sure that we understand the opposing conception—not just what it reports but what it means, the role it plays in culture X. Notice that as we genuinely bring ourselves to understand this explanation in culture X and as Smithe acquaints herself with wave theory and the concept of natural law, already all of us have broadened the range of concepts we can appeal to. Already, before we even think about drawing conclusions about the explanations, our perception of the world has acquired a new texture, a new dimension as it were, by acquainting ourselves with how the world appears to members of culture X. This in itself is no trivial achievement.

At this point, the much more difficult question appears. Are there compelling reasons to think that one explanation can be chosen over the other? Can Smithe and I, for example, decide what criterion we should use to judge the competing explanations? I, of course, can jump in with several helpful (i.e., Western) suggestions: Are the explanations logically sound or do they lead to contradictions? Do the explanations offer empirical and public means of verification?

Smithe might, as well, offer additional helpful suggestions: Do the explanations increase our understanding of the nature of God? Do they promote faith or undermine it? This does look like an impasse, but I don't think it has to be. Let's acknowledge Smithe's desire to uphold God's prominent role in her conceptual framework. Even in our culture many thinkers believe that God should be more visibly represented in our daily lives and thoughts. But I am thinking of introducing Smithe to the writing of Newton, for he articulates very vividly the conflict he experienced in holding dear his religious commitment while being irresistably drawn to secular scientific investigation. This, from our culture, comes the closest, so far as I know, to representing the dilemma that Smithe might face.

Smithe on the other hand, might wonder if "Logic" were a Western equivalent to "God." Upon learning they are not equivalent, she might ask, then, why I put so much faith in Logic. Well, I might reply, it's not faith but rationality. (But I might also stop and think: Why is it better for statements to be consistent and coherent than not? What can coherence show us about the world?) Notice that neither Smithe nor I have asked the other to abandon cultural values outright; but we have asked each other to critically extend ourselves beyond the mere acceptance of cultural beliefs.

Already, here, we have begun marking out an area of intercultural exchange. As we proceed it's quite likely that Smithe and I share a curiosity about how the world "really" is, or share a curiosity about which of our respective cultural beliefs might enable us to glimpse a world beyond our culture. She may be exhilerated as she acquires the skills of scientific investigation and I may find my life enriched as I acquire nonscientific skills of acceptance and trust.

But where does this leave us regarding our competing explanations? By now Smithe and I most likely can easily compare (1) which beliefs generate the greatest number of correct predictions, (2) which explanation seems to be most culturally neutral, (3) what mode of inquiry might accomplish our ends most appropriately (for we are both curious about the world we live in). And this comparison can yield a preference for one explanation over the other, *without* our needing to stubbornly and dogmatically cite the authority of our cultural biases.

* * * * *

Two brief conclusions will suggest how we might begin responding to the problem of achieving universal knowledge of an objective world in the face of cultural limitation. Notice that the language we are taught (whatever the language) is public and describes a public world, one shared by the speakers of the language. That the language is public and our instruction the same as others in our community guarantees intersubjective agreement, at least within this community. Since the language is public and can be acquired by instruction, we can conclude that *any* person is capable of acquiring it. Here, then, we see a possible road from intersubjectivity to universality: intersubjective agreement is guaranteed in any language since each person is using the same concepts to identify the same sorts of things in the world; a nonnative to our language, as Benedict shows us, is perfectly capable of acquiring our language *and* access to our culture, though his/her own language and culture may be radically different.

This capacity suggests, then, how humans can transcend cultural limitation. Not only can we come to know other "conceptual frameworks," but we see evidence in our own culture of being able to *create* such frameworks beyond the limitations of our ordinary, everday language. The abstract languages of physics, biology and computer technology, and the language of thought, feeling and sensation exemplify this ability.[1] We can talk to each other of chairs having seats and being capable of supporting weight. But to explain why this is so, to investigate the properties of chairs in any depth, we need concepts more sophisticated than those of our ordinary, everyday language. We need to enter (or construct) the conceptual framework of atomic or molecular theory to investigate the physical properties of objects. If I want to know how I come to know the physical properties of objects, we need a framework of sensation which includes concepts of tactile stimulation, retinal stimulation, etc. We are not talking here about three chairs, but about one chair—the chair I'm sitting on—and three modes in which it can be investigated.

Even though I am not really arguing for a particular analysis of language here beyond the claim that whatever the analysis it must include our dependence on language and culture, the brief description of language given thus far does suggest three answers to Cultural Relativism, answers which show the possibility of intercultural dialogue as well as the means for keeping objectivity and universality in knowledge.

The first answer to Cultural Relativism is this: language may influence the knowledge we have about the world, but, additionally, it also provides the very tools which enable us to seek knowledge about the world. Without a systematic way of classifying and codifying our experience, we could not posit or even conceive of underlying uniformities and patterns in the world.

1. The most comprehensive investigation into language, intersubjectivity and the creation of alternative conceptual frameworks is provided by Wilfrid Sellars. A good introduction to his work is his early book, *Science, Perception and Reality* (London: Routledge & Kegan Paul, 1963).

The fact that all human languages are not the same, that concepts and categories differ from group to group, may not have to mean that knowledge must be culturally relative. Such tools as metaphor and analogy,[2] for example, can enable us to reach beyond existing beliefs and enter or create conceptual frameworks unlike our own everyday framework. The work of Benjamin Whorf is a classic example of this. Much of his work seeks to reproduce for us the world of the Native American tribe of the Hopi as well as other, quite different, cultures. He uses linguistic categories as a basis for approximating the world as the Hopi sees it and experiences it.[3] That this is accomplished, that he can make comprehensible a world quite different from our own, reinforces the belief that we are not confined or condemned to the framework of dominant American concepts and conventions.

At this point we need to take a closer look at the insistence on relativism by social scientists such as Whorf and Benedict. They all, at some time in their work, explicitly state that their observations of culture show the folly of seeking universality. But when Benedict offers her conclusions—e.g., "Morality differs in every society and is a convenient term for socially approved habits" [4]—she asserts this claim universally. I doubt that any of the social scientists intend to suggest that claims to knowledge can be *both* universal and relative.

It's more likely that they are failing to distinguish cultures and persons as *objects of knowledge* from the *conditions under which knowledge is possible*. This brings us to our second answer to Cultural Relativism: descriptive statements about a culture are not the same as prescriptive statements about which beliefs one should accept or what one should do. Consider the sentence:

A: Material acquisition and consumption is the measure of success.

This statement would be true with respect to the dominant beliefs and practices in the contemporary United States, but would be false with respect to the beliefs and practices of members of an Amish community. If we want A to have a consistent truth value, as suggested in Chapter Three, we should restate the sentence more completely as:

A′: Material acquisition and consumption is the measure of success for the majority of people living in the United States in the twentieth century.

The truth conditions remain the same whether A′ is asserted by Rockefeller, a member of the Amish community or a Buddhist monk.

2. Jonathan Miller's book, *The Body in Question* (New York: Random House, 1979), offers a convincing argument for the role played by analogy in extending our knowledge.

3. A representative sample of Whorf's work can be found in *Language, Thought and Reality: Selected Writings of B. L. Whorf*, ed. J. B. Carroll (Cambridge: MIT Press, 1956). Also, for similar work in this area see Franz Boas, ed., *Handbook of American Indian Languages* (Washington, D.C.: Government Printing Office, 1911–22), and Edward Sapir, *Language: An Introduction to the Study of Speech* (New York: Harcourt Brace Co., 1921).

4. Margaret Mead, ed., *An Anthropologist at Work: Writings of Ruth Benedict* (Boston: Houghton Mifflin Co., 1959), p. 276.

A is ambiguous. Does it just mean to *describe* a dominant American practice or does it mean to suggest that material acquisition and consumption *should* constitute a measure of success for all people? A′, on the other hand, is clearly a descriptive statement of American culture and is included in our body of empirical knowledge as such. It is objective, for it depicts an actual practice in the world, and it is universal, for it is capable of being correctly asserted by any person.

If we want to talk about whether this is a good or desirable measure of success, we move out of the milieu of anthropology and into the world of philosophy. In other words, social scientists offer valuable methodological tools that can be universally applied as well as valuable insights into the actual workings of different cultures, groups and persons. But it is not within the purview of these disciplines to also formulate criteria by which to judge whether particular cultural practices and beliefs *should* be universally followed and adopted. Taking on this task was just the thing that got early anthropologists and others into trouble. And, as we have seen, Benedict and Marx themselves offer the very means of avoiding this difficulty by separating the descriptive work from the prescriptive.[5]

Philosophers themselves, as well, have failed to respond adequately to this distinction. The absence of inquiry into the problem of intersubjectivity [can the conventional "agreements" within a community inform us of a world beyond that community?] has had the effect of inviting Cultural Relativists to fill the gap. In other words, philosophy has traditionally failed to offer clear guidelines which we can use to assess our cultural dependence and begin to transcend it. (For the most part knowledge has been *assumed* to be culturally independent and most analyses forget to offer us the means by which we can begin untangling ourselves from cultural presupposition and prejudice.) Cultural Relativism, on the other hand, does acknowledge this dependence and though it may overstate the case (and generate unfortunate abuses as we have seen), we at least feel that relativism is talking about *our* world and *our* concerns.

Hence, the third answer to Cultural Relativism is this: it is not enough to say that we *are* culturally dependent; at best this can only promote "investigation" yielding a list of cultural beliefs; at the worst this

5. To reiterate briefly, "prescriptive" of course refers to prescribing, in this case telling members of a community what they *should* do, (whether or not they already perform these actions). Hence, part of the prescriptive work of philosophers is arguing for what is right or good, showing why one course of action is preferable to another, evaluating the worth of any code of action. That something is customarily the case does not, ideally, enter the analysis. The primary consideration in formulating prescriptions is to uncover the intrinsic worth of an action. In Section 17 above, we argued for the worth of the methodological prescriptions of Benedict and Marx and showed the value of universally applying their prescriptions. The descriptive work, as we've said, is simply a list of what is already being approved or done in a given culture. An interesting controversy known as the "is/ought" question is found throughout ethical literature: to put it in terms of our discussion, the question is whether the fact that there *is* an existing practice or belief carries any implication of whether there *ought* to be that practice or belief.

can further entrench harmful prejudices and practices. But showing the nature and extent of our dependence *does* bring philosophy face to face with the necessity of determining the *role* of culture in empirical knowledge.

If the philosopher takes up this challenge, does that mean then that we must abandon the quest for culturally independent empirical knowledge? Several points made thus far suggest not: Sellars, for example, shows us the possibility of extending ourselves conceptually without denying the role of culture; Whorf and others have been able to reconstruct for us "worlds" that are radically different from our own, worlds which offer us new means of evaluating our own beliefs and practices as well as new data with which to supplement our existing body of empirical knowledge; and, if we can keep confirmation and explanation intact as tools of evidence (without allowing them to be weakened by Cultural Relativism), we should be able to get a clearer picture of where cultural interest promotes investigation or inhibits it.

Here we anticipate a fourth answer to Cultural Relativism: we must give up too much valuable scientific knowledge (in subsuming such knowledge under cultural belief) to justify adopting relativism. Where it may be appropriate and desirable to scrutinize the cultural biases and presuppositions present in scientific investigation, it seems wholly inappropriate and undesirable to dismiss the results of such investigation out of hand.

Beyond the specific conclusions reached by scientists, beyond the range of hypotheses and experimentation, science is able to offer a great deal to us. The world around me, that I live in, appears to me reasonably stable, substantial and predictable. I depend to a large degree on this stability and continuity. As I drive to school, the road remains firmly and reassuringly solid. I expect that it will be so when I drive home this evening. My chair does not collapse under me, the colleague I greet coming down the hall stays embodied the entire distance, my bookshelves continue to hold my books where I put them, my typewriter remains positioned on my desk. In other words, I share with the scientist the presupposition that there is a world independent of my being, a world independent even from the fads and transitory fashions of culture, and a world that can be known.

I seem already to have acquired a fairly reliable and practical body of knowledge about this world: I can manipulate raw material—wood, clay—into enduring objects, I can reglue the rungs of my chair to strengthen it, I can put air into my bicycle tire and ride more comfortably down the road. This world independent of my being is neither alien nor mysterious (though there is a vast amount we don't know or understand in it). The investigation of scientists, the positing of molecules and quarks, does not alter or deprive me of my familiar world of chairs and bicycles, though the investigation may inspire me to understand how molecules generate sufficient strength to constitute dense, resistent physical objects.

The fact that scientific investigation proceeds with such tools as confirmation and explanation is also eminently reassuring. Confirmation provides some basis for my faith in the reliability of my beliefs about the world; that I am able to predict this event or that reassures me that there must be a world independent of myself that *can* be known (regardless of how accurate my actual beliefs are). Successful prediction must at least indicate that my beliefs aren't totally groundless.

Explanation enables me to experiment with competing theories and hypotheses about the world without disrupting the predictability of my own familiar world. For the present, in any case, confirmation and explanation provide some means other than outright prejudice or faith to uphold the beliefs on which we act. They are *capable* also of generating well-founded generalizations about uniformities in and characteristics of the world. I do not have to be helplessly dependent on popular cultural beliefs, but have the means—in confirmation and explanation—of *discriminating the worth* of one belief from the worth of another and *selecting on demonstrable grounds* one belief or hypothesis over another. In this way, whether our beliefs are ultimately right or wrong, we are freed from the indiscriminate acceptance of belief encouraged by relativism.

COMMENTS ■ QUESTIONS

1. There is, says Gifford, a way to choose between different fundamental beliefs held by people in different cultures that does not presuppose that the perspective of one culture or the other is correct. What we can do is ask "(1) which beliefs generate the greatest number of correct predictions, (2) which explanation seems to be most culturally neutral, (3) what mode of inquiry might accomplish our ends most appropriately (for we are both curious about the world we live in)". Do you have any reservations about the application of these three tests? If so, what are they? The third of the tests seems to appeal to the concept of what the world "really is in itself." Is Gifford's (apparent) appeal to this concept in any way problematic?
2. "We must give up too much valuable scientific knowledge (in subsuming such knowledge under cultural belief) to justify adopting relativism." Do you agree? If not, why not?

HENRY L. RUF

Cultural Pluralism: A Philosophical Investigation

For the last two centuries philosophers and social scientists have been trying to understand the significance of the fact that people in different communities speak different languages, have different social practices, seem to operate with different moral orientations, and have different religious traditions. Many philosophers have attempted to show that these differences are only surface superficialities, and that below the surface there are necessary, universal and unchanging structures, principles, and insights which guarantee that all people basically are the same—thinking with the same concepts, working with the same criteria of truth, knowledge, and reality. Other philosophers have charged that such an asocial and ahistorical approach fails to do justice to the social and historical character of the human form of life.

In this essay I am going to side with the historical pluralists against the ahistorical, asocial absolutists. I will present a sketch of an image of our human form of life in which social, cultural, conceptual, and cognitive pluralism is found to be as sound as it is inescapable. I will concentrate on sketching the social and historical character of human language and knowledge, and attempt to show that such a characterization does not lead to relativism or nihilism or a new absolutized deification of the social.

All people have been nurtured by their communities to think, perceive, feel and act in certain socially prescribed ways. We are trained to possess certain skills and to participate in certain social practices. By becoming certain sorts of social functionaries, we become certain sorts of people. By the time we are able to think for ourselves we already are representative examples of the social and cultural worlds into which we were thrown. Although our cultural heritage is not a prison enslaving us, it is a shadow from which we never fully escape because it provides the framework for all our thoughts, experiences and actions.

Most philosophers today would say that one of the most important areas of our cultural inheritance is our language. Communication presupposes and makes possible development of shared social practices. By training people to speak and write in a certain way we train them to think

Henry L. Ruf is a professor of philosophy at West Virginia University and the author of Moral Investigations. *He has taught philosophy in Japan as a Fulbright Fellow.*

Used by permission of the author.

in a certain way. Most of our concepts are acquired by acquiring our linguistic skills. Most of our thinking is expressible in language. Most of our beliefs, desires, intentions and feelings depend upon language. It is not accidental that we do our thinking in the privacy of our minds in the mother language we have been taught to speak.

Words are social institutions, cultural tools. They enable us to communicate to others knowledge of our beliefs, desires, intentions and emotions. We learn how to make statements, give directives, commit ourselves, and express our feelings. Only historically evolved and evolving social practices determine the correct way to use such words and perform such speech acts.

Our linguistic practices often have developed in very unsystematic ways. Things may be described correctly using a certain term even though these things only have a family resemblance to each other. Family groupings of things depend upon all the idiosyncratic factors which have determined how linguistic practices have historically developed in a certain community. Also, words seem to be systematically vague; boundary cases can be found whose correct description current social practices do not determine. Is this red or orange? Is this taxable income or not? Furthermore, since it is always in a certain kind of natural and social world that we acquire and exercise out linguistic and conceptual skills, linguistic and conceptual correctness always presuppose the natural and social background against which we speak and think. Talk about proving something beyond reasonable doubt has a certain meaning in a court of law only because legal practices determine what the legal rules of evidence are. Family resemblances, historical idiosyncracies, vague boundaries, multiple language games, different languages, cultures, and backgrounds—all of these factors require that we pay very close attention to the details in any case of using words, if we are to avoid false generalizations and confusion.

Since words and concepts are social institutions and cultural artifacts which exist within a network of many interrelated linguistic and nonlinguistic institutions and practices, understanding what a word or concept means involves understanding how it can and does function in a specific language community. Often words in one language have no good counterparts in another language. Also, linguistic institutions and practices are changeable like all social institutions and practices. The correct uses of words and concepts change over time.

The fact that the correct use of words and concepts is culturally variable and historically changeable has great significance for philosophical theories of knowledge in which normative words like "true" and "justified" play central roles. Does the fact that there are different languages which are historically changing mean that there is no objective knowledge? I think not. Just as social practices guarantee an objective difference between the correct use of words and their misuse, so they can guarantee objectivity in knowledge. However, this kind of objectivity, guaranteed as it is by intersubjectivity, is also compatible with conceptual and cognitive pluralism.

There are many different senses in which people know things—they know how to do things, that things are so and so, why things are so and so, and they understand people, works of literature, other cultures. All these concepts of knowledge and understanding involve the use of normative standards (of performance, truth, justification, adequacy, depth, and breadth). All of these norms are social and are constituted by social practices and shared forms of intersubjectivity.

When it comes to knowing that something is the case (propositional knowledge), it is expected that the person's beliefs go beyond that individual's personal biases and subjective points of view and that the objective correctness of the person's belief is something more than just a lucky guess. Propositional knowledge requires truth and authorization or justification. The social character of such knowledge comes from the social character of beliefs, truth, authorization, and justification. Consider the following sketches of the social nature of each.

1. The concepts used in our beliefs are social, cultural tools. Furthermore, beliefs exist only within a social network of beliefs and desires and against a background of social skills and practices.

2. Truth is a social ideal. Since beliefs conflict, it is not surprising that communities have developed the notion of correct or true beliefs. Truth, however, calls for more than the removal of conflict between our present beliefs. We want a concept of correctness which allows us to say tomorrow that our beliefs today were incorrect and that we were wrong even though we all agreed with each other. Built into our ideal of truth is the idea that true beliefs are those one won't ever have to say are incorrect; that a true belief is one which would be held without cancellation by the members of an ideal community of believers, where this ideal is specified in terms of procedures followed in settling conflicts among beliefs. Since the contents of perceptual beliefs, mathematical beliefs, scientific beliefs, and moral beliefs are so different, we would expect to use different criteria to specify what constitutes the truth of such beliefs. Likewise, we work with different notions of ideal communities—ideal scientific inquirers, ideal mathematicians, ideal moralists. Thus, when we say that a belief is true we are saying that it won't be displaced from that set of beliefs held in that community of inquirers which our cultural community takes as the ideal judges of what to believe in this area. Since different actual communities might be working with different concepts of ideal communities of inquirers, and since different ideal communities of inquirers might reconcile belief conflicts in different ways, this social notion of objective truth does not rule out the possibility of cognitive pluralism.

Is this social concept of truth relativistic and is it self-refuting? The answer to both questions is, "No." This social characterization of truth is not the claim that different people in different communities have different and incompatible sets of true beliefs about how things really are in the world. Saying "This is how things really are" is simply expressing one's belief about how things are, and expressing this in a context in which one intends to rule out some other suggestion about how things are. Defenders of a social characterization of truth believe that it makes no sense to talk about getting outside all social systems of concepts, beliefs, and truth ideals in order to see such systems as providing different perspectives on how things "really" are. These defenders certainly are not saying that they can see, from an absolutistic, asocial, and ahistorical point of view, that all concepts, beliefs, and ideals of truth are social. (One would have to be an absolutist in order to make such a charge of self-refuting relativism against this social characterization of truth.) Defenders of this social characterization simply claim that they believe that this characterization will be one of the beliefs held by the ideal community of inquirers in this area, with that ideal being part of the background against which they now are making this characterization.

Does this approach to truth and reality imply that we are locked hopelessly in a world of mere beliefs and that we cannot have knowledge of things which existed before beliefs or believers came into existence and which were, are and will be what they are regardless of what beliefs we have about them? Not at all. The social characterization of truth being given here rejects the intelligibility of the key presumption behind the question, the presumption that thoughts, beliefs, or statements are outside the world representing accurately or inaccurately the conditions of things in the world. Believers and their thoughts are in the world just as much as any of the objects of their beliefs. They don't have to "get to" the world because they cannot get out of the world. The reality of the world is not a thesis which can be intelligibly affirmed or denied. Natural and social worlds form the presupposed background of all beliefs and these worlds are far richer than our characterizations of them ever can capture.

3. Authorizing and justifying beliefs is also social. There is a need to offer justification only when there exists a reason in the community which it considers good enough to provide grounds for doubt. Our community treats people as the best authorities on their own pains and sensory states, and thus no justification of such beliefs is demanded. It also views perceptual and memory belief as being generally reliable and thus puts the burden of proof on any challenger of such beliefs. When conflicting beliefs do call for justification, the traditional practices in the various disciplines (law, science, medicine) are utilized in order to establish a reflective equilibrium among the community's beliefs. Justification is not the same as truth because we could say that we and our community yesterday were justified in our beliefs, but, on the basis of what we believe today, we now think that yesterday's beliefs are false. Of course, in our own case, we never would have any reason for saying that what we now believe is justified but not true.

Understanding oneself, other people, a work of literature or art, a historical period or a different culture, is a matter of exercising a learned ability. Some people do it better than others and each of us does it better with some things than with others. This is why understanding is never all or nothing; it always is a matter of more or less, being broad or narrow, deep or superficial. Understanding a person, oneself or someone else, involves knowing that person's beliefs, desires, emotions, intentions and actions, and seeing how they function within their personal integrated network of intentional states and against that background of natural conditions and social institutions and practices which they presuppose.

In some ways, understanding people who share our own cultural background is easier than understanding people from another culture. We know how to act in terms of the norms of the same community; we use many of the same concepts; we share many common beliefs and desires; we act in terms of the same social practices of justifying and evaluating. In some ways this shared familiarity makes it difficult to understand ourselves and our culture. It is difficult to see from inside our way of life that the way we are proceeding without questioning it is not the only way to proceed. This is especially difficult if in our community or in our personal lives we have built up defensive mechanisms to hide from ourselves our real beliefs, desires, emotions, intentions, or practices. Institutionalized racism or sexism and personal resentment often mask their existence in this way. It is in just such cases that at the individual level other people in our culture can understand us better than we understand ourselves, and people from other cultures can understand things about our culture and social practices which are hidden from the eyes of most of us.

It is vital to remember that we can gain some degree of understanding of other people in other cultures, people working with different social backgrounds and networks of intentionality. That we can see them as people with a culture, people who see us as foreign people seeing them, already demonstrates that we are not locked into any linguistic or cultural prisons. Even cultural misunderstanding can occur only because some degree of understanding exists, because some elements of a common form of life are shared.

That cross-cultural understanding is possible does not mean that it is easy or that it does not make special demands on us. In order to understand people from another culture, we must interpret their words, experiences and actions in terms of their network of intentions and their social background. This means that we must not absolutize our mode of life and force upon them our ways of conceiving, seeing, evaluating and judging. However, it also is useless to try to escape from our own network and background. Instead, we have to learn to listen, learn to engage in a form of cross-cultural dialogue in which we lose ourselves in the dialogue in the way we lose ourselves in a fast game of tennis, by trusting the other people, ourselves, and the event of dialogue itself. Seeking understanding through such dialogue is not a matter of passively picturing another tradition. That in fact would be superimposing our framework on their mode of life. Cross-cultural dialogue is a matter of opening up one's own form of life to creative expansion and reconstruction. After dialogue, people are not the same sorts of persons; their modes of life will have grown and overlapped in unplanned ways. Their separate identities will not have been lost, but neither any longer will they just be separate individuals; they will have been bonded together.

Cross-cultural understanding requires the use of a unique kind of ability which can be possessed only by people who are non-dogmatic, courageous, and adventuresome. One cannot predict what one will hear or how one's most precious cultural inheritance might be modified. It can and does cause painful and traumatic identity crises. Never, however, do we completely abandon our own cultural heritage. No one can do this. We remain tied to our historical past as people in other cultures remain tied to theirs, but we all become more than what we were. Cross-cultural dialogue, reconstruction, and understanding never eliminate cultural pluralism. It is dialogue and not homogenization which is needed and attainable.

Understanding of this sort requires that we do not absolutize our concepts, norms, and social practices. Does this mean that we cannot critically evaluate a community's social practices and mode of life? The answer to this question is "No". We can criticize our form of life internally in several ways. In the pursuit of a reflective equilibrium among our beliefs and practices we can claim that there is a need for reconstruction. Also, by examining the historical route which led to our present form of life, we may be able to see alternatives which were rejected in the past but which could be reconstructed now in a kind of renaissance revival, especially if remnants of these discarded options still remain in our current social life as minor, mini-practices which we can turn into saving remnants. Most importantly, we can draw on external resources in order to gain the understanding necessary to criticize self-deceptive and coercive practices. As one learns to hear voices from other cultures, one already is engaged in social criticism and reconstruction.

COMMENTS ■ QUESTIONS

1. The essential characteristic of *cultural pluralism* as described by Ruf is the claim that people belonging to different cultures may have different "criteria of truth, knowledge, and reality." Most of Ruf's paper is an expansion of this claim. Is the concept of cultural pluralism clear? Do you have any reason, or reasons, for rejecting the doctrine of cultural pluralism? If, before reading the present chapter you have read other chapters in this book, which (if any) of the selections in the chapters that you have read contain implicit arguments *against* cultural pluralism?
2. The premises for one of Ruf's arguments in defense of cultural

pluralism are the following. First premise: "Most of our beliefs, desires, intentions and feelings depend upon language." Second premise: "Words and concepts are social institutions and cultural artifacts which exist within a network of many interrelated linguistic and non-linguistic institutions and practices." Is this a good argument in defense of cultural pluralism?

3. "Defenders of a social characterization of truth believe that it makes no sense to talk about getting outside all social systems of concepts, beliefs and truth ideals in order to see such systems as providing different perspectives on how things 'really' are." Comment on this quotation. The quotation is part of an argument that Ruf makes to show that the "social concept of truth" that is part of cultural pluralism is not "self-refuting." Consider: a person who *rejects* cultural pluralism might say the following: "According to cultural pluralism all truth is relative; therefore the truth of cultural pluralism is relative to the culture that Ruf belongs to. Because I do not belong to that culture, I can reject cultural pluralism." Has Ruf shown that his version of cultural pluralism is not "self-refuting" in this way?
4. According to Ruf, if we are to understand people from another culture, we must have cross-cultural dialogue. As Ruf describes it, what are the important characteristics of cross-cultural dialogue? How is it different from dialogue with people from within one's culture? Is Ref's analogy with playing a fast game of tennis a good analogy?

JOHN STUART MILL

Necessity and Inconceivability

* * * * *

Although Dr. Whewell has naturally and properly employed a variety of phrases to bring his meaning more forcibly home, he would, I presume, allow that they are all equivalent, and that what he means by a necessary truth would be sufficiently defined, a proposition the negation of which is not only false but inconceivable. [One of the examples that Mill had in mind is the following proposition: "Two Straight lines cannot enclose a space."] I am unable to find in any of his expressions, turn them what way you will, a meaning beyond this, and I do not believe he would contend that they mean anything more.

* * * * *

Now I cannot but wonder that so much stress should be laid on the circumstance of inconceivableness when there is such ample experience to show that our capacity or incapacity of conceiving a thing has very little to do with the possibility of the thing in itself, but is, in truth, very much an affair of accident, and depends on the past history and habits of our own minds. There is no more generally acknowledged fact in human nature than the extreme difficulty at first felt in conceiving anything as possible, which is in contradiction to long established and familiar experience, or even to old familiar habits of thought. And this difficulty is a necessary result of the fundamental laws of the human mind. When we have often seen and thought of two things together and have never in any one instance either seen or thought of them separately, there is by the primary law of association an increasing difficulty, which may in the end become insuperable, of conceiving the two things apart. This is most of all conspicuous in uneducated persons who are, in general, utterly unable to separate any two ideas which have once become firmly associated in their minds; and if persons of cultivated intellect have any advantage on the point, it is only because, having seen and heard and read more, and being more accustomed to exercise their imagination, they have experienced their sensations and thoughts in more varied combinations and have been prevented from forming many of these inseparable associations. But this advantage has necessarily its limits. The most practiced intellect is not exempt from the universal laws of our conceptive faculty. If daily habit presents to

---

A biographical sketch of John Stuart Mill appears earlier in this chapter.

From *A System of Logic*. First published in 1843.

anyone for a long period two facts in combination, and if he is not led during that period either by accident or by his voluntary mental operations to think of them apart, he will probably in time become incapable of doing so even by the strongest effort, and the supposition that the two facts can be separated in nature will at last present itself to his mind with all the characters of an inconceivable phenomenon. There are remarkable instances of this in the history of science, instances in which the most instructed men rejected as impossible, because inconceivable, things which their posterity, by earlier practice and longer perseverance in the attempt, found it quite easy to conceive, and which everybody now knows to be true. There was a time when men of the most cultivated intellects and the most emancipated from the dominion of early prejudice could not credit the existence of antipodes, were unable to conceive, in opposition to old association, the force of gravity acting upward instead of downward. The Cartesians long rejected the Newtonian doctrine of the gravitation of all bodies toward one another, on the faith of a general proposition, the reverse of which seemed to them to be inconceivable—the proposition that a body cannot act where it is not. All the cumbrous machinery of imaginary vortices, assumed without the smallest particle of evidence, appeared to these philosophers a more rational mode of explaining the heavenly motions than one which involved what seemed to them so great an absurdity. And they no doubt found it as impossible to conceive that a body should act upon the earth from the distance of the sun or moon as we find it to conceive an end to space or time, or two straight lines inclosing a space. Newton himself had not been able to realize the conception or we should not have had his hypothesis of a subtle ether, the occult cause of gravitation, and his writings prove that though he deemed the particular nature of the intermediate agency a matter of conjecture, the necessity of *some* such agency appeared to him indubitable.

COMMENTS ■ QUESTIONS

1. Mill provides reasons for rejecting the "inconceivability test for necessary truth." What do you suppose Gifford would say in response to Mill? What would Ruf say?
2. Do you find any weaknesses in Mill's argument for rejecting the inconceivability test? If so, what are they?

ROGER TRIGG

The Sociobiological View of Man

What is the relation of the biological to the social sciences? Fierce battles are being currently fought over this question and much hangs on the answer. If society (or culture) is taken as an irreducible category which can only be understood in its own terms, the social sciences can feel safe from the sinister designs of other disciplines. Yet it is a commonplace that cultures vary, and we humans are prone to look at the differences rather than the similarities between them. The result can be a thoroughgoing relativism. If culture cannot be understood by means of any non-cultural categories, cultural differences themselves can be accepted as the ultimate truth about man. When everything is cultural, even the notion of a non-cultural category can seem to be a ludicrous contradiction in terms. The categories with which we think are the product of our culture, or so we are told. Instead of our being able to understand culture in terms of anything beyond itself, our understanding appears totally moulded by the society to which we belong. Any theory can thus be seen as merely the expression of the beliefs of a particular society.

Sociobiology has been defined by E. O. Wilson, one of its leading proponents, as "the systematic study of the biological basis of all social behaviour".[1] As such, it challenges at its roots the view that everything is cultural.[2] Yet it is equally possible for the discipline's opponents to argue that it is only the product of the concepts of a particular society at a particular time. Perhaps sociobiologists are merely projecting the norms of their own American capitalist society on to human society at large, and indeed even on to animal and insect society. Sociobiology, combining the insights of modern population genetics with the Darwinian theory of natural selection, has placed great importance on the

1. E. O. Wilson, *Sociobiology: the New Synthesis* (Cambridge, Mass.: Harvard University Press, 1975), 4.

2. See my book, *The Shaping of Man: Philosophical Aspects of Sociobiology* (Oxford: Blackwell, 1982).

Roger Trigg is chairman of the department of philosophy at the University of Warwick in England. He has published several books, including The Shaping of Man: Philosophical Aspects of Sociobiology, Understanding Social Science, *and* Reason and Commitment.

From "The Sociobiological View of Man" by Roger Trigg, in *Objectivity and Cultural Divergence*, edited by S. C. Brown, copyright (c) Cambridge University Press. Reprinted by permission of Cambridge University Press.

evolutionary importance of conflict between individuals. Those prone to self-sacrifice, for instance, will not be likely to have as many descendants as those who ruthlessly pursue their own genuine interests. Genes encouraging such self-sacrifice are not likely to spread. Indeed they will die out, as the families of more selfish individuals prosper. Some have argued that this is merely the selfishness endemic in the Western economic system writ large. The concepts of one society are given a universal application, which no concepts can ever have. The concepts of one society cannot be applied to others without the risk of grave misrepresentation.

This approach can soon induce paralysis. The sociology of knowledge, relating concepts to culture, is itself a cultural product with a validity which cannot, it seems, be applied beyond the frontiers of the society producing it. It can soon appear that nothing is ever stated objectively *about* societies. Everything is merely the cultural expression of a particular society. The possibility of any social theory, whether allied to or opposed to biology, is thereby removed. Yet once we step back from this conclusion, it must become an open question how far, if at all, society and biology are related. If everything is not automatically social, we are at liberty to examine how much is.

The extremism of some sociology of knowledge can be matched by that of some sociobiology. The discipline is exceedingly young, and it has been very tempting for some to claim that everything social can be reduced to the biological. In a quest for the genetic basis of social behaviour, the connection between genes and social phenomena can be made far too close. Accusations of "genetic determinism" have often been made. So far from sociobiology being irrelevant to the social sciences or even explicable in terms of them, it can make claim to take over from them. Edward Wilson suggested in his first book on the subject that the social sciences should in effect be superseded by biology. He wrote:

> Let us now consider man in the free spirit of natural history, as though we were zoologists from another planet completing a catalog of social species on Earth. In this macroscopic view, the humanities and social sciences shrink to specialized branches of biology.[3]

This position carries implications about the nature of man. Differences between him and other creatures are thought of little account. Biology can then hope to explain human behaviour as well as it tries to explain that of insects or of birds. Man may be more complicated, but he is not different in kind from other animals.

* * * * *

Sociobiology must prove an unrelenting opponent of any form of cultural relativism. The latter must uphold the utter distinctiveness of different cultures, coupled with the primacy of culture as a formative influence. Otherwise it reduces to uninteresting platitudes about people behaving differently in different circumstances. The bite of a relativist doctrine must lie in the view that different cultures shape man so differently that it is misleading to talk of any human nature common to them all. The cultural expression of

---

3. Op. cit. 547.

such a nature differs so widely, it may be held, that there is no way we can continue to posit it. There is no difference, it seems, between referring to radically different expressions in culture of the same human nature and denying that there is any common nature underlying human divergences. Both positions can be so obsessed with the undoubted differences between human cultures that any connection is either forgotten or deliberately repudiated. As a result we are left with a series of unrelated cultures which can only be understood in their own terms.

Sociobiology must be opposed to all this since its whole purpose is to examine what it believes is the same starting-point for all cultures. Human biology is taken to be the major influence on the moulding of culture. All cultures develop within the limits imposed by it and so they cannot be viewed as utterly distinct from each other. Studying culture in its own terms only leaves out what is for the sociobiologist the key factor. Biology is seen as not only creating the possibility of culture but as profoundly influencing its content. Thus any human culture must always possess some fundamental similarities with other cultures. The same needs have to be catered for. At times the link between culture and the biological base will be less straightforward. Nevertheless the fact that, according to sociobiologists, the link is there, provides a challenge to those who take cultural divergence at face value.

Treating culture as unconnected with biology can all too easily lead to relativism. The reason is that anyone faced with the multiplicity of human cultures is bound to be tempted by the view that their divergence is their most striking feature. Non-relativist explanations of divergence are harder to find once appeals to an underlying human nature are ruled out. This is one reason why social science does itself little good by ignoring the relevance of biology. Social scientists are clearly eager to preserve their territory from unwelcome encroachment, by limiting biology to talk about the general pre-conditions of culture. For example, human societies all use language and the ability to speak has a biological origin. How they use this ability together may be thought a matter for social science rather than biology. Talk of "human nature", if it takes place at all may then seem to be merely concerned with what makes culture possible. Different forms of culture are deemed irrelevant to biological research. This is, however, a very attenuated idea of human nature which can explain little of interest. It certainly has nothing to do with the question why we ever behave in one way rather than another. The latter can be regarded as an internal issue for whichever society is concerned. Society can then only be explained in social terms, and the concepts appropriate to one society may well be inappropriate to another. Losing our grip on the notion of human nature can easily lead us in this way into the paths of relativism.

Sociobiology does of course insist that human nature is a matter of *biological* concern. Many may agree that a social scientist jettisons the concept of human nature at his peril, but wonder whether that entails accepting a biological view of man. The emphasis on human society and man's social nature has often been made in order to avoid man being treated as a *mere* animal. Early sociobiology certainly seemed to reject anything distinctively human, which could not be assimilated to a recognizable type of animal behaviour. Even if it is accepted that some animals can possess elementary forms of culture, passed on through teaching, human culture is obviously far more complicated. It is crucial for the understanding of human behaviour in a way that animal "culture" could never be for the understanding of animals. Lumsden and Wilson have at last recognized this by allowing that *human* sociobiology is a subject in its own right. Humans are not merely one animal species amongst many. Account has to be taken of the positive role of culture and of human understanding. The idea of the zoologist from another planet, able to treat man as one social species amongst many, has had to be modified. Lumsden and Wilson now concede [4] that reference to the "canalization" of cultural evolution as a biological process need not involve treating it on a par with animal behaviour. Concept formation itself, they say, may be controlled in the last resort by biologically based "epigenetic rules". They go on, though, to say: [5]

> Such learning can be analyzed by gene-culture, theory, but not by direct comparison with animal species. The inseverable linkage between genes and culture does not also chain mankind to an animal level.

4. C. J. Lumsden, E. O. Wilson, *Genes Mird, and Culture*, (Cambridge, Mass.: Harvard University Press, 1981), 68.

5. Ibid. 345.

Reformed sociobiology can in fact join forces with social science rather than simply replace it. There will still be social scientists who will want nothing to do with biology, but this attitude cuts social science off totally from the rest of science and is bound to make its explanations seem suspect to many. In the end, indeed, social science can be made to appear a product of society rather than a dispassionate study of it. The choice can now be seen as less stark. It does not lie between physical science, including biology, and social science as competing modes of explanation. Each can illuminate the other. Social science cannot dismiss the insights of biology, if human society depends in any way on individual human nature. Lumsden and Wilson themselves say: "When cultural behaviour is treated as an ultimate product of biology instead of an independent stratigraphic layer above it, the social sciences can be connected more readily into a continuous explanatory system".[6] If this could be done without destroying the subject-matter of social science, the resulting integration of physical and social science would be of enormous importance.

The alternatives until now have often seemed to be a (literally) mindless reductionism and a refusal to allow that the social could be seen in any other than its own terms. This involved a very schizophrenic view of humanity. It could be seen in physical and chemical terms or in social ones. As a result of this split, man's "social essence" could appear to be something mysterious. Man becomes what he is through his par-

6. Op. cit. 350.

ticipation in society, and his biological make-up is irrelevant. This doctrine can reach the conclusion that man cannot have any desires that are not social in origin. It trades on the undoubted fact that all human tendencies and inclinations have to be expressed in the context of society. They can certainly be inhibited or even thwarted by a particular culture, but, according to sociobiology, this must always be at a cost. In the long run human nature will reassert itself. To take again the example of incest, humans may have inbuilt tendencies to avoid it, but it can still occur. What sociobiology denies is that incest could become a cultural norm, without inevitable and disastrous consequences, on individuals, and through them on their culture. The biological effects of culture cannot be ignored, any more than the biological origins of culture should be discounted.

Cultural divergence is no bar, in principle, to the attempt to explain society in a scientific way. In the tug between human biology and human culture, both elements have to be given weight. Humanity expresses itself in culture, but sociobiology points out that culture is not an arbitrary phenomenon. The demands of our biology give culture much of its point. There is a danger, though, in dealing with biology and culture in this way. There are not two competing types of explanation, biological and social. It is not a matter of one beating the other into submission. Much controversy is generated merely because of the false opposition of physical and social science. Human society will never be adequately understood as long as biologists and social scientists are in competition with each other. Each side has given credence to this idea by appealing to biological and environmental factors respectively. The emphasis was on either a "given" human nature or the myriad forms of human culture. The old battle between "physis" and "nomos" has been continually refought. This must be a false antithesis, since if human nature is expressed in a cultural context, we can never refer to it without bringing in the question of culture. Sociobiologists now, for the most part, see this.

The opposite danger, of studying culture without recognizing the underlying biological factors, is perhaps more seductive. It is a commonplace that the more similar people are to each other the more the differences between them seem to matter. Some of the fiercest battles are fought not between those with radically different ideologies but between those who have what would appear to the outsider to be very marginal differences. Different branches of Christianity or of Marxism find it harder to tolerate similar, but distinctive, views than a totally different outlook. So it is with human culture in general. We all notice and care about the differences, while taking for granted the similarities. Social science can become so obsessed with cultural divergence that it often takes it to be a basic fact about man, incapable of further explanation.

Sebastiano Timpanaro has attacked Marxists in particular for ignoring the biological underpinning of culture. He says:

> Marxists put themselves in a scientifically and polemically weak position if, after rejecting the idealist arguments

> which claim to show that the only reality is that of the Spirit and that cultural facts are in no way dependent on economic structures, they then borrow the same arguments to deny the dependence of man on nature.[7]

He likens the position of the contemporary Marxist to that of a person living on the first floor of a house who tells the tenant of the second floor that he is wrong if he thinks he is independent with no support from below. Yet at the same time he himself denies that the ground floor supports him, or rather says that the real ground floor is the first floor. In other words economic structures may underpin societies but they must themselves rest on biological facts about man. Non-Marxists, too, must recognize the biological basis of human society. Together the biological and social sciences can vastly increase our knowledge of man. Whether even in co-operation they can tell the whole story is another question.

7. S. Timpanaro, *On Materialism*, L. Garner (trans.) (London: New Left Books, 1975), 44.

C O M M E N T S ■ Q U E S T I O N S

1. "When it is stressed that there is a real connection between genes and behavior, sociobiologists often explain it in ways which make mind redundant." It may be instructive to relate this remark to the discussion in chapter 6 of the Identity Theory of Mind, according to which mind is nothing more than the activity of certain aspects of the nervous system. If you have read chapter 6 before reading this chapter, would you say that the sociobiological view of human nature commits one to some version of materialism in the philosophy of mind, or not?
2. According to Trigg, sociobiologists "have often argued that we do not need to be conscious of the reasons for our natural inclinations. We may even be programmed to delude ourselves as to the real reasons." What implications does this view of human nature have for the free will question (discussed in chapter 5)?
3. According to sociobiologists, morality "may be an elaborate system for furthering our own self-interest." What would the opponents of psychological egoism (discussed in chapter 9) say about this?
4. There is, says Trigg, something confused or paradoxical in the view that (a) human behavior is largely controlled by genes and (b) an understanding of the genetic basis of behavior can help us more effectively to control behavior. What response, if any, might the sociobiologist make to this criticism?

PO-KEUNG IP

Taoism and the Foundations of Environmental Ethics

I Introduction

I take it that the major task of environmental ethics is the construction of a system of normative guidelines governing man's attitudes, behavior, and action toward his natural environment. The central question to be asked is: how *ought* man, either as an individual or as a group, to behave, to act, toward nature? By *nature* I mean the nonhuman environment man finds himself in. Surely, a question of this sort presupposes the appropriateness of the application of moral, ethical concepts to nature, viz., stones, fish, bears, trees, water, and so on. Questions about the legitimacy and meaningfulness of such an application automatically arise. However, in the present paper I presume such legitimacy without arguing for it.[1]

Any viable environmental ethics, it seems to me, should provide adequate answers to three questions: (1) what is the nature of nature? (2) What is man's relationship to nature? (3) How should man relate himself to nature? In this paper I show that Taoism gives reasonably good answers to these questions and I argue that Taoism, in this sense, is capable of providing a metaphysical foundation for environmental ethics.

II Science and Ethics

Contemporary environmental crises, such as pollution of various sorts, overusage of natural resources, and extinction of rare species, force us to reconsider exactly what the relationships between man and nature are. At the same time they compel us to reflect once again on what sort of attitudes we ought to have toward nature. The kinds of questions raised here are both scientific and ethical. On the one hand, they are scientific because only recently has man come to realize how ignorant he is of the natural surrounding he is in. It is certainly an irony to twentieth-century man that even though modern science has made tremendous strides in probing both the very large and the very small, it has little to say

1. Tom Regan recently has given a detailed discussion on this issue in "The Nature and Possibility of an Environmental Ethic," *Environmental Ethics* 3 (1981): 19–34.

Po-keung Ip, who has a Ph.D. in the history and philosophy of science from the University of Western Ontario, has taught philosophy at Tunghai University and now teaches at Lingnan College in Hong Kong.

From *Environmental Ethics*, vol. 5 (1983). Reprinted by permission of *Environmental Ethics* and the author.

about the middle, i.e., our surrounding ecosphere. The still immature state of the environmental sciences, nonetheless, sadly bears this out. On the other hand, the questions envisaged here are clearly ethical both in the descriptive and the normative senses. First, we need to understand how man actually conceives his relationship with nature. This is clearly an empirical problem that invites both sociological as well as historical studies. However, we also need to go beyond these empirical questions and ask ourselves whether such attitudes are morally justified. This inevitably involves us in the problems of moral criteria.

I regard both the scientific and ethical approaches to our environmental problems to to be vitally important. Both should work closely with the other. Both need the help of the other. Without either, our understanding of environmental problems must remain very limited and incomplete. But what sort of relationship should science and ethics have? I do not try to enter into this thorny problem here.[2] It is important to note, however, that by urging a close working relationship between science and ethics, I am not attempting to *derive* ethics from science. I take the position, without arguing for it, that ethics can never be derived from science, if *derived* is understood in the logical sense of deduction. That this is so is due to the fact that one can never derive *ought* from *is*—a too familiar problem in moral philosophy. The sense in which I say that ethics should work closely with science is this: suppose we have a system of ethics, *E*, which is capable of generating a set of normative guidelines, *G*. Suppose that *G* in conjoining with the knowledge of the situation in which the agent is about to take action yields morally acceptable attitudes and actions. This set of attitudes and actions is not only morally acceptable, but is also according to the knowledge available at the time, workable or realizable. In other words, the relationship between science and ethics is an oblique one. Scientific knowledge only supports ethics indirectly in the way that it provides evidence that the set of actions and attitudes "derivable" from the ethical system in question is workable, realizable.

Let me give a brief example. Suppose we have an ethics which exhorts people to act selflessly regardless of causes and occasions. Scientific results may suggest, however, that self-interest is a primary motivation of human behavior and action. In this case, we have an ethics which runs counter to the evidences of human nature arrived at by scientific research. We say that such ethics is not supported by science and hence is not involved in the kind of working relationship that we hope for between the two. On the other hand, if we have an ethics which is not only compatible with science, but also receives support from it (in the sense explained), then we say that we have reason to believe that it is plausible.

Two concepts will be useful in my discussion. I take an ethics to be *minimally coherent* if and only if (1) it is coherent and (2) it is compatible with science. An ethics is *maximally*

---

2. See Don Marietta, Jr.'s "The Interrelationships between ecological Science and Environmental Ethics," *Environmental Ethics* 1 (1979): 195–207.

coherent if and only if (1) it is coherent and (2) it receives support from science. The minimally coherent ethics is a weak version of environmental ethics. The maximally coherent ethics, which requires more scientific data, and hence more research, presumably is harder to construct. Due to inadequate ecological information concerning the man-nature relation, nevertheless, I think the kind of ethics that is workable at present is the minimally coherent one. If such understanding is correct, the first step toward an adequate theory for environmental ethics depends on the possibility of establishing such minimally coherent ethics. In the light of such understanding, I show that Taosim, as chiefly represented by the teachings of Lao Tzu and Chuang Tzu, can provide us with such an ethic.

III *The Taoist Conception of Nature*

Recall the three questions posed at the beginning of the paper, viz., what is the nature of nature, of the man-nature relationship, of the right attitudes to nature? The first two questions are clearly metaphysical in nature and the last one ethical. Let us see how Taoism responds to these questions.

To understand the Taoist conception of nature, one must start with the notion of *Tao*. Using a mystical and poetical language, Lao Tzu in *Tao Té Ching* gives a rich but at times amorphous representation of how nature works. This is done by means of the notion of *Tao*. At the very beginning of *Tao Té Ching*, it is said:

> The Tao (Way) that can be told is not the eternal Tao,
> The name that can be named is not the eternal name,
> The nameless is the origin of Heaven and Earth .... (chap. 1)[3]

In other places, we are aslo told that "Tao is eternal and has no name" (chap. 32) and that

> There was something undifferentiated and yet complete,
> Which existed before Heaven and Earth.
> Soundless and formless, it depends on nothing and does not change,
> It operates everywhere and is free from danger,
> It may be considered the mother of the Universe,
> I do not know its name; I call it Tao. (chap. 25)

From similar utterances in *Tao Té Ching*, we gather that Tao has the following attributes: it is nameless, intangible, empty, simple, all-pervasive, eternal, life-sustaining, nourishing.[4] Indeed, for Lao Tzu, *Tao* stands for the ultimate reality of nature. Unlike *Tien* (Heaven) and *Ti* (God),[5] *Tao* is not anything like a

---

3. All quotations from *Tao Té Ching* are from Chan Wing-Tsit, *A Source Book in Chinese Philosophy*, (Princeton: Princeton University Press, 1963), pp. 139–173. They are identified in the text by chapter number.

4. See *Tao Té Ching*, chaps. 1, 74, 21, 35, 4, 6, 32.

5. The origins of the notions of *Ti* (God) and *Tien* (Heaven) were closely tied with ancestor worship in ancient China. *Ti* apparently represented a personal god and was supposed to be the perennial source of life. However, it was subsequently replaced by a less personalistic notion of *Tien*. The latter was a highly naturalistic notion which had no strong religious connotation, but was mainly used to stand for the physical sky. See Chang Chung-ying, "Chinese Philosophy: A Characterization," in A. Naess and A. Hannay, eds., *Introduction to Chinese Philosophy* (Oslo: Universitetsforlaget, 1972), pp. 141–165.

creator god. Rather it is a totally depersonalized concept of nature.

The namelessness of *Tao* is due to its infinite nature, since Lao Tzu believes that only finite things can be attached a name. To give a name to a thing is to individuate it and to give it a definite identity. However, *Tao* by virtue of its infinite nature certainly rejects all names. In other words, *Tao* cannot be exhaustively individuated in the domain of empirical beings, though the latter owe their existence to *Tao*. Hence, *Tao* is not characterizable in any finite manner. Therefore, although we can, in a sense, say we "know" *Tao* by knowing this or that finite being, yet the knowledge thus arrived at is very incomplete. In this way, the nature of *Tao* is at best indeterminable insofar as human knowledge is concerned.

There is also a dynamic side of *Tao*. We are told that "reversion is the action of *Tao*" (chap. 40). *Tao* is also depicted as a process of change and transformation. In fact, everything in the universe is the result of self- and mutual-transformations which are governed by the dialectical interactions of *Tao's* two cosmic principles—*Ying* and *Yang* [6]—which explain the rhythmic processes which constitute the natural world.

Since *Tao* nourishes, sustains, and tranforms beings, a natural relationship is built between them. This relationship is best understood if we understand the meaning of the *Té* of *Tao. Té* signifies the potency, the power, of *Tao* that nourishes, sustains, and transforms beings. As a result, the nourishment, development and fulfilment of beings are the consequence of *Té*. Because of the nature of *Té*, it is both a potency as well as a virtue, and by virtue of the possession of *Té, Tao* is itself virtuous as well. Since *Té* is internalized in all beings in the universe, there is no problem of relating beings in the world. Indeed, things are related to each other not only metaphysically but also morally. The *Té* of *Tao* provides the essential connections. Man, being a member of beings, is without exception internally linked to *Tao* as well as to everything else. Moreover, being endowed with *Té*, man is also endowed with the capacity of doing virtuous things toward his cosmic counterparts. Thus, a crucial metaphysical linkage between man and nature is established. In the Taoist world view, there is no unbridgeable chasm between man and nature, because everything is inherently connected to everything else. The *Tao* is not separated from the natural world of which it is the source. In Taoism, therefore, chaos is impossible.

The moral imperative to be virtuous toward nature is made possible by another feature of *Tao*, impartiality. According to Lao Tzu, *Tao* "being all embracing, is impartial" (chap. 16). *Tao* is impartial in the sense that everything is to be treated on an equal footing. To use a more apt term, everything is seen as being "ontologically equal." [7] Man receives no special attention or status from *Tao*. Homocentrism is simply

6. See Derk Bodde, "Harmony and Conflict in Chinese Philosophy," in A. F. Wright, ed., *Studies in Chinese Thought* (Chicago: University of Chicago Press, 1953), p. 121.

7. For more on the notion of ontological equality, see Chang, "Chinese Philosophy," p. 149.

an alien thing in the Taoist axiological ordering of beings. As a matter of fact, the Taoist holds that there is a kind of egalitarian axiology of beings. The notion of ontological and axiological equality of beings receives further elaborations in the hands of Chuang Tzu. For Chuang Tzu, beings are ontologically equal because they are formed as a result of a process of self- and mutal-transformations. The alleged individuality and uniqueness of beings can be determinable only in such process. Everything is related to everything else through these processes of self- and mutal-transformations.[8]

IV The Doctrine of Wu Wei

Acknowledging the fact that man-nature is an inherently connected whole, and that man and other beings, animated or otherwise, are ontologically as well as axiologically equal, the question of how man should behave or act toward his natural surroundings is readily answerable, for the Taoist would take the doctrine of *Wu Wei* as the proper answer to this question.

Although the doctrine of *Wu Wei* is relatively well-known, care must be taken as to how one construes the meaning of *wu wei*. I am taking a position which is at variance with the classical rendition. A majority of writers, to my knowledge, translate the meaning of *wu wei* as inaction,[9] but I think there is a better way of translating it which is more coherent with the system of thought presented in *Tao Té Ching* and other representative Taoist texts. Perhaps the translation of *wu wei* as nonaction is the result of relying too heavily on the literal understanding of the meanings of the words *wu* and *wei*. Literally, *wu* means "not"; *wei*, on the hand, means "action" or "endeavor." However, the meaning of *wu wei* need not literally be translated as "inaction." The reasons are as follows. Although we are told that "*Tao* invariably takes no action *[wu wei]*,[10] and yet there is nothing left undone" (chap 37), given that Tao nourishes, sustains, and fulfills, *Tao* is invariably action-in-itself. To say *Tao wu wei* here is tantamount to saying that *Tao* acts in accordance with its own nature. Since *Tao* is action-in-itself, it certainly requires no additional action to act. To say *Tao* takes no action can best be understood as *Tao* taking no *exogenous* action to act, since such action would be redundant.

This construal of *wu wei* indeed has other textual support as well. For example, in characterizing the sage, Lao Tzu says, that he

> Deal[s] with things before they appear.
> Put[s] things in order before disorder arises . . . .
> A tower of nine storeys begins with a heap of earth.
> The journey of a thousand *li* [1/3 mile] starts from where one stands,
> He who takes an action fails.
> He who grasps things loses them.
> For this reason the sage takes no action and therefore does not fail . . . . (chap. 64)

8. For more on the self- and mutual-transformation of beings, see *Chuang Tzu*, chapter two, in Chan, *Source Book*.

9. See Fung Yu-lan, *A History of Chinese Philosophy*, vol. 1, trans. D. Bodde (Princeton: Princeton University Press, 1952), p. 187; Chan, *Source Book*.

10. I systematically replaced *wu wei* in all places in Chan's original translations.

To make sense of the above paragraph, *wu wei* should not be interpreted as nonaction. To do otherwise would make it very difficult to make sense of the phrases, "Deal[s] with things before they appear. Put[s] things in order before disorder arises." Surely, not only are they not nonaction, they are indeed well-planned and deliberative actions. Moreover, when Lao Tzu says, "A tower of nine storeys begins with a heap of earth. The journey of a thousand *li* starts from where one stands," he seems to be saying that things simply work in accordance with the laws of nature. Anyone who tries to do things in violation of the laws of nature is doomed to failure. Therefore, the statements, "He who takes an action fails" and "the sage takes no action and therefore does not fail" can consistently be interpreted as "he who takes action in violation of the laws of nature fails" and "the sage acts in accordance with the laws of nature and therefore does not fail." The sage, being the ideal Taoist man, surely understands the *Tao* well and is thus capable of not acting against nature.[11]

The moral to be drawn from the doctrine of *Wu Wei* is clear and straightforward, given our interpretation of the meaning of *wu wei*. That is, insofar as ecological action is concerned, the Taoist's recommendation is so simple that it almost amounts to a truism: act in accordance with nature. However, one should be reminded of the fact that such a proposal is well supported both by the metaphysical and axiological conceptions of the man-nature relation. It is exactly this kind of metaphysical grounding that an environmental ethic needs.

V Conclusion—The Taoist Reversion

Western man inherited from the Enlightenment legacy a conception of nature which is patently anti-environmentalistic. The world is depicted, chiefly through the work of Descartes, as a big machine consisting only of extended matter. It has no life of its own and no value of it own. Its value can only be defined in terms of human needs and purposes. It does not have intrinsic value of any sort, but has only instrumental value defined in terms of human desires. Man, being the possessor of mind, can willfully subject this allegedly lifeless world to his desires and purposes. The extreme consequence of such homocentrism is the ruthless and unlimited exploitation of the environment.

Such an attitude assumes a clear dichtomy between subjectivity and objectivity. On the subjective side, we find man with his feels, desires, sentiments, passions, reasons, purposes, sensations etc., all of these regarded as needing to be satisfied, fulfilled or worthy of preserving and cultivating. On the objective side, we find the nonhuman world totally devoid of any sentience, functioning blindly according to mechanical laws. Such a machine-like world certainly cannot have any value and worth of its own except as a means to the satisfaction and fulfillment of human needs and wants. Such hu-

11. For other textual evidence to support my interpretation, see *Haai Nan Tzu*, quoted in J. Needham, *Science and Civilization in China*, vol. 2 (Cambridge: Cambridge University Press, 1956), p. 51 and *Chuang Tzu* in Chan, *Source Book*.

man needs and wants could range from the most noble to the most mean, from the purely aesthetic to the cognitively epistemic and to the practically technological. The physical world is there for us to comprehend (Greek philosophers), to experiment with (Francis Bacon), to transform into a humanized or human nature (Karl Marx), and to exploit for material goods (Adam Smith and Milton Friedman).

Nevertheless, the man-nature relationship envisaged here is at best an external and instrumental one. The world is simply something out there, ready to be subjected to human control and use. It is simply an "otherness." As the Enlightenment teaches us: there is no internal link between us and it. We do not feel that it is part of us, nor do we feel that we are part of it. We are, cast into a seemingly unsurpassable gap between subject and object, between man and nature.

To transcend this human predicament, we need a philosophy which can break this metaphysical barrier that separates man from his world, one which can reconnect the essential link which has been mistakenly severed for so long between human and nonhuman counterparts. We need a philosophy which can attribute values to nonhuman objects independently of human needs. That is, nonhuman beings should be regarded as having intrinsic values of their own rather than having only extrinsic or instrumental values. Moreover, we also need a philosophy which can tell us that we are part of a universe whose parts mutually nourish, support, and fulfil each other.

It seems to me that one philosophy which satisfies the above mentioned features is the Taoist philosophy we have been discussing. Most important of all, one cannot find in it the metaphysical schism that divides subject and object, for the supposed gap between man and nature simply has no place in the Taoist conception of the man-nature relationship. Subject and object, through self- and mutual-transformations, are metaphysically fused and unified. Moreover, the thesis of ontological equality of beings, and hence the axiological equality of beings, completely annihilates the kind of homocentrism at the center of the Enlightenment world view. In addition, it also opens up the possibility of ascribing values to nonhuman objects regardless of the latter's usefulness to human beings. Thus, a theory of intrinsic value for nature is indeed forthcoming within the Taoist framework. These features are vitally important to the construction of environmental ethics of any sort, and are, I believe, capable of providing the necessary metaphysical underpinnings upon which an environmental ethics has to rest.

Taoism, moreover, is compatible with science and is thus capable of providing a minimally coherent ethics. First, it is not anti-scientific, for despite all its mystical overtones, Taoism is in fact a version of naturalism. The doctrine of *Wu Wei* implicitly entails a notion of observation which is germane to science.[12] Second, ecology as a science teaches us the interdependence of all life

12. Needham incidentally holds such a view, see Colin A. Ronan, *The Shorter Science and Civilization in China*, vol. 1 (Cambridge: Cambridge University Press, 1978), p. 98.

forms and nonliving things. It takes man as only one part of the interdependent whole. Every member of this intricately integrated complex is, in a very real sense, ecologically equal because each member depends on all others for survival, sustenance, and fulfillment. Analogously, the Taoist concept of ontological equality undoubtedly expresses the same idea, although in a more metaphysical way.

Note also that in the Taoist metaphysics, the notion of axiological equality comes together with the notion of ontological equality. This is due to the fact that in Taoist metaphysics fact and value are fused together, just as subject and object are. Such metaphysical unification of value and fact is crucial in giving us a foundation upon which we can bring science and ethics together. It also makes it possible and meaningful to say that science and ethics cohere in this metaphysical sense. Although it seems presumptuous to assert that the Taoist ideas anticipate cognate concepts in modern ecology, nevertheless, one certainly cannot deny that the insights of the Taoist are explicitly acknowledged and endorsed by the latter.

C O M M E N T S ■ Q U E S T I O N S

1. According to Taoism, there is a "moral imperative to be virtuous toward nature," the foundation for which is the "ontological and axiological equality" of everything in nature. This means that everything in nature is, in some important way, on an equal footing, both in regard to its reality and its value. Is the Taoist view the correct one, or does it understate the value of human beings? Is it an advance over other ways of looking at nature, or does it carry egalitarianism too far?
2. "Insofar as ecological action is concerned, the Taoist's recommendation is so simple that it almost amounts to a Truism: act in accordance with nature." An unfriendly critic might say that the Taoists recommendation *is* a truism, and consequently is not worth saying. Do you agree with this criticism of Taoism? If you reject it, then what would you say is the value of a "Taoist ecology"? Is its message to live in "harmony with nature" foreign to Western ways of thinking or is its message one that people tend to agree is correct but have difficulty following? Put another way, does the Taoist message (if it is not a truism) teach us something new, or does it remind us of something that we already believe is true but need to be encouraged to put into practice?

AHMED M. ABOU-ZEID

The Concept of Time in Peasant Society

Peasant Behaviour

A study of the concept of time and systems of time-reckoning in traditional peasant societies is not an easy task. For one thing, time is seldom regarded by villagers in these societies as a mere tool that should be exploited in achieving certain well-defined objectives, or a mere means of measuring activity and productivity. It is also a means of consolidating existing social relationships and establishing new ones. Therefore any serious attempt to study the attitude of traditional peasants towards time should try to analyse the whole network of social relationships and understand the system of values prevailing in these societies. In fact, the relatively few sociologists and anthropologists who have studied the subject have been keen on emphasizing that peasants have, in general, a different outlook, and a different way of evaluating time and its role in organizing their activities and their life, from the outlook of urban people, especially in Western culture. They are sometimes described as people who seldom consider time as something actual, which passes, can be wasted or saved, and so on. Evans-Pritchard once asked whether the pastoralist Nuer "ever experienced the same feeling of fight against time or of having to co-ordinate activities with an abstract passage of time, because their points of reference are mainly the activities themselves, which are generally of a leisurely character". Similar ideas can be found in a number of writings about peasants in traditional societies. Peasant behaviour is often described as characterized mainly by indifference to time and not regulated according to a timetable. That is why peasants act and work without haste. "Haste is seen as a lack of decorum combined with diabolical ambition." They are masters of passing time, "or better, of taking one's time". Bourdieu thinks that the worst discourtesy in the eyes of peasants is "to come to the point and express oneself in as few words as possible. Sometimes one leaves with nothing settled". The notion of an exact appointment is not known. People may agree to meet, not at a certain precise hour, but just "in the morning" or "after the last prayer". In Algeria women are often seen waiting at the hospital or before the doctor's office two or three hours before it is due to open.

There is plenty of evidence from

Ahmed M. Abou-Zeid is a professor of sociology and anthropology at the University of Alexandria, Egypt.

Extracts from *Time and the Sciences*. Copyright (c) Unesco 1979. Reprinted by permission of Unesco.

peasant societies supporting these statements. Peasants in Egypt, for example, may spend the whole night at the railway station to catch the next morning's train, for, as they explain, one should wait for the train because the train does not wait for anyone. Villagers go to the village cafe mainly to meet each other. They chat freely for long hours about their daily life and their private problems. It would be discourteous of the waiter to come hurriedly to get their orders. A 'waiter' should 'wait' till he is called by the clients. Actually it is part of his duty to welcome the clients as if they were personal friends and guests, and to exchange friendly talk, including some jokes, with them. Even in economic transactions and exchanges, the same attitude prevails. One goes to the village store not only to buy whatever goods one may need, but also, and perhaps primarily, to "pay a visit" and have a chat with the storekeeper and other customers. Only at the end of the "visit" one may, or may not, buy the goods one wanted. Much haggling and bargaining takes place between merchant and client before they agree on the price of even the so-called fixed-price goods. Haggling is regarded as an art. It is a means of communication, and it establishes friendly relationships if conducted in the right way. A client who always knows what he wants and who always pays the price the merchant asks, and then leaves hastily, is not regarded as the ideal type of customer.

This leisurely attitude towards time may be the outcome of the very nature of agricultural life and activities, which are organized according to seasonal variations, rather than by hours or any other shorter time unit. Thus, time units tend to be less well-defined than they are in urban communities, and more particularly in Western societies. Keeping to a strict and precise timetable is of little significance.

* * * * *

The Peasant Future

The concept of time as something that recurs and repeats itself, and the inclination to see the future as another image of the past, raise some doubts about the ability, or even the willingness, of the peasant to plan for the future. The crucial question that imposes itself here is: If the future is so illusive and belongs entirely to God, and if man cannot take hold of the future, then to what extent can a peasant make a real and solid plan for the future?

Although sociologists and anthropologists who have dealt with this subject agree that peasants do make certain predictions about the future and arrange their life accordingly, they express very strong doubts about their ability to make far-reaching plans. Bailey, for example, says that peasants hardly think in terms of five-year plans, if that is what is meant by planning. He goes to the extent of arguing that "the idea of planning can exist only in those cognitive maps which include the idea of man in control of predictable and controllable impersonal forces". And since peasants give much weight to fate and to other supernatural or mystic forces, which they think do intervene in their actions, then "policy-making and planning are not part of their cognitive map of the world and human society. They do not reject the idea of planning as wicked; they simply do not have the category". It is true that peasants do plan the use of their resources, in the sense that they breed their cattle, or save for their marriages, or keep seed for next year's sowing, and so on. But these activities are not, so argues Bailey, planning in the way in which this word is used when one speaks about "five-year plans". Moreover, the policymaker sees a future that is different from the present because it will then be of a completely different kind from what it is now. This is something that falls far beyond the imagination of the peasant, who it seems cannot be interested in figuring a future state of affairs that is radically different from the present.

Bourdieu argues that traditional Algerian society does not try to transform the world but to transform its own attitude to the world. Indeed, he notices the absence of all effort to forecast the future and to master it, and he attributes this to the people's distrust of the future and to their feeling that they cannot take possession of it. The peasant usually refuses to sacrifice a tangible interest to an abstract one "which cannot be comprehended by concrete intuition". Thus he cannot sacrifice, for example, the pasture assured to his herds by the land to a mere abstract plan of agricultural development of which he does not know the outcome. Therefore, planning creates no incentive for him, because the plan is based on abstract calculation—which belongs to the realm of possibilities. The peasant certainly has foresight, but does not practise calculated planning; and between the two "lies the same gulf as between mathematical demonstration and practical demonstration by cutting and folding".

This scepticism about the peasant's capacity for planning and his interest in it comes from the very concept of time adopted by the peasants themselves. Most social scientists tend in their analysis to distinguish between two main concepts of time, which have been simply called, by Evans-Pritchard, ecological and structural. Ecological time is rather cyclical, as opposed to the structural progressive time. Other social scientists, such as Bailey and Bourdieu, whom we have quoted here, distinguish between what they call "the round of time" and "time's arrow" or "time as an arrow". The peasant plans for the round of time, in the sense that he allocates resources as if he holds the assumption that the coming year will be "this year over again", with very minor changes and trivial variations. Planning in the sense of making five-year plans envisages time as an arrow, envisages work as having a beginning and an end, and assumes that there is always a well-defined and clear target to be reached and an aim to be achieved. In other words, the plan for a future that is radically different from the present needs rational and deliberate calculation, thus falling beyond the scope of the peasant's mind or interest. Those who think in terms of the 'round of time' tend to see change as a result of the intervention of mystical and supernatural forces. This intervention makes it vain and hopeless for human beings to plan; it is useless to plan in the face of such forces.

COMMENTS ■ QUESTIONS

1. What lessons does a study of the concept of time in peasant societies teach us? Does it perhaps show, or tend to show, that anxiety about time in advanced societies is something that can be overcome? Or should we say instead that, because the overall way of life in advanced societies requires a view of time very different from the peasant view, people in advanced societies could never achieve the nonchalant peasant attitude toward time?
2. There are two quite different basic views about the nature of time. According to one, time is a reality "in itself," waiting to be discovered. The discovery of time may be more or less complete—more complete perhaps in advanced societies, less complete in peasant societies. According to the other basic view of the nature of time, there is no time "in itself"; rather, the structure of time is determined by the overall way of life that is to be found in a particular group of people who share a way of life—such as the members of a peasant society or the members of an advanced Western society. (Perhaps we should say that a third way of life is shared by the "society of mystics," whose view of time is briefly described by William James in chapter 3.) Which of the two basic views of time do you believe is most defensible? (For a discussion of philosophical questions about the nature of time, see chapter 14.)

READINGS

Blanshard, Brand. *Nature of Thought.* New York: Macmillan, 1941. Defends a version of the coherence theory of truth.

Caplan, Arthur L., ed. *The Sociobiology Debate: Readings on Ethical and Scientific Issues.* New York: Harper & Row, 1978. An excellent anthology.

James, William. *Pragmatism: A New Name for Some Old Ways of Thinking.* A classic defense of the pragmatic theory of truth.

Horton, Robin, and Ruth Finnegan, eds. *Modes of Thought: Essays on Thinking in Western and Non-Western Societies.* London: Faber, 1973. A very useful collection.

Korner, Stephan. *Categorical Frameworks.* Oxford: Basil Blackwell, 1974. Discusses the issue of conceptual relativism.

Rorty, Richard. *Philosophy and the Mirror of Nature.* Princeton: Princeton University Press, 1979. Contemporary, widely read, controversial examination of the problem of truth.

White, Alan R. *Truth.* New York: Doubleday, Anchor Books, 1970. A very careful analysis of the major theories of truth.

Wilson, E. O. *On Human Nature.* Cambridge, Mass.: Harvard University Press, 1975. One of the major presentations of sociobiology.

C H A P T E R T H I R T E E N

Since [the claims of parapsychology] contravene a substantial body of existing scientific knowledge, in order for us to modify our basic principles. . . the evidence must be extremely strong. But that it is, remains highly questionable.

—Paul Kurtz

Parapsychology has verified by relatively improved methods some old claims of powers that transcend the properties of material systems.

—J. B. Rhine

Science versus Pseudoscience

This chapter primarily concerns the question of whether some investigations into the existence of extrasensory perception (ESP), life after death, precognition, astrological influences of the stars, and so on belong to empirical science. If this question is to be answered, empirical science first must be defined. As a preliminary, we can say that it is a search for truth conducted essentially through observation and experiment.

For the sake of convenience, I will refer generally to such putative phenomena as ESP and life after death, as *paranormal phenomena*, or the paranormal. The word *paranormal* is probably the most nearly neutral term that can be chosen. (Paul Kurtz, in the second of the reading selections for this chapter, raises some objections to use of this word, but no better word can replace it in all of the contexts in which it may occur.) The use of a common term should not be understood to imply that attempts to establish the existence of ESP, life after death, and so on are all on an equal footing in regard to credibility. Instead, the intention is to leave open the question of whether any or all of these phenomena belong to empirical science proper, as opposed to pseudoscience. *Pseudoscience* is to be understood as any investigation that resembles empirical science but fails to meet at least one of the latter's criteria.

The primary question raised in this chapter has a twofold aspect. First, is the question regarding certain *actual* investigations into the existence of paranormal phenomena, particularly those that claim to successfully support the existence of paranormal phenomena. Do these investigations belong to empirical science or to pseudoscience? The second question is whether *any* investigation into the existence of paranormal phenomena can belong to empirical science.

If the second question is answered no, then necessarily the first question will also be answered no. Indeed, there would be no need to look at the methods and results of particular researchers if the investigation of paranormal phenomena as such could be shown to belong to pseudoscience. Still, the two questions above must be kept separate because a negative answer to the *first* does not entail a negative answer to the second. Much has been written about the shortcomings of actual attempts to establish the existence of various paranormal phenomena empirically. Paul Kurtz takes up this theme in his paper, reprinted here, entitled, "Is Parapsychology a Science?" Both those who want to say that the study of the paranormal does not belong to empirical science, such as Kurtz, and those who want to say the opposite, such as J. B. Rhine (also represented in this chapter), would agree that the actual history of efforts to study the paranormal empirically contains significant amounts of fraud as well as slipshod investigative procedures. But the most important philosophical question, and one that is also addressed by Kurtz and Rhine, is the second of the two given above—the question of whether any investigation of the paranormal *could* belong to empirical science, regardless of what actual attempts have been like.

The distinction between science and pseudoscience can perhaps be helpfully viewed from a broader perspective. Throughout its history, philosophy has been pulled in two very different directions. On the one hand, it has led the way in setting rigorous intellectual standards for logic and clarity; its job has been to root out confusion, wishful thinking, and illogical reasoning. Socrates, the ancient Greek philosopher, spent much of his life painstakingly analyzing people's beliefs in order to demonstrate that the people did not know as much as they thought they knew. Plato, the most famous pupil of Socrates, devoted much of his writing to a careful analysis of concepts and arguments. Aristotle, the most famous pupil of Plato, invented symbolic logic, a precise, formal system. All philosophers since the time of Aristotle have heeded the ancient Greeks' demand for philosophical *analysis*.

On the other hand, philosophy has also been pulled toward philosophical *speculation*—the endeavor to reach out beyond common and narrow ways of thinking to present a "large picture" of things. In contrast to philosophical analysis, philosophical speculation has a grand sweep. Its overall aim is to be bold and creative; one of its purposes is to remove any blinders that may be imposed by everyday routines, social prejudices, unexamined assumptions, and, in short, any type of narrow-minded thinking that may keep us from discovering the truth. Another purpose is to put together, or synthesize, our deepest and most comprehensive thoughts about ourselves and the world. The speculative side of philosophy is as well represented by the ancient Greeks as the analytical. Plato's philosophy, in particular, has much to say about "unseen realities" that transcend the world of common experience. (Some brief remarks about Plato's Theory of Forms are made in the opening essay for chapter 8.) The speculative bent of ancient Greek philosophy has been as influential on subsequent philosophers as its analytical bent.

Which of the two is the correct direction for philosophy? The answer is both; philosophy needs to insist upon being careful and rigorous, but just as much it needs to insist upon the broadest, most open and creative search for truth possible. It needs to he both analytical and speculative. It deeds to be tough-minded but not narrow-minded.

The same can be said about science, particularly when it overlaps philosophy, such as in areas that raise questions about the paranormal. Questions about the existence of paranormal phenomena have implications regarding the basic nature of the human mind, the nature of human life, and even the nature of reality as a whole. In reading the selections for this chapter, the need for philosophy and science to be both analytical and speculative should be kept in mind in order to avoid prejudice either for or against the claims of researchers in the area of the paranormal.

The disagreement between those who are sympathetic to paranormal research and those who are unsympathetic must not be seen in terms of a need for *choosing* between analysis and speculation. It would be quite wrong for the one side to say: "We want nothing to do with paranormal research because we believe that philosophy and science should primarily be tough-minded and analytical," or for the other side to say: "We are sympathetic to paranormal research because *we* believe that philosophy and science should be broad-minded and speculative." Instead, the essential questions concern how to be speculative in an intellectually responsible way, and how to apply criteria for analytical rigor fairly. Answering these questions is both difficult and complex.

Consider: should the very same criteria be applied in, say, ESP experiments that are applied in scientific experiments that deal with "normal" material processes? One criterion for an adequate scientific experiment is that it be repeatable under publicly verifiable conditions. Should ESP experiments be expected to meet this criterion if the study of ESP is to qualify as an empirical science? Should we say that otherwise it is a pseudoscience? Answering such questions is a controversial undertaking for several reasons. Let us look at just one of them. Some ESP researchers argue that it is unfair to require that ESP experiments be repeatable in the same way that, say, chemistry experiments need to be repeatable because ESP is a radically different sort of phenomenon. They argue that ESP by its very nature is a "subjective" phenomenon that depends upon the subject's state of mind in ways that are not publicly verifiable.

Opponents of this view may argue either (1) that such claims are merely attempts to cover up the fact that ESP experiments have had little or no success or (2) that the concept of a "subjective" phenomenon is impossible to make clear.

Investigation of the paranormal may be seen as a catch-22, namely, that until something is known about the nature of paranormal phenomena (assuming that any actually exist!) no one can say what the appropriate tough-minded analytical criteria for investigating them are, and no one can say what constitutes a responsible attempt to put together a grand, speculative picture of the world that contains a place for paranormal phenomena. But until agreement is reached on these matters (and some success achieved in applying what has been agreed upon), nothing *can* be known about the nature of paranormal phenomena!

Can this impasse be broken? Most philosophers would agree that, at least in theory, it can by building a *prima facie* defense. A *prima facie* case for the truth of a statement, p, does not show that p is true with certainty or even that p is more likely true than false. That is, a *prima facie* case for p falls short of embodying either a sound deductive or a successful inductive argument for the truth of p. It is weaker even than an inductive argument for p. (If you are not familiar with the concepts of deductive and inductive arguments, see the opening essay for chapter 3.) What, then, is a *prima facie* case? That is difficult to say, because there is no way to specify in a formally precise fashion what makes research in one area seem more *promising* than research in another. A *prima facie* case is one that holds out the rational promise of actual success.

Most philosophers would agree that there is not even a *prima facie* case for the existence of alleged astrological influences of stars and planets upon people's lives. The paper by John D. McGervey applies statistical tests to data relevant to certain claims in astrology for the purpose of showing that these claims are completely unfounded.

What about other paranormal phenomena? Here what one should say is not so clear. The main question to be asked is whether there is a need to suppose that paranormal phenomenan exist in order to explain certain events in the world—the results of ESP experiments, the experiences of people who think they have been "out of their bodies" or heard a "disembodied" voice speak to them, the prophecies that people may claim to have made, and so on. (These sorts of events and others are referred to in some of the reading selections for this chapter and chapter 7). Can these events readily be "explained away" by appealing to hypotheses that make *no* reference to the paranormal?

If you conclude that a *prima facie* case *can* be made for the truth of, say, an ESP claim, you probably should also conclude that the investigation of ESP either *is* (in the hands of certain researchers) or at least *could be* an empirical science—that is, that it could be an empirical science if researchers could devise experiments and methods of observation appropriate to the nature of ESP. If you conclude that not even a *prima facie* case can be made for the truth of any ESP claim or for claims in other areas of the paranormal, this will, of course, give you reason to believe that actual research into the existence of the paranormal that claims success belongs to pseudoscience, not empirical science. The question of whether *any* research into the existence of the paranormal could belong to empirical science will have been left open, but it probably will have lost its interest.

J. B. RHINE

The spontaneous, uncontrollable nature of ESP naturally bothers us all, parapsychologists as well as skeptics. But many other erratic, fugitive effects can be found in nature, more especially in the mental sciences, but even in biology and physics. And they are no less "natural" than the more reliable ones, for all man's inability to reproduce them at will.

—From an article in Science, 1956.

We are still so vastly ignorant about life and mind and their origin and functioning that I doubt that anyone has a reasonably close guess (or rational inference) as to the great ultimate universal truth about them. It is likely to be beyond present power to comprehend when and if eventually it is revealed to the sciences. What matters most today, in any case, is that we faithfully preserve this indescribably wonderful privilege of exploring as best we can.

—From an article in the Journal of Parapsychology, 1975.

J. B. Rhine (1895–1980) is widely regarded as the leading twentieth century parapsychologist. Originally interested in biology, Rhine became interested in the new field of psychic research and became associated with William McDougall, who founded at Duke the first psychic research laboratory in an American university. After studying at Chicago and Harvard, Rhine was associated with Duke University during most of his long and controversial career. He was aided in his work by his wife, Dr. Louisa Rhine, who shared her husband's commitment to parapsychology and, like J. B. Rhine, was the author of widely read studies in the field. J. B. Rhine's books include *The Reach of Mind* and *New Frontiers of the Mind.*

J. B. RHINE

The Science of Nonphysical Nature

Out of his sensory experience and its rational derivatives man has developed a general concept known as the physical universe. And out of the relationships that have been found to exist within this observed and inferred universe have emerged the recognized physical sciences and the physical bases of the other sciences. While from time to time there have been offered hypotheses of nonphysical factors in living organisms, none of these has ever become orthodox, either in biology or psychology. There are, therefore, no conventionally recognized nonphysical operations in the natural world, and, according to prevailing thought, any occurrence not fundamentally reducible to physical process would have either to be ignored or classed as supernatural (though such a category, too, is unacceptable in the sciences). Thus, even though many individual scientists have reservations on the point, nature has, in the sciences, come to be effectively synonymous with the physical universe.

There has been only one small branch of inquiry to make a scientific attack on the question of nonphysical causation in nature. This branch of inquiry logically is a division of psychological study and is known today as *parapsychology* (and by various other names such as psychical research, metaphysics, psychic science, etc.). Its problem-domain includes those natural occurrences (now called *psi* phenomena) which do not submit to classification as physical events. In more descriptive terms, parapsychology deals with the experiences and behavior of living organisms that fail to show regular relationships with time, space, mass, and other criteria of physicality.

Parapsychology began with the study of spontaneous psi (or psychic) experiences such as are fairly common throughout the world. These experiences appear to defy interpretation in terms of conventional principles. The more familiar of these were of cognitive nature, instances in which information was supplied to the person concerned, knowledge which he could not have acquired by way of the recognized sensory and rational channels. There were in such cases no adequate intermediating physical stimuli for interception by the sense organs. These spontaneous experiences, which had been familiar throughout the history of mankind, came to be identified as

---

A biographical sketch of J. B. Rhine appears on the preceding page.

From "The Science of Nonphysical Nature" by J. B. Rhine in *The Journal of Philosophy*, vol. II, no. 25 (1954). Reprinted by permission of the *Journal of Philosophy*.

instances of *telepathy* if they seemed to involve a transfer of thought or feeling from one person to another, and *clairvoyance* if there appeared to be an awareness of an objective event not present to the senses.

Such occurrences became of special interest during the latter half of the Nineteenth Century when the pressure of mechanistic thinking deriving from the rapid advancement of the physical sciences challenged the spiritual concept of man. An effort was made at first to collect and study the spontaneous experiences themselves, as evidence of an extrasensory mode of perception, but this attempt gave way in time to experimental research into the problems suggested. Early experiments based on these claims of extrasensory perception (ESP) were generally exploratory in character. They did not, as was eventually recognized, distinguish adequately between the two forms, telepathy and clairvoyance. Naturally, there was to begin with no very clear concept of the basic characteristics of parapsychological phenomena; that is, what common features would identify them. The field had not yet acquired general outlines. But these exploratory tests sustained interest and stimulated further research. Criticism and discussion followed and led in time to the refinement of the test procedures.

By the second quarter of the present century, however, the development of methods had produced a crucial order of tests for extrasensory perception. The occurrence of ESP had, by the midthirties, been tested under conditions that, even today, have not been seriously questioned. In the most definitive experiment conducted up to that time the best subject tested for ESP was able to identify the order of cards from shuffled packs located in another building, from 100 to 250 yards away, with a success of approximately 30% in a series of 1850 trials, tests in which the expectation on a theory of chance was but 20%. Since the theoretical probability of so great a result in such a series was of the order of 10^{-24}, it may be assumed that an effective relationship between subject and object had been demonstrated. In view of the distance involved and also other precautions against sensory cues, only an extrasensory mode of perception could have produced the results. With recurrent patterning from one pack of cards to the other eliminated, both by the shuffling and by the use of several decks of cards, rational inference on the part of the subject could not be considered as a reasonable alternative to ESP. With the provisions for independent recording (in duplicate) and even double surveillance during one section of the experiment, the hypothesis of error, whether deliberate or unconscious, was rendered improbable.

In the twenty years that have followed publication of those data many other series of experiments have been made by other investigators in the same and in other laboratories, some of them with even more elaborate precautions and more extensive design than the work described. Researches have also been conducted to distinguish between the types of ESP known as telepathy and clairvoyance. Both types of effects have been experimentally demonstrated, although in the case of telepathy it is not possible to say what the fundamental nature of the sender's operation is that constitutes the target. The mystery of the essential thought-brain relation for the present limits the investigation of the question of telepathy beyond this point.

If, as most serious scientific students who have followed the research developments will readily concede, the occurrence of ESP has been established, it will be allowable now to proceed to consider its challenge to physical explanation. In other words, assuming that extrasensory perception occurs, we may ask if it is extraphysical.

The very spontaneous experiences from which the experiments took their cue offered a challenge to physics in the first place. One of the most obvious features of these experiences is that two persons are as likely to have a telepathic experience when they are separated by thousands of miles as they are when only a short distance apart. In spontaneous experiences of clairvoyance, too, the distant scene is as likely to be perceived as that which is nearby. Moreover, a number of the exploratory tests of ESP, prior to the one described above, had involved considerable distances measured in miles, some of them even comparisons of different distances. The results failed to suggest any relationship of success in ESP to the proximity of the subject to the object.

The subject participating in the distance experiment mentioned above, in which 30% success was obtained at 100 to 250 yards, had, over a long series of previous tests, averaged approximately 32% successes with the target cards within a few feet of him. There was nothing, therefore, in the test results to indicate any lawful relationship whatever between distance and scoring rate. In the other experiments that involve distance, while it cannot be said that a nicely designed study, exhausting all possibilities, has ever yet been made, the results have been the same—there is no reliable relation indicated.

No hypothesis of a physical relationship in ESP has ever arisen from the research results. The spontaneous cases had given no suggestion of any effect of distance and the experimental evidence confirmed the impression. And yet, as a matter of course, there have been many types of conditions from which such an hypothesis could have emerged had the evidence suggested it. There have been many different barriers imposed incidentally in the experimental conditions, barriers such as walls, buildings, mountains, and thousands of miles of atmosphere. Also, the target objects have been presented at various angles. In most cases these objects were cards. They have been located in various positions, in some instances with the back of the card toward the subject, in other cases in such a position that only an edge would be turned in the direction of the subject. In addition, for any theory of radiation there is the difficulty of discriminating between numerous objects in close proximity. For example, in many ESP tests the problem involves the attempt to identify cards packed in a box in which all twenty-five are less than a quarter of an inch thick. This proximity would obviously become a limiting condition for a physical hypothesis. But in spite of all the varieties of physical conditions under which ESP tests have been conducted, the results have consistently been such that no hypothesis of a physical relationship has been suggested.

One of the most striking features of the spontaneous experiences of ESP is the fact that they are almost as likely to involve future events as contemporaneous ones. A dream of disaster occurring to a loved one may precede the tragic event itself or may merely precede the arrival of the news coming from the scene, which may be half way around the world. This suggestion that precognitive ESP might occur was reduced to experimental test following the definitive stage of ESP experiments mentioned above, and, so far as experimental comparisons have gone, the same relationship has been found as in the spontaneous cases; that is to say, time has not been found to be a limiting condition in the functioning of ESP. It is no handicap to ESP to be directed toward a target order of cards that is to be set up at a designated future time, as compared with a present order. This experimental result follows logically enough, not only from the spontaneous psi experiments but also from the results of the distance tests; it would be difficult to conceive of time as limiting a function that is independent of space. At least it will be difficult until science discovers an instance of time change involving no spatial change.

It would be too large an undertaking to recount here the steps through which the methods for testing precognitive ESP have progressed or to appraise the adequacy of the experimental design to meet the alternative hypotheses. As is natural in unfinished investigation, there still are those who have different degrees of confidence in the adequacy of the experiments thus far completed to establish a conclusive case for precognition. If, as now appears to many to be a reasonable conclusion, the case for precognitive ESP *has* been established, it will not be disputed that it is a radical development for psychology and for science in general. It introduces either an alternative to causation or a mode of causation independent of the time order.

* * * * *

Recoiling, however, as it naturally does from concepts it was more or less trained to reject, the educated mind demands a more developed rationale than mere statistical data on such a question as the actuality of ESP. This attitude has been frankly expressed by a number of scientific men. It is now happily possible to go far toward meeting this very human requirement and to offer a rationally cemented foundation of fact that is moderately extensive.

I have already referred to the consistency with which the various types of psi investigations have shown the same lack of a regular relation to physical conditions. This consistency extends into all the various areas of the research field, and these are too extensive to be effectively handled in a paper of this length.

Another of the tests of this lawfulness is the fact that it has been possible to use the standard scientific approach of hypothesis, prediction, and experimental verification to investigate psi. For example, on the strength of the distance tests of ESP it was possible to predict the results of the precognition tests. Again, it was inferred that if the law of reaction applied in ESP there should be some reaction upon the object (e.g., the card) when a cognitive perception of it occurred to the subject. This led to the designing of delicate tests of the direct influence of the subject upon the object, tests of psychokinesis (PK) based on the throwing of dice. After about 20 years of investigation the position may safely be taken that such a direct psychokinetic effect has been demonstrated and independently confirmed.

The overall relationship of these operations between subject and object, with ESP on the cognitive side and PK on the kinetic, indicates a reversible psychophysical interaction between subject and object, one that does not involve the sensorimotor system of the individual. In ESP the essential similarities observed between the conditions affecting telepathy, clairvoyance, and precognition seem to indicate that the various forms of ESP at least go back to one common perceptual function.

As psychological information concerning these various ESP effects accumulates it adds greatly to the rational understanding of the difficulties that have been encountered in the research. For example, when eventually it was recognized that psi is unconscious in all its types, it brought greater understanding of the puzzling effects encountered than had any other single discovery. Immediately the difficulties that had been found in controlling the capacity were more understandable. The peculiar experimental effects obtained, of which there had been many, fell at once into a more reasonable relationship. There was, for example, the well-known fact that sometimes a subject would score consistently below the chance average. This was for long a baffling occurrence, but psychologically such a performance on an unconscious level became understandable enough. The regular decline in the scoring rate which the subject had been found to show as he proceeded through his test run or other unit was at least partially clarified by the recognition of the unconsciousness of psi. Curious displacement effects and other distortions (preferential patterning, consistent missing, and the like) were no longer the puzzles they had been.

But the most recent extension of the rational network of psi relationships is that involving the investigation of psi in other animals, now that it has been established in man. Fifteen or more years ago the definite decision was taken to push the search for personality correlates of psi capacity. Surely, it was argued, some people have more of it than others. Quick identification of high-scoring subjects would revolutionize the investigation of the elusive capacity. A wide range of selective methods were utilized and much seining and sifting was done. Differences in performance were actually found and some significant correlations obtained, but more and more as the studies progressed it became apparent that the results were not revealing a tie-up of the extent of native psi capacity with the trait measured; instead, a relation to the more superficial quality of adaptability to the test situation was being demonstrated. Some of these correlates associated with scoring rate were even of transient nature as, for example, the subject's attitude of belief or scepticism toward ESP.

All this investigation was important; for one thing, it provided still more evidence of the occurrence of psi. But it was not leading the investigator to any group of subjects that had a monopoly on psi capacity or even a special amount of the gift. By the time the survey had extended to a considerable extent over the various classifications of abnormality and subnormality and into some of the racial subdivisions, it finally became evident that psi must be a capacity that, in evolutionary origin, antedated man himself. In order to check on this hypothesis it was necessary to look for psi in animals. Although this excursion into species other than man is a new and recent one, it has already brought up sufficient evidence to necessitate continuance and at least to permit the conclusion that man is, indeed, not the only species in possession of psi functions.

It is an important fact that two parallel lines of study are possible in parapsychology, based on the one hand on the comparative analysis of large collections of spontaneous psychic experiences, rich in suggestions for investigation, and, on the other, the experimental findings of the Laboratory on which the conclusions are more definitely based. The opportunity for checking findings from one to the other in these two very different lines of empirical study provides a special advantage and an exceptional quality of reassurance. Very little has been found thus far by the one that has not also been encountered in the other, except effects observed in the spontaneous material that cannot yet be brought to laboratory test.

And, finally, there are certain very general rational considerations that favor parapsychology as against the physicalistic philosophy that constitutes the main bar to its acceptance. First, as I have already stated, investigations of ESP arose from the need to explain actual reports of human experiences of types that have run persistently through all recorded cultures and that, essentially in the same patterns, still recur in our most sophisticated centers of human society today. No such basis in human experience can be claimed for any version of physicalism. Second, this concept of a nonphysical function in personality runs as a fundamental belief throughout the history of the social institutions of man, most conspicuously those dealing with his religious life. The only culture remotely approximating a physicalistic philosophy of man is that of communism. Whatever rational suport, then, may rightly be derived from the argument of long enduring social utility is against the philosophy that is opposed to psi.

While so brief a sketch of the growing rationale of the psi discoveries omits whole sections of data and relationships, it may serve to show that parapsychology at least is now past the point where its body of knowledge was composed of scattered, isolated, disconnected chunks of statistical findings. It now makes a great deal of sense.

* * * * *

It may more appropriately be the work of others than the parapsychologists to attempt a larger rational setting for psi in the scheme of knowledge. Any suggestions of this setting that may be made by the investigator as he proceeds are, of course, subject to the most careful reviewing. But they may serve the purpose of stimulating discussion on points that might otherwise be allowed to go undeveloped. It is always safe, at least, to raise questions.

For example, is it not the part of wisdom to try to fit the psi functions as far as possible into the familiar concept of causation even though the serial order of cause-effect relations as known from the physical world would not apply to precognition? One knows at least where the difficulty of squaring the new with the old is localized in such an approach, and in such a problem area one needs to take short and cautious steps.

Likewise, might not the same logic that has produced the concepts of the various energies involved in physical theory profitably be followed to the point of suggesting that a psi energy be hypothesized? It is true, there is not much use in setting up hypotheses unless they can be brought around to empirical test; but some initial thought is necessary to discover if this step is feasible.

It is no great jump from the broad concept of energy as it now prevails in physical theory over to the notion of a special state of energy that is not interceptible by any of the sense organs. Certain physical energies are already in that category. Psi energy would, of course, have to be a kind that does not regularly relate to time, space, and mass as do the better known forms of energy, but there is discussion among theoretical physicists of exceptions to this relationship in the operation of types of energies that are already recognized. For the most part physicists themselves do not balk at the notion of a state of energy operating out of the currently familiar framework of concepts. After all, the effects, the signs of "work being done," are there. It was for this that the concepts of the energies were invented.

Whatever it may be that is causing these psi manifestations has naturally to be a convertible sort of influence; for example, in PK the effect has to register in the motion of the target object (e.g., the falling die). In ESP the transition into consciousness, whatever the nature of that operation is, and from consciousness into a verbal or manual response, involves more interconversions, changes that are still for the most part unsolved mysteries in both psychology and physiology. It adds little burden to the rational mind, therefore, to recognize that the energy of psi has to be convertible to other forms in order to be detected as an occurrence in nature.

It may be tentatively proposed, then, that back of the phenomena of psi must exist an energy that interoperates with and interconverts to those other energetic states already familiar to physics. Psi energy is imperceptible by the sense organs and does not in any way yet discovered regularly function within the framework of time and space and mass, and yet does lawfully operate with intelligent purpose within the personality of the organism, though on an unconscious level. It probably belongs to the early evolutionary equipment of the organism and represents a more primitive relation between the organism and the environment. Possibly it antedates the sensorimotor system (which, of course, interacts with known energy forms and produces specific modalities of perception and behavior for the most part conscious, at least in man).

* * * * *

The key significance of the psi function lies, of course, in the fact that it can be measured and otherwise studied with respect to the criteria of physicality and demonstrated to depart from those criteria. Much of the rest of personality and the life functions of animals is, on this point, ambiguous and elusive and throughout the history of science has allowed completely opposite interpretations to prevail. Psi phenomena alone bring the issue into focus and allow a decision to be reached as to whether or not the organism possesses extraphysical powers. The investigation of psi has thus provided a scientific way of dealing with the question of the nature of man with respect to the physical world.

Without a reliable answer to this question of man's nature, it is not possible to solve intelligently the most important problems confronting mankind. To appreciate the importance of this issue of the bearing of physicalism on human life, it is necessary only to consider the consequences of a strict application of a thoroughly mechanistic theory of man.

The most far-reaching and revolting consequence lies in what would happen to volitional or mental freedom. Under a mechanistic determinism the cherished voluntarism of the individual would be nothing but idle fancy. Without the exercise of some freedom from physical law, the concepts of character, responsibility, moral judgment, and democracy would not survive critical analysis. The concept of a spiritual order, either in the individual or beyond him, would have no logical place whatever. In fact, little of the entire value system under which human society has developed would survive the establishment of a thoroughgoing philosophy of physicalism.

If the importance of the psi investigations is of this general order, it is urgent then not to lose the essential focus upon its principal advantage, the method of inquiry itself. It is always and perhaps unavoidably the case that new inquiries tend to generate excessive disputation over terms, interpretations, and significances. In the psi researches reviewed above there is not enough either of essential novelty or of anything approaching finality to justify taking a strongly formulated stand and holding out for any important decision at this particular point. Rather, the merit lies in the possibilities opened up: Parapsychology has verified by relatively improved methods some old claims of powers that transcend the properties of material systems. How much more can be found out about the properties of these nonphysical operations? What more can be done with and about them? What kind of a universe must it be that combines them and the physical world? One sees no end to questions, following one upon another. There is no time to lose over unessential issues and fruitless niceties.

One single well-established fact of parapsychology is enough to trigger such a program. Over against the iron wall of physical determinism one unmistakable sign of another order of reality is enough to justify a full-scale inquiry, a concentrated campaign of investigation to see what kind of world there is that could produce such a manifestation. Traces and faint signs have time and again in the history of discovery betokened the presence of hidden systems of reality.

Science still "moves but slowly, slowly, creeping on from point to point" as it did in Tennyson's day. But those who are most familiar with the halting, handicapped way in which radical scientific advances have been made in the past will understand the difficulties and delays. They will appreciate, too, the timely challenge the psi researches make to a philosophy of man that, over most of the world, across national and even ideological boundaries, dominates the scientific thinking of today. Tomorrow that philosophy may, unless challenged and effectively refuted, curtain the entire range of thought for mankind everywhere.

COMMENTS ■ QUESTIONS

1. A very important distinction belongs to the methodology of science that underlies the points made by Rhine. He refers to but does not elaborate upon it. It is the distinction between *scientific results* and *scientific understanding*. In the case of parapsychology, the results (which have been questioned by skeptics but endorsed by parapsychologists such as Rhine and other investigators of the paranormal) are primarily statistical correlations that cannot be explained in any normal way. For example, a person in an experiment guesses the sequence of cards being revealed in another building at a 30% success rate when "chance" would dictate a 20% success rate. Scientific *understanding* in these cases would consist of an explanation of the underlying reality that had produced the 30% success rate (assuming that there is no way to "explain away" the 30% rate). In the physical sciences, success and understanding usually go hand in hand; for example, when certain substances are heated, they expand at a specific rate (the results) that can be understood in terms of an account of their increased molecular motion. But in parapsychology, the results claimed by parapsychologists have not been matched by scientific understanding of those results. As a matter of fact, no one has been able to even begin to explain why the results occur. In regard to the question of whether parapsychology is a science or a pseudoscience, how important is the fact that parapsychology has produced no scientific understanding of its alleged results?
2. Since 1954, when Rhine wrote the paper reprinted here, much has been written by critics of parapsychology. They have argued that the experiments that appeared to produce significant sta-

tistical results had design flaws or else were simply fraudulent. The failure of parapsychology to provide a scientific understanding of its purported results has given critics the incentive to look for weaknesses in the experiments. But the very same failure has provided an incentive to those who are *sympathetic* to parapsychology to speculate on why the results of parapsychology have been so difficult, or impossible, to explain. Their general hypothesis has been that paranormal phenomena are *very* different from physical phenomena, and that that is why they are so difficult to explain. Which do you believe is the correct response to the failure in parapsychology to yield scientific understanding—the response of critics (who argue that there really are no bona fide results of properly designed experiments in need of explanation) or the response of those sympathetic to parapsychology (who hypothesize that the underlying phenomena must be so very different from ordinary phenomena that explanations of them would necessarily be extremely difficult to provide)?

3. Rhine makes reference to "spontaneous cases" of psi phenomena in addition to the statistical results from experiments. He describes the spontaneous cases as being "fairly common throughout the world." You may yourself have had some experience of the sort referred to by Rhine, or you may know someone who has. How important would you judge "spontaneous cases" to be? Is the fact that they appear to happen fairly frequently of any significance in regard to the question of whether parapsychology is a science or a pseudoscience?

PAUL KURTZ

Is Parapsychology a Science?

I

An observer of the current scene cannot help but be struck by the emergence of a bizarre new "paranormal world-view." How widely held this view is, whether it has penetrated science proper or is simply part of the popular passing fancy, is difficult to ascertain.

Many of those who are attracted to a paranormal universe express an antiscientific, even occult, approach. Others insist that their hypotheses have been "confirmed in the scientific laboratory." All seem to agree that existing scientific systems of thought do not allow for the paranormal and that these systems must be supplemented or overturned. The chief obstacle to the acceptance of paranormal truths is usually said to be skeptical scientists who dogmatically resist unconventional explanations. The "scientific establishment," we are told, is afraid to allow free inquiry because it would threaten its own position and bias. New Galileos are waiting in the wings, but again they are being suppressed by the establishment and labeled "pseudoscientific." Yet it is said that by rejecting the paranormal we are resisting a new paradigm of the universe (à la Thomas Kuhn) that will prevail in the future.

Unfortunately, the meaning of the term *paranormal* is often unclear. Literally, it refers to that which is "besides" or "beyond" the normal range of data or experience. Sometimes "the paranormal" is used as an equivalent of "the bizarre," "the mysterious," or "the unexpected." Some use it to refer to phenomena that have no known natural causes and that transcend normal experience and logic. The term here has been used synonymously with "the supernormal," "the supernatural," or "the miraculous." These definitions, of course, leave little room for science. They mark a limit to our knowing. Granted there are many areas at the present time that are unknown; yet one cannot on a priori grounds, antecedent to inquiry, seek to define the parameters of investigation by maintaining that some-

---

Paul Kurtz is professor of philosophy at the State University of New York at Buffalo and chairman of the Committee for the Scientific Investigation of Claims of the Paranormal. He has edited A Skeptics Handbook of Parapsychology *and is the author of* The Transcendental Temptation: A Critique of Religion and the Paranormal, *among other books.*

From "Is Parapsychology a Science?" by Paul Kurtz, in *Paranormal Borderlands of Science*, edited by Kendrick Frazier, 1981. Reprinted by permission of Prometheus Books.

thing is irreducibly unknowable or inexplicable in any conceivable scientific terms.

Some use the term *paranormal* to refer to that which is "abnormal" or "anomalous," that is, that which happens infrequently or rarely. But there are many accidental or rare events that we wouldn't ordinarily call paranormal—a freak trainwreck, a lightning strike, or a meteor shower.

Some use the term *paranormal* simply to refer to the fact that some phenomena cannot be given a physical or materialistic explanation. In some scientific inquiries, physicalist or reductionist explanations are, indeed, not helpful or directly relevant—as, for example, in many social-science studies, where we are concerned with the function of institutions, or in historical studies, where we may analyze the influence of ideas or values on human affairs. But this surely does not mean that they are "nonnatural," "unnatural," or "paranormal"; for ideas and values have a place in the executive order of nature, as do flowers, stones, and electrons. Although human institutions and cultural systems of beliefs and values may be physical at root, they are not necessarily explainable in function as such. There seem to be levels of organization; at least it is convenient to treat various subject matters in terms of concepts and hypotheses relative to the data at hand. To say this in no way contravenes the physical laws of nature as uncovered in the natural sciences.

The term *paranormal*, however, has also been used in parapsychology, where something seems to contradict some of the most basic assumptions and principles of the physical, biological, or social sciences and a body of expectations based on ordinary life and common sense. C. D. Broad has pointed out a number of principles that parapsychologists would apparently wish to overthrow [1]: (*a*) that future events cannot affect the present *before* they happen (backward causation); (*b*) that a person's mind cannot effect a change in the material world without the intervention of some physical energy or force; (*c*) that a person cannot know the content of another person's mind except by the use of inferences based on experience and drawn from observations of his speech or behavior; (*d*) that we cannot directly know what happens at distant points in space without some sensory perception or energy of it transmitted to us; (*e*) that discarnate beings do not exist as persons separable from physical bodies. These general principles have been built up from a mass of observations and should not be abandoned unless and until there is an overabundant degree of evidence that would make their rejection less likely than their acceptance—if I may paraphrase David Hume.[2] Nevertheless, those who refer to the "paranormal" believe that they have uncovered a body of empirical facts that call into question precisely those principles. Whether or not they do remains to be seen by the course of future inquiry. These scientific principles are not sacred and may one day need to

---

1. C. D. Broad, "The Relevance of Psychical Research to Philosophy," *Philosophy*, 24 (1949): 291–309.

2. David Hume, *Treatise on Human Nature*, 1739; *Essay Concerning Human Understanding*, 1748; *The Dialogues Concerning Natural Religion*, 1779.

be modified—but only if the empirical evidence makes it necessary.

Some who use the term *paranormal* refer to a range of anomalous events that are inexplicable in terms of our existing scientific concepts and theories. Of course, there are many events not now understood. For example, we do not know fully the cause of cancer, yet we would hardly call it paranormal. There have been many reports recently of loud explosions off the Atlantic coast that remain unexplained and that some have hinted are "paranormal." (These may be due to methane gas, test flights, or distant sonic booms.) If we were to use the term *paranormal* to refer to that which is inexplicable in terms of current scientific theory, with the addition that it cannot be explained without major revisions of our scientific theory, this would mean that any major advance in science, prior to its acceptance, might be considered to be "paranormal." But then new developments in quantum theory or relativity theory, the DNA breakthrough, or the germ theory of disease would have been paranormally related. But this is absurd. There are many puzzles in science and there is a constant need to revise our theories; each new stage in science waiting to be verified surely cannot be called "paranormal."

In actuality, the term *paranormal* is without clear or precise meaning; its use continues to suggest to many the operation of "hidden," "mysterious," or "occult" forces in the universe. But this, in the last analysis, may only be a substitute for our ignorance of the causes at work. Although I have used the term because others have done so, I think that it ought to be dispensed with as a meaningless concept.

* * * * *

III

What are we to say about parapsychology? Is it a science or a pseudoscience?

Interest in psychic phenomena appears throughout human history, with reports abounding from ancient times to the present. There is a fund of anecdotal material—premonitions that seem to come true, apparent telepathic communication between friends or relatives, reports of encounter with discarnate persons, and so on—that leads many people to believe that there is some basis in fact for psi phenomena. It has been almost a century since the Society for Psychical Research was founded in 1882 in England by a distinguished group of psychologists and philosophers (including William James and Henry Sidgwick) who were hopeful of the chance of getting results from their careful inquiries. In October 1909, William James, a president of the Society, wrote "The Last Report: Final Impressions of a Psychical Researcher," summarizing his experiences.[3] The Society, he said, was founded with the expectation that if the material of "psychic" research were treated rigorously and experimentally then objective truths would be elicited. James reported:

> . . . Like all founders, Sidgwick hoped for a certain promptitude of results; and I heard him say, the year before his death, that if anyone had

3. Gardner Murphy and Robert O. Ballou, eds., *William James on Psychical Research*, New York: Viking, 1960, p. 310.

told him at the outset that after twenty years he would be in the same identical state of doubt and balance that he started with, he would have deemed the prophecy incredible.

Yet James relates that his experiences had been similar to Sidgwick's:

> For twenty-five years I have been in touch with the literature of psychical research, and have had acquaintance with numerous "researchers." I have also spent a good many hours (though far fewer than I ought to have spent) in witnessing (or trying to witness) phenomena. Yet I am theoretically no "further" than I was at the beginning; and I confess that at times I have been tempted to believe that the Creator had eternally intended this department of nature to remain *baffling*, to prompt our curiosities and hopes and suspicions all in equal measure, so that, although ghosts and clairvoyances, and raps and messages from spirits, are always seeming to exist and can never be fully explained away, they also can never be susceptible of full corroboration.
>
> The peculiarity of the case is just that there are so many sources of possible deception in most of the observations that the whole lot of them *may* be worthless . . . Science meanwhile needs something more than bare possibilities to build upon; so your genuinely scientific inquirer . . . has to remain unsatisfied. . . . So my deeper belief is that we psychical researchers have been too precipitate with our hopes, and that we must expect to mark progress not by quarter-centuries, but by half-centuries or whole centuries.

Almost three-quarters of a century have elapsed since James's comments. Has any more progress been made? Since that time psychic research has given way to parapsychology, especially under the leadership of J. B. Rhine and the establishment of his experimental laboratory. Where there were before only a handful of researchers, now there are many more. We may ask, Where does parapsychology stand today? I must confess that for many researchers, both within and outside the field, not much further along than before.

One thing is clear: many researchers today at least attempt to apply experimental methods of investigation. This was not always the case; and the field today, as then, has been full of deception, conscious or unconscious—perhaps more than most fields of inquiry. There are a host of fraudulent psychics and researchers—including the Fox sisters (who were hailed as mediums, in whose presence raps were heard during seances, but who evidently admitted they had learned how to crack their toe knuckles), Blackburn and Smith (who deceived scientists into believing that telepathic communication occurred between them), Margery Crandon and Eustasia Palladino (both shown to be fraudulent mediums), the Soal-Goldney experiments on precognition (experiments now in disrepute), Walter J. Levy (who was exposed for faking the evidence on animal ESP at Durham in 1974), Uri Geller, Jean Girard, and Ted Serios (whose alleged abilities in psychokinesis and psychic photography are open to charges of trickery). Even some of the most sophisticated scientists have been taken in by illusionists posing as psychics. In spite of this there *are* many parapsychologists today who are committed to careful scientific inquiry—as Rhine's work illustrates—and the use of rigorous laboratory methods. Whether they ever achieve it is not always clear, and critics are constantly finding loopholes in their methodology.

What about the results? Are the hypotheses proposed by parapsychology testable? Have they been tested? Here there are also wide areas for dispute. Skeptics are especially unimpressed by the findings and believe that parapsychology has not adequately verified its claims—even though some parapsychologists believe that ESP, precognition, and PK have been demonstrated and need no further proof. I reiterate that, since the chief claims of parapsychology in these areas contravene the basic principles of both science and ordinary experience, it is not enough to point to a body of data that has been assembled over the years; the data must be *substantial.* This does not deny that there seems to be some evidence that certain individuals in some experiments are able to make correct guesses at above-chance expectations. The basic problem, however, is the *lack of replicability* by other experimenters. Apparently, some experimenters—a relative few—are able to get similar results, but most are unable to do so. The subject matter is elusive. It is rare for a skeptic to be able to replicate results, but it is even relatively rare for a *believer* in psi to get positive results. The problem of replicability has been dismissed by some parapsychologists who maintain that their findings *have* been replicated. But have they? For the point is that we cannot predict *when* or *under what conditions* above-chance calls will be made (with Zener cards, in precognitive dream labs, in remote-viewing testing situations); and one is much more likely to get negative results.

One explanation offered by parapsychologists for the difficulty in replication refers to the well-known "sheep/goat" distinction of Gertrude Schmeidler—that is, that those with a positive attitude toward psi (sheep) will get better results than those with a negative attitude (goats). Similar considerations are said to apply to the attitude of the experimenter. Is the explanation for this that when the experimenter is a believer he is often so committed to the reality of psi that he tends to weaken experimental controls? If so, perhaps we should distinguish between the donkey and the fox. The skeptic is accused of being so stringent that he dampens the enthusiasm of the subject. Yet parapsychologists Adrian Parker and John Beloff report on experiments at the University of Edinburgh by pro-psi experimenters that consistently score negative results. Most parapsychologists want positive results, but few receive them. Many or most people don't display ESP; or if they do, they do so infrequently. And those few that allegedly have the ability eventually seem to lose it.

According to John Beloff:

> There is still no repeatable experiment on the basis of which any competent investigator can verify a given phenomenon for himself.[4]
>
> The Rhine revolution . . . proved abortive. Rhine succeeded in giving

4. John Beloff, "Parapsychology and Philosophy," *Handbook of Parapsychology*, ed. by B. Wolman, New York: Van Nostrand, 1977, p. 759.

parapsychology everything it needed to become an accredited science except the essential: the know-how to produce results where required.[5]

Adrian Parker writes:

> The present crisis in parapsychology is that there appear to be few if any findings which are independent of the experimenter ... It still remains to be explained why, if the experiment can be determined by experimenter psi, only a few experiments are blessed with success. Most experimenters want positive results, but few obtain them.[6]

Charles Tart says:

> One of the major problems in attempting to study and understand paranormal (psi) phenomena is simply that the phenomena don't work strongly or reliably. The average subject seldom shows any individually significant evidence of psi in laboratory experiments, and even gifted subjects, while occasionally able to demonstrate important amounts of psi in the laboratory, are still very erratic and unpredictable in their performance.[7]

And Rhine himself says:

> Psi is an incredibly elusive function! This is not merely to say that ESP and PK have been hard phenomena to demonstrate, the hardest perhaps that science has ever encountered ... Psi has remained an unknown quantity so long ... because of a definite characteristic of elusiveness inherent in its psychological nature ... A number of those who have conducted ESP or PK experiments have reported that they found no evidence of psi capacity ... Then, too, experimenters who were once successful may even then lose their gift.... All of the highscoring subjects who have kept on very long have declined ...[8]

All of this means not only that parapsychology deals with anomalous events but that it may indeed be a uniquely anomalous science, for findings depend upon who the experimenter is. But even that is not reliable and cannot be depended upon. If any other science had the same contingent results, we would rule it out of court. For example, a chemist or biologist could not very well claim that he could get results in the laboratory because he believed in his findings, whereas his skeptical colleagues could not because they lacked this belief. We say in science that we search for conditional lawlike statements: namely, that if *a*, then *b*; whenever *a* is present, *b* will most likely occur. Yet in viewing the findings of parapsychology, the situation seems to be that we are not even certain that *b* occurs (there is a dispute about the reliability of the experiments). Moreover, we don't know what *a* is, or if it is present that *b* would occur; *b* may occur sometimes, but only infrequently. A high degree of replicability is essential to the further development of parapsychology. Some sciences may be exempt from the replicability criterion, but this is the case only if their findings do not contradict the general conceptual

5. ———, *Psychological Sciences: A Review of Modern Psychology*, New York: Barnes & Noble, 1973.

6. Adrian Parker, "A Holistic Methodology in Psi Research," *Parapsychology Review*, 9 (March–April 1978): 4–5.

7. Charles Tart, "Drug-Induced States of Consciousness," *Handbook of Parapsychology*, op. cit., p. 500.

8. J. B. Rhine, *The Reach of Mind*, New York: Wm. Sloane, 1947, pp. 187–189.

framework of scientific knowledge, which parapsychology seems to do. According to the parapsychologist, for example, ESP seems to be independent of space and does not weaken with distance; precognition presupposes backward causation; psychokinesis violates the conservation-of-energy law.

It is not enough for parapsychologists to tell the skeptic that *he*, the parapsychologist, on occasion has replicated the results. This would be like the American Tobacco Institute insisting that, based on its experiments, cigarette-smoking does not cause cancer. The neutral scientist needs to be able to replicate results in his own laboratory. Esoteric, private road-to-truth claims need to be rejected in science, and there needs to be an intersubjective basis for validation. Until any scientist under similar conditions can get the same results, then we must indeed be skeptical. Viewing what some parapsychologists have considered to be replication often raises all sorts of doubts. In the 1930s S. G. Soal attempted to replicate the findings of Dr. Rhine in Britain in regard to clairvoyance and telepathy. He tested 160 subjects, always with negative results, indeed with results far below mean chance expectations. After the tests were completed, he reviewed the data and thought he had found a displacement effect in two cases, which he considered evidence for precognition (that is, above-chance runs in regard to one or two cards before and after the target). Soal then went on to test these two subjects, Basil Shackleton and Mrs. Gloria Stewart, with what seemed to be amazing results. These results have often been cited in the parapsychological literature as providing strong proof for the existence of ESP. In 1941, in collaboration with the Society for Psychical Research, Soal designed an experiment with Shackleton that included 40 sittings over a two-year period. Among the people who participated were C. D. Broad, professor of philosophy at Cambridge, H. H. Price, of Oxford, C. A. Mace, C. E. M. Joad, and others. Broad described the experiment as follows:

> . . . Dr. Soal's results are outstanding. The precautions taken to prevent deliberate fraud or the unwitting conveyance of information by normal means . . . [are] seen to be absolutely water-tight.[9]
>
> . . . There can be no doubt that the events described happened and were correctly reported; that the odds against chance-coincidence piled up to billions to one . . .[10]

On the basis of his work in precognitive research, Soal was awarded a doctorate of science degree from the University of London. Even Rhine described the Soal-Goldney experiment as "one of the most outstanding researches yet made in the field . . . Soal's work was a milestone in ESP research."[11]

C. E. M. Hansel, in his work, found, on the contrary, that the Soal-Goldney experiments were full of holes, and he suggested the high results might be due to collusion between the experimenters and/or the

---

9. C. D. Broad, "The Experimental Establishment of Telepathic Precognition," *Philosophy*, 19 (1944): 261.

10. ———, "The Relevance of Psychical Research to Philosophy," reprinted in *Philosophy and Parapsychology*, ed. by Jan Ludwig, Buffalo, N.Y.: Prometheus, 1978, p. 44.

11. J. B. Rhine, op. cit., p. 168.

participants, especially in the scoring procedures.[12] Broad responded to "Hansel and Gretel," denying the possibility of fraud. It now seems clear that Hansel was correct. And even parapsychologists now doubt the authenticity of these famous experiments. In a recent publication of the Society for Psychical Research, Betty Markwick reported that there is substantial evidence that extra digits were inserted into the "random number" sequences prepared by Soal to determine the targets in the Shackleton tests. These insertions coincided with Shackleton's guesses and apparently accounted for the high scores on the record sheets. Interestingly, Soal was present at every session in which the subject recorded high scores. The only exception was when he was absent, at which time the results were null.[13]

Thus the classical tests usually cited as "proof" of ESP often employed improper shuffling and scoring techniques or had other flaws in the protocol. More recent developments in parapsychology have been more hopeful in this regard. Parapsychologists have attempted to tighten up test conditions, to automate the selection of targets, to use random-number generators and ganzfeld procedures, and to design ingenious dream research and remote-viewing experiments.

One might consider the use of random generators in testing situations to be an advance over previous methods, except for the fact that it is still the experimenter who designs and interprets the experiment. Walter J. Levy, who fudged his results, it may be noted, used machines in his testing work. No wonder the critic is still skeptical of some recent claims made in this area. Great results have been heralded in ESP dream research. Yet here, too, there are many examples of failed replication. For example, David Foulkes, R. E. L. Masters, and Jean Houston attempted to repeat the results obtained at the Maimonides laboratory with Robert van Castle, a high-scoring subject, but they met with no success at all. Charles Honorton has reported what he considers to be impressive results using ganzfeld techniques (where subjects are deprived of sensory stimulation). To date there have been upward of 25 published studies. Approximately a third have been significant, a third ambiguous, and a third nonsignificant. This may sound convincing. But given the sad experience in the past with other alleged breakthroughs, we should be cautious until we can replicate results ourselves. Moreover, we do not know how many negative results go unreported. (I should say that I have never had positive results in any testing of my students over the years.) Parker, Miller, and Beloff in 1976 used the ganzfeld method to test the relation of altered states of consciousness and ESP and reported nonsignificant results:

> A total of over 30 independent tests were conducted on the data without a single significance emerging. Whatever way we look at the results, they

---

12. C. E. M. Hansel, *ESP: A Scientific Evaluation*, New York: Scribner, 1966.

13. Betty Markwick, "The Soal-Goldney Experiments with Basil Shackleton: New Evidence of Data Manipulation," *Proceedings of the Society for Psychical Research*, 56 (1978): 250–278; D. J. West, "Checks on ESP Experimenters," *Journal of the Society for Psychical Research*, 49 (Sept. 1978): 897–899.

> not only detract from the reliability of the ganzfeld, but also argue against the view that psychological conditions are the sole mediating variable of the experimenter effect.[14]

Similarly, Targ and Puthoff at the Stanford Research Institute, in widely reported remote-viewing experiments, have allegedly achieved results that have been replicated. But the critic has many unanswered questions about the method of target selection and the procedures for grading "hits." Given their shockingly sloppy work with Uri Geller, Ingo Swann, and other "super-psychics" in the laboratory, the skeptic cannot help but be unconvinced about their claimed results.

IV

The accounts above have been introduced as a general comment on the field of parapsychological research: If parapsychology is to progress, then it will need to answer the concerns of its critics about the reliability of the evidence and the replicability of the results.

But difficulties become even more pronounced when we examine other kinds of inquiries that go on in this field; for the parapsychological literature contains the most incredibly naive research reports along with the most sophisticated. A perusal of the parapsychological literature reveals the following topics: clairvoyance, telepathy precognition, psychokinesis, levitation, poltergeists, materialization, demateralization, psychic healing, psychometry, psychic surgery, psychic photography, aura readings, out-of-body experiences, reincarnation, retrocognition, tape recordings of the voices of the dead, hauntings, apparitions, life after life, regression to an earlier age, and so on.

We now face a puzzling situation. There has been a marked proliferation of claims of the paranormal in recent years, many of them highly fanciful. Presumably, scientific researchers should not be held responsible for the dramatization of results by fiction writers. Yet in my view some parapsychologists have aided, whether consciously or unconsciously, the breakdown in critical judgment about the paranormal. I have not seen many parapsychologists attempt to discourage hasty generalizations based on their work. There are often extraordinary claims made about psychic phenomena, yet there are no easily determinable objective standards for testing them. Because parapsychologists are interested in a topic and do some research, it is said by some that, ipso facto, it is validated by science. (Lest one think that I am exaggerating, one should consult the *Handbook of Parapsychology*, the most recent comprehensive compilation in the field, which includes discussions of psychic photography, psychic healing, reincarnation, discarnate survival, and poltergeists, among other topics.) Professor Ian Stevenson, for example, of the University of Virginia, is well known for his work in reincarnation, which is of growing interest to many parapsychologists. After discussing the case of a young child who his parents think is a reincarnation of someone who had recently died, Stevenson says:

> Before 1960, few parapsychologists would have been willing to consider

14. Adrian Parker, op. cit., p. 4.

> reincarnation as a serious interpretation of cases of this type [recall] . . . Today probably most parapsychologists would agree that reincarnation is at least entitled to inclusion in any list of possible interpretations of the cases, but [he added] not many would believe it the most probable interpretation.[15]

Rhine is himself much more cautious in his judgment and implies that only clairvoyance, precognition, and psychokinesis have been established and that adequate test designs have not been worked out for other areas. If one asks if parapsychology is a genuine science or a pseudoscience, it is important that we know if one is referring to the overall field or to particular areas. Surely the critic is disturbed at the ready willingness to leap to "occult" explanations in the name of science in some kinds of inquiry.

Although I have no doubts that Rhine is committed to an objective experimental methodology, I have substantive doubts about his views on clairvoyance, precognition, and PK. The problem here is that one may question not simply the reliability and significance of the data but the conceptual framework itself. Rhine and others have performed tests in which they maintain that they have achieved above-chance runs. What are we to conclude at this point in history? Simply *that* and no more. ESP is not a proven fact, only a theory used to explain above-chance runs encountered in the laboratory. Here I submit that the most we can do is simply fall back on an operational definition: ESP is itself an elusive entity; it has no identifiable meaning beyond an operational interpretation. Some researchers prefer the more neutral term *psi*, but this still suggests a psychic reality. Of special concern here is the concept that is often referred to in trying to explain the fact that some subjects have significant below-chance runs—"negative ESP," or "psi-missing"—as if in some way there is a mysterious entity or faculty responsible for both above-chance and below-chance guessing. All this seems to me to beg the question. If ESP is some special function of the mind, then we need *independent* verification that it exists, that is, replicable predictions.

One of the problems with ESP is that parapsychologists have noted a "decline" effect; namely, that even gifted subjects in time lose their alleged "ESP" ability. At this point, I must confess that I am unable to explain why there are significant above-chance or below-chance runs: to maintain that these are due to psi, present or absent, is precisely what is at issue. A problem for me is how many validated cases we actually have of significant below-chance runs in the laboratory. Rhine mentions some. But are they as numerous as above-chance runs? If so, perhaps the overall statistical frequencies begin to reduce, particularly if parapsychologists stop testing those who have shown psychic ability once they lose their alleged powers. We still need to come up with possible alternative explanations. Some that have been suggested are bias, poor experimental design, fraud, and chance. There may be others.

---

15. Ian Stevenson, "Reincarnation: Field Studies and Theoretical Issues," *Handbook of Parapsychology*, op. cit., p. 657.

Rhine's reluctance to accept telepathy because of the difficulty in establishing test conditions is surprising to some. Of all the alleged psi abilities, this seems prima facie to be the most likely. Ordinary experience seems to suggest spontaneous telepathy, especially between persons who know each other very well or live together. If telepathy is ever established, I would want to find the mechanism for it—perhaps some form of energy transmission, though most parapsychologists reject this suggestion, possibly because they are already committed to a mentalistic interpretation of the phenomenon.

There are, as Rhine notes, very serious scientific objections to precognition—the notion that the future can be known beforehand (without reference to normal experience, inference, or imagination). The skeptical scientist believes that, where premonitions come true, coincidence is most likely the explanation. If one examines the number of times that premonitions do not come true, the statistics would flatten out. The conceptual difficulty with precognition is that, although we allegedly can know the future by precognition, we can also intervene so that it may not occur.

Louisa Rhine cites the following case to illustrate this:

> It concerns a mother who dreamed that two hours later a violent storm would loosen a heavy chandelier to fall directly on her baby's head lying in a crib below it; in the dream she saw her baby killed dead. She awoke her husband who said it was a silly dream and that she should go back to sleep as she then did. The weather was so calm the dream did appear ridiculous and she could have gone back to sleep. But she did not. She went and brought the baby back to her own bed. Two hours later just at the time she specified, a storm caused the heavy light fixture to fall right on where the baby's head had been—but the baby was not there to be killed by it.[16]

If the future is veridically precognized, how could one act to change it? There are profound logical difficulties with this concept. Some parapsychologists discuss a possible alternative explanation for the event: one parapsychologist suggests (without himself accepting it) that the dream itself might have contained enormous energy that forced the calm weather to change into a storm, which cracked the ceiling holding the light fixture. "This alternative, then, is not precognitive but of the mind-over-matter, or PK variety." [17]

This illustrates a basic problem endemic to parapsychology. The lack of a clearly worked out conceptual framework. Without such a causal theory, the parapsychologists can slip from one ad hoc explanation to another. In some cases we cannot say that telepathy is operating, it may be clairvoyance; and in others, if it is not precognition, then psychokinesis may be the culprit. (Even an ESP shuffle may be at work!) I fear that the central hypothesis of parapsychology, that mind is separable from body and that the "ghost in the ma-

---

16. L. E. Rhine, "Frequency of Types of Experience in Spontaneous Precognition," *Journal of Parapsychology*, 18(2) (1954): 199.

17. Douglas Dean, "Precognition and Retrocognition," in *Edgar D. Mitchell, Psychic Explorations: A Challenge for Science*, ed. by John White, New York: Putnam, 1974, p. 155.

chine" can act in uncanny ways, often makes it difficult to determine precisely what, if anything, is happening.

A number of familiar conceptual problems also concern psychokinesis. What would happen to the conservation-of-energy principle if PK were a fact? How can a mental entity cause a physical change in the state of matter? Comparing the alleged evidence for PK with the need to overthrow a basic, well-documented principle of physics is questionable. We read about Rhine's above-chance results in his die-rolling test: the results seem inconclusive. Recently a number of super-psychics, such as Uri Geller and Jean Girard, have made extraordinary claims for PK ability. Unfortunately, they have been uncritically welcomed by some parapsychologists and paraphysicists. Yet such super-psychics have been discredited, and what seems to be operating is probably magic and illusion, not psi.

Rhine at times expresses an underlying religious motive:

> What parapsychology has found out about man most directly affects religion. By supporting on the basis of experiment the psychocentric concept of personality which the religions have taken for granted, parapsychology has already demonstrated its importance for the field of religion ... If there were no ESP and PK capacities in human beings it would be hard to conceive of the possibility of survival and certainly its discovery would be impossible ... The only kind of perception that would be possible in a discarnate state would be extrasensory, and psychokinesis would be the only method of influencing any part of the physical universe ... Telepathy would seem to be the only means of intercommunication discarnate personalities would have.[18]

Unfortunately, many parapsychologists appear to be committed to belief in psi on the basis of a metaphysical or spiritualist worldview that they wish to vindicate. Charles Tart, a former president of the American Parapsychological Association, admits this motive. Giving an autobiographical account of why he became interested in parapsychology, he says:

> I found it hard to believe that science could have *totally* ignored the spiritual dimensions of human existence ... Parapsychology validated the existence of basic phenomena that could partially account for, and fit in with, some of the spiritual views of the universe.[19]

Of course, parapsychologists will accuse the skeptic of being biased in favor of a materialist or physicalist viewpoint and claim that this inhibits him from looking at the evidence for psi or accepting its revolutionary implications. Unfortunately, this has all too often been the case; for some skeptics have been unwilling to look at the evidence. This is indefensible. A priori negativism is as open to criticism as a priori wishfulfillment. On the other hand, some constructive skepticism is essential in science. All that a constructive skeptic asks of the parapsychologist is genuine confirmation of his findings and theories, no more and no less.

I should make it clear that I am not denying the possible existence of psi phenomena, remote viewing,

18. J. B. Rhine, op. cit., pp. 209, 214.
19. Charles Tart, *Psi: Scientific Studies of the Psychic Realm*, New York: E. P. Dutton, 1977, vii–viii.

precognition, or PK. I am merely saying that, since these claims contravene a substantial body of existing scientific knowledge, in order for us to modify our basic principles—and we must be prepared to do so—the evidence must be *extremely strong*. But that it *is*, remains highly questionable.

In the last analysis, the only resolution of the impasse between parapsychologists and their critics will come from the *evidence* itself. I submit that parapsychologists urgently need at this juncture to bring their claims to the most hard-headed group of skeptics they can find. In a recent review, C.P. Snow forcefully argues for this strategy. He admits that there are a good many natural phenomena that we don't begin to understand and ought to investigate. Moreover, phenomena exist that are not explained by natural science but which do not contradict it. It is when such phenomena allegedly do so that we should take a hard look. Snow says:

> An abnormal number of all reported paranormal phenomena appear to have happened to holy idiots, fools, or crooks. I say this brutally, for a precise reason. We ought to consider how a sensible and intelligent man would actually behave if he believed that he possessed genuine paranormal powers. He would realize that the matter was one of transcendental significance. He would want to establish his powers before persons whose opinions would be trusted by the intellectual world. If he was certain, for example, that his mind could, without any physical agency, lift a heavy table several feet, or his own body even more feet, or could twist a bar of metal, then he would want to prove this beyond, as they say in court, any reasonable doubt.
>
> What he would not do is set up as a magician or illusionist, and do conjuring tricks. He would desire to prove his case before the most severe enquiry achievable. It might take a long time before he was believed. But men with great powers often take a long time for those powers to be believed. If this man had the powers which I am stipulating, it probably wouldn't take him any longer to be accepted than it did Henry Moore to make his name as sculptor.
>
> Any intelligent man would realize that it was worth all the serious effort in the world. The rewards would be enormous—money would accrue, if he was interested in money, but in fact he would realize that that was trivial besides having the chance to change the thinking of mankind.
>
> It would now be entirely possible for such a man to have his claims considered with the utmost energy and rigor. For a number of eminent Americans of the highest reputation for integrity and intellectual achievement have set themselves to examine any part of the paranormal campaigns. The group includes first-class philosophers, astronomers, other kinds of scientists and professional illusionists. They are skeptical as they should be. This is too important a matter to leave to people who want to believe. So there they are, the challenge is down. It will be interesting to see if any sensible and intelligent man picks it up.[20]

This, then, is an invitation and a challenge to parapsychologists to bring their findings to the most thoroughgoing skeptics they can locate and have them examine their claims

20. C. P. Snow, "Passing Beyond Belief" (a review of *Natural and Supernatural: A History of the Paranormal*, by Brian Inglis), *Financial Times*, London (Jan. 28, 1978).

of the paranormal under the most stringent test conditions. If parapsychologists can convince the skeptics, then they will have satisfied an essential criterion of a genuine science: the ability to replicate hypotheses in any and all laboratories and under standard experimental conditions. Until they can do that, their claims will continue to be held suspect by a large body of scientists.

COMMENTS ■ QUESTIONS

1. Premise: Many of the important claims of parapsychology "contravene the basic principles of both science and ordinary experience." Conclusion: Therefore, if the claims made in parapsychology are to be supported, more than a body of data is needed; "the data must be substantial." Premise: The data are not substantial at all (in parapsychology it is much more difficult than in other areas to get reliable results). Conclusion: The claims made in parapsychology have not been supported. At which point, or points, in the foregoing argument by Kurtz would J. B. Rhine raise objections? (Which of the premises or logical steps would he object to?) Do you believe that the argument is sound?
2. As Kurtz points out, parapsychologists have great difficulty in being able to repeat the results of their experiments. Says Kurtz: "Some sciences may be exempt from the replicability criterion, but this is the case only if their findings do not contradict the general conceptual framework of scientific knowledge, which parapsychology seems to do." How can parapsychologists respond to this argument? Some supporters of parapsychology would say that just because the findings of parapsychology *do* contradict the general conceptual framework of scientific knowledge, we need to suppose that the reality that underlies the findings of parapsychology is very different from the reality that underlies ordinary phenomena and that this fact has made the replicability of experimental results difficult to achieve. Is this a defensible response to the points made by Kurtz? How would Kurtz respond to *it*?
3. "In the last analysis, the only resolution of the impasse between parapsychologists and their critics will come from the *evidence* itself. I submit that parapsychologists urgently need at this juncture to bring their claims to the most hard-headed group of skeptics they can find." Would it be best, do you believe, if the "hard-headed skeptics" initially had no sympathy whatsoever for the claims of parapsychology? Or would this instead prejudice them unduly against the claims of parapsychology?

PAUL E. MEEHL AND MICHAEL SCRIVEN

Compatibility of Science and ESP

As two of the people whose comments on an early draft of George Price's article on "Science and the Supernatural" he acknowledged in a footnote, we should like to clarify our position by presenting the following remarks.

Price's argument stands or falls on two hypotheses, only the first of which he appears to defend. They are (i) that extrasensory perception (ESP) is incompatible with modern science and (ii) that modern science is complete and correct.

If ESP is *not* incompatible with modern science, then the Humean skeptic has no opportunity to insist on believing modern science rather than the reports about ESP. If modern science is *not* believed to be complete or correct, then the skeptic is hardly justified in issuing a priori allegations of fraud about experimenters even when they claim that they have discovered a new phenomenon that requires reconsideration of the accepted theories.

In our view, both of Price's hypotheses are untenable. Whatever one may think about the comprehensiveness and finality of modern physics, it would surely be rash to insist that we can reject out of hand any claims of revolutionary discoveries in the field of psychology. Price is in exactly the position of a man who might have insisted that Michelson and Morley were liars because the evidence for the physical theory of that time was stronger than that for the veracity of these experimenters. The list of those who have insisted on the impossibility of fundamental changes in the current physical theory of their time is a rather sorry one. Moreover, unhappy though Price's position would be if this were his only commitment, he cannot even claim that specifiable laws of physics

Paul E. Meehl, Regents' Professor of Psychology at the University of Minnesota, has published widely in the areas of animal behavior, learning theory, psychometric theory, forensic psychology, and the philosophy of science. He was a co–founder and is a staff member of Minnesota Center for Philosophy of Science and engages in a part-time practice of psychotherapy. Michael Scriven holds the chair in Education at the University of Western Australia. Recent books include two on the theory and practice of evaluation and two on word processing and office automation.

From "Compatibility of Science and ESP" by P. E. Meehl and M. Scriven, in *Science*, vol. 123, pp. 14–15 (1956). Copyright 1956 by the American Association for the Advancement of Science. Reprinted by permission of *Science*.

are violated; it is only certain philosophical characteristics of such laws that are said to be absent from those governing the new phenomena.

It is true that Price attempted to give a specific account of the incompatibilities between ESP and modern science, rather than relying on Broad's philosophical analysis, but here the somewhat superficial nature of Price's considerations becomes clear. Of his eight charges, seven are unjustified.

(1) He claims that ESP is "unattenuated by distance" and hence is incompatible with modern science. But, as is pointed out in several of the books he refers to, since we have no knowledge of the minimum effective signal strength for extrasensory perception, the original signal may well be enormously attenuated by distance and still function at long range.

(2) He says that ESP is "apparently unaffected by shielding." But shielding may well have an effect: the evidence shows only that the kind of shielding appropriate to electromagnetic radiation is ineffectual; since detectors indicate that no such radiation reaches the percipient from the agent, this is scarcely surprising.

(3) He says "Dye patterns . . . are read in the dark; how does one detect a trace of dye without shining a light on it?" The two most obvious answers would be by chemical analysis and physical study of the impression (which is usually different for different colors).

(4) "Patterns on cards in the center of a pack are read without interference from other cards." The word *read* is hardly justified in view of the statistical nature of the results; however, this phenomenon is always used by parapsychologists as evidence against a simple radiation theory, which it is. But no simple radiation theory can explain the Pauli principle and one can no more refute it by saying "How could one electron possibly know what the others are doing?" than one can refute the ESP experiments by saying "How could one possibly read a card from the middle of the pack without interference from those next to it?" These questions are couched in prejudical terms.

(5) "We have found in the body no structure to associate with the alleged functions." Even if true, this hardly differentiates it from a good many other *known* functions; and among eminent neurophysiologists, J. C. Eccles is one who has denied Price's premise [originally in *Nature* 168 (1951)].

(6) "There is no learning but, instead, a tendency toward complete loss of ability" a characteristic which Price believes has "no parallel among established mental functions." Now it would be reasonable to expect, in a series of experiments intended to show that learning does not occur, some *trial-by-trial* differential reinforcement procedure. Mere continuation, with encouragement or condemnation after *runs of many trials* can hardly provide a conclusive proof of the absence of learning in a complex situation. We ourselves know of *no* experiments in which this condition has been met and which show *absence* of learning; certainly one could not claim that this absence was established. Furthermore, *even if it had been established*, it would be very dangerous to assert that there is "no parallel among established mental functions." In the

psychophysiological field particularly, there are several candidates. Finally, *even if it had been established and there were no parallel among mental functions*, there would be no essential difficulty in comparing it with one of the many familiar performances that exhibit no learning in adults—for example, reflex behavior.

(7) "Different investigators obtain highly different results." This is the most distressingly irresponsible comment of all. ESP is a capacity like any other human capacity such as memory, in that it varies in strength and characteristics from individual to individual and in the one individual from one set of circumstances to another. The sense in which Rhine and Soal (Price's example of "different investigators") have obtained "highly different results" is when they have been dealing with different subjects or markedly different circumstances—for example, different agents; and exactly the same would be true of an investigation of, for example, stenographers' speed in taking dictation or extreme color blindness.

There remains only statistical precognition, which is certainly not susceptible to the types of explanation currently appropriate in physics: but then it is not a phenomenon in physics. Even if it were, it is difficult to see why Price thinks that we properly accommodated our thought to the distressing and counterintuitive idea that the earth is rotating whereas we should not accept precognition. His test for distinguishing new phenomena from magic is hopeless from the start ("The test is to attempt to imagine a detailed mechanistic explanation") because (i) it is of the essence of the scientific method that one should have means for establishing the facts *whether or not* one has already conceived an explanation and (ii) it would have thrown out the Heisenberg uncertainty principle and action across a vacuum—that is, nuclear physics and the whole of electricity and magnetism—along with ESP.

Finally, Price's "ideal experiments" are only Rube Goldberg versions of the standard tests plus a skeptical jury. The mechanical contrivances would be welcome if only parapsychologists could afford them, and the jury is obviously superfluous because, according to Price's own test, we should rather believe that they lie than that the experiments succeed. However, in our experience, skeptics who are prepared to devote some time and hard work to the necessary preliminary study and experimenting are welcome in the laboratories at Duke and London. Without the training, one might as well have (as Price would say) twelve clergymen as judges at a cardsharps' convention.

The allegations of fraud are as helpful or as pointless here as they were when they were made of Freud and Galileo by the academics and others who honestly believed that they *must* be mistaken. They are irresponsible because Price has not made any attempt to verify them (as he admits), despite the unpleasantness they will cause, and because it has been obvious since the origin of science that any experimental results, witnessed by no matter how many people, *may* be fraudulent.

COMMENTS ■ QUESTIONS

1. This paper is a series of comments on a paper by George R. Price that first appeared in *Science* in 1955. Price's paper is too long to be reprinted here but can be found in *Philosophy and Parapsychology*, edited by Jan Ludwig (see complete citation at the end of this chapter).
2. In the third paragraph of their paper, Meehl and Scriven refer to the "Humean skeptic." In the context of their paper, this refers to someone who follows the eighteenth century philosopher David Hume in arguing that, because the existence of a "miraculous" event contradicts established laws of nature, it is more reasonable to suppose that stories reporting alleged miracles are erroneous than it is to believe that the event actually occurred. Hume was not thinking of ESP when he wrote about miracles, but ESP does appear to be the *sort* of occurrence that Hume had in mind. (Early in his paper, Paul Kurtz also refers to Hume's argument.) Is the position of the Humean skeptic regarding miracles defensible?
3. In contrast to some of the writers on parapsychology, such as J. B. Rhine, who emphasize the ways that ESP may be unlike physical phenomena, Meehl and Scriven emphasize what they take to be possible ways that the study of ESP could be placed on a continuum with established science. For example, they suggest that, contrary to some widely held views among parapsychologists, ESP may actually be attenuated by distance, if the distance is great enough, and it may be affected by an as yet undiscovered type of shielding. For those who are sympathetic to parapsychology, which do you suppose is the more fruitful approach to take—that of Rhine or that of Meehl and Scriven?

JOHN D. McGERVEY

A Statistical Test of Sun-Sign Astrology

It has been said that the basic premise of astrology is that the stars and planets can influence terrestrial processes. If astrology did indeed develop from such a premise by careful observations followed by testing of results against predictions in a scientific way, one could have no quarrel with it. Nobody denies that extraterrestrial influences exist.

We could even accept the fact that astrologers can identify no known physical mechanism on which to base their predictions. If the predictions of astrology come true, then the subject cannot be dismissed, even though the basis of the prediction is not understood. However, the bases of astrological predictions are so far removed from any logical cause-and-effect relationship that it becomes difficult for any logical thinker to remain open-minded. The predictions are not based on any observable or even hypothetical physical *process*; instead they are often based on superficial aspects of the appearance of celestial objects. For example, Mars is red and blood is red, so Mars has something to do with blood, and by extension, Mars governs (in some vague sense) warfare and combat.

If we try to discredit astrology simply by pointing to the stupidity of this sort of reasoning, we run the risk of being considered closed-minded. Since advances in science are often based on ideas that seem stupid when they are first proposed, we should apply unbiased tests to the *results* of a theory and not apply value judgments to the reasoning that leads to these results. Who knows? Maybe by some curious coincidence the planet Mars does have something to do with warfare.

Unfortunately it is hard to evaluate the various "one-shot" predictions that astrologers make, because nobody knows what would be a good percentage of successful predictions; there are no standards of performance, and any particular failure can be attributed to an individual astrologer's mistake rather than to the "science" of astrology. However, there are some predictions, applicable to the entire population, that result from the drawing up of horoscopes. A number of tests of planetary and solar influences in horoscopes

---

John D. McGervey is a professor of physics at Case Western Reserve University whose research is in the area of positron annihilation. He has written two books, Introduction to Modern Physics *and* Probabilities in Everyday Life.

From "A Statistical Test of Sun-Sign Astrology" by John D. McGervey, in *Paranormal Borderlands of Science*, edited by Kendrick Frazier, 1981. Reprinted by permission of Prometheus Books.

have been reported, but all appear to suffer from either a small sample or the possibility that the cause-and-effect relation has been incorrectly diagnosed. For example, effects claimed to be associated with the rising of one of the planets could be, and probably are, the result of the fact that more people are born in the morning hours than in the evening hours (Jerome 1976).

Tests of planetary influence are difficult because of the necessity of knowing the exact time of birth as well as the date, so such tests always involve a relatively small population. It is clear that in a small number of people one can always find common traits that one can then attribute to some astrological phenomenon; even Adolf Hitler and Julie Andrews probably have some traits in common. But one element of a horoscope that can be tested with good statistics using readily available information is the effect of the "sun sign." Although "serious" astrologers say that the sun sign is simply one component of a horoscope and that the "ascendant" and planetary influences are equally or even more important, to my knowledge they have never said that the sun sign has no influence whatsoever. They may say, for example, that sun-sign astrology as given in newspapers does not *completely* determine one's destiny, but they still refer to the *influence* of the sun. Clearly, if the sun has any influence at all, it should be detectable in a large enough population.

To test the effect of the sun sign, we need a characteristic that can be determined unambiguously for each member of a large population. A person's occupation is ideal for such a study, because it can be determined unambiguously by using standard reference books. For example, Americans who have done sufficient work in science to be listed in *American Men of Science* (1965) are scientists, and others are not. Although various astrologers may disagree on the specific effects of a given sign and may even define the signs differently (some of them have now become aware of the precession of the equinoxes), virtually all of them claim some connection between one's sun sign and one's chances of success in (or aptitude for) a given occupation.[1]

In searching for such a correlation I have tabulated the birthdates of 16,634 persons listed in *American Men of Science* and of 6,475 persons listed in *Who's Who in American Politics* (1973). The results are summarized in Table 1. Because the starting and ending dates of a given sign vary from year to year, I have tabulated the totals for the central 27 dates of each sign. The dates not included in these signs show no significant deviation from the flat pattern observed in the dates that were used, as can be seen by referring to the complete tabulation in Table 2.

---

1. For a summary of such claims see M. Zeilik II, *American Journal of Physics* 42 (1974): 538–42, or L. E. Jerome, *Leonardo* 6 (1973): 121–30.

Table 1.
Number of births by astrological sign

Sign	*Dates (inclusive)*	*Scientists* *	*Politicians* **
Capricorn	Dec. 24–Jan. 19	1241	462
Aquarius	Jan. 23–Feb. 18	1217	445
Pisces	Feb. 21–Mar. 19 ***	1193	480
Aries	Mar. 23–Apr. 18	1158	452
Taurus	Apr. 23–May 19	1185	471
Gemini	May 24–Jun. 19	1153	471
Cancer	Jun. 24–Jul. 20	1245	514
Leo	Jul. 25–Aug. 20	1263	504
Virgo	Aug. 25–Sept. 20	1292	507
Libra	Sept. 25–Oct. 21	1267	513
Scorpio	Oct. 25–Nov. 20	1246	488
Sagittarius	Nov. 24–Dec. 20	1202	453

* Birthdays taken from consecutive pages in two different volumes listed in *American Men of Science* (1965). A small percentage of scientists (less than 1 percent, in my estimation) may choose not to be listed in this directory, but elimination of this small number from the sample can hardly have a significant effect on the overall distribution. Some of those listed may also pursue other occupations, but this does not nullify the fact that they have achieved something in science to set them apart from nonscientists.

** Virtually all of the birthdays in *Who's Who in American Politics* (1973) were used. About 1 percent of the IBM cards were punched incorrectly and not redone.

*** February 29 not included.

Table 2.
Number of births on each date

Scientists	*Politicians*
46 40 52 50 50 51 49 31 50 39	26 14 17 18 23 19 16 08 11 15
48 48 40 28 47 45 63 45 43 36	15 20 23 18 12 16 20 14 22 24
40 55 47 53 52 47 39 47 47 36 44	20 23 15 17 15 19 11 14 16 13 15
48 59 48 41 45 43 39 34 49 35	17 16 17 12 25 20 19 14 25 14
48 46 42 49 42 48 54 35 48 52	17 19 19 19 13 09 21 14 21 23
33 47 50 43 58 41 36 55 10	11 17 18 20 21 15 18 20 07
50 47 37 26 42 38 45 45 41 38	21 13 14 15 19 20 16 21 17 19
45 44 54 48 40 44 61 46 39 42	24 14 20 20 16 19 21 12 19 20
51 52 36 45 48 43 41 43 40 42 45	19 18 16 13 11 22 19 24 12 19 12
43 38 36 46 37 45 43 41 34 49	21 13 13 13 18 16 15 18 17 20
43 36 46 54 40 51 43 50 48 58	16 24 20 14 14 18 20 14 18 16
44 51 47 56 40 43 45 40 44 31	17 18 14 16 18 15 20 11 18 16
48 43 34 44 46 47 51 50 38 36	15 17 13 16 15 16 17 20 16 20
37 57 48 48 38 42 45 35 52 53	14 21 21 22 22 22 15 18 23 13
52 48 50 46 47 44 40 54 40 50 41	17 15 10 13 19 10 11 19 10 12 16

46 32 45 33 47 47 43 44 46 45	18 18 17 23 10 12 20 20 18 18
48 37 36 34 38 40 54 36 40 49	13 31 17 16 21 26 22 17 24 13
39 52 51 44 46 45 42 46 34 52	21 19 14 15 13 17 19 20 31 19
53 49 53 52 39 43 56 37 42 39	19 12 21 24 14 21 18 19 22 26
49 45 50 44 58 53 31 57 51 35	19 17 16 21 12 24 20 21 16 18
50 42 54 38 46 42 37 52 31 45 33	10 30 20 25 23 23 25 13 19 12 17
56 52 46 45 54 50 47 44 60 47	13 16 21 33 20 16 21 18 21 22
52 52 33 46 56 43 51 46 41 56	09 17 21 18 19 18 18 12 22 17
50 58 45 55 49 53 43 42 47 43 51	24 21 13 24 16 22 24 18 17 17 28
59 56 57 39 35 56 56 57 40 40	28 24 23 18 22 17 22 14 19 17
47 39 56 55 40 44 60 40 43 45	11 23 20 18 13 21 12 12 11 20
50 49 49 47 45 57 46 38 38 34	24 27 17 21 17 16 28 16 17 18
42 57 52 55 46 57 43 57 49 52	25 22 13 17 19 14 24 15 23 28
47 51 44 46 48 52 38 54 41 45	15 21 16 09 26 17 17 19 25 18
33 61 46 37 50 43 44 69 44 48 53	18 11 15 18 16 14 19 24 23 13 12
43 42 45 34 38 40 43 47 48 42	20 21 15 15 19 18 25 13 17 20
45 43 45 49 53 58 42 39 44 55	22 17 21 21 19 16 17 15 20 16
45 49 51 51 45 53 48 33 51 48	18 17 24 17 14 23 15 17 18 20
52 30 43 33 52 48 33 40 39 48	14 17 19 17 19 13 13 08 16 20
42 47 36 45 40 43 40 57 54 51	22 20 15 12 17 20 11 21 19 16
44 42 47 53 51 39 45 46 44 51 47	22 14 22 13 06 20 20 14 20 24 18

The number of scientists born under each sign lies between 1,153 and 1,292; the mean (m) is 1,220 and the standard deviation is 45.6. The theoretical standard deviation for a binomial distribution of this size with randomly selected signs would be 33.4. The maximum deviation observed is 2.1 times the theoretical binomial standard deviation. Corresponding numbers for the politicians are: $m = 474$, $\sigma = 26.2$, and binomial $\sigma = 20.8$. The value of the reduced chi-squared for a fit to a flat distribution is 1.70 for scientists and 1.45 for politicians. These values are slightly high, and careful study of the numbers in Table 1 shows that there is a definite trend in the dates. *Both* sets shows an excess of births in late summer and a corresponding deficiency in the spring. These deviations are somewhat too large to be random fluctuations, even though they are a small percentage (less than 5 percent) of the mean. But there is no need to invoke astrological influences for this effect; the same pattern appears in "live births by month" in the U.S. population, where an excess of about 5 percent in July, August, and September occurs (*Vital Statistics of the United States 1968–69*). Thus any effect of one's sun sign on one's choice of occupation must be considerably less than 5 percent, hardly enough to justify the vast literature on the subject.

No effect was observed in the individual dates, either; for scientists, the mean number per day was 45.6, the maximum observed was 69, and the minimum 26. One hundred twelve dates, or 30.7 percent of the total of 365 dates, had more than 52 or fewer than 39 scientists' birthdays; that is, there were 253 cases within one standard deviation of the mean—just about what one would expect for a random normal distribution. In other words, a table of birthdates serves reasonably well as a random number generator (unless a pair of twins is listed).

An astrologer might argue that the class of scientists and the class of political figures is too broad and that subsets of these groups (e.g., microbiologists, paleontologists) might favor certain signs, but that these sets would distribute themselves among the various signs so that no overall effect is seen. However, books on astrology consistently insist that "scientists" or "politicians" are favored by one sign or another. Furthermore, it is highly improbable that the various scientific disciplines could be favored by certain signs in such a way that when the groups are added together no effect of the sun sign remains. By breaking the population up into sufficiently small subsets one can undoubtedly find, in one subset or another, a surprisingly large deviation from the mean in some range of birthdates. But the significance of such a deviation must be viewed in the light of the large number of possible subsets that could be chosen, as well as the large number of ranges of dates that could be used. If an astrologer chooses the occupation and the range of dates *before* looking at the data and correctly *predicts* a large deviation on the basis of his "science," then the result might be significant. However, that has not yet happened.

In the face of this negative result some astrologers might be tempted to claim that they never attached *any* significance to sun signs. But they are then faced with the task of explaining (1) why their "science," thousands of years old, suddenly has lost one of the elements that has appeared in every book on the subject, (2) how the positions of the planets can have an influence if the sun's position does not, and (3) how the time of day when one is born can have an influence which varies with the seasons and planets if the date of the year has no influence in itself. If logic had any place in astrology, they would be faced with a hopeless task.

References

American Men of Science 1965, 11th ed. *The Physical and Biological Sciences.* New York: R. R. Bowker.

Jerome, L. E. 1976. *The Humanist*, March/April 1976, pp. 52–53.

Vital Statistics of the United States 1968–69, Public Health Service, Department of Health, Education, and Welfare; and *Vital Statistics of the United States* 1937–39, Census Bureau, U.S. Department of Commerce.

Who's Who in American Politics 1973, 4th ed. New York: R. R. Bowker.

COMMENTS ■ QUESTIONS

1. Most scientists and philosophers of science place a high value on the *predictive success* of scientific hypotheses; they believe that, other things being equal, one hypothesis is more strongly supported, or confirmed, than another if more successful predictions are made on the basis of the one than the other. Predictive success is to be distinguished from *explanatory success*, which means, roughly, how well the hypothesis "fits" with the data. McGervey argues that, while sun-sign astrology is lacking in both kinds of success, it is lacking more in predictive success than in explanatory success. One reason for this is that *after the fact* it may be possible, by selecting the right group of people, to find some correlations between, say, people's occupation and the time and date of their birth relative to the position of the sun. *Before the fact*, however, it is not possible to predict where such correlations will be found. What possible response might astrologers make in their own behalf regarding these points? Or is McGervey simply correct in saying that the lack of predictive success counts heavily against accepting the conclusions of astrology?
2. If astrology is scientifically unsound, what explanation can be given for its popularity?

READINGS

Bok, Bart J., and Lawrence E. Jerome, eds. *Objections to Astrology.* Buffalo: Prometheus Books, 1975. A good collection.

Broad, C. D. *Lectures on Psychical Research.* New York: Humanities Press, 1962. A sympathetic treatment of psychical research.

Gardner, Martin. *Fads and Fallacies in the Name of Science.* New York: Dover, 1957. Analyses examples of pseudoscience.

Hansel, C. E. M. *ESP: A Scientific Evaluation.* New York: Scribners, 1966. An unsympathetic view of parapsychology.

Koestler, Arthur. *The Roots of Coincidence.* New York: Random House, 1972. Strongly sympathetic to the view that parapsychology is a science.

Ludwig, Jan, ed. *Philosophy and Parapsychology.* Buffalo: Prometheus Books, 1978. A good collection of papers on conceptual issues in parapsychology.

Murphy, Gardner, and Robert O. Ballou, eds. *William James on Psychical Research.* New York: Viking, 1960. Well chosen selections from James.

Rhine, J. B. *The Reach of Mind.* New York: William Sloan, 1947. A sympathetic view of parapsychology.

CHAPTER FOURTEEN

How is it that there are the two times, past and future, when even the past is now no longer and the future is now not yet?
—*St. Augustine*

"Scientific people," proceeded the Time Traveller. . . , know very well that Time is only a kind of Space.
—*H. G. Wells*

Time

The philosophy of time is perhaps the best illustration in all of the areas of philosophy of the extensive influence that contemporary science has had on the development of philosophical theories. I am referring primarily to Einstein's special theory of relativity and its impact upon philosophical theories of time—particularly the "static view" of time, which is discussed below. One of the remarkable things about the special theory of relativity is that its impact has been felt both by professional philosophers and by the general public. Nearly everyone has become aware that the nature of time is very puzzling.

The best way to orient oneself to the philosophical treatment of time is to look at the major competing philosophical concepts and theories that have to do with time. A brief description of each follows.

1. *Absolute time* versus *relative time*. According to philosophers who defend the absolute theory of time, time exists independently of things in time. That is, time would pass even if nothing was happening in the universe. The best known defense of the absolute theory of time was given by Sir Isaac Newton (1642–1727): "Absolute, true, and mathematical time, of itself, and from its own nature, flows equably without relation to anything external, and by another name is called duration." [1]

In contrast, according to the relative theory, time could not exist independently of the existence of changing things. For the relative theory, time should be thought of as a kind of dimension of changing things, or as a way of looking at the temporal relations of things, and not as a reality over and above the series of changing things that exist in the world. Gottfried Wilhelm Leibniz defended the relative theory of time against Newton's theory of absolute time. (A biographical sketch of Leibniz is to be found in chapter 4.) Leibniz defined time as an "order of successions." [2]

A parallel controversy regarding the nature of space is worth noting. Is space absolute—a vast "empty box" existing independently of things in space, which was Newton's view—or is it an "order of coexistences" dependent upon relations among things, which was Leibniz's view? Were things in the universe created *in* time and space, or were time and space created *along with* (we cannot say *at the same time as*) things? Or were things perhaps not created at all? This last question is discussed in chapter 3 and is referred to below.

2. *Infinite time* versus *finite time*. Has time always gone on? Will time always go on? Or is it instead the case that time is finite, with a beginning in the past and an ending to come sometime in the future? Immanuel Kant believed that the concepts of *both* infinite and finite time presented serious philosophical problems. (A biographical sketch of Kant is to be found in chapter 8.) In the first place, let us suppose he said that time was infinite in the direction of the past. Then, said Kant:

> Up to every given moment an eternity has elapsed, and there has passed away in the world an infinite series of successive states of things. [Kant is assuming here that the relative theory of time is correct.] Now the infinity of a series consists in the fact that it can never be completed through successive synthesis. It thus follows that it is impossible for an infinite world-series to have passed away.[3]

If Kant is correct in saying that an infinite series cannot be completed, then time cannot be infinite in the direction of the past. Let us suppose instead that past time is *finite*. Then, said Kant, we need to think of past time as having a boundary. But to think of this is to think of more time beyond the boundary (a "time before there was time"), which is impossible. It appears to follow that past time cannot be finite either.

Kant's solution to the above dilemma was to conclude that time does not exist apart from the mind; time, he said, is not a mind-independent reality that is *either* finite or infinite. The question of whether time in any sense exists apart from the mind brings us to the next pair of contrasting theories.

3. *The phenomenal theory of time* versus *the realistic theory*. The phenomenal theory is simply the idea that time *is* mind-dependent, while the realistic theory holds that time is not mind-dependent. Kant, as we have seen, defends the former theory of time in order to escape the dilemma posed by having to choose between finite and infinite real time. Kant had other reasons as well for defending the phenomenal theory, but it would take us too far afield to discuss them here.

Another philosopher who defended the phenomenal theory, but for quite different reasons from those of Kant, was Saint Augustine, who is represented in this chapter. Augustine maintained that an essential feature of time was its passage (a view that is quite controversial; see below). However, Augustine claimed, the passage of time cannot make sense unless we suppose that time is mind-dependent. This is because the passage of time requires that past, present, and future all be linked together—time passes as future events move into the present and recede into the past. But, said Augustine, if we think of time as existing apart from the mind, then only the present exists. Augustine thought it was obvious that, apart from the mind, the past no longer exists and the future does not yet exist. The past is retained only in our memories—things past are gone but not forgotten—while the future has reality only in our anticipation. Thus, according to Augustine, the passage or flow of time is mind-dependent. Only the "eternal present" exists independently of the mind.

The phenomenal theory of time defended by Augustine stands in contrast, we said, to the realistic theory, according to which time is not mind-dependent. To understand the realistic theory, we must look at the following pair of contrasting theories.

4. The *passage view of time* (the A-theory of time) versus *the static view of time* (the B-theory of time). Each provides an answer to the question, What sort of reality is time when time is understood to exist apart from the mind? The conflict between these two theories is without doubt the most difficult to understand of all the controversies in the philosophy of time. It is also almost surely the most significant as regards our understanding of ourselves and the world around us. In the reading selections for this chapter, the distinction between the two theories is discussed by James Otten.

A good way to approach the controversy between the A- and B-theories of time is to think first about the idea of "time travel" that is to be found in science fiction, such as H. G. Wells's *The Time Machine*, an excerpt from which is included in the present chapter. Even though time travel as described by Wells is not an entirely clear concept, we all have a clear enough idea of what some of the requirements are for time travel. Most important, if time travel of the sort described by Wells were possible, the past and future would have to "exist out there" (not just in our minds) *along with* the present. If past events are completely gone from existence, no one can "travel" to them, and the same would have to be true regarding future events.

Thinking about "time travel" should help us understand what the B-theory of time entails, because B-theorists *do* want to say that in some sense past and future exist "out there." Defenders of the B-theory deny that only the present exists. They assign no privileged status at all to the present, in contrast to A-theorists who *do* say that only the present exists.

The controversy between the A- and B-theories of time has been much written about by contemporary philosophers but is very difficult to understand clearly. Quoting some of the phrases used by contemporary philosophers in describing the two theories may therefore be helpful. For example, George Schlesinger distinguishes between A-theorists who affirm, and B-theorists who deny, that events in the future "keep approaching the Now and, after momentarily coinciding with it, keep receding into the past." [4]

Some defenders of the B-theory say that they are defending the "time/space continuum," "the four-dimensional fabric of juxtaposed actualities," [5] "the four-dimensional manifold of events," [6] or the "mind-dependence of becoming." [7] The B-theory is often associated with the special theory of relativity, according to which time may be thought of as a "fourth dimension" of things, and accordingly as belonging to them in just as real a sense as the three spatial dimensions do. (A different, but related, implication of relativity theory for the concept of time is explored by Nigel Calder in the selection reprinted here from *Einstein's Universe*.)

It may be helpful to think of the universe according to the B-theory as a gigantic sausage, with each day, minute, or year being a thicker or thinner slice. We just happen to live in the twentieth century slice, while Abraham Lincoln, for example, happens to live in the nineteenth century slice. Notice that I used the present tense in saying that Lincoln *lives* in the nineteenth century slice. Because all times coexist in a fundamental way for the B-theorist, all can be referred to by using a single tense (or better yet by using a tenseless language such as that of symbolic logic).

In contrast, real time for the A-theorist is not at all like a gigantic static sausage in which all times exist together. Instead, time really does flow and pass away. Time is *passage*. The present is very special, not simply "one time among many times." Because the existence of the world "out there" depends so crucially upon the present, the pair of contrasting theories discussed below is of special interest to the A-theorist.

Before turning our attention to these theories, one last point regarding the B-theory must be made. In saying earlier that the concept of "time travel" in Wells's *The Time Machine* presupposes the B-theory of time or something close to it, I did not mean to imply that defenders of the B-theory would say that Wells's concept of time travel is really possible. The story requires that *at one and the same time* conflicting things be true, for example, that the Time Machine both be and not be at a given time in the garden behind the Time Traveller's house. One of the things that is especially remarkable about *The Time Machine* is that the story makes sense even though it appears to be impossible!

5. *The view that the present has a duration, or length*, versus *the view that the present has no duration*. A-theorists are particularly interested in this controversy because their view of time commits them to saying that only the present exists. But if (a) only the present exists and (b) the present has *no* duration, it may be difficult to understand where our concept of duration comes from. If only the present exists, it would seem that time (or the concept of time) must be "built up" out of a "series of presents." However, if each present moment fails to have duration, then it is difficult to see how any *series* of such moments could have duration. How could something come from nothing?

On the other hand, if the present *is* said to have duration—if the present moment really does "last for a little bit of time"—the present could be subdivided into its own past, present, and future. That is, if the present has duration, part of it will come first, part will come after the first part has become past, and finally part will come that has not yet occurred. If the present can be subdivided into its own past, present, and future, however, the "present" is not the true present! We will need to ask if the true present (the present part of the present) has duration, and we will be right back where we started.

Notes

1. Isaac Newton, *Mathematical Principles of Natural Philosophy* in *Sir Isaac Newton's Mathematical Principles of Natural Philosophy and His System of the World*, Florian Cajori edition (Berkeley: University of California Press, 1934).

2. See *The Leibniz-Clarke Correspondence*, ed. H. G. Alexander (Manchester, England: Manchester University Press, 1956).

3. Immanuel Kant, *Critique of Pure Reason*, trans. Norman Kemp Smith (New York: St. Martin's Press, 1965), 397.

4. George Schlesinger, "How Time Flies," *Mind*, 91 (1982): 502.

5. Donald C. Williams, "The Myth of Passage," *Journal of Philosophy*, 48 (1951); reprinted in *The Philosophy of Time*, ed. Richard M. Gale (Garden City, N.Y.: Anchor Books, 1967), 98–116.

6. David Lewis, "The Paradoxes of Time Travel," *American Philosophical Quarterly*, 13 (April 1976): 145.

7. Adolf Grunbaum, "The Status of Temporal Becoming," in Gale, *Philosophy of Time*, 322–354.

SAINT AUGUSTINE

Who shall ... catch the glory of that ever-standing eternity [of God] and compare it with the times which never stand, and see that it is incomparable; and that a long time cannot become long, save from the many motions that pass by, which cannot at the same instant be prolonged; but that in the Eternal nothing passeth away, but that the whole is present ... ?
—*Confessions*

We all certainly desire to live happily; and there is no human being but assents to this statement almost before it is made. But the title happy cannot, in my opinion, belong either to him who has not what he loves, whatever it may be, or to him who has what he loves if it is hurtful, or to him who does not love what he has, although it is good in perfection.
—*Moral Behavior of the Catholic Church*

Saint Augustine (354–430) was the most important philosopher who lived during the decline of the Roman Empire. His writings have influenced Christian thought more than any others except for the *Bible*. Augustine's primary contribution was in the development of Christian thought from its roots in classical Greek and Roman philosophy, and especially the philosophy of Plato.

Although Augustine's mother was a Christian, and played a very influential role in his life, Augustine himself was not converted to Christianity until he was 32 years old. His conversion was a very dramatic event in Augustine's life. He had lived a "worldly" life as a teacher of rhetoric and as a father who cared very much for a son born to a mistress with whom Augustine had lived for several years. After his conversion, Augustine became a priest and then Bishop of Hippo in North Africa. His major works are *The City of God* and *Confessions*.

SAINT AUGUSTINE

What Is Time?

* * * * *

There was no time, therefore, when thou hadst not made anything, because thou hadst made time itself. And there are no times that are coeternal with thee, because thou dost abide forever; but if times should abide, they would not be times.

For what is time? Who can easily and briefly explain it? Who can even comprehend it in thought or put the answer into words? Yet is it not true that in conversation we refer to nothing more familiarly or knowingly than time? And surely we understand it when we speak of it; we understand it also when we hear another speak of it.

What, then, is time? If no one asks me, I know what it is. If I wish to explain it to him who asks me, I do not know. Yet I say with confidence that I know that if nothing passed away, there would be no past time; and if nothing were still coming, there would be no future time; and if there were nothing at all, there would be no present time.

But, then, how is it that there are the two times, past and future, when even the past is now no longer and the future is now not yet? But if the present were always present, and did not pass into past time, it obviously would not be time but eternity. If, then, time present—if it be time—comes into existence only because it passes into time past, how can we say that even this *is*, since the cause of its being is that it will cease to be? Thus, can we not truly say that time *is* only as it tends toward nonbeing?

18. And yet we speak of a long time and a short time; but never speak this way except of time past and future. We call a hundred years ago, for example, a long time past. In like manner, we should call a hundred years hence a long time to come. But we call ten days ago a short time past; and ten days hence a short time to come. But in what sense is something long or short that is nonexistent? For the past is not now, and the future is not yet. Therefore, let us not say, "It *is* long"; instead, let us say of the past, "It *was* long," and of the future, "It *will be* long." And yet, O Lord, my Light, shall not thy truth make mockery of man even here? For that long time past: was it long when it was already past, or when it was still pre-

A biographical sketch of Saint Augustine appears on the preceding page.

Reprinted from *Augustine: Confessions and Enchiridion*, translated and edited by Albert C. Outler (Volume VII: The Library of Christian Classics). First published MCMLV, Great Britain: SCM Press, Ltd., London and USA: The Westminster Press, Philadelphia. Reprinted by permission.

sent? For it might have been long when there was a period that could be long, but when it was past, it no longer was. In that case, that which was not at all could not be long. Let us not, therefore, say, "Time past was long," for we shall not discover what it was that was long because, since it is past, it no longer exists. Rather, let us say that "time *present* was long, because when it was present it *was* long." For then it had not yet passed on so as not to be, and therefore it still was in a state that could be called long. But after it passed, it ceased to be long simply because it ceased to be.

19. Let us, therefore, O human soul, see whether present time can be long, for it has been given you to feel and measure the periods of time. How, then, will you answer me?

Is a hundred years when present a long time? But, first, see whether a hundred years can be present at once. For if the first year in the century is current, then it is present time, and the other ninety and nine are still future. Therefore, they are not yet. But, then, if the second year is current, one year is already past, the second present, and all the rest are future. And thus, if we fix on any middle year of this century as present, those before it are past, those after it are future. Therefore, a hundred years cannot be present all at once.

Let us see, then, whether the year that is now current can be present. For if its first month is current, then the rest are future; if the second, the first is already past, and the remainder are not yet. Therefore, the current year is not present all at once. And if it is not present as a whole, then the year is not present. For it takes twelve months to make the year, from which each individual month which is current is itself present one at a time, but the rest are either past or future.

20. Thus it comes out that time present, which we found was the only time that could be called "long," has been cut down to the space of scarcely a single day. But let us examine even that, for one day is never present as a whole. For it is made up of twenty-four hours, divided between night and day. The first of these hours has the rest of them as future, and the last of them has the rest as past; but any of those between has those that preceded it as past and those that succeed it as future. And that one hour itself passes away in fleeting fractions. The part of it that has fled is past; what remains is still future. If any fraction of time be conceived that cannot now be divided even into the most minute momentary point, this alone is what we may call time present. But this flies so rapidly from future to past that it cannot be extended by any delay. For if it is extended, it is then divided into past and future. But the present has no extension whatever.

Where, therefore, is that time which we may call "long"? Is it future? Actually we do not say of the future, "It is long," for it has not yet come to be, so as to be long. Instead, we say, "It will be long." *When* will it be? For since it is future, it will not be long, for what may be long is not yet. It will be long only when it passes from the future which is not as yet, and will have begun to be present, so that there can be something that may be long. But in that case, time present cries aloud, in the words we have already heard, that it cannot be "long."

21. And yet, O Lord, we do perceive intervals of time, and we compare them with each other, and we say that some are longer and others are shorter. We even measure how much longer or shorter this time may be than that time. And we say that this time is twice as long, or three times as long, while this other time is only just as long as that other. But we measure the passage of time when we measure the intervals of perception. But who can measure times past which now are no longer, or times future which are not yet—unless perhaps someone will dare to say that what does not exist can be measured? Therefore, while time is passing, it can be perceived and measured; but when it is past, it cannot, since it is not.

22. I am seeking the truth, O Father; I am not affirming it. O my God, direct and rule me.

Who is there who will tell me that there are not three times—as we learned when boys and as we have also taught boys—time past, time present, and time future? Who can say that there is only time present because the other two do not exist? Or do they also exist; but when, from the future, time becomes present, it proceeds from some secret place; and when, from times present, it becomes past, it recedes into some secret place? For where have those men who have foretold the future seen the things foretold, if then they were not yet existing? For what does not exist cannot be seen. And those who tell of things past could not speak of them as if they were true, if they did not see them in their minds. These things could in no way be discerned if they did not exist. There are therefore times present and times past.

23. Give me leave, O Lord, to seek still further. O my Hope, let not my purpose be confounded. For if there are times past and future, I wish to know where they are. But if I have not yet succeeded in this, I still know that wherever they are, they are not there as future or past, but as present. For if they are there as future, they are there as "not yet"; if they are there as past, they are there as "no longer." Wherever they are and whatever they are they exist therefore only as present. Although we tell of past things as true, they are drawn out of the memory—not the things themselves, which have already passed, but words constructed from the images of the perceptions which were formed in the mind, like footprints in their passage through the senses. My childhood, for instance, which is no longer, still exists in time past, which does not now exist. But when I call to mind its image and speak of it, I see it in the present because it is still in my memory. Whether there is a similar explanation for the foretelling of future events—that is, of the images of things which are not yet seen as if they were already existing—I confess, O my God, I do not know. But this I certainly do know: that we generally think ahead about our future actions, and this premeditation is in time present; but that the action which we premeditate is not yet, because it is still future. When we shall have started the action and have begun to do what we were premeditat-

ing, then that action will be in time present, because then it is no longer in time future.

24. Whatever may be the manner of this secret foreseeing of future things, nothing can be seen except what exists. But what exists now is not future, but present. When, therefore, they say that future events are seen, it is not the events themselves, for they do not exist as yet (that is, they are still in time future), but perhaps, instead, their causes and their signs are seen, which already do exist. Therefore, to those already beholding these causes and signs, they are not future, but present, and from them future things are predicted because they are conceived in the mind. These conceptions, however, exist *now*, and those who predict those things see these conceptions before them in time present.

Let me take an example from the vast multitude and variety of such things. I see the dawn; I predict that the sun is about to rise. What I see is in time present, what I predict is in time future—not that the sun is future, for it already exists; but its rising is future, because it is not yet. Yet I could not predict even its rising, unless I had an image of it in my mind; as, indeed, I do even now as I speak. But that dawn which I see in the sky is not the rising of the sun (though it does precede it), nor is it a conception in my mind. These two are seen in time present, in order that the event which is in time future may be predicted.

Future events, therefore, are not yet. And if they are not yet, they do not exist. And if they do not exist, they cannot be seen at all, but they can be predicted from things present, which now are and are seen.

25. Now, therefore, O Ruler of thy creatures, what is the mode by which thou teachest souls those things which are still future? For thou hast taught thy prophets. How dost thou, to whom nothing is future, teach future things—or rather teach things present from the signs of things future? For what does not exist certainly cannot be taught. This way of thine is too far from my sight; it is too great for me, I cannot attain to it. But I shall be enabled by thee, when thou wilt grant it, O sweet Light of my secret eyes.

26. But even now it is manifest and clear that there are neither times future nor times past. Thus it is not properly said that there are three times, past, present, and future. Perhaps it might be said rightly that there are three times: a time present of things past; a time present of things present; and a time present of things future. For these three do coexist somehow in the soul, for otherwise I could not see them. The time present of things past is memory; the time present of things present is direct experience; the time present of things future is expectation. If we are allowed to speak of these things so, I see three times, and I grant that there are three. Let it still be said, then, as our misapplied custom has it: "There are three times, past, present, and future." I shall not be troubled by it, nor argue, nor object—always provided that what is said is understood, so that neither the future nor the past is said to exist now. There are but few things about which we speak properly—and many more about which we speak improperly—though we understand one another's meaning.

COMMENTS ■ QUESTIONS

1. "What, then, is time? If no one asks me, I know what it is. If I wish to explain it to him who asks me, I do not know." Has Augustine described your own experience with the phenomenon of time?
2. Is Augustine correct in saying as he does, in effect, that the essence of time is passage?
3. According to Augustine, time apart from the mind (that is, apart from memory and anticipation) has being "only as it tends toward nonbeing." Augustine would be the first to acknowledge that he is saying something that is not entirely clear. Is it nevertheless something that needs to be said? Does it come as close as may seem possible to expressing an important truth about time?
4. Is Augustine correct in saying that "the present has no extension whatever"?

H. G. WELLS

The Time Machine

The Time Traveller (for so it will be convenient to speak of him) was expounding a recondite matter to us. His grey eyes shone and twinkled, and his usually pale face was flushed and animated. The fire burned brightly, and the soft radiance of the incandescent lights in the lilies of silver caught the bubbles that flashed and passed in our glasses. Our chairs, being his patents, embraced and caressed us rather than submitted to be sat upon, and there was that luxurious after-dinner atmosphere when thought runs gracefully free of the trammels of precision. And he put it to us in this way—marking the points with a lean fore-

H. G. Wells (1866–1946) was a very popular English novelist who also was a historian and sociologist. He was one of the first writers of science fiction stories.

From *The Time Machine*. First published in 1895.

finger—as we sat and lazily admired his earnestness over this new paradox (as we thought it) and his fecundity.

"You must follow me carefully. I shall have to controvert one or two ideas that are almost universally accepted. The geometry, for instance, they taught you at school is founded on a misconception."

"Is not that rather a large thing to expect us to begin upon?" said Filby, an argumentative person with red hair.

"I do not mean to ask you to accept anything without reasonable ground for it. You will soon admit as much as I need from you. You know of course that a mathematical line, a line of thickness *nil.* has no real existence. They taught you that? Neither has a mathematical plane. These things are mere abstractions."

"That is all right," said the Psychologist.

"Nor, having only length, breadth, and thickness, can a cube have a real existence."

"There I object," said Filby. "Of course a solid body may exist. All real things—"

"So most people think. But wait a moment. Can an *instantaneous* cube exist?"

"Don't follow you," said Filby.

"Can a cube that does not last for any time at all, have a real existence?"

Filby became pensive. "Clearly," the Time Traveller proceeded, "any real body must have extension in *four* directions: it must have Length, Breadth, Thickness, and—Duration. But through a natural infirmity of the flesh, which I will explain to you in a moment, we incline to overlook this fact. There are really four dimensions, three which we call the three planes of Space, and a fourth, Time. There is, however, a tendency to draw an unreal distinction between the former three dimensions and the latter, because it happens that our consciousness moves intermittently in one direction along the latter from the beginning to the end of our lives."

"That," said a very young man, making spasmodic efforts to relight his cigar over the lamp; "that . . . very clear indeed."

"Now, it is very remarkable that this is so extensively overlooked," continued the Time Traveller, with a slight accession of cheerfulness. "Really this is what is meant by the Fourth Dimension, though some people who talk about the Fourth Dimension do not know they mean it. It is only another way of looking at Time. *There is no difference between Time and any of the three dimensions of Space except that our consciousness moves along it.* But some foolish people have got hold of the wrong side of that idea. You have all heard what they have to say about this Fourth Dimension?"

"*I* have not," said the Provincial Mayor.

"It is simply this. That Space, as our mathematicians have it, is spoken of as having three dimensions, which one may call Length, Breadth, and Thickness, and is always definable by reference to three planes, each at right angles to the others. But some philosophical people have been asking why *three* dimensions particularly—why not another direction at right angles to the other three?—and have even tried to construct a Four-Dimensional geometry. Professor Simon Newcomb was expounding this to the New York Mathematical Society only a month or so ago. You know how on a flat surface, which has only two dimensions, we can represent a figure of a three-dimensional solid, and similarly they think that by models of three dimensions they could represent one of four—if they could master the perspective of the thing. See?"

"I think so," murmured the Provincial Mayor; and, knitting his brows, he lapsed into an introspective state, his lips moving as one who repeats mystic words. "Yes, I think I see it now," he said after some time, brightening in a quite transitory manner.

"Well, I do not mind telling you I have been at work upon this geometry of Four Dimensions for some time. Some of my results are curious. For instance, here is a portrait of a man at eight years old, another at fifteen, another at seventeen, another at twenty-three, and so on. All these are evidently sections, as it were, Three-Dimensional representations of his Four-Dimensioned being, which is a fixed and unalterable thing."

"Scientific people," proceeded the Time Traveller, after the pause required for the proper assimilation of this, "know very well that Time is only a kind of Space. Here is a popular scientific diagram, a weather record. This line I trace with my finger shows the movement of the barometer. Yesterday it was so high, yesterday night it fell, then this morning it rose again, and so gently upward to here. Surely the mercury did not trace this line in any of the dimensions of Space generally recognized? But certainly it traced such a line, and that line, therefore, we must conclude was along the Time-Dimension."

"But," said the Medical Man, staring hard at a coal in the fire, "if Time is really only a fourth dimension of Space, why is it, and why has it always been, regarded as something different? And why cannot we move in Time as we move about in the other dimensions of Space?"

The Time Traveller smiled. "Are you so sure we can move freely in Space? Right and left we can go, backward and forward freely enough, and men always have done so. I admit we move freely in two dimensions. But how about up and down? Gravitation limits us there."

"Not exactly," said the Medical Man. "There are balloons."

"But before the balloons, save for spasmodic jumping and the inequalities of the surface, man had no freedom of vertical movement."

"Still they could move a little up and down," said the Medical Man.

"Easier, far easier down than up."

"And you cannot move at all in Time, you cannot get away from the present moment."

"My dear sir, that is just where you are wrong. That is just where the whole world has gone wrong. We are always getting away from the present moment. Our mental existences, which are immaterial and have no dimensions, are passing along the Time-Dimension with a uniform velocity from the cradle to the grave. Just as we should travel *down* if we began our existence fifty miles above the earth's surface."

"But the great difficulty is this," interrupted the Psychologist. "You *can* move about in all directions of Space, but you cannot move about in Time."

"That is the germ of my great discovery. But you are wrong to say that we cannot move about in Time. For instance, if I am recalling an incident very vividly I go back to the instant of its occurrence: I become absent-minded, as you say. I jump back for a moment. Of course we have no means of staying back for any length of Time, any more than a savage or an animal has of staying six feet above the ground. But a civilized man is better off than the savage in this respect. He can go up against gravitation in a balloon, and why should he not hope that ultimately he may be able to stop or accelerate his drift along the Time-Dimension, or even turn about and travel the other way?"

"Oh, *this*," began Filby, "is all—"

"Why not?" said the Time Traveller.

"It's against reason," said Filby.

"What reason?" said the Time Traveller.

"You can show black is white by argument," said Filby, "but you will never convince me."

"Possibly not," said the Time Traveller. "But now you begin to see the object of my investigations into the geometry of Four Dimensions. Long ago I had a vague inkling of a machine—"

"To travel through Time!" exclaimed the Very Young Man.

"That shall travel indifferently in any direction of Space and Time, as the driver determines."

Filby contented himself with laughter.

"But I have experimental verification," said the Time Traveller.

"It would be remarkably convenient for the historian," the Psychologist suggested. "One might travel back and verify the accepted account of the Battle of Hastings, for instance!"

"Don't you think you would attract attention?" said the Medical Man. "Our ancestors had no great tolerance for anachronisms."

"One might get one's Greek from the very lips of Homer and Plato," the Very Young Man thought.

"In which case they would certainly plough you for the Little-go. The German scholars have improved Greek so much."

"Then there is the future," said the Very Young Man. "Just think! One might invest all one's money, leave it to accumulate at interest, and hurry on ahead!"

"To discover a society," said I, "erected on a strictly communistic basis."

"Of all the wild extravagant theories!" began the Psychologist.

"Yes, so it seemed to me, and so I never talked of it until—"

"Experimental verification!" cried I. "You are going to verify *that*?"

"The experiment!" cried Filby, who was getting brain-weary.

"Let's see your experiment anyhow," said the Psychologist, "though it's all humbug, you know."

The Time Traveller smiled round at us. Then, still smiling faintly, and with his hands deep in his trousers pockets, he walked slowly out of the room, and we heard his slippers shuffling down the long passage to his laboratory.

The Psychologist looked at us. "I wonder what he's got?"

"Some sleight-of-hand trick or other," said the Medical Man, and Filby tried to tell us about a conjurer he had seen at Burslem; but before he had finished his preface the Time Traveller came back, and Filby's anecdote collapsed.

The thing the Time Traveller held in his hand was a glittering metallic framework, scarcely larger than a small clock, and very delicately made. There was ivory in it, and some transparent crystalline substance. And now I must be explicit, for this that follows—unless his explanation is to be accepted—is an absolutely unaccountable thing. He took one of the small octagonal tables that were scattered about the room, and set it in front of the fire, with two legs on the hearthrug. On this table he placed the mechanism. Then he drew up a chair, and sat down. The only other object on the table was a small shaded lamp, the bright light of which fell full upon the model. There were also perhaps a dozen candles about, two in brass candlesticks upon the mantel and several in sconces, so that the room was brilliantly illuminated. I sat in a low arm-chair nearest the fire, and I drew this forward so as to be almost between the Time Traveller and the fire-place. Filby sat behind him, looking over his shoulder. The Medical Man and the Provincial Mayor watched him in profile from the right, the Psychologist from the left. The Very Young Man stood behind the Psychologist. We were all on the alert. It appears incredible to me that any kind of trick, however subtly conceived and however adroitly done, could have been played upon us under these conditions.

The Time Traveller looked at us, and then at the mechanism. "Well?" said the Psychologist.

"This little affair," said the Time Traveller, resting his elbows upon the table and pressing his hands together above the apparatus, "is only a model. It is my plan for a machine to travel through time. You will notice that it looks singularly askew, and that there is an odd twinkling appearance about this bar, as though it was in some way unreal." He pointed to the part with his finger. "Also, here is one little white lever, and here is another."

The Medical Man got up out of his chair and peered into the thing. "It's beautifully made," he said.

"It took two years to make," retorted the Time Traveller. Then, when we had all imitated the action of the Medical Man, he said: "Now I want you clearly to understand that this lever, being pressed over, sends the machine gliding into the future, and this other reverses the motion. This saddle represents the seat of a time traveller. Presently I am going to press the lever, and off the machine will go. It will vanish, pass into future Time, and disappear. Have a good look at the thing. Look at the table too, and satisfy yourselves there is no trickery. I don't want to waste this model, and then be told I'm a quack."

There was a minute's pause perhaps. The Psychologist seemed about to speak to me, but changed his mind. Then the Time Traveller put forth his finger towards the lever. "No," he said suddenly. "Lend me your hand." And turning to the Psychologist, he took that individual's hand in his own and told him to put out his forefinger. So that it was the Psychologist himself who sent forth the model Time Machine on its interminable voyage. We all saw the lever turn. I am absolutely certain there was no trickery. There was a breath of wind, and the lamp flame jumped. One of the candles on the mantel was blown out, and the little machine suddenly swung round, became indistinct, was seen as a ghost for a second perhaps, as an eddy of faintly glittering brass and ivory; and it was gone—vanished! Save for the lamp the table was bare.

Every one was silent for a minute. Then Filby said he was damned.

The Psychologist recovered from his stupor, and suddenly looked under the table. At that the Time Traveller laughed cheerfully "Well?" he said, with a reminiscence of the Psychologist. Then, getting up, he went to the tobacco jar on the mantel, and with his back to us began to fill his pipe.

We stared at each other. "Look here," said the Medical Man, "are you in earnest about this? Do you seriously believe that that machine has travelled into time?"

"Certainly," said the Time Traveller, stooping to light a spill at the fire. Then he turned, lighting his pipe, to look at the Psychologist's face. (The Psychologist, to show that he was not unhinged, helped himself to a cigar and tried to light it uncut.) "What is more, I have a big machine nearly finished in there"—he indicated the laboratory—"and when that is put together I mean to have a journey on my own account."

"You mean to say that that machine has travelled into the future?" said Filby.

"Into the future or the past—I don't, for certain, know which."

After an interval the Psychologist had an inspiration. "It must have gone into the past if it has gone anywhere," he said.

"Why?" said the Time Traveller.

"Because I presume that it has not moved in space, and if it travelled into the future it would still be here all this time, since it must have travelled through this time."

"But," said I, "if it travelled into the past it would have been visible when we came first into this room; and last Thursday when we were here: and the Thursday before that; and so forth!"

"Serious objections," remarked the Provincial Mayor, with an air of impartiality, turning towards the Time Traveller.

"Not a bit," said the Time Traveller, and, to the Psychologist: "You think. *You* can explain that. It's presentation below the threshold, you know, diluted presentation."

"Of course," said the Psychologist, and reassured us. "That's a simple point of psychology. I should have thought of it. It's plain enough, and helps the paradox delightfully. We cannot see it, nor can we appreciate this machine, any more than we can the spoke of a wheel spinning, or a bullet flying through the air. If it is travelling through time fifty times or a hundred times faster than we are, if it gets through a minute while we get through a second, the impression it creates will of course be only one-fiftieth or one-hundreth of what it would make if it were not travelling in time. That's plain enough." He passed his hand through the space in which the machine had been. "You see?" he said, laughing.

We sat and stared at the vacant table for a minute or so. Then the Time Traveller asked us what we thought of it all.

"It sounds plausible enough to-night," said the Medical Man; "but wait until to-morrow. Wait for the common sense of the morning."

"Would you like to see the Time Machine itself?" asked the Time Traveller. And therewith, taking the lamp in his hand, he led the way down the long, draughty corridor to his laboratory. I remember vividly the flickering light, his queer, broad head in silhouette, the dance of the shadows, how we all followed him, puzzled but incredulous, and how there in the laboratory we beheld a larger edition of the little mechanism which we had seen vanish from before our eyes. Parts were of nickel, parts of ivory, parts had certainly been filed or sawn out of rock crystal. The thing was generally complete, but the twisted crystalline bars lay unfinished upon the bench beside some sheets of drawings, and I took one up for a better look at it. Quartz it seemed to be.

"Look here," said the Medical Man, "are you perfectly serious? Or is this a trick—like that ghost you showed us last Christmas?"

"Upon that machine," said the Time Traveller, holding the lamp aloft, "I intend to explore time, Is that plain? I was never more serious in my life."

None of us quite knew how to take it.

I caught Filby's eye over the shoulder of the Medical Man, and he winked at me solemnly.

COMMENTS ■ QUESTIONS

1. The selection that you have just read constitutes the opening pages of Wells's *The Time Machine*, a book that was immensely popular when it first appeared in 1895 and which has continued to be read and talked about ever since. Does the popularity of *The Time Machine* tell us anything of interest about the way people perceive time? About the way that they *wish* time could be experienced? Why have stories about time travel been so popular?
2. As a fictional device, the concept of time travel can be employed in ways quite different from that employed by Wells. One can, for example, imagine that people visit past or future time as "mere spectators" who have no effect upon events (this device is employed in a story by Daphne DeMaurier). From the point of view of logical coherence, what would you say is the most plausible concept of time travel? Which concept is most satisfying from the point of view of constructing a good story?
3. The Time Traveller says that "scientific people know very well that Time is only a kind of Space." What would be Saint Augustine's reply to this?

N I G E L C A L D E R

Methuselah in a Spaceship

Are you ready to grasp firmly the nettle of einsteinian time? The more thoroughly the theory of General Relativity is borne out by experiments, the less avoidable its implications become. So long as one is talking of a microsecond here or there, relativistic effects on time may seem to be of no great consequence. But the modern theory of gravity makes it quite clear that significant time-travel into the future is possible in principle. The idea that time stands still at the edge of a black hole has to be taken quite literally. A black hole could be used to stretch a person's life and let him survive for thousands of years into the future.

It would be a one-way journey. This is not time-travel of the kind described in science fiction, where you can visit the past and interfere with history, or go off into the future and then return to tell your friends what it will be like. Passing back and forth through time like that entails horrendous logical problems in the workings of the universe, which Einstein himself would abhor. But no contradictions arise when relativity allows events to unfold more slowly for one observer than for another, including the events of a person's living, ageing and dying. The moment has come to affirm that everything I have said about changes in the rates of atomic clocks applies in full measure to the rates of life itself.

The operations of atomic clocks show that atoms certainly run slowly under strong gravity, compared with the rate at which they run in empty space. The colours of light emitted by atoms in natural circumstances testify to the same effect. But the human body is a collection of atoms reacting endlessly together in the elaborate molecular dance of life. The rates of all the essential living processes are governed by the rates of atomic action. Under strong gravity brain impulses, for example, will pass less rapidly and hearts will beat more slowly. Einstein would rightly regard this as needless elaboration. For him all energy diminishes, or slows down, in the presence of gravity. Anything that feels the effects of gravity is subject also to the effects on time.

When the propositions about time in General Relativity are interpreted

Nigel Calder is a British television producer and writer on scientific topics. He has written many popular books on the themes of his programs.

From *Einstein's Universe* by Nigel Calder. Copyright (c) 1979 by Nigel Calder. Reprinted by permission of Viking Penguin Inc.

at face value, the practical consequences on the Earth are utterly trivial compared with the philosophical shock induced in pre-einsteinian man, by the realisation that the recording of time is a private or parochial matter. Even when all the arguments have been rehearsed, the mind looks for an escape, back to absolute time. If theory and experiment agree that clocks run more slowly "there" than they do "here", some people still suspect that it is an illusion—that real time is "here" and familiar and anyone I know who goes "there" will in a certain sense always be adding the same number of minutes and years to his age as I do. The conclusion from relativity is that by going "there" a person can in principle slow down his clock, his calendar and his life-rate and so outlive those who remain "here", travelling effortlessly into their future. He will experience time passing at a rate that seems quite normal to him, and yet is much slower than "here".

A more promising escape route might be to suppose that there remains some absolute cosmic time, marching steadily on, which different observers—including ourselves—measure falsely and differently because our clocks are less than perfect. For example, if you took an atomic clock far enough away into empty space, it would cease to feel the gravity of the Earth or the Sun and might then be said to be approximate to the "true" cosmic rate. While there may be some practical sense in such a notion, it runs counter to the spirit of Einstein's theory, which takes the democratic view that everyone's assessment of events is equally valid. If a time-traveller looks out and sees the universe apparently speeded up, because time for him is running slowly compared with time in the "outside world", his description of the universe is just as correct as yours or mine.

The would-be time-traveller, in my opinion, should be discouraged from diving into the black hole. Despite optimistic speculations about hopping through a black hole to another region of space and time, or even into another universe, it seems improbable (to put it mildly) that the diver would avoid destruction. No, what he should do is to take his spaceship into orbit around a black hole, as closely as he dares, in a timeshell where his clocks—atomic and biological—run very slowly as judged by a distant onlooker. In practice, the tidal stresses would be formidably great, unless the black hole were a very large one, and he would in any case have to keep his motor running to avoid being driven in. The nearest stable orbit, where an unpowered spaceship could survive, lies at six times the radius of a non-rotating black hole; there the slowing of time is only a few months per year. But let us imagine that, against all odds, the time-traveller succeeds in skimming around and around the black hole so close to the surface that he is in a timeshell where clocks run at one thousandth of their rate at the Earth's surface. Purists please note: I am ignoring the effects of motion; in powered flight a fictional traveller can go arbitrarily slowly.

One way of judging whether or not the effect on time is illusory is to imagine signals passing between the astronaut and base. If both parties had the impression that the other's clock was running slow—as they would have, for example, were the spaceship simply travelling away from the Earth at a very high speed—then it might well be dismissed as a self-contradictory illusion. But in fact the time-traveller and his friends at base will agree on what is happening.

The signals coming from the Earth to the spaceship circling close around the black hole will appear to be running fast. In the jargon, they will show an enormous gravitational blueshift and the radio frequency of the transmissions will appear in a completely different, high-frequency band in the receiver; to understand them the astronaut will have to record them and play them back in a much-slowed form. But the information they carry will be arriving thick and fast, too. The time-traveller will receive a daily news bulletin from the Earth every 90 seconds and he will witness a US presidential election five times a week. If his friends transmit their heartbeats to the time-traveller, he will hear them as a high-pitched hum.

Going the other way, the time-traveller's signals will be registered on the Earth with an enormous gravitational redshift. His friends at base will have to tune their receivers to a low-frequency band, and be prepared to record and speed-up the messages to make them intelligible. But they will not have to work very hard at it: the time-traveller's daily reports will come in once every three years and a ten-minute greeting will take a week to record. As for the time-traveller's heartbeat, that will come to Earth about once every twenty minutes. If he sends them a television picture of himself, one blink of his eye will seem similarly protracted in time.

Yet back in his spaceship, going around and around the black hole, the time-traveller is not aware of any peculiarity about time within his own surroundings. If he feels his pulse, his heart is beating at the normal rate. In each camp, time seems to pass normally—physically, biologically and psychologically. But there also is complete consistency in the discrepancy in time between the two camps. Within a few weeks, the time-traveller will receive news that all his friends are dead. If he continues to circle the black hole for ten years and then flies back to the Earth, he will find 10,000 years have passed, into a period when his "own" era rates only a few lines in the archaeological textbooks. But he will never be able to return to his former time. In relativity theory there is no method for any real object or individual or information to travel backwards in time.

High-speed travel, too, can keep you young. Our astronaut does not need to find a black hole in order to engage in time-travel and so outlive his colleagues on Earth. In empty space, he can plan a flight in such a way as to make the atomic clocks in his spaceship and his body run, on average, slower than the clocks at home. The plan turns out to be a very simple one: all that he has to do is to go off at a high speed in any direction, then turn around and come home again. The faster he goes, and the longer he travels, the greater his advantage in time will be.

The possibility of time-travel in empty space was among Einstein's early discoveries. It was one of the principal conclusions of Special Relativity, which he formulated in 1905, and his first strong clue that physicists would have to abandon the old notion of absolute time, ticking away everywhere at the same rate. The theory of Special Relativity is the main subject of this and the next few chapters. As its name implies, it deals with relative motion in "special" circumstances: in empty space far removed from any strong sources of gravity. The world of Special Relativity is mathematically much simpler than the gravity-ridden world of General Relativity, but it is conceptually more confusing. Everything is footloose and there are no definite points of reference like the gravitational centres of stars and planets. I have reversed the order of presentation of Einstein's ideas, as compared with the history of their discovery: we are proceeding from General Relativity and gravity to Special Relativity and high-speed travel. Supplying links between the two theories are (1) the similarities between acceleration and gravity and (2) the effects of high-speed travel on time.

Gravity is not very strong on the Earth, or indeed in most places in the universe. As a result, the conclusions of Special Relativity apply almost exactly in all normal circumstances, and most precisely within spaceships—*Skylab*, for instance—falling freely under gravity. Although the gravitational redshift and the associated behaviour of atomic clocks may be crucial for understanding gravity, it is usually small compared with the possible effects on time of relative motion at very high speeds.

In the case of gravity slowing down clocks there is, though, a palpable cause. That a massive body such as the Earth, the Sun or a black hole should influence time and space in its environment in a peculiar way is not altogether surprising. What makes Special Relativity somewhat difficult to grasp is that, when effects of gravity are explicitly ruled out, motion alone deforms space and time. That has puzzled many eminent physicists as well as laymen.

The same is true of a central theme of Special Relativity, that the speed of light is always the same for everyone, regardless of their motions or the motions of the sources of light. This, too, is a correct though bewildering concept. A later chapter will consider it in detail. For the moment, please take it as a fact that whenever anyone travelling at a steady speed measures the speed of light in empty space he always gets the same answer, 186,000 miles a second, regardless of his own speed. With that information an effect upon time is deducible at once, taking us to the heart of Special Relativity.

If I am travelling at a high speed past you, you will judge my clock to be running more slowly than yours is. The reason becomes apparent if I am an astronaut in one of a pair of spaceships flying side by side, and you are watching us dashing past the Earth. Looking out of my window I see the other ship at rest in our little world, while the Earth rushes past in the background. But I decide to check my separation from the other ship by radar or laser beam. I send out a pulse travelling at the speed of light and time the return of the echo by my atomic clock. As far as I am concerned the pulse goes directly to my sister-ship by the shortest possible route and comes straight back to me.

That is not how it looks to you. During the short time in which the pulse is travelling from my ship, you see the other ship continuing to move forward. From your point of view the pulse has to travel at a forward-slanting angle to reach the second ship. Similarly, the returning echo has to slant forward to reach my ship, which is also still forging ahead. In other words the pulse, in your estimation, has farther to travel.

At low speeds the difference is negligible but when the ships are travelling at, say, half the speed of light you will reckon the path of the pulse to be about fifteen per cent longer than I do. But if the speed of light is the same for both of us, your estimate of the time for my pulse to go out and come back to me is about fifteen per cent greater than mine is. Yet it is one and the same radar pulse making one and the same journey and something is out of joint in our figuring of space and time.

Einstein decided that what had to "give" in this case was the usual reckoning of time, and all subsequent investigations have justified his decision. His theory reconciles the discrepancy in distance for the travel time of the pulse by declaring that you (watching from the Earth) are entitled to suppose that my clock (in the spaceship) is running slow to just the extent needed to reconcile our two opinions about the distance travelled by the light.

Suppose that I report that the pulse echo took 100 nanoseconds (billionths of a second) to return to me—putting the ships about 100 feet apart. You will say to me: "Aha, your spaceship's clock is running slow and it 'really' took 115 nanoseconds."

Our roles are completely interchangeable in this argument. From my spaceship I can see the Earth rushing past me, and I can watch you measuring the distance from your house to your local pub by radar. By my reckoning both you and your pub are hurrying along at half the speed of light and again your direct to-and-fro radar echo becomes a slanting, longer track in my estimation. So by my reckoning, it is *your* clock that must be running slow. The effect is reciprocal and contradictory: both clocks cannot be running more slowly than the other. This effect of high-speed motion on time is therefore in the nature of a visual illusion.

But then an amazing thing happens. If I continue past the Earth and then swing my spaceship around and fly back to you, it turns out that only the slow running of *your* clock was illusory—the slow running of *mine* was real and I have spent less time on my journey than you think. It has nothing to do with the direction of travel, because the effect of high-speed motion on clocks is quite independent of that. The distinction arises simply because I am the traveller and you are the stay-at-home.

This prediction of Special Relativity is often known as the "twin paradox", because it is cast in the form of the story of the astronaut who leaves his twin brother on the Earth while he flies off at high speed for a long journey to the stars. On his return home he finds his twin is an old man while he, the astronaut, is still in his prime. The astronaut's clocks, atomic and biological, have registered fewer hours and years than the clocks on the Earth have done. With an appropriate flight-plan the astronaut can survive for as many Earth-years as Methuselah who, the Old Testament tells us, lived 969 years.

COMMENTS ■ QUESTIONS

1. The concept of time travel described by Nigel Calder is obviously different from the concept of time travel presented by Wells in *The Time Machine*. One important difference is that "Einsteinian time travel," as it may be called, would be "a one-way journey," in contrast to Wells's time travel. For this reason, it might be said that the Einsteinian type of time travel is not time travel at all. What is perhaps most important is that Einsteinian time travel may appear to be conceptually possible, or logically coherent, in contrast to Wells's concept of time travel. Do you believe that Einsteinian time travel *is* conceptually possible?
2. Does Einsteinian time travel entail the B-theory of time? The A-theory? Or is it compatible with either theory?
3. Does Einsteinian time travel entail the absolute theory of time as a way of accounting for the "different rates" at which time may pass for people on earth in relation to someone travelling close to a black hole? Does Einsteinian time travel instead entail the relative theory of time? Or is it compatible with both the absolute and relative theories?

JAMES OTTEN

The Passage of Time

One of the seemingly brute facts of our existence is the inexorable passage of time. We commonly express this supposed fact in a variety of colorful ways. Time advances, we say. It flows by, marches on, moves along, pushes on, passes by. No matter what may happen, even if the heavens fall, time does not stop. Things that are once future come to be present and then vanish into the emptiness of the past. While they exist, things steadily grow older, but never does their age freeze and never do they become younger. Presentness perpetually journeys along the time axis in the direction of the future. Or, at least, so it all seems.

Among philosophers there exists a fascinating dispute about the passage of time, involving two conflicting views. The *passage view* maintains that the passage of time is something real; the *static view* claims that it only seems to take place, that it is illusory. I shall first examine the dispute between these two views, and then I shall defend the passage view against two objections commonly brought to bear on it by adherents to the static view.

The Meaning of "the Passage of Time"

At the outset we need to determine what the meaning of "the passage of time" is in this dispute. Conceivably it could mean any one of a number of different things. Three possible meanings immediately come to mind.

First, by speaking of the passage of time one could mean that *time itself* is the subject of passage or motion—that it flows like a river, or that it moves along like a locomotive. However, there is a devastating objection to construing the passage of time in this way. The concept of motion is a relational concept. That is, to say that something moves is to imply that it moves in relation to something else. But what is this something else that time is supposed to move in relation to? Unless this question can be satisfactorily answered, and I am sure that it cannot be, then certainly we must conclude that time itself cannot move and that therefore this first meaning is completely unintelligible.

Second, by speaking of the passage of time one could mean, not necessarily that anything in particular is the subject of passage or motion, but rather that one's appre-

James Otten, who has a Ph.D. in philosophy from the University of Rochester and who taught philosophy at Purdue University, is a vice president of Bryant and Stratton Business Institute, Inc.

Reprinted by permission of the author. First published in *Introductory Readings in Metaphysics*, edited by Richard Taylor, 1978.

hension of the duration of things matches to some extent the actual duration of those things. For instance, it might be remarked in the midst of a football game that time is passing quickly or slowly, that it is flying by or creeping along. This means that the game, or a certain segment of it, seems to be of shorter or longer duration than it in fact is. In such contexts, one's judgments about the passage of time are comparative judgments concerning perceived duration and real duration. Indeed, we sometimes do have this second meaning in mind when talking of the passage of time.

And, third, by speaking of the passage of time one could mean that *things in time* are the subject of passage or motion through time—that they move through time in a fashion similar to that in which they move through space, except that things move through time only in *one* direction and always at the *same* rate. Perhaps this meaning would be expressed more clearly if we were to speak, not of the *passage of time*, but rather of the *passageway of time* through which things move, or, even better, of the *passage through time* of things.

At any rate, it is precisely this third meaning that "the passage of time" has in the dispute between the two views of time. In other words, both views are in total agreement that the idea of the passage of time is equivalent to the idea that things move through time, the passage view claiming that they do, and the static view claiming they do not.

The Two Views of Time

Let us now examine the two views of time in greater depth so that we can see more clearly the difference between them. Interestingly enough, these views are rooted in two fundamental but starkly different ways in which we conceive of things as temporal.

On the one hand, we conceive of things as having the "transitory temporal properties" of *being past, being present*, and *being future*. These temporal properties are transitory in the obvious sense that anything once possessing such a property necessarily lacks it at some other time. For instance, if the Third World War is indeed a real event in the future, then at some time yet to come it must lose its status as a future event by becoming present and then past.

On the other hand, we conceive of things as bearing to each other the "static temporal relations" of *being earlier than, being simultaneous with*, and *being later than*. Of course, these temporal relations are static inasmuch as anything once bearing such a relation to another thing necessarily bears that relation to it forever. Thus, since Caesar's birth was once earlier than Napoleon's death, his birth must once and forever be earlier than Napoleon's death.

Quite in line with our commonsense beliefs, the passage view of time maintains that not only do things bear the "static temporal relations" to each other, but they also possess the "transitory temporal properties." To put it more simply, things not only are earlier than, simultaneous with, and later than other things, according to the passage view, but they also are, at diverse times, in the past, present, and future.

Now the static view of time asserts that things do bear the "static temporal relations" to each other, but that, contrary to our commonsense beliefs, things do not possess the "transitory temporal properties." In other words, the static view admits that things are earlier than, simultaneous with, and later than other things, but it denies that things really are past, present, or future in any nonrelative sense.

Thus, the difference between the two views of time amounts simply to this: whereas the passage view holds that it is a *fact* that things possess the "transitory temporal properties" of *being past, being present*, and *being future*, the static view holds that it is a *myth*. It hardly needs mentioning here that the passage view's notion that the passage of time is something real is equivalent to the notion that things actually do possess the "transitory temporal properties." As the passage view would have it, things move relentlessly through time on the onrushing wave of the present, constantly encroaching on the future and leaving behind ever larger expanses of the past.

Metaphors Employed by the Two Views

Time is an amazingly difficult thing to understand, and an even more difficult thing to explain in words. Because of this, we often resort to metaphors in our attempts to express the nature of time. Each of the two views that we are considering uses its own peculiar type of metaphor to explain time.

Consider an example of a metaphor that the passage view would employ to express the idea of the passage of time—or, what comes to the same thing, the idea that things move through time. Such an example would be the metaphor that *things move through time much as ships move through a waterway*. Naturally the static view would maintain that the motion of things through time in the sense expressed by this metaphor does not actually occur and is simply an illusion.

However, according to the static view, things can be said to "pass" through time in a static sense. This is not the same as the motion of things through time, but rather it is a kind of extendedness of things through time. It is aptly expressed by the metaphor that *things pass through time much as the planks of a fence pass through a field in which the fence is situated.*

By elaborating upon these metaphors, we can see how both views are able to explain our seeming awareness of the passage of time. For the passage view, a person is like a ship passing through a waterway, a person's awareness of the passage of time is like a spotlight on a ship that can focus on other ships located on either side of it but not on ships located in front of or behind it. And, for the static view, a person is like a plank (or a cross section of many planks) on a fence situated in a field, and a person's awareness of the passage of time is like a spotlight that seemingly can focus successively on different planks of the fence, thus giving rise to the illusion that the planks themselves are in motion.

The First Objection: Conceptual Confusion

At this point we have a fairly complete picture of the two views of time, and so we are ready to consider the two objections raised by the static view against the passage view.

Probably the most challenging objection is that the passage view is at bottom the result of conceptual confusion over the concept of motion through time. Once this concept is gotten straight, the objection says, it becomes apparent that there can be no such phenomenon as the passage of time. In detail, the objection runs this way. In order to explicate the obscure concept of motion through time, we need to appeal to the relatively clear concept of motion through space. Now obviously *something moves through space only if it varies in spatial position over time*—that is, only if it is in different places at different times. To derive the temporal analogue of this, we need to substitute temporal for spatial terms and vice versa. Accordingly, we find that *something moves through time only if it varies in temporal position over space*—that is, only if it is in different places at different times. But then motion through time is one and the same thing as motion through space. And therefore, just as motion through space must be motion through space from one place to another, so also motion through time must be motion through time from one present moment to another only if present moments are places, which, of course, is totally absurd. The objection concludes that there can be no motion through time from one present moment to another, or, in simpler terms, that the passage of time cannot be real.

Indeed, this is a powerful objection, for unless it can be met, the passage view must be forsaken as a conceptual hodgepodge. However, it is not very difficult to discover the point at which the objection goes wrong: its description of something moving through time is incorrect, and because of this the whole objection collapses.

A correct description would be that *something moves through time if and only if it varies in temporal position over time*. One can see that this is a correct description from the following considerations. Motion is essentially variation in some respect over time. Thus, to say that Jones moves from one income bracket to another is to imply that his income varies over time. Similarly, to say that something moves from one temporal position to another is to imply that its temporal position varies over time. In generating the description of something moving through time from the description of something moving through space, the static view erred by replacing variation in some respect over *time* with variation in some respect over *space*. Ironically enough, the static view rather than the passage view falls prey to conceptual confusion here.

Finally, we should observe that there is no more difficulty in the idea that things move through time from one present moment to another, than there is in the perfectly harmless idea that things move through space from one here to another.

The Second Objection: How Fast?

The second objection to consider is a very simple one, which can be expressed in the following way. If something moves through a certain frame of reference, then it must make sense to ask how fast or at what rate it is moving. For instance, if a satellite moves through space, it must make sense to ask how fast it is moving through space. However, says the objection, it does not make any sense at all to ask how fast things move through time. Therefore, it must be concluded that things do not move through time.

Now this objection seems to be plainly mistaken in its claim that it makes no sense to ask the question, How fast or at what rate do things move through time? For we do know at least two general facts about the rate at which things move through time. First, we know that things move through time at some rate or other, since if they were at a standstill in time then change would not take place, but quite obviously it *does* take place. Second, we know that all things move through time at the same rate. So, we can answer the above question by saying that things move through time at some rate or other, and that all things move through time at one and the same rate. Hence, the second objection, like the first, carries no weight against the passage view.

An Unnoticed Implication

Finally, I want to point out a very surprising implication of the passage view of time, which I believe has gone unnoticed until now. If the passage view of time is correct, and we have not found any reason to think otherwise, then we may not be nearly so alone in the vast expanse of time as we previously thought ourselves to be.

Recall the metaphor that was used earlier to explain the passage view. According to that metaphor, things are like ships passing through a waterway, and a person's awareness of the passage of time is like a spotlight on a ship that can focus on the other ships located on either side of it but not on ships located in front of or behind it. Of course, the area on the sides of a ship represents its present, the area in front represents its future, and the area behind represents its past. We would represent the universe as we know it by a fleet of ships lined up side by side across the width of the waterway at some point; like a line of soldiers, this fleet would march down the waterway.

Now the surprising implication I have in mind is that, besides the fleet that comprises the universe as we know it, there very well may be numerous other fleets floating down the waterway. Perhaps the different fleets are packed in like sardines. Perhaps they are moving at different speeds and will sometime collide. Perhaps some are standing still. At any rate, the novel possibilities that the passage view implies are enormous.

COMMENTS ■ QUESTIONS

1. According to Otten, two major objections are raised by the passage view of time against the static view. The first objection is that the concept of moving through time is conceptually confused (that is, it makes no sense). Otten argues that it *does* make sense. Has he shown that this is the case?
2. Has Otten successfully refuted the second objection against the passage view of time (that, if there is movement through time, it would have to make sense to ask how fast the movement is, but that this does *not* make sense)? Is Otten correct in his claim that it makes sense to say that "things move through time at some rate or other"? If not, why not?
3. Do you believe that the passage view of time really is, as Otten says, the view of common sense?
4. Otten would have us conceive of the passage view of time in terms of the image of a fleet of ships moving down a waterway. Imagine, he says, that the universe we live in corresponds to "a fleet of ships lined up side by side across the width of the waterway at some point." Then, he says, we might imagine that there could be *other* fleets of ships. Does this make sense? Does this image of "possible universes" commit us to any "larger-scale" version of the static view of time?

READINGS

Gale, Richard M., ed. *The Philosophy of Time.* New York: Doubleday, Anchor Books, 1967. A very useful collection of papers and excerpts, both historical and contemporary.

Griffin, David Ray, ed. *Physics and the Ultimate Significance of Time.* Albany, N.Y.: State University of New York Press, 1986. Excellent collection from the perspective of process philosophy.

Grünbaum, Adolf. *Philosophical Problems of Space and Time.* New York: Alfred A. Knopf, 1963. Grünbaum is one of the best known defenders of the B-theory of time.

Oaklander, L. Nathan. *Temporal Relations and Temporal Becoming.* Lanham, Md.: University Press of America, 1984. One of the best defenses of the B-theory of time.

Russell, Bertrand. *The ABC of Relativity.* New York: Signet, 1959. A very readable account of Einstein's theories of relativity.

Schlesinger, George N. *Aspects of Time.* Indianapolis: Hackett, 1980. One of the best defenses of the A-theory of time.

Sklar, Lawrence. *Space, Time, and Spacetime.* Berkeley: University of California Press, 1974. Discusses the

Newtonian and Einsteinian theories and the question of the "direction of time."

Smart, J. J. C., ed. *Problems of Space and Time.* New York: Macmillan, 1964. An excellent collection, both historical and contemporary.

Van Fraassen, Bas/C. *An Introduction to the Philosophy of Time and Space.* New York: Random House, 1970. An excellent but sometimes difficult introduction.

GLOSSARY

A posteriori truth A statement dependent upon experience and therefore judged to be not necessary. To be contrasted with *a priori truth*. See also *necessary truth*.

A priori truth A statement independent of experience and therefore judged to be necessary. To be contrasted with *a posteriori truth*. See also *necessary truth*.

Absolute Nonrelative, unconditioned, certain. See also *ethical absolutism*.

Abstraction The mental separation of one concept from another concept or from a percept. An example is thinking of the general concept of color as distinct from particular colors.

Act morality The moral quality of a person's acts. To be contrasted with *agent morality*.

Act utilitarianism The view that everyone should seek to perform individual acts that, when all of their consequences are considered, will or most probably will bring about the greatest good for the greatest number of people.

Ad hominem reasoning Reasoning addressed to persons rather than to claims made by the persons. Such reasoning is fallacious when it implies that what a person says should be rejected because the person is in some way objectionable.

Aesthetics Philosophical study of the nature of art and beauty.

Agent morality The moral quality of the *persons* who are performing acts. To be contrasted with *act morality*.

Agnosticism The view that we cannot know whether God exists. To be contrasted with *atheism* and *theism*.

Altruistic ethics Ethical theories based on the principle that overall one should put concern for others above concern for oneself.

Amoral Neither moral nor immoral. Falling outside the moral domain.

Analytic truth A statement whose denial is a contradiction; or, a statement whose truth is wholly dependent upon the definitions of its terms; or, a statement whose subject concept includes its predicate concept. To be contrasted with *synthetic truth*.

Antecedent See *conditional statement*.

Anthropomorphic Attributing human qualities to that which is not human, such as animals, natural phenomena, and especially God.

Antithesis See *dialectical reasoning*.

Apodictic Necessary. Absolutely certain.

Argument A piece of reasoning. In an argument, premises are intended to provide support for the conclusion. See *deductive argument* and *inductive argument*.

Asceticism The view that the best life is one of self-denial and simplicity.

Atheism The view that God does not exist. To be contrasted with *agnosticism* and *theism*.

Atomism The view that all things are composed of atoms. In classical thought atoms were held to be indivisible and unanalyzable. In contemporary thought, atoms are judged to be composed of subatomic particles.

Autonomy The capacity to live according to one's own decisions. Self-determination. Freedom.

Axiology Value theory. The philosophical study of the nature of values. Axiology is one of the major branches of philosophy, the others being *epistemology*, *logic*, and *metaphysics*.

Axiom A fundamental, self-evident principle from which other principles may be deduced but which cannot itself be deduced from other principles.

Behaviorism The view that all essential aspects and functions of a human being can be explained in terms of observable behavior and without reference to concepts of consciousness, soul, the inner or private self, mind, or spirit.

Cartesian Pertaining to the philosophical views of René Descartes.

The Categorical Imperative (From Immanuel Kant) "I ought never to act except in such a way that I can also will that the maxim of my action be universal law." What Kant means, approximately, is that it is wrong for one person to do something unless that person is willing to have everyone else in similar circumstances do the same thing. See also *deontological ethics*.

Causality The relation between a cause, or that which produces an event, and an effect, or that which is produced.

Certain Necessarily true. What cannot be doubted. Unavoidable.

Chance event 1. An event occurring at random. 2. An event that is uncaused. 3. An event that is not predictable.

Cognition Knowledge, or more broadly, awareness, perception, or thought about something.

Cognitivism The view that moral judgments are capable of being true or false, and thereby capable of expressing knowledge, and are not merely the expression of feeling or the giving of a command. To be contrasted with *noncognitivism.*

Coherence theory of truth The view that a statement is true if it is consistent with, or coheres with, other statements that together constitute an accepted or acceptable system of beliefs. To be contrasted with the *correspondence theory of truth* and the *pragmatic theory of truth.*

Coherent Not contradictory.

Common sense A faculty for acquiring knowledge that is presumed to be available to most people.

Compatibilism The view that determinism is consistent with, or compatible with, a belief in human freedom and moral responsibility.

Conceivable Capable of being thought. Consistent.

Concept A general idea, as opposed to a mental image or sensory impression of a particular thing. An idea of the nature, character, property, or quality of something. To be contrasted with *percept.*

Conclusion See *argument.*

Conditional statement A statement of the form "if A then B," asserting that the truth of A implies the truth of B. A symbolizes the *antecedent* and B symbolizes the *consequent* of a conditional statement.

Consequent See *conditional statement.*

Consistent Not containing or implying a contradiction. If two statements are consistent, they can both be true together. If they are not consistent, at least one must be false.

Contingent event An event that is causally dependent on or conditioned by another event.

Contingent truth A statement that is true but whose falsehood is conceivable or logically possible. To be contrasted with *necessary truth.*

Contradiction One statement is the contradiction of another statement when both cannot be true or false together.

Contrary One statement is the contrary of another statement when both cannot be true together but both can be false together.

Conventional rights Rights that human beings are said to possess as a consequence of legislation, social convention, or social practice. To be distinguished from *natural rights.*

Correspondence theory of truth The view that a statement is true if it represents, or in some way corresponds to, the way things are. To be contrasted with the *coherence theory of truth* and the *pragmatic theory of truth.*

Cosmological argument The argument that God must exist as the first cause of the material world and the objects in it. Otherwise, they would be inexplicable.

Cosmology The study of the origin and nature of the universe.

Cynicism A philosophical outlook that discounts the value of many things, particularly those having traditional values.

Deductive argument An argument in which the premises are intended to guarantee the truth of the conclusion. To be contrasted with *inductive argument.*

De facto Existent or actual in regard to a specific time or circumstance.

Deism The view that God created the world but then withdrew, allowing created things to take their own course in accordance with laws of nature.

Demonstration The truth of a statement has been demonstrated when it is shown to be the conclusion of a sound deductive argument.

Deontological ethics A family of ethical theories according to which the rightness or wrongness of an individual act is determined primarily by something other than the consequences of the act.

Determinism The view that every event in the universe (including human action) has a cause or causes and could not have happened differently unless it had had a different cause or causes.

Dialectical reasoning A method of reasoning that compares and contrasts opposing points of view in order to find a new point of view that will incorporate whatever is true in the originals. The opposing points of views in dialectical reasoning are sometimes referred to as the *thesis* and *antithesis*; the new point of view is sometimes referred to as the *synthesis.*

Disjunction A statement of the logical form A or B.

Distributive justice Justice that concerns the distribution of things that have value in life. Some theories of distributive justice maintain that the good things in life should be distributed as equally as possible. Others place emphasis on the question of who is entitled to receive benefits. To be contrasted with *procedural justice* and *retributive justice.* (See *retribution.*)

Disvalue Negative value. Badness.

Divine command morality The view that what makes an act morally right or wrong is whether God has commanded us to do it or not to do it.

Dogma A belief that is held irrationally, without good reason, and possibly even in spite of good reasons for rejecting it.

Dualism The view that within a given domain there are two fundamental explanatory principles that cannot be explained in terms of any single more fundamental principle. For example, a dualistic account of human nature holds that a human being is composed of both body and soul. To be contrasted with *monism.*

Duty When used broadly, any moral obligation. The expression *duty-based ethics*, which is more restrictive, usually means deontological ethics.

Efficient cause The force, action, or agent that brings about an effect.

To be contrasted with *formal cause, final cause*, and *material cause*.

Egoism See *ethical egoism, psychological egoism*, and *rational self-interest*.

Emotivism See *noncognitivism*.

Empirical science Investigation and study of the universe that is based upon conducting experiments and observation.

Empiricism A philosophical orientation that places special emphasis on sensory experience as the foundation for knowledge. To be contrasted with *rationalism*.

Epiphenomenalism The view that mental events, which may be causally influenced by material events, do not themselves influence material events.

Epistemology The branch of philosophy that examines basic questions about the nature and scope of knowledge. The other branches are *axiology, metaphysics*, and *logic*.

Ethical absolutism The view that certain moral principles apply equally to everyone under circumstances that are relevantly similar. The opposite of *relativism*.

Ethical egoism The view that everyone should be selfish, that is, act for the sake of self-interest regardless of the needs or supposed rights of others. According to ethical egoism, a person should recognize the rights and needs of others only when it is in the person's self-interest to do so.

Ethical hedonism The position that pleasure is the only thing that is good in itself and pain is the only thing that is bad in itself.

Ethical relativism The position that values are relative either to individuals—personal ethical relativism,—or to the dominant beliefs of cultures—cultural ethical relativism.

Ethics The branch of philosophy that studies moral values and controversies.

Existentialism A school of twentieth century philosophy associated with Jean-Paul Sartre, Albert Camus, Gabriel Marcel, and others. A central claim of existentialism is that human existence precedes essence.

Faith Belief in the truth or value of something that is not supported by facts or argument.

Fallacious reasoning Reasoning that may appear to be valid, sound, or successful but in reality is not.

Fatalism The view that human beings can do little or nothing to change the course of events, whose outcome is causally determined.

Final cause The purpose that is served by an effect. To be contrasted with *efficient cause, formal cause*, and *material cause*.

Form (in logic) The structure or pattern of a statement or argument. Formal logic is the study of such patterns for the purpose of showing that some arguments are valid in virtue of their forms while other arguments are invalid in virtue of their forms.

Form (in metaphysics) The essence, character, structure, or nature of some thing or class of things. According to the Platonic tradition, the forms of material things have an existence independent of those things. According to the Aristotelian tradition, the forms of material things do not exist independently of the things.

Formal cause The form (or shape, structure, essence, or character) that determines the nature of an effect. To be contrasted with *efficient cause, final cause*, and *material cause*.

Formal logic See *form (in logic)*.

Free will 1. The capacity to make choices and act upon them. 2. The capacity to make choices and act upon them in such a way that the choices or actions could have been different from what they are even if all of the causes for the choices or actions had been the same. *Libertarians* believe in free will in this sense.

Functionalism The view that mental states or processes are functions of the human nervous system or of any other type of system, such as that possibly found in a computer, that could duplicate the function of the human nervous system.

Generalization A statement that applies to more than one individual, such as "all crows are black" or "some swans are white."

Golden mean A moderate position between two extemes.

Greatest happiness principle The claim that the most basic moral obligation is to bring about the greatest good for the greatest number.

Hedonism See *ethical hedonism*.

Heuristic Helpful in the process of discovery. Serving to stimulate investigation.

Hypothesis An explanation or theory that is assumed to be true for the purpose of testing it.

Idealism In metaphysics, the view that everything in existence is mind-dependent, that is, everything either is a mind or is the content of a mind. To be contrasted with *realism*.

Identity theory The view that mental states are identical with states of the nervous system.

Ideology A set of beliefs representative of a particular school of thought or political or social group.

Immanent Dwelling within. For example, it may be said that God is immanent, or present in the world. To be contrasted with *transcendent*.

Immortality The survival of one's soul or sense of self after the death of the body.

Imply Statement A imples statement B when the truth of A necessitates the truth of B, or when the inference from A to B is valid.

Inductive argument In an inductive argument, the premises are intended to make the conclusion more probably true than false but not to guarantee the truth of the conclusion.

To be contrasted with *deductive argument.*

Inference 1. A statement that is implied by other statements or is made more probable by other statements. 2. The process of determining that a statement is implied or made more probable by other statements. 3. An argument, either deductive or inductive.

Innate idea An idea that is not derived entirely from sensory experience but instead is present in a partial or rudimentary form at birth.

Instrumental good Something that is not good in itself but is good because it will lead to something else that is good.

Intention 1. The reference of consciousness to an object. 2. The determination to act as one has chosen.

Intuition A direct or immediate type of cognition. To claim that something is known through intuition is to say that knowledge of it was not arrived at by any type of inference.

Ipso facto By virtue of the facts. By the very nature of the case.

Judgment The assertion that something is the case. A statement or proposition.

Justice See *distributive justice, procedural justice*, and *retributive justice* (which is discussed under *retribution*).

Law of nature A principle that specifies the behavior of certain things in nature in a way that is understood to have no exceptions.

Libertarianism See *free will.*

Logic The branch of philosophy that studies arguments and formulates rules for good thinking. The other branches are *axiology, epistemology*, and *metaphysics.*

Logically false False in virtue of logical considerations alone. Necessarily false.

Logical positivism A school of philosophy whose central tenet is that all assertions that are either true or false (as opposed to being expressions of feeling or imperatives) are *analytic a priori* or *synthetic a posteriori.*

Logically true True in virtue of logical considerations alone. Necessarily true.

Logos The principle of order and purpose that some philosophers have said governs the universe.

Material cause The material from which an effect is made. To be contrasted with *efficient cause, final cause*, and *formal cause.*

Materialism The view that everything that exists is made only of matter.

Matter That which exists in space, has mass, and is open in principle to the investigative methods of empirical science. That which is not spiritual.

Mechanism The view that all events can be explained in terms of principles of matter and motion, and that the universe as a whole has no design or purpose. To be contrasted with *teleology.*

Metaethics The study of basic questions about the nature of moral values in general, as opposed to the study of specific moral principles or controversies. Metaethics investigates the meanings of moral terms and the nature of moral reasoning.

Metaphilosophy The philosophical study of philosophy itself.

Metaphysics The branch of philosophy that examines basic questions about the nature of reality. The other branches are *axiology, epistemology*, and *logic.*

Miracle An event that violates a law of nature.

Modus operandi The method or mode of operating or proceeding.

Monism The view that within a given domain there is a single fundamental explanatory principle. To be contrasted with *dualism.*

Mysticism The view that God, the supernatural, or the basic nature of the universe can be known through a kind of direct experience that is different from ordinary sensory experience and from logical reasoning.

Naive realism The view that the world is in all or most respects just as it is perceived.

Natural rights Rights that all people are said to possess because of their natures as human beings. Natural rights are held independently of anyone's voluntary agreement to recognize them. Some theories of natural rights place special emphasis on the claim that our human natures were given to us by God.

Naturalism 1. The metaphysical view that everything in nature can be explained in terms of processes such as those of the material world. To be contrasted with *supernaturalism* and certain versions of *dualism.* 2. The ethical view that moral properties such as goodness are not radically different from the properties of material things. To be contrasted with *nonnaturalism.*

Necessary condition A condition that is required for the occurrence of something or for a statement to be true. To be contrasted with *sufficient condition.*

Necessary truth A statement that is true and whose falsehood is not conceivable or logically possible. To be contrasted with *contingent truth.*

Nomological Pertaining to laws.

Noncognitivism The view (also referred to as *emotivism*) that moral judgments are neither true or false, but instead are commands or the expression of feelings.

Nonnaturalism The rejection of ethical *naturalism.*

Non sequitur An invalid inference.

Normative A normative judgment or statement tells people what is good or what they ought to do, as opposed to a descriptive judgment or statement, which tells the way things are.

Omnipotent All-powerful.

Omniscient All-knowing.

Ontology Metaphysics.

Panpsychism The view that the property of being a mind or resembling a mind belongs to all existing things.

Pantheism The view that God is in all things or that the entire universe is God.

Paradox An apparent contradiction in which all of the contradictory elements appear to be true.

Percept An idea or mental content that is of a particular thing or event or a particular aspect of a thing or event. A mental image is an example of a percept. To be contrasted with *concept*.

Perception Experience of the world through one or more of the five senses.

Phenomenalism The view that all of human knowledge can be analyzed in terms of statements that describe perceptual experiences.

Phenomenon 1. Any observable fact or event. That which is explained by a scientific theory. 2. An object of sensory experience, as opposed to an object of thought.

Phenomenology A school of twentieth century philosophy associated with Edmund Husserl, Martin Heidegger, Maurice Merleau-Ponty, and others. A central aim of phenomenology is to describe phenomena (in the second sense) wholly apart from any presuppositions about them.

Positivism A philosophical perspective that emphasizes scientific knowledge at the expense of metaphysics.

Postulate A basic statement from which other statements may be deduced. Unlike an axiom, a postulate is not presumed to be self-evident. It is like an axiom in being unproven.

Pragmatic theory of truth The view that a statement is true if its acceptance leads to success in our dealings with the world. To be contrasted with the *coherence theory of truth* and the *correspondence theory of truth*.

Predestination The view that everything that happens is the inevitable unfolding of God's plan for the universe.

Premise See *argument*.

Primary quality 1. A perceivable quality that is actually possessed by the object perceived. 2. A quality that can be specified mathematically. Many philosophers would say that shape, size, and motion are primary qualities. To be contrasted with *secondary quality*.

Prime mover The first cause of all motion. God.

Probable More likely than not to occur or to be true.

Procedural justice 1. Propriety or fairness in a set of rules or procedures. 2. Propriety or fairness in following some set of rules, laws, or procedures.

Property Any attribute or characteristic of a thing.

Proposition 1. Statement. An assertion that is either true or false. 2. An idea or thought that is expressed by a statement.

Psychological egoism The view that all human beings do everything for selfish reasons.

Rational self-interest Self-interest that is understood in the broadest and most defensible way to include everything that is of benefit to a person, especially self-interest that is understood to include the need to live in society, have friends, conduct business, and in general cooperate with other people.

Rationalism A philosophical orientation that places special emphasis on reason as the foundation for knowledge. To be contrasted with *empiricism*.

Rationalization Attempting "after the fact" to justify an action or belief with arguments that may appear sound or successful but which in reality are not sound or successful.

Realism 1. In metaphysics, the view that reality is not mind-dependent. To be contrasted with *idealism*. 2. In epistemology, the view that objects of perception exist independently of acts of perception. See also *naive realism* and *representative realism*.

Reason 1. The capacity to form ideas or concepts. 2. The capacity to think logically and with a certain degree of impartiality.

Reductio ad absurdum Indirect proof. A method of showing that A is true by showing that not-A leads to a contradiction.

Reductive explanation The attempt to explain one set of phenomena by claiming that they are "nothing but" some other type of phenomena.

Relativism See *ethical relativism*.

Representative realism The view that some or all percepts represent aspects of perceived objects.

Retribution Punishing someone simply because the person has done something wrong and not for any other reason. Also called retributive justice.

Rule utilitarianism The view that everyone should follow those rules that would bring about the greatest good for the greatest number of people if all or most people obeyed them.

Scepticism See *skepticism*.

Secondary quality A perceivable quality that is not actually possessed by an object but instead is produced in the mind as a consequence of perception of the object. Many philosophers would say that colors, sounds, tastes, and smells are secondary qualities. To be contrasted with *primary quality*.

Self-contradiction A statement that contains a contradiction within it.

Self-evident Known to be true without proof or reasoning.

Semantics The meaning of a sentence. The philosophical study of such meaning.

Sense datum Percept.

Sensum Percept.

Sexism An attitude of bias toward members of one gender, usually one's own. Often associated with the attitudes of men toward women. Actions, policies, and social circumstances that reflect such an attitude are sexist.

Skepticism The view that knowledge as a whole or knowledge within a particular field is impossible or severely restricted.

Sociological value relativism The theory from sociology or anthropology that different cultures or societies in fact have differing fundamental ethical beliefs or practices.

Solipsism The view that nothing exists apart from oneself and one's own thoughts.

Sound A deductive argument is sound when it has only true premises and also is valid.

Substance 1. That which is capable of existing by itself independently of everything else except possibly God. 2. That which has qualities, properties, or attributes but which itself is not a quality, property, or attribute. An individual material or spiritual entity.

Substratum Substance in the second sense.

Successful argument An inductive argument is successful if its premises make its conclusion probable.

Sufficient condition A condition such that if it obtains then some event will occur or some statement will be true. To be contrasted with *necessary condition.*

Sui generis Unique, one of a kind. Pertaining to his, her, or its own kind.

Summum bonum The highest or final good, from which everything else that is good is derived.

Supernaturalism The rejection of metaphysical *naturalism.*

Syllogism A deductive argument having two premises and a conclusion. In an Aristotelian syllogism, at least one of the premises is a generalization of the form "every A is a B" or "no A is a B." In a disjunctive syllogism, one premise has the form "either A is the case or B is the case."

Sympathy Felt concern for the well-being of others.

Syntax The grammar or logical form of a sentence.

Synthesis See *dialectical reasoning.*

Synthetic truth A true statement whose denial is not a contraction, whose subject term does not include its predicate term, and whose truth is not wholly dependent upon the definitions of its terms. To be contrasted with *analytic truth.*

Tautology A statement that is an analytic truth.

Teleological argument An argument intended to prove God's existence by appealing to evidence of design or purpose in nature.

Teleological ethics A family of ethical theories according to which the rightness or wrongness of an individual act is to be determined primarily by the consequences of the act.

Teleology The view that the universe as a whole has a purpose or a design. To be contrasted with *mechanism.*

Theism The view that God exists distinct from the material world. To be contrasted with *atheism* and *agnosticism.* See also *deism* and *pantheism.*

Theodicy The attempt to reconcile the existence of evil with the goodness of God.

Theology The study of God's existence, nature, and relationship to the world.

Thesis See *dialectical reasoning.*

Transcendent That which lies beyond or above something else. For example, it is often said that God transcends nature. To be contrasted with *immanent.*

Truth See *coherence theory of truth, correspondence theory of truth,* and *pragmatic theory of truth.*

Utilitarianism An ethical theory according to which everyone should always act to bring about the greatest good for the greatest number. See also *act utilitarianism* and *rule utilitarianism.*

Valid A deductive argument is valid when it is impossible for its premises to be true but its conclusion false.

Virtue A moral excellence. Specifically, a disposition or capacity for doing the morally right thing.

Will The capacity to make one's own choices and either to act upon them or attempt to act upon them.